UPSSSC

Uttar Pradesh Subordinate Service Selection Commission

PET

Preliminary Eligibility Test

2022

Group-C

Sheelwant Singh and Sarika Krishna

Includes

3 Model Test Papers &
UP PET 2021 (Shift 1 & Shift 2)

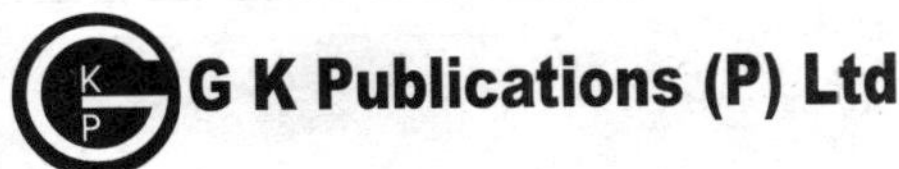

Title : UPSSSC 2022 : PET - Group C - Guide

Language : English

Author's Name : Sheelwant Singh and Sarika Krishna

Typeset & Published by :

Career Launcher Infrastructure (P) Ltd.

A-45, Mohan Cooperative Industrial Area, Near Mohan Estate Metro Station, New Delhi - 110044

Marketed by :

G.K. Publications (P) Ltd.

Plot No. 9A, Sector-27A, Mathura Road, Faridabad, Haryana-121003

ISBN : **978-93-95101-70-7**

Printer's Details: Printed in India, New Delhi.

For product information :
Visit ***www.gkpublications.com*** or email to ***gkp@gkpublications.com***

CONTENTS

INDIAN HISTORY & INDIAN NATIONAL MOVEMENT

GEOGRAPHY

INDIAN ECONOMY

INDIAN POLITY & CONSTITUTION

GENERAL SCIENCE

REASONING

GENERAL HINDI

GENERAL ENGLISH

GENERAL AWARENESS

MODEL TEST PAPERS

UP PET PAPERS

INDIAN HISTORY &
INDIAN NATIONAL MOVEMENT

1
Chapter

Ancient Indian History

INDUS VALLEY CIVILISATION (2500 BC - 1500 BC)

- From the beginning of 4th millennium BC, the individuality of early village cultures began to be replaced by a more homogenous style of existence.
- By the middle of 3rd millennium, a uniform culture had developed at settlements spread across nearly 500,000 square miles, including parts of Punjab, Uttar Pradesh, Gujarat, Baluchistan, Sindh and the Makran coast. It was a highly developed civilisation and derived its name from the main river of that region-river Indus.
- The cities were far more advanced than their counterparts in pre-historic Egypt, Mesopotamia or anywhere else in Western Asia.

Script and Language

- Harappan script is regarded as pictographic since its signs represent birds, fish and a variety of human forms. The script was boustrophedon, written from right to left in one line and then from left to right in the next line. The number of signs of the Harappan script is known to be between 400 and 600. The language of the Harappans is still unknown and will remain so until the Harappan script is deciphered.

Religion

- The chief male deity was Pashupati Mahadeva (proto-Siva), represented in seals as sitting in a yogic posture on a low throne, and having three faces and two horns. He is surrounded by four animals (elephant, tiger, rhino and buffalo), each facing a different direction, and two deers appear at his feet.
- The chief female deity was Mother Goddess, who has been depicted in various forms.
- There is sufficient evidence for the prevalence of phallic worship also.
- The worship of fire is proved by the discovery of fire altars at Lothal, Kalibangan and Harappa. Indus people also worshipped Gods in the form of trees (pipal, etc.) and animals (unicorn, etc). Further, they believed in ghosts and evil forces and used amulets as protection against them.

Important Harappan Sites

Site	Excavator	Present Location
Harappa	Dayaram Shahani (1921)	Montogomery (Punjab) Pakistan
Mohenjodaro	Rakhal Das Banerjee (1922)	Sindh (Pakistan)
Kalibanga	Amlananda Ghosh, B.B. Lal	Hanumangarh (Rajasthan)
Lothal	S.R. Rao (1957)	Ahmedabad (Gujarat)
Banwali	R.S. Bist (1973)	Hissar (Haryana)
Rangpur	M.S. Vatsa (1931)	Gujarat (near Madar river)
Ropar	Y.D. Sharma (1955-56)	Punjab (Sutlej Bank)
Alamgirpur	Y.D. Sharma	Meerut (Hindon river)
Sutkagendor	A. Stein, George Dales	Baluchistan (Dashak river)
Surkotada	J.P. Joshi (1964)	Gujarat (Kuchchh Plain)
Dabarkot	Macay (1935)	Baluchistan
Chanhudaro	N.G. Majumdar (1931)	Sindh (Pakistan)
Ali Murad	K.M. Kazzak	Sindh (Pakistan)
Mitathal	Punjab University	Bhiwani
Rakhi Garhi	Suraj Bhan	Jind (Haryana)
Sutkakoh	Dales (1962)	8 km from Perin
Manda	Jagpati Joshi	Akhnur

Burial Practices

- Three forms of burials are found at Mohenjodaro, viz. complete burials, fractional burials (burial of some bones after the exposure of the-body to wild beasts and birds) and post-cremation burials.
- The general practice was extended inhumation - the body lying on its back with the head generally to the north.

Trade and Commerce

- Inter-regional trade was carried on with Rajasthan, Saurashtra, Maharashtra, South India, parts of Western Uttar Pradesh and Bihar.
- Foreign trade was conducted mainly with Mesopotamia and Bahrain.
- Trade was carried on by land as well as overseas transport.

- Bullock carts and pack-oxen were employed for land transport.
- There is evidence of sea and river transport by ships and boats in several seals and terracotta models, apart from the dockyard at Lothal.
- The Sumerian texts refer to trade relations with 'Meluha' which was the ancient name given to the Indus region and they also speak of two intermediate stations called Dilmun (identified with Bahrain) and Makan (Makran coast).

Decline

- After 2000 BC, the Indus culture slowly declined and gradually faded away.
- Some ascribe this to the decreasing fertility of the soil on account of increasing salinity caused by expansion of the neighbouring desert.
- Others attribute it to some kind of depression in land. which caused floods.
- Still others point out that the Aryans destroyed it.
- According to some scholars, decline of trade, particularly oceanic trade with Sumerians, must have contributed partly to the decline.
- Even though there are various theories for the downfall of this civilisation, the most accepted version is that of ecological imbalance.

Pottery

- Harappan pottery is bright or dark red and is uniformly sturdy and well-baked.
- It is chiefly wheel-made, and consists of both plain and painted ware, the plain variety being more common.
- Harappan people used different types of pottery such as glazed, polychrome, incised, perforated and knobbed. The glazed Harappan pottery is the earliest example of its kind in the ancient world.
- On the whole, Harappan pottery was highly utilitarian in character, though the painted designs on some pieces show a remarkable artistic touch.

Seals

- They are the greatest artistic creations of the Indus people.
- Most commonly made of Steatite (soft stone).
- Majority of the seals have an animal engraved on them with a short inscription.
- Unicorn is the animal most frequently represented on the seals.
- Main type - (a) the square type with a carved animal and inscription. (b) the rectangular type with inscription only.

Towns near River Banks

Town	River
Mohenjodaro	Indus
Banwali	Ghagghar
Lothal	Bhogava
Malavan	Tapti
Sutkagendor	Dashak
Bhagtrav	Kissagar confluence
Rangpur	Bhadar
Harappa	Ravi
Kalibanga	Ghagghar
Rojdi	Bhadar
Sutkakoh	Shadi Kaur
Chanhudaro	Indus
Alamgirpur	Hindon
Kot Diji	Indus

Theories of decline of the Harappan Civilisation

Cause	Historian
Aryan invasion	Wheeler, Gordon, Childe
Ecological disturbance	Fair service
Change in river course	Dales, M.S. Vatsa
Low rainfall	Stein
Flood	Macay, S.R. Rao
Drying of Ghaghar	D.P. Agrawal and Sood
Earthquake	Raikes and Dales

Major Sites

Harappa

- The Great Granary is the largest and the most remarkable structure found at Harappa.
- So far, 891 seals have been recovered from Harappa, that is 40% of the total number of seals belonging to the Indus Valley Civilisation which have been found.
- A red sandstone naked male torso has been found, which shows traces of Jainism.
- Between the granary and the citadel. there have been found a series of circular platforms, probably for the pounding of grain.

- At a lower level below the granary, platforms and the citadel, were crowded one-room dwellings, which suggest slave habitats.

Mohenjodaro

- In Sindhi language, the word Mohenjodaro means 'mound of the dead'.
- It is the largest of all Indus cities.
- The Great Bath is the most important public place, located at the centre of the citadel. It is remarkable for beautiful brickwork. Its floor is made of burnt bricks set in gypsum and mortar. It must have served as a ritual-bathing site.
- Remains have been found of an oblong multi-pillared assembly hall and a big rectangular building, which must have served administrative purposes.
- Most of Mohenjodaro houses are built of kiln-fired bricks.
- The major streets are 33 feet wide 1 and run north-south, intersecting , subordinate ones, running east-west at right angles.
- The evidence of Indian ships (figured on a seal) and a piece of woven cloth have been discovered from here.
- Parallel rows of two-roomed cottages found. The workmen or poor sections,of the society perhaps used these cottages.
- A bronze dancing girl, Steatite statue of a priest and a seal bearing Pashupati have been found here.
- Excavation reveals that the city was flooded more than seven times.

Kalibangan

- Has pre-Harappan as well as Harappan cultural phases.
- Less developed compared to Mohenjodaro.
- There is evidence of mud-brick fortification.
- Pre-Harappan phase here shows that the fields were ploughed, unlike the Harappan period.
- Archaeologists have discovered two platforms (within the citadel) with fire altars suggesting the practice of cult sacrifice.
- The existence of wheel conveyance is proved by a cartwheel having a single hub.

Important Discoveries

Year	Site	Discovered by
1921	Harappa	Dayaram Sahni
1922	Mohenjodaro	R. D. Banerjee
1927	Sutkagendor	R. L. Staine
1931	Chanhudaro	N. G. Majumdar
1953	Rangpur	M. Vats
1953	Kalibangan	A. Ghosh
1955-56	Ropar	Y. D. Sharma
1957	Lothal	S. R. Rao
1972-75	Surkotada	J. Joshi
1973-74	Banwali	R. S. Bisht

Chanhudaro

- The only Indus city without a citadel.
- Existence of Pre-Harappan as well as Harappan cultural phase.
- A small pot was discovered here, which was probably an ink pot.
- Excavations reveal that the people of Chanhudaro were expert craftsmen. Archaeologists have discovered, 'metal-workers', 'shell-ornament makers' and bead-makers' shops here.

Banwali

- Like Kalibangan, Amri, Kot Diji and Harappa, Banwali also saw two cultural phases- pre-Harappan and Harappan.
- Here, we find large quantity of barely, sesamum and mustard.

Surkotada

- Excavations reveal a citadel and a lower town, both of which were fortified.
- It is the only Indus site where the actual remains of a horse have been found. Kot Diji Pre-Harappan and Harappan phases found.
- According to excavations, the city was probably destroyed due to fire.
- Wheel-made painted pottery, traces of a defensive wall and well-aligned streets, knowledge of metallurgy, artistic toys, etc.
- Five figurines of Mother Goddess discovered.

Ropar

- The excavations have yielded five-fold sequence of cultures-Harappan, Painted Grey Ware (PGW), Northern Black Painted Ware (NBP), Kushana-Gupta and Medieval.

- The evidence of burying a dog below the human burial is very interesting.
- One example of rectangular mud brick chamber was noticed.

Dholavira

- It is the latest and one of the two largest Harappan settlements in India, the other being Rakhigarhi in Haryana.
- The other Harappan towns were divided into two parts - Citadel and the Lower Town, but Dholavira was divided into three principal divisions, two of which were strongly protected by rectangular fortifications.
- There are two inner enclosures - the first one hemmed in the citadel (which probably housed the highest authority) and the second one protected the middle town (meant for the close relatives of the rulers and other officials). The existence of this middle town, apart from the lower town, is the exclusive feature of this city.

Lothal

- The only Indus site with an artificial brick dockyard. It must have served as the main seaport of the Indus people. It was surrounded by a massive brick wall, probably for flood protection.
- Lothal has evidence of the earliest cultivation of rice (1800 BC). The only other Indus site where rice husk has been found is Rangpur near Ahmedabad.
- Fire altars, indicating the probable existence of a fire cult, have been found.
- A terracotta figurine of a horse is found here.

THE VEDIC AGE (1500 - 600 B.C.)

The Early Vedic Period (1500-1000 B.C.)

- It is also known as the Rig Vedic Age.
- The earliest Aryans lived in the land of 'Sapta Saindhava' i.e., land of seven rivers.
- The early vedic society was pastoral.
- Cattle was the chief measure of wealth and wealthy man was called 'Gomat'.
- The Raja or Chief is called 'Gopati'.
- In the Rig Veda, Godhuli is used as a term for a measure of time.
- Apart from Yava or Barley, no other grain is mentioned.
- Indra was the greatest God of Aryans, Agni occupied the second position.
- Varuna occupied the third position and he personified water.
- The Battle of Ten Kings ended with the victory of the Bharatas led by Sudas.
- Gayatri Mantra is attributed to Savitri.
- Aditi was the goddess of eternity.
- Important functionaries were Purohita, Senani, and Gramini.
- Important tribal assemblies were Sabha, Samiti, Vidhatha and Gana.
- Sabha performed judicial and administrative functions.
- The King attended Sabha but was not elected by it.
- Samiti is mentioned nine-times in the Rig veda.
- Samiti was presided over by the king.
- King was elected in Samiti.
- 'Gana' is mentioned in 46 places in Rig veda.
- Leader of Gana was called as 'Ganapati'.
- Dasyus were the most bitter enemies of the Rig vedic people.
- Rig vedic people were not aware of iron.
- Indra was the most important God.
- Indra was known as Purandar, Vritrahan and Marutavant.
- Varuna uphold the natural or cosmic and moral order (Riti).
- Varuna was the punisher of sin.
- Agni was called as Bhuvan-Chakshu.
- IXth book is devoted to Soma.
- Gayatri Mantra is mentioned in III Mandal of Rig veda.
- Asvins and Nasatyas were divine physicians.
- Yama was the Lord of the dead.
- Aditi is the mother of Surya.
- Varuna bears the title 'Asura'.

The Later Vedic Period (1000-600 B.C.)

- The communities of this period used a particular kind of pottery called the **Painted Grey Ware (PGW).**
- More then 700 PGW sites have been found in the Upper Ganga Basin. Some important PGW sites are Atranji Khera, Ahichhatra, Noh, Hastinapur, Kurukshetra, Bhagwanpura and Jakhera.
- Iron objects are common to most PGW sites. This metal was introduced around 1000-800 B.C. It is mentioned as Ayas.

- Society was clearly divided into four Varnas namely- Brahmin, Kshatriya, Vaishya and Sudra.
- The upper three classes were known as Dvij (twice born).
- Education began with investiture ceremony (upanayana).
- Gotra first appeared in Atharva veda with the meaning of clan.
- There was practice of class exogamy.
- There was reference to sati but not in common fashion.
- There were instances of child marriage.
- Indra and Agni lost their importance. Prajapati (the creator) became Supreme.
- Vishnu came to be conceived as the preserver and protector of the people.
- Sacrifices became more important.
- There were 33 deities during the Later Vedic Period.
- The king's influence was strengthened by rituals.
- Rajasuya conferred supreme power on king.
- Vajapeya was a samayojan which was the symbol of strength. It had a chariot race.
- Aswamedha was the horse sacrifice.
- Kings were known with different names in different regions.
- Eastern Kings were called Samrat.
- Western Kings were called Svarat.
- Northern Kings were called Virat.
- Southern Kings were called Bhoja.
- Kings of the middle country were called Raja.
- Earliest evidence of medicine comes from Atharvaveda.
- Parikshit has been called as the king of 'Mrityuloka' in Atharvaveda.
- King used to visit the house of each Ratnin in Ratnavimshi ceremony.
- Atharvaveda mentions Sabha and Samiti as daughters of Prajapati.
- According to Kathak Samhita, 24 oxen were employed for agriculture.
- During the Later Vedic Period, Prajapati came to occupy the Supreme position.
- Pushan was the God of Sudras.
- Rudra was the God of animals.
- Institution of Gotra appeared during the later vedic period.
- Duties of four varnas are given in **"Aitreya Brahamana"**.
- Three-roomed mud house has been discovered at Bhagwanpura.
- Largest deposits of iron tools and weapons have been found at Atranjikhera.
- Two furnaces for iron smelting have been found at Suneri village in Jhunjhunu district.
- Legend of 'Videha Madhav' is mentioned in Satapatha Brahamana.
- Eight forms of marriages are given in Ashvalahayan Grihyasutra.
- Satapatha Brahamana says that 'wife is half of her husband'.
- Earliest clear reference to the four ashramas is given in Jabala Upanishad.

The Vedic Literature

- The word Veda is has been taken from the Sanskrit word 'Vid' which reflects 'to know' or 'knowledge par excellence'.
- Vedic literature is divided between Sruti which was (based on hearing), which is distinct from Smriti (something which is based on memory).
- The four Vedas and their Samhitas, the Brahmanas, the Aranyakas and the Upanishads form a class of literature known as Sruti.

Rig Veda

- The Rig Veda is divided into 10 Books or Mandalas.
- The books II to VII are defined as the oldest one and are also called as family books.
- The book I, VIII and X are assumed to be later additions.
- The collection of approx 1028 hymns are from a number of priestly families.
- They are written between 1700-1500 B.C. when Aryans were still in Punjab.
- They are attributed to Gritsamada, Visvamitra, Vasudeva, Atri, Bhardwaj, Vashishtha, Kanva and Angiras.
- The IX Mandala is devoted completely to Soma.
- The Xth Mandala has the famous Purushsukta hymn that describes about the origin of four Varnas.
- Gayatri Mantra is the most sacred hymn of the Rig Veda.

Yajur Veda

- It is a ritualistic Veda.
- Yajur Veda is divided into Shukla Yajurveda and Krishna Yajurveda.

- Atharvaveda includes beliefs and practices of non-Aryans.
- Yajur Veda is written in prose, it deals with process for performance of sacrifices and contains rituals as well as hymns.

Sama Veda

- Sama Veda acquired its roots from Saman, which reflects a melody.
- So, it can be said that Soma Veda is a collection of melodies.
- It consists of 1603 hymns. Except 99, all others were derived from the Rig Veda.

Atharva Veda

- It is a collection of 711 hymns and it is divided into 20 khandas.
- It is the newest written Veda.
- Atharva Veda is a book which's consists of magical formulae.
- It contains charms and spell to ward off evil and disease.
- Its content describes the practices of non-Aryans.

The Mahajanapadas

- Around 6th century BC, iron began to be used widely.
- As iron equipments helped clear the dense forests of the Gangetic plains, civilisation expanded eastwards.
- The new agricultural tools improved the knowledge of cultivation.
- This helped in the production of surplus food grains, which could be collected by the Kings to meet their military and administrative needs.
- Establishment of an agrarian economy enabled the people to lead, a settled life, to stick to their land, and also to expand at the cost of the neighbouring virgin areas.
- Around this time, sixteen Mahajanapadas or kingdoms rose to pre-imminence in India.
- According to Anguttara Nikaya, they were - Kashi, Kosala, Anga, Magadha, Vajji, Malla, Chedi, Vatsa, Kuru, Panchala, Matsya, Surasena, Assaka, Avanti, Gandhara and Kamboja.
- These Mahajanapadas were either monarchical or republican in character.
- The Mahajanapadas of Anga, Kashi, Kosala, Chedi, Vatsa, Matsya, Shursen, Ashmak, Avanti, Gandhara and Magadha were ruled by kings or monarchs.
- The kings in these states had the supreme authority.
- The Mahajanapadas of Vrijji, Malla, Kuru, Panchal and Kamboj were republican states and so were other smaller states, like Lichhavi, Shakya, Koliya, Bhagga and Moriya.
- These republican states had a Gana-parishad or an Assembly of senior and responsible citizens.
- This Gana-parishad had the supreme authority in the state.

Magadhan Ascendancy

- Of the sixteen Mahajanapadas, Magadha, Kosala, Vatsa and Avanti were more powerful.
- They fought amongst themselves for political pre-eminence for about hundred years.
- Ultimately, Magadha, under the leadership of Bimbisara (542 BC- 493 BC) and Ajatshatru (493 BC - 461 BC) emerged victorious.
- The victory of Magadha was a victory for the monarchical system, which was now firmly established in the Ganges plain.
- Magadhan ascendancy began with Bimbisara of the Haryanka dynasty.
- He married the princesses of Kosala, Vaishali and Madra, which helped him in his expansionist policy.
- His one and only conquest was that of Anga. He also gained a part of Kashi as dowry in his marriage with the sister of King Prasenajit of Kosala.
- Bimbisara was murdered by his own son, Ajatasatru (492-460 BC).
- He defeated Prasenajit, married his daughter, and annexed Kashi. Ajatasatru was succeeded by Udayin (460-444 BC), who founded the new capital at Pataliputra.
- The Haryanka dynasty was succeeded by the Sisunaga dynasty, which destroyed the power of Avanti and incorporated it in the Magadhan empire.
- Thus, the 100-year-old rivalry between Avanti and Magadha came to an end.
- The Sisunagas were succeeded by the Nandas, who annexed Kalinga to the empire.
- Mahapadma Nanda was the most important king of his dynasty.
- The Nandas are said to have checked Alexander's army from advancing towards Magadha.
- Their rule was supplanted by that of the Mauryas.

Religious Movements

Buddhism

- Buddhism was founded by Gautam Buddha.
- Buddha was born on the Vaisakh Purnima day in 563 B.C.
- He belonged to the Sakya clan of Kshatriyas.
- His father was Suddhodana, the Sakya ruler of Kapilvastu.
- He was born in Lumbini in Kapilvastu **in Nepal**.
- His mother was Mahamaya of the Kosala dynasty.
- Buddha got Nirvana at the age of 35 years at Uruvela on the bank of river Niranjana.
- Buddha gave his first sermon at Sarnath.
- Buddha's first sermon is called as "Dharma Chakrapravartana".
- Buddha died in 483 B.C. at Kushinagar.
- Kushinagar has been identified with village Kasia in Deoria district of U.P.
- Buddha's last words were "All composite things, strive diligently".
- Buddha was brought up by his stepmother Gautami because his mother died just after 7 days of his birth.
- Buddha got married at 16 years to the Princess Yashodhara.
- He enjoyed the married life only for 13 years and had a son named Rahula.
- After seeing an old man, a sick man, a corpse and an ascetic, Buddha decided to become a wanderer.
- He left his palace at just the age of 29 (with Channa, the charioteer and his favourite horse, Kanthaka) in search of truth of life (also called 'Mahabhinishkr-amana' or 'The Great Renunciation') and wandered for 6 years.
- He attained 'Enlightenment' at 35 at Gaya in Magadha (Bihar) under the Pipal tree.
- Asvajit, Upali, Mogallana, Sariputra and Ananda were the five disciples of Buddha.

Five Great Events of Buddha's Life and their Symbols

1. Birth : Lotus and Bull
2. Great Renunciation : Horse
3. Nirvana : Bodhi tree
4. First Sermon : Dharmachakra or wheel
5. Mahaparinirvana or Death : Stupa

Four Noble Truths

1. The world is full of sorrows.
2. Desire is the root cause of sorrow.
3. If desire is conquered, all sorrows can be removed.
4. Desire can be removed by following the eight-fold path.

Eight Fold Path

The mnemonic for remembering the 8-fold path is SLUM CATE :

1. Right understanding	**S** = Speech
2. Right speech	**L** = Livelihood
3. Right livelihood	**U** = Understanding
4. Right mindfulness	**M** = Mindfulness
5. Right thought	**C** = Concentration
6. Right action	**A** = Action
7. Right effort and	**T** = Thought
8. Right concentration	**E** = Effort

Three Ratnas

- Buddha
- Dhamma
- Sangha

Important Facts related to Buddha

Tathagata, Sakyamuni	Titles of Buddha
Sakya	Clan to which Buddha belong
Gautama	Gotra of Buddha
Suddhodana	Buddha's Father
Mahamaya	Buddha's Mother
Prajapati Gautami	Foster Mother
Yasodhara	Buddha's Wife
Rahula	Buddha's Son
Kanthaka	Buddha's Horse
Channa	Buddha's Charioteer
Alara Kalam	Buddha's Teacher
Sujata	Girl who offered rice and milk
Niranjana	River on the bank of which Buddha attained Nirvana
Mara	King of spirit who troubled Buddha during meditation
Chunda	The person who offered pork of Buddha
Sravasti	Buddha preached most of his sermons here

Buddhist Councils

Council	Period	Place	Purpose	Chairman	Patron
I	483 B.C.	Saptaparni cave near Rajagriha	• To compile the teachings of Buddha into two Pitakas - Dhamma Pitaka and Vinaya Pitaka. • Upali recited the Vinaya Pitaka and Ananda recited the Sutta Pitaka.	Mahakassapa	Ajatsatru
II	383 B.C.	Vaishali	• The monks of Vaisali wanted to mark some change in the rites. • So, the followers got divided into Sthaviravadins and Mahasanghikas.	Sabakami	Kalasoka
III	250 B.C.	Pataliputra	• The main objective of the council was to revise the scriptures. • The third part of the Tripitaka was coded in the Pali language.	Moggliputta Tissa	Ashoka
IV	72 A.D.	Kashmir (Kundalvan)	• In this Council, Budhhism was divided into Mahayana and Hinayana sects.	Vasumitra, (helped by vice-Chairman Ashvaghosha)	Kanishka

Sects of Buddhism

Hinayana

(a) Its followers believed in the oldest teachings of Buddha without any changes.

(b) They propagated individual salvation through self-discipline and meditation.

(c) They did not trust idol-worship.

(d) Hinayana, like Jainism, became the religion without God, and the Karma of individual taking the place of God.

Mahayana

(a) The followers of Mahayana believed in the heavenliness of Buddha and sought the salvation of all through the grace and help of Buddha and Bodhisattvas.

(b) They believed in idol worship.

(c) They believed that Nirvana is not a negative cessation of misery but a positive state of bliss.

(d) Later on, the Mahayana had two chief philosophical schools: the Madhyamika and the Yogachara.

Vajrayana

(a) The followers of vajrayana believed that salvation could be best attained by obtaining the magical power, which they called Vajra.

(b) The chief divinities of this new sect were the Taras.

(c) It became popular in Eastern India, particularly Bengal and Bihar, including the neighbouring country Tibet.

Buddhist Literature

- The Buddhist scriptures in Pali are commonly referred to as Tripitaka, i.e. Three-fold Basket.
- **Tripitaka** includes Vinaya Pitaka, Sutta Pitaka, and Abhidhamma Pitaka.
- The Vinayapitaka comprises of Suttavibhanga, Khandakas and Parivarpatha.
- The Vinay Pitaka:
  (a) Deals with rules and regulations of Buddha which he promulgated.
  (b) It elaborates in detail the gradual development of the Sangha.
  (c) An account of the life and teaching of the Buddha is also given.
- The **Sutta Pitaka** is divided into five Nikayas.
- The 5 Nikayas are:
  1. Digha Nikaya
  2. Majjhima Nikaya
  3. Samyutta Nikaya
  4. Anguttara Nikaya and
  5. Khuddaka Nikaya.

- The Khuddaka Nikaya consists of large number of miscellaneous works.
- The Jatakas are a part of Khuddaka Nikaya of Sutta Pitaka.
- The Sutta Pitaka consists chiefly of :
  - (a) The preachings delivered by Buddha himself on different places and moments.
  - (b) Few discourses delivered by Sariputta, Ananda, Moggallana and others are also included in it.
  - (c) It lays down the principles of Buddhism.
- The **Abhidhamma Pitaka** is written in the form of questions and answers.
- It is made-up of seven books of which Kathavattu is the most important.
- Kathavattu is attributed to Tissa Moggaliputta
- The Abhidhamma Pitaka:
  - (a) Contains the deep philosophy of the Buddha's teachings.
  - (b) It investigates mind and matter to help the understanding of things as they truly are.

Buddhist Architecture

- Buddhist architecture developed essentially in to three forms viz:
  - (a) Stupa (relics of the Buddha or some prominent Buddhist monks are preserved)
  - (b) Chaitya (prayer hall)
  - (c) Vihara (residence)

Eight Holy Places (Ashtamahasthanas)

1. Lumbini	2. Bodh Gaya
3. Kusinagar	4. Sravasti
5. Sankasya	6. Rajgriha
7. Vaisali	8. Sarnath

Buddhist Sects and their Areas of Influence

Mahayana	India, Sri Lanka, Burma, Bangladesh, Malaysia, Nepal, Singapore.
Hinayana	India, China, Nepal, Singapore, Japan, Korea, Taiwan, Vietnam.
Vajrayana	India, Nepal, Tibet, Mongolia, Bhutan.

Jainism

- Jainism was founded by Vardhamana Mahavira.
- Mahavira was born in 540 B.C.
- Mahavira's birth place was Kundagram in Vaishali.
- He belonged to the Jnatrika Kshatriya clan.
- His father's name was Siddhartha and mother's name was Trishala, who was a sister of the Lichchavi prince Chetak of Vaishali.
- Mahavira was married to Yashoda.
- He left home at the age of 30 and wandered for 12 years.
- Mahavira is regarded as the 24th Tirthankara.
- Rishabha was the 1st Tirthankara.
- Parsavanath was the 23rd Tirthankara.
- Mahavira's first disciple was Jamali.
- Mahavira attained Kaivalya on the bank of river Rijupalika near Jrimbhikgrama.
- The names of two Jain Tirthankaras - Rishabha and Aristanemi - are found in the Rigveda.
- Many Jain followers went to south under the leadership of Bhadrabahu.
- These southern followers later formed the Digambra sect.
- Those who remained at Magadha, under the leadership of Sthulabahu formed the Shvetambar sect.

Five Main Teachings

1. Non-injury (ahimsa)
2. Non-lying
3. Non-stealing (asteya)
4. Non-possession (aparigraha)
5. Observe continence (Brahmacharya). It was added by Mahavira.

Important Facts about Jainism

Mahavira, Arhat	Titles of Vardhamana
Vardhamana	Original name of Mahavira
Kundagram	Mahavira's birth place
Trisala	Mahavira's mother
Yashoda	Mahavira's wife
Jamali	Mahavira's son-in-law
Jnatrika	Clan to which Mahavira belonged
Rajupalika	River on the bank of which Mahavira got Kaivalya
Sal tree	The tree under which Mahavira got Kaivalya
Pava	Place where Mahavira died

Jain Literature

- Most of the literature is written in Prakrit.
- The Jain literature includes:
  1. The 12 Angas
  2. The 12 Upangas
  3. The 10 Prakirna
  4. The 6 Chhedsutras
  5. The 4 Mulasutras

Jain Councils

- **First Council** was conducted at Pataliputra by Sthulabahu in the beginning of the third century B.C. and resulted in the compilation of 12 Angas to replace the lost 14 Purvas.
- **Second Council** was held at Valabhi in the 6th (513 A.D.) century under the leadership of Devaridhi Kshamasramana and resulted in final compilation of 12 Angas and 12 Upangas.

24 Tirthankaras and their Symbols

S.No.	Name	Symbol
1.	Rishabha	Bull
2.	Ajitnath	Elephant
3.	Sambharnath	Horse
4.	Abhianandam Swamy	Monkey
5.	Sumathinath	Curlew
6.	Padamprabhu	Red Lotus
7.	Suparsavanath	Swastik
8.	Chandraji Prabhu	Moon
9.	Suvidhinath	Crocodile
10.	Shitalnath	Srivatsa
11.	Shreganesnath	Rhinoceros
12.	Vasupujya	Buffalo
13.	Vimalnath	Boar
14.	Ananthnath	Falcon
15.	Dharamnath	Vajra
16.	Shantinath	Deer
17.	Kuntunath	He-Goat
18.	Arath	Fish
19.	Mallinath	Water Pot
20.	Muniswasth	Tortoise
21.	Naminath	Blue Lotus
22.	Neminath	Conch Shell
23.	Parsavanath	Serpent
24.	Mahavir	Lion

Rise of Magadha

Haryanka Dynasty

- The epic Mahabharata has provided information about the early period of Magadha.
- Jarasandh and Brihdrath were the rulers during the period of Mahabharata.
- Girivraja was the Magadhan capital during the early period.

Bimbisara (544-492 B.C.)

- Bimbisara established the Haryanka dynasty.
- Bimbisara ascended the throne in 544 B.C.
- In Jain literature, he has been called as 'Shrenik'.
- Bimbisara had three wives - Mahakosala, Chellana and Khema.
- Mahakosala was the sister of Kosal ruler Prasenjit.
- Chellana was a Lichchhavi Princess.
- Bimbisara defeated Anga and annexed it.
- Bimbisara send his physician Jivak to treat Chand Pradyot of Avanti.
- Bimbisara was prisoned by his son Ajatshatru and died in 493 B.C.

Ajatshatru (492-460 B.C.)

- Ajatshatru sat on Magadha throne in 492 B.C.
- Ajatshatru followed an expansionist policy.
- After a long struggle, he defeated Kasi and Vajji confederacy.
- Ajatshatru took the services of his minister Vassakar to divide the Vajji confederacy.
- Ajatshatru got a large stupa constructed in Rajgriha.
- Ajatshatru constructed a fort around Rajgriha to protect it from Lichcchavi attack.
- Ajatshatru was killed by his son Udayin in 461 B.C.
- Udayin transferred the Capital to Patliputra.
- Udayin was a follower of Jainism.
- The last Haryanka ruler was Nagdasak.

Shisunaga Dynasty (412-344 B.C.)

- Nagdasak was killed by his amatya Shisunaga.
- Shisunaga established Shisunaga dynasty in 412 B.C.
- Shisunaga annexed Avanti to Magadha.
- Shisunaga established his capital at Vaishali.
- Kalashoka came to the throne in 344 B.C.
- Kalashoka again transferred the capital to Pataliputra.

- During the reign of Kalashoka the second Buddhist council was organised at Vaishali.
- Nandivardhan was the last Shisunaga ruler.

Nanda Dynasty

- Nanda Dynasty was established by Mahapadmananda.
- According to Puranas, he was not a Kshatriya.
- Mahapadmananda was known as Ekarat and Sarvakshatrantaka.
- Mahapadmananda conquered Kalinga.
- The last Nanda ruler was Dhanananda.
- Dhanananda was the contemporary of Alexander.
- Nanda Dynasty was destroyed by Chandragupta Maurya and Chanakya.
- Nandas have been termed as the first empire builders of India.

Factors for the Rise of Magadha

- Magadha enjoyed an advantageous geographical position.
- Iron deposits were situated close to Rajgir, the earliest capital of Magadha.
- Rajgir and Pataliputra were situated at very strategic points.
- Pataliputra was surrounded by rivers from all sides, it was called as Jaladurga (water-fort).
- Magadha lay at the centre of the middle Gangetic plain.
- Magadha for the first time used elephants on a large-scale in wars.
- Greek sources have mentioned that the Nandas maintained 6000 elephants.
- Magadha society was unorthodox and was recently Aryanised.
- Ambitious rulers like Bimbisara, Ajatshatru and Mahapadmananda established Magadha as a powerful kingdom.

Foreign Invasions

- North-West India was ruled by smaller principalities like Kambojas, Gandharas and Madras.
- The period of 6th B.C. was marked by political instability in North-West India.
- In 516 B.C. the Iranian ruler Darius penetrated into North-West India.
- Darius annexed Punjab, west of Indus and Sindh.
- This area constituted the 20th kshatrapy (province) of Iran.
- The Indian kshatrapy included Sindh, the North-West Frontier and part of Punjab.
- The Indian Kshatrapy paid a tribute of 360 talents of Gold.
- Xerxes, the successor of Darius, employed Indians in the long war against the Greeks.
- The Iranian scribes brought into India Kharoshti script.
- Under the leadership of Alexander of Macedonia, the Greeks destroyed the Iranian Empire.
- Alexander marched to India through the Khyber Pass in 326 B.C.
- Ambhi was the king of Taxila.
- Porus ruled between Jhelum and Ravi.
- Porus provided a strong resistance to Alexander.
- Alexander remained in India for 19 months (326-325 B.C.)
- Alexander's campaign opened up four distinct routes by land and sea.
- Alexandria and Boukephala were Greek settlements which were established in the North West.
- Alexander's historian Nearchus has left valuable geographical accounts.
- Battle of Hydaspes was fought between Porus and Alexander.
- Alexander sent 20,000 oxen to Macedonia for use in Greece.
- The Sati system and slave trade was prevalent in the society.
- Alexander's invasion paved the way for the expansion of Mauryan Empire in North-West India.
- Alexander's campaign opened up four distinct routes by land and sea.

THE MAURYAN EMPIRE (321 BC - 289 BC)

Chandragupta Maurya (322-295 B.C.)

- The Mauryan dynasty was founded by Chandragupta Maurya with the help of Chanakya or Kautilya.
- Brahamanical texts say he was born of Mura, a sudra women in the court of the Nandas.
- An earlier Buddhist tradition says he belonged to the Moriya Kshatriya clan.
- In some texts, he is referred to as Vrishala and Kulahina.

- He fought Seleucus in 305 B.C.
- Seleucus surrendered a large territory including Paropanisadai (Kabul), Aria (Herat), Arachosia (Gandhara) and Gedrosia (Baluchistan), in return for 500 elephants.
- According to Jaina tradition, Chandragupta was converted to Jainism.
- Chandragupta Maurya passed his last days at Sravanbelagola near Mysore.
- Seleucus sent an ambassador Megasthenes to the Mauryan court.
- Megasthenes wrote the text 'Indica'.

Bindusara (298-272 B.C.)

- Bindusara succeeded Chandragupta Maurya.
- In Jain literature, he has been called as 'Simhasen'.
- Antiochus sent Daimachus as an ambassador to Bindusara's court.
- Ptolemy Philadelphus of Egypt sent Dionysius as ambassador.
- He was known as Amitraghata. He was also known as Amitrochates.
- He wrote to Antiochus-I of Syria and asked for some sweet, wine, dry figs and a sophist.
- He sent his son Ashoka to quell a rebellion in Taxila.
- He was a follower of Ajivika sect.
- The Syrian ambassador Demiachus was sent to his court.

Ashoka (273-232 B.C.)

- Ashoka (273-232 B.C.) succeeded Bindusara.
- He held vice-royalty of Taxila and Ujjain during his fathers lifetime.
- After his father's death he ascended the throne but formal consecration was delayed for 4 years.
- A Buddhist text says he usurped the throne after killing his 99 brothers.
- He fought the Kalinga war in 260 B.C. in the 9th year of his reign.
- In course of his second Dharmayatra tour (in 21st year of his reign), he visited Lumbini.
- In the 14th year of his reign, he started the institution of Dharma Mahamatras.
- The reverberation of the war drum (Bheri Ghosha) was to become the reverberation of the law (Dhamma Ghosha).
- His Hellenistic contemporaries were Antiochus-II of Syria, Ptolemy-II of Egypt, Antigonus of Macedonia, Magas of Cyrene and Alexander of Epirus.
- He organised the third Buddhist council in the 18th year of his reign at Pataliputra.
- Ashoka banned animal sacrifice, regulated the slaughter of animals for food.
- According to his Maski and Gurjara inscriptions, he was known as Devanam Priya Priyadarshi.
- He was converted to Buddhism by Nigrodh.

Names and Titles of Ashoka

Ashoka	Personal name
Piyadassi	Official name
Ashoka	Maski edit and Gurjara edict
King of Magadha	Bhabru edict
Ashoka Vardhan	Puranas
Ashoka Maurya	Junagarh inscription
Piyadassi	Dipavamsa, Kandhar inscription
Piyadassi Raja	Barabar hill cave inscription

The Mauryan Administration

The King

- The Mauryan government was a centralised bureaucracy in which the nucleus was the king.

The Mantri Parishad

- The king was assisted by Mantri Parishad, whose members included - (i) The Yuvaraj, the crown prince (ii) The Purohita, the chief priest (iii) The Senapati, the commander-in-chief of the army (iv) a few other ministers.

Important officials

Amatyas	: The Secretaries
Sannidhata	: Chief treasury officer
Samaharta	: The collector general of Revenue
Durgapala	: Governor of fort
Antapala	: Governor of the frontier
Akshapatala	: Accountant General
Vachabhumika	: Officer in charge of the rest houses, groves and wells, etc.
Dhammamahamatras	: A new post created by Asoka, empowered with the dual functions of propagating Dhamma and taking care of the common folk for their material well-being.

Lip ikaras : Scribes

Prativedikas : Reporters

Kumaras : The viceroys in charge of a province. In order to check the growing power of the viceroys, the provincial ministers were empowered sufficiently.

Pradesikas : They were the modern district magistrates and in charge of district. They were to make tours once in every 5 years to inspect the entire administration of the areas under control.

Rajukas : They were the later day Patwaris. They were responsible for surveying and assessing the land. In rural areas, they were the judicial officers.

Yukta : A subordinate revenue officer of the district level. He was responsible for the secretarial work of accounting.

Gopa : Responsible for accounts.

Sthanika : The tax collecting officer directly under the control of the Pradesikas.

The village level officers

Gramika : Head of a village. He was generally elected by the people. He was not a paid servant.

Gramvriddhas : Village elders (To assist the Gramika in his work). Every village had its own Panchayat to settle the disputes.

The municipal administration

Nagaraka : The officer in charge of, the city administration.

Sitaadhyaksha : Supervised agriculture.

Panyaadhyaksha : Superintendent of commerce.

Samsthadhyaksha : Superintendent of market.

Pauthavadhyaksha : Superintendent of weight and measures.

Navadhyaksha : Superintendent of Ships.

Sulkadhyaksha : Collector of tolls.

Akaradhyaksha : Superintendent of mines.

Lohadhyaksha : Superintendent of Iron.

Army

- The most striking feature of the Mauryan administration was maintanence of a huge.army They also maintained a Navy.
- According to Megasthenes, the administration of the Army was carried by a board of 30 officers divided into six committees, each committee consisting of 5 members. They are: (i) Army (ii) Cavalry(iii) Elephants (iv) Chariots (v) Navy (vi) Transport.
- The state controlled almost all economic activities.
- Tax collected from peasants varied from 1/4 to 1/6 of the produce.
- The state also provided irrigation facilities and charged water-tax.
- Tolls were also levied on commodities brought to town for sale and they were collected at gate.
- The state enjoyed monopoly in mining, sale of liquor, manufacture of arms, etc.

Location of Important Ashokan Edicts

Location of Major Rock Edicts

1. Kalsi (Dehradun)
2. Manshera (Hazara District Pakistan)
3. Shahbazgarhi (Peshawar)
4. Girnar (Gujarat)
5. Sopara (Near Mumbai)
6. Dhauli (Orissa)
7. Jaugada (Orissa)
8. Maski (Andhra Pradesh)
9. Yerragudi (Andhra Pradesh)

Location of Minor Rock Edicts

1. Bairat
2. Rupnath
3. Sahsaram
4. Brahmagiri
5. Gavimath
6. Jatinga Rameshwar
7. Maski
8. Palkigundu
9. Rajula-Mandagiri
10. Suvarnagiri
11. Yerragudi
12. Gurjara
13. Ahraura

Location of Pillar Edicts

1. Allahabad
2. Delhi-Topra
3. Delhi-Meerut
4. Nigalisagar
5. Lauriya-Araraj
6. Lauriya-Nandangarh
7. Rampurva

Information about Ashokan Edicts

1. 1st major rock edict declares prohibition of animal sacrifice.
2. 2nd major rock edict mentions medical treatment of human and animals.
3. 3rd major rock edict mentions Pradeshikas, Rajukas and Yukta.
4. 4th major rock edict mentions that Bheri Ghosha is replaced by Dhamma Ghosha.
5. 5th major rock edict mentions the appointment of Dhamma Mahamatras.
6. 6th major rock edict mentions Mantri Parishad and officers like Pulisani and Prativedikar.
7. 7th major rock edict mentions religious toleration amongst all sects.
8. 8th major rock edict mentions that he went to Sambodhi in Bodh Gaya.
9. 9th major rock edict mentions the uselessness of various ceremonies.
10. 10th major rock edict mentions that the king desires no more fame.
11. 11th major rock edict explains the policy of Dhamma.
12. 12th major rock edict appeals for toleration amongst sects.
13. 13th major rock edict mentions Kalinga war.
14. 14th major rock edict mentions the purpose of the rock edicts.

Information about Seve Pillar Edicts

1. In the first pillar edict, social code has been mentioned.
2. In the 2nd pillar edict, eye donation has been mentioned.
3. In the 3rd pillar edict, soul and sin has been mentioned.
4. In the 4th pillar edict, Rajukas have been mentioned.
5. In the 5th pillar edict, animal killing is mentioned.
6. The 6th pillar edict mentions the welfare of people.
7. The 7th pillar edict mentions the Dhamma Mahamatras.

Facts about Ashokan Inscriptions

- Maski edict discovered in 1915 is the only edict which mentions the name Ashoka.
- The Topra and Meerut pillars were brought to Delhi by Feroz Shah Tughlaq.
- Ashokan edicts were deciphered by James Princep in 1837.
- The Kaushambi pillar was brought to Calcutta by Jahangir.
- The Bairat inscription was brought to Allahabad by Cunnigham.
- Two major rock edicts at Mansehra and Sahbazgarhi are in Kharoshti script.
- The Qandhar inscription is bilingual - Greek and Aramaic.
- The most of the Ashokan edicts have been written in Brahmi script.
- The language of Ashokan edicts except Qandhar is Prakrit.
- The inscriptions in fragmentary condition found at Lampak / Lamghan are in Aramaic.
- In all the edicts, except the Maski edict, Ashoka refers himself by his title Devanampriya Priyadassi.
- The Allahabad pillar (brought from Kausambi) contains the inscription of Samudragupta and Jahangir also.
- Major rock edicts are fourteen in number.
- Total number of pillar edicts is thirteen, they are inscribed in ten pillars. Out of thirteen, seven are major pillar edicts, four are minor pillar edicts and two are commemorative pillar edicts.
- Of the four minor pillars edicts, one is known as Queen's edict and it is on Allahabad pillar.
- Schism edicts (one each) are found in Allahabad, Sanchi and Sarnath Pillars.
- The commemorative pillar edicts are Rumeindei and Nigalisagar (both in Nepal).
- The longest among the major rock edict is 13th rock edict (in Orissa).
- 7th pillar edict is longest among all the edicts.
- The Allahabad pillar contains first six pillar edicts, Queen's edict, Kosam Schism edicts, Prasasti of Samudragupta written by Harisena and some decrees of Jahangir.
- Kharosthi script was derived from Persian Aramaic.

18 Tirthas as mentioned in Arthashastra

1.	Mantrin	Chief Minister
2.	Purohita	Chief Priest
3.	Senapati	Commader-in-Chief
4.	Yuvaraja	Crown prince (These four were the highest functionaries among the tirthas)
5.	Dauvarika	Chamberlain
6.	Antarvesika	Chief of the Harem
7.	Prasastri	Inspector General of Prisons
8.	Samaharta	Collector General
9.	Sanidhata	Treasury Chief
10.	Pradeshtri	Divisional Commissioner
11.	Nayaka	City Constable
12.	Paura	Governor of the City
13.	Vyavaharika	Chief Judge
14.	Karmantika	Chief of the Mines
15.	Mantri	President of the Council. Parishadhyaksha
16.	Dandapal	Police Chief
17.	Dvarapala	Chief of the Home Defence
18.	Antapal	Chief of the Frontier Defence

South Indian Dynasties

The Chalukyas of Badami (543-757 A.D.)

- The Vakatakas in the Deccan were followed by the Chalukyas of Badami.
- The Chalukyas established their base at Badami (Vatapi) in Bijapur district of Karnataka .
- The Chalukyas claimed their descent either from Manu or Moon .
- Pulakesin-I (543-66), founder of the Chalukya dynasty, established a small kingdom with Badami / Vatapi in Bijapur District as its capital .
- Kirtivarman-I expanded the kingdom by wars against the Kadambas of Banavasi and the Nalas of Bastar.
- Pulakesin-II was able to check Harsha's design to conquer Deccan .
- Aihole inscription is a compliment written by his court poet Ravikirti.
- He sent an ambassador to Persian king Khusrau II in 625 A.D. and also received one from him .
- The Chinese pilgrim Hiuen-Tsang visited his kingdom.
- Pallava ruler Narsimhavarman I invaded the Chalukya kingdom, killed Pulakesin II and captured Badami.
- Vishnu Vardhan, son of Pulakesin II , founded the eastern branch of the Chalukyas with its capital at Vengi.

The Pallavas (560–803 A.D.)

- The Pallavas played an important role after the fall of Satvahanas in 3rd century A.D. until the rise of the Cholas.
- The origin of Pallavas is a debatable issue.
- Pallava dynasty was founded by **Simhavishnu** in 560 A.D.
- Mahendravarman-I was defeated by Pulakesin-II.
- Narasimhavarman was the greatest king. He defeated Pulakesin II and captured Badami/Vatapi, so took the title of Vatapikonda.
- Narsimhavarman also defeated Cholas, Cheras and Pandyas, thus became supreme in South India.
- Narsimhavarman was a great builder having constructed Mamallapuram and the various buildings here. During his reign, Hieun Tsang visited Kanchi.
- Narsimhavarman II constructed the shore temple of Mamallapuram and the Kailasnath temple of Kanchi. He sent embassies to China to encourage maritime trade.
- The Chalukya Vikramadita-II attacked the Pallava capital during the reign of Paramesvarman.
- Nandivarman-II was a worshipper of Vishnu. He built Vaikuntaperumal temple at Kanchi.
- The last Pallava ruler, Aparajita Pallava, was defeated by Aditya Chola.
- Kanchi, tha Pallava capital, was a great centre of Sanskrit learning.
- Both Bharavi and Dandin, the authors of 'Kirtarjuniyam'' and 'Dashkumarcharitam', respectively lived in the Pallava court.
- The scientific works of Varahamihira and the poetry of Kalidasa were well-known in the Pallava country.
- Most of the kings were accomplished scholars and Mahendravarman- I himself wrote the famous 'Mattavilasa Prahasana'.

The Gangas

- The Gangas were the contemporaries of the Chalukyas and the Pallavas.
- They ruled over a large part of modern Mysore.

- The region was called after them as Gangavadi.
- The founder of the Ganga dynasty was Konkanivarman Dharmamahadhiraja.
- The Gangas had matrimonial alliances with the Pallavas, Chalukyas and Rashtrakutas.

The Kadambas

- The Kadamba dynasty was founded by Mayur Sarman.
- The Kadambas ruled from Banvasi from 345 A.D. to 365 AD.
- Kakusthavarman (435-455 AD.) was the most powerful ruler of the dynasty.
- Kakusthavarman established matrimonial relations with the Gangas and the Guptas.

The Cholas

- The Cholas were the feudatories of the Pallavas.
- The originator of Chola dynasty was Vijayalaya, who was at first a feudatory of the Pallavas. He captured Tanjore in 850 AD.
- The prominent Chola rulers were Rajaraja (985-1014 AD.) and his son Rajendra I (1014-1044 AD.)
- Raja built the Saiva temple of Rajarajeshwara at Tanjore.
- Rajendra I assumed the title of Gangaikondachola and built a city called Gangaikondacholapuram.
- The Chola empire was distributed into Mandalams or provinces and these in turn were divided into Valanadu and Nadu.
- Chola rulers marked their victories by erecting a number of Shiva and Vishnu temples.
- During the reign of Rajendra I, a naval expedition was sent against the Sri Vijaya empire.
- The Bay of Bengal was converted into a 'Chola lake'.
- The Chola rulers fought constantly with the Chalukyas of Kalyani.
- Rajaraja I granted a village for the maintenance of Buddhist vihara at Nagapattam.
- The king was the most important person in the Chola administration .
- The Cholas maintained a large army consisting of elephants, cavalry and infantry .
- Rajaraja gave his daughter Kundavai to Vimaladitya (Eastern Chalukya of Vengi) and restored Vengi to him.
- Rajaraja-I sent his son Rajendra-I to capture Banavasi and sack Manyakhet of Western Chalukyas .
- During the reign of Rajaraja, Maldives was captured.
- Rajaraja conferred the title of 'Mahadandanayaka' upon Rajendra-I for his victory over Pandyas and Keralas .
- Rajaraja-I started the system of land survey called 'kadamb'.
- Adhirajendra was murdered in a public revolt.
- Kulotunga-I of Vengi united the kingdom of Eastern Chalukyas of Vengi and Chola kingdom. His other name was Rajendra-II. He was given the title of Sangam Tavirtta (he who abolished tolls).
- Rajendra II was crowned in the battle field of Koppam. He was given the title of Prakesari .
- Vira Rajendra Rajakesari defeated Western Chalukyas king Someswara-I Ahvamalla in the battle of Kudal Sangman (Kurnool district). He foiled all efforts of Vijayabahu of Sri Lanka to extend his authority and drive away the Cholas from Sri Lanka.
- After the decline of Cholas, their place was taken by the Hoysalas of Dwarsamudra and Pandyas of Madurai.

Tripartite Struggle

(Palas, Pratiharas and Rashtrakutas)

- A number of powerful empires arose in Northern India and the Deccan between 756 A.D.-1000 A.D.
- The Gurjara Pratiharas, the Palas and the Rastrakutas emerged almost at the same time.
- These three powers fought for the supremacy over Kannauj.

The Pratiharas

- The Pratiharas emerged from Gurjarata or South West Rajasthan.
- They resisted Arab incursions from Sindh into Rajasthan.
- Pratihara dynasty was founded by Nagabhatta-I.
- Pratihara power revived under Nagabhatta-II. He defeated Dharmapala near Monghyr (Mudgir).
- Pratiharas traced their descent from Lakshamana (the solar race).
- Their capital was at Mahodaya (Kannauj).
- The real founder and the greatest king was Bhoja (836-885 AD.).
- Bhoja is also called Mihir Bhoja. He defeated Devapala and got Kannauj back.
- Bhoja was a devotee of Vishnu and adopted the title of Adivaraha.

Important Pratihara Rulers

- Vatsaraja 773-793
- Nagabhata I 793-833
- Bhoja 836-885
- Mahipala 908-942

The Palas

- The pala empire was founded by Gopala in 750 AD.
- Gopala was elected as the king by the notable men of the area.
- Gopala was succeeded by his son Dharmapala in 770 AD.
- Palas established their rule in Bengal and Bihar.
- Dharmapala (770-810) was defeated by Dhruva (Rashtrakuta) and Nagabhatt II (Pratihara).
- During Dharmapala, two brothers Indra and Chakra clashed for Kannauj.
- Dharmapala revived the Nalanda University, which had been famous all over the eastern world.
- He also founded the Vikramshila University.

The Rashtrakutas

- Founded by Dantidurga in the Deccan.
- Their capital was at Manyakhet or Malkhed near modern day Sholapur (earlier at Ellora).
- Amoghvarsha rulled for 68 years.
- Amoghvarsha wrote 'Kavirajamarga', a book on Poetics Kannada.
- Amoghavarsha first transferred capital from Ellora to Manyakhet or Malkhed.
- Indira III (915-927) defeated Mahipala (Pratihara) and sacked Kannauj in 915. Indra was the most powerful ruler of his time.
- Rashtrakutas imported horses from Arabia, West-Asia and central Asia.
- In the Rashtrakuta kingdom, the directly administered areas were divided into Rashtras (provinces), Visaya and Bhukti.
- The last ruler Karka was overthrown by Tailap, the founder of Chalukyas of Kalyani.
- Dantidurga built the Dasavatara temple at Ellora.
- Krishna-I built the Kailasa or Shiva temple at Ellora in the 9th century A.D.
- The great Apabhramsha poet Svayambhu and his son lived at the Rashtrakuta court.

The Parmaras

- The Parmaras ruled in the Malwa region.
- The Parmaras initially had their capital at Ujjain.
- The Parmaras later transferred their capital to Dhara.
- Vakpati Munj was the founder of the Parmara dynasty.
- Vakpati was a great patron of art and literature.
- Padmagupta, Dhananjya, graced the court of Vakpati.
- The greatest ruler of dynasty was Bhoja.
- Bhoja built the city of Bhojapur.
- Bhoja founded a college, Bhojshala near Dhara.

The Gahadavalas

- The Gahadavala dynasty was founded by Chandradeva.
- The capital of Gahadavalas was Kannauj.
- Govindchandra conquered east Malwa.
- Govindchandra's minister for peace and war, Lakshmidhara, wrote Krityakalpataru.
- Jaychandra was defeated by Lakshman Sena of Bengal.
- In the Battle of Chandawar (1194 A.D.), Muhammad Ghori defeated Jaichandra.
- Harischandra was the last ruler of Gahadavala dynasty.

The Chauhans

- The Chahamana (Chauhan) dynasty emerged near Sakambhari (Ajmer).
- The Chauhans were the feudatories of Pratiharas.
- Simharaja declared independence in the middle of 10th century.
- Ajayraja founded the city of Ajayameru (Ajmer).
- Prithviraj Chauhan ascended to the throne in 1177 A.D.
- Prithviraja Chauhan defeated Muhammad Ghori in the first battle of Tarain (1191 A.D.).
- In the second battle of Tarain (1192 A.D.), Muhammad Ghori defeated Prithviraj Chauhan.

Kashmir

- Three dynasties Karkota, Utpala and Lohar ruled Kashmir during 800 A.D. to 1200 A.D.
- Karkota dynasty was founded by Durlabh Vardhana.
- Lalitaditya Muktapida defeated Yasovarman of Kannauj.
- Lalitaditya built the famous Sun temple at Martand.

- Utpala dynasty was founded by Avantivarman.
- Queen Didda ruled from 980 A.D. to 1003 A.D.
- Sangramraja founded the Lohara dynasty.
- King Harsha belonged to Lohara dynasty.
- Kalhana wrote 'Rajatarangini' in 12th century.

The Chandellas

- The dynasty was founded by Nanuka in the early years of 9th century and his capital was Khajuraho.
- Dhanga was the first independent king of the Chandella dynasty and assumed the title Maharajadhiraja.
- He was succeeded by Ganda who in turn was succeeded by Vidyadhara.
- During Vidyadhara's reign Mahmud of Ghazni invaded Kalinjar in 1019 and again in l022.
- In 1165, Parmardideva was defeated by Prithviraj Chauhan.
- Qutub-ud-din Aibak defeated Parmadideva and occupied greater part of Bundelkhand.
- Alauddin Khalji captured the whole of the kingdom.
- Temples of Khajuraho were built by Chandellas.
- The most prominent among the Khajuraho temples are the Kandariya Mahadeva, Devi Jagadamba, Parsvanatha, Lakshamana and the Viswanatha temples.

The Senas

- The Senas supplanted the Palas in Bengal.
- The Senas called themselves 'Brahma Kshatriya'.
- Vijaysena ascended the throne in l095 A.D. and enlarged the frontiers off senas.
- Vijayapuri and Vikrampuri were two capitals of Senas.
- Vijayasena was succeed by his son Ballalsena.
- Ballalsena established the tradition of 'Kulinism.'
- Ballalsena wrote 'Adbhutsagar' and 'Dansagar',
- Ballalsena was succeeded by Lakshmanasena.
- Bakhtiyar Khalji invaded Bengal during the reign of Lakshmanasena.
- Jayadeva, Dhoyi, Halayudha adorned Lakshmana sena's court.

Famous Scholars and their Patrons

Scholar	Patron
Udayraja	: Mahmud Begrha (Gujarat)
Hemchandra	: Kumarpala (Chalukyas of Anhilwara)
Nagarjuna	: Kanishka
Amar Singh	: Chandragupta Vikramaditya
Ravikirti	: Pulkesin-II
Vakpatiraj	: Yashovarman of Kannauj
Bhav Bhuti	: Yashovarman of Kannuaj
Harishena	: Samudragupta
Rajshekhar	: Mahendrapala and Mahipala
Somadeva	: Prithviraja-III
Chandrabardai	: Prithviraja-III
Banabhatta	: Harshavardhana
Dandin	: Narsinghavarman (Pallava)
Bharvi	: Simhavishnu (Pallav)
Gunadhya	: Hala (Satvahana)
Mahaviracharya	: Amoghvarsha (Rashtrakuta)
Jinasen	: Amoghvarsha (Rashtrakuta)
Sakatyayan	: Amoghvarsha (Rashtrakuta)
Jayadeva	: Lakshmanasena (Bengal)
Bilhan	: Vikramaditya VI (Chalukya of Kalyani)
Vijnaneshwar	: Vikramaditya VI
Lakshmidhar	: Govind Chandra
Shri Harsha	: Jaychand
Firdausi	: Mahmud Ghazni
Amir Khusro	: Balban to Alauddin Khalji

Chapter 2 Medieval Indian History

MUSLIM INVASIONS

The Ghaznavids

- Alaptagin established an independent kingdom with its capital at Ghazni.
- Mahmud ascended the throne (998-1030) at Ghazni.
- Firdausi was the poet laureate at the court of Mahmud.
- Firdausi wrote 'Shah Namah'.
- Mahmud claimed descent from Iranian legendary king Afrasiyab.
- Mahmud is said to have made 17 raids into India.
- The initial raids were directed against the Hindustani rulers.
- In 1001 Jayapala, the Hindushahi ruler was defeated.
- Jaypala's son 'Anandpal' succeeded him to the throne.
- The Battle of Waihind (1008-1009) was fought between Mahmud and Ananda.
- After the battle, Punjab passed into the hands of Ghaznavis.
- The subsequent raids of Mahmud into India were aimed at plundering the rich temples and cities.
- Mahmud invaded Kannauj in 1018 and Somnath in 1025 A.D.
- Mahmud died at Ghazni in 1030 A.D.

Mahmud Ghazni's 17 Attacks

1.	1000-1001	(against Jaipal of Peshawar) Sindh.
2.	1001	(against Anandpal of Peshawar) Sindh
3.	1002-1004	Multan
4.	1005-1006	Multan
5.	1007-1008	Nawasa Shah of Multan
6.	1008-1009	Anandpal of Hindushahi of Sind
7.	1009-1010	Narayanpur (Rajasthan)
8.	1010-1011	Daud of Multan
9.	1012-1013	Thaneswar (The Mecca of Hindus)
10.	1013-1014	Nandana (against Anandpal)
11.	10-15-1016	Kashmir valley (unsuccessful)
12.	1016-1018	Kannauj, Mathura
13.	1020-1021	Kalinjar
14.	1021-1022	Lahore
15.	1025-1026	Somnath
16.	1026-1027	Jats of Sind
17.	1027	Khokars of Punjab

The Turkish Conquest

- The Ghurid empire rose into prominence in North-West Afghanistan.
- The Ghurids had started as vassals of Ghazni, but had soon thrown off its yoke.
- The power of the Ghurids increased under Sultan Alauddin who earned the title of 'jahan-soz'.
- In 1173, Shahabuddin Muhammad (Muhammad Ghori) ascended the throne at Ghazni.
- By 1190, Muhammad Ghori had conquered Peshawar, Lahore and Sialkot.
- In India, Chauhans had captured Delhi from the Tomars.
- Conflict between Muhammad Ghori and Prithviraj Chauhan started with rival claims for Tabarhinda (Bhatinda).
- The First Battle of Tarain was fought in 1191 A.D.
- In this battle, the Ghuri forces were completely routed. Muhammad Ghori's life was saved by a young Khalji horseman.
- The second battle of Tarain was fought in 1192 A.D.
- This battle is considered as one of the turning points in Indian history.
- Prithviraj Chauhan escaped but was captured near Saraswati.
- After Tarain, Muhammad Ghori returned to Ghazni.
- He left the affairs in India in the hands of his trusted slave Qutubuddin Aibak.
- In 1194 A.D., Muhammad Ghori returned to India.
- The battle of Chandawar (1194 A.D.) was fought between Muhammad Ghori and Jai Chandra.
- Jai Chandra was defeated in the battle of Chandawar.
- The battles of Tarain and Chandawar laid the foundations of Turkish rule in India.

Important Literary Works of Ancient India

Literary Work		Author
Ashthadhyayi	:	Panini
Mahabhashya	:	Patanjali
Manu Smriti	:	Manu
Arthshastra	:	Kautilya
Chhanda-Sutra	:	Pingala
Buddhacharita	:	Ashvaghosha
Saripurta Prakarna	:	Ashvaghosha
Saundaranand	:	Ashvaghosha
Kumarsambhavam	:	Kalidasa
Raghuvansa	:	Kalidasa
Malvikagnimitram	:	Kalidasa
Sisupalvadha	:	Magha
Natyashastram	:	Bharat Muni
Ratnavali	:	Harshavardhana
Nagananda	:	Harshavardhana
Maltimadhav	:	Bhavabhuti
Uttararamcharita	:	Bhavabhuti
Meghaduta	:	Kalidas
Gita Govinda	:	Jayadeva
Harshacharita	:	Banabhatta
Ramcharita	:	Sandhyakar Nandi
Gaudvaho	:	Vakpati Raj
Daskumarcharita	:	Dandin
Vashvadatta	:	Subandhu
Kathasaritsagar	:	Somdeva
Panchatantra	:	Vishnu Sharma
Hitopdesha	:	Narayan Pandit
Kamasutra	:	Vatsayan
Mattavilasa Prahasana	:	Mahendravarman-I
Nitisara	:	Kamandaka
Charak Samhita	:	Charak
Dayabhaga	:	Jimutavahana
Nighantu	:	Yaska
Mitakshara	:	Vijneshvra
Brihat Kathamanjari	:	Kshemendra
Mahaviracharita	:	Bhavabhuti

DELHI SULTANATE (1206-1526 A.D.)

The Slave Dynasty (1206-1290 A.D.)

- After the death of Muhammad Ghori, his slave, Qutub-ud-din Aibak laid the foundation of Slave dynasty in 1206 A.D.
- Qutub-ud-din Aibak ruled from Lahore.
- Qutub-ud-din Aibak was known as Lakh Baksh for his magnanimity.
- He built Quwwattul Islam mosque in Delhi and Adhai Din Ka Jhopda in Ajmer.
- He laid the foundation of Qutub Minar, in memory of famous sufi saint Khwaja Qutbuddin Bakhtiyar Kaki in 1199 A.D.
- Aibak was a Turk of 'Aibak tribe' which means in Turkish language 'Lord of the Moon'.
- He began his reign with the modest title **'malik'** and **'siphasalar'** which had been conferred upon him by Muhammad Ghori.
- Under Ghori, he was 'amir-i-akhur', the master of stables.
- He made Indraprastha near Delhi, his military headquarters.
- After Qutub-ud-din, Aram Shah ascended the throne.
- **Iltutmish** ruled from 1211-1236 A.D.
- Iltutmish was the real founder of the Sultanate.
- First appointed by Aibak as Amir-i-Shikar.
- He was governor of the iqtas of Gwalior and Baran (Bulandshahar) in succession.
- At the time of Aibak's death, he was the Governor of Badaun.
- He was the son-in-law of Aibak.
- He made Delhi as capital of his empire.
- He was nominated by Aibak in 1206 at the instance of Muhammad Ghori.
- Defeated Aram Shah and took the throne in 1211.
- Iltutmish defeated Tajuddin Yaldoz, the sultan of Ghazni in 1216 at Tarain (third battle of Tarain).
- In 1217, he defeated Nasiruddin Qabacha, the governor of Lahore at Mansura.
- Introduced the silver tanka and the copper jital, two basic coins of the Sultanate period.
- He reconquered Multan and Bengal in 1227-1228, reasserted his authority in Bengal and Bihar in 1229.
- In 1229, he received a deed of investiture from the ***'Abassid Caliph of Baghdad'***.
- In 1226, Iltutmish wrested Ranthambhor and Mandor. In 1233, he attacked Malwa and captured Bhilsa. He also conquered Gwalior and Jalore.
- He issued a purely arabic coinage of silver and was the first to do so.
- He organised the Yurkan-i-Chahalgani.
- Minhas-us-Siraj, his contemporary historian, has praised him.

- Iltutmish declared **Razia** to be his successor.
- The amirs put Ruknuddin Firoz Shah on the throne.
- He was killed and Razia became the Sultan.
- She was the first and the last Muslim woman ruler of the Delhi Sultanate.
- Iltutmish's Wazir, Nizamul Mulk Junayadi rebelled and was defeated.
- Muhazabuddin (a Tajik) was made Deputy Wazir.
- Yakut (Ethiopian/Abyssinian) was made Amir-i-Akhur.
- Raziya's reign marked the beginning of a struggle for power between the monarchy and the Turkish nobles called 'forty' or the 'chahalgani'.
- She discarded the female apparel and started holding court with her face unveiled.
- Raziya and Altunia were killed at Kaithal in 1240.
- The contemporary historian Minhaj described her as a great sovereign, endowed with all the admirable characteristics and qualifications necessary of kings.
- Khutba was read and coins struck in Raziya's name.
- The successor of Razia (1236-1240 were Muizuddin Bahram Shah (1240-1242) and Alauddin Masud Shah (1242-1246).
- In 1246, Nasiruddin Mahmud (1246-1265) ascended the throne, but the real power was in the hands of Balban.
- **Balban or Ulugh Khan** (1246-1286) was a member of the chahalgani founded by Iltutmish. In 1250, the Balban married his daughter to the Sultan.
- Balban became Naib-i-Mamlakat and got the title of Ulugh Khan (Great Khan) by Sultan.

Balban

- Started Iranian practice of Sijda (bowing before Sultan) and paibos (kissing of monarch's feat) -an unislamic trace.
- Abolished Chalisa or Chehalgani.
- Held darbar (court) on Iranian model.
- Sought to increase the prestige and power of the monarchy by curbing nobles.
- No jokes and laughter in courts.
- Stopped drinking wine and made nobles to do so.
- Called himself the Nasir Amir-ul Momin or Caliph's right hand man.
- Claimed descent from Afrasiyab (the legend of Iranian hero).
- Real organiser or consolidator of the Delhi Sultanate.
- First Sultan to propound the theory of kingship. According to it, king is the shadow of God. (Zil-i-Ilahi)
- He separated finance department from military department.
- He reorganised the Diwan-i-Arz (military department).
- Built strong forts at Kampil, Patiali, and Bhojpur to suppress Hindu rebels.
- Bhatinda, Sunam and Samana forts strengthened as frontier outposts.
- Kept friendly relations with Halaku and received his envoys.
- In 1279, Chaghatai Mongols defeated by Prince Mahmud, Bughra Khan and Malik Bektars.
- In 1285, Mongols under Taimur invaded India and killed Prince Mahmud (Khan Sahid).
- After Balban's death in 1286, Kaiqubad (1287-1290) and Kaimurs became Sultans for a brief period.
- After 3 months, Kaimurs, the last ilbari was killed and Jalaluddin ascended the throne.

The Khalji Dynasty (1290-1320 A.D.)

- The Khalji Dynasty was founded by Jalaluddin Khalji.
- Jalaluddin began to rule from Kilkhori.
- Malik Chhajju (Balban's nephew and governor of Kara) rebelled, but was pardoned and Kara was given to Ali Gurshap (Alauddin Khalji).
- A gang of thugs were banished to Bengal showing leniency.
- In 1291-1292, Mongols under Abdulla were defeated at Dipalpur.
- Ulghus (descendent of Changez) embraced Islam and these new mussalmans settled near Delhi.
- In 1292, Ranthambhor was beseized, but later abandoned.
- Sidi Maula, a darvesh of Delhi was accused of conspiracy by Maydari Qalandars was trampled by an elephant ordered by prince Arkali Khan.
- Jalaluddin was assassinated in 1296 at Kara by Alauddin Khalji.
- Alauddin Khalji's original name was Ali Gurshap.
- Alauddin Khalji was the Governor of Kara.
- Mongols under Kadar were repulsed by Zafar Khan (Rustam-i- Hind).
- In 1299, Mongol leader Qutugh Khawaja was repulsed by Alauddin Khalji and Jafar Khan. the latter was killed at Kili near Delhi.
- In 1303 Mongols under Targhil were defeated near Siri, (near Delhi).
- In 1304-1305, Alibegh and Khwaja Tash and Tartag were defeated.

- During Jalaluddin's reign, Alauddin had captured Bhilsa, Devagiri (Ramchandra) and Chanderi.
- The Mongol incursions were repulsed by Zafar Khan during the reign of Alauddin Khalji. The new mussalmans were slaughtered.
- Alauddin captured Gujarat in 1297 A.D. During that time it was ruled by Rai Karan. He sacked Anhilwara and Somnath and married to the queen of Rai karan Named Kamla Devi. He also captured Malik Kafur and took him to the royal court.
- In 1300, he captured Ranthambhor which was under Hamirdeva.
- During Gujarat campaign, Malik Kafur (Hazar dinari) was captured from Cambay.
- Alp Khan was made the Governor of Gujarat.
- In 1303, Chittor under Ratan Singh was captured.
- Khizr Khan was made the Governor of Chittor.
- Chittor was renamed as Khizarabad.
- In the Deccan, Malik Kafur attacked Devagiri in 1306-1307.
- Ramchandradeva was given title the 'Rai-i-Rayan'.
- Warangal under Pratap Rudra Deva was attacked in 1309 (Kakatiya).
- In 1310. Dwarasamudra under Vir Balala Deva III (Hoysala) was invaded.
- In 1311, Mabar/Madura under Vira Pandya was attacked. But none of the southern states were annexed.
- For successful Deccan campaigns, Kafur was awarded title Malik Naib (Regent).
- Malik Kafur was a Eunuch.
- During south campaigns, Kafur reached up to Rameshwaram where he built a mosque.

Alauddin Khalji

- New land settlement was introduced.
- Cultivators were brought under direct control of states and middlemen (Khut, Chaudhari, Mukaddams) were deprived of powers and privileges.
- Organised standing army, first Sultan to do so. Soldiers were paid in cash.
- Appointed Diwan-i-Mustakharaj to collect arrears.
- Ghari (house tax) and Charai (grazing tax) levied.
- All Patwari accounts were audited.
- Kismat-i-Khuti (headmen's cess) was abolished.
- Market reforms for the maintenance of a large army cheaply.
- Prices of goods were fixed on the principle of Bar Award (Production cost).
- Land revenue from Khalisa village was paid in cash.
- Diwan-i-Riyasat, ministry of commerce, was organised under Malik Yakub.
- Three types of markets:
  (i) Sahna-i-mandi (grain market)
  (ii) Sarai Adl (cloth and groceries market)
  (iii) Market for horses, cattle and slaves.
- Malik Qabul looked after grain market.
- Sarai Adl was near Badaun gate under Rais Parwana.
- Nayaks were grain merchants.
- Multanis traded mainly in cloth.
- Alauddin Khalji paid his soldiers in cash.
- Cavalry was the main stay, 234 tankas per year for maintaining one horse (Yak Aspa) and 78 more for two (Do Aspa).
- Dagh or branding of horses was introduced. Chehra or descriptive role of soldier was also introduced.
- Diwan-i-Arz as military department. Arz-i-Mumalik was the commander in chief.
- Alauddin Khalji adopted title Sikandar-i-Saini (the second Alexander) inscribed in his coins.
- After Alauddin's death, his son Mubarak Khalji ascended the throne. He declared himself the caliph and took the title 'Al wasiq Billah'. He was killed and succeeded by Nasiruddin Khusrau Shah. He was the only Hindu to sit on the throne of Delhi.

The Tughlaq Dynasty (1320-1414 A.D.)

- Ghiyasuddin Tughlaq ascended the throne after murdering Khusrau Shah.
- Ghiyasuddin Tughlaq ruled from 1320-1325.A.D.
- Ghiyasuddin Tughlaq belonged to the Qarauna Tribe.
- He was first Sultan to use the term Ghazi with his name.
- He banned sale and production of wine.
- He exempted Khuts, Mukaddams from tax.
- He encouraged cultivation by digging canals, first to do so.
- He laid the foundation of Tughlaqabad Fort.
- His relation with Nizamuddin Auliya soured because he wanted gift and money back given by Khusrau Khan to Auliya.
- Prince Jauna Khan's (title Ulugh Khan) Warangal campaign (1321) against Kakatiya ruler failed with rumours of the sultan's death.
- In 1323, second Warangal campaign of Jauna Khan succeeded and Telengana was annexed.
- In 1324-1325, Ghiyasuddin invaded Bengal and defeated Ghiasuddin Bahadur. On return journey, Tirhut, under Raja Harpal Deva was annexed.

- Died in the collapse of the victory pavilion for the Bengal campaign built by Jauna Khan at Afghanpur near Delhi.
- Ibn Batuta accused Jauna Khan of patricide. Barani says that a had stage collapsed due to lightening or parade of elephants.
- Muhammad bin Tughlaq is one of the most controversial figures in Sultanate history.
- Muhammad bin Tughlaq's original name was Jauna Khan.
- Muhammad bin Tughlaq ruled from 1325-1351.A.D.

Muhammad-Bin-Tughlaq

- Had discussion with Jain saint Jinaprabha Suri and enjoyed playing hockey.
- Allowed Indians into services, even son of gardeners, cooks, musicians and weavers.
- In1325, Mongol under Tamrashirin reached Meerut but were repelled.
- Bahauddin Gurshap, Governor of Sagar (M.P.) rebelled and was flayed alive in 1326.
- Believed in 'Divine rights of kings'.
- First sultan to grant loans to farmers (sondhar).
- Increased land tax 1/2 in Doab.
- Neglected religion in matters of politics.
- Created agriculture department diwan-i-kohi.
- Organised army on decimal model of Mongols.
- Made centrally located Devagiri (Daulatabad) his capital in 1328-1329.
- He launched token currency.
- After repulsing an attack of Mongols he aimed to captured Khurasan and Iraq. He organised a huge army but later disbanded it.
- His Qarachill expedition 'was launched in the Kumaon hills to counter Chinese incursions. His army suffered heavy setbacks.
- He also organised the Kangra expedition.
- He instituted agricultural reforms. He fixed the land revenue at half the produce and not on the basis of produce.
- When a large part of India was ravaged by famine and plague, he shifted to Swargdwari, 100km east of Delhi.
- Harihara and Bukka founded the Vijaynagar kingdom in 1336.
- Hasan founded the Bahmani kingdom in Deccan in 1347.
- His end came when he was in Thatta to quell one of the many rebellions that took place during his reign.
- Muhammad Bin Tughlaq was succeeded by Firoz Shah Tughlaq.
- Firoz Tughlaq ruled from 1351 A.D. to 1388 A.D.
- Firoz Tughlaq has been described as "not even a mediocre military leader".

Firoz Shah Tughlaq

- Irrigation extended massively by digging canals and wells.
- Gardens and orchard's planted. Established 1200 gardens around Delhi for grapes.
- As well as 23 taxes were abolished. Only 4 taxes sanctioned by shariat were levied.
  - Kharaj (1/1 Oth of produce)
  - Zakat (Alms for poor Muslims)
  - Jaziya (poll tax on non-Muslims)
  - Khams (1/15th of the spoils of war)
- Jaziya was separated from land tax, earlier it was part of land tax.
- Jaziya was also imposed on Brahmins (earlier exempted) were exempted from the tax.
- Sharb (Irrigation tax), 1/ 10th of produce was imposed.
- Free hospitals (Dar-ul-Shafa), marriage bureau and employment bureau were set-up.
- Officials were paid by iqta grants, very few were paid in cash.
- Soldiers and higher officials post became hereditary.
- In 1353, led campaign against Haji Illyas of Bengal but failed siege of lkadalamud fort.
- In 1358, second Bengal campaign against Sikandar Shah Ilyas who accepted Firoz's suzerainty.
- Raja Gajpati of Jajnagar (Orissa) was attacked and Jagannath temple of Puri was sacked .
- In 1365, Nagarkot campaign was successful. 1300 Sanskrit manuscripts from Jawalamukhi temple were collected and got translated into Persian as the Dalai-i-Firoz Shahi (by Azizudin Khan).
- He had 180,000 slaves and setup Diwan-i-Bandagan (for slaves).
- Founded towns of Jaunpur named after Jauna Khan, Hisar Firoza, Fatehabad and Firozabad (Firoz Shah Kotla, the 5th city of Delhi).
- Topara and Meerut pillars of Ashoka were brought to Delhi.
- Diwan-i-Khairat, the chairty bureau, was formed.
- Introduced new coins Adha (1/2 Jital) and Bikh (1/4th Jital), Shashgani was 6 jitals and Hastgani 8 jitals.
- Firoz Shahi Madrasa was built at Firozabad,
- Banned unislamic practices e.g., prohibiting women to pray graves of sun saints.

- He erased palace paintings.
- He repaired the Qutub minar which had been struck by lightening.
- The chief architect of Firoz was Ghazi Shahna.
- He wrote Fautuhat-i-Firoz Shahi.
- He had great regard for the Caliph of Egypt and styled himself as his deputy.
- He revived the jagir system which had been abolished by Alauddin.
- After Firoz Shah Tughlaq, Muhammad Khan, Ghiyasuddin Tughlaq Shah-II. Abu Baqr, Nasiruddin Muhammad, Humayun and finally Nasiruddin Mahmud ascended the throne.
- Taimur invaded Delhi in 1398 A.D.
- Nasiruddin Mahmud fled to Gujarat.
- Nasiruddin Mahmud died in Kaithal.

The Sayyids and The Lodhis

- The Sayyids occupied the throne of Delhi in 1414 A.D.
- Yahya Sirhindi claims that the founder of the Sayyid dynasty was a descendant of the Prophet.
- **Khizr Khan,** the founder of Sayyid dynasty, had collaboration with Taimur.
- As a reward for his service Taimur gave him governorship of Lahore, Multan and Dipalpur.
- After Taimur's departure, he declared himself the Viceroy of Taimur in north-western India.
- Later, he invaded Delhi and became its master.
- Khizr Khan did not rule as a sovereign ruler but professed to rule as the deputy of Taimur's son and successor, Shah Rukh.
- Khizr Khan's three successors Mubarakshah (1421-1433), Muhammad Shah (1434-1443) and Alauddin Alam Shah (1443- 1451) assumed the royal title of Sultan and ruled as sovereign rulers.
- Bahlol Lodhi, the most prominent noble of the State, got the control of Delhi.
- Bahlol Lodhi deposed Shah Alam (or Alam Shah) the last Sayyid sultan, and laid the foundation of the Lodhi dynasty.
- All Sayyid rulers had to face stiff resistance from the Khokhars led by Jasrath.
- The Sayyid dynasty had the shortest lifespan of all Sultanate ruling houses, excluding that of Khaljis.
- The Lodhi's were the first 'Afghans to rule Delhi'.
- **Bahlol Lodhi**, the founder of Lodhi dynasty. (1451-1489).
- He annexed the Sharqi kingdom of Jaunpur in 1484.
- His government was like a tribal confederacy of Afghans on high positions.
- He introduced copper Bahloli coins.
- He was succeeded by **Sikandar Shah Lodi** (Nijam Khan).
- He introduced Gazz-i-sikandari a new yard for land measurement.
- He conquered South Bihar and concluded a treaty of friendship with Alauddin Hussain Shah, ruler of Bengal.
- In 1506, he established the city of Agra (original name Yoginipur) and made it his capital.
- He wrote verses in Persian (130 verses) under the pen name of Gulrukhi.
- Prices of commodities were made cheap by him.
- He forbade unislamic practices because he was a bigoted ruler. Forbade women from visiting graves of saints, prohibition of processions in their memory.
- Jaziya was reimposed by him.

Important Departments and Officials under Delhi Sultanate

Officials	Departments
Wakil-i-Dar	: Royal palace
Diwan-i-Istikak	: Head of pension department
Sahna-i-Mandi	: Head of grain market
Mufti	: Interpreter of shariat
Diwan-i-Mawalim	: Head of administrative tribunal
Sar-Jandar	: Head of royal bodyguards
Sar-i-Jamadar	: Looked after royal garments
Hajib	: An officer under Barbak
Diwan-i-Khas	: Head of royal correspondence department
Barbek/Amir-i-Hajib	: Royal ceremonies
Amir-i-Koh	: Head of agriculture department
Amir-i-Shikar	: Looked after royal hunting
Barid-i-Mamalik	: Head of intelligence department
Ariz	: Military needs, recruitment, horses
Dabiri-Mamalik	: Chief Secretary
Shiqdar	: Head of Shiq
Qazi ul-Qazat	: Chief Justice
Amir	: Officer of Sipalsalar
Amirdad/Dadbau	: Head of Diwan-i-majlis in absence of sultan
Amiran-i-Tuman	: Head of 10,000 soldiers
Amiran-i-Hazara	: Officer of 1000 soldiers
Amiran-i-Sada	: Head of 100 soldiers
Amir-i-Punjah	: Head of 50 soldiers
Amil	: Land revenue collection in Paragana
Qazi	: Justice
Kargun	: Land record keeper
Kotwal	: Law and order
Kharitdar	: Dispatcher of orders
Dabir	: Officer of royal correspondence

Naib Barbak	: Head of royal court
Barid	: Spionage, Intelligence
Malik	: Head of Sipalsalari and Amirs
Mutsarif	: Head of royal Karkhana
Mushrif	: Accountant General
Mustaufi	: Auditor General
Muhatasib	: Public morals

Sultanate Rulers : At a Glance

Slave Dynasty	
Qutb-ud-din Aibak	: 1206-1210 AD
Aram Shah	: 1211 AD
Shamsuddin Iltutmish	: 1211-1236 AD
Ruknuddin Feroz	: 1236 AD
Razia Sultan	: 1236-1240 AD
Muizuddin Behram	: 1242 AD
Alauddin Masud	: 1246 AD
Naseeruddin Mahmud	: 1246-1266 AD
Ghiyasuddin Balban	: 1266-1286 AD
Muizuddin Kaikubad	: 1290 AD
Kaimur	: 1290 AD
Khalji Dynasty	
Jalaluddin Khalji	: 1290-1296 AD
Alauddin Khalji	: 1296-1316 AD
Shihabuddin Omar	: 1316 AD
Mubarak Khalji	: 1316-1320 AD
Khusro Khan	: 1320 AD
Tughlaq Dynasty	
Ghiyasuddin Tughlaq	: 1320-1324 AD
Muhammad Tughlaq	: 1324-1351 AD
Firoz Shah Tughlaq	: 1351-1388 AD
Mohammad Khan	: 1388 AD
Ghiyasuddin Tughlaq Shah-II	:
Abu Baqr	: 1389-1390 AD
Naseeruddin Muhammad	: 1390-1394 AD
Humayun	: 1394-1395 AD
Naseeruddin Mahmud	: 1345-1412 AD
Sayyid Dynasty	
Khizr Khan	: 1414-1420 AD
Mubarak Shah	: 1421-1433 AD
Muhammad Shah	: 1434-1451 AD
Alauddin Alam Shah	: 1443-1451 AD
Lodhi Dynasty	
Bahlol Lodhi	: 1451-1489 AD
Sikander Lodhi	: 1489-1517 AD
Ibrahim Lodhi	: 1517-1526 AD

THE VIJAY NAGAR EMPIRE

- The VIjayanagar Empire was founded by Harihara-I and Bukka-I in 1336 A.D.
- Earlier, they had served under the Kakatiya ruler of Warangal, Prataprudra-II.
- The first dynasty was named (Sangama) after founders' father Sangama.
- Capital city Vijayanagar (The city of victory) was named after their Guru Vidyaranya.
- City of Vijayanagar was located on the bank of Tungabhadra river.
- There are four dynasties in the history of the Vijayanagar empire.
- The first was Sangama dynasty founded by Harihara-I and Bukka in 1336.
- The second was Saluva dynasty founded by Saluva Narasimha in 1485.
- The third was Tuluva dynasty, founded by Vira Narashimha in 1505.
- The fourth was Aravidu dynasty, founded by Tirumala in 1570.
- Raichur Doab was the area of contention between the Vijaynagar and Bahmani rulers.
- Bukka-I fought with the Bahmani Sultan Muhammad Shah-I and signed a treaty with him.
- Harihara-II repulsed the attack of Bahmani Sultan Muzahid Shah.
- Devaraya-I had to face invasion by the Bahmani ruler Firoz Shah and he had to surrender the fort of Bankapur.
- In 1410, Devaraya-I constructed a barrage across the Tungabhadra. He also encouraged the construction of a dam of the river Harihara.
- The famous Telugu poet Srinatha, the author of 'Harivilasam', adorned Devaraya-I's court. The "Pearl Hall" of the palace honoured the men of eminence.
- Devaraya-II was called Immadi Devaraya and Proudha Devaraya. The inscriptions call him as Gajabetekara (the elephant hunter).
- Devaraya-II was the greatest king of Sangama dynasty.
- In order to strengthen his army, Devaraya-II employed muslims in his army and asked his soldiers and officers to learn the archery from them.
- In 1442, Devaraya-II sent a naval expedition against Srilanka and defeated them.
- Devaraya-II wrote two sanskrit works-'Mahanataka Sudhanidhi' and a commentary on the Brahma Sutras of Badarayana.

- The history of the Sangama dynasty ended with the murder of Virupaksha by his own son in 1485.
- **Krishna Deva Raya** (of Tuluva dynasty) was regarded as the greatest of all the Vijayanagar rulers for his military as well as other achievements.
- In battle of Diwani, Krishna Deva Raya defeated Bahmani forces and murdered Yusuf Adil Shah of Bijapur.
- Krishna Deva Raya defeated the rebellious chief of Ummattur, the Gajapati king Prataprudra of Orissa, the Adil Shahi sultan Yusuf Adil Shah and his son Ismail Adil Shah.
- Krishna Deva Raya restored Bahmani sultan Mahmud on the throne of Bidar.
- His political ideas are contained in his Telugu work "Amuktamalayada" . He was known as 'Andhra Bhoja' and 'Abhinava Bhoja'.
- Ashta Diggajas (eight eminent luminaries in literature) adorned his court.
- He built the famous temples of Krishna Swami, Hazara Ramaswami and Vitthala Swami at the capital.
- He built a new city called 'Nagalpura' in memory of his mother Nagalmba.
- He built a large number of Rayagopurams (towers).
- During Sadashiva Raya's reign the obsolute power laid in the hands of **Rama Raya**.
- The Deccan sultans except Berar's joined hands to defeat Vijayanagar in the **Battle of Talikota** (1565).
- After the battle of Talikota, Vijayanagar Government was shifted first to Penukonda and then to Chandragiri.
- King was considered equal to God.
- Achyutadeva Raya had his coronation performed in the Tirupati temple.
- The Vijayanagar kings generally nominated their heirs, usually the eldest prince as appointed Yuvaraja.
- The king had a council of ministers who met in a hall called 'Venkatavilas Mandapa'.
- The Pradhani was the Prime Minister.
- Ministers bore the title of 'Dandanayaka'.
- The Rayasani was an officer who recorded the oral orders of the king.
- The Karanikam was an accountant.
- Nayakara System: In this system, the king distributed land to his dependents called Nayaks.They enjoyed great freedom.
- Amaram: The feudatories bounded by military obligation held amaram (tenure) and were known as Amar Nayaks.
- Harihara-I issued Hanuman type coins. Bukka-I also issued Hanuman-inscribed coins.
- Krishna Deva Raya issued Venkatesha and BalaKrishna-inscribed coins.
- Achyuta Raya issued Garuda type coins.
- Tirumala issued Varaha-inscribed coins.
- Land tax was also called 'cist'.
- Krishna Deva Raya got the land surveyed.

ESTABLISHMENT OF THE MUGHAL RULE

Babur Suri (1526-1530 A.D.)

- **Zahiruddin Muhammad Babur** was the founder of the Mughal empire in India.
- Babur was the king of Farghana in Afghanistan.
- Taking advantage of the political conditions prevailing in India, Babur marched towards India.
- Babur defeated Ibrahim Lodi in the first Battle of Panipat in 1526 A.D.
- Before the Battle of Panipat (1526 A.D.), Babur had made **four expeditions** to India.
- In 1519 (**first**-Indian expedition) he used gun powder for the first time in India to storm fort of Bhira.
- His **second** expedition was in 1519 when he captured Peshawar.
- **Third** expedition in 1520 occupied Bajaur, Bhira, Sialkot and Sayyadpur.
- **4th** expedition in 1524-Daulat Khan Lodi (Governor of Lahore) sent his son Dilawar Khan and Alam Khan Lodi to join Babur.
- Rana Sanga sent a message to Kabul inviting him.
- **5th** expedition was in 1526, Battle of Panipat against Ibrahim Lodi. He used Rumi (ottoman) device and Tulugama tactics.
- In 1527, he defeated Rana Sanga of Mewar in battle of Khanwa.
- In 1529 he conquered Ibrahim Lodi's younger brother. Mahmud Lodi in battle of Ghaghara.

Humayun (1530-1540 and 1555-1556 AD)

- **Nasiruddin Muhammad Humayun** succeeded Babur.
- Humayun ruled from 1530 A.D. to 1540 A.D. and again from 1555- 1556 A.D.
- Humayun built Dinpanah at Delhi as his second capital.
- In 1532, defeated Afghans udner Mahmud Lodhi at Daurah.
- In 1530, attacked Kalinjar.

- In 1539, Afghan leader Sher Shah defeated him at Chausa (Bihar).
- In 1540, Sher Shah again defeated him in battle of Kannauj.
- After the battle of Kannauj (1540) Humayun fled and took shelter for a few days at Amarkot (ruler-Rana Virsala)
- In 1545, he went to Shah Tahmasp's court in Persia (Iran) who aided him in conquering Kandhar.
- In 1551, Askari was exiled to Mecca.
- In 1553, Kabul was occupied and Kamran was blinded and sent to Mecca.
- Captured Lahore in 1555 from Sikandar Sur, Governor of Punjab, then Delhi and Agra.
- Humayun died in 1556 A.D. of falling from his library Sher Mandal.
- Humayun's tomb is situated in Delhi.

Sher Shah (1540-1545 A.D.)

- Sher Shah's childhood name was Farid.
- Sher Shah was born to Hasan, the Jagirdar of Sasaram.
- He received the title of Sher Shah from Bahar Khan Lohani, the Afghan Governor of South Bihar,
- Sher Shah gained Chunar by marrying the widow, Malika.
- He defeated Humayun in the battle of Chausa. He adopted the title of Sher Shah and proclaimed himself the emperor of Hindustan.
- He again defeated Humayun in the battle of Kannauj or Bilgram.
- Sher Shah's last campaign was against Kalinjar; he succeeded, but died from an explosion in 1545.
- He was succeeded by his son Islam Shah.
- Humayun defeated Sikandar Suri and occupied Delhi in 1555.
- Sher Shah established a highly centralised government.
- He divided his empire into 47 Sarkars (districts) which were divided into several parganas (sub-districts). Village was the lowest unit of administration. He made the local village headmen (muqaddams) and Zamindars responsible for local crime.
- He built many sarais.
- He built the grand trunk road from Sonargaon to Attock.
- He improved the land revenue system by adopting Zabti-i-Har-Sal.
- Sher Shah abolished all internal customs and duties.
- Sher Shah built three important roads, Agra-Jodhpur-Chittor, Lahore-Multan, and Agra-Burhanpur.
- Sher Shah built 1700 sarais which also worked as dak chaukis.
- Sher Shah ascended the throne of Delhi at the ripe age of 67.
- Abbas Khan Sarwani was the historian of Sher Shah.
- Sher Shah's roads and sarais have been called "The arteries of the Empire".

Akbar (1556-1605 A.D.)

- Akbar was born in Amarkot in the palace of Virasal in 1542 A.D.
- Akbar's full name was Jalaluddin Muhammad Akbar.
- He was crowned at Kalanaur at the age of 13 years.
- Akbar conquered Hemu in the second battle of Panipat in 1556 A.D.
- Bairam Khan was his regent from 1556 to 1560. Bairam Khan was a Shia.
- Bairam Khan was assassinated by Mubarak Khan at Patan (Gujarat) on his way to Mecca.
- Bairam's widow Salima Begum was married to Akbar and her son (from Bairam) Abdur Rahim, joined the court of Akbar and later became the Khan-i-Khanan.
- His chief advisor was Mir Abdul Latif.
- In 1562, he abolished the system of making war captives as slaves.
- In 1563, he abolished pilgrim tax.
- In 1564, he abolished Jaziya.
- His tomb was at Sikandara, near Agra.
- Laid the foundation of Fatehpur Sikri as his capital.
- Learnt the principles of Sulah-i-Kul from his teacher Mir Abdul Latif.
- In 1564, Garh Katanga was attacked. It was under the regency of Durgavati, the Chandella princess of Mahoba on behalf of her minor son Vir Narayan. Her capital Chauragarh was stormed by Asaf Khan.
- In 1668, Chittor under Rana Udai Singh of Mewar was invaded. Here, two Rajput warriors fought bravely against Akbar-Jaimal and Patta.
- Akbar had the statues of Jaimal and Patta installed at Agra fort.
- In 1569, campaign against Ranthambhor, Rao Surajan Hara submitted and joined the imperial service.
- In 1569-1570, campaign against Kalinjar, Ramchandra offered submission to Majnun Khan.
- In 1601, captured fortress of Asirgarh- his last conquest in Khandesh (1601).
- In 1582, Tauhid-i-Ilahi (Divine monothesim) was initiated. 80 years later it came to be called Din-i-Ilahi. It was sufistic.
- After returning from Gujarat campaign, Akbar appointed officials called Karoris.

- Akbar divided the empire into 12 Subas in 1580.
- In 1585, Akbar moved to Lahore and remained there for 12 years.
- Akbar nominated Salim as his successor who ascended the throne with the title of Jahangir.
- In 1605, Akbar died of dysentery.
- Hakim Ali was his personal physician, while Raja Salivahan was his court physician.
- Akbar was buried at Sikandra.
- Sheikh Farid Bukhari was his last Mir Bakshi.
- Started giving loans from royal treasury as Musadat.
- Loan to farmers was called takavi.
- Started worshipping light (Prakash Pujas) in court.
- With the help of Raja Todarmal (revenue minister), he began land settlement and launched Ain-i-Dahsala system.
- Issued round and square size silver coins called Rupaya and Jalali.
- Adopted Persian as court language.
- Laid foundation of Fatehpur Sikri in 1572-1580. Here, main buildings include-Buland Darwaza, Diwan-i-Am, Diwan-i-Khas, palace of Sultana, Panch Mahal, etc.
- Expert exponent of music. He played Nakkara (drum).
- His court musicians-Tansen, Baba Ramdas, Baz Bahadur, etc.
- Famous painters in his court included Khwaja Abdus Samad, Daswant, Basawan, etc.
- Akbar set up a department of painting headed by Khwaja Abdus Samad with the title Shirin Kalam.
- Got Mahabharata translated into Persian as ***'Razmnama'***.
- Contemporary Hindu scholars- Ramdas, Suradas, Tulsidas, Raskhan, Abdur Rahim Khan-Khanan and Birbal (Raja Mahesh Das).
- Famous Persian scholars-Abul-Fazaal, Faizi, Budayuni, Abbas Khan Sarwani, Utbi, and Naziri.
- Organised army and started Mansabdari system in 1575-1576.
- Todar Mal, Abul Fazal, Faizi, Birbal, Tansen, Abdur Rahim Khan- i-Khanan, Mullah do Pyaza and Man Singh were gems of his court.

Jahangir (1605-1627 A.D.)

- Jahangir was born at Lahore in 1569 A.D.
- Jahangir's full name was Nuruddin Muhammad Jahangir.
- Jahangir was popularly known as Salim.
- Jahangir banned slaughter of animals on Sunday and Thursday.
- He founded Zanjir-i-Adal at Agra Fort for the seekers of royal justice.
- His son Khusrau, who accepted patronage of Guru Arjun Dev, revolted against Jahangir. The fifth Sikh Guru Arjun Dev was later condemned to death for his blessings to the rebel prince.
- Khurram (Shahjahan) supported by his father-in-law, Asaf Khan, also revolted against Jahangir but the two soon resolved all issues.
- His military general, Mahabat Khan revolted and abducted him, but Nurjahan saved him by using her diplomatic efforts.
- Jahangir was well-read and wrote his memoirs Tuzuk-i-Jahangiri in Persian.
- Jahangir's sons-Khusrau, Parvez, Khurram, Shahriyar and Jahandar.
- Shahryar married Ladli Begum.
- James-I sent Captain Hawkins and Sir Thomas Roe to Jahangir's court to get concession in trade for British.
- Laid many gardens, like Shalimar Bagh in Kashmir.
- Jahangir built a mosque in Lahore, Itmad-ud-daula's tomb in Agra (first building to have Pietra Deura), completed Akbar's tomb in Sikandara.
- During Jahangir, Mughal painting was on climax.
- Portrait painting and paintings of animals and birds started. Mansur was expert in this style.
- He was himself expert painter and claimed to recognise painting of a particular painter at a glance.
- Introduced Du-Aspa and Sih-Aspa systems in Mansabdari system.
- Lover of music, painting and arts.
- Jahangir met Nur Jahan on Nauroz (new years day) in Mina Bazar of Agra, married her in 1611.
- Ladli Begum was the daughter of Nur Jahan from Sher Afghan.
- In 1613 Nur Jahan was made Padshah Begum (the first lady).
- In 1616, Nur Jahan got the title Nur Mahal.
- Farmans had signature and coins were struck in her name.
- Itmad-ud Daula (father of Nur Jahan) was given mansabdari of 7000 Zats.
- Nur Jahan's brother, Abul Hasan was appointed Mir-i-Saman (in charge of the royal household).

- Khusrau was blinded and in 1620 he was killed on the orders of Khurram at Burhanpur.
- John Hawkins inhabited Agra for two years (1609-1611). He was given the mansab of 400.
- Sir Thomas Roe (1615-1618) was ambassador of James-I.

Shahjahan (1628-1657 A.D.)

- Shahjahan was born in Lahore in 1592 A.D.
- Shahjahan's childhood name was Khurram.
- Shahjahan's full name was Shihabuddin Muhammad Shah Jahan.
- Shahjahan was born to Jagat Gosain, daughter of Mota Raja Udai Singh of Jodhpur.
- Shahjahan married Arzumand Banu Begum in 1612. She became famous as Mumtaz Mahal.
- Mahabat Khan was given 7000 Zat and Sawar and title Khan-i- Khanan.
- In 1628, Pir Khan Khani-i-Jahan, Lodi governor of the Deccan, rebelled and joined the Nizam Shahis but was defeated at Tal Sahonda.
- In 1628-1629, Jujhar Singh Bundella of Orchha rebelled, but later submitted. He again rebelled in 1635 by attacking Prem Narain of Chauragarh (Gondwana) and was defeated by Aurangzeb. Devi Singh was installed at Orchha.
- Cham-pat Rai of Mahoba also rebelled. His son Chhatrasal rebeled during Aurangzeb's reign.
- The 1630 Deccan famine, witnessed by Peter Mundi, led to large-scale relief measures by the state.
- In 1631, Mumtaz Mahal died during child birth at Burhan Pur. She was first buried at Burhan Pur but later transferred to Agra (Taj Mahal).
- Shah Jahan's six children from Mumtaj Begum-Jahanara Begum were Dara Shikoh, Shah Shuja, Roshan Ara Begum, Aurangzeb (born at Daulatabad) and Murad Baksh.
- Shah Jahan introduced 1/3, 1/4, 1/5 method in Mansabadari system. According to this, a mansabdar had to keep horsemen 1/3, 1/4, 1/5 of his sawar rank.
- Jagannath Pandit was his court poet.
- Shah Jahan was an expert musician and his voice was very melodious.
- Appointed Amins whose main function was to assess revenue.
- Constructed the Peacock throne (1628-1635).
- Attacked Hooghly against the Portuguese and captured it in 1632.
- Foreign travellers who visit his court were Bernier (France), Travernier (France) and Manucci (Italy).
- His period was the climax of Mughal architecture.

Aurangzeb (1658-1707 A.D.)

- Aurangzeb's full name was Muinuddin Muhammad Aurangzeb.
- Aurangzeb was the third son of Mumtaz Mahal.
- Aurangzeb had to fight war of succession to gain the throne.
- He took the title of 'Alamgir' in 1659.
- He was known as Zinda Pir, the living saint.
- In 1662, Mir Jumla, Aurangzeb's ablest general led the expedition against Ahoms.
- He forbaded inscription of Kalma on the coins.
- He ended the celebration of Navroz festival.
- Mutasib (regulator of moral conduct) was appointed.
- He ended Jharokha darshan, use of almanacs and weighing of the emperor.
- Aurangzeb assembled Fatwa-i-Alamgiri.
- Jaziya was re-introduced.
- Built Moti Masjid (Pearl Mosque) in Red Fort of Delhi.
- No new temples were to be constructed. But old ones were not to be destroyed and they were allowed to be repaired.
- In 1669, the Vishwanath temple of Banaras and the Keshav Raj temple of Bir Singh Bundela at Mathura were destroyed.
- The proportion of Hindu mansabdars was highest in Aurangzeb's reign.
- Guru Govind Singh wrote letters to Aurangzeb, their collection is called Zafarnama.
- Guru Govind Singh died at Nanded, on way to meet Aurangzeb, Aurangzeb had died earlier.
- Shambhaji (son of Shivaji) was captured at Sanghameshwar (1689) and executed.
- Bijapur (1686) and Golconda (1687) were annexed.
- His tomb is located in Aurangabad.
- He was an expert veena player.
- Banned singing in court, but allowed Royal Band (Naubat).
- He restarted Pilgrim tax.
- He disallowed cultivation of Hemp (Bhang).
- In 1669, Jats under Gokla revolted.

- In 1672, Satnamis, nick-named Mundiya Sadhus, founded by Birbhan near Narnaul revolted.
- In 1685, second Jat rebellion took place under Raja Ram and his successor Churaman.
- In 1667, Yusufzai tribe of Afghans, under the Raushanai movement led by Bhagu rebelled.
- In 1672, second Afghan rebellion took place by the-Afridi tribe led by Akmal Khan.

Mughal Administration

Provincial Administration

- Mughal empire was divided into subas which was further sub-divided into sarkar, parganas and villages.
- However, it also had other territorial units as 'Khalisa', (royal land), Jagirs (autonomous rajas) and Inams (gifted lands, mainly waste lands).
- There were 15 territorial units (subas) during Akbar's reign, which later increased to 20 under Aurangzeb's reign.

Province (Suba)

- Sipahsalar—The Head Executive (under Akbar and later he was known Nizam or Subedar)
- Diwan—Incharge of revenue department
- Bakshi—Incharge of military department.

District/Sarakar

- Fauzdar—Administrative head
- Amal/Amalguzar—Revenue collection
- Kotwal—Maintenance of law and order, trial of criminal cases and price regulation.

Pargana

- Shiqdar—Administrative head combined in himself the duties of 'fauzdar and kotwal'
- Amin, Qanungo—Revenue officials of Village
- Muqaddam—Headman
- Patwari—Accountant
- Chowkidar—Watchman

Mughal Central Administration

- Wazir: Akbar abolished the post of the all-powerful Wazir. He became the head of the revenue department, also known as Diwan-i-ala.
- Diwan: Responsible for all income and expenditure and had control over Khalisa and jagir land.
- Mir Bakshi: Headed military department, nobility information and intelligence agencies.
- Mir Saman: Incharge of Imperial household and Karkhanas.
- Diwan-i-Bayutot: Maintained roads, government buildings, etc. and worked under Mir Saman.
- Mir Munshi: Incharge of royal correspondence
- Sadr us Sadr: Incharge of charitable and religious endowments
- Qazi ul Quzat: Headed the Judiciary department
- Muhtasib: Censor of Public Morals.

Mughal Rulers : At a Glance

Zahiruddin Babur	:	1526-1530
Nasiruddin Humayun	:	1530-1540
Nasiruddin Humayun	:	1555-1556
Jalaluddin Akbar	:	1556-1605
Nuruddin Jahangir	:	1605-1627
Shihabuddin Shajahan	:	1628-1657
Aurangzeb Alamgir	:	1658-1707
Azam Shah	:	1707
Kam Bakhsh (in the Deccan)	:	1707
Shah Alam-I	:	1707-1712
Azim-ush-Shah	:	1712
Muizz-ud-din Jahandar	:	1712-1713
Farrukhsiyar	:	1713-1719
Shams-ud-din Rafi-ud-Darajat	:	1719
Nikusiyar	:	1719
Nasir-ud-din Muhammad	:	17191748
Ahmad Shah Bahadur	:	1748-1754
Aziz-du-din Muhammad	:	1754-1760
Shah Jahan-III	:	1760
Shah Alam-II (First reign)	:	1760-1788
Bidar Bakht	:	1788
Shah Alam-II (Second reign)	:	1788-1806
Muin-ud-bin Akbar-II	:	1806-1837
Siraj-ud-bin Bahadur Shah-II	:	1837-1857

Mughal Architecture

Babar

- Babar built two mosques-one at Kabulibagh in Panipat and the other at Sambhal in Rohilkhand.

Humayun

- Humayun laid the foundation of the city 'Din Panah' at Delhi.
- Humayun's tomb is called the proto-type of Taj Mahal. It has a double dome of marble, while the central dome is octagonal. It was built by his widow Haji Begum.
- The garden and the gateway are to be found in all Mughal-style tombs.

Akbar

- Buildings built by Akbar are Agra Fort (1565), Lahore Palace (1572), Fatehpur Sikri, Buland Darwaza and Allahabad Fort (1583).
- The architecture at Fatehpur Sikri is an excellent blend of Persian, Central Asian and various Indian (Bengal and Gujarat) styles. It is also known as Epic poem in red sandstone. Indian tradition includes deep eaves, balconies and Kiosks.
- Central Asian Style is evident in the use of glazed blue tiles.
- Two unusual buildings at Fatehpur Sikri are Panch Mahal and Diwan-i-Khas.
- The Panch Mahal had the plan of Buddhist Vihara.
- The Jodhabai's Palace, Diwan-i-Aam, Diwan-i-Khas are Indian in their plan.
- Buland Darwaja, built after Gujarat victory, formed the main entrance to Fatehpur Sikri. It is built in the Iranian style of half dome portal.
- Salim Chisti's tomb (redone in Marble by Jahangir is the first Mughal building in pure marble); palaces of Birbal, Anup Talao, and Mariyam Mahal are also inside the Fatehpur Sikri.
- He built the Jahangiri Mahal in Agra fort according to Hindu design based on Man Mandir.
- Haroon Minar-Tower built by Akbar in memory of his elephant (Haroon).
- He also began to build his own tomb at Sikandara which, was later completed by Jahangir.

Jahangir

- The style of architecture used by both Jahangir and Shahjahan is known as Indo-Persian. Important features of this style are curved lines, bulbous dome, foliated arches vigorous use of marble instead of red sand stone and use of pietre dura for decorative purposes.
- Nurjahan built Itimad-ud-Daula's (another name of Mirza Ghiyas Beg) marble tomb at Agra, which is noticeable for the first use of pietra dura (floral designs made-up of semi-precious stones) technique.
- He built Moti Masjid in Lahore and his own mausoleum at Shandara (Lahore).
- He also changed the plan of Akbar's tomb at Sikandara. It is an unusual tomb as it is not surmounted by a dome and built on the model of a Buddhist Pagoda.

Shahajahan

- Mosque-building activity reached its climax in Taj Mahal. He also built the Jama Masjid (sand stone).
- Some of the important buildings built by Shahajahan at Agra are Moti Masjid (only mosque of marble) in Agra, Khaas Mahal, Musamman Burz (Jasmine Palace where he spent his last years in captivity) and Sheesh Mahal with mosaic glasses on walls and ceilings.
- Many stone buildings were destroyed by him and replaced by marble.
- He laid the foundations of Shahjahanabad in 1637 where he built the Red Fort and Taqt-i-taus (Peacock throne).
- Most richly ornamented building in Red Fort was the Diwan-i-Khas or Rang Mahal.
- He laid the Shalimar Gardens in Lahore.
- Shahjahan built Nahar-i-Faiz.

Aurangzeb

- Only building built by Aurangzeb in the Red Fort is Moti Masjid.
- Only monument associated with Aurangzeb is Bibi ka Makbara which is the tomb of his wife Rabbia-ud-daura in Aurangabad.
- He also built the Badshahi mosque in Lahore.

Regional Architecture

Jaunpur

- Tughlaq influence on the Sharqi architecture is seen in the use of arch and beam, and battering walls.
- Propylons (huge recessed arch framed by tapering square minars divided into registers) have been used in Atala Masjid (Ibrahim Shah) and Jami Masjid (Hussain Shah).

Malwa

- It is notable for the excellent combination of arch and lintel, construction of stairs of flight, the use of coloured tiles and lofty plinth for the buildings.

- Malwa boasts of Hussain Shah's tomb, Jami Masjid, Jahaz Mandal, Hindola Mahal and the palaces of Baaz Bahadur and Rupmati.
- In Chanderi, Shahzadi Ka Rauza, Kushak Mahal and the Badal Mahal are located.

Bengal

- Adina Masjid was built by Sikandar Shah and the Eklakhi tomb of Mahmud Shah was constructed. Some other monuments are Dakhil Darwaza, Tantipura Masjid, the Bara Sona Masjid, etc.

Kashmir

- Wood was the principle building material and the roofs are pyramidal.
- Kashmir has two buildings of prominence: Sajjid Ali Hamadani's Mosque and Jami Masjid of Sikandar Shah.

Gujarat

- Notable monuments are Jami Masjid of Ahmedabad, Nagina Masjid of Champaner and the cities of Mahmudabad and Mustafabad founded by Mohammed Beghara.

Sur Architecture

- Sur Architecture forms the climax of Pre-Mughal style of Architecture.
- Surs built tombs at Sasaram which were octagonal but most outstanding was Sher Shah's Mausoleum built on a huge plinth, amidst a lake and is multi-storeyed.
- He also built the Purana Qila whose surviving monuments are Qila-i-Kuhna Masjid and the Sher Mandal library.

Mughal Painting

- The Mughals introduced new themes depicting the court, battle scenes and the chase and added new colours (Peacock blue and Indian red).
- Humayun had taken into his service two master painters- Mir Syed All and Abdus Samad.
- Jaswant and Dasawan were two famous painters of Akbar's court.
- Apart from illustrating Persian books of fables (Hamzanama), the painters illustrated Razamnama (Mahabharta) and Akbaranama.
- Jahangir claims that he could distinguish the work of each artist in a picture.

During Akbar

- European painting was introduced at the court by the Portuguese priests.
- Humayun brought Mir Sayyid All of Tabriz and Khwaja Abdus Samad of Shiraz to instruct Akbar, influenced by Bihzads schools of Hearts. Abdus Samad was Akbar's tutor, who enjoyed painting.
- Akbar had the Tuti Nama illustrated and then the Hamza Nama (1004 illustrated pages), Tarikh-i-Khandan-i-Timuriyya-(more like a photographic biography, it has pictures of Akbar's birth), Babul Nama, Akbar Nama, Razm Nama (Persian Mahabharat), Ramayan, Ayiar Danish, Nal Damyanti and Kalil were Dimfria. They created a new style, a blend of Persian and Indian, but different from both.
- Most of the paintings are the result of the joint work of artists: the designer or master. The flat effect of the Persian style is replaced by the roundness of the Indian brush. It leans towards naturalism, with sweeping movement and bright colours. There is a striving for delicacy and refinement.
- European painting was introduced in the last years of Akbars reign. Elements of mysticism, suspense and mystery are present. Important painters were: Mir Sayyid All and Abdus Samad in the early period, (Tuti Nama and Hamza Nama) and in the later- Dasawant (a potters son) who did the Razm Nama and Basavan.

During Jahangir

- Painting was his favourite art and was influenced by European painting, especially the minature portrait by Isaac Oliver, presented by James I, through ambassador Sir Thomas Roe, Miskin, who painted the story of the unfaithful wife in the Bharistan was influenced by 16th c. Italian style.
- Father Jerome Xavier presented the Dastan-i-Ahwali-Hawariyan (lives of the apostles) painted in India in Italian style. Naturalism was pre-dominant. Textbook illustration gradually disappeared, with emphasis on portraiture and studies of birds and animals. Parts of the bodies were painted by specialists and Jahangir could distinguish who painted which part.
- Darbar pictures were essentially an aggloromation of portraits. Colours were subdued. The divine nature of kingship emphasised by use of European moties: hour glass, globe, cherubs among Europeanised clouds, golden rays depicting divine light, haloes making him super human like Italian saints.

- Main painters Abdul Hasan, Ustad Mansur (specialist in animals) Bishandas (portraits). Other was Manohar, son of Basawan, Goverdhan, and Daulat, etc.

During Shah Jahan

- Composition are static and symmetrical, colour is heavier, texture and ornamentation are sumptuous and lack freshness, and an emphasis on royal glory by having a mass of humanity in the background attendent to the king.
- Important painters: Kalyan Das (Alias Chaturman) Anup Chitr, Raj Anup, and Mohammed Nadir Samargandi, etc. Dara Shikoh had an album of pictures, mainly bird and Vegetal, with strong European influence.

During Aurangzeb

- Antipathy to art is exaggerated. Mughal painting was essentially a court nurtured art, and the long absence of the Emperor from Delhi withdrew imperial patronage, forcing artists to work for nobles who didn't pay well, and therefore, these artists later migrated. There is stylistic debasement.
- Aurangzeb had many paintings plastered due to the animals present, yet, he had his own portraits with haloes around him.
- During Muhammad Shah Rangila, there was a brief revival, but the state was in decline.

Rajsthani School

- It developed around the same time as the Mughal School, as a direct natural evolution from the western Indian style.
- Though there were contacts, for the most part the Rajasthani Schools remained unaffected from Mughal influence till the 17th century.
- The subject matter is essentially Hindu, the primary concern being the Radha-Krishna myth, and also inspired from Puranas, Mahabharata, Ramayan and Shiva's dance.
- The style had different schools based in states: Mewar (Shahibdin was the best painter), Bundi, Kota, Marwar, Jaipur Amber, Bikaner (as an exception it was heavily influenced by Mughals), etc. The style, unlike Mughal naturalism, is abstract and heretic, the language mythical and symbolic. Musical modes were symbolically represented.
- The Ragamala (Garland of songs) painting depict Ragas and Raginis in their emotive setting. Each melodic mood was symbolically assigned a specific colour. Bikaner was highly influenced by Mughal naturalism; Bundi slightly less. Kishangarh style is full of lyrical mysticism. Amber is of rather formal style.

Pahari Style

- Prevalent in the Himalayas roughly from Jammu to Garhwal. The earliest is the Basholi style (named after a state) marked by bold colour, vigorous drawings and a primitive and intense expression.
- The themes are similar to the Rajsthan Schools: Radha-Krishna myth, love, erotica, the seasons, etc.
- The later phase of the Pahari style, called the Kangra School, begins from the late 18th century.
- It is characterised by a sentimental and lyrical mood, smooth rhytms carried by curving lines, and cool and refreshing colour. This dramatic change is due to the immigration of Mughal court painters, but the influence was radically transformed in the process of assimilation.

Deccan Style

- It evolves as a combination of foreign (Persian and Turkish) and strong indigenous element inherited chiefly from the Vijayanagar tradition.
- Ibrahim Adil Shah II patronised it. Aurangzeb after conquest had them plastered, hence not much remain.
- The Bijapur version is marked by a very poetic quality.

RELIGIOUS MOVEMENTS

- The Bhakti Movement began in South India in the 7th Century.
- The Alvars (Vaishnavites) and Naynnars (Shaivites) popularised the Bhakti cult in South India.
- There were 12 Alvar Vaishnavite and 63 Naynar Saivite Saints.
- The Saivite Saint Appar is said to have converted the Pallava king, Mahendravarman, to Saivism.
- Sambandar and Manikkavasagar were other great Bhakti Saints.
- The writings of these saints were collected in the Tirumurai.
- The Tirumurai has been called as the Tamil Veda.
- Periya Puranam was composed by Shekkilar in the reign of the Chola king Kulottunga-I.
- Ramananda was the first great Bhakti saint of North India.
- Raidas, Kabir, Dhanna, Pipa were his disciples.
- Kabir (1440-1518) belonged to a family of weavers.
- Kabir spent greater part of his life in Banaras.

- Kabir's verses were included in Adi Granth.
- Raidas was a tanner.
- Dhanna was a Jat peasant from Rajasthan.
- Guru Nanak (1469-1539) was born at Nankana Sahib.
- Kabir and Nanak were Nirguna Bhakti saints.
- Vallabhacharya was a Telugu Brahmana.
- Vallabhacharya was the founder of Pushti Marga (way of grace).
- Chaitnya (1486-1533) was the most prominent Vaishnav saint of Bengal.
- Chaitanya popularised Krishna Bhakti. Chaitanya was looked upon as living Krishna.
- Jnaneswar (1275-1296) was the pioneer Bhakti Saint of Maharashtra.
- Jnaneswar wrote Jnaneswari.
- Jnaneswari is a commentary on Bhagavad Gita.
- Jnaneswar was the author of many hymns called Abhangas.
- Namdeva (1270-1350) was a tailor by caste.
- Namdeva travelled to North India and Punjab.
- Namdev's Bhakti songs have been included in the Adi Granth.
- Namdeva is considered to be a part of the Varkari tradition.
- Lal Dev was a Saiva Bhakti saint of Kashmir.
- In Assam, Sankaradeva (1449-1568) introduced bhakti.
- Sankaradeva's sect is called Mahapurushiya dharma.
- Dadu (1544-1603) was inspired by Kabir's doctrine.
- Tukaram's tarlings are in the form of Abhangas or dohas.
- Tukaram founded the Varkari Sect.
- Ramdasa wrote Dasabodha.
- Ramdasa was the Guru of Shivaji.
- The Lingayat Sect was founded by Basava.
- The biography of Chaitanya is 'Chaitanya Charitra'.
- The biography of Chaitanya was written by Krishnadas Kaviraj.
- The disciples of Kabir later formed the Kabirpanthi sect.
- Jagjivan Das founded the Satnami sect.
- Tulsidas wrote Ramcharitmanas, Vinaypatrika, Kavitavali.
- Surdas wrote Sur Surawali, Sahitya Ratna, Sursagar.
- Mirabai was a Rajput Princes of Merta.
- Mirabai married to Bhojraja, son of Rana Sanga.
- Mirabai was famous for her devotion to Krishna.
- Mirabai advocated image-worship and observance of special fasts.
- Mirabai wrote several poems like Padavali.
- Ramanuja advocated the philsophy of Vishista Advaitavada.
- Madhvacharya founded the Dvaita philosophy.
- Nimbarka propounded the Dvaitadvaita philosophy.
- Nimbarka founded the Sanak Sampradaya.

The Marathas

- Shivaji was born in the fort of Shivner in Poona in 1627.
- Shivaji belonged to the Bhonsle clan.
- Shivaji's father Shahji Bhonsle was in the service of Ahmadnagar.
- Dadaji Kondadeo and Guru Ramdas had great influence on the life of Shivaji.
- Guru Ramdas wrote 'Dasabodh'.
- Shahji gave Shivaji the jagir of Poona.
- Shivaji first captured Torna 1646 A.D.
- Shivaji began his real career of conquest in 1656 when he conquered Javli from the Maratha Chief Chandra Rao More.
- The conquest of Javli made him the master of the Mavalis, Mavali foot soldiers became a strong part of his army.
- He murdered Afzal Khan of Adil Shahi kingdom of Bijapur with baghnakh (tiger claw) in 1659.
- In 1663, Shivaji injured Shaista Khan, the Mughal Governor.
- In 1664, Shivaji sacked Surat for the first time.
- The treaty of Purandhar was signed on June 24, 1665 A.D.
- Shivaji surrendered 23 out of the 35 forts to Mughals.
- Shivaji's son Sambhaji was awarded a Mansab of 5000.
- Shivaji visited Agra in 1666.
- On August 29, 1666, Shivaji escaped from Agra.
- On October, 1670 Shivaji sacked Surat a second time.
- Shivaji was coronated at Rajgarh in 1674.
- Shivaji assumed the title of Chhatrapati Hindeva Dharmodharak.
- Shivaji died in 1680 at the age of 53.

- Shivaji was succeeded by Sambhaji (1680-89).
- Shivaji introduced various administrative and revenue reforms.
- Shivaji's Council of Ministers was called Ashtapradhan.
- Shivaji maintained a regular standing army.
- The cavalry was divided into two classes : the Bargis and Silahdar.
- Bargis were supplied with horses and arms by the State.
- Silahdars had to keep their own equipment.
- Chauth was 1/4 of the land revenue paid to the Marathas for the land not be sullied by the Maratha raids.
- Sardeshmukhi was an additional levy of 10% which Shivaji demanded on the basis of being the hereditary Sardeshmukh.
- Shivaji discouraged reveneue farming system.
- Kathi was measurment in rods.
- Annaji Datto introduced various reforms in revenue in 1679.
- Chauth and Sardeshmukhi both were land taxes collected from Mughal territory.

Ashtapradhana

1.	Peshwa	General Administration; like Prime Minister
2.	Sar-i-Naubat	Senapati
3.	Mazumdar	Accountant
4.	Waqia-i-nivas	Intelligence, posts and household affairs
5.	Surnavis or Chitins	Correspondence
6.	Dabir/Sumant	Foreign affairs and master of ceremonies
7.	Nyayadhis	Justice
8.	Panditrao	Religious affairs

Maratha Peshwas (1714-1818 A.D.)

1714-1720	:	Balaji Vishwanath
1720-1740	:	Baji Rao-I
1740-1761	:	Balaji Baji Rao
1761-1772	:	Madhava Rao Ballal
1772-1773	:	Narayan Rao
1773-1774	:	Raghunath Rao
1774-1796	:	Madhava Rao Narayan
1796-1818	:	Baji Rao-II

Decline of the Mughal Empire

- After the death of Aurangzeb, Muaazam emerged victorious in the war of succession.
- Muazzam conquered the throne with the name of Bahadur Shah-I in 1707 at the age of 67.
- During Bahadur Shah's reign, Jaziya was abolished.
- Bahadur Shah gave a high Mansab to Guru Govind Singh.
- Bahadur Shah released the Maratha Prince Sahu.
- Jahandar Shah came to the throne in 1712 A.D.
- He was dominated by his mistress Lal Kunwar. She imitated the style of Nur Jahan.
- Administration was virtually in the hands of Zulfiqar Khan.
- Jahandar Shah was the first later Mughal ruler to get the throne with the help of nobles.
- The policies of Aurangzeb were reversed.
- Jai Singh of Amber was given the title of Mirza Raja Sawai and appointed as the Governor of Malwa.
- Ajit Singh of Marwar was awarded by the title of Maharaja and appointed governor of Gujarat.
- Sahu was granted Chauth and Sardeshmukhi of Deccan.
- Farrukh Siyar came to the throne in 1713 A.D. with the help of Sayyid Brothers.
- Sayyid brothers were known as King-makers.
- Sayyid brothers dominated the mughal court and empire from 1713 to 1719. The elder brother Abdullah Khan was Wazir and the younger, Hussain Ali Khan was Mir Bakshi.
- Sayyid brothers belonged to Hindustani group of Mughal nobility.
- In 1719, the Sayyid brothers deposed Farrukh Siyar and killed him.
- After Farrukh Siyar, Sayyid brothers placed Rafi-ud-darajat on the throne, but he died soon.
- Muhammad Shah came to the throne in 1719 A.D.
- Muhammad Shah was known as "Rangila"',
- Nadir Shah, the Napoleon of Iran invaded India and inflicted a crushing defeat on Mughal army at Karnal on Feb 13, 1739.
- Nadir Shah captured Delhi and Muhammad Shah was imprisoned. He plundered Delhi.
- Nadir Shah's total plunder has been estimated at Rs. 70 crores, He also carried away the famous Koh-i-Noor diamond and the jewel-studded Peacock Throne of Shah Jahan.

- Various provinces became independent like Bengal, Hyderabad, Awadh, Carnatic, etc.
- The Jats under Badan Singh established themselves in the districts of Agra and Mathura and founded the Jat state of Bharatpur.
- Sayyid brothers were murdered in 1720 A.D.
- Ahmad Shah came to the throne in 1748 A.D.
- Safdar Jang, the Nawab of Awadh became the wazir of the Empire.
- His wazir (after Safdar Jang), Imad-ul-Mulk, blinded him and placed Alamgir-II on the throne.
- Ahmad Shah Abdali invaded India thrice during his reign.
- Alamgir-II came to the throne in 1754 A.D.
- Ahmad Shah Abdali invaded fourth time in his reign in 1755.
- The Marathas were invited by his wazir to safeguard the empire against Abdali.
- In 1759 he was murdered by his wazir, Imad-ul-mulk.
- Real name of Shah Alam II was Ali Gauhar.
- Along with Mir Qasim and Shuja-ud-daulah he was defeated by the English at the battle of Buxar in 1764.
- He lived for several years at Allahabad as a pensioner of the East India Company.
- He regained the throne of Delhi with the help of Maratha sardar Mahadji Scindhia in 1772.
- British under Lord Lake captured Delhi and Agra in 1803.
- He was killed by Ghulam Qadir in 1806.
- English concluded treaty of Allahabad (1765).
- Bahadur Shah Zafar was the last Mughal Emperor.

3 Chapter Indian National Movement

THE ADVENT OF THE EUROPEANS

Portuguese

- **Discovery of the New Sea Route**: Vasco da Gama discovered the cape route from Europe to India. He arrived at the port of Calicut on the May 17, 1498, and was received by the Hindu ruler of Calicut known by the title of Zamorin. This led to the establishment of trading stations at Calicut, Cochin and Cannanore. Cochin was the early capital of the Portuguese in India which was relocked by Goa.
- **Alfonso d'Albuquerque** arrived in India in 1503 as the governor of the Portuguese in India. He captured Goa from the ruler of Bijapur in duration of 1510.

Other Governors

- **Nino da Cunha (1529-38)**: He transferred his capital from Cochin to Goa (1530) and obtained Diu and Bassein (1534) from Bahadur Shah.
- **Martin Alfonso de Souza (1542-45)**: He was came to India with the famous Jesuit saint Francisco Xavier.

Dutch

- The formation of Company in March, 1602, by a charter of Dutch parliament which formed Dutch East India Company with powers to make wars, conclude treaties, acquire territories and build fortresses.
- After the. Charter of Dutch Parliament, the Dutch factories at Masulipatam (1605), Pulicat (1610), Surat (1616), Bimil ipatam(1641), Karikal(1645), Chinsura (1653), Kasimbazar, Baranagore, Patna, Balasore, Negapatam , (all in 1658) and Cochin (1663).
- Dutch replaced Portuguese and became the most controlling power in European trade with the East, including India. Pulicat was their main centre in India till 1690, and later on, the Negapatam replaced it.
- The Dutch was replaced by English after their failure in the war of Bedera in 1759.

English

- John Mildenhall, a merchant adventurer, was the first Englishman who reached India in 1599 by the land route, ostensibly for the purpose of trade with Indian merchants.
- The Company, known as the 'English East India Company', was setup by a group of merchants in 1599.
- The East India Company started a factory at Surat in 1608.
- Captain Hawkins arrived at Jahangir's court (1609) to get permission. A farman was passed by Jahangir permitting the English to build a factory at Surat in 1613.
- Sir Thomas Roe reached to India as an ambassador of James I to Jahangir's court in 1615 to get the permission to trade and to set up factories in different parts of the empire.

Danish

- The Danes established an East India Company and arrived India in the year 1616. They established settlements at Tranquebar in Tamil Nadu in 1620 and at Serampore Bengal in 1676. Their headquarters was at Serampore in India. They were compelled to sell all their settlements in India to the British in 1854.

French

- The formation of the East India Company of French was set up by Colbert under state patronage in 1664. The first French factory was set up at Surat by Francois Caron in 1668. A factory at Masulipatam was established in 1669.
- The French power in India was revived under Lenoir and Dumas, they both were the governors between 1720 and 1742. They captured Mahe in the Malabar, Yanam in Coromandal and Karikal in Tamil Nadu during the year, 1739.
- Dupleix arrived in India as French governor in 1742. He saw the beginning of Anglo-French conflict (Carnatic wars) that resulted in their final defeat in India.

Establishment of Factories

- The East India Company obtained Bombay from Charles II on lease. In this duration, Gerald Aungier was the governor from 1669 to 1677 of the company.
- In 1639, Francis Day acquired the site of Madras from Raja of Chandragiri with permission to build a fortified factory, which was named as Fort St. George.
- Soon Madras was replaced by Masulipatam and converted as the headquarters of the English on the Coromandal coast.

- In 1690, Job Charnock set up a factory at Sutanuti and the zamindari of the three villages of Sutanuti, Kalikata and Govindpur was obtained by the British in 1698. These villages turned into the city of Calcutta.
- The factory at Sutanuti was fortified in 1696 and this new fortified settlement was named as 'Fort William' in 1700.
- In 1694, the British Parliament approved a resolution which gave equal rights to all Englishmen to trade in the East. A new rival company, called as the 'English Company of Merchants Trading to the East Indies' in 1698 came in existence.
- The final amalgamation of the company formed in 1708 under the title of 'The United Company of Merchants of England Trading to the East Indies'. The new company continued its existence till the 1858.

SOCIAL AND RELIGIOUS MOVEMENTS

Brahmo Samaj

Rammohan Roy (1771-1833)

- Roy was born at Radhanagar in Bengal in 1772.
- He is known as the first great leader of modern India.
- He opposed the idol worshipping and gave the Doctrine of the Unity of God.
- He believed that basically all religions preach common message.
- Roy was influenced by monotheism, anti-idolatry of Islam, Sufism, and ethical teachings of Christianity and liberal and rationalist doctrines of the west.
- He belonged the group of the earliest propagators of modern education.
- He initiated the Atmiya Sabha in 1814.
- Later on, the Brahma Samaj was started in 1829, it was based on two philosophies of the Vedas and the Upanishads. It laid emphasis on human dignity, opposed idolatry, and criticised social evils. Succeeded in persuading Lord Bentick to abolish Sati in 1829.
- He provided enthusiastic assistance to David Hare, who was the founder of the famous Hindu college in Calcutta.
- He established a Vedanta College during (1825) which both Indian and western social and physical sciences courses were offered.
- His famous work has been written in Persian language which is a Gift to Monotheists or Tuhafat-ul-Muwahidin published in, 1809.
- He launched a movement for the abolition of Sati through his journal named Sambad Kamudi in 1819.
- Published his Precepts of Jesus in 1820.
- He believed in the philosophy of Vedanta, according to him it was based on the principle of reason.
- Was opposed to the Sanskrit system of education.

Brahmo Ideas

- The purpose of Brahmo Samaj was to purify Hinduism and to preach monotheism.
- It laid emphasis on human dignity, opposed idolatry and criticised such social evils as the practice of Sati.
- Preached by Raja Rama Mohan Roy and later went through some changes.
- Opposed idol worship, priesthood and the ritualistic worship.
- Emphasised on worship through prayer, meditation and reading from Upanishads.
- It emphasised on higher human qualities like piety, virtue and benevolence.

The Brahmo Samaj

- The earliest reform movement of modern type.
- Founded by Raja Rammohan Roy in 1828 under the name 'Brahmo Sabha'.
- 1848- Devendranath Tagore joined the Samaj.
- 1858- Keshab Chandra Sen joined the Samaj.
- 1866-Adi Brahmo Samaj (under Devendranath Tagore's leadership) -Brahmo Samaj of India (under Keshab Chandra Sen's leadership)

Sadharan Brahmo Samaj

- (Led by the disgruntled followers of Keshab Chandra Sen)
- It was based on democratic principles and gave equal rights to all members in management of Samaj.
- Important members of the Samaj were Sivnath Shastri, Anand Mohan Bose, Bipin Chandra Pal, Dwarka Nath Ganguly and Sir Surendra Nath Bannerjee.
- They contributed highly to the growth of the spirit of nationalism in India.
- It initiated many new journals to educate the masses, such as Tattva-Kaumudi, Brahmo Public Opinion, Indian Messenger, Sanjibani, Nabhyabharat, Modern Review and Prabase.

Dharma Sabha

- The orthodox Hindus organised the Dharma Sabha under the leadership of Raja Radhakant Dev.
- The main objective of all the activities of the Dharma Sabha was only to oppose the propaganda of the Brahmo Samaj.

The Paramahansa Mandali

- Founded by Dadoha Pandurang and Bal Shastri Jambhekar in 1849.
- Founders of the Mandali believed in one god and were against caste rules.
- The members ate the food cooked by lower caste people.
- They trusted in permitting widow remarriage and in women education.

The Prarthana Samaj

- Founded in 1867 by M. G. Ranade.
- Prominent leaders were Dr. Atmaram Pandurang and R. G. Bhandarkar and N. G. Chandavarkar.
- Along with its reformist attitudes, the Prarthana Samaj was also very much attached with the Maharashtrian Bhakti Cult.
- The two main objectives of the Samaj were worship and social reform.
- It denied idolatry and the Vedas, but they adopted the method of congregational worship.

Arya Samaj

Arya Samaj

- The first Arya Samaj conference was conducted in Bombay in 1875, by Swami Dayanand Saraswati.
- They supported the four-fold varna system which was determined by merit and not by birth.
- They stood for equal rights for both men and women in social and educational matters.
- They were against the practice of untouchability, caste discrimination, child marriage, and supported widow remarriage and inter-caste marriages.
- The headquarters of Arya Samaj were later shifted to Lahore.
- They adopted the authority of the Vedas (sanctioned by rationalism and utilitarianism). They believed and disseminated, father-hood of God and brotherhood of man, equality of sexes, love and charity towards all.
- The DAV School was opened at Lahore, in 1886, by the effort of Lala Hansraj.
- Later in 1902 in Hardwar, the Gurukul Pathsala was also established.
- After the death of Dayanand in 1883, differences came in the Gurukul section led by Swami Shradhananda and DAV Section led by Lala Lajpat Rai and Lala Hansraj. The Gurkul section laid emphasis on the traditional pattern of education while the Dayanand-Anglo-Vedic section supported the dissemination of English education, which become the cause of the split of Arya Samaj in 1892.
- The Anglo- Vedic school set-up at Lahore in the year 1886 provided the nucleus for Arya Samaj movement. Lala Hansraj initiated the Gurukulnear Hardwar to promote the more traditional ideals of education.
- The Samaj started the shuddhi movement to convert non-Hindus to Hinduism. It became a factor in the development of communalism in India in the duration of 20th century,

Swami Dayananda

- Swami Dayanand Saraswati (or Mula shankar) was born in 1824 in Gujarat. He received education from Swami Virajonanda at Mathura. Formally conducted the first Arya Samaj unit at Bombay in 1875.
- He was known as the earliest Neo-nationalist.
- His motive was to unite India religiously, socially and nationally. He considered the Vedas as India's "Rock of Ages," the genuine seed of Hinduism. His objective was "Go back to Vedas".
- He was against of idol worship and spread the unity of God.
- He decried untouchability and casteism and advocated remarriage and an equal status of woman in society. He criticised infinite number of meaningless rights and launched a crusade against all religious superstitions.
- He was the first hindu reformer who converted from defence to attack, from protecting hindu faith from assaults.
- He was the writer of three books "Satyartha Prakash" in Hindi", Veda-Bhashya Bhumika in Hindi and Sanskrit and Veda Bhashya in Sanskrit.

Rama Krishna Paramhansa and Swami Vivekanand

Rama Krishna (1836-1886)

- His real name was Gadoidhar Chattopadhyay. He was born in 1836 in Kamarpukar village in Hooghly district of West Bengal.
- He worked as a priest in Dakshineshwar temple of Goddess Kali near in Calcutta.
- He found the religious salvation in traditional ways of renunciation, meditation and devotion
- He believed in the philosophy that service to man was service to god.
- He firmly believed in Indian thought and culture although he insisted on the truth in all religions.

Ram Krishna Mission

- The Ram Krishna monastic order (1887) and mission (in 1897) were established by Swami Vivekananda to carry on humanitarian relief and social work.
- It laid stress not on personal salvation, but on a social good or social service. Many schools, hospitals and dispensaries, orphanages, libraries were opened by it.

Swami Vivekananda (1863-1902)

- The real name of Swami Vivekanand was Narendranath Dutta and he was born at Calcutta in 1863. He was a disciple of Ramakrishna Paramhansa.
- He attended the Parliament of Religions held at Chicago in 1893 and published two papers- Prabhudha Bharata in English and Udbodhana in Bengali.

Social ideas

- He emphasised on social action and proclaimed the essential oneness of all religions and opposed any narrowness in religious matters.
- He trusted that only in uplifting the masses lay the vitality of the nation. He requested people to imbibe spirit of liberty, equality and free-thinking.
- He wanted to create a new social order based on freedom and equality.
- He was champion of emancipation of women and was of the view that "no social progress is possible without improving condition of women, who were most important instrument of social change".
- He said, "So long as millions live in hunger and ignorance, I hold every man a traitor who, having been educated at their expense, pays not the least heed to them."

Religious ideas

- Felt Hinduism needs reinterpretation.
- He subscribed to Vedanta, which he declared to be a fully rational system and reinterpreted the vedant which led to Neo-Vedantism.
- Denied the caste system and the Hindu emphasis on rituals and superstitions.
- He preached humanistic religion and was of the view that best form of worship was service to humanity.

Nationalism

- He contributed to the development of nationalism. His nationalism was based on 4 pillars of :
  - * Awakening of masses
  - * Development of physical and moral strength
  - * Unity based on common spirtual ideas
  - * Pride in ancient Indian glory.
- He focused on modernisation of India through Science and Technology.
- In 1897, founded of Ramakrishna Mission to carry on humanitarian relief and social work. Belur was the headquarter of his mission and Matha. An Irish woman Margaret Noble popularised the teachings of the Mission.
- In the year 1902, Swami Vivekananda was died.

Social and Cultural Awakening - Socio-religious Movements

Year	Place	Name of the Organisation	Founder
1815	Calcutta	Atmiya Samaj	Rammohan Roy
1828	Calcutta	Brahmo Samaj	Rammohan Roy
1829	Calcutta	Dharma Sabha	Radhakanta Dev
1839	Calcutta	Tattvabodhini Sabha	Debendranath Tagore
1840	Punjab	Nirankaris	Dayal Das, Darbara Singh, Rattan Chand, etc.
1844	Surat	Manav Dharma Sabha	Durgararn Manchharam
1849	Bombay	Parmahansa Mandli	Dadoba Panderung
1857	Punjab	Namdharis	Ram Singh
1861	Agra	Radha Sowami Satsang	Tulsi Ram
1866	Calcutta	Brahmo Samaj of India	Keshab Chandra Sen
1866	Deoband	Dar-ul-Ulurn	Maulana Hussain Ahmed
1867	Bombay	Prarthna Samaj	Dr Atmaram Pandurung
1875	Bombay	Arya Samaj	Swami Dayanand Saraswati
1875	New York (USA)	Theosophical Society	Madame HP Blavastky and Col H. S. Olcott
1878	Calcutta	Sudharam Brahmo Samaj	Anand Mohan Bose

1884	Pune (Poona)	Deccan Education Society	G G Agarkar
1886	Aligarh	Muhammadan Educational Conference	Sir Syed Ahmad Khan
1887	Bombay	Indian National Conference	M. G. Ranade
1887	Lahore	Deva Sarnaj	Shivnarayan Agnihotri
1894	Lucknow	Nadwah-ul-Ulama	Maulana Shibli Numani
1897	Belur	Ramakrishna Mission	Swami Vivekanand
1905	Bombay	Servents of Indian Society	Gopalakrishan Gokhale
1909	Pune (Poona)	Poona Seva Sadan	Mrs Ramabai Ranade and G. K. Devadhar
1911	Bombay	Social Service League	N. M. Joshi
1914	Allahabad	Seva Samiti	H. N. Kunzru

Tricks to Remember Socio-Religious Movements in India

B - Braho Samaj

P - Prarthna Samaj

A - Arya Samaj

R - Ramkrishna Mission

T - Theosophical Society

Y - Young Bengal Movement

Trick - Be Practical at Religious Topic in this year.

THE REVOLT OF 1857

- The revolt was basically anti-imperialist and both the sepoys and the civilians wanted to throw out the British imperialists.
- In 1856, the government decided to replace the old fashioned musket 'Brown Bess' by the 'Enfield rifle'. The training for the new weapon was to be imparted at Dum Dum, Ambala and Sialkot.
- On March 29, 1857 the sepoys at Barrackpur refused to use the greased cartridges and, Mangal Pandey, a Brahmin sepoy attacked the Sergeant Major.
- On 10th May, 1857, the sepoys of the 3rd cavalry at Meerut also refused to use the greased cartridges and broke out in open rebellion. They were immediately joined by the 11th and 20th Native infantries
- On May 12, 1857, Delhi was seized and Bahadur Shah-II of the Mughal dynasty was proclaimed the emperor of India. The real command was in the hands of Bakht Khan who had led the revolt at Bareilly and brought the troops to Delhi.
- In Kanpur the revolt was led by Nana Saheb, who proclaimed himself the Peshwa. He was assisted by Tantia Tope. The Rebels defeated General Windham outside Kanpur. Azimullah Khan also led to Kanpur.
- In Lucknow, Begum Hazrat Mahal and Ahmadullah led the revolt. Hazrat Mahal proclaimed Birjis Qadir as the nawab of Awadh against the wishes of the British. Henry Lawrence, the British resident was killed.
- In Jhansi, Rani Laxmibai assumed the leadership of the mutiny.
- In Bareilly, Khan Bahadur proclaimed himself as the Nawab and revolted there.
- In Arrah, Kunwar Singh led the revolt.
- In Faizabad, Maulavi Ahmadullah led the revolt.
- In Delhi, the revolt was suppressed by Colonel Nicholson and Hudson.
- In Kanpur and Lucknow, the revolt was suppressed by Campbell.
- In Jhansi, the revolt was suppressed by Hugh Rose.
- In Allahabad and Banaras, the revolt was suppressed by Colonel Neil.
- In Arrah, the revolt was suppressed by William Taylor and Vincent Eyre.
- Bahadur Shah 'Zafar' was arrested and departed to Rangoon where he died in 1862.
- Nana Sahib and Begum Hazrat Mahal escaped to Nepal.
- The revolt was poorly organised and restricted in its scope, and there was no unity among its leaders.
- There was no impact of rebellion beyond Narmada. Even in north India, Rajasthan, Punjab and Sind remained quiet.
- The Indian princes, such as Scindia of Gwalior, Nizam of Hyderabad, Gulab Singh of Kashmir, and princes of Rajasthan remained loyal to the British.
- The Indian intelligentsia or modern educated class kept away from the revolt.

- The control of the Indian administration was transferred from the East India Company to the crown by the Government of India Act, 1858.
- The Indian Civil Services Act was passed which provided for an annual competitive examination to be held in London for recruitment to the most coveted civil services in 1861.
- The Army Amalgamation Scheme of 1861 transferred the company's European troops to the service of crown. The general formula used to reorganise the army was that in Bengal presidency, the proportion between the European and Indian troops should be 1:2, while for Bombay and Madras presidency it should be 1:3.

Causes of the Revolt

Political

- Nana Sahib was refused pension, as he was the adopted son of Peshwa Baji Rao II.
- Lucknow was annexed in 1856, on charges of maladministration and Jhansi was annexed owing to Doctrine of Lapse.

Military Discrimination

- Indian soldiers were paid low salaries; they could not rise above the rank ofsubedar and were racially insulted. The soldiers were also distressed by the fact that their cherished Awadh state had been annexed by the British.

Religious Discrimination

- British social reforms (widow remaniage, abolition of Sati, school for girls, Christian missionaries)
- Rumours that Enfield rifles used greased (by pork or beef) cartridges.

Economic Grievances

- Heavy taxation, summary evictions, discriminatory tariff policy against Indian products and destruction of traditional handicrafts that hit peasants, artisans and small zamindars.

Impact of the Mutiny

- In August 1858, the British Parliament passed an Act, which put an end to the rule of the Company. The control of the British government in India was transferred to the British Crown.
- A minister of the British government, called the Secretary of State, who was made responsible for the government of India.
- The British Governor-General of India was now also given the title of Viceroy, who was also the representative of the monarch.
- Marked the end of British Imperialism and Princely states where assured against annexation. Doctrine of lapse was withdrawn
- After the revolt, the British pursued the policy of divide and rule.
- Far-reaching changes were made in the administration and increase of white soldiers in the army.
- Total expense of the suppression was borne by Indians.

Who Said What about 1857 Revolt

- British Historians - A mutiny, due to the use of greased cartridges.
- Disraeli (Opposition Leader) - A national revolt rooted in deep mistrust.
- V D Savarkar- First War of Independence.
- S B Choudhary- Civil Rebellion.
- R C Majumdar- Neither 'first' nor 'national' nor 'a war of independence'.
- S N Sen - An effort by the conservative elements to turn the clock back.
- Marxists - A soldier-peasant struggle against foreign and feudal bondage.
- Malleson - Sepoy Mutiny.

Fate of the Leaders

- Bahadur Shah II - Deported to Rangoon, where he died in 1862. His sons were shot dead.
- Nana Sahib and Begun Hazrat Mahal- Escaped to Nepal.
- Rani Jhansi - Died in the battle field.
- Tantia Tope - Was captured and executed on 15th April, 1859.

Suppression of the Revolt

- **Delhi** : Recaptured on 20 September, 1857 by John Nicholson
- **Kanpur** : Recaptured on 6 December, 1857 by Colin Campbell
- **Lucknow** : Recaptured on 21 March ,1858 by Colin Campbell.
- **Jhansi** : Recaptured by Hugh Rose
- **Arrah** : William Taylor and Eyre suppressed the revolt

THE INDIAN NATIONAL CONGRESS

Political Associations Before 1885

- Association of Landholders: Landholders Society (1837), Bengal British India Society (1843). In 1851, the two were merged to form the British Indian Association.

- Bombay Association and Madras Native Association were established in 1852. They sent petitions suggesting changes in EIC's charter to end company's monopoly of salt and indigo.
- Associations like Poona Sarvjanik Sabha were established to promote reform and political consciousness.
- 1876- Indian Association was founded In Calcutta by Surendranath Banerjee, Anand Mohan Bose.
- Madras Mahajan Sabha and Bombay Presidency Association were established in 1884.
- In December 1883. the Indian Association of Surendra Nath Bannerjee and Anand Mohan Bose decided to invite prominent public men and associations to discuss questions of general concern. This was referred to as the National
- Conference (in 1883) and is described as the 'dress rehearsal' for the Indian National Congress (INC).
- National Conference and Indian National Union (by A O Hume in 1884) merged to form the Indian National Congress in 1885.

Indian National Congress

- The first meeting of the INC was organised by A O Hume at Gokaldas Tejpal Sanskrit College on 28th December 1885 (Bombay). Its first president was W C Bonnerjee. It was the first organised expression of the Indian National movement on an all-India scale.
- Hume's main purpose in encouraging the foundation of the Congress was probably to provide a "safety valve" to the growing discontent among the educated Indians.

Aims and Objectives of Congress

- Promotion of friendship amongst the countrymen.
- Development and consolidation of feeling of national unity, irrespective of race, caste, religion or provinces.
- Formulation of popular demands and presentation before the Government through petitions.
- Training and organisation of public opinion.
- Consolidation of sentiments of national unity.
- Recording of the opinions of educated classes on pressing problems.
- Laying down lines for future course of action in public interest.

The Methods of Work

- Early Congressmen had faith in peaceful and constitutional agitation.
- Prayers and petitions were the instruments.
- Congress sessions lasted only for three days a year. It had no machinery to carry on the work in the interval.
- They believed in the goodness of the British nation and believed that all would be well if the British could be acquainted with the true state of affairs in India. Deputations of Indians were sent to inform the British public.
- In 1889, a British Committee of INC was founded.

Important Sessions of INC

Year	Presidents	Venue
1. 1885	W.C. Bonnerjee	Bombay
2. 1886	Dadabhai Naroji	Calcutta
3. 1887	Badruddin Tyabji	Madras
4. 1888	George Yule	Allahabad
5. 1889	Sir William Wedderburn	Bombay
6. 1890	Pherozshah Mehta	Calcutta
7. 1891	P. Ananda Charlu	Nagpur
8. 1892	W.C. Bonnerjee	Allabad
9. 1893	Dadabhai Naroji	Lahore
10. 1894	Alfred Webb	Madras
11. 1895	S. N. Banerjea	Poona
12. 1896	Rahimtulla M Sayani	Calcutta
13. 1897	C.Sankaran Nair.	Amravati
14. 1898	Ananda Mohan Bose	Madras
15. 1899	R.C. Dutt	Lucknow
16. 1900	N.G Chandavarkar	Lahore
17. 1901	D.E. Wacha	Calcutta
18. 1902	Hasan Imam	Bombay
	S.N. Bonerjea	Ahmedabad
19. 1903	Lal Mohan Ghose	Madras
20. 1904	Sir Henry Cotton	Bombay
21. 1905	G.K. Gokhale	Benaras
22. 1906	Dadabhai Naoroji	Calcutta
23. 1907	Dr. Rash Behari Ghosh (Suspended)	Surat
1908	Dr. Rash Behari Ghosh	Madras
24. 1909	Pandit Madan Mohan Malaviya	Lahore
25. 1910	Sir William Wedderburn	Allahabad
26. 1911	Pandit B.N. Dhar.	Calcutta
27. 1912	R.N. Modholkar	Bankipore
28. 1913	Nawab Syed Mohammad Bahadur	Karachi
29. 1914	Bhupendranath Basu	Madras
30. 1915	Sir Satyendra Prasad Sinha	Bombay
31. 1916	Ambika Charan Majumdar	Lucknow

Year	Presidents	Venue
32. 1917	Mrs. Annie Besant	Calcutta
1918	Hassan Imam (Special session)	
33. 1918	Pandit Madan Mohan Malaviya	Delhi
34. 1919	Motilal Nehru	Amritsar
35. 1920	Lala Lajpat Rai (Suspended)	Calcutta
	C.Vijayraghavachariar (annual)	Nagpur
36. 1921	C.R. Das (in prison)	Ahmedabad
	Hakim Ajmal Khan (Acting)	
37. 1922	C.R. Das	Gaya
38. 1923	Maulana Abul Kalam Azad (suspended)	Delhi
	Maulana Mahamlnad Ali (Annual)	Golconda
39. 1924	Mahatma Gandhi	Belgaun
40. 1925	Mrs Sarojini Naidu.	Cawnpore
41. 1926	S. Srinivasa Iyengar.	Guwahati
42. 1927	Dr. M.A. Ansari	Madras
43. 1928	Pandit Motilal Nehru.	Calcutta
44. 1929	Jawaharial Nehru.	Lahore
1930	(No session) but Independence Day Pledge was adopted on 26th Jan, 1930.	
45. 1931	Vallabhabhai Patel	Karachi
46. 1932	R. Amritlal (session was banned)	
47. 1933	Mrs. J.M. Sen Gupta (session was banned)	Calcutta
48. 1934	Rajendra Prasad (Continued again for 1935)	Bombay
49. 1936	Jawahar lal Nehru	Lucknow
50. 1937	Jawahar lal Nehru	Faizpur
51. 1938	S.C. Bose	Haripura
52. 1939	S.C. Bose (Re-elected for 1939)	Tripuri
53. 1940	Maulana Abul Kalam Azad	Ramgarh
1941-45	(No sessions, caused by arrests and jailing)	
54. 1946	Acharya J. B. Kripalani	Meerut
55. 1948	B. Pattabhi Sitaramayya	Jaipur

SWADESHI MOVEMENT

- It started as an anti-partition agitation in Bengal and boycott was first suggested by Krishnakumar Mitra in Sanjivni in 1905.
- The boycott of British products was followed by the advocacy of swadeshi and to buy indigenously produced goods as a patriotic duty.

Stages of Swadeshi Movement

- 1905-1909- Movement was limited to Bengal and launched as a protest movement.
- In the year 1909-1910, the movement was spread out all over the country and launching of anticolonial movement.
- 1910-1911 Swadeshi movement merged with revolutionary terrorist movement of 1st phase and led to foundation of numerous secret associations.
- To promote the indigeneous industries, some Swadeshi Enterprises were set-up, viz. Calcutta Potteries, Bengal Chemicals and Bengal Lakshmi Cotton Mills. Swadeshi melas or fairs were also organised for selling handicrafts.
- Charkha (spinning wheel) became to typify the popular concern for country's economic self-sufficiency.
- The 'Carlyle Circular' withdrew grants and scholarships to educational institutions. Therefore the nationalist educational institutes were founded, e.g. Bengal Technical Institute, Bengal National College and School with Aurobindo Ghosh as its principal.
- Rabindranath Tagore called for the observance of Rakshabandhan as a symbol of brotherhood.
- A numours of volunteer bodies or Samitis were founded in that duration. Swadesh Bandhav Samiti of Barisal founded by Ashwini Dutt was the largest.
- The Anushilan Society was having two branches. **1.** Pulin Das led the Dacca branch. **2.** Birendra Ghosh and Jatin Banerjee led the Calcutta Branch.

Impact of Swadeshi Movement

- Swadeshi movement was stepping stone of the Nationalist movement, which led to beginning of organized political movement in India.
- It created the rise of Neo-Nationalist movement.
- It became the reason of the Surat split.
- Revival of indigenous industries.
- It led to the boycott of foreign goods.
- Revival and emergence of nationalist art and literature.
- It focused on developing the concept of national education.

Regional Variations

- Bihar and United Provinces were quiet.
- B C Pal in Madras led Vande Matram Movement.
- Lala Lajpat Rai and Ajit Singh led the movement in Punjab.
- Tilak began the Swadesh Vastra Pracharini Sabha.
- Vinayak Savarkar and Ganesh Savarkar founded the Mitra Mela was a kind of revolutionary secret society in Nasik.
- Tilak was imprisoned for 6 years in Mandalay jail and was released in 1914.

Failure of Swadeshi Movement by 1908

- Severe government repression.
- Lack of effective organisation of all leaders
- Split in nationalist ranks.
- The Swadeshi leaders refrained from rallying the peasants.
- Narrow social base.

Acts Passed by the Government to Suppress the Movement

- Prevention of Seditious Meetings Act (1907)
- Crinlinal Law (Amendment) Act (1908)
- Indian Newspapers (Incitement to Offences) Act (1908)
- Explosive Substances Act (1908)
- Indian Press Act (1910)

The Moderates

- The Congress programme during the first phase of the Freedom Movement (1885-1905) was very moderate.
- It asked for the mild constitutional reforms, economic relief, administrative reorganisation and protection of civil rights.
- The strongest fact made by the nationalists during this phase was about the economic drain of India.
- The methods for political reformation of moderates were constitutional agitations within four walls.
- The Moderates firmly believed that the British people and the parliament wanted to be just to India but did not know the true state of affairs.

The other important demands were:

- The organisation of the provincial councils,
- Simultaneous holding of examinations for the I.C.S in India and England.
- The reconstitution of Indian Council, 1892.
- The separation of the judiciary from the executive, and the abolishment of the Arms Act.
- The appointment of Indians to the commissioned ranks in the Army,
- The cutting back of military expenditure, etc.
- Indianisation of higher grades of the admini-strative services on economic, political and moral grounds, During the first twenty years (1885-1905) there was practically no change in the Congress programme.

The leaders were careful in their demands. They did not want to annoy the govermnent and increase the risk of suppression.

To them, the government was forced to pass the Indian Councils Act, 1892 but the moderates raised the slogan 'No taxation without representation'.

Therefore in this period a general impression grew that the Moderates were political mendicants, only petitioning and praying to the British Government for petty concessions. The thinking of moderates behind such requests was that, their belief in British Government and administration they felt that it is important for continued political progress in India.

The Extremists

Ideological Basis of Extremism

- The attachment to rationalism and western ideals had almost alienated the 'Liberal' (Moderate) school from the masses in India.

Socio-religious reform influenced the extremists ideology tremendously

- The socio-religious movements was start by Swami Vivekananda like Ramakrishna Paramahamsa and his disciple.
- Swami Dayananda, founded and the Arya Samaj with a strong emphasis in native pride, played a vital role in the birth of extremist philosophy.
- They derived inspiration from their traditional cultural values and wanted to have relations with other countries in terms of quality and self-respect.
- They all were aganist the Moderates who were considered by them to be servile and respectful to the British.
- They gave a call for passive resistance in addition to Swadeshi and boycott.
- Social Reform Movements like Arya Sămaj and Theosophical Society gave impetus to political radicalism. The political radicals derived inspiration from their traditional cultural values.

Main Extremist Leaders

- There were three groups of extremists- **1.** The Maharashtra Group (headed by Bal Gangadhar Tilak), **2.** The Bengal Group (represented by B C Pal and Aurobindo) and **3.** The Punjab group (led by Lala Lajpat Rai,)

- Shri Aurobindo published New Lamps for Old in the Indu Prakash in 1853-94. It was the first systematic critique of the Moderates.
- Bal Gangadhar Tilak resented any interference by foreigners or British government into the domestic and private life of the people. He argued with the reformers over the Age of Consent Bill in 1891.
- Tilak asserted, "Swaraj is My Birth Right and I will have it". He was also the editor of the Maratta (English) and the Kesari (Marathi).

Reasons for the Emergence of Extremists

1. The realisation that the true nature of British rule was exploitative.
2. International influences and events, which abolished the myth of European supremacy. These included -
   - Abyssinia's (Ethiopia) victory over Italy
   - Boer Wars (1899-1802) in which the British faced reverses
   - Japan's victory over Russia (1905)
   - Nationalist movements worldwide
3. Lack of satisfaction with the achievements of Moderates.
4. Reactionary policies of Curzon such as the Calcutta Corporation Act (1899), the Official Secrets Act (1904), the Indian Universities Act (1904) and Partition of Bengal (1905).
5. Existence of a militant school of thought and the emergence of a trained leadership.

Conflict and the Surat Split

- Tilak was unpopular with the Moderate group of Bombay.
- At the Calcutta Congress (1906), Bipin Chandra Pal and Aurobindo wanted Tilak to become the President of the Congress.
- But the Moderates were not ready to accept him because of Tilak's revolutionary nature.
- Pheroj Shah Mehta, MM Malaviya and Gokha le were heckled and booed.
- Ultimately a compromise was hurriedly made and the agreeable resolutions on the partition of Bengal, Swadeshi and Boycott were phrased and they secured a smooth passage in the open session.
- With the foundation of the Deccan Sabha, the division between the Extremists and the Moderates in Maharashtra was complete.
- The Congress split in 1907 at Surat under the presidentship of Rash Behari Ghosh.

Morley-Minto Reforms

There were following reforms made by Morley-Minto.

- Number of elected members in Imperial and Provincial Legislative Councils increased-elected non-officials still in minority.
- Separate electorates introduced for Muslims.
- Elected non-officials to be elected indirectly-thus, elections introduced for the first time.
- Legislatures could pass resolutions, ask questions and supplementaries, vote separate items of the budget. No responsibility entrusted to the legislators.
- One Indian to be on viceroy's executive council.
- Aimed at dividing the nationalist ranks and at rallying the Moderates and the Muslims to the Government's side.

HOME RULE MOVEMENT

- After Tilak's return, having served sentence of six years in Mandalay, he tried securing the readmission of himself and other Extremists into the Indian National Congress.
- With the need being felt for popular pressure to attain concessions, disillusionment with Morley-Minto Reforms and wartime miseries, Tilak and Annie Besant readied to assume leadership.
- The Home Rule League was pioneered on lines of a similar movement in Ireland.

Objective

The main objective of Home Rule League was:

- To have the self government for India in British Empire.
- To work for National Education, Social and Political reforms.

Tilak asked for the swaraj with the demand for the formation of linguistic states and education in vernacular. He also used Home Rule to put an end to caste feeling among the common people and advocated abolition of untouchability.

- Tilak (April) and Annie Besant and S. Subramaniam Iyer (September) established Home Rule Leagues in 1916.
- Tilak's League was to work in Maharashtra, Karnataka, Central Provinces and Berar and Annie Besant's in the rest of India.
- Annie Besant set up the newspapers-New India, Commonweal and Young India (1914)
- Tilak published -Mahratta and Kesari.
- Jamnadas Dwarkadas, Shankarlal Banker, Indulal Yagnik, George Arundale, B P Wadia and L P Ramaswamy Iyer were in Besant's League.

- Home Rule Movement declined after Besant accepted the proposed Montford Reforms and Tilak went to Britain to fight the Libel suit against Valentine Chirol's Indian Unrest.

Methods

- The tactics of this movement were to create public opinion in favour of Home Rule through public meeting, also organising discussions, reading rooms propaganda through public meetings, newspapers, pamphlets, posters, etc.
- Positive Gains Emphasis shifted to the masses permanently organisational link established between town and country they efforted to prepared a generation of ardent nationalists, influenced Moderate-Extremist reunion at Lucknow (1916).
- Lucknow Session-1916 (Presided by Ambika Charan Mazumdar) Lucknow Pact (1916) was signed between the INC and the Muslim League. The main provisions of this pact were as following:

  (a) Principle of separate electorates was accepted, (b) Demand for a representative government and Dominion Status for India.

Results

- The movement can be understood as the starting for attainment of Swaraj.
- It discredited moderates of INC and created condition for readmission of Neo-Nationalists in 1916.
- The biggest result of this movement was the Montague Declaration of 1917-Greatest political achievement.
- The Education Programme was started.

Rowlatt Satyagrah

The 1919 Sedition Committee, headed by Justice Rowlatt, led to the Rowlatt Act (18 March, 1919) whereby war time 'restrictions of civil rights were to be made permanent by:

(a) System of special courts

(b) Detention without trial for 2 years maximum

(c) Greater police powers.

- This Act authorised the Government to imprison any person without trial and conviction of the court of law.
- This law provided the authentication to the Government to suspend the right of Habeas Corpus, which had been the foundation of civil liberties in Britain.
- Anti-Rowlatt Satyagraha intended to mobilise public opinion against the Act.
- It was first countrywide agitation by Gandhi and marked the foundation of Non Cooperation Movement.
- During March and April 1919, the country witnessed a significant political awakening in India. There were hartals, strikes, processions and demonstrations.
- On April 13-1919 (Baisakhr Day), Dr. Saifuddin Kitchlew and Satyapal were addressing a peaceful rally in Jallianwala Bagh when General Dyer ordered for the infamous massacre.
- The Hunter Commission's report on the Punjab disturbances was described by Gandhi as a 'white wash'.
- In the result of this cruelty, Tagore returned his knighthood in protest.
- Sardar Udham Singh who took the name of Ram Mohammed Singh murdered Dyer in England.

Freedom Struggle Phase-1

The Earlier Phase

South Africa : (a) In 1907, Satyagraha began against compulsory registration and passes for Indians (b) 1910 Satyagraha against immigration restrictions, de-recognition of non-christian Indian marriages while deciding the cases of new entrants and (c) tax on ex-indentured labourers.

Literary Influences on Gandhi : John Ruskin's Unto the Zast, Emerson, Thoreau, Leo Tolstoy, the Bible and the Bhagvad Gita.

Appeal of Gandhi :

(1) He was already a leader of action who had achieved results in South Africa.

(2) The social composition of Indians in S. Africa made him an all-India figure while the Lal-Bal- Pal, trio were essentially regional leaders.

(3) The principle of ahimsa mediated internal diffferences contributing. to a joint nationalist struggle.

(4) Gandhi's social utopia was a critique of Industrialism, and appealed to those alienated by it.

(5) The use of the Indian idiom (eg Ram Rajya) helped in communication.

(6) Rumours greatly enhanced his stature.

Gandhi in Champaran, Ahmedabad and Kheda

- Champaran is in (Bihar) and the chaos began in the early 19th century when European planters had involved the cultivators in agreements that forced them to cultivate indigo in 3/20th of their holdings (Tin-Kathia).
- But when indigo became unremunerative, the European planters imposed higher taxes to compensate their losses in the international trade at that time.

- Gandhi (in July 1917) ji successfuly abolished the Tin-Kathia system and refund was made to the cultivators in wages.
- In the year 1918 March, the dispute occurred between the mill owners at Ahmedabad and employees over the 'plague bonus' which the former wanted to withdraw once the epidemic was over.
- The workers troubled by inflation wanted adequate compensation.
- From this typical situation, Gandhi initially persuaded the mill owners and workers to agree to arbitration by a tribunal, but the mill owners withdrew after commitment.
- Gandhi then advised the worker to go on strike and he under took hunger strike after which the mill owners were pressurised into accepting the tribunal award of 35 percent increase in wages.
- In 1917-1918, the peasants of Kheda district were extremely disappointed by the failure of crops and the government ignored their appeals for the remission of land revenue.
- The peasants of Kheda were already hard pressed because of plague, high prices and drought.
- Appeals and petition having failed, Gandhi advised the withholding of revenue and asked the peasants to fight unto death.
- After this long hardship process, the Government directed that revenue should be recovered only from those peasants who could pay, the movement was withdrawn.
- Gandhi observed his first hunger strike at Ahmedabad (1918) for the mill workers for increasing the wages.
- His first Civil Disobedience movement was the Champaran Satyagraha.
- His first all-India Satyagraha was the Rowlatt Satyagraha.
- His first Non-Cooperation Movement was started from Kheda Satyagraha.

Khilafat and The NCM

In the period of First World War, Turkey was allied with Germany and Austria against the British. The Indian Muslims regarded the Sultan of Turkey as their spiritual leader, Khalifa, so naturally they sympathised with Turkey. After the War, the British removed the Khalifa from power and fragmented Turkey. Therefore, the Muslims started the Khilafat movement in India for the restoration of the Khalifa's position. The demands were:

- Khalifa's control should be retained over the Muslim sacred places.
- After the post-war territorial adjustments, the Khalifa should be left with sufficient territories.

Khilafat Movement in India

- The Khilafat issue was not directly linked with politics in India but the Khilafat leaders (Ali Brothers, Maulana Azad, Hakim Ajmal Khan and Hasrat Mohani) were eager in enlisting the support of Hindus.
- Gandhi turned this situation in positive way as to bring about Hindu-Muslim unity against the British.
- The publication of the terms of the Treaty with Turkey, which were very harsh, and also the publication of the Hunter Committee Report on 'Punjab disturbances' in May 1920 infuriated the Indians.
- Thus, at one level, the Indian political situation also merged with the issue of Khilafat.
- Initially the Khilafat leaders limited their actions to meetings, petitions, and deputations in favour of the Khilafat.
- Later a militant trend emerged, demanding an active agitation such as stopping all cooperation with the British.
- The Central Khilafat Committee met at Allahabad.
- The meeting was attended by a number of Congress and Khilafat leaders.
- The result of this meeting was thay non-cooperation was declared against the government and it also included the rejection of all the government titles.
- Boycott of civil services, army and police, i.e. all government jobs.
- Non-payment of taxes to the Govemment.
- August 1, 1920 was fixed as the date to start the movement.

THE NON-COOPERATION MOVEMENT

- The movement was the first huge political compaign against Britishers polices and the first India mass-based cooperation under Gandhi Ji.
- The Movement was launched as per resolution of Calcutta session and ratified in Nagpur session in Dec 1920. Anti-Rowlatt Agitation, Jalianwala Bagh tragedy, Khilafat Movement, General economic, distress during and after the war were the reasons of Non-Cooperation Movement.

- The Tilak Swarajya Fund was started to finance the Non-Cooperation Movement.
- The main objective of the movement was on rejection of schools, colleges, law courts and advocacy of the use of Charkha. There was widespread student unrest and top lawyers, like C. R. Das and Motilal Nehru gave up their legal practice. Afterwards, the stress was on boycott of foreign cloth and boycott of the forthcoming visit of the Prince of Wales in November, 1921; popularisation of Charkha and Khadi and Jail Bharo by Congress volunteers.
- Swaraj or self-rule, Redressal of Punjab wrongs and Khilafat issue were demanded through Non-Cooperation Movement.
- The Non-Cooperation Movement raised very powerfully from January 1920 to early February 1922.
- But soon, the attack on a local police station by angry peasants at Chauri Chaura, in Gorakhpur district of UP on February 5, 1922, changed the complete situation. This made Gandhi, disturbed by this incident and he withdrew the Non- Cooperation Movement.

Spread of NCM

United Provinces

- It became a strong base of the Gandhian Non-Cooperation Movement.
- Organised non-cooperation was an affair of cities and small towns.
- In the countryside, the movement engaged with the Kisan movement.
- The peasants in the movement aroused in revolt not only against Talukdars, but also, against merchants with widespread agrarian-riots under the leadership of Baba Ram Chandra.
- In late 1921, the 'Eka' movement under Madari Pasi started. Demand was conversion of produce rents into cash.

Punjab

- The Akali movement for reform and control of the Gurudwaras got closely identified with non-cooperation.
- Udasi Sikh Mahants, who managed Gurudwaras, had issued Hukumnamas against Ghadrites and honoured Dyer.
- Akalis were led by Kartar Singh Jhabbar, Master Tara Singh and Baba Kharak Singh (head of SGPC).
- The Shiromani Gurudwara Prabandhak Committee was founded by the Shiromani Akali Dal.

Andhra

- The Non-Cooperation Movement got the success in the Andhra delta area.
- Alluri Sitaram Raju united the tribals in Andhra and merge their demands with those of the Non-Cooperation Movement.
- Temple entry for Ezhavas and Pulayas was led by Sri Narayan Guru, NK Asan and TK Madhavan. In 1924, Vaikom Satyagraha in Travancore was led by KP Kesava Menon.

Revolutionary Terrorism

The youth of India had played a vital role in the Swadeshi movement in the hope and belief that Extremist methods of agitation, such as boycott and passive resistance would take the national movement out of its elitist groove. The Extremist leadership did not analyse adequately the weaknesses of the movement and their failure to suggest new ways out of the impasse further strengthened revolutionary ideas of assassination and dacoities. Brutal repression of the Swadeshi movement by the Government, too added to the trend of revolutionary terrorism. The youth drew inspiration from Irish nationalists and the Russian Nihilists.

Bengal

1902 First revolutionary groups in Midnapore and Calcutta (The Anushilan Samiti).

1906 Yugantar and Sandhya in Bengal and Kal in Maharastra.

1908 Prafulla Chaki and Khudiram Bose attempt to murder Muzaffarpur Judge, Kingsford. Alipore conspiracy case involving Aurobindo Ghosh, Barindra Kumar Ghosh and others.

1912 Bomb thrown at Viceroy Hardinge by Rashbehari Bose and Sachin Sanyal.

Anushilan Committee (a secret society) whose Dhaka section had 500 branches.

Sandhya, Yugantar newspapers advocating revolutionary activity.

Punjab

Revolutionary activity by Lala Lajpat Rai, Ajit Singh, Aga Haidar Syed Haidar Raza, Bhai Pannanand, Lalchand 'Falak', Sufi Ambaprassad.

Maharashtra

1879 Ramosi Peasant Force by Vasudev Balwant Phadke.

1890s Tilak's attempts to propagate militancy among the youth through Shivaji and Ganapati festivals and journals Kesri and Maharatta.

1897 Chapeker brothers assassinated two unpopular British Officials Rand, the Plague commissioner of Poona and Lt. Ayerst.

1899 V.D. Savarkar and his brother Ganesh organised a secret society Mitra Mela. They were co-accused in Nasik and Gwalior Conspiracy cases).

1904 Mitramela and Abhinav Bharat were merged.

1909 Jackson, District Magistrate of Nasik was assasinated.

Abroad

1905 Shyamji Krishnavarma set up Indian Home Rule Society and India House and brought out a journal 'the Sociologist' in London.

1909 Madan Lal Dhingra murdered Curzon- Wyllie; Madame Bhikaji Cama operated from Paris and Geneva and brought out journal Bande Mataram.

FREEDOM STRUGGLE PHASE-2

Influences on Revolutionary

Terrorism

- Upsurge of working class trade unionism after the war; the revolutionaries wanted to harness the revolutionary potential of the new emergent class for nationalist revolution
- Russian revolution, 1917
- Newly sprouting communist groups with their emphasis on Marxism, socialism and proleteriat
- Journals extolling the self-sacrifice of revolutionaries

Hindustan Republican Army (HRA)

- In October, 1924 Hindustan Republican Army was founded by Sachin Sanyal, Jogesh Chatterjee and Ramprasad Bismil (HRA) near Kanpur.
- HRA aimed at organising an armed revolution and establishing a Federal Republic of the USA with a government elected on the basis of adult franchise.
- Sachin Sanyal wrote 'Bandi Jivari'. Hindustan Republican Army was later renamed Hindustan Socialist Republican Association (HSRA).
- The remarkable action of Hindustan Republican Army was Kakori Robbery in August 1925.

Hindustan Socialist Republican Association (HSRA)

- Under the leadership of Chandra Shekhar Azaad, it was founded in September 1928 at Feroz Shah Kotla,
- They were also influenced by socialist ideas.

Miscellaneous

- Bhagat Singh, Azad and Rajguru shot dead Saunders, the police official responsible for the lathicharge in Lahore.
- Bhagat Singh and B. K. Dutt threw bombs in the Central Legislative Assembly on 8 April, 1929 to protest against the passage of the Public Safety Bill and the Trade Disputes Bill. The objective was not to kill but to make the deaf hear.
- Bhagat Singh wrote: Why I Am An Atheist.
- Jatin Das (Sept, 1929) died after a prolonged fast in jail.
- After raiding Chittagong Armoury, Surya Sen proclaimed the formation of Provisional Revolutionary Government and the Indian Republican Army, which fought at Jalalabad.
- Bina Das fired point blank at the governor while receiving her degree 'at the convocation.
- Kalpana Datta was arrested and tried along with Surya Sen.
- Udham Singh assassinated General Dowyer.
- After the debacle of Non-Cooperation Movement in 1922, a group of leaders (No-changers: Ansari, Rajapogalachari, Kasturiranga Iyengar, Rajendra Prasad and Vallabh Bhai Patel) who still believed in Gandhian methods advocated on continuing Gandhian constructive rural work while another group, the Pro-changers with such stalwarts like, Motilal Nehru, C. R. Das demanded Congress participation in council politics.
- The Gaya session (1922) rejected council entry.
- A compromise was struck by which Pro-changers were allowed to stand for elections even as their faith in the constructive programme was reiterated.
- Their immediate objective was 'speedy attainment of full Dominion Status-Swaraj', including 'the right to frame a constitution with provincial autonomy.
- During the elections of 1923, the Das-Nehru group under the banner of the Swaraj Party became the single largest party in the Central Assembly, Bombay and Bengal Councils.
- The Swarajists pursued an obstructionist strategy to defeat all proposals for legislative enactments.
- C. R. Das died in 1925 and a section of Swarajists (NC Kelkar, MR Jayakar, Lajpat Rai and Malaviya) converted as responsivists . Madan Mohan Malviya and Lala Lajpat Rai founded the Independent Congress Party and rallied the Hindus. In 1933, it was reorganised as Congress Nationalist Party.

- In 1930, the Swarajists walked out of the Assemblies in accordance to the Lahore resolution. The Swaraj Party now merged with the Congress as the country started to prepare for the second round of direct mass action to achieve complete independence.

Towards Civil Disobedience Movement

Simon Commission

- The British (Lord Birkenhead was the Secy. Of State) decided in 1927 to appoint a commission to recommend further constitutional reforms.
- The Indian protest was on the grounds that the commission headed by Sir John Simon was an "all white" commission.
- Lord Birkenhead believed that Indians are notable to arrive at any consensus and that the British did not find anyone from among the Indians fit enough to serve in a body that would make recommendation about India's political future.
- The arrival of Simon Commission in India led to a powerful protest movement in which nationalist enthusiasm and unity reached new heights.
- On 3rd February, the commissions was greeted with hartals and black flag demonstrations.
- They could not carry on with their coalition partners because of conflicting ideas

Nehru Report

- To measure up to the challenge of the British, the Report was tabled in 1928.
- Since there it is considered as the first major Indian effort to draft a constitutional framework for India, complete with lists of central and provincial subjects and fundamental rights.
- It asked for responsible government both in the center and in the provinces. But, it advocated Dominion Status and not complete independence.
- It demanded universal adult suffrage.
- It denied to separate communal electorates. It proposed reservation for the Muslims at the center and in provinces in which they were in minority.
- The report suggested equal rights for women, freedom to from unions, and disconnection of the state from religion in any form.
- The session of Calcutta of INC in 1928 approved the report. INC now wanted the English government to either accept or reject the recommendations of the suggested constitution, based on Dominion status. By Swaraj, the Congress leaders had so far meant the Dominion Status for India within the-ambit of the British Empire.

Irwin Offer of 1929

- The Dominion Status (OS) was a natural issue of Indian constitutional progress.
- A proposed Round Table Conference (RTC) after the publication of the Simon Report.

Lahore Session (Dec 1929)

The discussion with Irwin broke down on the issue of Dominion Status, which the British were reluctant to concede immediately. Jawaharlal Nehru replaced Motilal Nehru as the INC President at Lahore and the major decisions taken at the Lahore session -

- The Round Table Conference to be boycotted.
- The Purna-Swaraj or complete independence as the main objective of Congress.
- The launch a programme of civil disobedience, including non payment of taxes.
- January, 26th 1930 became the certain date as the 1st Independence day to be celebrated everywhere.
- On the December 31, 1929 the tricolour was hoisted on the banks of Ravi.

CIVIL DISOBEDIENCE MOVEMENT

Beginning

- After the INC authorised Gandhiji to start CDM, he placed Eleven Point Ultimatum to Irwin (31 Jan 1930) for administrative reforms and stated that if Lord Irwirn accepted them, there would be no need for agitation.
- The Civil Disobedience Movement began with the Dandi March on 12th March.

Programme

Salt production had geographical limitations. So, in other parts of the country the movement included- (a) Picketing of liquor shops and auctions (b) No revenue campaign in Bardoli (c) Forest Satyagrahas (d) Large-scale resignation of rural officials (e) Refusal of chaukidari tax (f) Prabhat Pheris-singing of national songs (g) Patrikas- distribution of illegal pamphlets

Regional Spread

- **Chittagong**: 18th April, armoury raid by Surya Sen.
- **Peshawar**: 23 April, Khan Abdul Ghaffar Khan's Khudai Khidmatgar activated the NWFP leading to rioting where the Hindu Gharwal rifles refused to fire on Muslim masses.
- **Sholapur**: News of Gandhi's arrest (4th May) led to working class strike form 7th to 17th May.

- **Darshana** salt works (21 May) satyagraha led by Sarojini Naidu, Imam Sabeb and Maniklal Gandhi.
- **Madras**: Rajagopala Chari led the march from Trichinopoly to Vedaranniyam.
- **Kerala**: K. Kelappan marched from Calicut to Payannur. Central Provinces held forest satyagrahas.

Pause

- With occasion of rising violence and with majority of leading Congress leaders behind bars, Gandhiji called for rather sudden retreat. He started a talk with Irwin, which culminated in the Delhi Pact of 5th March, popularly called the Gandhi-Irwin pact.

Delhi Pact (Gandhi-Irwin Pact) (1931)

- Irwin agreed to release all political prisoners, except those who were engaged in violence.
- Right to make salt in coastal villages for personal consumption.
- Gandhi agreed to suspend CDM and participate in 2nd RTC.

Second Round Table Conference

Gandhi ji agreed to attend the second Round Table Conference, scheduled to be held in September 1931. He asked control over defence and foreign affairs. Hindu Mahasabha demanded federal responsibility which was opposed by Muslim League and the Princes. Ambedkar asked separate electorates for Dalits, which was opposed by Gandhi.

The Government denied to accept the basic nationalist demand of freedom on the basis of immediate grant of dominion status.

Communal Award and Poona Pact

On August 16, 1932 McDonald announced the proposal on minority representation, known as the "Communal Award" which recommended:

- to double the existing seats in provincial legislatures
- to keep the system of separate electorate for the minorities intact
- to provide weightage to Muslims in provinces where they were in minority
- to reserve 3% seats for women in all provincial legislatures, except in NWFP
- to recognise depressed classes as minority community and make them entitled to the right of separate electorte, and
- to disseminate seats to labour, landlords, and traders and industrialists

Gandhi's objections

Gandhi responded very strongly to the proposal of granting the right of separate electorates to the Depressed Classes. He regarded the Depressed Classes as an integral part of Hindu society. He felt what was required was not protection of the depressed classes but root eradication of untouchability. He had the firm belief that the Hindus would do full social justice to fully integrate them within their fold. He wanted that the depressed classes be elected through a joint and if possible, a wider electorate through universal franchise.

To persuade the recalcitrant Ambedkar to accept his approach, Gandhi, then in the Yarvada Jail, resorted to fast unto death. To save his life, the Poona Pact with the following main terms resulted between him and Ambedkar on 25 September, 1932.

- 147 seats were to be allotted to the depressed classes in the provincial legislatures as against 71 promised by the Communal Award and 18% of the total in central legislature.
- The adequate representation for the depressed classes in the civil services.
- Ambedkar also accepted the principle of joint electorate.

CDM compared to NCM

- Launched to attain Poorna Swaraj and not merely the selections of wrongs.
- It has the complete deliberate violation of law and not merely non-cooperation.
- In the initial phase urban people participated, but it spread to rural areas where it gained its maximum strength.
- Lack of Muslims and labour participation.
- Women participated in a huge numbers of picket shops.

Impact of CDM

- The Congress swept the polls in most provinces in 1937.
- The Left objective emerged, for the Movement had aroused expectations, which Gandhian strategy could not fulfill.
- At the level of leadership, Nehru and Bose voiced the new mood, forcing the need to combine nationalism with radical social and economic programmes.
- Few Congress activists formed a socialist group within the party in 1934.
- The Kisan Sabhas with anti-zamindar programmes developed rapidly in provinces, like Bihar and Andhra.

Towards Qutt India Movement

Following the withdrawal of the CDM, Gandhi wanted to focus upon his village reconstruction programme and Harijan Campaign while many other party members wanted to fight the elections.

In October 1934, Gandhi separated himself from the Indian National Congress.

In the elections to the Central Legislative Assembly in November 1934, the Congress won 45 seats out of 75. The government announced the holding of elections to the provincial legislatures in February 1937 under the Government of India Act 1935, which promised provincial autonomy. At the Lucknow session (April 1936), the Congress pronounced to contest them. The Congress framed a detailed political and economic programme at the Faizpur session (December 1936) under the Presidentship of Jawaharlal Nehru.

Provincial Elections under the GoI Act, 1935

The Congress won an immense mandate. It formed ministries in 8 provinces-Madras, Bombay, Central Provinces, Orissa, Bihar, UP, NWFP and Assam.

- The Haripura Session (Feb 1938) declared Purna Swaraj ideal to cover Princely States.
- Tripuri Congress (Mar 1939) supported active participation in the Princely States because of the federal structure of the 1935 Act and due to assumption of office by the Congress after the 1937 elections.
- The Tripuri Session witnessed Bose vs. Sitaramyya (Gandhi's nominee) conflict. Bose resigned to form the Forward Bloc.

August Offer, 1940

The Viceroy (Linlithgow) put forward a proposal that was having following things:

- The Dominion Status in the unspecified future.
- A post-war body to enact the Constitution.
- The expansion of Governor-General's Council with representation of the Indians.
- Establishing a War Advisory Council. In this offer, he promised the Muslim League and other minorities that the British Government would never agree a Constitution or government in India, to which did not enjoy their support (the Muslim League had demanded Pakistan in its Lahore session of 1940). The Congress rejected this offer because:
- There was no suggestion for a national government and the demand for Dominion Status was already discarded in favour of Purna Swaraj.
- It uplifted the anti-Congress forces, like the Muslim League.

Individual Satyagraha

With the failure ot the British government to measure up to the demands, there were two opinions in Congress about the launching of civil disobedience. Gandhi felt that the atmosphere was not in favour of civil disobedience as there were differences and indiscipline within the Congress. However, the Congress Socialists and the All India Kisan Sabha were in favour of immediate struggle.

Convinced that the British would not modify their policy in India, (the Congress having rejected the August Offer), Gandhi was determined to start the Individual Satyagraha.

The reason for confining the movement to individual participation was that neither Gandhi nor the Congress wanted to hamper the War effort and this was not possible in a a mass movement. Even the aim of the Satyagraha was a limited one, i.e. to disprove the British claim of India supporting the War effort whole-heartedly.

On 17 October, 1940 Vinoba Bhave became the first satyagrahi, followed by Nehru.

The Cripps Mission: March-April 1942

Under the pressure of Allies and the need for gestures to win over Indian public opinion, the British were forced to offer reconciliatory measures. After the fall of Rangoon to the Japanese, the British decided to send the Cripps Mission to India for constitutional proposals, which included:

- The dominion status to be provided after the war with the right to secede (Any province could, if it so desired, remain outside the Indian Union and negotiate directly with Britain).
- Consitution-making body to be elected from Provincial Assemblies and Princes' nominees after the War.
- Individual princes could sign a separate agreement with the British which in effect accommodated the Pakistan demand.
- British would however, control the defence for war period.

The Congress did not want to rely upon future promises. It asked for a responsible government with full powers and also a control over the country's defence. Gandhi defined the proposals as a post-dated cheque in a crashing bank. Cripps Mission failed to satisfy Indian nationalists and turned out to be merely a propaganda device for US and Chinese consumption.

But above all, the Cripps Proposals to brought in "Pakistan" through the backdoor via the "local option" clause. Though the Cripps Mission failed, Cripps' proposals provided legitimacy to the Pakistan demand by accommodating it in their provision for provincial autonomy.

QUTT INDIA MOVEMENT

Beginning

- After the failure of the Cripps Mission. Japanese tried to innate in India, they threaten India, as they wanted to having more presence in Asia.
- The auger against the world war II that was meaningless war for Indian. The quit India resolution was passed on 8th August, 1942 at Gowalia Tank Bombay (now Mumbai).
- Gandhi informed British to quit and "leave India in God's hand". His message was 'Do or Die'.
- In the begining stages, the movement was based on non-violent lines.
- Repressive policy of the government and indiscriminate arrests of the leaders provoked people to violence. (Nehru was lodged in Almora jail, Maulana Azad in Bankura and Gandhi in Agha Khan's palace, Poona).
- Further, it was the only all-India movement, which was leaderless. In many areas, the government lost all control and the people established Swaraj.

Public Participation

- Parallel governments were set-up in Satara- (Prati Sarkar under Nana Patil), Talcher (Orissa), parts of eastern U.P and Bihar.
- In Bengal, Tamluk Jatiya Sarkar functioned in Midnapore district. This national government had various departments, like law and order, Health, Education, Agriculture, etc. along with a postal system of its own and arbitration courts.
- The revolutionary activity also started in this phase. Jaya Prakash Narain and Ramnandan Misra escaped from Hazaribagh Jail and organised an underground movement.
- In Bombay, the Socialist leaders continued their underground activities under leaders, like Aruna Asaf Ali. The most challenging act of the underground movement was the establishment of Congress Radio with Usha Mehta as its announcer.
- The participation was on many levels. School and College students remained in the forefront, women actively participated and workers went on strikes. Though, peasants focused on their offence on symbols of authority, there was complete absence of anti-zamindar violence. There were no communal clashes during the movement. Repression was severe.
- The movement did not evoke much response from the merchant community. In fact, most of the Capitalists and merchants had profited heavily during the War.
- The Muslim League kept aloof and the Hindu Mahasabha condemned the Movement. The Communist Party of India due to its "People's War" line did not support the movement.
- The Indian Princes and the landlords were contributing the War effort and hence, did not sympathise with the movement.
- Few main Congress leaders, like Rajagopalachari also did not participate.

Towards Freedom

Rajagopalachari Formula (1944)

- In 1944, C. Rajagopalachari offered that after the termination of the war, a Commission could be appointed for' demarcating contiguous districts in the north-west and east where Muslims were in absolute majority. In the areas thus demarcated, a plebiscite would be held on the basis of adult suffrage that would ultimately decide the issue of division from Hindustan. If the majority decided in favour of forming a separate Sovereign State, such decision could be accepted.
- In situation of acceptance of partition, agreement to be made jointly for safeguarding defence, commerce, communications, etc. The discussed terms would to be operative only if England transferred full powers to India.
- The Muslim League was expected to endorse the Congress demand for independence and co-operate with it in the formation of provisional government for the intrerim period.
- The Jinnah objected, as he demanded congress to accept two-nation theory and wanted only Muslims of the north-west and east of India to vote in the plebiscite. The Hindu leaders led by Y.D. Savarkar criticised the plan.

Shimla Conference (June-July 1945)

- It was proposed by Wavell.
- Discussion suggested setting up of a new Executive council with only Indian members. The Viceroy and the Commander-in-chief would be the only non-Indian members of the council

- The 'Caste Hindus' and Muslims would have parallel representation, The executive would work within the existing constitution (i.e., not responsible to the Central Assembly), but the door was kept open for discussions on a new constitution.
- The Congress, headed by Maulana Azad, resented being characterised as a caste Hindu organisation.
- The discussion failed due to Jinnah's demand for the Muslim League to have absolute choice in choosing all Muslim members and a demand for communal veto, though it had ministries only in Assam and Sind.
- The termination of the conference gave Jinnah the Communal Veto in effect. Thereafter, the satisfaction of the League became a pre-requisite to any major settlement.

Royal Indian Vavey (RIN) Mutiny (1946)

- In 18 Feb, 1946, Bombay Ratings of HMS Talwar affected work due to flagrant racial discrimination, unpalatable food and abuse after the arrest of BC Dutt who lad scrawled Quit India on the ship. On 19th Feb. HMS Hindustan, in Karachi also mutinied.
- The seventy-four ships, four flotillas and twenty shore establishments in Bombay, Karachi, Cochin, Vizag, Calcutta and Delhi had come under the influence of a Naval Central Strike Committee (headed by M. S. Khan). In Bombay, the mutineers hoisted the tricolour on their shipmasts together with a portrait of Subhash Bose and shouted Jai Hind in the barracks. Their requirement included release of all political prisoners, including those belonging to the Indian National Army.
- Vallabhbhai Patel and Jinnah jointly persuaded the ratings to surrender on 23rd February, 1946.

Cabinet Mission (March-June 1946)

- The Members-Pethwick Lawrence (secretary of State), Stafford Cripps and Alexander.
- The Mission denied all the demand for a full-fledged Pakistan (Comprising the whole of all the Muslim majority areas). The Mission reasoned that the right of communal self-determination, if conceded to Muslims, also had to be granted to non-Muslims, who were in majority in West Bengal and Eastern Punjab, as well as in Assam. The 'truncated' or smaller Pakistan was unacceptable to the League.

The Plan proposed

- For a very loose union of all the Indian territories under a centre that would control merely the defence, the Foreign Affairs and the Communications, leaving all other subjects to the existing provincial legislatures.
- Provincial legislatures would elect a Constituent Assembly. The members would divide up into three sections- A, B and C while electing the constitutent Assembly. All these sections would have the authority to draw up provincial constitutions and even group constitutions.

  Section A- Non-Muslim majority provinces (Bombay, United Provinces, Bihar, Central Provinces, Orissa, Madras)

  Section B - Muslim majority provinces in the north-west (Sind, NWFP and Punjab)

  Section C - Muslim majority provinces in north-east (Bengal, Assam)
- The communal questions in Central legislature were to be decided by a simple majority in both communities.
- The provinces were to have full autonomy and residual powers.
- Princely states were no longer to be under paramountcy of British. Government.
- After the first general elections, a province could come out of a group and after 10 years a province could call for reconsideration of the group or union constitution.
- Each group had powers to establish intermediate level legislature and executive on their own.
- The plan failed on the issue of the nature of grouping - Jinnah was for compulsory grouping while Nehru was for grouping only till the formation of a constituent assembly. On the 29th July, 1946 Jinnah withdrew his earlier acceptance of the plan and fixed 16 August, 1946 as Direct Action Day. Calcutta, Noakhali, Garmukteshwar were the storm centres. The communal massacre weakened the Congress position in the NWFP.
- It came into existence on 2nd September, 1946, in accordance with Cabinet Mission's proposal and was headed by J L Nehru. Muslim League refused to join it initially.
- Wavell persuaded the League leaders to join on 26 October, 1946.

- 8th December, 1946 - The Constituent Assembly began its session with Liaqat Ali Khan of Muslim League as the Finance Minister.
- The Interim government, obstructed by its League members and bureaucracy, was decreased to a figurehead and was unable to control the communal carnage.

Attlee's Announcement (February 1947)

- British Prime Minister Atlee on 20 February, 1947 announced that the British would take a backseat from India by 30 June, 1948 and that Lord Mountbatten would replace Wavell. The British powers and obligations vis-a-vis the princely states would lapse with transfer of power, but these would not be transferred to any successor Government in British India. Partition of the country was implicit in the provision that if the Constituent Assembly was not fully representative, then power would be transferred to more than one central governmentt.

Mountbatten Plan (3rd June Plan)

- His earlier Plan Balkan was abandoned for the 3rd June Plan.
- The Plan announced that power would be handed over by 15 August, 1947 on the basis of dominion status to India and Pakistan.
- Mountbatten supported the Congress stand that the princely states must not be given the option of independence. They would either join India or Pakistan,
- They Boundary Commission was to be headed by Radcliffe and the award was to be announced after Republic day (which was a major cause of massacres).
- Punjab and Bengal Legislative Assemblies would meet in two groups, Hindus and Muslims, to vote for partition. If a general majority of either group voted for partition, then these provinces would be partitioned. In case of partition, two dominions and two constituent assemblies would be created.

Indian Independence Act, 1947

- Implemented on 15th August, 1947 and Sovereignty of British Parliament was abolished. The dominions of India and Pakistan were created. Each dominion to have a Governor-General. Pakistan was to comprise Sind, British Baluchistan, NWFP, West Punjab and East Bengal.

GEOGRAPHY

Chapter 1

Physiography

LOCATION

- India is located in the northern and eastern hemisphere of the globe between 8° 4' N and 37° 6' N latitudes and 68°7' E and 97°25'E longitudes.
- The southern range goes upto 6°45' N latitudes to cover the last island of the Nicobar group of islands. The southern extremity is known as Pygmalion Point or Indira Point.
- Its entire land frontier of 15,200 kilometers passes through marshy lands, desert, level plains, rugged mountains, snow covered areas and thick forests.
- There is a maritime boundary of 6,100 kilometers along the main land mass which increases to 7,516 kilometers if the coastlines of Andaman-Nicobar and Lakshadweep Island are added to it.
- India-Afghanistan and Pakistan-Afghanistan international boundary is called Durand Line, determined as a "militarily strategic border" between British India and Afghanistan.
- The India-China boundary (4,225 km) is a natural boundary parallel along the Himalayan ranges and is based on various treaties. Its eastern part (1,140 km) is known as the Mc Mahon Line.
- The boundary with Pakistan and Bangladesh (the East Pakistan) was drawn at the duration of partition in 1947 through the 'Radcliffe Award'.
- India is the only country which has given its name to an ocean, i.e. Indian Ocean encircled by 46 countries (27 littoral including Australia, 7 island states and 12 land locked countries).

Size and Shape

- India has a total geographical area of 32,87,263 sq. km which is approximately 0.57% of the area of the earth and 2.4% of the total area of the land hemisphere.
- After Russia, China, Canada, USA, Brazil and Australia, India is the seventh largest country of the world. Its area is almost equal to the area of Europe (Excluding Russia), one-third of Canada, one-fifth of Russia, eight times of Japan and twelve times of United Kingdom.
- In population-size, India (1210 million in 2011) is the second largest country in the world after China (1344 million in 2010).
- Its total population is more than the combined population of USA, Russia, Australia, Canada and Japan.

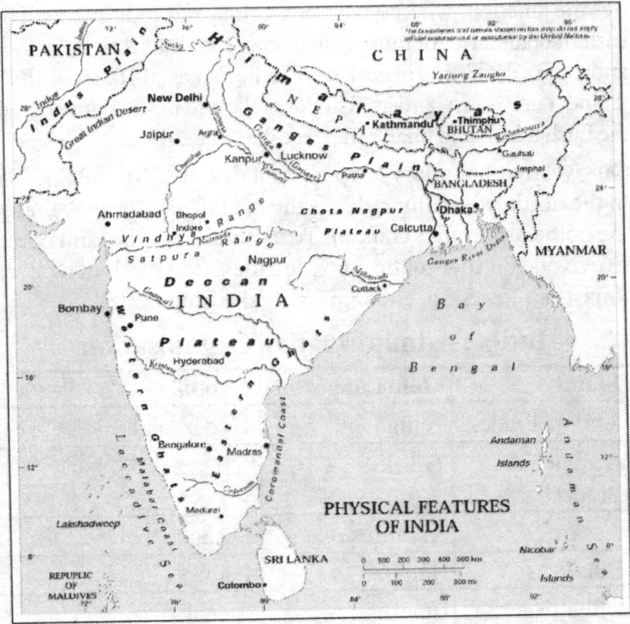

- India has roughly a quadrangular shape. It measures about 3,214 km from north to south and about 2,933 km from east to west, the difference between the two being just 281km.

Neighbouring Countries

The borderline of India are mostly natural and historically determined. There are some countries having a similar boundries with India are- Afghanistan and Pakistan to the north-west, China and Nepal to the north, Burma (Myanmar) to the east and Bangladesh to the east of West Bengal.

The closests neighbours across the seas is Sri Lanka- the two countries are separated by the narrow Palk Strait. Across the eastern borders of India and Bay of Bengal lie Myanmar (Burma), Malaysia, Indonesia, Thailand, Cambodia (Kampuchea), Laos and Vietnam. The West Asian neighbours are Pakistan, India, Iraq and the Arab countries. In the west across the Indian Ocean lie Egypt, Sudan, Ethiopia, Somalia, Kenya and Tanzania. The Maldives lie to the south of the Lakshadweep. The Himalayan mountains guard our northern frontiers. Across the mountains lies the Sinkiang (Xinjiang) region of China-the Tarim Basin. To the west of Sinkiang and divided from India by the narrow Wakhan territory of Afghanistan, is situated Tajikistan. Tibet, the land of the sacred Kailash and the Mansarovar stretches to the east and north of the Indian frontiers. To our north lies the Himalayan Kingdom of Nepal.

Bhutan, famous for its beauty it is situated further east along our northern frontiers. To the east of Bhutan, the crest of the high Himalayas works as the dividing line between India and China. Across this boundary line, known as the Mc Mahon Line, lies Tibet.

The Indian boundary stretches eastwards along the region of voluminous forests and complex mountainous terrain. Here lies the junction, where Myanmar, China and India meets. The eastern boundaries of India with almost continuous chain of hills and ranges consisting of the Mishmi, the Patkai and the Naga hills defines our eastern borders. They are followed by the Barail range, the Lushat hills and finally, the majestic Arakan Yoma.

Our western boundary keep us on a distance from Pakistan. In the north, adjoining India, is the land of the sturdy Pathans, the home of Frontier Gandhi. To its south, lies the land of the five rivers. Further south, adjoining the desert sands of western Rajasthan lies Sind, encompassing the Indus delta.

India : Administrative Organisation

States	Main Language	Capital
Andhra Pradesh	Telugu	Hyderabad
Arunachal Pradesh	Tribal	Itanagar
Assam	Assamese	Dispur
Bihar	Hindi	Patna
Chhattisgarh	Hindi	Raipur
Goa	Marathi,Konkani	Panaji
Gujarat	Gujarati	Gandhinagar
Haryana	Hindi	Chandigarh
Himachal Pradesh	Hindi	Shimla
Jammu & Kashmir	Kashmiri	Srinagar (in Summer) Jammu (in Winter)
Jharkhand	Hindi	Ranchi
Karnataka	Kannada	Bangalore
Kerala	Malayalam	Thiruvananthapuram
Madhya Pradesh	Hindi	Bhopal
Maharashtra	Marathi	Mumbai
Manipur	Manipuri	Imphal
Meghalaya	Khasi, Garo, English	Shilong
Mizoram	Mizo, English	Aizawl
Nagaland	Naga	Kohima
Odisha	Oriya	Bhubaneswar
Punjab	Punjabi	Chandigarh
Rajasthan	Rajasthani, Hindi	Jaipur
Sikkim	Lepcha, Bhutia	Gangtok
Tamil Nadu	Tamil	Chennai
Telangana	Telugu	Hyderabad
Tripura	Bengali, Tripuri	Agartala
Uttar Pradesh	Hindi	Lucknow
Uttaranchal	Hindi	Dehradun
West Bengal	Bengali	Kolkata

Union Territories

Andaman	Andamanese, & Nicobar	Port Blair Nicobarese
Chandigarh	Punjabi, Hindi	Chandigarh
Dadra & Nagar Haveli	Gujarati, Marathi	Silvassa
Daman & Diu	Gujarati	Daman
Delhi	Hindi	Delhi
Lakshadweep	Malayalam	Kavaratti
Pondicherry	Tamil, French	Puducherry
India	**Hindi**	**New Delhi**

PHYSIOGRAPHY

- The 10.6% is occupied by mountains, 18.5% by hills, 27.7% by plateaus and 43.2% by the plains.
- In can be understood by dividing into four major physiographic regions, viz., 1. The Northern Mountains, 2. The Great Plains, 3. The Peninsular Uplands and 4. The Indian Coasts and Islands.

1. **The Northern Mountains**
   - The region spread all along the northern frontier of the country, for about 2500km, with a varying width of 240 to 320 km and a total area of about 5,00,000 km^2.
   - The Himalayas represent the youngest and the highest folded mountains on the earth, rising to over 8000 m above sea level and consisting of three parallel ranges: (a) Himadri (Greater Himalayas), (b) Himanchal (Lesser Himalayas), and (c) the Siwalks (Outer Himalayas).
   - The Valley of Kashmir, about 135 km long and 40 km broad, is the only large level strip of land in the Himalayas.
   - In the Himalayas, snow fields cover about 40,000 sq. km of area from Kashmir to Assam.
   - The height of snow line deviate between 4000-5800m in the east and 4500-6000m in the west.
   - The Himalayas are divided by numerous valleys like Kashmir valley, the Karewas, the Doon valley, the Kangra and Kullu valley (Himachal Pradesh), Kathmandu valley (Nepal), Bhagirathi valley (near Gangotri) and Mandakini valley (near Kedarnath).

- The Himalayas range can be easily understood by the following fou r parallel zones.
  - *(a)* ***The Tibetan Zone:*** This is about 40 km wide and consists of fossil bearning marine sediments which are underlain by 'Tertiary granite'.
  - *(b)* ***The Greater Himalayan Zone:*** This zone rises abruptly like a wall north of the Lesser Himalayas. It is about 25 km wide with average height above 5000m.
  - *(c)* ***The Lesser Himalayan Zone:*** It is about 80 km wide with average height between 1300 to 5000 m. It generally consists of unfossiliferous sediments or metamorphosed crystallines, constituting the main nappe zone in the Kashmir, Himachal and Garhwal sections.
  - *(d)* ***The sub-Himalayan Zone:*** This is a 8 to 45 km wide zone with average height below 1300 m. The Siwalik Range forms the southern part of the zone and the intervening area is generally occupied by the tectonic longitudinal valley called the Duns, viz., Dehra, Kotah, Patli, Kothri, Chumbi and Kyarda.

Longitudinal Division of the Himalayas

(a) ***The sub-Himalaya or Siwaliks:*** The range has a total length of about 2400 km from the Indus gorge to the Brahmaputra valley. It is recognised by various local names, i.e. the Jammu hills (Jammu & Kashmir), the Dundwa range (Uttaranchal), the Churia Muria hills (Nepal), the Daffla, Miri, Abor and Mishmi hills (Arunachal Pradesh).

(b) ***The Lesser Himalaya or Himachal:*** Important ranges having the Dhauladhar, Pirpanjal, Nag Tiba, Mahabharat range and Mussoorie range. The famous hill resorts like Shimla, Chail, Ranikhet, Chakrata, Mussoorie, Nainital, Almora and Darjeeling, etc, are situated over this range.

(c) ***The Greater Himalaya or Himadri:*** The Burzil pass and Zoji La in Kashmir, Bara Lapcha La and Shipki La in Himachal Pradesh, Thaga La, Niti Pass and Lipu Lekh Pass in Uttaranchal and Nathu La, Jelep La in Sikkim are worthy of mention.

- The hill ranges running in north-south direction along the Burmese border and crossing through Arunachal Pradesh (Tirap division), Nagaland, Manipur and Mizoram are collectively called Purvanchal. Their local names are i.e. Patkai Bum (Arunachal Pradesh), Naga hills, Kohima hills, Manipur hills, Mizo hills, Tripura hills and Barail range.
- The highest peak of Naga hills is Saramati peak (3826 m).

2. The Great Plains

- It is an aggradational plain formed by the alluvial deposits of the Indus, Ganga and the Brahmaputra and their tributaries.
- The plain is spread out over from the west (from the banks of the Ravi and Satluj) to east (the Ganga delta) to a length of 2400 km.
- The plain converges into the Thar Desert in the south-west. A low watershed of the Delhi ridge (278 m) along the right bank of the Yamuna river separates the Satluj plains (a part of the Indus plain) from the Ganga plains.

Divisions of the Great Plains

- The Great Plains are divided into many smaller ranges on the basis of their characteristics of the alluvium, surface gradient, drainage channels and regional traits.
- **Bhabar Plains:** It stretches all along the foot of the Siwaliks range with a noticeable continuity from the Indus to the Tista. The wide belt approximately 87016 km, consists of gravel and unassorted sediments deposited by the Himalayan rivers in the foreland zone due to sudden break of slope.
- The porosity is so high that all streams disappear in the Bhabar tract leaving out only dry channels.
- **Terai Plains:** South of the Bhabar is a 15-30 km wide marshy tract known as *terai* where streams reappear to the surface.
- The Terai is more significant in the eastern part than in the west due to higher degree of rainfall. It is a zone of excessive dampness, voluminous forests, rich wild life and malarial climate.
- **Bangar or Bhangar Plains:** The Bhangar represents the uplands (alluvial terrace) made up of the deposition of the older alluvium and lie above the flood-limit of the plains. The main element of Bhangar is clay which at places gives way to loam and sandy-loam.
- **Khadar Plains:** The small alluvium of the flood plains of the numerous rivers is called the Khadar or Bet (in Punjab).
- Its alluvium is floaty and poor in calcareous matter consisting of deposition of sand, silt, mud and clay.
- **Delta Plains:** The deltaic plain is an expansion of the Khadar plain. It covers about 1,86 lakh sq km of area in the lower reaches of the Ganga river (West Bengal). It primarily consists of old mud, new mud and marsh.
- In can be divided on the basis of regional characteristic, It has four meso regions:

1. **The Rajasthan Plains:** This includes Marusthali and Rajasthan Bagar areas (Steppe lands) to the west of the Aravalli mountains.

Longitudinal Division of the Himalayas

Area-wise

Administrative Units	Area '000 km2
Rajasthan	342.2
Madhya Pradesh	308.2
Maharashtra	307.7
Andhra Pradesh	160.2
Uttar Paradesh	238.6
Jammu & Kashmir	222.2
Gujarat	196
Karnataka	191.8
Orissa	155.7
Chhattisgarh	135.2
Tamil Nadu	130.1
Telangana	114.8
Bihar	94.2
West Bengal	88.8
Arunachal Pradesh	83.7
Jharkhand	79.7
Assam	78.4
Uttaranchal	55.8
Himachal Pradesh	55.7
Punjab	50.4
Haryana	44.2
Kerala	38.9
Maghalaya	22.4
Manipur	22.3
Mizoram	21.1
Negaland	16.6
Tripura	10.5
Andaman & Nicobar	8.2
Sikkim	7.1
Goa	3.7
Delhi	1.5
Dadra &Nagar Haveli	0.5
Pondicherry	0.5
Chandigarh	0.1
Daman & Diu	0.1
Lakshadweep	0.03
India	**3287.3**

Population_wise states (2011)

INDIA	1,21,01,93,422
Uttar Pradesh	19,95,81,477
Maharashtra	11,23,72,972
Bihar	10,38,04,637
West Bengal	9,13,47,736
Andhra pradesh	4,93,86,799
Madhya Pradesh	7,25,97,565
Tamil Nadu	7,21,38,958
Telangana	3,52,86,757
Rajasthan	6,86,21,012
Karnataka	6,11,30,704
Gujarat	6,03,83,628
Odisha	4,19,47,358
Kerala	3,33,87,677
Jharkhand	3,29,66,238
Assam	3,11,69,272
Punjab	2,77,04,236
Chhattisgarh	2,55,40,196
Haryana	2,53,53,081
NCT of Delhi	1,67,53,235
J & K	1,25,48,926
Uttarakhand	1,01,16,725
Himachal Pradesh1	68,56,509
Tripura	36,71,032
Meghalaya	29,64,007
Manipur	27,21,765
Nagaland	19,80,602
Goa	14,57,723
Arunachal Pradesh	13,82,611
Puducherry	12,44,464
Mizoram	10,91,014
Chandigarh	10,54,686
Sikkim	6,07,688
Andaman & Nicobar Islands	3,79,944
Dadra & Nagar Haveli	3,42,853
Daman & Diu	2,42,911
Lakshadweep	64,429

- The plain area has been made by the recession of the sea as is evident by the occurrence of several brackish water lakes in the region, i.e. Sambhar, Degana, Kuchaman, Pachpadra, Didwana and Lunkaransar Tal from which table salt is obtained. At present, Luni is the only flowing river which reaches the sea.

2. **The Punjab-Haryana Plains:** The Punjab-Haryana Plains owe their origin to the aggradational activity of the Satluj, the Beas and the Ravi rivers.
   - The region has two regional slopes, westward towards the Indus river and southwards the Rann of Kachchh.

3. **The Ganga Plains:** The Ganga Plains expanded from the Yamuna river in the west to the western borders of Bangladesh covering a distance of about 1,400 km and an average width of 300 km. The maximum height is located near Saharanpur (276m) from where it goes on decreasing towards the Sagar Islands (3 m).

   (a) The Upper Ganga Plain: It covers a total area of 1,49,029 sq km.

   Besides the Ganga and Yamuna, other important rivers of the region include Ramganga, Gomti, Ghaghara and Tapti, etc.

   Upper Ganga Plains is divided into three micro units: (i) the Ganga-Yamuna Doab, (ii) the Rohilkhand Plain and (iii) the Avadh Plain.

   (b) The Middle Ganga Plain: The Middle Ganga Plain is a part of eastern Uttar Pradesh and the Bihar Plains.

   There are two large troughs, which may be called Gorakhpur trough and Raxaul-Motihari trough of over 8,000 m deep.

   Besides Ganga, Gomti, Ghaghara, Rapti, Gandak, Kosi (in the north), and Son (in the south) are other important rivers of the region.

   (c) The Lower Ganga Plain: The Lower Ganga Plain adjusting an area of 80,968 sq km, expands from the foot of the Darjeeling Himalaya in the north to the Bay of Bengal in the South.

   (d) The Brahmaputra Plain: The Brahmaputra Plains, also known as Assam Valley, are the easternmost part of the Great Plains drained by the Brahmaputra and its triburaties.

   These plains from Sadiya (in the east) to Dhubri (near Bangladesh border in the west) are about 720 km long and about 80 km wide, covering a total area of about 56,274 sq km.

Density-wise States 2011

States	Density(persons per km)
NCT of Delhi	11,297
Chandigarh	9,252
Punducherry	2,598
Daman & Diu	2,169
Lakshadweep	2,013
Bihar	1,102
West Bengal	1,029
Kerala	859
Uttar Pradesh	828
Dadra & Nagar Haveli	698
Haryana	573
Tamil Nadu	555
Telangana	307
Punjab	550
Jharkhand	414
Assam	397
Goa	394
Maharashtra	365
Tripura	350
Karnataka	319
Andhra Pradesh	308
Gujarat	308
Odisha	269
Madhya Pradesh	236
Rajasthan	201
Uttarakhand	189
Chhattisgarh	189
Meghalaya	132
Jammu & Kashmir	124
Himachal Pradesh	123
Manipur	122
Nagaland	119
Sikkim	86
Mizoram	52
Andaman & Nicobar Islands	46
Arunachal Pradesh	17

3. **The Peninsular Uplands**

- It is covering an area of 16 lakh sq km, the Peninsular Uplands form the largest physiographic division of India.
- The fault in which the Narmada river flows divides the region into two unequal parts; the smaller one in the north being called as the Central Highlands.
- It is slightly titled towards north. The southern part has been tilted east with bold heights to the west. It is commonly called as the Deccan Plateau comprising the Satpuras, Western and Eastern Ghats and a large number of plateaus.
- On the behalf of its physiographic characteristics, the Peninsular Upland may be divided into a number of sub units. These having hill ranges like Aravallis, Vindhyas, Satpuras, Sahyadris, the Eastern Ghats, plateaus like Chotanagpur, Meghalaya, Deccan, Karnataka, Tamil Nadu, Andhra, Bundelkhand; and fertile plains like Malwa, Chhattisgarh, etc.
- The Aravalli which runs from north-east to south-west for about 800 km between Delhi and Palanpur (Gujarat) represents a relict of one of the world's oldest fold mountain systems.
- The range becomes more sustainable and arising to above 900 m in the south. Its highest peak lies in Abu hills (Gurushikhar Peak 1722m).

The Malwa Plateau

- Malwa Plateau with a length of 530 km and a width of 390 km, captures an area of about 15,000 sq. km. It is covered by the Aravallis in the north, the Vindhyan range in the south and the Bundelkhand Plateau in the east.
- The region has two drainage systems-one towards the Arabian Sea (Narmada, Tapi and Mahi), and another towards the Bay of Bengal (Chambal and Betwa joining the Yamuna).
- The Western Vindhyas is a downhill which varies in character and height.
- The Western Satpuras divide the Narmada and the Tapi river basins.
- South-west of Pachmarhi is Dhupgarh (1350 m), which is the highest peak of the Satpuras.

Bundelkhand Uplands

- Bundelkhand Uplands is bound by the Yamuna river in the north, the Vindhyan Plateau in the south, the Chambal in the north-west and Panna-Ajaigarh ranges in the south-east.
- The region is featured by 'senile topography'.
- The streams like Betwa, Dhasan and Ken have carved out steep gorges.

Chhotanagpur Plateau

- The Chhotanagpur Plateau is composed of Archaean granite and gneiss rocks with patches of Dharwar rocks. The Dalma range marks the belt of Archaean lava flows.
- Chhotanagpur is made up of a series of plateaus situated at different levels of elevation; the highest general elevation of about 1100m in the mid-western portion known as the Pat lands.
- Hazaribag and Ranchi plateaus are situated at same general elevation (600m) but divided by the Damodar trough.
- Chhotanagpur is drained in different directions by numerous rivers and streams, of which the Damodar, Barakar, Subarnarekha, North Koel, South Koel rivers have developed extensive drainage basins.

Meghalaya-Mikir Uplands

- The Meghalaya-Mikir Uplands having the Garo, Khasi, Jaintia and the outlying Mikir and Rengma hills is a tableland which has been detached from the Indian Peninsula by the Malda Gap.
- It is bordered by the Dhansiri river in the east and the Singimari in the west.
- The Shillong peak (1961m) is the highest peak of the area.
- The southern ranges known as the Rengma Hills have an average elevation of 900m. The area is characterised by radial drainage with Dhansiri and Jamuna being the main rivers.

Maharashtra Plateau

- The thickness of basaltic sheet is approximately 2000 metere and has been formed by the consolidation of the lava that erupted sub-aerially about 60 to 65 million years ago.
- Sometimes it becomes tough to distinguish the Deccan Plateau from the Sahyadri.

Mahanadi Basin

- The Basin of Mahanadi is also known as Chhattisgarh. The Mahanadi with its tributaries like Seonath, Hasdo, Mand, etc., drain, this area and form the radial pattern. The area is characterised by red and yellow soils which are suitable for rice cultivation.
- The Durg Uplands are surrounded by rolling granitic and gneissic areas. The southern rimland includes the Rajhara Hills in southern Durg district and the Raipur Uplands in south-eastern Raipur district (300-500m). The Rajhara Hills contain Dharwarian rocks in which iron ore is mined for Bhilai steel plant.

Dandakaranya Region

- Its Abujhmar hills gives one of the richest iron-ore deposits at Bailadilla Range.

Karnataka Plateau

- The region consists with an average elevation between 600-900m. Mulangiri (1923m) is the highest peak (Baba Budan hills) followed by Kudremukh (1892 m).

Telangana Plateau

- The region is made up of small physiographic units: (i) Telangana, and (ii) Rayalaseema Upland. The Telangana is a long belt of peneplains mainly developed over the gneissic rocks. Its northern and north-eastern margin is occupied by the Godavari valley which is distinct due to its faulted structure.
- The Rayalaseema Uplands is divided by the Penner.
- The Rayalaseema Plateau is a vast highland making the northward extension of the Karnataka Plateau.

The Sahyadris

- The Sahyadris or Western Ghats run parallel to the western coast for about 1,600 km in north south direction from the mouth of the Tapi river to Cape Camorin.
- These are block mountains formed due to the downwarping of a part of the land into the Arabian Sea. Sahyadris form the real watershed of the Peninsula.
- In the Nilgiris, the Eastern Ghats join the Sahyadris to form a mountain knot whose highest point is Doddabetta (2637m).

The Eastern Ghats

- The Eastern Ghats start from the eastern boundary of the Deccan Plateau.
- These are the series of detached hills of heterogeneous composition which are known by various local names.
- Their average elevation is 1100m. They depict true mountain characteristic between the Mahanadi and Godavari.
- The Nilgiris also called as Blue Mountains provide the converging site for three mountain ranges: the Sahyadri joining opposite of the Makurti peak; the southern Ghats across the Palghat in the south and the Eastern Ghats at the north-eastern corner.

The Vindhyan Range

- The Vindhyan Range expanding from Jobat in Gujarat to Sasaram in Bihar runs for about 1,050 kms.
- The Maikal range, forming a connecting link between the Vindhyas and the Satpuras, is a large plateau.
- The Vindhyan range together with Satpura forms the watershed of Betwa, Tons, Ken, Son and other rivers some of which flow into the Ganga and other into the Godavari and Mahanadi.

The Satpura Range

The Satpura range is parallel to the Vindhyas between the valleys of the Narmada in the north and that of the Tapi in the south, lies the Satpura range which extends from Ratanpur in the west to Amarkantak in the east. It has a total length of about 900km and average height of 770 m. The Satpura range is divided into three parts which are as following. (i) Rajpipla hills (width 60 km), in the western part with steep slopes. (ii) The Mahadeo hills are composed of quartzites of the Gondwana systems and pink sandstones. (iii) The eastern part consisting of Maikal range is composed of Gondwana and Archaean gneisses.

The Indian Coasts and Islands

- The Peninsular Uplands are surrounded by coastal plains of varied width stretching from Kachchh to Orissa.
- With the notable exception of Gujarat, the west coast has a narrow alluvial margin interspersed by hilly terrain and characterised by more wet climate.
- It is sub-merged coast.
- The backwaters are the significant features of this coast.
- From Kachchh to Cape Camorin, it has a total length of 1840 km.
- The East Coast Plains are broader, associated with depositional activity of rivers.
- It strectches about 1800 km from Mahanadi mouth to Cape Camorin. It is a coast of emergency in which the deltas of Mahanadi, the Godavari, the Krishna, the Kaveri, etc. are characteristic features of the coast.

The Indian Islands

- India consists of a total of 247 islands of which 204 lie in the Bay of Bengal and remaining in the Arabian Sea.
- The Andaman and Nicobar group of islands have a crescentic shape and denote the peaks of submerged teriary mountain ranges – a continuation of the Arakan Yoma fold axis.
- The Arabian Sea islands have a coral origin and are surrounded by fringing reefs.
- Besides, there are a number of offshore islands along the Ganga-mouth, eastern and western coasts and in the Gulf of Mannar.
- *(a) Arabian Sea Island:* The Arabian Sea islands comprise 36 islands of Lakshadweep Group.
- Only 25% of the area is inhabited.

- The southern most island (Minicoy) is divided from the rest of the group by the 9° channel.
- The northern most group is collectively called as Amindivi Islands. Same as that, the central group is collectively called as Laccadive Islands.
- In the south the Lakshadweep is divided from Maldive Island by Eight Degree Channel.
- *(b) Bay of Bengal Island:* The Andaman and Nicobar group of islands are distinguished from each other by the 10° Channel. The extreme southernmost point is the Indira Point. (Pygmalion Point or La Henching) at 6.7° N and 93.8° E.
- The Andaman Group of Islands conisists of 204 islands. There are two volcanic islands, e.g. Barren and Narcondam.
- The Nicobar Group of Islands comprise of 18 islands. These are separated from the Andaman Group of islands through the 10° Channel which represent a fracture zone. Some of the Nicobar islands like Chowra, Car Nicobar and Pulo Milo are essentially coral, while Katchall, Nancowry and Great Nicobar are hilly as are the Andamans.
- *(C) Offshore Islands:* India has a number of islands along the Western, Eastern Coasts. Among Western coast islands, mention may be made of Piram, Bhaisala (Kathiawar); Diu, Vaida, Nora (Kachchh coast); Aliabet (Narmada-Tapi mouth); Elephanta, Salsette, (near Mumbai); Pamban, Crocodile (Gulf of Mannar); Sri Harikota (mouth of Pulicat lake); Parikud (mouth of Chilka lake) and New Moore and Sagar (Ganga delta).

Forest

DISTRIBUTION OF FOREST AREA

- In India, 24.01% area was under forests and trees in 2013.
- India's total forest is nearly 2% of the total forest in the world.
- Minimum desired area for a tropical country like India is about 33%. Further, it should be about 60% in mountainous region and 20% in the plain region.
- Per capita forest area in India is 0.06 hectares.
- Forests meet about 40% of energy need of the country including 80% of the rural energy requirements.
- Main forest products are timber, fuelwood, hardwood, softwood, etc.
- Jammu and Kashmir is the largest producer of timber wood, followed by Punjab and Madhya Pradesh (1999-2000).

Statewise forest's share to their geographical area in 2013

State	(%) Share
Mizoram	90.38
Lakshadweep	84.56
Nagaland	78.68
Andaman & Nicobar	81.36
Arunachal Pradesh	80.39
Manipur	76.10
West Bengal	1,029
Kerala	859

States with lowest forest area (2013)

State	(%) Share
Punjab	3.52
Haryana	3.59
Rajasthan	4.70
Daman & Diu	8.28
Uttar Pradesh	5.96

State-wise lac production

State	(%) Share
Jharkhand	40
Chhattisgarh	30
West Bengal	15
Maharashtra	5

States/UTs with Forest Cover more than 33 percent

State/UTs	Forest Cover(%)
Mizoram	90.38
Lakshadweep	84.56
Andaman & Nicobar	81.36
Arunachal Pradesh	80.39
Nagaland	78.68
Meghalaya	77.08
Manipur	76.10
Tripura	75.01
Goa	59.94
Sikkim	47.32
Kerala	46.2
Uttarakhand	45.82
Dadra & Nagar Haveli	43.38
Chhattisgarh	41.14
Assam	35.28

Statewise total forest (2013)

State	Total Forest (Sq km)
Madhya Pradesh	77,522
Arunachal Predesh	67,321
Chhattisgarh	55,621
Maharashtra	50,632
Odisha	50,347
Andhra Pradesh	46,116
Karnataka	36,132
Assam	27,671
Uttarakhand	24,508
Tamil Nadu	23,844
Jharkhand	23,473
Jammu & Kashmir	22,538
Mizoram	19,054
Kerala	17,922
Meghalaya	17,288
Manipur	16,990
Rajasthan	16,086
Himachal Pradesh	14,683
Gujarat	14,653
Uttar Pradesh	14,349
Nagaland	13,044

West Bengal	16,805
Tripura	7,866
Bihar	7,291
Andaman & Nicobar	6,711
Sikkim	3,358
Goa	2,219
Punjab	1,772
Haryana	1,586
Dadra & Nagar Haveli	213
Delhi	179,81
Puducherry	50.06
Lakshadweep	27.06
Chandigarh	17.26
Daman & Diu	9.27
Grand Total	**697,898**

- Karnataka is the largest producer of fuelwood in India followed by West Bengal, Maharashtra and Bihar.
- Madhya Pradesh, followed by Maharashtra and Andhra Pradesh, is the largest producers of 'gums' in India.
- The main producer of Resin are Arunachal Pradesh, Punjab and Jammu & Kashmir.
- In Tendu leaves, Madhya Pradesh is the largest producer followed by Bihar, Andhra Pradesh and Maharashtra.
- India holds a monopoly in the production of lac.

  In lac production, Jharkhand leads all the states, followed by Chhattisgarh, West Bengal and Maharashtra.

Chapter 3

Drainage System

- The annual yield of water in the rivers of the country is 1,858,100 million cubic meters:

River	Contribution (%)
Brahmaputra	33.8
Ganga	25.2
Godavari	6.4
Indus	4.3
Mahanadi	3.6
Krishna	3.4
Narmada	2.9

- Major river basins with catchment area of 20,000 sq km and above, account for 58% of the total run-off of all the rivers of India. They are 14 in number.

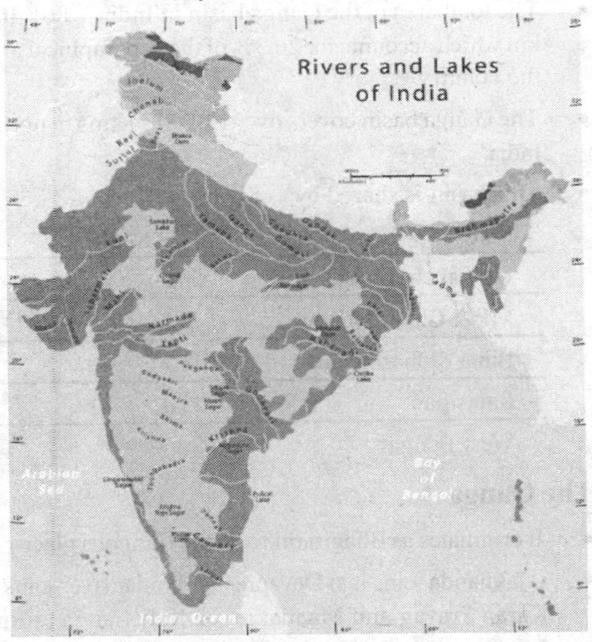

- Medium river basins with a catchment area between 2000 sq km and 20,000 sq km account for 7% of the total run off of all the rivers. They are 49 in number.
- Minor river basins with a catchment area below 2000 sq km account for 8% of the total run off of all the rivers of India.
- On the basis of origin, the drainage system of India is divided into 'Himalayan rivers' and 'Peninsular rivers'.
- About 77% of the drainage area of the country is oriented towards the Bay of Bengal.
- Arabian Sea drainage spreads over 23% of the country's surface flow area.

Himalayan Rivers

- Indus, Ganga, Brahmaputra, Satluj, Alaknanda, Gandak, Kosi, etc. are Himalayan rivers.
- Some rivers are older than the mountain themselves. Their gorges are the evidence of it. So, they are also examples of antecedent rivers.
- Antecedent rivers in respect of all three parallel ranges of Himalayas – Indus, Satlej, Ganga, Ghaghra, Kosi, Brahmaputra.

Antecedent rivers in respect of Himalayan ranges

Himalayan ranges	(Rivers Antecedent)
All three ranges (Greater, Lesser and Outer)	Indus, Sutlej, Ganga, Ghaghra, Kosi, Brahmaputra
Two ranges (Lesser and Outer)	Jhelum, Yamuna, Ravi, Ramganga
Outer range	Kamala, Rapti, Gola

Indus River System

- Indus along with its tributaries forms one of the largest drainage systems of the world.
- Indus river enters India at an elevation of 4206m and continues to flow in the north-west direction between the ladakh and the Zaskar Ranges.
- About 50 km before Skardu, it is joined by the Shyok river.
- Indus river ends its mountainous journey at Attock and is joined by the Kabul river from Afghanistan.
- Just above Mithankot, it receives accumulated waters of Panjhad-Jhelum, Chenab, Ravi, Beas and Satluj.
- Finally, it empties itself in the Arabian Sea, making a big delta.
- Indus has total catchment area of 1,178,440 sq km, out of which about 321,290 sq km lies within India.

The Jhelum

- It rises in a spring at Verinag.
- Lidar, Sind and Pohru are the tributaries of Jhelum in Kashmir.

- At Muzaffarabad, the river takes a sharp hairpin swing southward and the Kishanganga joins it on its right banks.
- Thereafter, it forms the India-Pakistan boundary for 170 km and emerges at the Potwar Plateau near Mirpur.
- It joins the Chenab at Trimmu.

The Chenab

- It originates from near the Bara Lacha Pass in the Lahul-Spiti part of the Zaskar Range. The united stream-Chandra and Bhaga-called the Chandrabhaga flows in the north-west direction through Himachal Pradesh and enters Jammu & Kashmir as Chenab.
- It enters the plain area near Akhnur in J&K.
- It cuts a deep gorge near Kishtwar.
- It receives water of Jhelum and Ravi rivers.

The Ravi

- It originates form Kullu hills near the Rohtang Pass in Himachal Pradesh.
- It cuts a deep gorge in the Dhaola Dhar range after crossing Chamba.
- It enters Punjab Plains near Madhopur and later enters Pakistan 26 km below Amritsar.
- It debounches into the Chenab a little above Rangpur.

The Beas

- It also originates near Rohtang Pass, close to the source of the Ravi.
- It crosses the Dhaola Dhar range through a deep gorge from Lorji to Talwara.
- It debouches on the plain near Pong and meets the Satluj river at Harike.
- It lies entirely within the Indian territory.

The Satluj

- It rises from the Manasarovar – Rakas Lake near Darma Pass.
- In Nari Khorsan province of Tibet, it has created an extraordinary canyon.
- It is joined by the Spiti river at Namgia near the Shipki La.
- Before entering the Punjab Plain, it cuts a gorge in Naina Devi Dhar (Bhakra Dam has been constructed here).
- It enters the plain at Rupnagar (Ropar).
- It is joined by the Beas at Harike.
- From near Ferozepur to Fazilka, it forms the boundary between India and Pakistan for nearly 120 km.
- It joins the Indus a few kilometers above Mithankot.

Indus Drainage System

Name of the river Length in km	Source Area drained (Sq km)
Indus 2,880 (709 in India)	Near Manasarover Lake 1,178,440 (321,290 in at 5,182m elevation India
Jhelum 724	Verinag at 4,900m altitude 34,775 upto Indo-Pak boarder
Chenab 1,180	Bara Lacha Pass 26,155 upto Indo-Pak Boder
Ravi 725	Near Rohtang Pass 14,442 (5,957 in India)
Beas 460	Near Rohtang Pass 20,303 at 4,062m height
Satluj 1,450 (1,050 in	Manasarovar-Rakas 25,900 Lakes at 4,570 m altitude India

The Ganga River System

- The total area of the Ganga basin in India is 861,404 sq km which accounts for 26.3% of the geographical area of the country.
- The Ganga basin covers over 12,500 sq kms in northern India.
- This basin is shared by:

State	(%) Share
Uttaranchal & UP	34.2
MP & Chhattisgarh	23.1
Bihar & Jharkhand	16.7
Rajasthan	13.0
West Bengal	8.3

The Ganga

- It originates as Bhagirathi from the Gangotri glacier.
- Alaknanda joins it at Devaprayag. Pindar river joins it at Karan Prayag and Mandakini or Kali Ganga at Rudra Prayag.
- The combined water of Bhagirathi and Alaknanda flows in the name of the Ganga, below Devprayag.
- It debouches on plain from hills in Haridwar.
- It is joined by Yamuna in Allahabad.
- Beyond Farakka, it is known as Padma in Bangladesh.
- It bifurcates itself into Bhagirathi-Hooghly in West Bengal and Padma-Meghna in Bangladesh.

- The Brahmaputra as the Jamuna joins it at Goalundo.
- Padma receives Meghna to the north of Chandpur.
- The delta formed by the Ganga-Brahmaputra is the largest delta of the world covering an area of 58,752 sq km.
- The total length, 2525 km, is distributed among states:

States	KM
Uttar Pradesh	1140
West Bengal	520
Bihar	445
Uttaranchal	310

The Yamuna

- It is the largest and the most important tributary of the Ganga.
- It originates from the Yamunotri glacier on the Bandarpunch Peak in Garhwal in Uttaranchal.
- It enters the plains near Tajewala.
- Tons, a tributary of it, join it below Kalsi. At this site, the water carried by the Tons is twice the water carried by the Yamuna.
- It takes a southerly course upto Mathura and south easterly in its onward journey upto Allahabad, where it unites with the Ganga.

The Chambal

- It rises near Mhow in the highlands of Janapao Hills.
- It enters a gorge at Chaurasigarh.
- It joins Yamuna in Etawah district of Uttar Pradesh.
- Banas joins it near Sawai Madhopur.
- Betwa, rising in Bhopal, joins the Yamuna near Hamirpur. Dhasan is also a tributary.

The Son

- The Son river springs from the Amarkantak Plateau.
- It joins the Ganga near Danapur in Patna district.
- Its catchment area is 71,259 sq km.
- Almost all the tributaries join it on its right bank.
- Tributaries are Johilla, Rihand, Kanhar and north Koel.

The Damodar

- It rises in the hills of the Chotanagpur plateau and flows through a rift valley.
- It is also called 'Sorrow of Bengal'.
- It joins the Hugli 48 km below Kolkata.
- The total length of the river is 541 km.
- Its catchment area is 25,820 sq km.

The Ramganga

- It rises in the Garhwal district of Uttaranchal.
- It enters the Ganga plain near Kalagarh.
- It joins the Ganga at Kannauj.
- Its basin covers 32,493 sq km.

The Ghaghra

- It originates near the Gurla Mandhota peak, south of Manasarovar in Tibet.
- It is known as the Karnaili in Western Nepal.
- It joins Ganga a few kilometers downstream of Chapra in Bihar.
- The total catchment area of the river is 127,950 sq km out of which 45% is in India.

The Kali

- It forms the boundary between Nepal and Kumaon.
- It is known as the Sarda or Chauka after it reaches the plains near Tanakpur.

The Ganga Drainage System

Name of the river	Source	Length in Km	Area drained (sq km)
Ganga	Gangotri Glacier at 7,010 m	2,525	861,404
Yamuna	Yamnotri Glacier at 6,330	1,376	366.223
Chambal	Near Mhow	1,050	139,468
Ramganga	Garhwal district at 3,110m	596	32,493
Ghaghara	Near Gurla Mandhota Peak south of manasarovar	1,080	127,950
Gandak	Tibet-Nepal border at 7,620	425 in India	46,300 (7,620 In India)
Kosi	Sikkim-Nepal-Tibet Himalaya	730 in India	86,900 (21,500 In India)

The Gandak

- It originates near the Tibet-Nepal border.
- Kali Gandak, Mayangadi, Bari and Trishuli are the major tributaries of it.
- Its drainage area is 46,300 sq km out of which 7620 sq km is in India.

The Burhi Gandak

- Originates from the western slopes of Sumerar hills near the India-Nepal border, it joins the Ganga opposite Monghyr town.
- Its length is 610 km and drainage area is 12,200 sq km.

The Kosi

- The Kosi river consists of seven streams, namely, Sut Kosi, Tamba Kosi, Talkha, Doodh Kosi, Botia Kosi, Arun and Tamber and is popularly known as Saptkaushiki.
- Seven rivers mingle with each other to form three streams named the Tumar, Arun and Sun Kosi.
- Then all three streams unite at Triveni to the north of the Mahabharat Range to form the Kosi.

The Brahmaputra River System

- The Brahmaputra rises in the great Chemayundung glacier in the Kailas range.
- It flows eastward from its source region.
- Mariam La separates the source of the Brahmaputra from the Manasarovar lake.
- With the total length of 2900 km, it is one of the longest rivers of the world.
- It is known as Tsangpo in Tibet and Yarlung Zangbo Jiangin in Chinese language.
- It is one of the most remarkable navigable waterways of the world with boats sailing at an altitude of about 4000 metre above sea-level.
- It turns suddenly south and south-west near Namcha Barwa.
- It emerges from the foothills under the name of Siang and then the Dihang.
- It enters India West of Sadiya town near Passighat, where it receives the Dibang and the Lohit. From here, it is known as the Brahmaputra.
- Near Gwalpara, it enters Bangladesh as Yamuna and meets Padma at Goalundo.
- It has a braided channel along most of its length in Assam.
- It is among the four largest rivers of the world in terms of volume of discharge at the mouth.
- The look is like a **delta in reverse,** where Dibang and Lohit rivers meet the Brahmaputra river.
- Tista, a tributary of the Brahmaputra, was a tributary of the Ganga prior to the devastating floods of 1787.
- Majuli is the river island of the river Brahmaputra (area-1250 sq km).
- National waterways – 2 is on the Brahmaputra river from Sadiya to Dhubri.

The Peninsular River System

- Three main directions of flow:
  - Mahanadi, Godavari, Krishna, Cauvery and several smaller rivers draining south-east into the Bay of Bengal.
  - The Narmada and the Tapi flowing west as well as several small rivers originates from the Western Ghats flow westwards into the Arabian Sea.
  - Tributaries of Ganga and Yamuna such as Chambal, Betwa, Ken, Son and Damodar flow in the north-easterly direction.

The East Flowing Rivers

The Mahanadi

- It has its source in Dandakaranya near Sihawa in Raipur district of Chhattisgarh.
- Its upper course lies in the saucer-shaped basin called the 'Chhattisgarh Plains'
- Hirakud dam is built on this river.

The Godavari

- It is the largest river system of the peninsular India.
- It is held in reverence as 'Vridha Ganga' or 'Dakshina Ganga'.
- It has a catchment area of 312,812 sq km which covers about 10% of the area of India.
- Percentage-wise distribution of its catchment area:

State	(%) Share
Maharashtra	48.6
Andhra pradesh	23.8
Madhya Pradesh (Chhattisgarh also)	20.7
Orissa	5.5
Karnataka	1.4

- The source of the river is in the Trimbak Plateau of North Sahyadri near Nashik in Maharashtra.
- Manjira is the only important right bank tributary which joins the Godavari near Kondalwadi.
- Below Rajahmundry, the river Godavari divides itself into two main streams – the Gautami Godavari on the east and the Vashishta Godavari on the west – and forms a large delta of lobate type with a round bulge and many distributraries.

The Krishna

- It is the second largest east flowing river of peninsular in India.
- It rises in Western Ghats near Mahabaleshwar.
- It debouches into the Bay of Bengal, forming a big delta in arcute shape.
- Koyna Dam is made on the Koyana river, a tributary of the Krishna river.

The Cauvery

- It is designated as "the Ganga of the South".
- Its source lies at Taal Cauvery on the Brahmagiri range of hills in the Western Ghat.
- Its upper catchment area gets the rainfall in the duration of summer from the south-west monsoon and the lower catchment area receives rainfall during winter season by the retreating north-east monsoon.
- It is one of the best regulated rivers and 90 to 95% of its irrigation and power potential already stands harnessed.
- Sivasamudram waterfall is on this river.
- The river divides itself into two distinct channels at Srirangam, the northern channel is called Kollidam and the southern one retains the Cauvery.
- Cauvery river also forms a big delta in a quadrilateral shape.

The Subarnarekha

- It originates from the Ranchi Plateau.
- It forms the boundary between West Bengal and Orissa in its lower course.
- Its total length is 395 km.

The Brahmani

- It comes into existence by the confluence of Koel and the Sankh rivers near Rourkela in Orissa.
- It has total length of 800 km.
- Its main tributaries are Kura, Sankhad and Tikra.

The Penneru

- It springs from the Nandi Durg peak in Karnataka.
- The total length is 597 km.
- The principal tributaries are the Jayamangli, the Kunderu, the Chitravari, the Papagani and the Cheyeru.

The West Flowing Rivers of the Peninsula

The Narmada

- It is the largest of all the west flowing rivers of the Peninsula.
- It rises from the Amarkantak plateau in Shahdol district of Madhya Pradesh.
- It flows through a rift valley between the Vindhyan Range on the north and the Satpura Range on the South.
- The Duan Dhar falls is formed by the Narmada river in Jabalpur.
- It makes an estuary studded with several islands. Aliabet is the largest island.

The Tapi

- It is the second largest west flowing river of the Indian peninsula.
- It is also known as 'the twin' or 'the handmaid' of the Narmada.
- It originates from Multai in Betul district of Madhya Pradesh.

The Sabarmati

- This, 320 km long river is the name given to the combined streams - the Sabar and the Hathmati.
- It rises from the hills of Mewar in the Aravali range.
- Its tributaries are Hatmati, Sedhi, Wakul, Meshwa, Vatrak, etc.

The Mahi

- It rises in the Vindhyan range and debouches into the Gulf of Khamabhat.
- Its length is 533 km.
- It drains an area of 34, 862 sq km.
- The main tributaries are Som, Anas, Panam.

The Luni

- Its water is brackish below Balotra.
- Its source lies to the west of Ajmer in the Aravalli.
- The river is known as the Sagarmati in its upper course and from Govindgarh, where Sarsuti joins, it, becomes Luni. Finally, it is lost in the Rann of Kuchchh.

River Basins with the Largest Catchment Area

River	Catchment Area (Sq Km)
Ganga	8,61,452
Indus	3,21,289
Godavari	3,12,812
Krishna	2,58,948
Brahmaputra	1,94,413
Mahanadi	1,41,589

Major Rivers of the Peninsular India

Name of the river	Source	Leangth in Km	Area drained (sq km)
Mahanadi	Dandakaranya near Sihawa in Raipur district of Chhattisgarh	877	141,600
Godavari	Trimbak Plateau near Nashik in Maharashtra	1,465	312,812
Krishna	Near Mahabaleshwar in Maharashtra	1,400	258,948
Cauvery	Taal Cauvery Western Ghats	800	87,900
Narmada	Amarkantak Plateau	1,310	98,796
Tapi	Multai in Betul Distt, of MP	730	65,145

Rivers	Left Bank tributaries	Right Bank tributaries
Indus	Zaskar, Panjnad, Nubra	Shyok, Gilgit, Kabul
Mahanadi	Ib, Mand, Hasdo, Sheonath	Ong, Jonk, Tel
Godavari	Penganga, Wardha, Wainganga, Indravati and Sabari	Manjira
Krishna	Bhima, Doni, Musi, Muneru	Malprabha, Ghatprabha, Tungabhadra
Cauvery	Herangi, Hemavati, Lokpavani, Srimsha and Arkavati	Laksmantirtha, Kabani, Suvarnavati, Bhavani, and Amravati
Narmada	Burhner, Banjar, Shar, Shakkar, Tawa and Kundi	Hiran, Barna, Kolar
Tapi	Sipra, Kapra, Khursi, Mona, Girna, Bori, Amravati	Purna, Betul, Patki, Suki, More, Arunavati, Gomai
Ganga	Gomati, Ghaghara, Gandak, Burhi Gandak, Kosi, etc.	Yamuna, Son, Punpun, etc.
Yamuna	Tons	Chambal, Sind, Betwa, Ken

Longest Rivers

River	Length (Km)
Ganga	2510
Godavari	1465
Satluj	1440
Krishna	1400
Yamuna	1376
Narmada	1289

Highest Waterfalls and Name of River

Waterfalls	Height (m)	River	State
Gersoppa	260	Sharavati	Karnataka
Yenna	180		Maharashtra
Rakim Kund	168	Gaighat	Bihar
Chachai	127	Bihad	Madhya Pradesh
Kevti	98	Mahana	Madhya Pradesh
Sivasamudram	90	Cauvery	Karanataka

4 Chapter Climate

- Climate of a country includes the study of temperature, rainfall, atmospheric pressure, as well as the direction and velocity of winds over a long period of time.
- These elements of climate are largely influenced by latitudinal extent, relief and areal distribution of land and water.
- The Tropic of Cancer passes through the middle of the country.
- The whole of India, south of the Himalayas is climatically treated as a tropical country.
- India is par excellence, a tropical monsoon country.
- Mawsynram in Meghalaya receives as high as 1,221 cm of annual rainfall, while at Jaisalmer (Rajasthan) the annual rainfall rarely exceeds 12 cm.

Factors influencing the climate of India

- Location and latitudinal extent
- Distance from the sea
- The Northern mountain ranges
- Physiography
- Monsoon winds
- Upper air circulation
- Jet stream
- Tropical Cyclones
- Western Disturbances
- El-Nino
- La Nina
- Southern Oscillation
- The changes in the upper air circulation over the Indian landmass influences the climate of India to a great extent. Jet streams in the upper air system influence the Indian climate.
- Jet stream is a band of fast moving air from west to east usually found in the middle latitudes in the upper troposphere at a height of about 12 km. The wind speeds in a westerly jet stream are commonly 150 to 300 kmph.
- *Tropical Cyclones and Western Disturbances:* Tropical cyclones originate in the Bay of Bengal and Arabian Sea and influence large parts of the peninsular India.
- *El-Nino Effect*: El-Nino is a narrow warm current which occasionally appears off the coast of Peru in December.
- *La Nina*: La Nina is the complete opposition of El Nino. It is the harbinger of heavy monsoon shower in India.
- *Southern Oscillation*: Whenever the surface level pressure is high over the Indian Ocean, there is low pressure over the Pacific Ocean and vice-versa. This inter-relation of high and low pressure over the Pacific and the Indian Ocean is called Southern Oscillation.

Mechanism of the Monson

- *Classical Theory:* The credit for first scientific studies of the monsoon winds goes to the Arabs. Al Masudi, an Arab explorer from Baghdad, gave an account of the reversal of ocean currents and the monsoon winds over the north Indian Ocean.
- In 1668, the famous Englishman Sir Edmund Halley explained the monsoon as resulting from thermal contrasts between continents and oceans due to their differential heating.
- *Modern Theories:*
  - Thermal Concept of Halley
  - Air Mass Theory
  - Jet Stream Theory
  - MONEX – 1979
  - Southern Oscillation (SO)

Seasonal Rhythm

- Indian Meteorological Department (IMD) has recognised the following four distinct seasons:
  - The cold weather season or winter season
  - The hot weather season or summer season
  - The south-west monsoon season or rainy season, and
  - The season of the retreating monsoon or cool season.

The Cold Weather Season or Winter Season

Temperature

- The northern two-thirds of the country have mean temperature below 21°C, with afternoon temperatures of 27°C. January is the coldest month.

- Dras Valley in Kashmir is the coldest place in India.
- The southern one-third has rather warm conditions and does not have a distinctly defined winter weather. The isotherm of 20°C runs in east-west direction, roughly parallel to the Tropic of Cancer and divides India climatically in the northern and southern parts.

Pressure and winds

- High air pressure prevails over large parts of north-west India due to low temperature conditions there. Normally, the pressure varies from 1015 to 1020 mb. However, pressure is comparatively lower in south India. The isobar of 1019 mb is seen in north-west India while the isobar of 1013 mb touches the southern tip of the country. The winds start blowing from high pressure area of north-west to low pressure area of south-east. The velocity of wind is low because of the low pressure gradient.

Western Disturbances and Tropical Cyclones

- However, sky is generally clear, the spell of fine weather is often broken due to inflow of depressions from the west. These low pressure depressions are called western disturbances. They originate in the Mediterranean sea and enter India after crossing over Iraq, Iran, Afghanistan and Pakistan.
- Their moisture content is expanded from the Caspian sea and the Persian Gulf.
- They turn to eastwards across the sub-Himalayan belt and reach right upto Arunachal Pradesh, and becomes the reason of light rain in the Indo-Gangetic plains and snowfall in the Himalayan belt.
- The recurrence of the western disturbances changes from year to year, but on an average 3 to 5 disturbances are experienced.
- The jet streams are very essential in bringing these disturbances to India.

Precipitation

- The retreating winter monsoons blow from land to sea and do not cause much rainfall. These winds lift some moisture while crossing the Bay of Bengal and cause winter rainfall in Tamil Nadu, south Andhra Pradesh, south-east Karnataka and south-east Kerala. The higher seasonal rainfall of about 75 cm between October and December occurs along the south-eastern coast of Tamil Nadu and adjoining parts of South Andhra Pradesh.
- The western disturbances makes a reason for a little rainfall in north-west India.

The Summer Season

Temperature

- High temperature and low humidity are the chief characteristics of this season.
- The highest temperatures so far recorded are 50.5°C at Alwar but in certain areas, June is the month of the highest temperatures.
- The diurnal range of temperature is also very high.
- The temperature along the west coast are comparatively lower than those prevailing on the east coast due to the prevailing westerly winds.
- Northern and central parts of India experience heat waves in the season.

Pressure and Winds

- The atmospheric pressure is low all over the country due to high temperature.
- Hot, dust laden and strong wind known as *loo* blows.
- The strong dust storm resulting from the convective phenomena are locally known as andhis which literally mean blinding storms.
- The velocity often reaches 50-60 kms per hour and the visibility is reduced to a few metres.
- Norwesters are often very violent with squall speeds of 60 to 80 km per hour.
- The period of maximum occurrence of these storms is the month of *Vaisakh* (mid-April). They are locally known as *Kalabaishakhis,* the *black storms* or a *mass of dark clouds of Vaisasakha.*

Western Disturbances and Tropical Cyclones

- Disturbances cause change in weather conditions by bringing cloudiness and convective activity in this part of the country.
- About three-fourth of the tropical cyclones are born in the Bay of Bengal and the rest originate in the Arabian Sea.
- Most of the depressions in April originate to the south of 10°N while those originating in May are born to the north of this latitude.

Precipitation

- This is a dry season.
- But this is not a totally rainless season although only one per cent of the annual rainfall of India is received during this season.
- The rainfall brought by the Norwesters bring storm showers.

- In Assam, the rainfall received in May is about two-thirds of the rainfall received in June.
- This small amount of rainfall is very useful for the cultivation of tea, jute and rice and is known as tea showers in Assam.
- Thuderstorms also cause about 10 cm of rainfall in the interior of south India.
- Such showers are called *mango showers* in Tamil Nadu and Andhra Pradesh because they are very beneficial to mango. In Karnataka, they are known as cherry blossom due to the salutary effect on the coffee plantations.

The Rainy Season

- This season is also called as *monsoon season,* the *south-west monsoon season,* the *wet season* and the *hot-west season.*
- The main characteristics of this season are as following: High heat, high humidity, extensive clouding and several spells of moderate to heavy rain with strong surface winds are.

Temperature

- There is an important fall in temperature with the beginning of rainy season.
- However, the temperature increases again in during the month of September with the pause of rains and secondary maximum temperature is experienced all over the country.
- Also, there is rise on temperature whenever there is cessation in the monsoons and rainfall does not fall for a number of days. The night temperatures are more stable than the day temperatures. The day to day range of temperature is small due to clouds and rains.
- In the Thar desert of Rajasthan. The highest temperatures of over 32°C are experienced.
- The temperatures are experienced very low, all over the Western Ghats due to high elevation and also because of heavy rainfall, but the rainshadow area is comparatively warmer on account of low elevation and scanty rainfall.

Pressure and Winds

- In the north-west India, the temperatures are still very high as a result of which, low pressure conditions prevail there. The most conspicuous feature of the surface pressure distribution during this season is an elongated trough across the Ganga basin right upto the head of Bay of Bengal. This is called the monsoon trough.
- In southwest to north-west winds blow from Arabian Sea and Bay of Bengal. They maintain this direction throughout peninsular India. But their direction undergoes a change in Indo-Gangetic plain where they move from east to west.

Rainfall

- India's three fourths of the total annual rainfall is received during this season.
- The normal rainfall over the plains of India in this season is about 92 cm, or about 87 per cent whereas during the remaining part of the year, only 14 cm of rainfall occurs.
- The rainfall during this season all over the country is due to southwest monsoons coming from the Indian Ocean.
- The advance of the monsoon is much more in the Bay of Bengal than in the Arabian Sea.
- The monsoons advance with startling suddenness, accompanied with a lot of thunder, lightning and heavy downpour. This sudden onset of rain is termed as monsoon burst.
- It is very fascinating to know that the Arabian Sea branch of the monsoon is much more powerful than the Bay of Bengal branch for two reasons:
    - The Arabian Sea is wider than the Bay of Bengal.
    - The entire Arabian Sea current advances towards India, whereas only a part of the Bay of Bengal current enters India, the remainder proceeding to Myanmar, Thailand and Malaysia.

The Cool Season

- The cool season starts with the commencement of the withdrawal of southwest monsoon in the middle of September and continues up to November, after which the winter season starts.
- The south-west monsoons reach north-west India in th last and withdraw from there first.
- Therefore, the duration of the southwest monsoon period is minimum there.

Temperature

- With the digress retreat of the monsoons, the clouds disappear and the sky becomes clear.
- The nights are cool with lowest temperatures varying from 20° to 25°C.
- The general temperature in most parts of the country alters from 25° to 30°C.
- The day to day range of temperature increments due to lack of cloud cover.

Pressure and Winds

- As the monsoon retreat, the elongated trough of the low pressure across the Indo-Gangetic plains weakens and gradually shifts southward.
- The surface pressure in most parts of the country varies from 1,010 to 1,012 mb. Consequently, the pressure gradient is low.

- The onset of the north-east monsoon is not clearly defined.
- The direction of winds over large parts of the country is influenced by the local pressure conditions.

Cyclones

- This is the season of the most severe and devastating tropical cyclones originating in the Indian seas, especially in the Bay of Bengal.
- The highest frequency of the cyclones is in the month of October and the first half of November.
- More cyclones are born in October and then in November, and more cyclones originate in the Bay of Bengal than in the Arabian Sea.

Precipitation

- The humidity and cloud cover is much reduced with the retreat of the southwest monsoons and most parts of the country remains without much rainfall. However, October-November is the main rainy season in Tamil Nadu and adjoining areas of Andhra Pradesh to the south of the Krishna delta as well as a secondary rainy period for Kerala.
- In fact, Kerala has bi-modal pattern of rainfall with main rains in the south-west monsoon season and subsidiary rains in this season.

Annual Rainfall

- The average annual rainfall of India is about 118 cm. There are large spatial and temporal variations.
- India can be divided into the following regions based on annual average rainfall.

Distribution Of Rainfall

(%) of the total Land area	Amount of annual rainfall (cm)
11	Above 200
21	125 to 200
37	75 to 125
24	35 to 75
7	Below 35

Distribution of Rainfall Table

- *Areas of very high rainfall:* Areas receiving an annual rainfall of 200 cm and above are termed as areas of very high rainfall.
- *Areas of high rainfall:* These areas receive 100-200 cm annual rainfall.
- *Areas of lower rainfall:* These areas receive 50-100 cm annual rainfall.
- *Areas of very low rainfall:* These are desert and semi-desert areas receiving less than 50 cm of annual rainfall.

Variability of Annual Rainfall:

- Variability of annual rainfall is computed with the help of the following formula:
- Coefficient of Variability (CV)

$$= \frac{S\tan dardDeviation}{Mean} \times 100$$

- In general, the variability increases from west into the interior of the plateau as from Orissa and West Bengal towards the north and north-west.
- The variability is highest where the amount of rainfall is the lowest.
- The rainfall variability is inverse to total amount of rainfall and reliability of rainfall is inversely proportional to the coefficient of variability.

Peculiarities and Significance of Indian climate

- Of the country's total rainfall, about 75 per cent is received in the monsoon months from June to September, 13 per cent comes in the post-monsoon season, 10 per cent in the pre-monsoon season and the remaining 2 per cent in the winter season.
- In January and February, north-west India gets rainfall from the western disturbances.
- Coromandel Coast receives rainfall by the north-east monsoons in the winter season.
- The highest record, as already mentioned, is 103.6 cm in 24 hours at Cherrapunji in Meghalaya.

Chapter 5 Agriculture

1. According to recent data "The net sown area is 141.1 million hac and gross cropped area is 19.5 million hac.
2. Agriculture and allied sectors contribute about 17.32% of GDP.
3. All India average consumption of fertilisers per hectare is 165.12 (kg).
4. India is the second largest producer of fertilisers in the world after China.
5. India is the world's second largest fertilisers consumer accounting for 25.5% of total consumption.
6. NPK consumption ratio in India has increased to 16.2%.
7. India is self-sufficient in respect of urea while 95% self-sufficient in DAP.

Contribution of Agriculture and Allied Sectors in GVA (At the Current Price of 2011-12)

Year	Agriculture & Alleied Sector % in GVA
2013-14	18.6
2014-15	18.2
2015-16	17.7
2016-17	17.9
2017-18 (PE)	17.1

Food Grains Production (in Million Tonnes)

Year	Food Grains Production (in Mullion Tonnes)
2013-14	265.04
2014-15	252.02
2015-16	252.22
2016-17	275.11
2017-18	284.83

3 Largest Producer of States (2017-18)

Crope	Largest Producer States
Rice	1. West Bengal, 2. U.P., 3. Punjab
Wheat	1. U.P., 2. Madhya Pradesh, 3. Punjab
Maize	1. Maharashtra, 2. Karnataka, 3. Madhya Pradesh
Grams	1. Madhya Pradesh, 2. Maharashtra, 3. Rajasthan
Tar	1. Maharashtra, 2. Karnataka, 3. Madhya Pradesh
Sugarcane	1. U.P., 2. Maharashtra, 3. Karnataka
Cotton	1. Maharashtra, 2. Gujarat, 3. Telengana
Total Food Grains	1. U.P., 2. Madhya Pradesh, 3. Panjab
Total Pulses	1. Madhya Pradesh, 2. Maharashtra, 3. Rajasthan

Production of Crops (Million Tonnes)

Crope	2016-17	2017-18	(IVth Advance Estimates, 28 August 2018)
Rice	109.70	112.92	(Record Production)
Wheat	98.51	99.70	(Record Production)
Maize	25.90	28.72	(Record Production)
Pulses	23.13	25.23	(Record Production)
Gram	9.38	11.23	(Record Production)
Tur	4.87	4.25	
Soyabean	13.16	10.98	
Sugarcane	306.07	376.91	(Record Production)
Total Pulses	23.13	25.23	(Record Production)
Total Food Grains	275.11	284.83	(Record Production)

MSP of Kharif Crops (₹/ Quintile)

Crops	MSP of 2018-19	MSP of 2017-18	MSP increase in ₹
Rice	1750	1550	200
Tur	5675	5450	225
Seasamum	6249	5300	949
Soyabeans	3399	3050	349
Niger Seed	5877	4050	1827

MSP of Rabi Crops (₹/Quintile)

Crops	MSP of 2018-19	MSP of 2017-18	MSP increase in ₹
Wheat	1840	1735	105
Jao	1440	1410	30
Gram	4620	4400	220
Rapeseed and Mustard	4200	4000	200

Agriculture Credit (₹ in Crore)

Year	Target	Real Achievement of Target	Target achievement in %
2014-15	8,00,000	845328.23	105.67
2015-16	8,50,000	915509.92	107.71
2016-17	9,00,000	1065755.67	118.42
2017-18	10,00,000	1168507.84	116.85
2018-19	11,00,000	–	–

Agriculture Credit Distributed by Agencies (in %)

Name of the Agencies	2016-17	2017-18
1. Commercial Banks	75.04	75.07
2. Cooperative Banks	13.40	12.87
3. Regional Rural Banks	11.56	12.07
Total	**100.00**	**100.00**

Horticulture in India

Year	Area (Million Hectare)	Total Producation (in Mullion Tonnes)
2016-17	24.9	300.6
2017-18	25.7	306.8

Note: 29 August 2018

Livestocks:

1. India ranks first in milk production and third in egg production in the world.
2. India is endowed with the largest livestock population in the world and accounts for 57% of the world's buffalo population.

Major Crops in India

Indian Crops can be divided into mainly two categories

(i) Food Crops : Rice, Wheat, Maize, Bajra.

(ii) Cash/Commercial Crops:

(a) Oilseeds : Groundnut, Castor, Mustard, Sunflower

(b) Sugar Crops : Sugarcane

(c) Fiber Crops : Jute, Mesta, Sunnhemp, Cotton

(d) Narcotic Crops : Tabacco

(e) Beverage Crops : Tea, Coffee

Irrigation

The All India percentage of net irrigated area to total cropped area was 34.5 percent in 2014-15 which makes a large part of agriculture in India dependent on rainfall. Irrigation means watering the fields by any means others than rain.

Need for Irrigation in India is given below:

(i) India is a big country and stands next to China when we talk about population and so irrigation facilities are needed to grow more food to feed the teaming millions.

(ii) The distribution in rainfall is uneven and uncertain which either causes famines or drought by means of irrigation we can check both the problems.

(iii) Different water requirements of different crops can only by met through irrigation facilities.

(vi) India, being a tropical country the temperature is high and evaporation more rapid, so artificial irrigation is necessary for ample supply of water and also to prevent water scarcity in the long dry winter season.

Types of Irrigation:

Mainly 3 types of irrigation practiced in India are as follows:

1. Tanks, 2. Well,

3. Canals

Oilseeds production (2015-16)

State	Production (Millon Tonnes)
Madhya Pradesh	6.24
Rajasthan	5.71
Gujarat	4.10
All India	25.30

States with the Highest Milk Production (2017-18)

State	(000 Million Tonnes)
Uttar Pradesh	23.23
Rajasthan	13.94
Andhra Pradesh	12.762
Punjab	10.315

States with the Highest Egg Production (2017-18)

- The production of egg is largely contributed by commercial poultry farms with nearly 75.75% and remaining production is from household/backyard poultry.

State

1. Andhra Pradesh
2. Tamil Nadu
3. Telangana
4. West Bengal

States with the Highest Meat Production

- According to ICRA's estimation, per capita meat Conscription is around 3.6 kg per annum.

State

1. Uttar Pradesh
2. Maharashtra
3. West Bengal
4. Andhra Pradesh

Major Crops

- Indian crops can be divided into following categories:
- Food crops – Rice, wheat, maize, millets-jowar, bajra, etc.
- Cash crops – Cotton, jute, sugarcane, tobacco, groundnut, etc.
- Plantation crops – Tea, coffee, spices, coconut, rubber, etc.
- Horticulture crops – Apple, mango, banana, citrus, etc.

Food Crops

- It covers about three-fourth of the total cropped area in the country.
- It includes: Rice, wheat, maize; millets-jowar, bajra, ragi; pulses-gram, tur (Arhar)

Rice

- It covers ¼ of the total cropped area in India.
- It requires high temperature (about 24°C monthly) and high rainfall (about 150 cm annually).
- One hundred (100 cm) isohyet forms the limit of rice production in rainfed area.
- About 40% of rice crop is raised under irrigation.
- Rice culture is also called 'hoe-culture'.

Production

- India is the 2nd largest producer and consumer of rice in the world after China.
- India produces 21% of the world's total rice production.
- Three largest rice production states – West Bengal, Uttar Pradesh, Andhra Pradesh – in descending order.

Rice Production (2013-14)

State	Production (Million Tonnes)
West Bengal	15.75
Uttar Pradesh	12.5
Punjab	11.82

- Highest yield of rice is in Punjab.
- West Godavari, East Godavari and Krishna district of Andhra Pradesh account for over 12% of the total rice production of the country.
- Tanjavur in the Cauvery delta (Tamil Nadu) is the second largest rice production district of the country and is called as the "Rice bowl of Tamil Nadu".
- Chhattisgarh is known as the 'Rice Bowl of India.'
- India occupies second position in rice exports, next to Thailand.

Wheat

- It accounts for 27 per cent of the total area and 37 per cent of the tatal production of cereals in the country.
- India stands second in the production of wheat in the world contributing over 13 per cent of the total area and 12 per cent of the total production of wheat in the world.

Wheat Production

State in India	Production (in Lakh Tonnes)
Uttar Pradesh	300.010
Punjab	164.720
Haryana	116.30

- The highest yield is in Punjab (45 quintal/hectare) and in Haryana (44 quintal/hectare)
- India is self-sufficient in wheat.

Maize

- In India, it is characterised by 'inter-culture'.
- The minimum temprature for maize is between 21°c and 27°c.

Maize producting States in India

1. Karnataka
2. Uttar Pradesh
3. Bihar
4. Andhra Pradesh

Jowar

- It is rainfed crop of dry farming.
- The major quality of this crop is that it can be cultivated in both Kharif and Rabi season.

Jowar producing states and their share (2011-12)

Maharashtra

Karnataka

Andhra Pradesh

Madhya Pradesh

- The highest yield is in Madhya Pradesh and Andhra Pradesh.
- The largest area under the crop is in Maharashtra followed by Karnataka.

Bajra

- It is a crop of dry and warm climate.
- It grows very well on the sandy soil and shallower black soil.

Major States in Bajra production

State

1. Rajasthan
2. Uttar Pradesh
3. Gujrat
4. Haryana

- The largest area under the crop is in Rajasthan (43.69%) followed by Uttar Pradesh (22.03%).
- The highest yield is in Uttar Pradesh (1638 kg/hect.).

Ragi

- It is also known as 'Buck wheat'.
- Karnataka is the largest producer.

Pulses

- In total pulses, Madhya Pradesh is the largest producer followed by Uttar Pradesh.
- Gram accounts for 37% of the total pulses production and 28.28% of the total area under pulses in India.
- In Tur, Madhya Pradesh and Maharashtra are the major producing states.

States with the Highest Pulses Prodution

1. Madhya Pradesh	**32.97%**
2. Maharashtra	**18.36%**
3. Tamil Nadu	**4.97%**

Cash crops

- The cash crop is a crop which generates revenue for a country.

Cotton

- It is a fibre crop of tropical and sub-tropical areas.
- About one-third of the total area under it is irrigated.
- Cotton is categorised into three groups- long staple, medium staple and short staple.
- But the highest yield is in Punjab and then in Haryana.
- It is also known as 'White Gold'.
- India is both and exporter as well as importer of cotton.

State share in cotton production (2018-19)

State	Production (Million Bales of 170 kg)
Andhra Pradesh	20.38
Gujarat	126.37
Haryana	16.26

Jute

- Currently, India accounts for about 70% of world's total jute production.
- The largest producers are West Bengal, Bihar and Assam.
- The largest area under jute is in West Bengal.
- But, the highest yield is in West Bengal and Assam.

Sugarcane

- India has the largest area under sugarcane cultivation in the world and the second largest producer next only to Brazil.
- Sugarcane Research Institute is located at Coimbatore in Tamil Nadu.
- UP is the leading producer, followed by Tamil Nadu, Maharashtra and Andhra Pradesh.

Sugarcane producing states in India

Uttar Pradesh

Maharashtra

Tamil Nadu

- The highest yield is in Tamil Nadu and then in Karnataka.

Tobacco

- It was brought to India by the Portuguese.
- Two types of tobacco are grown in India – Nicotiana Tabacum (90%) and Nicotiana Rustica (10%).
- Andhra Pradesh accounts for 45%, Karnataka (26%) and Gujarat for 14.6% of India's total production.
- UP has the highest yield.
- India is the world's fourth largest exporter of tobacco.

Oilseeds

- In total oilseeds production, Madhya Pradesh (6.24 Million Tonnes) is the leading producer followed by Rajasthan and Gujarat.
- India has the largest area and production in the world.
- Oilseeds occupy about 20% of the net sown area in India.
- In groundnut production, India produces 18% of the world's production.

Groundnut production and share of states (2016)

State	Million Tonnes
Gujarat	2.36
Tamil Nadu	0.88
Rajasthan	1.06

- In Rapeseed and Mustard production, India has the largest area and the highest production in the world.
- Rajasthan is the largest producer followed by Haryana, in Rapeseed and Mustard production.
- India, being the third largest producer of linseed in the world, accounts for about 10% of the world's total production. Madhya Pradesh is the largest producer in India.
- In castor seed, Gujarat is the largest producer in India which accounts for two-third of the total production, while India is the second largest producer next to Brazil in the world.
- In soyabean output, Madhya Pradesh is the largest producer succeeded by Maharashtra and Rajasthan.
- In sunflower, Karnataka leads the states in production.

Miscellaneous

- In onion production, Maharashtra ranks first followed by Karnataka.
- In potato production, Uttar Pradesh is the leader among major producers, followed by West Bengal and Bihar.

Plantation Crop

Tea

- India is the second largest producer and consumer of tea after China and accounts for about 24% of world production.
- It is a labour intensive tropical and sub-tropical crop, wherein women constitute over 50% of the total workforce.
- The leading states are Assam, West Bengal and Tamil Nadu.
- The highest yield is in Karnataka, while the largest number of tea gardens is in Tamil Nadu followed by Kerala.

Coffee

- India is the third largest producer of Coffee in Asia. It is indigenous to Abyssinia (Ethiopia).
- Coffee Robusta and coffee Arabica are the two varieties grown in India wherein, the former has a large demand in the international market.
- India contributes around four percent (4%) of the world production.
- The largest producer is Karnataka (71%) followed by Kerala (21%) and Tamil Nadu.
- In fact, Karnataka leads in production, area coverage and yield of coffee.

Rubber

- India is the fourth largest natural rubber producer next to Thailand, Indonesia and Malayasia and accounts for about 8% of the world's total production.
- Kerala is the leading state in production, area coverage and yield, followed by Tamil Nadu and Karnataka.
- Kerala produces around 90% of India's total production.

Spices

- India is the second largest producer of pepper.
- India is the largest producer of ginger, cardamom and arecanut.
- India is the third largest producer of coconut next to Philippines and Indonesia.
- Kerala leads in the production of pepper, cardamom, ginger, arecanut and coconut among Indian states.
- Andhra Pradesh is the largest producer of chillies and turmeric.

- India is the largest producer, processor, consumer and exporter of cashew nut in the world.

Horticulture crops

- India is the second largest producer of fruits and vegetables.
- India leads the world in the production of mango, banana, sapota and acid lime and has recorded highest productivity in grape.
- Mango, citrus and banana ranks first, second and third respectively, in area in India.
- Banana ranks first in fruits production followed by mango.
- India is next to China in area and production of vegetables, contributing 13% of world production.
- India occupies first, second rank and third rank in the production of cauliflower, onion and cabbage, respectively.

Fisheries

- Fish catch in India is of two types – marine fisheries and inland fisheries.
- India is the second largest producer of fish and second largest producer of inland fishing in the world.
- It accounts for about one per cent of the total agricultural production in India.
- The production of fish reached 10.07 Million Metric Tonnes and in present time 65% contribution from inland sector.
- About 75% of marine fish landings are on the west coast and only 25% in the east coast.
- Important fish caught along the coast are shark, sardine, herring, Mumbai duck, fly fish ribbon fish and Mackerrel.
- In the year 2001, the Govt. of India declared "10th of July" as the "National Fish Farmers Day."
- Fish and fish products have presently emerged as the largest group in agricultural exports of India, with 10.51 lakh tonnes in terms of quantity and Rs. 33.442 crores in value. This accounts for around 10% of the total exports of the country and nearly 20% of the agricultural exports. More than 50 different types of fish and shellfish products are exported to 75 countries around the world.

Indian Fisheries

Global position	:	**3rd in Fisheries 2nd in Aquaculture**
Contribution of Fisheries to GDP (%)	:	1.07
Contribution to Agril. GDP (%)	:	5.15
Per capita fish availability (Kg.)	:	9.0
Annual Export earnings (Rs. In Crore)	:	33,441.61
Employment in sector (million)	:	14.0

Resources

Coastline	:	8129 kms
Exclusive Economic Zone	:	2.02 million sq. km
Continental Shelf	:	0.506 million sq. km
Rivers and Canals	:	1,91,024 km
Reservoirs	:	3.25 million ha
Ponds and Tanks	:	3.15 million ha
Oxbow lakes and derelict waters	:	1.3 million ha
Brackishwaters	:	1.24 million ha
Estuaries	:	0.29 million ha

Some Facts

Present fish production	:	6.4 mmt
Inland	:	3.4 mmt
Marine	:	3.0 mmt
Potential fish production	:	8.4 mmt
Fish seed production	:	21,000 million fry

7 Chapter

Manufacturing Industry

- On the basis of source of raw material, industries are classified as:
- Agro-based industries
- Mineral-based industries
- Forest-based industries
- First successful venture to start an industry took place in 1854 at Mumbai with the establishment of cotton textile industry.
- The first jute mill was set up at Rishra near Kolkata in 1855.
- The first Industrial Policy was brought in 1948.
- Industrial Policy, 1956 is called the 'Magna-carta' or 'semi-constutution' of the Indian industrial development.
- BHEL was establishment at Bhopal during the second Five Year Plan (1956-61).
- SAIL was constituted during the fifth Five Year Plan (1974-79).

Textile Industries

- It contributes about 5% to the GDP.
- It includes cotton, jute, wool, silk and synthetic fibre textiles. The textile industry employs about 40 million workers and 60 million indirectly. India's overall textile exports during FY-2015-16 stood at US $ 40 billion.

Cotton textiles

- The first modern cotton textile mill was set up in 1818 a Fort Glaster near Kolkata, but could not become successful.
- The first successful modern cotton textile mill was established in Mumbai in 1854.
- The cotton textile industry is the largest modern industry of India.
- About 20% of the industrial labour of the country is engaged in this industry.
- Cotton cloth is produced in mills, powerlooms and handlooms.
- Cotton yarn and fabrics exports accounts for about 23 percent of India's total textiles and apparel exports.
- In the year 2017-18, India's cotton production was 34.86 million bales of 170 kgs each.
- In the production of Yarn, Tamil Nadu is the largest producer and accounts for 44% of the total yarn production of the country.
- Coimbatore is the most important centre in Tamil Nadu and known as the Manchester of South India.
- Kanpur is the Manchester of Uttar Pradesh.
- In the duration of April 2017 to August 2017, India's powerloom production was 16,119 million square meters.
- Powerloom sector contributes to 24% of the total cloth production.

Jute

- The first jute mill was started in 1855 at Rishra near Kolkata.
- West Bengal produces the highest quantity of jute goods.
- Assam is the second in jute goods production.

Woollen textile

- The modern woollen textile industry was started with the establishment of Lal Imli at Kanpur in 1876.
- Punjab leads all other states in manufacturing woollen goods, Dhariwal is the largest centre.
- Maharashtra is the second largest producer of woollen textiles, followed by Uttar Pradesh.
- Mirzapur, Bhadoni, Agra and Khamana are important centres for woollen carpet production in Uttar Pradesh.
- Ludhiana is the largest centre of hosiery manufacturing in India.
- India is an important exporter of woollen goods.

Silk Industry

- India is the only country producing all the five known commercial varieties of silk, viz. Mulberry, Tasar (Tropical), Oak Tasar, Eri and Muga.
- India is the second largest producer of raw silk, accounting for 20% of the world production, next to China.

Share of silk varieties in total production of silk in India (2016-17)

Mulberry	70.09%
Eri	18.58%
Tasar	10.77%
Muga	0.56%

- Karnataka is the foremost silk producing state in India, which accounts for one-third of the Indian silk production.

Metallurgical Industries

- These industries form the economic backbone of a developing country.

Iron and Steel Industry

- The first iron and steel unit on modern lines was established in 1830 at Porto Novo in Tamil Nadu.
- But the real beginning of modern iron and steel industry was made in 1907 when TISCO was set up at Sakchi, Jamshedpur.
- IISCO was set up in 1919 at Burnpur.
- Mysore steel works at Bhadravati came into extistence in 1923.
- SAIL was established in 1973.
- India is now the second largest producer of steel in the world.
- The first on-shore steel plant in India was set up at Vishakhapatnam (Andhra Pradesh).
- Mysore Steel plant was the first plant based on wood and was built by Indian Engineers.
- India is the leading county in the production of sponge iron.

Different Steel Plants and their mineral resources places:

TISCO (in Jharkhand)

- Haematite iron ore – Noamundi and Gurumahisani
- Coal – Jharia and Raniganj
- Manganese – Joda mines (Kendujhar, Orissa)
- Water – Subarnarekha
- Dolomite and Limestone – Sundargarh (Orissa)

IISCO

- Iron are – Guna mines in Singhbhum
- Coal – Jharia
- Electricity – Damodar Valley Corporation
- Dolomite and Limestone – Sundargarh

Visweswaraya Steel Plant (in Karnataka)

- Iron ore – Kemmangundi mines
- Electricity – Sharavati Power Plant
- Limestone – Bhundiguda
- Manganese – Shimoga and Chitradurga

Bhilai Steel Plant (in Chhattisgarh)

- Iron ore – Dalli – Rajhara
- Coal – Korba, Kargali coal fields
- Limestone – Nandini
- Electricity – Korba Thermal Power Plant
- Manganese – Bhandara and Balaghat

Bokaro Steel Plant (in Jharkhand)

- Iron ore – Kiriburu
- Coal – Jharia
- Limestone – Palamu
- Electricity – DVC (Hydro power)

Rourkela Steel Plant (in Orissa)

- Iron ore – Sundargarh and Keonjhar
- Coal – Jharia
- Electricity – Hirakud Hydro Power Plant
- Manganese – Barajmda
- Limestone – Purnapani

Durgapur Steel Plant (in West Bengal)

- Iron ore – Bolani mines
- Coal – Jharia and Raniganj
- Limestone – Birmitrapur
- Manganese – Keonjhar
- Electricity – DVC

Aluminium Smelting

- Manufacturing of aluminium metal commenced in 1886.
- Indian Aluminium Corporation Ltd was formed in 1937 and started its production in 1938.
- BALCO came into being in 1965, NALCO in 1981
- Integrated Aluminium Plant of NALCO at Damanjodi near Jeypur in Koraput district of Orissa is the largest complex in India.
- NALCO, the lowest cost producer of aluminium in the world, at present ranked among the top 10 global companies and is the second to HINDALCO in India.

Company	*Its Plant*
INDAL	Alupuram (Kerala), Hirakud (Orissa)
HINDALCO	Renukut (Uttar Pradesh)
BALCO	Korba (Chhattisgarh), Ratnagiri (Maharashtra)
NALCO	Damanjodi (Orissa), Angul (Orissa)

- Aluminium companies with the highest sales in descending order: HINDALCO, NALCO, INDAL, MALCO

Copper Smelting

- Indian Copper Corporation was set up in 1924 which was taken over by Hindustan Copper Ltd (established in 1967), in 1972.
- At present, copper is produced at only two centres – Maubhandar (Ghatsila) and Khetri (Jhunjhunu).

Lead and Zinc smelting

- The first lead smelting plant was set up at Tundoo near Dhanbad (Jharkhand) which was later occupied by Hindustan Zinc Ltd in 1965.
- HZL's another plant is at Vishakhapatnam.
- The lead-zinc complex was constructed at Chanderiya (Rajasthan) in 1991 under the British aid programme.
- Presently, there are four zinc smelters in country-Alwaye (Kerala), Debari and Chanderi (Rajasthan) and Vishakhapatnam (Andhra Pradesh).
- Alwaye Plant is wholly dependent upon imported supplies of zinc concentrates.

Engineering Industries

- These industries contribute about 12.8% of total exports of the country in 2017-18.
- Heavy Engineering Corporation Ltd was set up at Ranchi (Jharkhand) in 1958.
- Drills for drilling holes in rocky areas are manufactured at Naroda (Ahmedabad).
- Kirloskar Brothers Ltd is the pioneer company in the manufacturing of machine tools.
- HMT is the largest manufacturer of machine tools in the country.
- HMT's plants: Bangalore, Pinjore, Kalamassery (Kerala), Hyderabad, Sri Nagar and Ajmer.
- Locomotive Works: Chittaranjan Locomotive Works, Diesel Locomotive Works (Varanasi), Tata Engineering and Locomotive Works (Jamshedpur).
- BHEL, Bhopal has been developed to manufacture electric locomotive for the Indian railways.
- Wheel and Axle Plant was set up at Bangalore in 1984.
- The Integral Coach Factory at Perampur near Chennai was set up in 1955 with Swiss collaboration.
- Rail Coach Factory at Kapurthala (Punjab) was set up in 1988.
- Bharat Movers Limited at Bangalore also produces railways coaches.
- Most of wagons are produced in private sector. About 60% of wagons are produced in West Bengal.

Automobile Industry

- Auto industry became the 4th largest in the world and the 7th manufacturer of largest commercial vehicles in 2017.
- Top six automobile companies with the highest sales:
  1. Tata Motors
  2. Mahindra & Mahindra Ltd
  3. Maruti Udyog Ltd
  4. Hero Motocorp Ltd.
  5. Bajaja Auto Ltd.
  6. Ashok Leyland Ltd.
- In medium and heavy commercial vehicles, TELCO is the leading Maruti Udyog Ltd is at top position.
- Almost the entire production of jeeps comes from Mahindra, Mumbai.
- Indian two-wheeler market is the second largest market in the world after that of China.

Ship-building Industry

- India ranks second among the Asian countries next only to Japan in terms of shipping tonnage.
- There are four main centres of ship-building industry at Vishakapatnam, Kolkata, Kochi and Mumbai.
- Hindustan Shipyard Ltd, Vishakapatnam set up in 1941, is the first-ship-building yard in the country to receive ISO-9001 certification.
- Cochin Shipyard Ltd, Kochi was incorporated in 1972. It also manufactures ships for the Indian Navy.
- Mazgaon Dock at Mumbai builds cargo ships, passenger ships, dredgers etc. for Indian Navy. Recently, it has started constructing submarines, missiles boats, destroyers of the Navy and off-shore supply vessels for ONGC.
- Goa Shipyard Ltd at Vasco-da-Gama undertakes the manufacture of fibre glass boats, trawlers, etc. and also constructs or refits variety of vessels for Indian Navy and coast-guard.
- Shipping Corporation of India Ltd has the highest sales followed by Great Eastern Shipping Company Ltd.

Air Craft Industry

- The first aircraft industry was set up at Bangalore in 1940 under the name of Hindustan Aircraft Ltd.
- Later, Hindustan Aircraft Ltd was merged into Aeronautics India Ltd in 1964 to form Hindustan Aeronautics Ltd, Bangalore.
- Different Division of HAL and production:
- Nashik division – MIG airframe
- Koraput division – Engine of MIG aircraft
- Hyderabad division – Electronic equipment of MIG.
- Transport aircrafts are manufactured at Kanpur.
- Recently, a factory was set up at Lucknow for producing equipment for aircraft.

Fertiliser Industry

- The first super-phosphate factory was set up at Ranipet in Tamil Nadu in 1906.
- India is now the third largest producer of nitrogenous fertilisers in the world.
- At present, there are 11 public sector undertakings under the department of fertilisers.
- Fertilisers companies with the highest sales are – National Fertilisers Ltd, Tata Chemicals Ltd, Rashtriya Chemicals & Fertilisers Ltd (in descending order).
- India is the third largest producer and consumer of fertilisers in the world.

Cement Industry

- The first successful attempt was made in 1912-13 when the Indian Cement Co Ltd set up a plant in Porbander (Gujarat).
- In 1934, 10 out of 11 existing companies were merged into the Association Cement Co Ltd (ACC).
- The industry was totally decontrolled in 1989.
- The Indian Cement industry is the second largest in the world after that of China.
- The industry is the second contributor to the exchequer, producing 1335.70 lakh tonnes (2004-05)
- Indian Cement industry produces 11 varieties of cement:

Portland cement – 71% of Indian output
Portland Pozzolana cement – 18% of Indian output
Portland Blast furnace slag cement – 10% of Indian output

- Madhya Pradesh and Chhattisgarh, together, are the leading producers, which account for 22.5% of total cement production in India (2003-04).
- India has emerged as a major exporter of cement in the international market.
- States with the largest cement capacity are Andhra Pradesh, Rajasthan, Madhya Pradesh and Gujarat (in descending order).
- States with the highest cement consumption are Maharashtra, Uttar Pradesh, Tamil Nadu and Gujarat (in descending order).
- States with the highest number of large cement plants are Andhra Pradesh, Rajasthan and Tamil Nadu and Gujarat and Madhya Pradesh (in descending order).

Leather and Leather Goods

- The industry is divided into two parts – tanning and leather goods.
- For tanning, Kanpur, (1st tannery centre), Chennai, and Kolkata are three largest centres.
- The Central Leather Research Institute at Chennai is the largest of its kind in the world.
- India is now one of the top ten producers of footwear in the world.
- Leather and leather products companies with the highest sales are Bata Ind. Ltd, Mirza Tanners Ltd and Relaxo Footwear Ltd (in descending order).

Glass Industry

- The main raw for the industry is silica sand.
- Uttar Pradesh is the leading producer of glass in India followed by West Bengal and Maharashtra.
- Firozabad in Agra district is the largest producer of glass.The other major centres are Bahjoi, Naini, Hathras, Sasni and Allahabad in Uttar Pradesh.

Paper Industry

- The first abortive attempt to begin this industry was made in 1816 at Chennai.
- The first successful effort was made in 1870 with the setting up of the Royal Bengal Paper Mills at Ballyganj near Kolkata.
- The important centres for paper products are Lucknow, Titagarh, Raniganj, Pune, Naihati, etc.
- Per capita consumption of paper in India is 5.5 kg.
- Of the total installed capacity, 43% is dependent on forest-based raw materials, 28% on agro-based raw materials and the remaining 29% on other materials, including waste paper.
- Raw materials are – Bamboo, Sabai Grass, Bagasses, etc.
- Maharashtra is the largest producer of paper and accounts for 18% of the paper produced in India. Ballarpur has the largest paper mill in Maharashtra.
- Andhra Pradesh is the second largest producer followed by Gujarat, Uttar Pradesh and West Bengal.
- Uttar Pradesh has the largest number of paper mills.
- National Newsprint and Paper Mills is at Nepanagar.
- Paper companies with the highest sales are Ballarpur Industries Ltd, Orient Paper & Industries Ltd and Tamil Nadu Newsprint & Papers Ltd (in descending order).

Lac Industry

- Lac is obtained from an insect named Cerria lacca which lives on trees.
- India's share in the world production of lac has fallen to 50-60% due to increased production in Thailand, Myanmar and Indo-China.
- In India, Jharkhand is the largest producer of Lac (50%), followed by Madhya Pradesh (25%) and Chhattisgarh (15%).
- India is the largest exporter in the world.

Sugar Industry

- It is the second largest agro-based industry in India after cotton textile industry.
- India is world's largest producer of sugarcane and sugar as well.
- Maharashtra is the largest sugar producer.
- Uttar Pradesh is placed on second position in sugar production followed by Karnataka.
- The highest yield of sugar per hectare is in Tamil Nadu followed by Gujarat.

8 Chapter

Minerals

- There are 3,108 mines in India, out of which 570 are fuel mines, 563 metallic mineral mines and 1975 non-metallic mines.
- Mineral sector accounts for 11.5% of the country's industrial output and nearly 8% of GDP.
- The high rainfall areas of India lack in limestones, gypsum and salts which are soluble in water.
- The Himalayas have a variety of rocks, but its geological structure is too complex.
- The exploitation of minerals in this mountainous terrain is not economically viable because of:
- Small quantity available at any one location;
- Difficult terrain;
- Lack of transportation;
- Sparse population; and
- Adverse climate conditions
- Chhotanagpur Plateau is known as the mineral heart land of India.

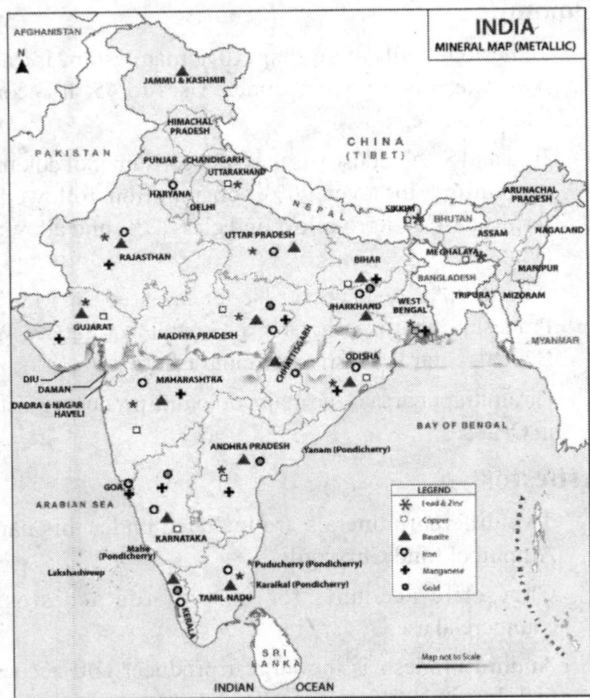

- It is the backbone of modern civilisation.
- Varieties of iron ore:
- Magnetite- the best quality of iron ore and contains 72% pure iron.
- Haematite- contains 60 to 70% pure iron.
- Limonite- contains 40 to 60% pure iron.
- Siderite- contains many impurities and has just 40 to 50% pure iron.
- Jharkhand has the largest reserves accounting for about 25% of the total reserves of iron ore in India.
- High grade ore deposits in Karnataka are in Kemmangundi (in Bababuden hills) and Sandur and Hospet (Bellary district).
- India's richest haematite deposits are located in Barabil-Koira valley in Orissa.
- Other important iron ore production centres are Gorumahisani, Badampahar, Kiriburu, Daitari hills (in Orissa), Bailadila and Dalli-Rajhara (in Chhattisgarh) and north Goa.
- The Bailadila mine is the largest mechanised mine in Asia from where iron ore is exported to Japan through Vishakhapatnam. Most of Goa's iron ore is exported to Japan as well.
- India is the fifth largest exporter of iron ore in the world.
- Japan is the biggest buyer of Indian iron ore accounting for about three-fourth of our total expor
- India has the second largest manganese ore reserves in the world after Zimbabwe.
- India is the fifth largest producer in the world after Brazil, Gabon, South Africa and Australia.
- The main reserve are found in Karnataka, followed by Orissa, Madhya Pradesh, Maharashtra and Goa.
- The belt comprising Nagpur-Bhandara districts of Maharashtra and Balaghat-Chhindwara districts of MP is the important region for manganese ore production.
- Srikakulam (in Andhra) is considered to be the earliest producer of manganese ore in India (1892).
- India exported manganese ore less than one fifth of the total production.
- Japan is the largest buyer of Indian manganese, accounting for about two-thirds of our total exports.

Chromite

- Most of the reserves are concentrated in Orissa, Bihar, Karnataka, Maharashtra and Andhra Pradesh.
- Orissa is the largest producer, accounting for 99% of the total production, followed by Karnataka.

Copper

- Major copper ore deposits are located in Singhbhum district (Jharkhand), Balaghat district (MP) and Jhunjhunu and Alwar districts (Rajasthan)
- Malanjkhand belt of Balaghat (MP) and Khetri-Singhana belt of Jhunjhunu, Kho-Dariba and Delwara-Kirovli area are very well-known mining centres.

Bauxite

- Kalahandi and Koraput belt of Orissa is the largest bauxite bearing region of the country.

Gold

- India's contribution to gold production across the world is less than one percent (.75%).
- There are mainly three gold fields in India:
- Kolar gold field in Karnataka
- Hutti gold field in Karnataka
- Ramgiri gold field in Anantapur district of Andhra Pradesh
- Karnataka is the largest producer of gold followed by Andhra Pradesh.

Miscellaneous: Other Minerals

- Silver is mainly produced from Zawar mines of Udaipur district in Rajasthan.
- Wolfram is the ore of 'Tungsten'. Over 95% of the wolfram is used by the steel industry. Wolfram deposits are mainly in Degana (Rajasthan) and Chendpathai in Bankura district (West Bengal).
- More than 99% of the total zinc in India is produced in Zawar area in Udaipur district of Rajasthan.
- The ore of lead is galena. Over 94% of it is produced the Rajasthan, followed by Andhra Pradesh.
- Orissa has the largest deposits of Nickel.
- Karnataka is the leading state in Lead and Zinc reserves followed by Rajasthan, Maharashtra and West Bengal.

Non-Metallic Minerals

- India also produces a large number of non-metallic minerals.

Mica

- The three major types of mica found in India are – Muscovite, Phlogopite and Biotite.
- The total in situ reserves of mica are placed at 59,065 tonnes out of which –
- Andhra Pradesh has 42,626 tonnes
- Bihar and Jharkhand have 14,431 tonnes
- Rajasthan has 2006 tonnes.
- India is the world's leading producer of sheet mica and accounts for about 60% of global mica trade due to which India is the largest exporter of mica in the world.
- About 95% of India's mica is found in just three states of Andhra Pradesh, Rajasthan and Jharkhand.
- Nellore Belt of Andhra Pradesh and Gaya-Hazaribagh (Jharkhand-Bihar), Giridih and Munger to Bhagalpur belt are important centres of mica production. The richest deposit of high quality ruby mica is found in Bihar-Jharkhand mica belt.
- Most of the mica exports are routed through the ports of Kolkata and Vishakapatnam.
- Japan (19%) and USA (17%) are the major buyer of our mica.

Limestone

- Limestone deposits are of sedimentary origin and exist in almost all the geological sequences from pre-cambrain to recent except in Gondwana.
- The total in-situ reserves of all categories and grades are placed at 1,69,941 million tonnes.

Dolomite

- Limestone with more than 10% magnesium is called dolomite, when the percentage rises to 45, it becomes true dolomite.
- Iron and Steel industry is the chief consumer of dolomite, accounting for over 90% consumption followed by fertiliser (4%), ferro-alloys and glass (2%) and alloy steel (1%).
- About 90% reserves are concentrated in Madhya Pradesh, Chhattisgarh, Orissa, Gujarat, Karnataka, West Bengal, Uttar Pradesh and Maharashtra.
- Biramitrapur area is the major dolomite producing district in Orissa.

Asbestos

- Two different minerals are included under this name: Amphibole and Chrysotile.
- Chrysotile accounts for 80% of the asbestos of commercial use.
- Andhra Pradesh is the largest producer and accounts for almost 100% of the total production in India in 2010-11.

- Andhra Pradesh is the second largest producer followed by Karnataka.

Gypsum

- It is mainly used in making ammonia sulphate fertiliser and in cement industry.
- Rajasthan is the main producer followed by Jammu and Kashmir. Rajasthan produces 99% of the total production in (2010-11)

Magnesite

- Major deposits of magnesite are found in Uttranchal, Tamil Nadu, Rajasthan.
- Chalk Hills near Salem in the major centre for the production of magnesite in India.

Other Non-Metallic Minerals

- India has the largest deposits of kyanite in the world.
- Jharkhand is the largest producer of Kyanite in India followed by Maharashtra and Karnataka (in descending order).
- In Sillimanite production, Orissa contributes 55.87% of the total production, followed by Kerala (32.21%) and Maharashtra (11.70%) (2002-03).
- The main diamond bearing area are Panna belt in MP, Wajrakarur Kiberlite in Anantpur district and the gravels of the Krishna river basin in Andhra Pradesh.
- In salt production, rock salt is taken out in Mandi district of Himachal Pradesh. Sambhar lake in Rajasthan produces about 10% of annual production. Gujarat coast produces nearly half of our salt.
- Uranium deposits occur in Jadugoda of Singhbhum and Hazaribagh district of Jharkhand.
- The largest concentration of monazite sand is on the Kerala coast. Thorium is also derived from monazite. Zirconium is also found in Kerala coast.

Coal (Black Gold)

- It constitutes about 70% of total commercial energy consumed in India. And, the power sector and industries account for 94% of total consumption.
- Coal has been described as the bridge into the furture.
- India ranks third in the world after China and USA in coal production.
- Coal occurs in rock sequences mainly of two geological ages – Gondwana and tertiary deposits.
- Gondwana coal are located in coalfields occupying the Indian heartland, while tertiary coal occurs in Assam, Arunachal Pradesh, Meghalaya and Nagaland.

Varieties of Coal

- Anthracite Coal – the best quality of coal and conatains 80 to 95% carbon. It is found only in Jammu and Kahsmir in small quantity.
- Bituminous Coal – the most widely used coal and contains 40 to 80% carbon. It is found in Jharkhand, Orissa, West Bengal, Chhattisgarh and Madhya Pradesh.
- Lignite – also known as brown coal. It is a lower grade coal and contains about 40 to 55% carbon. It is found in Palna of Rajasthan, Neyveli of Tamil Nadu, Lakhimpur of Assam and Karewa of Jammu and Kashmir.
- Peat – it is the first stage of transformation of wood into coal and contains less than 40 to 55% carbon.
- The coal reserves of India as on 1 January, 2004 have been estimated at 2,45,693 million tonnes.
- Resource-wise, coalfields of Orissa contain the largest reserves.
- Over 90% of the lignite reserves are concentrated in Tamil Nadu. The main areas of lignite in Tamil Nadu are Neyveli, Jayamkondacholapuram and Mannargudi.
- The major coal-fields of Jharkhand are Jharia, Bokaro, Giridih and Karanpura. Jharia has been recognised as the stor house of the best metallurgical coal in the country.
- Korba, Birampur, Chirimiri, Hasdo-Arand, Johilla, Jhilmili and Tatapani-Ramkola are some important coal fields of Chhattisgarh.
- Singrauli, Sohagpur, Umaria and Pench-Kanhan-Tawa are important coal fields of Madhya Pradesh.
- Jhingurda with a total thickness of 130 m is the richest coal seam of the country (in MP).
- The Talcher coal fields in Orissa ranks second in reserves after Raniganj coal field.
- Tamil Nadu accounts for 71% of the total lignite production in India followed by Gujarat (26%).
- Coal India Ltd produces the largest quantity of coal in India followed by Singareni Collieries Comp Ltd.

Petroleum

- In 2012-13, India produced 37.862 million tonnes of crude oil out of which 16.4 million tonnes came from on-shore sources and 21.4 million from off-shore oilfields.
- Andhra Pradesh has both on-shore and off-shore oil reserves.

Oilfields in India

- Assam is the oldest oil producing state in India.
- Digboi is the oldest oil field of India.
- Naharkatiya field, Moran-Hugriyan field are other oil-producing fields in Assam.

- Ankleshwar, Lunej, Kalol etc are important oil fields of Gujarat.
- Pt Jawahar Lal Nehru called Ankleshwar oil field the 'fountain of prosperity'.
- Saraswati and Rajeshwari are two on-shore oil blocks in Barmer (Rajasthan) discovered recently.
- Mumbai High, Bassein and Aliabet are important off-shore oilfields in India.
- Oil Refineries with the largest refining capacity-
- Reliance Petroleum Ltd.
- Indian Oil Corp Ltd.

Natural Gas

- Recent discoveries of Krishna-Godavari off-shore basin and Ravva field will have a big contribution in the field of gas production in India.
- The production of natural gas has reached to 1330.26 BCM in 2011-12 in India.
- Krishna-Godavari off-shore basin is reported to be the largest discovery of natural gas in the world in the year 2002. The wells are being drilled at depths of 1350-2700 metres which is the deepest oil exploration in India.

Chapter 9

Electricity

Conventional Energy

- Power development in India commenced with the commissioning of electricity supply in Darjeeling during 1897, followed by a hydropower station at Sivasamudram in Karnataka during 1902.
- The installed power generation capacity in the country has increased to 228721.73 MW (30 Sept 2013) comprising 155968.9 MW thermal, 39788.4 MW hydro, 28184.3 MW Renewable and 4780 MW nuclear.
- Power generation during 2012-13 was 912 billion units.
- Plant load factor has increased to 72.21% in 2013.
- The per capita consumption was only 917.8 kwh in 2012-13.

Hydroelectricity

- National Hydroelectric Power Corporation (NHPC) was set up in 1975.
- Total installed capacity of hydro-electricity is 39,788 MW (Sept, 2013).
- Total electricity generation of hydro sector increased to 130510 GWH in 2011-12.
- Himachal Pradesh, Meghalaya, Nagaland, Sikkim and Uttranchal wholly depend upon hydro-electricity.
- Punjab has the largest share in hydro electricity generation followed by Karnataka, Maharashtra and Kerala in 2002-03.

Important Hydroelectric Plants in Different States of India

State	Name of Hydroelectric Plants
Jammu and Kashmir	Lower Jhelum, Salal on Chenab, Dool Hasti, Karrah and Banihar.
Punjab and Himachal Pradesh	Bhakra-Nangal on Satluj, Dehar on Beas, Giri Bata, Andhra, Binwa, Rukti, Rongtong, Bhabanagar, Bassi, Baira Siul, Chamera, Nathpa-Jhakri on Satluj (Biggest Hydel Power project in India).
Uttar Pradesh	Rihand, Khodri, Chibro on Tons.
Uttaranchal	Tehri dam on Bhagirathi.
Rajasthan	Ranapratap Sagar and Jawahar Sagar on Chambal.
Madhya Pradesh	Gandhi Sagar on Chambal, Pench, Bargi on Narmada, Bansagar-Tons.
Bihar	Kosi.
Jharkhand	Subarnarekha, Maithon, Panchet, Tilaiya (all three under DVC).
West Bengal	Panchet.
Orissa	Hirakud on Mahanadi, Balimela.
North-eastern states	Dikhu, Doyang (both in Nagaland), Gomuti (Tripura), Loktak (Manipur), Kopili (Assam), Khandong and Kyrdemkulai (Meghalaya), Serlui and Barabi (Mizoram), Ranganadi (Arunachal Pradesh).
Gujarat	Ukai (Tapi), Kadana (Mahi).
Maharashtra	Koyana, Bhivpuri (Tata Hydro-electric Works), Khopoli, Bhola, Bhira, Puma, Vaitema, Paithon, Bhatnagar Beed.
Andhra Pradesh	Lower Sileru, Upper Sileru, Machkund, Nizam Sagar, Nagarijun Sagar, Srisailam (Krishna).
Karnataka	Tungabhadra, Saravati, Kalinadi, Mahatma Gandhi (Jog fall), Bhadra, Sivasamudram (Kaveri), Shimasapura, Munirabad, Lungnamakki.
Kerala	Kallada, Neriamangalam, Parambikulum Aliyar, Poringal, Ponniar.
Tamil Nadu	Pykara, Mettur, Kodayar, Sholayar, Aliayar, Sakarpathi, Moyar, Suruliyar, Papanasam.

Thermal electricity

- The installed capacity reached a level of 137936.18 MW.
- In the year 2010-11, thermal power accounted for over 66% of the total power generation.

Major Thermal Power Stations in India

State	Thermal Power Stations
Maharashtra	Karadi, Nashik, Kaparkheda, Paras, Bhusawal, Parli, Uran, Ballarshah, Chola, Trombay, Kolhapur, Dhobal, Ujjaini.
Gujarat	Banas, Gandhinagar, Kachchh, Sabarmati, Wanskbori, Kawas, Sikka, Mahuva, Utran, Shapur, Porbandar, Kandla, Ahmedabad, Dhuvaram, Ukai.
Andhra Pradesh	Ramagudam, Kothagudam, Nellore, Vijayawada, Bhadrachalam, Manuguru.
West Bengal	Bundel, Kolkata, Durgapur, Farakka, Murshidabad, Birbhum, Kalaghat, Titagarh, Mejia, Santaldih, Gauripur.
Tamil Nadu	Neyveli, Methur, Ennore, Tuticorin.
Uttar Pradesh	Obra, Harduganj, Renusagar, Rosa, Jawaharpur, Unchohar, Rihand, Kanpur, Mau, Gorakhpur, Dohrighat, Moradabad, Tundla, Bahraich.
Madhya Pradesh	Singrauli, Satpura, Amarkantak.
Jharkhand	Durgapur, Subarnarekha, Chandrapur.
Chhattisgarh	Korba.
Haryana	Faridabad, Panipat, Yamunanagar.
Punjab	Bhatinda, Roopnagar.
Delhi	Indraprastha, Rajghat, Badarpur.
Rajasthan	Kota, Polana, Sawai Madhavpur, Banswara, Anta.
Assam	Namrup, Bongaigaon, Chandarput.
Orissa	Talcher, Balimela.
Bihar	Barauni, Kahalgaon.

- NTPC was set up in 1975.
- NTPC has 16 coal-based super thermal power projects and seven gas/liquid based combined cycle projects.
- The commissioned capacity of NTPC (March 2012) is 36014 MW.
- Maharashtra is the largest producer of thermal electricity and accounts for about 16% in India.
- Gujarat is the second largest producer of thermal electricity in India followed by Andhra Pradesh and West Bengal.

Nuclear Energy

- Nuclear energy is obtained from Uranium and Thorium.
- India has vast deposits of Thorium amounting to about 50% of the world's total.
- It contributes a little over 3% of our total power generation.
- Atomic Energy Institute at Trombay, set up in 1954, was renamed as the Bhabha Atomic Research Centre (BARC) in 1967.
- The first nuclear power station with 320 MW capacity was set up at Tarapur in 1969.
- At present, nuclear energy is produced from ten units located at six centres.
- Nuclear Fuel Complex is in Hyderabad.
- Heavy Water Plants are in Vadodra, Tuticorin, Kota, Thal, Hazira, Manuguru. Ther first heavy water plant was set up in Nangal (1962).

Nuclear Plant	State
Tarapur	Maharashtra
Rawatbhata	Rajasthan
Narora	Uttar Pradesh
Kalpakkam	Tamil Nadu
Kaiga	Karanataka
Kakrapara	Gujarat

- India has become the sixth nation having technology to build and operate a Fast Breeder Nuclear Reactor after USA, UK, France, Japan and USSR.
- States with the highest energy consumption – Maharashtra, Tamil Nadu, Andhra Pradesh, Gujarat and Uttar Pradesh (in descending order).

Non-conventional energy sources

- The renewable energy programme started with the establishment of the Department of Non-Conventional Energy Sources in 1982.
- Indian Renewable Energy Development Agency was set up in 1987.
- In 1992, DNES was converted into the Ministry of Non-conventional Energy Sources.
- According to energy experts, India's non-conventional energy potential is estimated at about 1,95,000 MW.

Energy Sources	% share in total potential
Sun	31
Ocean thermal	30
Bio-fuel	26
Wind	13

Renewable energy potential

Surces	Potential
Solar Photovoltaic Power	20000 MW
Wind Power	100000 MW
Small Hydro Power (upto 25 MW)	15000 MW
Biomass Power	16881 MW
Biomass Cogeneration	2500 MW
Miomass Gasifier	16000 MW
Urban and Industrial Wastes Energy	1700 MW
Solar Water Heating	140 (Million)
Biogas Plant	12 (Million)

Wind Energy

- The first wind farms in India were installed in 1986 in coastal areas of Tamil Nadu, Gujarat, Maharashtra and Orissa.
- The largest installation of wind turbines in country so far has been in Muppandal-Perungudi near Kanyakumari in Tamil Nadu. It is one of the largest concentrations of wind farm capacity (425 MW) at a single location next only to that of California.
- Another wind turbine has been set up at Kayattar in Tamil Nadu.
- There is a commercial wind power projects in Satara (200 MW) in Maharashtra.
- Jogimatti wind power project is in Karnataka.
- Gujarat has also wind farms at Lamba and Mandvi, of 28 MW capacity.
- India has been placed on fifth position globally in wind energy production (2483 MW) after China, USA, Germany and Spain.
- Technical potential in wind power is the highest in Maharashtra followed by Gujarat and Tamil Nadu.

Other energy sources

- In Biogas, Uttar Pradesh has the highest estimated potential followed by Madhya Pradesh and Andhra Pradesh.
- In Biogas, the highest number of installed plants is in Maharashtra followed by Uttar Pradesh and Gujarat.
- A five KW, geothermal pilot power plant has been commissioned at Manikaran in Kullu district of Himachal Pradesh. Puga valley in Ladakh and Tattapani in Chhattisgarh have been finalised for geothermal plant.
- In tidal energy, India has the potential of 8000-9000 MW. The Gulf of Khambhat (7000 MW), followed by Gulf of Kachchh (1000 MW) and Sunderbans (100 MW) are significant sites for tidal power. The feasibility of a tidal power project at Durgaduani creek in Sunderbans area of West Bengal is also being examined.
- One wave energy power plant has been installed at Vizhinjam near Thirubananthapuram. And Another plant is being set up in the Andaman and Nicobar Islands.
- The first plant of ocean thermal energy conversion of 100 MW is proposed to be set up off the coast of Tamil Nadu.

Source of Energy	Potential (in MW)
Tidal Energy	8000-9000
Wave Energy	40000
Ocean Thermal Energy Conversion	50000
Energy From Waste	27000

- Solar cooking system has been installed in Shirdi.
- World's largest system with a capacity to prepare food for 15,000 pilgrims was also set up by the Tirumala Tirupati Devasthanam in October 2002.

10
Chapter

Transport

Railways

- The first railway line in India was opened for public traffic on 16 April, 1853 between Mumbai and Thane over a distance of 34 km.
- The first section of the East Indian Railways, from Hoara to Hugli, was inaugurated on 15 August, 1854.
- In the southern part of India, the first railway line was started in 1856 from Royapuram to Arcot.
- India has the second largest railway network in Asia and the fourth largest in the world after the USA, Russia, and China.
- India tops world's leading countries with regard to passenger/kilometre carried.
- It is the largest public sector undertaking of the country.
- Indian railway is world's second largest rail network under a single management.
- Of the two main segments-freight and passenger – the freight segment accounts for roughly two-thirds of revenues.

Railway Zones

Zone	Headquarters
Central Railway	Mumbai(CST)
Eastern Railway	Kolkata
Northern Railway	New Delhi
North Eastern Railway	Gorakhpur
Northeast Frontier Railway	Maligaon (Guwahati)
Southern Railway	Chennai
South Central Railway	Secunderabad
South Eastern Railway	Kolkata
Western Railway	Mumbai(Church Gate)
East Central Railway	Hajipur
East Coast Railway	Bhubaneswar
North Central Railway	Allahabad
North Western Railway	Jaipur
South East Central Railway	Bilaspur
South Western Railway	Hubli
West Central Railway	Jabalpur

- The total route length is 64,460 km with 7133 stations. (2011-12)
- Railway zones with the highest earning are South East Central, Northern, South Eastern and Western (in descending order).
- Indian railways comprise three gauges, i.e. Broad gauge (1.675 metre), Metre gauge (1.0 m) and narrow gauge (0.762 m and 0.610 m)
- Track electrification was introduced in early 1920s.
- The first two sections from Victoria Terminus to Kurla and from Victoria Terminus to Bandra were electrified in 1925.
- Total electrified route is about 19607 km (2010-11). About 30.41% of railway lines has been electrified.

Roadways

- Nagpur Plan of 1943 classified roads into four categories:
  - National Highways
  - State Highways
  - District roads, and
  - Village roads
- National Highways are constructed and maintained by CPWD.
- The length of NH has increased from 19,811 km in 1951 to 79,116 km in 2012-13.
- The percentage share of the National Highways to the total length of roads has decreased to 2%. But they carry nearly 40% of the total traffic of India.
- The National Highways Development Project consists of the following components-
- Golden quadrilateral (5846 km) connecting four major cities of Delhi, Mumbai, Chennai and Kolkata.
- North-South and East-West corridor (7300 km) connecting Srinagar in the north to Kanyakumari in the south and Silcher in the east to Porbander in the West.
- Indian road network is the third largest in the world with about 4.69 million km of road.

National Highways	76,818 km
State Highways	1,63,898 km
Major district roads	4,70,000 km

- Out of the total length of NH, about 23% is of single lane/intermediate lane width, about 54% is 2-lane standard and balance about 23% is 4-lane standard or more.
- States with longest surfaced roads are Maharashtra, Uttar Pradesh, Tamil Nadu and Andhra Pradesh (in descending order) (2011).
- NH-7 is the longest National Highway in India.
- NH-5 and 17 run along the eastern and western coasts, respectively.
- NH-15 represents the border road in Rajasthan desert.
- Kerala has the highest density of roads, followed by West Bengal and Tripura.

Air Transport

- Air transport was started in 1911 between Allahabad and Naini.
- International Airports Authority of India and National Airports Authority were merged on 1 April, 1995 to form Airports Authority of India.
- There are around 449 airports/airstrips in the country in various stages of development.
- The top six airports account for 70% of the domestic air traffic.
- Delhi and Mumbai airports are being given to private sector for modernisation and upgradation.
- Private airlines now account for 68.9% of domestic traffic.
- Mumbai airport is on the top position in all respects in India.

Water Transport

- Waterways provide only one percent on total transport in India.
- The total length of navigable waterways in India comprising rivers, canals, backwaters, etc. is 14,500 km, out of which only 3700 km is navigable by mechanised boats.
- Only 2000 km is actually used in India.
- National waterways:
- Ganga river between Allahabad and Haldia (1620 km)–NW–1
- Brahmaputra river from Sadiya to Dhubri (891 km) –NW–2
- Kollam – Kottapuram in west coast canal – (168 km)
- Inland waterways Authority of India was set up in 1986.

Shipping

- About 90% of India's trade volume is moved by sea.
- India has the largest merchant shipping fleet among the developing countries.
- 7516.6 km long coastline of India is studded with 12 major and 185 non-major ports.
- 12 major ports handle about 90% of our foreign trade.
- Ports with the highest cargo traffic handling are Vishakapatnam, Kandla, Chennai, Haldia (in descending order).
- *12 major ports are:*
- Mumbai – handles one-fifth of India's foreign trade. It is the biggest port of India.
- Jawaharlal Nehru Port
- Kandla
- Marmago – handles export of iron-ore from Goa.
- New Mangalore
- Kochi
- Kolkata – Haldia
- Paradip – deep water and all weather port
- Vishakapatnam – deepest land locked port
- Chennai – an oldest artificial port in India
- Ennore
- Tuticorin
- Port Blair – It is the latest addition to the major port on June 2010, the 13th port in the country.

Chapter 11
Indian Beaches

India is a land with a long coastline measuring over 6,700 km, washed by the Arabian Sea to the west, the Bay of Bengal to the east and the Indian Ocean to the south. Flanking the Konkan / Malabar Coast of Maharashtra, Kerala, Karnataka and Goa, are the Western Ghats. While on the Eastern side, a wider area stretches between Bay of Bengal and Eastern Ghats, called as the Coromondal Coast. The Indian States and Union Territories having coastal boundaries are Gujarat, Maharashtra, Goa, Karnataka, Kerala, Daman & Diu and Lakshadweep Islands facing the Arabian Sea and West Bengal, Orissa, Andhra Pradesh, Tamil Nadu, Pondicherry and Andaman & Nicobar Islands facing the Bay of Bengal.

Of all these States and Union Territories, Gujarat has the longest coastline. India is endowed with several beautiful beaches, dotting its long coastline. Here, we have given information about some of the beautiful beaches of India.

Andhra Pradesh	Rishikonda Beach, Bheemunipatnam, Manginapudi Beach, Vodarevu Beach, Mypad Beach
Goa	Colva Beach, Dona Paula, Miramar, Anjuna, Vagator Beach, Arambol Beach, Agonda.
Gujarat	Porbandar Beach, Chorwad Beach, Beyt Dwarka, Somnath and Veraval Beach, Mandvi Beach, Gopanath Beach.
Karnataka	Devbagh Beach, Om Beach and the Kutle Beach, Parambur Beach, Ullal Beach, Murudeshwar, Malpe Beach, Maravanthe, Karwar Beach.
Kerala	Lighthouse Beach, Rockholm Beach, Samudra Beach, Ashoka Beach, Kappad, Kovalam, Varkala, Thirumullavaram, Vypeen and Gundu Island, Cheria Beach, Alleppey Beach, Veli Beach, Bekal Beach, Shangumugham Beach, Kovalam Beach.
Lakshadweep	Kavratti, Minicoy, Kadamat, Bangaram.
Maharashtra	Ganapatipule, Velneshwar, Marve, Manori and Gorai, Juhu, Chowaptty, Bassien, Alibag Murud Janjira, Dahanu, Mandwa, Kihim Beach, Shriwardhan, Harihareshwar, Vijaydurg and Sindhudurg, Vengurla, Malvan.
Orissa	Prui, Chandipur, Gopalpur-on-sea, Gahirmatha Beach, Paradeep, Bolighai Beach, Konark Beach.
Andaman & Nicobar	Corbyn's Cove, Beaches of Havelock Island, Beaches of Neil Island, Beaches of Chiriya Tapu, Wandoor.
Puducherry	Beaches of Puducherry.
Tamil Nadu	Pulicat, Covelong, Marina Beach, Pichavaram, Kurusada Islands, Vattikotai, Sadurangapattinam, Beach, Mandapam, Mahabalipuram.
West Bengal	Digha Beach, Shankarpur Beach, Frazerganj, Ganga Sagar.
Daman	Devka (or Dwarka beach), Jaypore Beach.
Diu	Jallandhar Beach, Chakratith Beach, Nagoa Beach.

12 Chapter Biosphere Reserves

- Biosphere Reserves are areas of terrestrial and coastal ecosystems which are internationally recognised within the framework of UNESCO's Man and Biosphere (MAB) programme.
- These Reserves are required to meet a minimal set of criteria and adhere to a minimal set of conditions before being admitted to the World Network of Biosphere Reserves designated by UNESCO.
- 18 ecosystems are recognized in India as Biosphere Reserves till date.
- The Central Government provides 100% Grants-in-Aid for management and promoting research and development in these reserves.
- Seshachalam Hills in 2010, and Panna Biosphere Reserve in 2011 have been to the Network.

Biosphere Reserves in india

S. No.	Name of the Reserve and Area in km²	Year of Notification	Type/Region	Location
1	Nilgiri (5520)	1986	Western Ghats	Kerala, Karnataka, Tamil Nadu
2	Nanda Devi (5861)	1988	Western Himalayas	Uttarakhand
3	Nokrek (820)	1988	Eastern Himalayas	Meghalaya
4	Manas (2837)	1989	Eastern Himalayas	Assam
5	Sunderbans (9630)	1989	Delta, Mangroves	West Bengal
6	Gulf of Mannar (10500)	1989	Coastal	Tamil Nadu
7	Great Nicobar (885) Nicobar Islands	1989	Island/Coastal	Andaman &
8	Simlipal (4373)	1994	Deccan Peninsula	Odisha
9	Dibru Saikhowa (765)	1997	Eastern Himalayas	Assam
10	Dehang Debang (5112)	1998	Eastern Himalayas	Arunachal Pradesh
11	Pachmari (4926)	1999	Semi Arid	Madhya Pradesh
12	Khangchend zonga (2620)	2000	Eastern Himalayas	Sikkim
13	Agasthyamalai 3506	2001	Western Ghats	Kerala
14	Achanakmar Amarkantak (3835)	2005	Semi Arid	Chhattisgarh, (M.P.)
15	Rann of Kachchh (12454)	2008	Semi Arid	Gujarat
16	Cold Desert (7770)	2009	Western Himalayas	Himachal Pradesh
17	Sheshachalam (4755)	2010	Eastern Ghats (A.P.)	
18	Panna (2998.98)	2011	Semi Arid	Madhya Pradesh

Biodiversity Conservation

- **Biodiversity** is the variability among living organisms and ecological complexes of which they are part, including diversity within and between species and ecosystem.
- Under the scheme for **biodiversity conservation** in India, there are **two components:**
- **Biodiversity:** It includes activities related to Convention on Biological Diversity and support to National Biodiversity Authority; and

- **Biosafety:** It includes activities relating to Cartagena Protocol on Biosafety and issues relating to Genetic Engineering Appraisal Committee.
- **Convention on Biological Diversity**
- One of the key agreements adopted during the **Earth Summit in Rio de Janerio, 1992.**
- Three **main goals:**
- The conservation of biological diversity;
- The sustainable use of its components; and the fair and equitable sharing of the benefits arising out of resources.

Wildlife Conservation

- A National Board for Wildlife (NBWL), chaired by the Prime Minister of India provides for policy framework for wildlife conservation in the country.
- The National Wildlife Action Plan (2002-2016) was adopted in 2002, emphasising the people's participation and their support for wildlife conservation.
- India's conservation planning is based on the philosophy of identifying and protecting representative wild habitats across all the ecosystems. The Indian Constitution entails the subject of forests and wildlife in the Concurrent list. The Federal Ministry acts as a guiding torch dealing with the policies and planning on wildlife conservation, while the provincial Forest Departments are vested with the responsibility of implementation of national policies and plans.
- A network of 668 Protected Areas (PAs) has been established, extending over 1,61,221.57 sq. kms. (4.90% of total geographic area), comprising 102 National Parks, 515 Wildlife Sanctuaries, 47 Conservation Reserves and
- 4 Community Reserves.
- As the ecosystems and species do not recognise political borders, the concept of Transboundary Protected Areas has been initiated for coordinated conservation of ecological units and corridors with bilateral and/or multilateral cooperation of the neighbouring nations.
- There are 4 categories of the Protected Areas viz:

Sanctuary	National Park	Conservation Reserve	Community
		Reason for declaration	
An area of adequate ecological, faunal, floral, natural geomorphological, or zoological significance	An area of adequate ecological, faunal, floral, natural, geomorphological, or zoological significance	Can be declared by the State in any area Governments owned by the Government, particularly the areas adjacent to National Parks and Sanctuaries and those areas which link one Protected Area with another	Can be declared by the State Government in any private or community land, not comprised within a National Park, Sanctuary or a Conservation Reserve, where an individual or a community has volunteered to conserve wildlife and its habitat.
		Purpose of declaration	
Protecting, propagating or developing wildlife or its environment conservation	Protecting, propagating or developing wildlife or of a Sanctuary	Protecting landscapes, seascapes, flora and fauna its environment, like that and their habitat	Protecting fauna, flora and traditional or cultural values and practices
		Affect on rights of people residing in the area	
Certain rights of people living inside the Sanctuary could be permitted.	The people living inside the National Park are allowed no rights. are not affected.	The rights of people living inside a Conservation Reserve are not affected.	The rights of people living inside a Community Reserve

Biosphere Reserves

State/UT Community	No. Of National Parks	No. of Wildlife Sanctuaries	No. of Conservation Reserves	No. of Reserves
Andhra Pradesh	6	21	0	0
Arunachal Pradesh	2	11	0	0
Assam	5	18	0	0
Bihar	1	12	0	0
Chhatisgarh	3	11	0	0
Goa	1	6	0	0
Gujarat	4	23	1	0
Haryana	2	8	2	0
Himachal Pradesh	5	32	0	0
Jammu & Kashmir	4	15	34	0
Jharkhand	1	11	0	0
Karnataka	5	22	2	1
Kerala	6	16	0	0
Madhya Pradesh	9	25	0	0
Maharashtra	6	35	1	0
Manipur	1	1	0	0
Meghalaya	2	3	0	0
Mizoram	2	8	0	0
Mizoram	2	8	0	0
Nagaland	1	3	0	0
Orissa	2	18	0	0
Punjab	0	12	1	2
Rajasthan	5	25	3	0
Sikkim	1	7	0	0
Tamil Nadu	5	21	1	0
Tripura	2	4	0	0
Uttar Pradesh	1	23	0	0
Uttarakhand	6	6	2	0
West Bengal	5	15	0	0
Andaman & Nicobar	9	96	0	0
Chandigarh	0	2	0	0
Dadar & Nagar Haveli	1	0	0	0
Lakshadweep	0	1	0	0
Daman & Diu	0	1	0	0
Delhi	0	1	0	0
Puducherry	0	1	0	0
Total	**102**	**515**	**47**	**4**

Protected Area Network in India

- India is one of the 17 mega diverse countries of the world.
- With only 2.4% of the world's land area, 16.7% of the world's human population and 18% livestock, it contributes about 8% of the known global biodiversity, however, putting enormous demands on our natural resources.
- India is home to world's largest wild tigers population and has got unique assemblage of globally important endangered species like Asiatic lion, Asian Elephant, One-horned Rhinoceros, Gangetic River Dolphin, Snow Leopard, Kashmir Stag, Dugong, Gharial, Great Indian Bustard, Lion Tailed Macaque, etc.

Autonomous Bodies/PROJECTS

National Tiger Conservation Authority

- NTCA is a statutory body under the Ministry of Environment and Forests, constituted under enabling provisions of the Wildlife (Protection) Act, 1972 for strengthening tiger conservation, as per powers and functions assigned to it under the said Act. It was set up to facilitate the Project Tiger .

Project Tiger

- Project Tiger was launched in 1973.
- Objective " to ensure maintenance of a viable population of Tigers in India for scientific, economic, aesthetic, cultural and ecological values, and to preserve for all times, areas of biological importance as a national heritage for the benefit, education and enjoyment of the people."
- Total tiger reserves in India currently are 41 (January 2013).
- In-principle approval has been accorded to the following new tiger reserves:
- Ratapani – Madhya Pradesh
- Sunabheda – Odisha
- Pilibhit – Uttar Pradesh
- Mukundara Hills – Rajasthan
- New areas suggested for tiger reserves:
- Satyamangalam – Tamil Nadu
- Nagzira-Navegaon – Maharashtra
- Bor – Maharashtra
- Suhelwa – Uttar Pradesh

Central Zoo Authority

It was established in 1992 through an amendment to the Wildlife (Protection) Act, 1972.

- It oversees the functioning of Zoos and enforces minimum standards and norms for upkeep and health care of animals in Indian Zoos and restrain mushrooming of unplanned and ill-conceived zoos.

Wildlife Institute of India

- Established in 1986
- A premier training institute and research institution in the field of wildlifeand protected area management in South and South East Asia.

National Zoological Park

- Established in 1992, under the provisions of the Wildlife Protection Act, 1972 to oversee the functioning of zoos in the country with the view to enhance their role in conservation.

Wildlife Crime Control Board

- Constituted as statutory body under the Wildlife Protection Act, 1972, in June 2007 at New Delhi, to combat wildlife crime in the country.

Project Elephant

- Launched in 1991-92.

Objective:

- To protect elephants, their habitat and corridors;
- To address the issues of man-animal conflict; and
- welfare of domesticated elephants.
- Task force under chairmanship of Prof. Mahesh Rangrajan, constituted in April 2010 to provide detailed recommendations to upgrade the project to bring about more effective conservation and management regime for the species in India, submitted report in August 2010.
- Persuant to the task force recommendation, Elephant notified as National Heritage Animal.
- Action initiated to constitute statutory "National Elephant Conservation Authority".

Project Snow Leopard

- The Himalayas in northern India are home to about 200 to 600 snow leopards. The 'Project Snow Leopard' has been launched by the GOI in January 2009 for conservation of snow leopard and its habitat. It aims to promote a knowledge-based and adaptive conservation framework that fully involves the local communities who share the snow leopard's range. This project is being undertaken to create 12 Snow-Leopard Reserves throughout the Himalayas.

Crocodile Breeding Project

- The project started from a proposal for development of a crocodile farming industry in India Crocodile husbandry work was undertaken with a view to develop sanctuary. A total of 16 crocodile rearing centres have been developed in the country in eight States. Eleven sanctuaries have been declared under the project.

Rhino Breeding Project

- The centrally-sponsored scheme for conservation of rhinos in Assam was introduced in 1987 and was continued for effective and intensive management of rhino habitat.
- In 2007, the total population was estimated to be 2,575 individuals, of which 2,200 lived in Indian protected areas.

Chiru Conservation

- The concern about chiru mainly started in 1992 when George Schaller, a wildlife expert, claimed that the chiru was shot and then fleeced, to make Shahtoosh shawls. This shawl is as soft as a baby's skin, it can be passed through a ring.

Olive Ridley Turtle Conservation Project

- A significant proportion of the World's Olive Ridley turtle population nests at nesting sites along the eastern coast of India India has five species of sea turtles and the world's largest known turtle breeding beaches for the Olive Ridley Sea Turtle (Gahrimatha, Devi and Rushikulya River mouths in Odisha). Mechanised fishing trawlers have created new problems for these sea creatures as they have to come to the beach to lay eggs, sometimes twice a year.

National Museum of Natural History

- Opened in 1978 with the main objective of creating public awareness in preservation and conservation of environment and nature through museum exhibitions, educational programmes, outreach activities, etc.
- Over the years, the Museum has extended its activities in different regions of the country and set up three Regional Museums—one each at Mysore (Karnataka), Bhopal (Madhya Pradesh) and Bhubaneswar (Odisha). These museums have been established to depict flora, fauna, forests, wildlife and other environmental aspects of the respective regions.

Centres of Excellence

- The MoEF started the scheme in 1983 to strengthen awareness, research and training in priority areas of Environmental science and management. Ten Centres of Excellence set up so far by the Ministry with a view to strengthening awareness, research and training in priority areas of environmental science and management.

Fellowships and Awards

- The Ministry of Environment, Forest and Climate Change, in the year 1987, instituted an award called the Indira Gandhi Paryavaran Puraskar to give recognition to those having made or have the potential to make measurable and major impact in the protection of environment.
- Indira Priyadarshini Vriksha Mitra Awards – given annually to recognise the pioneering and innovative contribution made by individuals and institutions in the field of afforestation/wasteland development every year.
- Pitambar Pant National Environment Fellowship – awarded annually to encourage and recognise excellence in any branch of research related to environmental sciences.
- (b) P.Pal National Environment Fellowship for Biodiversity –awarded with a view to further develop, deepen and strengthen the expertise on bio-diversity available in the country.
- National Awards for Prevention of Pollution and Rajiv Gandhi Environment Award for Clean Technology
- Amrita Devi Bishnoi Wildlife Protection Act – instituted by MoEF for protecting wildlife, carries a cash reward of 1 lakh rupees and is given to an individual/institution pertaining to rural communities.
- Rajiv Gandhi Wildlife Conservation Award.
- Medini Puraskar – awarded with a view to encourage writing of original books in Hindi, on the subject related to environment.

Environmental Information

- **Environmental Information System (ENVIS)**
- Set up in 1983 by MoEF as a plan programme with a comprehensive network in environmental information collection, collation, storage, retrieval and dissemination to varying users, which include decision-makers, researchers, academicians, policy planners, research scientists,etc.

- Indian State Level Basic Environmental Information Database (ISBEID) – developed by ENVIS in collaboration with National Informatics Centre.
- State of Environment Reporting (SoER) Scheme
- NGO Cell has been set-up in the MoEF to handle various NGOs working in diverses fields of environment.

International Cooperation

- The Ministry of Environment and Forest is the nodal Ministry in the Government of India for all Multilateral Environmental Agreements. These include:
- Vienna Convention for the Protection of the Ozone Layer;
- Montreal Protocol on substances that deplete the Ozone Layer;
- UN Conventions on Biological Diversity;
- UN Framework convention on Climate Change;
- UN Convention to Combat Desertification;
- Kyoto Protocol;
- the Basel Convention on Trans-boundary Movement of Hazardous Substances;
- Stockholm Convention on Persistent Organic Pollutants;
- Rotterdam Conventions;
- Ramsar Convention, etc.
- International Co-operation & Sustainable Development Division is the nodal point within the Ministry to coordinate all international environmental cooperation and sustainable development issues. It is the nodal Division for United Nation Environment Programme (UNEP); UNCP; World Bank; UNIDO; UN Commission for Sustainable Development (CSD); Global Environment Facility (GEF) and regional bodies like Economic & Social Commission for Asia & Pacific ((ESCAP); South Asian Association for Regional Cooperation (SAARC); South Asia Cooperative Environment Programme (SACEP); ADB; and European Union (EU). The Division also handles bilateral and country to country co-operation in the areas of environment protection and sustainable development.

Indian council of forestry research and education (icfre)

S. N.	Research Institute	Location
1.	Forest Research Institute	Dehradun
2.	Institute of Forest Genetics and Tree Breeding	Coimbatore
3.	Institute of Wood Science and Technology	Bengaluru
4.	Tropical Forest Research Institute	Jabalpur
5.	Rain Forest Research Institute	Jorhat
6.	Arid Forest Research Institute	Jodhpur
7.	Himalayan Forest Research Institute	Shimla
8	Institute of Forest Productivity	Ranchi

S. N.	Advanced Research Centre	Location
1.	Centre for Social Forestry and Eco-Rehabilitation	Allahabad
2.	Centre for Forestry Research and Human Resource Development	Chhindwara
3.	Forest Research Centre	Hyderabad
4.	Advanced Research Centre for Bamboo and Rattans	Aizwal

Centers of Excellence under the Ministry of Environment on forest (MoEF)

S. N.	Centre of Excellence	Location
1.	Centre for Environmental Education	Ahmadabad
2.	CPR Environmental Education Centre	Chennai
3.	Centre for Ecological Science	IISc, Bengaluru
4.	Centre for Mining Environment	ISM, Dhanbad
5.	Salim Ali Centre for Ornithology and Natural History	Coimbatore
6.	Centre for Environment of Degraded Ecosystem	University of Management Delhi
7.	Madras School of Economics	Chennai
8.	Foundation for Revitalisation of Local Health Traditions	Bengaluru
9.	The Tropical Botanic Garden and Research Institute	Thiruvananthapuram
10.	Centre for Animals and Environment	Bengaluru

13 Chapter Water Pollution

Nature has taken hundreds and thousands of years to shape this world up. And we, the human beings, are determined to destroy the earth at the earliest. Water is being contaminated and polluted like anything.

Geographically, 70 % of the earth is made up of water and the rest is made up of land. But as a matter of fact, human beings are bringing the entire 70 % of water under peril and intoxicating it through a careless attitude to the environment. Industrial effluents, sewage and farm wastes are the major pollutants threatening the sanctity of our water resources.

The organic and inorganic contaminants are acids, alkalis, carbohydrates, dyes, fats, soaps, waxes, gases, suspended matter, oil, toxic metals and pesticides, including radioactive materials and heated effluents that impose thermal load on receiving waters. Biological pollutants include bacteria, viruses, plants and animals. The other main contaminants are:

Acids

Both organic and inorganic acids are discharged into rivers as industrial wastes. Sulphuric acid is the main constituents with nitric acid, hydrochloric acid and phosphoric acid. These acids can damage metals or concrete structures by their corrosive action.

Alkalis

Alkalis alter the pH value in rivers resulting in the break off of the natural buffer system. Alkalis too, destroy bacterial and other micro-organisms to restrict the self-purification of the stream. Fishes and other aquatic life are also affected in the process.

Suspended Impurities

Insoluble matter in suspension is the common form of pollution as it is present in sewage and industrial waste waters reducing the photosynthetic activity of water-plants. Suspended matter chokes the gills of fish and destroys aquatic life.

Gaseous Pollutants

It includes ammonia, free chlorine, hydrogen sulphide, ozone and phospine. Ammonia produces a spasm of the glottis leading to death and acts like poison to fishes when it enters their body through gills.

Oils

Replacement of coal by oil as a fuel has aggravated the problem of pollution. Oil spreads over the surface of water, thus inhibiting the diffusion of oxygen into water thereby coating the gills of fishes and affecting their respiration.

Pollutants in Oceans

Many of the pollution problems affect rivers and lakes and the coastal zones where the land meets the ocean. Thus, the cumulative effects of pollutants affect oceans too, as about 85 per cent of pollution of the oceans have its origin on land. Not only chemicals, but also plastics which are of recent origin and man-made garbage cause ocean contamination.

Pollution in ground-water

Storage of liquid wastes in factory premises allows it to seep into the nearby wells. A typical example is the distillery. Intrusion of sea-water-due to over-pumping is a common phenomenon in coastal areas. Excess withdrawal of ground water results in the flooding of sea-water through the cavities.

The difference between other types of pollution and ground-water pollution is that the ground water cannot be cured and treated if affected. While surface water flushes away the pollutants, the latter cannot be flushed away from the ground water due to which the effects continue for indefinite periods.

Industrial Pollutants

Industrial activities generate various waste products which are discharged into water. During the past four decades, industries discharge effluents of varied nature of which some are poisonous and responsible for long-term effects. As technology develops, new wastes are generated making the control of pollutants very difficult.

More than 66,000 compounds are used, of which less than 2 per cent which are tested cause side-effects. Many of these untested chemicals end up as industrial waste, dumped or buried in a secluded but hazardous dump site. Inorganic wastes include acids, alkalis, dyes, heavy metals, toxic substances such as cyaninde and gaseous pollutants. Organic compounds also constitute a larger proportion of industrial wastes.

Agricultural Pollutants

Sewage is not the only source of excess nutrients. Modern techniques in agriculture and use of synthetic fertilisers and pesticides have contributed to environmental degradation, especially to water pollution. Increase in the number of cattle and poultry farming also cause water pollution. The wash-waters from cattle sheds and poultry farms contain phosphates, organic matter, bacteria and other micro-organisms, which cause eutrophication.

Prevention and Control of Water Pollution

Water pollution are contributed due to industrial effluents and sewage. The time has came to avert major disaster. Effluent treatment systems have to be incorporated in industry. Industries, where it is already in existence, need to operate their plants regularly without looking for savings.

- New techniques that need no water is highly beneficial. Some of the wet processes is replaced by the dry processes. For example, metal pickling once carried out by acids is replaced by sand blasting in which no liquid effluent is generated.
- To minimise the volume of effluents, the waste water that is less polluted may be used in rinsing. For instance, in the mercerising of yarn, the final rinse water containing little alkali is used for the first and second rinsing of yarn containing excess alkali.
- Concentrated wastes, low in volume, are mingled with diluted waste for treatment or disposal. It can be segregated from other streams of diluted wastes, for reduction in pollution load and the diluted wastes after minor treatment is utilised for irrigation. This method is used for treating tannery effluents.
- Small industries cannot afford treatment plants as they frequently discharge their effluents, near agricultural lands and on roads. It can be avoided by setting up a common effluent treatment plant where industries are located.
- Waste can be converted into wealth. For instance, in our country distilleries can set up bio-gas plants which are fed by their effluents resulting in reduction in fuel costs and decrease in effluent's strength.

Air Pollution

A man can live without food for a month, without water for two or three days, but he cannot live without breathing even for a minute. According to research, it is estimated that an average adult male breathes in 15 kg of air a day, in comparison to about 1.5 kg of the food consumed and 2.5 kg of water intake. Hence, it is obvious that the quantum of pollutants that enter our body through respiration would be manifold in comparison to those taken in through polluted water or contaminated food.

Air is a mixture of gases comprising 78 per cent nitrogen, 21 per cent oxygen and a little less than 1 per cent argon, together with 0.03 per cent carbon dioxide. These elements make upto 99.9 per cent of dry air. As long as this composition is maintained, the air is pure. If this composition is altered, i.e. the oxygen level gets reduces or other harmful gases enter the atmosphere, then the air is said to be polluted and inhalation of this polluted air can lead to respiratory disorders.

Origin of Pollutants

Industries, especially where coal and oil are used.

Effects

Irritation to eyes and respiratory system, increased mucus production, cough and difficulty while breathing.

Effects of Air Pollution

1. Air pollution affects human health, animals, and plants causing global effects.
2. Lung cancer is a disease caused by polluted air which leads to death. It is mostly associated with respiratory diseases ranging from common cold to lung cancer.
3. Gaseous and particulate pollutants cause emphysema, bronchitis and asthma. Polluted air irritates the eyes and pollutants like lead accumulates in the body.
4. The prominent gaseous pollutants are carbon monoxide, sulphur dioxide, oxides of nitrogen, hydrogen sulphide, certain acid, aldehydes and hydrocarbons.
5. The particulate pollutants include dust, silicious matter and asbestos. Carbon monoxide reacts with the haemoglobin reducing the oxygen-carrying capacity of blood. Persons suffering from anaemia are more prone to get affected as carbon monoxide leads serious injuries.
6. Sulphur dioxide is the most serious and widespread air pollutant as lower levels of sulphur dioxide cause temporary spasm of the smooth muscles of the bronchia.
7. Higher concentration of sulphur dioxide induces increased mucus production. The cilia protecting respiratory system is affected by it causing cough, shortness of breath, spasm of the larynx, acute irritation of the eye membranes resulting in tears and redness.
8. Oxides of nitrogen are pulmonary irritants and excess concentration lead to pulmonary haemorrhage.
9. Hydrogen sulphide is well known for its characteristic rotten-egg odour. Hydrocarbons emitted from automobile exhaust cause lung cancer.
10. Lead is a cumulative poison causing brain damage in children. It develops and matures with red blood cells. The amount of lead in blood is higher in smokers than in non-smokers.

11. Among the particular pollutants, asbestos during the last 30 years is used as roofing material for buildings, and for insulating brake and clutch linings in automobiles, that increased asbestos content in the air. Asbestosis is scarring of the lungs led by accumulation of asbestos.
12. Another dreaded disease caused by polluted air is silicosis which is the most common dust, related disease. It results from inhaling dust particles of silica-containing rocks. Workers in mines, and in industries of pottery, ceramics, granite carving and sand blasting, have a risk of contacting this disease which in the early stages shows no symptoms but leads to cough and shortness of breath. Silicosis is often combined with tuberculosis which is gradually progressive and death occurs due to heart failure or pulmonary tuberculosis.
13. Other serious dust diseases include block lung disease from inhaling coal dust, berylliosis from beryllium dust, byssinosis that is cotton dust.

Prevention and Control of Air Pollution

Prevention and control of air pollution is the need of the hour as both the animal and human population is endangered. It is not feasible to provide for the growing needs and amenities of modern life without paying the price of air pollution. However, much of the pollution can be averted through careful planning and setting-up of industries, better-designed equipments and proper operation of the equipments.

Complete Combustion

The first and foremost rule is to ensure that there is no incomplete combustion, i.e. by ensuring complete burning, so that poisonous carbon monoxide gets converted to harmless carbon dioxide. The combustion can be increased by reducing the size of the fuel and adjusting the ratio of air to fuel. For example, coal may be pulverised and then used.

Tree plantation

More and more trees need to be planted in and around an industry and also along the roadsides and in the houses located in the vicinity of the industry. Trees are capable of absorbing more of carbon dioxide and help reduce the atmospheric carbon dioxide levels, thus maintaining equilibrium in the air composition.

Preventing vehicle pollution

Many techniques for the control of automobile emissions have been developed. These include tune-ups, catalytic reactors and engine modification. A tune-up has a significant effect on emission compounds. The catalytic reactor oxidizes toxic carbon monoxide to the innocuous carbon dioxide, thereby reducing the nitrogen oxides to nitrogen.

Be ozone-friendly

There is no easy solution to the depleting ozone layer. Even if a ban on the production of CFC (chlorofluorocarbons) is imposed with immediate effect, the effects of the CFC produced till date will continue to harm the atmosphere for coming years. However, if all the nations work unitedly, the further deterioration of the ozone layer can be prevented.

Noise pollution

1. **Sounds of Normal Conversations**

   Sound Intensity : 40-60 db

   Health Hazard : Sound, less than 80 db, is safe for the ear.

2. **Sounds emanating from Tape recorders or an Orchestra**

   Sound Intensity : 70 db

   Health Hazard : It is safe for ear.

3. **Sounds of Heavy Traffic**

   Sound Intensity : 90 db

   Health Hazard : Constant hearing of sound, greater than 80 db, causes temporary hearing loss and if they are not treated immediately, causes permanent impairment.

4. **Sounds of Pneumatic Drills and other machines**

   Sound Intensity : 100 db

   Health Hazard : Constant hearing causes temporary hearing loss and if they are not treated immediately, causes permanent impairment.

5. **Sounds of Aircraft Engine**

   Sound Intensity : 100-200 db

   Health Hazard : Higher noise level of 160 db cause total deafness, rupturing eardrums, damaging inner ear. It also causes high blood pressure, ulcer in stomach, palpitation, nervous problems, irritation, anger, and affects pregnant women's embryo.

6. **Sounds of Rockets during Take Off**

   Sound Intensity : 200 db

   Health Hazard : It is dangerously causing total deafness by rupturing the eardrums and damaging the inner ear. It also causes high blood pressure, ulcer in stomach, palpitation, nervous problems, irritation, anger and affects pregnant women's embryo.

Hazards of Noise Pollution

1. Eardrum is damaged when exposed to very loud and sudden noises. The hair cells in the inner ear are chronically damaged. Prolonged exposure to noise of certain frequency pattern leads to hearing loss.

2. According to Kryter in 1970, noise causes heart output to decrease with fluctuations in arterial blood pressure and vaso-constriction of peripheral blood vessels.
3. Recently, report indicates that blood is thickened by excessive noise. Eosinophilia, hyperglycaemia, hypokalaemia and hypoglycaemia are caused by alteration in the blood due to noise.
4. Noise affects sleep and work performance, especially of watch-repairers and others where precision is called for.

Solid Wastes and the Pollution

Massive mountains of solid wastes are disposed each day by our consumer society. It is estimated that about 10 billion tones of solid wastes are produced every year in the world and are dumped into the surroundings. Solid wastes are an integral part of our life as they devour our precious landscape spoiling the aesthetics of the surroundings.

Solid wastes are unwanted materials thrown away in solid form, arising from the normal community activity. It includes garbage, i.e. kitchen and food wastes, rubbish materials like paper, rag, glass bottles, metallic cans, plastics, fibers, residues from home fuels, street sweeping, building debris, rubbles and abandoned vehicles.

Useful Wastes

The two main useful wastes are Cow dung and Press mud. Cow dung is utilised for producing biogas and the used dung slurry is reused as manure. Press mud on the other hand is a waste obtained during the manufacture of cane sugar and is a valuable manure used in dry lands as it conserves the moisture and releases plant nutrients.

Recycling

Recycling is utilising wastes as raw materials in the manufacturing of new products. Wallboard, organic fertiliser and cellulose plastics are some end products of recycling. Recycling has two distinct advantages:

- Recycling conserves existing natural resources. For instance, recovery of 1 tonne of paper saves 17 trees from the axe, and are the virgin sources of paper.
- Sufficient reduction in the volume of waste.

Harmful Effects

Industrial solid wastes are disposed from coal and mineral industries, mining industries, metal industries, engineering industries and thermal power stations.

Biomedical waste includes anatomical waste, syringes, gauze, absorbents, glass. Serious health problems are caused by such disposals. Rotting of it in front of clinics, street corners is not uncommon due to which rag pickers, mostly children are attacked by the hepatitis virus or jaundice-causing virus. The dumping of solid wastes spoils the beauty of cities and towns, causing health problems.

The garbage becomes breeding grounds for disease-carrying vectors such as flies, mosquitoes, rats and cockroaches. Reports say that about 8,00,000 flies is produced in one cubic meter of garbage, which carry pathogenic organisms, causing dysentery, diarrhea, etc. Rats, carriers of insects and bio-organisms, cause plague.

Present mode of management collects the garbage from the city, transporting to a remote place, where it is incinerated or dumped again. The easiest solution is recycling the waste as it yields revenue, compensating for the expenditure on its collection and transportation. Metallic wastes, metallic scraps, disposed metallic cans and wrecked automobiles are reprocessed and utilised while plastic materials are melted to mould into useful articles.

Chapter 14

Soil

Soils in India display wide diversity because of the variations in the climate and relief. The soil-forming components which include parent material, relief, climate and natural vegetation vary spatially. The soil can be classified under various criteria, most acceptable being based on horizon development and its relationship with climatic condition.

The factors that affect the soil formation are:

1. **Parent Material:** The parent material, of which the soils are formed, is derived from the weathering of the rocks exposed on surface. For example, the soil derived from lava and rocks is generally black in colour.
2. **Relief Features:** They influence the process of soil formation through various ways. The variation in relief features like slope, underground water, etc. affect the colour, composition and properties of soil.
3. **Climate:** Climate is the most important single factor in soil formation. It affects the conditions of soil formation through the amount and seasonal distribution of temperature and rainfall. It also affects soil formation indirectly by affecting other genetic factors like parent material, relief features, natural vegetation, etc.
4. **Natural Vegetation:** The decayed leaf material adds to the fertility of soil by providing to it the much needed content of humus. That is why, the densely forested areas contain some of the best soils.

Soil Types

The Indian Council of Agricultural Research (ICAR) has divided the Soils of India into 8 major groups.

1. **Alluvial Soils including the coastal and deltaic alluvium:** Agriculturally the most important soils. It covers 24% of the country's total and is mainly found in Central plains extending from Punjab to Assam, Eastern and Western Coastal plains and deltaic region. Alluvial soil is transported or interzonal soil. It is divided into Khadar (newer) and Bhabar (older). This soil is, however, deficient in nitrogen and humus content; unsuitable for water retentive plantation, e.g. cotton. It is suitable for the cultivation of rice, wheat, sugarcane and vegetables.

   Khadar: Finer and newer alluvium. Its texture varies from clayey to sandy loam. It is light in colour and is formed in the flood-plains of rivers and is generally acidic, deficient in lime, phosphorus and humus.

   Kankar: They are found only few feet below the surface of Bhangar which is a bed of lime nodules known as kankar. Kankars are collected near Dadri in Haryana for making cement.

   Bhangar: They are older alluvium or coarse gravel, high level soils above 30 m above flood level where flood water cannot reach. Its texture is more clayey and the colour is darker.

   Alluvial texture varies from sand and loam to silts and heavy clays that are ill drained and sometimes injurious accumulations of salt and produces a sterile surface called ***"Lisar"***.

   In the sub-mountain belts on the foot hills of Siwalik, alluvial forms with coarse often pebbly soils known as **"Bhabhar"**. To its south occurs swampy lowland with silty soils known as "Terai".

2. **Black Cotton Soils:** This is also called regur soil. Main areas include Deccan Trap, Maharashtra, Gujarat, Madhya Pradesh, Karnataka, Andhra Pradesh, Tamil Nadu, U.P. and Rajasthan. Black soils are usually deficient in nitrogen, phosphate and humus but rich in potash, lime, aluminum, calcium and magnesium. The soil is moisture retentive and it has a high degree of fertility. It is suitable for the cultivation of cotton, cereals, oilseeds, tobacco, groundnut and citrus fruits.

   Black soils develop under semi-arid condition, in area covered with basalt. Colour of the black soils varies from deep black to light black or chestnut. The black colour is added due to the presence of "Titaniferous magnetite".

   They become sticky when wet due to high percentage of clay and develop cracks in hot-sunny weather. Black soils are well-known for their fertility. Since, the content of water soluble salt is high they are not suitable for heavy irrigation. Black soil regions are ideal for dry forming due to their moisture retentive quality.

3. **Red Soils:** Occupies about 70% of the total area in Tamil Nadu, Chhotanagpur, few parts of Andhra Pradesh and Orissa.

   Red soils develop generally on crystalline and metamorphic rocks rich in ferromagnesium minerals. Hence, they are more sandy and less clayey. Red soils are found in area of comparatively low rainfall and so are less leached than the laterite soils. Red soils have a concentration of iron, absence of lime, Kankar, carbonates, humus, phosphoric acid and are neutral to acid reactions.

   They are not retentive to moisture so cultivated mostly during the rainy season. These are favorable for the cultivation of pulses and coarse grains.

   Crops: Rice, Ragi, Tobacco, Vegetables, Groundnut etc. on coarse soil for higher level; Sugarcane on heavy clay at lower level.

4. **Laterite Soils:** They are formed under the conditions of high rainfall and temperature with alternate wet and dry periods. These soils are rich in oxides of iron and aluminum but poor in nitrogen, potash, phosphoric acid and lime content due to leaching; highly acidic in nature. These soils are concentrated in Vindhyan Plateau, Satpura, Mahadeo and Maikal ranges in Madhya Pradesh, Malabar Coast, Orissa coast and Meghalaya.

   Laterite soils develop in the tropical regions which receive heavy seasonal rainfall. Heavy rainfall promotes leaching whereby lime and silica are leached away and soils rich in oxides of iron and aluminum are left behind. If the oxide of aluminum predominates the laterite soils, they are called "Bauxite", the chief industrial ore of aluminum.

   Laterite soils are red due to the presence of oxides of iron. They are poor in lime content, hence acidic in nature. Laterite soils of high areas are very poor and least retentive to moisture. Sometimes they form the barren land topography. Laterite soils of low level areas hinder the process of laterisation due to regular addition of soil washed down from the neighbouring high areas.

   Crops: Rice, Ragi, Sugarcane, Tapioca, Chestnut, etc.

5. **Forest Soils:** Humus predominates in forest soil but it is deficient in potash, phosphorous and lime. It is distributed over the Himalayan and other ranges in the north, Western Ghats, Eastern Ghats and Peninsula. Favourable for plantation crops, e.g. tea, coffee spices and tropical fruits.

   (i) **Podzols (At high Level):** They are formed under high acidic condition and found on higher slopes of Himachal Pradesh and, Jammu & Kashmir. They are covered by coniferous forests. They are highly leached due to excessive moisture and are greyish brown in colour.

   (ii) **Brown Forest Soil (In warm temperate belt):** They are less acidic than podzol with high base status. They are rich in humus and fertile and extensively used for crop cultivation.

   (iii) **Alpine Meadow (In alpine zone of Himalayas):** They are dark coloured, either sandy clay or sandy-loam. They contain mostly undecomposed plants.

6. **Arid and Desert Soils:** These soils, characterised by high salt and low humus content, are found in Rajasthan, Haryana, Punjab, Rann of Kutch, and other rain-shadow regions, since these soils consist of high phosphate, fertility increases with irrigation and by adding nutrients.

   Desert soils are found in and arid and semi-arid conditions in north-western part of India, west of Aravalli range. They are mostly friable and low in moisture content. They are rich in phosphate, but poor in nitrogen and clay content (only 8%).

   Crops: Very few crops especially Millets, Jowar, Bajra are growing for want of water supply.

7. **Saline and Alkali Soils:** Develop along arid region in small patches. These are also called Reh, Keller and Usar. They are infertile, but can be reclaimed by good drainage. These soils are found in Rajasthan, Punjab, Haryana, U.P. and Bihar.

   Saline and alkaline soils develop at places where desert condition prevails because of high rate of evaporation and very little leaching. Saline soils contain free sodium and other salts while alkaline soils have sodium chloride. Alkaline soils are deficient in calcium and nitrogen and are highly impervious and have very low water holding capacity.

   Crops: Rice, wheat, cotton, sugarcane, tobacco, etc. supported by irrigation. For better fertility application of lime and gypsum and cultivation of salt resistant crops like rice, sugarcane can be used.

8. **Peaty and Organic Soils:** Develop under result of accumulation of large quantity of organic matter. Highly saline and deficient in phosphate and potash and occur in central Orissa, Central Bihar, West Bengal and Tamil Nadu.

Peaty and marshy soils originate in humid regions as a result of an accumulation of large amount of organic matters. They may contain considerable soluble salt and is called as "Kari".

These areas are submerged under water during the monsoon season and as soon as rain ceases the land is put under paddy cultivation. These soils are black, heavy and highly acidic.

Soil Erosion

The destruction of soil cover is known as soil erosion. The main reasons of soil erosion are:

(a) Deforestation

(b) Overgrazing

(c) Irrational cultivation (e.g., Jhoom cultivation in North Eastern India)

(d) Floods

(e) Winds

Soil Erosion in India: The areas which have suffered soil erosion in India are generally tracts having sparse vegetation cover like the badlands of lower Chambal and the Yamuna. The vegetation cover in these areas is sparse; hence, the running water cuts easily into the soil forming deep ravines. In many parts of the plain a high degree of slope induces similar erosion. The dry areas of Rajasthan and Haryana, on the other hand, lose their soil cover through wind erosion.

Soil Conservation: Soil conservation depends on the existing conditions. The most common methods, however, include afforestation, contour cultivation and scientific methods of cultivation keeping in view landform characteristics.

Rain water washes the calcium compounds and consequently it causes the lime deficiency in soils. Such soils are acidic and develop in area of heavy rainfall. Oxygen combining with iron compounds produces iron-oxide, red in colour and it gives the red colour to the soils.

15

Chapter

Irrigation

Irrigation in India

The process of supplying water to the crops by artificial means such as canals, wells, tube-wells from the source of water such as river, tanks, ponds or ground water is called irrigation. The monsoon rainfall in India is uncertain highly variable. The temporal and spatial variability of rainfall accentuates the need for artificial supply of water to the crops. Hence, irrigation in India becomes indispensable.

Apart from vagaries of monsoon, the cropping pattern in India also enhances the need for irrigation in the areas with sufficient rainfall. Certain crops like rice, sugarcane, jute, cotton, chalks require irrigational water. It is estimated that production of irrigation crops is 50 to 100 percent higher than that of unirrigated crops under similar geographical conditions. Introduction of HYV seeds and green revolution have further increased the need for irrigation.

Reasons for Water Scarcity

- The rainfall is highly variable.
- 18% of water available is polluted and unfit for drinking.
- Almost all parts of India are affected either by flood or drought.
- Demand for water is increasing due to rapid increase in population.
- The management of available water resources is not proper.
- The storage facilities are very poor.
- Over-exploitation of ground water often results in the intrusion of saline sea water in coastal areas.
- Cultivation of hybrid varieties of paddy, wheat, cotton, sugarcane and tobacco which consume more water.
- Evaporation loss of water stored in large reservoirs and loss by seepage in long canal systems.
- Dumping of various types of pollutants into water bodies reduce its usability.

The source of irrigation depends upon the water availability, topography, relief, availability of soil and moisture, requirements of crop. Important sources of irrigation in India include:

(i) **Wells:** Wells are the most basic sources of irrigation in India. It depends upon the availability of ground water. The Great Plains, the deltaic regions of the Mahanadi, Godavari, Krishna and Cauvery are important regions of well irrigation.

(ii) Tanks: Located in the rocky region of the Peninsula, the tanks are non-perennial in nature and additional water is needed in summer. About 11% of the net irrigated area in India is under tank irrigation. The Karnataka plateau, coastal Maharashtra, Andhra Pradesh, Tamil Nadu have this kind of irrigation.

(iii) Canals: India has one of the world's largest areas under canal irrigation. About 40% of the net irrigated area comes under canal irrigation. Uttar Pradesh, Punjab, Haryana, Rajasthan, Bihar, Andhra Pradesh are the main regions.

Multi-purpose projects aim at:

(a) Flood Control

(b) Promotion and operation of irrigation schemes, water supply

(c) Generation and Transmission of electric power

(d) Promotion and control of irrigation

(e) Afforestation and other economic activity generation

For the better utilisation of the total potential the irrigation schemes have been divided into:

(1) Major Projects: Cultivable command area of more than 10,000 hectare, (including canal irrigation).

(2) Medium Project: Cultivable command area between 2000 and 10000 hectare.

(3) Minor Projects: Cultivable command area less than 2000 hectare, includes mainly well-irrigation.

(4) Micro Projects: Drip irrigation and the use of sprinklers.

Major Irrigation and Power Projects:

1. **Bhakra-Nangal Project:** Joint venture of Punjab, Haryana and Rajasthan; on river Sutlej; Bhalua Dam is the highest straightway gravity dam in the world with a reservoir named 'Govind Sagar lake'. Nangal Dam is 13 km downstream of Bhakra dam. It has four power houses (total 120 Mw) at Gonguwal, Kotta, Left Bank and Right Bank.

2. **Rihand-Dam Project:** Across river Rihand on MP-UP border in Mirzapur District. Rihand is the largest man-made lake in India; reservoir is known as 'Govind Ballabh Pant Sagar'.
3. **Chambal Project:** A joint venture of Rajasthan and MP; on river Chambal comprises there dams Gandhi Sagar Dam (MP), Rana Pratap Sagar (Rajasthan), Jawahar Sagar (Rajasthan).
4. **Gandak Project:** A joint venture of UP and Bihar and Nepal; on Gandak river; a barrage near Valmiki Nagar.
5. **Nagarjuna Sagar Project:** On Krishna River near Nandikonda village in Andhra.
6. **Kosi-Project:** On River Kosi; a joint venture of Bihar and Nepal, a barrage near Hanuman Nagar in Nepal.
7. **Tungabhadra Project: A joint** venture of Andhra and Karnataka; on river Tungabhadra.
8. **Beas Project:** A joint venture of Punjab, Haryana and Rajasthan; on river Beas; a dam at 'Pang'.
9. **Hirakund Project:** On Mahanadi in Orissa, its dam is longest in the world.
10. **Damodar Valley Project :** (W. Bengal and Bihar) have a series of small dams on the tributaries of river Damodar i.e. Tilaiya (R. Barakar), Konar (R. Konar), Maithan (R. Barakar), Panchet (R. Damodar) and 3 Thermal Power stations at Bokaro, Chandrapura and Durgapur.
11. **Kakrapara Project:** on river Tapi in Gujarat.
12. **Machkund Project:** on river Machkund Andhra and Orissa joint venture.
13. **Malprabha Project:** On river Malprabha in Karnataka.
14. **Mayurakshi Project:** On river Mayurakshi in W. Bengal.
15. **Hansdeo Bango Project:** On river Hansdeo in MP.
16. **Bhima Project:** have two dams Pawna dam at river Pawna and Ujjaini dam on river Krishna in Maharashtra.
17. **Jaikawadi Project:** On river Godavari in Maharashtra.
18. **Tawa irrigation Project:** on river Tawa, a tributary of Narmada in M.P.
19. **Tihri Dam Project:** On river Bhagirathi near Dev Prayag in UP.

Important Hydro Electric Projects

1. **Tata HEP:** On Nila-Mulas River in Maharashtra; power to Bombay.
2. **Pykara HEP:** T.N. on Pykara river in Nilgiri; 1st HEP in T.N.
3. **Mandi HEP:** 1st in Himalayan region on a tributary of Beas.
4. **Balimela HEP: Orissa.**
5. **Ukai HEP:** Maharashtra on river Tapi.
6. **Salal HEP: J & K.**
7. **Chukha HEP:** Bhutan-constructed by India and surplus energy is purchased by India.
8. **Koyna HEP:** Maharashtra on Koyna river at Deshmukhwadi.
9. **Sivasarrindrant Scheme:** In Karnataka, at Sivasamudram falls on Cauvery.
10. **Sharavati HEP:** Karnataka across Sharavati near Jog fall in Shimoga district.
11. **Mettar HEP:** T.N. Stanley Darn on river Cauvery.
12. **Papanasam. Scheme:** T.N. On Tamraparni river in Tirunelveli district.
13. **Sabrigiri HEP:** Kerala; Dam across Pamba river.
14. **Sarda HEP:** U.P. across Sarda river in Nainital district.
15. **Idukki HEP:** Kerala have three storage dams on rivers Periyar, Cherutheni, Idukki.
16. **Kalinadi HEP:** Karnataka on Kalinadi river in N. Kanara district.

India's potential of HEP: 5th after Zaire, Former USSR, Canada and USA.

North-Eastern India has 30% of India HEP potential Himalayan region has 30% of India HEP Potential.

Peninsular India has 40% of India HEP potential (1/2 in the east flowing rivers rising in the Western Ghats). We have developed only 40% of the total potential till now.

16 Chapter

Atmosphere

- The gaseous envelope that surrounds the Earth extending upto 1600 km is called the Atmosphere. But 99% of the total mass of the atmosphere is found within 32 km due to gravitational pull of the earth.
- Gas, Water Vapour and Dust particles compose the atmosphere.

Composition of Atmosphere Gas

1. Nitrogen (78%) 2. Oxygen (21%) 3. Argon (0.93%) 4. Carbondioxide (0.03%) 5. Neon (0.0018%) 6. Helium (0.0005%) 7. Ozone (0.0006%)

- Cabondioxide (0.03%) is an important constituent of air that causes Green House Effect (i.e. absorb heat and keep the atmosphere warm, thereby balancing the heat of the Earth).
- Water Vapour accounts for 4% of the air by volume in the warm and wet tropics and is the source of all clouds and precipitation.
- By absorbing parts of the insolation from the Sun and the Earth's radiated heat, it acts like a blanket protecting the Earth from becoming neither too cold nor too hot.
- Dust particles intercept and reflect incoming insolation. Dust in the atmosphere causes the red and orange color of the sunrise and sunset.

Structure of the Atmosphere

The atmosphere is made up of almost concentric layers of air with varying density and temperature.

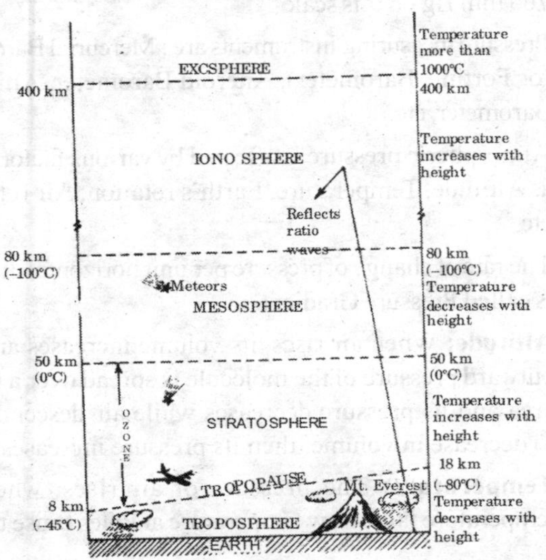

1. **Troposphere**
   - It is the lowest layer of the atmosphere.
   - This layer is 16 km thick over the Equator and 8 km at the Poles.
   - All weather phenomena are confined to the Troposphere (e.g. fog, cloud, frost, rainfall, storms, etc.)
   - The temperature of the atmosphere decreases with height in this layer roughly at the rate of 6.5° per km, which is called Normal Lapse Rate.
   - The upper limit of the Troposphere is known as Tropopause which separates Troposphere from Stratosphere.

2. **Stratosphere**
   - The stratosphere is almost vacant, but there is circulation of feeble winds and Cirrus cloud in the lower stratosphere.
   - This layer extends upto 30-40 km.
   - Jet planes fly from the lower stratosphere as this layer is free from dust particles and atmospheric turbulences.
   - The ozone layer persists within the Stratosphere mostly at the altitude of 15 to 35 km above earth's surface.
   - The ozone layer acts as a protective cover as it absorbs Ultra-Voilet rays of solar radiation.
   - The depletion of ozone can increase the temperature of ground surface and lower atmosphere.
   - In Stratosphere, the temperature increases with increase in height due to absorption of the Ultraviolet radiation of the Sun by Ozone layer present in this layer. This phenomenon is known as Temperature Inversion.
   - The upper most limit of the Stratosphere is known as Stratopause.

3. **Mesosphere**
   - Mesosphere streches to the height of 50-60 km.
   - In this layer, temperature decreases with increase in the height and reaches -80°C at an altitude of 80-90km.

- The Mesosphere is the coldest of the atmospheric layers. It is colder than Antarctica. It is cold enough to freeze water vapour into Ice Clouds (Noctiulucent clouds).
- It is the upper layer of the Mesosphere which is known as Mesopause which separates Mesosphere from Thermosphere.

4. Thermosphere

- It persists at 80 km to 640 km above the earth's surface.
- This layer is called the Ionosphere.
- The temperature of this layer increases rapidly with increasing height.
- It is an electrically charged layer. At height of 80 km (50 miles), the gas is so thin that free electrons can exist for short periods of time before they are captured by a nearby positive ion. This portion of the atmosphere is ionised and build up plasma which is referred to as the ionosphere. The Ultraviolet (UV), X Ray and shorter wavelengths of solar radiation ionises the atmosphere.
- Aurorae occur in this layer.
- There are four layers in Thermosphere e.g., D-layer, E-layer, F-layer and G-layer.
- Radio waves transmitted from Earth are reflected back to the Earth by these layers.
- In Ionosphere, a lot of meteors burn up while entering the Earth's atmosphere. By watching from the earth, they seems as shooting stars.

5. Exosphere

- This is the uppermost layer of the atmosphere extending upto 10000 km beyond the Ionosphere.
- The density is very low and temperature becomes 5568°C.
- This layer merges with the outer space. In this region of atmosphere, hydrogen and helium are the prime components.

Insolations (Solar Radiation)

- The Sun releases tremendous amount of energy by Nuclear Fusion in all directions due to the presence of Hydrogen and Helium gases (in proportion of 3:1 present in Sun).
- Because of its small size in relation to Sun, the Earth intercepts only a small part of Sun's radiant energy known as Insolation. It is received in the form of short waves.
- Insolation is measured with the help of Pyranometers.
- The average energy received of 1.94 Calories per sq. cm per minute varies slightly throughout the year because of the altering distance between the Earth and the Sun.
- The amount of Insolation depends on following factors:
  1. The rotation of Earth on its axis
  2. The angle of incidence of the Sun's rays
  3. The length of the day
  4. The transparency of the atmosphere
  5. The area and nature of the surface
- The Earth's surface does not absorb all the energy that it receives. The proportion of the solar radiation reflected from the surface is called Albedo.
- On an average, Insolation is highest near the Equator, marginally lower at the Tropics and lowest at the Poles.
- Earth receives solar radiations of short wavelength, but radiates energy in the form of long waves and this process is called terrestrial radiation.

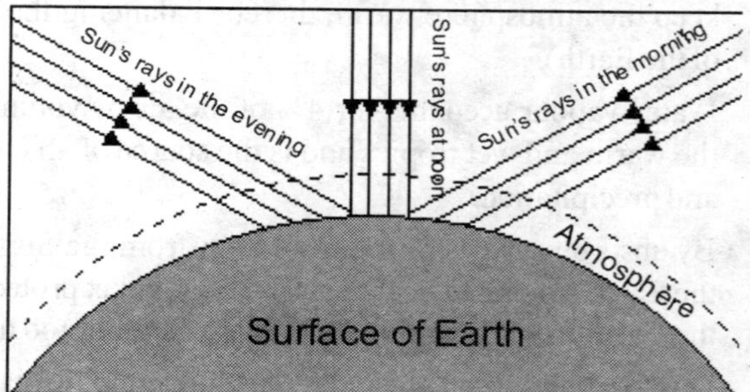

Atmospheric Pressure

- Atmospheric pressure is the pressure at any point on the surface of the Earth due to the weight of the column of air above that point.
- Standard sea level pressure is 76 cm or 29.92 inches or 760 mm Hg on this scale.
- Pressure measuring instruments are : Mercurial Barometer (or Fortin's Barometer), Aneroid Barometer, Altimeter Barometer, etc.
- Atmospheric pressure is affected by various factors such as Altitude, Temperature, Earth's rotation; Air rotation, etc.
- The rate of change of pressure per unit horizontal distance is called Pressure Gradient.
- **Altitude:** When air rises, its volume increases and the outward pressure of the molecule is spread over a larger area and its pressure decreases while air descends due to decrease in volume, then its pressure increases.
- **Temperature:** The pressure of air rises, when its temperature falls. Low temperature at Poles cause the air

to contract and high pressure develops, whereas the high temperature along the Equator causes the air to expand and low pressure develops.

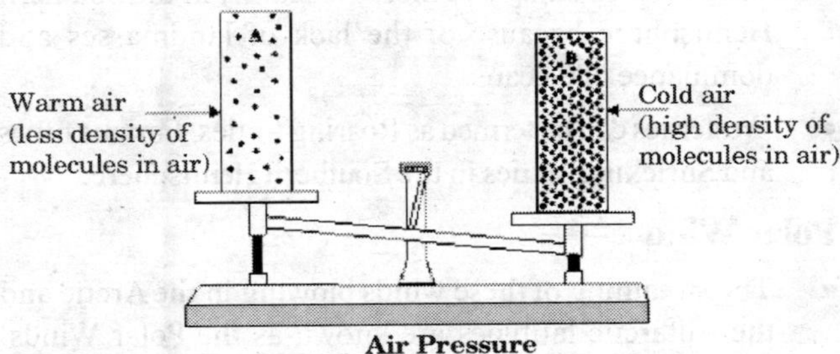

Air Pressure

The Global Pressure Belts

1. **Equatorial Low Pressure Belt**
   - It is located on either side of the Equator in a zone extending between 5°N and 5°S latitudes and may shift to higher latitudes during Summers in each hemisphere.
   - This belt is the result of intense heat leading to low pressure regions.
   - It represents the Zone of Convergence of North-East and South-East Trade Winds and characterised by light and feeble winds.
   - Because of the frequent calm conditions, this belt is called as a Belt of Calm or Doldrums.
2. **Sub-tropical High Pressure Belt**
   - It extends between 30° to 35° in both the Hemispheres.
   - This Zone of high pressure is also called as Horse Latitude and is characterised by anti-cyclonic conditions.
3. **Sub-Polar Low Pressure Belt**
   - It extends between 60° to 65° in both the hemispheres.
   - It is more developed and regular in Southern hemisphere than in the Northern hemisphere because of the over dominance of water (Ocean) in the Southern hemisphere.
4. **Polar High Pressure Belt**
   - It persists at Poles throughout the year because of the prevalence of very low temperature throughout the year.
   - Apparent movement of the Sun guides the movement of Pressure belts. In Northern hemisphere, Pressure belts shift to North in Summer and towards South in Winter.

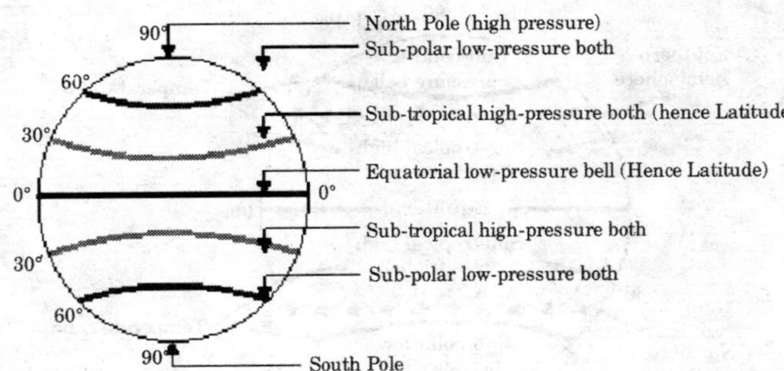

Wind System

- When the movement of the air in the atmosphere is in horizontal direction over the surface of the earth, it is known as Wind. The air moves from high pressure to low pressure.
- The pressure difference is the major cause of the genesis of the wind system.
- The slope of pressure from high to low is called a pressure gradient or Barometric slope.
- Anemometer measures the wind velocity.
- **Isobars:** The imaginary line joining the points having same pressure.

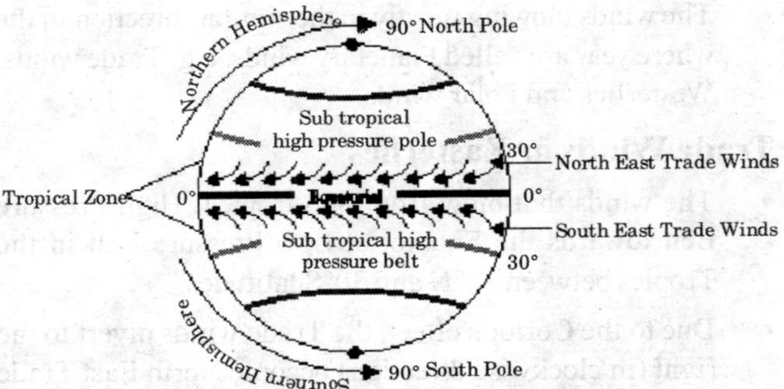

Trade winds and its position

- The winds blowing parallel to the Isobars at the height of 600 m is called Geostropic wind.
- Wind circulation around a low pressure is called Cyclonic circulation and around a high pressure is called Anti-cyclonic circulation.
- The factors that control the air motion or atmospheric circulation are:
  (a) Pressure Gradient
  (b) Rotation of Earth and Coriolis Force
  (c) Frictional Force
  (d) Centrifugal action of wind

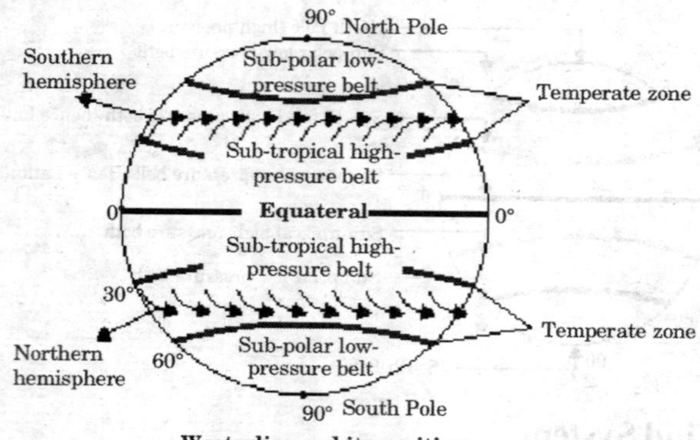

Westerlies and its position

Coriolis Force

- The rotation of the Earth generates force, called as Coriolis force, which works as a deflective force to the wind direction. Put to the Coriolis force, wind is deflected to the right of its path in Northern Hemisphere, while in the Southern Hemisphere it is deflected to the left. This is referred to as Farrel's Law. Coriolis force is absent at the Equator, and its strength rises as one approaches either Pole. Besides it, an increase in wind speed results in a stronger Coriolis force, and thus in greater deflection of the wind.

Planetary Winds

- The winds blowing mostly in the similar direction in the where year are called Planetary winds, e.g. Trade winds, Westerlies and Polar winds.

Trade Winds or Easterlies

- The winds that blow from Sub-tropical High Pressure Belt towards the Equatorial Low Pressure Belt in the Tropics between 30°N and 30°S latitudes.
- Due to the Coriolis effect, the Trade winds divert to the right (in clockwise direction) become North East Trade Wind in the Northern hemisphere and when deflected to the left become South East Trade Wind in the Southern hemisphere, i.e. blow from South-East.
- The western margins of the Continents have dry hot deserts because those High Pressure Belts cause these regions to remain dry throughout the years.
- The Doldrums are regions of low pressure and calm weather located in the Inter Tropical Convergence Zone (ITCZ) and extending upto 5° to the North and South of the Equator.

Westerlies

- The permanent winds blowing from the Sub Tropical High Pressure Belt to the Sub Polar Low Pressure Belt in the Temperature latitudes between 30° and 60°, on either side of the Equator in both the hemisphere is called Westerlies.
- The general direction of the Westerlies is South-West to North-East in the Northern Hemisphere and North-West to South-East in the Southern Hemisphere.
- They blow strongly and more constantly in the Southern Hemisphere because of the lack of landmasses and dominance of Oceans.
- Westerlies can be termed as Roaring forties, Furious fifties and Shrieking sixties in the Southern Hemisphere.

Polar Wind

- The streaming of these winds blowing in the Arctic and the Antarctic latitudes are known as the Polar Winds. They have been called as the 'Polar Easterlies', as they stream from the Polar High Pressure Belt towards the Sub-Polar Low Pressure Belts. In the Northern Hemisphere, they blow in general from the North-East, and are known as the North-East Polar Winds; and in the Southern Hemisphere, they blow from the South-East and are called the South-East Polar Winds. As these winds blow from the ice-capped landmass, they are extremely cold. They are more regular in the Southern Hemisphere than in the Northern Hemisphere.

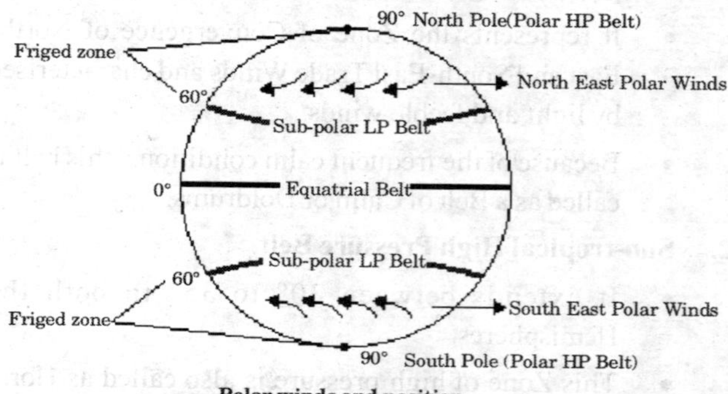

Polar winds and position

Periodic Seasonal Winds

Following are periodic winds:

(a) Monsoon winds
(b) Land and Sea Breezes
(c) Mountain and Valley Breezes
(d) Land and Sea Breezes occur daily, whereas the occurrence of Monsoon winds is seasonal.

(a) Monsoon Winds

- They are seasonal winds that blow from sea to land in summer and from land to sea in winter (*i.e.* complete reversal of direction) because of the differential heating of land and water.
- These winds originate in the belt of Trade Winds lying between the Tropic of Cancer and the Tropic of Capricorn. These winds are widely found in South East Asia.

(b) Land and Sea Breezes

- During the day, land heated quickly than nearby sea. As a result, the low pressure area is built over land and a high pressure over the nearby sea. The pressure gradient causes the air to blow from high pressure to low pressure areas, *i.e.* from the sea to the land. This is known as Sea Breeze.

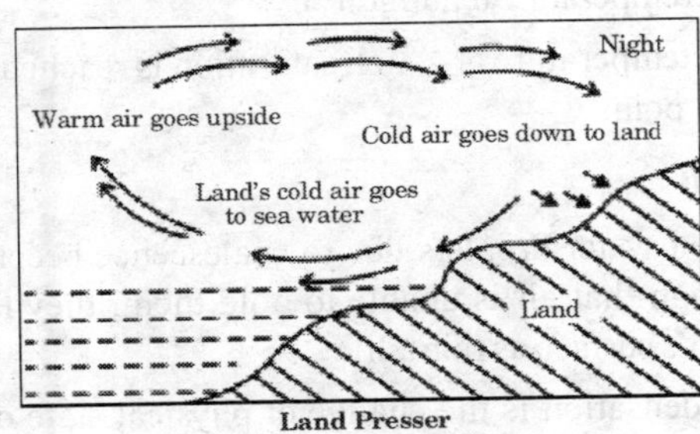

Land Presser

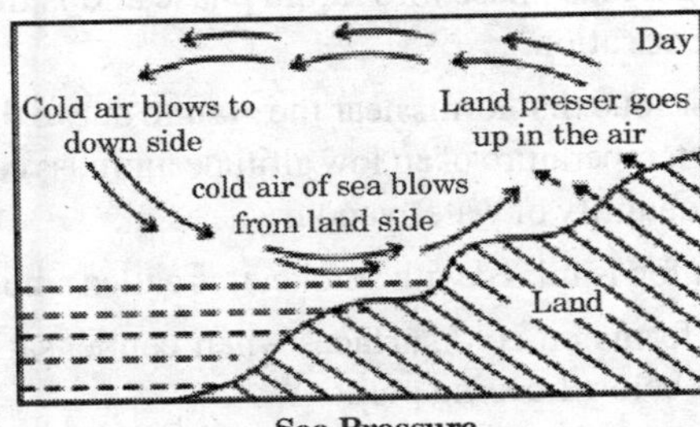

Sea Pressure

- In the night, land becomes cooler than the nearby sea as loss of heat is faster for solids than for liquids (water). Hence, a high pressure area in built over the adjacent land and the winds starts blowing from land to sea. It is called Land Breeze.

(c) Katabatic Wind (Valley Breezes) and Anabatic Wind (Mountain Winds)

- Mountain wind is an upslope wind. In mountainous regions, during the day, the slopes of the mountain gets heated and air starts to move upslope. To fill the resulting gap, the air at the bottom of the valley blows up.
- Valley breeze is the downslope wind, usually cold, which blows down valleys at night. At night, mountain slopes get cooled, as a result of which the dense air descends into the valley as a mountain wind.

Local Winds

Local winds blow in the various region of the world.

- Sirocco – Sahara Desert
- Leveche – Spain
- Khamsin – Egypt
- Harmattan – Sahara Desert
- Santa Ana – USA
- Zonda – Argentina
- Brick fielder – Australia
- Mistral – Spain and France
- Bora – Adriatic coast
- Pampero – Argentina
- Buran – Siberia

Jet-Streams

- The jet streams found in the upper Troposphere are bands of high speed Westerly winds (95-190 km/hr). In 1947 the large-scale motions of the atmosphere in terms of fluid mechanics was explained by Carl Gustaf Rossby. The two significant types of Jet Streams are the Polar Jet Streams and the Subtropical Jet Streams.
- Their circulation path is wavy and meandering.

Cyclones

- Cyclones are well-developed low-pressure systems occupy by closed isobars having increasing pressure outside and closed air circulation, towards the centre of low atmospheric pressure such that the air blows inward in anti-clockwise direction in the Northern Hemisphere and clockwise in the Southern Hemisphere.

Tropical Cyclones

- Tropical cyclones are intense cyclonic storms that develop only over the warm Oceans of the Tropics near ITCZ in Summer.
- They are found in the Trade Wind belt between 8°-20° North and South. There are not found between 0° to 8° as there is no CoriolisForce. It travels from East to West in the Easterly Wind belt and non-frontal in nature. Tropical cyclone can form only in Summer does not have definite cycle.

Temperate Cyclones

- Temperate cyclones, also termed as middle latitude or extra Tropical cyclones are found between 35°-65° latitudes North and South in the Sub Polar frontal zones where cold Polar air mass meets the warm Tropical air mass.
- It moves from West to East under the influence of Westerly Wind belts.
- These cyclones travel at an average speed of 32-48 km/h over a much large area with the diameter 300 to 1500 km and frontal in nature.
- They can form both in summer as well as in winter over Continents or Oceans.

Comparision of Tropical and Temperate Cyclones

- Tropical cyclones develop only over the ocean during summer while Temperate cyclones develop on land and sea during winter and summer both.
- The Isobars of Tropical cyclones are complete Circles, while that of Temperate cyclones are V-shaped.
- Limited to small area, Tropical cyclones travel from East to West while Temperate cyclones occupy thousands of kilometers and travel from West to East.
- Tropical cyclone causes heavy rainfall but does not last beyond a few hours, while Temperate cyclone continues for many days causing comparatively less rainfall.
- In a Temperate cyclone, wind speed is low while it may reach upto 1200km/h for Tropical cyclone.
- Latent heat of condensation and air mass density difference provides energy to the Tropical cyclone while the energy of Temperate cyclone depends only on the densities of air masses.

Name of Cyclone	Country
• Hurricanes	USA
• Typhoon	China
• Willy-Willy	Western Australia
• Baguio	Philippines
• Taifu	Japan

Anti-Cyclones

- They are high pressure systems surrounded by low pressure areas on all sides, where wind blows from the Centre to outside region in clockwise direction in Northern Hemisphere and anti-clockwise in Southern Hemisphere. They are common in Sub-Tropical Belts and practically absent in the Equator region.
- Average velocity of anti-cyclones is 30-50 km/h and they do not form fronts.
- Anti-cyclones are generally associated with rainless fair weather and that's why they are called as weatherless phenomena.

Thunderstroms

- Thunderstroms are local storms characterised by swift upward movement of air and heavy rainfall with cloud, thuder and lightening.

Tornado

- Tornado are very strong tropical cyclones of smaller size. In the Mississippi Valley (USA), they are called Twister.
- Formed over land, tornadoes are more destructive than cyclones as wind an exceed 320 km/h. Water spout is formed when tornado passes over a sea or lake and suck up the water towards its center.

Humidity

- Humidity of air refers to the content of the water vapour present in the air at a particular time and space.
- Humidity is measured by an instrument called Hygrometer.
- Higher the temperature, higher the humidity capacity of air (Temperature α humidity).
- The temperature at which saturation is reached is called Dew point.

Rainfall

- When water droplets due to coalescence become large enough that air is unable to hold them, they fall on to earth's surface as rainfall.
- Condensation is the change of physical state of matter from gaseous phase into liquid phase and is the reverse of Vaporisation.
- Fog is cloud that forms near the ground due to the sudden fall in temperature of an low altitude air mass containing large quantity of water vapour.
- When fog is mixed with smoke, it is called smog.
- Frost forms on cold surfaces when condensation takes places below freezing point.

Clouds

- Cloud is a mass of very tiny water droplets or ice crystals, formed when water vapour condenses in free air at a considerable elevation.
- Due to the lifting of surface air, it cools down adiabatically and condenses around the hydroscopic nuclei to form cloud.

Types of Clouds

- Cirrus means looking like a feather and form at high altitudes of 8000 to 12000m.
- Cumulus means looking like a heap or cotton wool and form at altitudes of 4000 to 7000 m.
- Stratus means lying in layers and cover a large portion of the sky.
- Nimbus are rain carrying clouds. They are black or dark grey in colour and form at the middle altitudes or very near to the surface of earth.

  Combining these basic types give the following types of clouds-
- Cirrostratus and Cirrocumulus (High altitude), Altrostratus and Altocumulus (Middle latitude), Stratocumulus and Nimbostratus (Low altitude) and Vertical clouds, such as Cumulus and Cumulonimbus.
- Cumulonimbus is characterised by convectional rain, lightning and thunder.

Hydrosphere Oceanography

- The water component of Earth is called hydrosphere which covers about 70% of the surface of Earth.
- Out of all water on Earth, saline water in oceans, seas and saline groundwater makeup about 97% of it. Only 2.5-2.75% is fresh water including 1.75-2% frozen in glaciers, ice and snow (68%) 0.5-0.75% as found in ground-water (30%) and less than 0.01% of it as surface water in lakes, swamps and rivers.
- Most of the water on earth is in Oceans. It is divided into 5 smaller Oceans (Pacific, Atlantic, Indian, Southern and Arctic Oceans – arranged in descending order of their size).

Indian Ocean

- Only Ocean named after a country and is deeper than the Atlantic ocean.
- 3rd largest body of water in the world.
- Scientist have found a lost Continent '(Mauritia) whose remains exist in the depth of the Indian Ocean.'
- It contains numerous continental islands of volcanic origin (e.g. Mauritius, Seychelles, Andaman and Nicobar). Lakshadweep and Maldives are of Coral origin.
- The Indian ocean's deepest point is the Sunda Deep, which located in the Java Trench (Indonesia).
- About 40% of world's oil supply is sourced from the depths of the Indian ocean.
- World's most important ports are in Indian Ocean, *e.g.* Durban and Richards Bay in South Africa, Kolkata, Chennai and Mumbai in India, Melbourne in Australia, Jakarta in Indonesia and Colombo in Sri Lanka.
- The Indian Ocean is known as the warmest ocean and has lowest oxygen content in the world.
- The Persian Gulf, Arabian Sea and the Red Sea are the most pollution prone areas in the Indian ocean.
- Indian ocean is bordered by Asia to the North, Antarctica to South, Australia to the East and Africa to the West.
- Several rivers like Indus, Ganges, Zambezi, Narmada, Brahmaputra, Jubba and Irrawady rivers flow into the Indian Ocean (Hind Mahasagar).

Pacific Ocean

- It is the largest and deepest ocean of the world.
- It borders four Continents: North America, South America, Australia and Asia.
- The ocean is split into two parts that are divided by the Equator.
- The Deepest Trench of the Ocean and world is Mariana Trench.
- The Pacific 'Ring of fire' is the world's biggest chain of volcanoes.
- Many seas sit along the western part of the Pacific Ocean like the Sulu sea, Celebes sea, East China sea, South China sea, Yellow sea.
- The Pacific ocean is connected to the Arctic ocean by Bering Strait.
- The Strait of Magellan and Drake passage join the Pacific to the Atlantic ocean and the Strait of Malacca joins the Pacific ocean to the Indian ocean.
- About 50.1% of the ocean water on Earth is in the Pacific Ocean.
- Fishing is common activity in Pacific Ocean.
- Magellan gave the ocean its name "Mar Pacifico", i.e. the peaceful sea.

Arctic Ocean

- Arctic ocean is the smallest and shallowest of the world's five oceans, but has the widest Continental Shaft among them all.
- Continents that border the Arctic include Europe, Asia and North America.
- Arctic contains less salt than other four oceans due to its low evaporation rates and the large amount of fresh water that is contributed to the ocean by rivers and streams.
- Phytoplankton are the only plant types that live in the Arctic ocean.
- Polar Bears, the largest land predators in the world, can only be found in Arctic but not Penguins.
- There are lots of petroleum reserves under the Arctic ocean.
- Huge part of the Arctic ocean is covered by sea ice. Therefore, the Arctic ocean is also called as the 'Frozen ocean'. It is the least saline ocean.
- All of the Arctic ocean is located within the Arctic Circle. North Pole lies in the middle of the Arctic ocean.

Atlantic Ocean

- It is the second largest ocean in world and has the longest coastal line.
- It is a life-giver ocean and has been a source of food and livelihood for a large number of cultures around the world for thousands of years.
- Atlantic ocean is home to the world's most fertile fishing grounds.
- The lowest point in the Atlantic ocean is Puerto Rico Trench, located near the boundary of the Atlantic ocean and the Caribbean sea.

- Greenland is the largest island in the Atlantic ocean.
- Bermuda Triangle is located in the Atlantic ocean.
- Atlantic ocean is the world's saltiest sea and has abundant number of natural petroleum deposits and gas fields.
- There are four Trenches in Atlantic beyond the ocean's depth: Puerto Rico Trench, the Laurentian Abyss, Romanche Trench and South Sandwich Trench.
- The Atlantic ocean is bordered in the North by Arctic ocean, Sourthern ocean in the South and Indian ocean in the South-East.
- The man made Panama canal connects the Atlantic ocean and the Pacific ocean. Its entrance can be found in the Carribean sea.
- The Sargasso sea (sea without a shore) is located completely within the Atlantic.
- Amelia Earhart is the first woman to have crossed the Atlantic.
- Sinking of Titanic in 1912 in Atlantic ocean.
- The Great Maya Reef, the second largest barrier reef is located in Atlantic.
- The highest tides in the world are experienced in the Atlantic ocean near the Bay of Fundy in Canada.
- It is the busiest ocean for trade and commerce since its sea routes connect Western Europe and North Eastern America.
- Atlantic Ridge (twice as large as Andes mountain) is located in the Atlantic ocean.
- The Atlantic ocean is home to the Walvis Ridge, a giant volcanic underwater mountain range.
- The Atlantic ocean borders a total of 91 countries.
- Tropical cyclone originate in the Atlantic ocean are responsible for the Hurricane season that effects Central America, Eastern USA and Carribean.
- Gulf stream in Atlantic ocean resembles an underwater river running beneath the ocean.
- The Atlantic is both a polar and equatorial ocean. It is bisected by the Equator.
- Cuba, Jamaica and Puerto Rice are Volcanic islands. Iceland is the largest island of volcanic origin.

Southern Ocean

- The Southern Ocean is located in the Southern hemisphere on the 60° latitude and is the 4th largest ocean.
- It encircles the entire Antarctic continent and the South Pole.
- Its deepest point is the South Sandwich Trench.
- Its temperature ranges from -2° to 10°C.
- The Southern ocean is home to Albatrosses, Fur Seals and Blue Whales.
- The Emperor Penguin (largest Penguin) on our planet is found in the Antarctica.
- Giant Squid (largest invertebrates on our planet) is found in the Southern Ocean.
- The Southernmost port in the Southern ocean is McMurdo Station. Other ports belong to research stations and include Palmer Station (USA), Rothera Station (British) and Mawson Station (Australia).
- Krill (Shrimp like creatures) are found in the freezing Southern ocean's Antarctic waters.
- The circumpolar currents of the Southern ocean flow clockwise from West to East.
- Icebergs can be found in the Southern Ocean during any season.
- The first explorers to get in contact with Southern ocean cold waters were Bartolomeo Diaz and Ferdinand Magellan.

Ocean Currents

- The Ocean Currents are horizontal flow of mass of water generated by the winds, density differences in ocean waters due to differences in temperatures and salinity, gravity and tides caused by gravitation pull of the Moon and Sun.
- The direction of movement of an ocean current is mainly influenced by the rotation of the earth (Due to Coriolis force, most ocean currents in Northern hemisphere move in Clockwise manner (towards right) and in Southern hemisphere move in an Anti-Clockwise manner (towards left).

Cyre, Drift and Stream

- Any large system of rotating ocean current, specifically those which having the large wind movement is called as Gyre. They are generated by the Coriolis force.
- When ocean water moves forward under the influence of Prevailing wind, it is called Drift. (the term 'Drift' is also used to refer the speed of an ocean current which is measured in knots). *E.g.* North Atlantic Drift.
- When a large mass of the ocean water moves in a definite path just like a river on the Continent, it is called a Stream. They have greater speed than Drift, *e.g.* Gulf Stream.

Types of Ocean Currents

1. Warm Currents

- Those ocean currents which flow from equatorial regions (lower latitude) towards poles (higher latitudes) have a higher surface temperature and are called Warm current.
- They bring warm water to the cold regions and are usually observed on the East Coast of the Continents in the lower and middle latitudes of both the hemispheres.
- In the Northern hemisphere, they are also found on West Coast of the Continents in the higher latitudes, *e.g.* Alaska and Norwegian currents.

2. Cold Currents

- Those currents which blow from polar regions (higher latitude) towards the equator (lower latitude) have a lower surface temperature and are called cold currents.
- They bring cold waters to warm areas and usually found in West Coast of the continents in the lower and middle latitudes of both the hemispheres.
- In the Northern hemisphere, they are also found on the East Coast of continents in the higher latitudes, *e.g.* Labrador, East Greenland and Oyashio currents.

Current	Nature
Northe Pacific Ocean	
North Equatorial current	Warm
Kuroshio current	Warm
Alaska current	Warm
Oyashio current	Cold
Kuril current	Cold
West wind drift	Cold
Californian current	Cold
Sourth Pacific Ocean	
East Australian current or Great Barrier current	Warm
South Equatorial current	Warm
Counter Equatorial current	Warm
Peruvian/Humboldt current	Cold
West Wind Drift current	Cold
North Atlantic Ocean	
North Equatorial current	Warm
Florida current	Warm
Antilles current	Warm
Cayenne current	Warm
Gulf stream	Warm
North Atlantic drift	Warm
Labrador current	Cold
Irminger current of East Greenland current	Cold
Canarie current	Cold
West Wind drift	Cold
South Atlantic Ocean	
South Equatorial current	Warm
Brazilian current	Warm
Falkland current	Cold
Benguela current	Cold
West Wind drift	Cold
Guinea current	Cold
Indian Ocean	
South Equatorial current	Warm
North East Monsoon current	Warm
South West Mansoon current	Warm
Mozambique current	Warm
Madagascar current	Warm
Agulhas current	Warm
West Australian current	Cold
Somalia current	Cold/Warm
Antarctic drift	Cold

Coral Reefs

- Coral reefs are formed due to accumulation and the compaction of skeletons of lime secreting organisms known as Coral Polyps.
- Corals are found mainly in the Tropical oceans and seas because they require high mean annual temperature of ranging between 20° to 25°.
- Corals do not live in deeper waters due to lack of sufficient sunlight and oxygen.
- Coral reefs are formed mainly along western coast.
- When Corals are stressed by changes in temperatures, light or pollution, they expel the symbiotic algae (Zooxanthellae) living in their tissues them to turn completely them to turn completely white. This phenomenon is known as Coral Bleaching.

Types of Coral Reefs

The coral Reefs is classified into 4 types:

1. **Fringing Reefs:** develop along the continental margins or along the islands. This type of reef found in Rameshwaram in the Gulf of Mannar and Andamans.
2. **Barrier Reef** *e.g.* The Great Barrier Reef of Australia is the largest Barrier Reef in the world. In India, found in Nicobar & Lakshadweep.
3. **Patch Reef** found in Palk Bay, Gulf of Mannar, Gulf of Kutch.
4. **Atoll:** A reef of narrow growing corals of horse- shoe shape and crowned with palm tree is called an Atoll, *e.g.* Funafuti atoll of Ellice islands is famous atoll, also found in Nicobar and Lakshadweep.

Salinity

- Average salinity of ocean water is 35 parts per thousand.
- Average salinity in Southern hemisphere is more than that of Northern hemisphere.
- Temperature, Rainfall, Evaporation and Influx of river are controlling factors of salinity.
- Isohalines are the lines joining places have an equal degree of salinity.
- The main source of salinity is dissolution of rocks of oceanic crust which contains salts.
- Salinity decreases from Equator to Poles. The highest salinity is recorded near the Tropics rather than the Equator because of the heavy precipitation in the equatorial region.

Most Saline Water Bodies

Water Body	% Composition
Lake Assal (Djibouti)	34.8%
Lake Van (Turkey)	33%
Dead Sea (West Asia)	33.7%
Gread Salt Lake (USA)	32.0%

World Continents Continenets of the World

- Asia, Africa, North America, South America, Europe, Australia and Antarctica are the Seven Continents.

Continents	% of Earth Area
Asia	29.5
Africa	20.4
North America	16.3
South America	11.8
Antarctica	9.6
Europe	7.1
Australia	5.3

INDIAN ECONOMY

1
Chapter

Indian Economy

BASIC CONCEPTS OF ECONOMY

What is ECONOMICS?

- Economics is regarded as the queen of social science. The term "Economics" comes from the Greek term **OIKONOMIA,** which is composed of **Oikos** (house) and **Nemein** (Custom or law), meaning **Rules of the household.**
- Economics is the social science that studies economic activities to gain an understanding of process that governs the production, distribution and consumption of goods and services in an economy.

What is an ECONOMY?

- An economy is a system of organisations and institutions that either facilitate or play a role in the production and distribution of goods and services in a society.
- Economies determine how resources are distributed among members of a society, they determine the value of goods or services and they even determine what sort of thing can be traded or bartered for those services and goods.

Economy before British Rule

- Before the advent of British rule, India had an independent economy. It was largely primary sector economy and the major occupations were agriculture, handicrafts, and many other primary sector works.

Economy during British Rule

- During the British rule, India's economy became a net raw material supplier and a net importer of finished products.
- No British economist attempted to measure the per capita income and national income of India.
- Some of the Indian economists **Dadabhai Naoroji, V.K.R.V. Rao, Desai and British Findlay Shirras and William Digby** attempted to measure India's national income. Among all, V.K.R.V. Rao was the most successful.

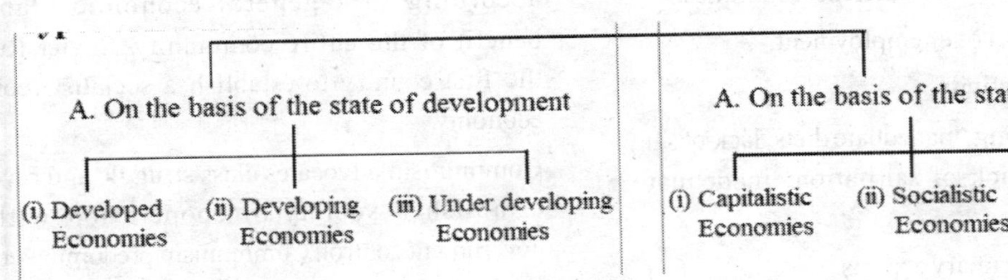

A. On the basis of the stage of development

From the viewpoint of economic development, economies of the world are divided into 3 categories:

(i) Developed Economies
(ii) Developing Economies
(iii) Under-developed Economies

(i) Developed Economies: - Characteristics of developed economies are given below:-

- The dependency of developed economies is on industrial and service sector rather than agriculture sector.
- Human capital is very skilled, that's why physical goods like railway, super computer, and infrastructure of the economy is in advance stage.
- High per capita income.
- High standard of living.
- Low incidence of poverty.
- Higher contribution of industrial and service sectors in national Income.
- Low rate of population growth.
- High rate of saving and capital formation.

- Use of modern and advance techniques of production.
- Better quality of human capital, high literacy rate, adequate availability of health and sanitation facilities.
- Exports of largely industrial products and services.

DO YOU KNOW: The best example of developed economy is G-7. The group of G-7 is group of 7 countries named as-USA, Canada (North America), UK, France, Germany, Italy(Europe), Japan (Asia).

(ii) Developing Economies:- Characteristics of developing economies are given below:

- Predominance of agriculture as a source of income and employment.
- Higher contribution of agriculture in national income.
- Human capital is unskilled.
- Low per capita income.
- Existence of widespread poverty.
- Large income inequalities.
- High growth rate of population.
- Saving and capital formation rate is low.
- Use of traditional and less efficient techniques.
- High and rising level of unemployment.
- Low level of productivity.
- Low standard of living, inadequate diets, lack of safe drinking water, lack of sanitation, inadequate housing, etc.
- Pre-dominance of primary exports.

(iii) Under/Less Developed Economies: - According to United Nations a country having lowest indicator of socio-economic developments with the lowest HDI ratings are called as underdeveloped or less developed Economies. Some characteristics of underdeveloped Economies are: low quality of life-low life expectancy and high infant mortality, underdeveloped infrastructure in terms of shortage of transport, communication and power supply, lack of financial institutions like bank and NBFCs.

B. On the basis of Nature of Economic System:

From the point of view of the nature of economic system, Economies of the world can be classified into 3 categories:

(i) Capitalistic Economies

(ii) Socialistic Economies

(iii) Mixed Economies

(i) Capitalistic Economies: Capitalism is the economy system based on private or corporate ownership, production and distribution of goods. Capitalists favour a system of free enterprise which means the government does not interfere in the economy that the laws of supply and demand will make sure that the capitalism is characterised by competition in which there is rivalry in supplying or getting an economic service or goods.

(ii) **Socialistic Economies:** "Socialism" is a very elusive and confusing term. As professor Joad comments, **"Socialism is like a hat which has lost its shape because too many people have worn it."** There is no standard model of a socialistic economy. Socialistic economic system is defined as an economic system in which the means of production are owned by the entire society and operate by the public authority according to a general economic plan for the benefit of the entire community. Soviet Russia was the first country to establish a socialist (communist) economy.

Communism advocates class struggle and revolution to establish a society of cooperation with strong government control. Communism predominated informer Soviet Union and much of Eastern Europe at one time. Today, it pre-dominates in China and Cuba, but its influence has lessened.

(iii) **Mixed Economies:-** A mixed economy is an economy which combines elements of both the capitalist and the socialist economies. This type of economy consists of a combination of public sector and private sectors units. Here, the government is the decision-maker for the public sector and individuals, and businessman make decision for the private sector. It basically incorporates governmental involvement in a market-based economy.

- **Difference between Capitalistic, Socialistic and Mixed Economies**

Basics	Capitalistic Economies	Socialistic Economies	Mixed Economies
Owned by	The fundamental feature of capitalistic economy is that productive resources like-land, factories, mines, machinery and other resources are owned by private individuals	All the productive resources such as land, mines, mills, bank, trade, etc. are owned and controlled by the state.	The main feature of mixed economy is the coexistence of public and private sector.
Objective	Maximisation of profit is the principle objective of producers.	Maximization of social welfare is the chief motivating force behind all economic activities	Promotion of social welfare is the objective of state and other hand profit maximisation is the objective of private sector.
Decision-making	Price or market mechanism is the basic coordinating mechanism. All economic decisions are taken through price mechanism.	Planning takes the place of market mechanism. All important economic decisions are taken by the Central Planning Authority.	Economic planning is essential to promote economic development, to ensure smooth and systematic operation of the economy to regulate the entire economy and to have coordinated operation of the public and private sectors.
Competition	Competition is an essential part of capitalistic economy.	Competition of all types is absent in a socialistic economy.	Healthy competition prevails in mixed economy.
Distribution of Income	There exist large inequalities in the distribution of income and wealth.	Equality in income distribution is main aim of socialistic economy.	Income equality and inequality both situations exist in mixed economy.
Class struggle	A capitalist economy has led to class struggle among various groups, particularly between the capitalists and the workers.	A socialist society is a classless society. Therefore, there is no scope of class struggle in such a society.	No class struggle found in mixed economy.
Power	Economic power is concentrated in the hands of capitalist class.	Economic and political powers are concentrated in the hands of government.	Power is decentralised in mixed economy.
Example	USA	Russia	India

Classification of the countries by the World Bank

The World Bank prepares the World Development Report (WDR) 2016. The WDR as in July, 2016 classified the different countries on the basis of their per capita income.

Categories Based on Per Capita Income:

1. Low income countries	:	\$ 1025 and Less.
2. Lower-middle Income countries	:	Above \$1026 to \$ 4035
3. Upper-middle Income countries	:	Above \$ 4036 to \$ 12,475
4. High income countries	:	Above \$ 12476 and above

Meaning of Parallel Economy

Imagine in our economy where everything is smooth. We pay taxes, everything is on paper, etc. The RBI and the government have great control on the economy by it monetary and fiscal policy. Now, on the other hand, there is market and ultimately an economy created by black money. This flow of money in our system which is beyond the purview of the RBI and government is called parallel economy. The major pitfall in such economy is that it is beyond the control of the apex bodies or the regulatory bodies.

DO YOU KNOW? The word "parallel economy" is an alternative term use for black money.

Meaning of Dual Economy

At present, the Indian economy is characterized by dualistic economic structure where a modern economy is existing along with a primitive traditional economy. Dualism is one of the important characteristics of an under-developed economy. Thus, under dualism, two sectors, i.e., modern or advanced sector and traditional or backward sector exist and operate side by side. Under this dualism, advanced sector is capital-intensive and backward sector is labour-intensive.

In a less developed country like India, the economy is represented by traditional rural sector characterised by peasant agriculture, small and cottage industries and handicrafts which are largely adopting labour-intensive techniques of production. On the other hand, the economy is also supporting an advanced modern sector consisting of large scale industries, like mining industries, iron and steel and power plants etc., which are characterized by fixed technical co-efficients, lower degree of substitutability of factors and largely adopting capital-intensive techniques of production.

Other Important Concepts

Capital

All the man-made things which are involved in production but are not destroyed during the production are known as such as machine, plant and building, etc. Related to capital, one thing must be clean, currency of own country is not capital but medium of exchange and foreign currencies are capital.

Capital Formation

Capital formation refers to the increase in the stock of real capital in an economy during an accounting period. In other words, the creation of things that help us produce more. However, the term capital formation is used both in broader as well as narrow sense. In narrow sense, capital formation indicates physical capital stock, i.e., machines, tools, etc., but in a broader sense it includes non-physical capital or human resources which include visible and invisible capital, human efficiency , craft, public health, etc.

Capital-Output Ratio

The concept of capital-output ratio expresses the relationship between the value of capital invested and the value of output. Capital-output ratio is the amount of capital needed to produce one unit of output. For example, suppose that investment in an economy, investment is 32% (of GDP), and the economic growth corresponding to this level of investment is 8%.

Here Rs. 32 investment produces an output of 8 units.

Capital		Output
32	:	8

Capital-output ratio is 32/8 or 4. In other words, to produce one unit of output, 4 units of capital is needed.

ICOR & LCOR [Incremental capital output ratio and lower capital output ratio]

Example of ICOR

Capital		Output
10	:	2 [each cost in Rs. 5]
20	:	2 [each cost in Rs. 10]

NOTE: This situation (ICOR) is not good for economy. It is proves an inefficiency of an economy.

Example of LCO

Capital	:	Output
10	:	2 [each cost in Rs. 5]
8	:	2 [each cost in Rs. 4]

NOTE: LCOR is good for economy and lower capital output ratio shows that capital is very productive.

Final and Intermediate Goods

Final goods refer to those goods which are used either for consumption or for investment.

Final goods include: Goods purchased by consumer household as they are meant for final consumption like milk purchased by household. Goods purchased by firm for capital formation or investment, like machinery purchased by firm.

It must be noted that final goods are neither resold nor used for any further transformation in the process of production.

Intermediate goods refer to those goods which are used either for resale or for further production in same year.

Intermediate goods include:

(i) Goods purchased for resale like milk purchased by a dairy shop.

(ii) Goods used for further production like milk used by for making sweets.

It must be noted that, the price of intermediate goods are added in final goods.

Example:- Cake is a final but sugar, cream, chocolate powder etc. called intermediate goods.

Economical Growth and Economical Development

Economical Growth	Economical Development
• Economical growth refers to an increase over time in a country's real output of goods and services (GNP).	• Economical development implies an upward movement of the entire economic social system in terms of income, saving and investment along with progressive changes in socio-economic structure of country.
• Growth related to gradual increase is one of the components of GDP: consumption; government spending investment, net exports.	• Development related to growth of human capital index, a decrease in inequality figures and structural changes that improve the general population's quality of life.
• It is quantitative in nature and measured through increase in real GDP.	• It is both qualitative and quantitative measured through HDI, GHI, MPI.
• It is concerned with increase in the economy's output.	• It is concerned with structural changes in economy.
• Growth is positive and negative both.	• Development is always positive.

Development is depended on growth, but every growth is converted indevelopment is not necessary.

DO YOU KNOW?

HDI (Human Development Index) :

Released by : UNDP in the year of 1990

Developed by : Amartyasen Sen & Mehbub Ul Haq

Criteria of Ranking : 1. Life Expectancy Ratio, 2. Education, 3. PCI

GHI (Global Hunger Index)

Released by : International Food Policy Research Institute & Welthungerhilfe in the year of 2006

Importance of GHI : The GHI is tool that measures and tracks hunger globally by region and by country.

MPI (Multidimensional Poverty Index).

Developed and Released by : UNDP in the year 2010

Criteria to Measure MPI : 1. Health 2. Education 3. Living Standard.

Purchasing Powr Parity (PPP)

PPP approach was given by the economist Gustav Casella in 1918. The concept is based on the law of one price, where, in the absence of trade and non-trade barriers, identical goods will have same price in different countries, when the prices are expressed in the same currency.

The PPP is defined as the number of units of a country's currency required to buy the same amount of goods and services in the domestic market as $1 would buy in the United States. For e.g. if we have to spend Rs. 30 for purchasing the same amount of goods and services as are purchased in spending $1 in USA, then the exchange rate in PPP approach is $1 = Rs. 30.

Example: In the year 2017-18, national income of USA $5000 and in the same year, the national income of India Rs. 9000. According to PPP-

$1 = Rs. 30

= Rs. 9,000

Rs. 30

= $300

Nations with highest PPP 1. USA 2. China 3. India 4. Japan 5. Germany

Durable and Non-Durable Goods

	Durable Goods	Non-Durable Goods
Meaning	Durable goods or hard goods are the goods that do not quickly wear out and last over a long period of time.	Non-durable goods or soft goods are those goods that have a short life cycle.
Example	TV, AC, Car	Bread, Butter, Vegetables

Giffen Goods and Veblen Goods

A Giffen good is a good for which demand increases as the price increases, and falls when the price decreases. Veblen goods violate the law of demand, because people actually "prefer" goods to be more expensive as a status symbol.

Note: Giffen goods are inferior goods, while Veblen goods are not.

2 Chapter National Income

- **Meaning of National Income**

  National income in defined as the monetary value of all final goods and services produced in a country over a period of time, usually one year. National income is calculated for a specified period, normally a financial year. (In India, financial year) means April 1 to March 31 of the next year).

- **According to the National Income Committee (1949)**

  "A national income estimate measures the volume of commodities and services turned out during a given period counted without duplication." Country + Financial year + Monetary Value of Final Goods and Services + Total = NI

  Note: The Government of India appointed the National Income Committee in August 1949 for the purpose of compile a national income estimates rationally on a scientific basis, under the chairmanship of Prof. P.C. Mahalnobis and two other members Prof. D.R. Gadgil and Dr. V.K.R.V. Rao.

- **Concepts of National Income**

  These 4 ways to look upon "Income of an economy", although different from each other in some way, are the concepts of GDP, NDP, GNP, and NNP. All are forms of the national income, but are different from one other. They all say a different story about the income of a nation in their own specific way. Here, we will discuss them in a very objective way.

- **Gross Domestic Product (GDP)**

  GDP is the value of the all final goods and services produced within the boundary of a nation during one year. In GDP, income generated by foreigners in a country is included, but income generated by nationals of a country outside the country, in not included. It means in the concept of GDP, "Place" (domestic boundary) is important, not a person:

- **In equation form**

  Country + Financial Year + Final Goods and Services produced with in the Domestic Boundary + Sum of Monetary Value = GDP.

- **Uses of GDP**

  The different uses of the concept of GDP are as given below:

1. Per annum percentage change in it is the "growth rate" of an economy. For example, if a country has a GDP of Rs. 110 which is 10 rupees higher than the last year, it has a growth rate of 10 percent. When we use the term "a growing" economy, it means that the economy is adding up its income, i.e., in quantitative terms.
2. It is a "Quantitative" concept and its volume/size indicates the 'internal' strength of the economy. But, it does not say anything about the "Qualitative" aspects of the produced goods and services by the economy.
3. It is used by the IMF/WB in the comparative analyses of its member nations.

Meaning of Domestic Boundary

Domestic boundary is a very important concept in national income accounting. In layman's language, domestic boundary means the political frontiers of a country. However, for the purpose of national income accounting, it is used in a wider sense.

1. Ships and aircrafts owned and operated by normal residents between two or more countries. For example, planes operated by Air India between Russia and Japan are part of the domestic boundary of India. Similarly, planes operated by Singapore Airways between India and Japan are a part of the domestic boundary of Singapore.
2. Fishing vessels, oil and natural gas rigs and floating platforms operated by the residents of a country in the international waters, where they have exclusive rights of operation. For example, fishing boats operated by Indian fishermen in international waters of Indian ocean will be considered a part of domestic boundary of India.
3. Embassies, consulates and military establishments of a country located abroad. For example, Indian Embassy in Russia is a part of the domestic boundary of India.

According to the United Nations, economic boundary or

domestic boundary is the geographical territory, administered by a government within which, persons, goods and capital circulate freely.

- Net Domestic Product:

  It is the net value of GDP after deducting depreciation of plant and machinery from GDP.

- In equation form:

  GDP – Depreciation = NDP

  This way, NDP of an economy has to be always lower than its GDP for the same year, since there is no way to cut depreciation to zero. But, mankind has achieved too much in this area by the developments such as "ball-bearing," lubricants," etc., all innovated to minimise the levels of depreciation.

Uses of NDP

The different uses of the concept of NDP are as given below:

- The concept of GDP is only used for domestic level. It means NDP is not used in comparative economics, i.e., to compare the economics of the world. Why this is so? This is due to different rate of depreciation which is set by the different economics of the world.
- To show the achievements of the economy in the area of research and development which have tried cutting levels of the depreciation in a historical time period.

Meaning of Depreciation

Depreciation is the total value of the "wear and tear". Every asset (except human beings) goes for depreciation in the process of these uses.

The governments of the economics decide and announce the rates by which assets depreciate (done in India by the Ministry of Commerce and Industry) and a list published, which is used by the different sections of the economy to determine the real levels of depreciations in different assets.

Gross National Product (GNP)

GNP is the value of the all final goods and services produced by the nationals of a country during a given period of time, generally a year. In GNP, income generated by foreigners in a country is excluded but we include all final goods and services, produced by nationals of a country during a year in the calculation of GNP, we include the money value of goods and services produced by nationals outside the country in calculating GNP.

In equation form:

GDP + X – M = GNP

Where,

X = Income earned and received by nationals within the boundaries of foreign countries.

M = Income received by foreign nationals within the boundary.

Uses of GNP

The different uses of the concept of GNP are as given below:

- GNP is the more exhaustive concept of national income than the GDP as it indicates about the "quantitative" as well as the "Qualitative" aspect of the economy, i.e., the "internal" as well as "external" strength of the economy.

  In the concept of GNP, income received from abroad is added. On the other hand, foreigners who received income within a country in not included. It means, GNP shows the strength of an economy.
- It enables us to learn several facts about the production behavior and patterns of an economy, such as, how much the outside world is dependent on its product and how much it depends on the world for the same (numerically shown by the size and net flow of its "trade balance"), what is the standard of its human resource in international parlance (shown by the size and the net flow of its 'private remittance'), what position it holds regarding financial support from and to the world economics (shown by the net flow of interest on external lending / borrowing).
- **Net National Product (NNP):**

  NNP is obtained by subtracting depreciation value from GNP.

  In equation form:

  GNP – Depreciation = NNP

Uses of NNP:

The different uses of the NNP are as given below:

- NNP is the purest form of the income of a nation.
- In reality, NNP is the national income of an economy.
- In the concept of NNP, money value of depreciation in subtracted and money value of final goods and services which is produced by nationals of a country is added.
- Method of measuring National Income at Market Price and Factor Cost:

National income is estimated either at Market Price (MP) or at Factor Cost (FC).

Market Price:

Market price is the price that customers actually pay. It includes the component of indirect taxes and the subsidies.

In equation form:

Cost of production + Indirect tax + Subsidy = Market Price.

Factor Cost:

Factor Cost refers to the Cost of 'factors of production' viz., rent of land, interest of capital, wages of the labour and profit of the entrepreneurship. Basically "Factor Cost" is the "input cost" the producer has to incur in process of producing something. This is also termed as "factory price" or production cost/price. This is nothing but 'price' of the commodity from the producers side.

In equation form:

Market price – Indirect Tax + Subsides = Factor Cost. When NNP is obtained at factor cost, it is known as NATIONAL INCOME. In India, Income is calculated at factor cost, and so is the case with most of the developing countries. The reason are lack of uniformity in taxes, goods are not printed with their prices, etc.

- Graphical Presentation of National Income:

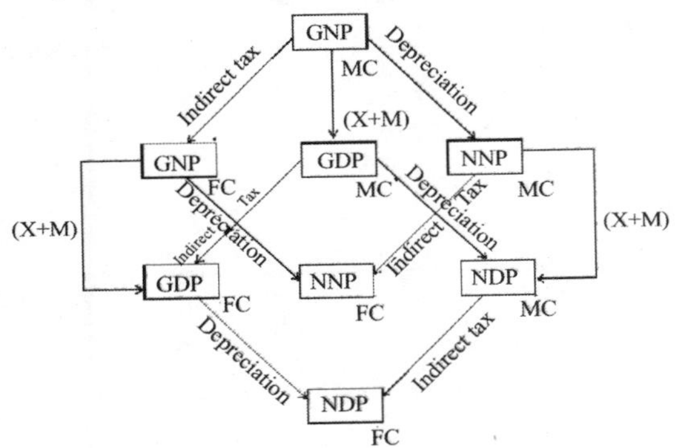

- Method of Measuring National Income at Current Price & Constant Price:

  National Income can be measured in terms of money in two ways – at current prices and constant prices.

- National Income at Current Price:

  When goods and services produced by normal resident of a country in a given year are estimated at current prices, it is called national income at current prices. Current prices refer to the prices prevailing during the year for which estimates are made. Thus, it is the estimation of goods and services produced during a year on the basis of the prices of the year. For national income at current prices, we use same year's output and same year's market prices. Such date reflects the state of economic affairs of that year, but does not show real change in national income because prices keep on changing.

National Income at Constant Prices

When goods and services produce by normal residents of a country during a year are valued at fixed prices, i.e., prices of the base year, it is called national income at constant prices; constant prices refer to the prices prevailing in the base year. Every country measures national income both at current prices and constant prices, but it is the latter which indicates real change in national income.

Different between GDP and GNP

Gross Domestic Product (GDP)	Gross National Product (GNP)
• Domestic boundary plays an important role in GDP	• No need of Domestic boundary
• In GDP, goods and services are produced by residents of the country or foreigners	• In GNP, the production of foreigners in the country is not included while the production of nationals outside the country is included.
• "Place" is important for GDP, persons are not.	• Persons are important for GNP, place is not.
• GDP is a quantitative concept and its volume economy.	• GNP is the more exhaustive concept of national size indicates the internal strength of the income than the GDP as it indicates about the "Quantitative" as well as the "Qualitative" aspect of the economy.

Who is bigger-GDP or GNP ?

In respect of India, GNP is always lower than it GDP.

For example:

Suppose,

Income received by an Indian who lives in India	=	Rs. 10,000
Including the Income from Abroad	=	Rs. 5,000

Subtracting the Income received by Foreigners who live in domestic boundary of India- = Rs. 6,000

India's GNP = 10,000 + 5000 − 6000 = 9000

Suppose,

- Income received by an Indian who lives in India = Rs. 10,000
- Include the Income received by Foreigners who live in domestic boundary of India. = Rs. 6,000
- Subtracting the income from Abroad = Rs. 5,000

  India's GDP = 1000 + 6000 − 5000 = 11000

  India's GDP is greater than GNP of India, because foreigners who live in India are more skilled competition of those Indians who live abroad.

Indian Economy is divided into 3 Sectors:

The economic activities of any economy is broadly classified into three broad categories which are known as the "Three sectors" of the economy: (i) Primary Sector (ii) Secondary Sector (iii) Tertiary Sector.

Sector	Meaning and Example	In equation form
Primary Sector	This sector includes all those economicactivities where there is the direct use of natural resources' as agriculture, forestry, fishing, etc. **Note:** This sector also known as AGRICULTURAL SECTOR.	Agriculture + Forestry + Fishing = Primary Sector
Secondary Sector	The secondary sector of the economy is involved in the production of finished goods. This sector is rightly called the manufacturing sector which uses the produce of the primary sector as its raw materials. Since the manufacturing is done by the industries as-automobiles, textiles, ship-building, bread, biscuits and cake, etc. **Note:** This sector also known as INDUSTRIAL SECTOR.	Mining and Quarrying + Manufacturing + construction + Electricity, Gas and water Supply = Secondary Sector.
Tertiary Sector	This sector includes all those economic activities where different "Services" are produced, such as education, banking, insurance, tourism, etc. Note: This sector is also known as SERVICE SECTOR.	Trade, Hotel, Transportation, Communication + Finance, In surance, Real Estate and Professional Services + Public Administration, Defence and other Services = Tertiary Sector.

Sometime, two more sectors i.e., Quaternary and Quandary are defined separately, even though these can also be considered as part of the services sector itself.

Quaternary Sector: This sector consists of the intellectual and knowledge based activities. Examples of activities associated with this sector are research and development, cultures, information technology, consulting, financial planning, education, etc.

Quandary Sector: This sector consists of the highest levels of decision – making in a country. This includes the top officials of government, media, universities, etc.

- Items to be excluded in national income with reason

  Some of the major items excluded in national income are as follows:

- Winning of lottery prize: It will not be included in the national income as it does not add to flow of goods and services in the economy.

- Increase in the prices of storks lying with a trades: It will included in the national income as it does not be amount to any flow of goods.
- Profit earned by foreign banks in India: It is not included in the national income as it is part of the factor income paid abroad. It is subtracted from domestic income to get national income.
- Old age pension: It will not be included in the national income as it is a transfer payment mode by the government and a transfer income for the receiver.

  Note: Old age pension must not be confused with retirement pension. Old age pension is not included in national income as it is a transfer payment. On the other hand, retirement pension in included in national income.
- Earnings of shareholders from the sale of shares: It will not be included in the national income as it is a financial clam and does not contribute to any productive activity.
- Expenditure on advertisement by a firm/Commodities used in scientific research: It will not be included in the national income as it is a part of intermediate consumption expenditure.
- Financial help received by flood victims: It will not be included in the national income as it is a transfer income.
- Money received from sale of secondhand goods: It will not included in the national income because receipts from the sale of secondhand goods are by virtue of transfer of an already existing object.
- Growing vegetables in a kitchen garden of the house: It will not included in the national income as it is difficult estimate the value of production (It is non-market transaction).
- Transport expenses by a firm: It will not be included in the national income as it is a part of intermediate consumption expenditure.
- Harish works in USA and sends money to his family in India: It will not be included in the national income as it is a transfer payment.
- Expenditure by father on marriage of his daughter: It will not be included in the national income as it does not add to current flow of goods and services.
- Expenditure by the government on scholarships to student: It will not be included in the national income as it is a transfer payment.
- Expenditure on maintenance by a firm: It will be not be included in the national income as it is a part of intermediate consumption expenditure.
- Payment of excise duty by a firm: It will not be included in the national income as it is an indirect tax paid by the firm.
- Payment of wealth tax/payment of death duty/ Entertainment tax received by the government: It will not be included in the national income as it is an indirect tax and a compulsory transfer payment received by the government.

Types of Income

Per Capita Income (PCI)

It is the average income (per-person) of a country

$$PCI = \frac{\text{National Income}}{\text{Population of the year}}$$

Personal Income (PI)

It is the income of the residents (individuals) of a country. To be calculated in personal income, transfer payments of the individuals are added to National Income, while social security contributions, corporate tax and undistributed profits are subtracted.

PI = National Income + Transfer payments – Social security contributions – Corporate tax – Undistributed profit.

- **Disposable Income (DI)**

  It is the income of individuals at their disposal after paying direct tax liabilities.

  DI = Personal income – Direct tax liabilities.
- **Some Important Concepts:**

  Nominal GDP

  It is the market value (Money Value) of all final goods and services produced within the country.

  Real GDP

  It is the value of national income adjusted for inflation calculated from some reference point (base year).

  Green GNP

  The net value after deducting consumption of natural resources and degradation of environment from GNP is called green GNP.

  Green Economy

  In this economy, which deals with the environmental risks and ecological scarcity and also an economy that aims for sustainable development without degrading the environment.

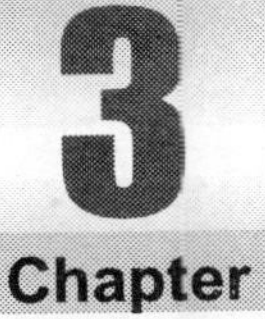

Tax

Meaning of Tax and Fee: Tax is a compulsory payment given by citizens to the government. The purpose of taxation is to abolish socio-economic disparities and finance the government's expenditure. In other words, taxes are the basic source of revenue to the government. But fee is the compulsory charge given by people when they use government services like, passport fee, PAN Card fee, etc. It means, fee is specifically applied for the use of a service.

Classification of Taxes:

Tax	Meaning	Example	Diagram
Proportional Tax	A proportional tax, also referred to as a flat tax, impacts low, middle and high income earners relatively equally. Under a proportional tax system, individual tax payers pay a set percentage of their income, regardless of the total income earned.	In India, Corporate Tax is a good example of proportional tax. At present the Government of India charges a flat rate of 25% on the income earned by the companies.	Y; Tax Rate 25 (in %); Proportional Tax/Flat Tax; A; B; X; 0 1 2 3 4; Income
Progressive Tax	Progressive tax means rate of tax increases for increasing values or volumes on which the tax is levied.	Income Tax is a progressive tax as it has exemptions for very small incomes, low rates for the first slab of taxable income and higher rates for the largest incomes.	Y; B; 30; Tax Rate (in%) 20; 5; Progressive Tax; A; X; 0; 2.5 to 5; 5 to 10; 10↑; Income (in Lakh)
Regressive Tax	Regressive taxes are those that have a greater impact on low income individuals or entities than high income earners.	To promote the growth and development of the small scale industries, India at one time, had regressive excise duty on their production, with increasing slabs of volume they produced, the burden of tax used to go on decreasing.	Y; A; Tax Rate (in %) 20% 15% 10% 5%; Regressive Tax; B; X; 0 5 10 15 20; Income (in Lakh)
Digressive Tax	Under this system of taxation, characteristics of progressive and proportional tax is found in the concept of tax.	In India, an individual income tax is the good example of digressive tax.	Y; Tax Rate; A; Progressive; Proportional = Digressive; X

Types of Tax : Tax can be direct or indirect: income tax, wealth tax, gift tax, etc. are the examples of direct taxes and sales taxes, excise duty, custom duty, etc. are the examples of indirect taxes.

Direct Tax : A direct tax refers to any levy that is both imposed and collected on a specific group of people or organisations. An example of direct tax is the income tax collected from the people who actually earn.

Indirect Tax : Indirect taxes are imposed on one person or organisation, but collected from some other person or organisation.

Difference between Direct and Indirect Tax

Basis for comparison	Direct Tax	Indirect Tax
Meaning	Direct tax is referred to as the tax levied on a person's income and is paid by the same person to the government.	Indirect tax is referred to as the tax levied on a person who consumes the goods and services and is paid by other person to the government.
Nature	Progressive in nature because tax slab rate increase with increase in income.	Regressive in nature. A particular commodity is taxed at the same rate. A poor person with limited resources finds it difficult to purchase the commodity when compared to the rich.
Incidence and impact	Falls on the same person.	Falls on different persons.
Examples	Wealth tax, income tax, property tax, corporate tax.	Goods and services Tax (GST), Security Transaction Tax (STT), excise duty, custom duty.
Evasion	Tax evasion is possible.	Tax evasion is difficult because the taxes on commodity are included in the price of that commodity.
Inflation	Direct tax helps in reducing inflation.	Indirect taxes promote inflation.
Event	Taxable income or wealth of the person.	Purchase/sale/manufacture of goods and delivery of services.

Some important Direct Taxes

- Personal Income Tax
- Corporate Tax / Corporation Tax

Some Important Indirect Taxes

- Central Excise Duty
- Service Tax
- Custom Duty
- Personal Income Tax: It is the tax levied directly on the income of individuals by the Central Government. The various types of incomes covered under income tax are as follows:
- Salary
- Business or profession profits
- Rental income from property
- Gains arising from sale of asset (Capital gains)
- Interest income, etc.
- Corporate Tax / Corporation Tax: It is levied on the profit of the companies or corporations.
- **Central Excise Duty:** Central excise duties are imposed by the Central Government on the goods produced within the country, except certain goods on which State Governments are empowered to impose tax. These goods include liquor, drugs, etc.
- **Service Tax :** It is a tax imposed on the person, who avails any specified service. Service tax is an indirect tax paid on the sale of service in the case of goods. There are two separate events of production and sale, whereas in the case of services, the production and sale of services occur simultaneously. In case of goods, excise duty is levied on manufacture, and sales tax is levied on sale of goods. In case of services, single tax is levied, namely, service tax.
- **Custom Duty :** It is the tax imposed on commodities imparted imported into India (Import duty) or those exported from India (export duty). In other words, when a goods cross the political boundary of a country or come from other countries, custom duties are imposed. Like excise duties, customs duties also contribute largely to the government revenue.

4 Chapter

Planning

Meaning of Economic Planning:

Economic Planning means a development strategy taking into consideration limited resources to achieve long-term objective in the economy. It is different from Laissez Faire in which there is no external force guiding the economic agents to achieve some per-decided goals for the benefit of all. According to H.D. Dickinson—"Economic planning is taking major economic decisions, what and how much is to be produced, how, when and where it is to be produced, and to whom it is to be allocated by the comprehensive survey of the economic system as whole."

Objectives of Planning

The broad objectives of the five year plans in India are as follows:

- A high rate of growth with a view to improvement in the standard of living.
- Modernization of economy in terms of adoption of new technologies and social outlook.
- Economic self-reliance, meaning avoiding import of the products that can be produced in India.
- Equity, implying equitable distribution of wealth with social justice.
- Economic stability, which means controlling inflation and unemployment.
- Poverty alleviation was the important issue which polarised the member of the NPC (National Planning Commission) as well as the Constituent Assembly that a highly emphatic decision in favour of a planned economy evolved ever before independence. Several programmes have been launched in India directing the cause of poverty alleviation by all the governments till date and the process continues even today.
- Providing employment to the poor has been the best tool of economics to alleviate poverty. Thus, this objective of planning in India comes naturally once it committed itself to alleviate poverty. Employment generation in India has been, therefore, part and parcel of the objective of the poverty alleviation in India. General programmes and schemes have been launched by the governments from time to time in this direction, some based on the wage employment, still others based on self-employment.

History of Planning in India:

Mr. Visvesvaraya, a noted engineer and politician, is regarded as the pioneer of economic planning in India. In 1934, he introduced the concept of economic planning through his book, "Planned Economy for India."

In 1938, National planning Commission was set up under the chairmanship of Jawaharlal Nehru by the Indian National Congress.

Due to the beginning of the World War II and changes in the Indian political situation, its (NPC) is recommendations could not be implemented.

It recommended that the objective of planning should be to ensure an adequate living standard for the masses. Also, it emphasised heavy industrialisation and land reforms. However, its recommendations could not be implemented due to beginning of the World

War II and changes in the Indian political situation.

Later in 1944, the Bombay Plan was presented by 8 leading industrialists including JRD Tata, G.D. Birla and others. It envisaged future economic progress, based on textile and consumer industries. It also acknowledged an important role for the state in post independent India.

Moreover, in 1945, "People's Plan" was given by M N Roy. In 1950, Jai Prakash narayan gave 'Sarvodaya Plan'. And finally, Planning Commission' was set up on 15th March, 1950. The state holds complete control over the entire private industrial and agricultural sectors, along with banking and transport. Imperative planning ensures the target of optimum planning. As a result, there is least place for oligopolistic and monopolistic tendencies.

Types of Economic Planning

1. Role of the Government

A. Imperative Planning

There is one central authority which plans, directs and orders the execution of the plan. Market forces are not allowed to operate freely. Both saving and investment are strictly controlled by the planning authority. The state holds the commanding posts in its hands by taking over entire private industrial and agricultural sectors and banking and transport. "Without such concentration, the state would lack the means to carry out the tasks of the plan. Provisions in the plan would be mere pious wishes without any guarantee of realisation attached to them." Under such planning, the targets for optimum planning can be ensured. Oligopolistic and monopolistic tendencies can easily be eliminated. **Note:-** Russia provides the best example of Imperative Planning. The Indian government also adapted imperative planning for the first five year plan to the end of the seventh five year plan.

B. Indicative Planning/Inducement Planning

Planning by inducement is consistent with democratic planning. It refers to the planning by manipulating the market. There is no compulsion and direction, but only persuasion. Therefore, in planning by inducement, the state manipulates the market economy not by command but by providing inducement to secure its objectives. The planning authority induces the people through monetary and fiscal measures and through appropriate price policies to act in certain desired ways. In case planning authority wishes to raise the level of production, it can do so by granting subsidies. Similarly, price control and rationing can be adopted in case of scarcity. Furthermore, in order to increase the rate of capital formation, planning authority can undertake public investment or encourage private investment. In a real sense, qualitative methods of credit control can help in long way in maintaining the price level, while qualitative method of credit control can help is diverting investment into desired channels.

Note : India adapted Indicative Planning since the 8th Five Year Plan.

2 Extent of People's Participation

A. Centralized Planning

All economic decisions are taken by the central authority. The Government formulates economic plans, determines objectives, sets targets and priorities.

B. Decentralized Planning

Connected with capitalistic economies. Implemented through market mechanism. Empowers peoples as planning operates from bottom to top.

3. On the basis of Time Period

A. Short-term Plan

Main objectives of short-term plans are: raise revenue, attain short-term economic target, bring price stability and remove balance of payment deficit.

Note: Short-term Plan is also known as Annual Plan.

B. Medium-term Plan

Main objectives of medium-term plans are raise per capita income, raise level of employment, create self sufficiency, reduce dependence over foreign aid and raise revenues through domestic sources and to remove regional and inter regional disparity.

Note: Medium-term plan is made for 5 years.

C. Long-term plan

Main objectives of long-term plans are structural changes in the economy.

Note : Long-term plan is made for 10 to 30 years, for example: MDGs (2000 to 2015), SDGs (2015 to 2030), and Indian Vision 2020.

Model of Planning

Model of Planning	Focus Areas
Harrod Domar Model	• The first five year plan (1951-56) was based on this strategy. This strategy emphasised the role of capital accumulation's dual character, which on the one hand, increased the national income (demand side role) and on the other hand, increased the production capacity (supply side role). • According to this growth model, the rate of economic growth in an economy is dependent on the level of saving and capital output ratio.

Nehru-Mahalanobis Model	• This strategy was a two-sector model, that is, consumer good sectors and capital goods sector. The strategy emphasised investment in heavy industry to achieve industrialisation for rapid economic development. It was based on the Russian experience. • The objective was to become self- reliant and overcome capital constraint. This strategy was adopted in the second five year plan (1956-61) and with minor modifications, up to the fifth plan. it was a long-term strategy. • It is also suffered to as planning by inducement as against imperative planning.
Gandhian Model	• It was enunciated by Acharya Shriam Naryan Agarwal in his "Gandhian Plan" in 1944. This basic objective of the Gandhian Model is to raise the material as well as cultural level of the masses so as to provide a basic standard of life. • It laid emphasis on the scientific development of agriculture and rapid growth of cottage and village indsutires. Moreover, Gandhian strategy emphasised on employment-oriented planning rather than production-oriented planning of Nehru.
Singh-Rao Model	• Liberalisation, Privatisation and Globalisation (LPG) strategy of planning was introduced by the Finance Minister Dr. Manmohan Singh under the Narasimha Rao government. • The strategy ended the "License-permit raj" and opened the hitherto areas reserved for the public sector to private sector. It allowed for foreign direct investment and followed an export promotion policy to boost economic growth. In all, it changed the nature of planning from centralised to "Indicative", wherein planning was to play a facilitating role. • It is also referred to as, planning by inducement, as against imperative planning.

The Planning Commission

- The Planning Commission was set-up through an executive order on 15th March, 1950. It is essentially a non-political and non-constitutional advisory body. Pt. Jawaharlal Nehru was its first chairperson. It was basically designed to formulate plans for the economic development of the country.
- However, it has been replaced by the NITI Aayog.

National Development Council

- The National Development Council was set-up in 1952 through an executive order.
- It is neither a constitutional body nor a statutory body. Rather, it is mainly concerned with approval of five years plan.
- It is chaired by the Prime Minister. It consists of the central ministers, chief ministers of the state, Lt. governors of the UTs, etc.
- The security of the Planning Commision also acts as the Secretary of the council. Overall, it is essentially an advisory body.

NITI Aayog

- The government of India set-up NITI Aayog on 1st January, 2015. It was replaced by the Planning Commission.
- The institution will serve as the "Think-Tank" of the government.
- It is designed to provide relevant strategic and technical advice to the government on key element of policy.
- These area of advice include maters of national and international importance on the economic front, dissemination of best parties and infusion of new policy ideas.

Composition

Unlike the Planning Commission, the NITI Aayog consists of part-time members and full-time members.

1. Prime Minister : Ex-officio chairperson
2. Vice-Chairperson
3. Chief Executive officer
4. 5 Full-time members and
5. 2 Part-time members
6. 4 Central government ministers.

New Structure under the NITI Aayog

- The Governing Council headed by the Prime Minister has replaced the xxx National Development Council.
- It includes Chief Ministers of all the states and heads of all Union Territories as members.

- In addition, there will be a 'Regional Council' comprising of Chief Ministers and Governors of UTs. It will be mandated to develop region-specific plan.
- The current structure of the Aayog comprises 7-8 full-time members, 2 well-known part-time members drawn from leading research organisation and major universities.
- Moverover, the PM also nominates four Union Ministers in ex-officio capacity. Besides, specialists across domain, on PM's invitation, will be invited to share knowledge and add value to the planning process.
- The Centre expected the recommendations of the 14th Finance Commission for racing the share of states from 32% to 42% in the Union's tax revenue.
- The hike (32% to 42%) was the single largest increase ever recommended.
- This increase has given more power to states in determining how they spend, on the other hand, it has reduced the fiscal resources available to the centre.
- For the Commission, the increased devolution is a 'compositional shift in transfers' from grants to tax devolution.
- Grants to states have been divided into two parts. One, grants to duly constituted Gram Panchayats and second to duly constituted municipal bodies.
- Further, there are basic grant and performance grant for Gram Panchayats and Municipal bodies. And, the ratio between basic to performance grant is 90:10 and 80:20 for panchayats and municipalities, respectively.

Inter-State Council

Article 263 provides for the constitution of Inter State council.

According to Article 263, "the President can constitute an institution to facilitate co-ordination of policies and their implementation between the union and states."

In 1990, on the recommendation of the Sarkaria Commission, the President constituted the Inter-State Council.

Functions

- To inquire and advise upon disputes which may have been arisen between states.
- Investigating and discussing subjects in which some or more states are involved.
- Making recommendation for the better co-ordination of policies and actions with respect to that subject.
- Generating 50 million new work opportunities in non-farm sector and providing to equivalent numbers.
- Increasing infrastructure investment to 9% of GDP.
- Financial inclusion of 90% of GDP.
- Achieving universal road connectivity and access to power for all villages, increasing the up gradation of national and state highways to minimum two lane attended.

India Vision 2020

- India Vision 2020 was released by Planning Commission on 23rd January, 2003. This document was prepared by Mr. Shyam Prasad Gupta, a member of the Planning Commission.

Salient Features

- Achieving growth rate by 2020 to be 9%.
- Elimination of unemployment, illiteracy and property by 2020.
- Per capita income to get doubled by 2020.
- Urban population density from 25% to 40%.

The Finance Commission

- According to Article 280 of the Constitution, the President appoints a Finance Commission after every 5 years. This provision is also a fundamental feature of the Indian Constitution, which is not found in any other Constitution. The Finance Commission was appointed 2 years after the implementation of the Constitution and every 5 years thereafter.
- The President has the power to appoint a new Finance Commission even before the expiry of 5 years, if he deems it necessary. In other words, the appointment of the Finance Commission is a continuous process according to our Constitution.
- The Finance Commission generally presents its recommendations regarding the allocation of revenue between the Centre and the states, so that, there is no discord between the Centre and the States.
- Main objective of the Finance commission is to access the financial requirements of the states to determine amount of grants-in-aid to be given to various states and to strengthen the federal financial system.

Objective of the Finance Commission

- To determine the basis for the allocation of funds collected from the taxes, which are divisible between the center and states.
- To formulate the principles regarding the grants to the states from the Centre.
- To continue the agreements made between the Government of India and the states or to recommend changes in them.
- To consider any other financial matter in the interest of the country, on being notified by the President to do so.
- On the basis of this arrangement, 15th Finance Commission have been set-up so far.

Finance Commission	Year of Establishment	Chairman	Operational Duration
First	1951	K. C. Neogy	1952–57
Second	1956	K. Santhanam	1957–62
Third	1960	A. K. Chanda	1962–66
Fourth	1964	P. V. Rajamannar	1966–69
Fifth	1968	Mahaveer Tyagi	1969–74
Sixth	1972	K. Brahmananda Reddy	1974–79
Seventh	1977	J. M. Shelat	1979–84
Eighth	1983	Y. B. Chavan	1984–89
Ninth	1987	N. K. P. Salve	1989–95
Tenth	1992	K. C. Pant	1995–2000
Eleventh	1998	A. M. Khusro	2000–2005
Twelfth	2002	C. Rangarajan	2005–2010
Thirteenth	2007	Dr. Vijay L. Kelkar	2010–2015
Fourteenth	2013	Dr. Y. V Reddy	2015–2020
Fifteenth	2017	N.K. Singh	2020-2025

14th Finance Commission

- The 14th Finance Commission, headed by the former RBI Governor YV Reddy, has endorsed the compensation road map for the goods and service tax finalized by Centre, but has called for an autonomous and independent GST compensation fund.
- Members of the 14th Finance Commission-YV Reddy, Abhijit Sen, M Govinda Rao, Sushama Nath and Sudipto Mundle.
- The Government of India on 24th February, 2015 accepted recommendations of the 14th Finance Commission for increasing share of stats in centre taxes to 42%.
- The Commission recommended increase in the share of states in the centre's tax revenue from the current 32% to 42%, the single largest increase ever recommended.
- The recommendation will give more power to states in determining how they spend this money (it also correspondingly reduces the fiscal resources available to the centre).

Recommendation of the 14th Finance Commissions

- The 14th Finance Commission is of the view that tax devolution should be the primary route for transfer of resources to the states.
- In understanding the states needs, it has ignored the plan and non-plan distinctions.

- According to the Commission, the increased devolution of the divisible pool of taxes is a 'compositional shift in transfers' from grants to tax devolution.
- In recommending an horizontal distribution, it has used broad parameters population (1971), changes in population since then, income distance, forest cover and area, among others.
- It has recommended distribution of grants to states for local bodies using 2011population data with weight of 90% and area with weight of 10%.
- Grants to states are divided into two. One, grant to duly constituted Gram Panchayats and two, grant to duly constituted municipal bodies.
- It has divided grants into two parts. A basic grant and a performance one for Gram panchayats and Municipal, bodies.
- The ratio of basic to performance grant is 90 : 10 for panchayats and 80 : 20 for municipalities.

Industrial Sector

Importance of Industry is an economy

- The industrial sector plays an equally important role as it accelerates growth of economies, provides self-reliance, employment, creates a demand for the agricultural produce and creates "ripple effect".
- Industries can create townships around them, thereby creating indirect employment.
- Industrialisation is all about focusing on the industries, allowing them to meet the requirement of the economy besides providing linkages to the agricultural sector and also employment opportunities in the economy. This can be achieved only through higher industrial growth which can provide momentum to the overall growth and also make it sustainable in future.

There has been a missing link in India of the industrial/ manufacturing sector, despite policies and governmental focus, not playing its role of creating linkages with agricultural sector and also creating desired employment opportunities. The service sector is becoming a major contributor to output rather than manufacturing or the industrial sector. Such sectoral composition in favour of services does happen, but once industrial sector supporting higher levels of growth of economies, which has not happened in India.

Categorisation of Industries

Industries can also be categorised across the following features:

Features : On basis of Products industries.

Example :

- Basic industries, for example: steel, cement and fertiliser
- Capital goods industries, for example: manufacturing of plant and machineries.
- Intermediate goods industries for example: manufacturing of dyes, tools, etc.
- Consumer goods industries for example: manufacture of cars, scooters, fridges, readymade garments, etc.

Features : On Basis of Ownership

Example :

- Public sector
- Private sector
- Joint Sector [Public and Private both]

Features : On Basis of Capital/Labour intensity

Example :

- Capital intensive industries [larger capital intensive in relation to labour]
- Labour intensive industries [larger labour intensive in relation to capital]

Industrial Policy

- Industrial policy is a tool to provide effective co-ordination of the activities in various sections of the economy.
- The Industrial policy was devised to realise the goal of planned development.
- After independence, a national consensus was in favor of rapid industrialisation of the economy.
- The industrial policy is not only the key to economic development, but also to economic sovereignty.
- The evolution of industrial policy took place through successive resolutions and statements.

Industrial Policy Resolution, 1948

Announcement Date : On April 8, 1948

Presented By : Industrial Minister, Late SP Mukherjee

Objective : In the policy resolution of 1948, importance of both, public sector and private sector (Mixed Economy) was recognised, but considering the the limited resources of private sector, leading role was given to the public sector.

Categories of Industries : 4 categories

Categories of Industries	Related Industries	Undertaking
First Category (3 Industries) Note:- This category is known as the "Public Sector".	1. Arms and Ammunition 2. Atomic energy 3. Rail Transport	These areas were under state monopoly and private entities were not allowed to enter into these areas.

Categories of Industries	Related Industries	Undertaking
Second Category (6 Industries) Note: This category is known as the "Mixed Sector".	1. Coal 2. Iron and Steel 3. Aircraft manufacture 4. Ship-building 5. Manufacture of telephone, telegraphs and wireless apparatus (excluding radio sets) 6. Mineral oils	New units were to be set up by the public sector only, but existing private sector units were allowed for 10 years. The government announced that the status of exiting private units in this category will be reviewed after 10 years.
Third Category (18 Industries) Note: This category known as the "Controlled Private Sector".	Some of the industries in this category were: machine tools, heavy machinery, automobiles, electrical engineering, cement, etc.	Private sector was allowed to set-up units in areas, but considering the importance, the government decided to direct and regulate these industries.
Fourth category Note: This category known as the "Private and Co-operative sector".	Industries not included in these three categories were put in the fourth category.	Private sector was allowed to set-up units.

Industrial Policy Revolution, 1956

Announced Date: On April 1, 1956

Presented By: PM Pandit Jawaharlal Nehru

Objective: The Industrial Policy 1956 laid down broad objective too be achieved through the industrial policy. These are:

- To accelerate the growth rate and industrialisation
- Expansion of the public sector
- Development of the cooperative sector
- To develop heavy and machine-making industries
- To reduce inequalities in income and wealth
- To control concentration of economic power and monopolistic tendencies in the industrial sector.

Categories of Industries : 3 Categories

Categories of Industries	Related Industries	Undertaking
First Category Schedule-A	Arms and ammunition, atomic energy, rail transport and air transport.	This schedule had 17 industrial areas in which the centre of was given complete monopoly. The industries setup under this provision were known as the Central Public Undertaking (CPSUs) later getting popularity as the 'PSUs'.
Second Category Schedule-B	Road transport, sea transport, machine tools, fertilizers, drugs, etc.	In the second category 12 industries were included. This was mixed sector of public and private enterprises. The government policy was to increase the participation of public sector units, but private participation was not denied. Many important industries were placed under this category.
Third category Schedule-C	Industries not included in Scheduled 'A' and Schedule 'B' were placed in the third category and responsibility for the development of these was left for the private sector.	

New Industrial Policy, 1991

Announced Date : On July 24, 1991

Presented By : PV Narsimha Rao

Objective :

- The main objective of this policy is to unshackle the Indian industrial economy from administrative and legal control. It main aim is to raise industrial efficiency to the international level through substantial deregulation of this industrial sector of the country.
- To maintain a sustained growth in productivity.
- To enhance gainful employment.
- To achieve optimum utilisation of human resources.
- To attain international competiveness.
- To transform India into a major player in the global arena.

Policy measures :

- Liberalisation of Industrial Licensing Policy.
- Liberalisation of Locational Policy.
- At present, only 2 sectors reserved for public sector, i.e. atomic energy, atomic minerals, etc.
- Liberalised policy for FDI. It means up to 51% foreign equity in high priority industries requiring large investments and advanced technology was permitted.
- Abolition of the MRTP limit.
- FERA was replaced by highly liberal FEMA.
- Set-up Foreign Investment Promotion Board (FIPB). It was established to expeditiously clear foreign investment proposals. It serves as a single window clearing agency for the FDI proposals.

The Industrial Policy, 1991 is related to period of Economical Reforms in India. Economical Reforms are known as LPG Policy.

Liberalization : Literally, 'Liberalisation' means removal of barrens and restrictions to promote free trades in the area of social, political and economic domain.

Privatization : Privatisation is a process to transfer ownership and control of public sector units to private individual entities.

Globalization : It is a platform for integration of social, cultural and technological development across the globe.

Monopolies & Restrictive Trade Practices Act, 1969 (MRTP):

The Industries (Development & Regulation) Act, 1951, empowered the government to issue licenses for the setting up of new industries, expansion of existing ones and for diversification of products. The main aims of the Industrial Licensing Policy were the development and control of industrial investment and production as per national priorities, checking the concentration of industries and ensuring balance regional development. However, from time-to-time, many deficiencies in the licensing system came to light. The government set-up several committees for the study of the licensing system and giving suggestions for its improvement.

On the basis of the Subimal Dutt Committee (1967) recommendations, the enacted gov. the MRTP Act 1969.

Main features of the MRTP Act 1969 given below:

- The MRTP Act was enacted in 1969 and The MRTP Commission was constituted in 1970, to prevent the concentration of economic power and to prohibit restrictive or unfair trade practices.
- Under the Act, Companies having assets beyond the threshold limit (i.e. 20 crore rupees in 1985) were placed under the purview of the act.
- Certain restrictions are imposed on such companies, like prior approval of the MRTP, Commission for establishment of new undertakings, expansion of undertakings, mergers and acquisitions.

The Micro, Small and Medium Enterprises (MSMEs)

- The small-scale industries have a prominence place in the Indian economy. It has played significant role in the growth of GDP, employment generation and imports.
- Presently, this sector not only includes small-scale industries, but also small services and business enterprises.

Enterprises	Manufacturing sector (Investment in plant and Machineries)	Services Sector (Investment in Equipments)
Micro Enterprises	Does not exceed Rs. 25 lakh	Does not exceed Rs. 10 lakh
Small Enterprises	More than Rs. 25 lakh, but does not exceed	More than Rs. 10 lakh, but does not exceed Rs. 2 crore.
Medium Enterprises	More than Rs. 5 crore, but does not exceed Rs. 10 crore	More than Rs. 2 crore, but does not exceed Rs. 5 crore

Cottage and village industries

Cottage industries: This focuses on hand-made production and is run by family members on full or part time basis. It has negligible capital investment.

Village industries: It is established in rural areas, having population below 10,000. Here, the capital investment per worker is less than 15,000.

Difference between Cottage and Small-scale Industries

- Cottage industries are mostly in rural areas, while small industries are mostly in urban areas.
- Cottage industries are run by family members, while small industries have hired labourers.
- Cottage industries have very little capital investment, while small industries can have upto Rs. 5 crore invested.
- Cottage industries produce mostly traditional goods, while small industries produce many modern goods also.
- Collage industries are located in the homes of workers, while small industries are not located in home.

Problems of Small-scale Industries

This sector faces a number of problems and a large number of units turn sick and closed down every year. Some of the problems are as under:

- The problem in getting credit is the main obstacle in the development of this sector. For very small units, this problem is even more severe;
- These units face a number of infrastructural constraints. Power constraint is the most severe.
- Small units using imported raw material, often face inverted tariff structure which means that tariff is higher on imported raw material as compared to finished goods.
- Units procuring local raw material face exploitation by traders as they get the raw material on the condition that finished goods will be sold to these traders only. In the process, they are subjected to double exploitation. This is due to the problem of adequate working capital.
- Many units face the problem of obsolescence as they are still using old machines and losing in competition because of technological backwardness;
- These units also face problem of marketing. Without the brand name, they often fail to get fair price for their produce;
- After globalisation, many units are facing the heat of global competition and in some cases, it has forced the units to close down.

Government Policy

Role of small-scale sector in the Indian economy was recognized and appreciated from the very beginning. Even before the announcement of first Industrial Policy in 1948, the Cottage Industries Board was set up in 1947. Later on, during the first five year plan, a number of boards were set-up to plan and support the development of small-scale sector.

Some important institutions are as under:

- All Indian Handloom Board (1952);
- All Indian Handicraft Board (1952);
- All Indian Khadi and Village Industries Board (1953);
- Small Industries Board (1954);
- Khadi and Village Industries Commission (Second five year plan);
- Small Industries Development Organization (SIDO) (1954);
- National Small Industries Corporation (NSIC) (1955);
- District Industries Centers (1979);
- Council for Advancement of Rural Technology (CART) (1982)

Other than these institutions, allocation for small-scale sector was increased. It was just 42 Crore rupes considerable in every plan and in the eleventh five year plan it was 10,168 crore rupees.

To protect small-scale units from competition from large units, the government announced the policy of reservation of items in 1967. The list was expanded during the plans and by 1984, 873 items were reserved for small-scale units.

For financial assistance to this sector, Small Industries Development Bank of India (SIDBI) was set-up in 1990, which is the apex financial institution in the small-scale sector.

Small-scale sector was included in the priority sector to facilitate institutional lending;

Other measures, like price and purchase preference to products manufactured in small-scale units and excise concessions on the basis of specified turnover, etc.

New Small Enterprises Policy 1991

Investment limit for tiny units was raised from 2 lakh rupees to 5 lakh rupees and further to Rs 25 lakh on the recommendation of the Abid Hussain Committee Report. On the recommendations of the same committee, investment limit for small industries, ancillary units and export oriented units increased to 1 crore rupees.

- Small units in services sector were included in the small-scale sector;
- Other units were allowed to investment up to 24 percent in the equity of small units.
- A new legal form of organisation was announced which was named 'Limited Liability Partnership'.

Maharatna, Navratna and Miniratna

In order to provide more managerial and financial autonomy to the public sector management, the government announced the policy of MoU. The policy provided for autonomy to selected PSEs. Classified Navratna and Miniratna. Recently, one more class has been added and named of Maharatna. The status is granted on the basis of various parameters and level of autonomy depends on the status individual enterprises.

Maharatna

Status : In 2009, the government announced the Maharatna status.

Eligibility : The 6 point criteria for eligibility as Mahartna are:

- Having Navratna status
- Listed on India Stock Exchange with minimum prescribed public shareholding under SEBI regulations.
- An average annual turnover of more than Rs. 25,000 crore during the last 3 year.
- An average annual net worth more than Rs. 15,000 crore.
- An average annual net profit after tax more than Rs. 5,000 crore during the last 3 years.
- Should have significant global presence/international operations.

Investment freedom : Maharatna companies could invest up to Rs. 5,000 crore without government approvals.

List of Maharatna

Name of the Company	Established Year	Head Office
1. Bharat Heavy Electricals Limited (BHEL)	1964	New Delhi
2. Gas Authority of India Limited (GAIL)	1984	New Delhi
3. National Thermal Power Corporation (NTPC)	1975	New Delhi
4. Steel Authority of India Limited (SAIL)	1954	New Delhi
5. Oil and Natural Gas Corporation Limited (ONGC)	1956	Dehradun (Uttarakhand)
6. Indian Oil Corporation (IOC)	1959	New Delhi
7. Coal India Limited (CIL)	1975	Kolkata (West Bengal)
8. Bharat Petroleum Corporation Limited (BPCL) (Sep 2017)	1977	Mumbai (Maharashtra)

Navratna

Status: This title was given originally to 9 PSEs identified by the Government of India in 1997.

Eligibility : Having Miniratna category I status

Investment freedom : Navratna companies could invest up Rs. 1000 crore without government approvals.

List of Navratna :

1. Bharat Electronics Limited (1954, Bengalore, Karnataka)
2. Container Corporation of India Limited (1988, New Delhi)
3. Engineers India Limited (1965, New Delhi)
4. Hindustan Aeronautics Limited (1940, Bengaluru, Karnataka)
5. Hindustan Petroleum Corporation Limited (1974, Mumbai)
6. Mahanagar Telephone Nigam Limited (1986, New Delhi)
7. National Aluminium Company Limited (1981, Bhubaneswar, Odisha)
8. National Buildings Construction Corporation Limited (1960, Delhi)
9. NMDC Limited (1958, Hyderabad)
10. Neyveli Lignite Corporation Limited (1956, Neyveli, Tamil Nadu)
11. Oil India Limited (1959, Duliajan Assam)
12. Power Finance Corporation Limited (1986, New Delhi)
13. Power Grid Corporation of India Limited (1989, Gurgaon, Haryana)
14. Rashtriya Ispat Nigam Limited (1982, Visakhapatnam)
15. Rural Electrification Corporation Limited (1969, New Delhi)
16. Shipping Corporation of India Limited (1961, Mumbai)

Miniratna

The Government has also accorded the status of Miniratna to some profit-making PSEs. There are two types of Miniratnas.

Category I Miniratna

- There are companies, which have made a profit in each of last 3 years and earned a profit of Rs.30 crore in at least one of the 3 years.
- They are allowed to incur capital expenditure without government approval of upto Rs.500 crore or equal to their net worth, whichever is lower.

  Note : There are 60 Miniratna of this category at present (April 2018).

Category II Miniratna

- There are companies, which have made profits for the last 3 years continuously and have a positive net worth.
- They can incur capital expenditure up to Rs. 300 crores or 50% of their net worth, whichever is lower.

Note : There are 15 Miniratna of this category at present (April 2018).

Industrial Sickness

Industrial sickness is one of the major problems of the Indian industrial sector. Industrial sickness creates problem of wasting financial resources, puts a burden on banks and also enhances the public expenditure.

In 1985, the Tiwari Committee was appointed to probe into the problems of industrial sickness. On the basis of recommendations given by the committee, the government introduced Sick Industrial Companies Act. (SICA) and later on in January 1987, a statutory institution named the Board for Industrial and Financial Reconstruction (BIFR) was set-up. Primary of industrial sickness is vested in the Board for Industrial and Financial Reconstruction (BIFR).

During the phase of liberalisation in 1991, it was felt essential to take some preventive steps to check growing industrial sickness in the country. In April 1993, a committee on industrial sickness and corporate restructuring was constituted and Dr. Omkar Goswami of the Indian Statistical Institute was appointed the chairman of this committee. The committee submitted its report to the Ministry of Finance on July 13,1993.

The committee suggested a new definition of industrial sickness and also gave recommendations to modify SICA and the role of BIFR.

Industrial Finance

Indian Industries need 3 types of finances:-

Types	Objective of finance
Long-term	Long-term finance are required to purchase permanent assets like land, building, machinery, etc. industrial units also need long-term finance for their extension and re-establishment.
Medium-term	Medium-term finance is generally a part of long-term finance.
Short-term	Industrial unit has to arrange raw material, intermediate goods and to meet out daily expenses short-term finance is required for all these purposes.

Source of Industrial Finance:

Sources of industrial finance are divided into 2 types:

(i) Internal Sources

Internal sources include shares, debentures and reinvestment of profit.

The major industrial finance institutions are:

(ii) External Sources

External sources are public despoits, loan from commercial banks and institutional finance.

All India Development Finance Institutions:

Example:

- Industrial Finance Corporation of India (IFCI)
- Industrial Development Bank of India (IDBI)
- Small Industrial Development Bank of India (SIDBI)
- Indian Credit and Investment Corporation of India Limited (ICICI)

Specialized Financial Institutions:

- Export-Import Bank (EXIM Bank)
- Tourism Finance Corporation of India (TFCI)
- Infrastructure Development Finance Company Limited (IDFC), etc.

Investment Institutions:

- Life Insurance Corporation of India (LIC)
- Unit Trust of India (UTI)
- General Insurance Corporation of India (GIC)

Refinance Institutions

- National Housing Bank (NHB)
- National Bank for Agricultural and Rural Development (NABARD)

State-level Institutions

- State Finance Corporation (SFCs)
- State Industrial Development Corporation (SIDC)

Competition Act, 2002

In the present era of LPG (Liberalisation, Privatisation and Globalisation), it was felt that the existing Monopolies and Restrictive Trade Practices Act, 1969 has become hurdle in certain respects and there is a need to shift our focus from curbing monopolies to promoting competition. Hence a new law, the Competition Act has been enacted and published in gazette of India on January 14, 2003 for brining competition in the Indian market. The main objectives of the Act are to establish a commission to prevent practices having adverse effect on competition, to promote the sustain competition in markets in India, to protect the interests of consumer and to ensure freedom of trade carried on by participants in market in India and for related matters.

The Act mainly covers the following aspects:

(i) Prohibition of anti competitive agreements;

(ii) Prohibition of abuse of dominance;

(iii) Regulation of combination (acquisitions, merger and amalgamations of certain size);

(iv) Establishment of Competition Commission of India (CCI).

(v) Functions and power of the CCI.

Competition (Amendment) Act, 2007

On September 10, 2007 the Parliament finally passed the long-pending Competition (Amendment) Bill, 2007 that empowers the Competition Commission of India (CCI) to act as the competition regulator and to deal with a host of contemporary economic issues including monopolies and take-over's of corporate firms.

According to the Bill's provision, the CCI replaced Monopolies and Restrictive Trade Practice Commission (MRTPC). The CCI was established in 2003. Under new provisions, the MRTPC continued for two years after the Constitution of CCI for dealing with pending cases but after two years MRTPC was dissolved.

However, MRTPC could not entertain any new cases after the CCI wad constituted. Cases pending with MRTPC after two years of setting up of CCI were transferred to the latter.

Structure of PSEs in India

The PSEs in India are basically categorized under four broad types based on their ownership structure. These include:

(i) Departmental undertakings

(ii) Statutory Corporations

(iii) Government-owned companies

(iv) Autonomous bodies set up as registered societies

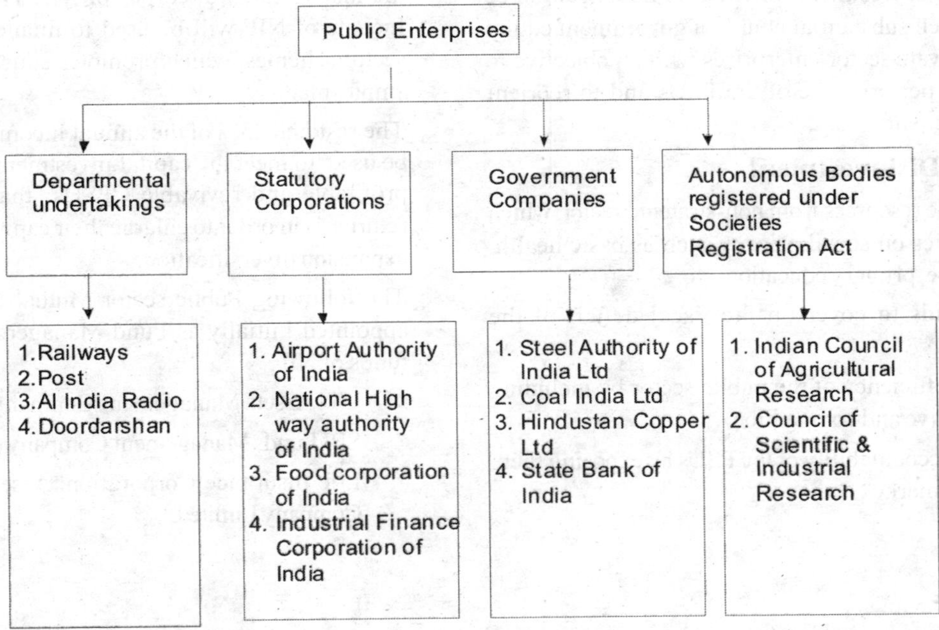

(i) Departmental undertakings : Departmental undertakings are primarily meant to provide essential services such as railways. They function under the control of the respective ministries of Government of India (GOI). A departmental undertakings structure is considered suitable for activities the government aims to keep in its control in view of the public interest.

(ii) Statutory corporations : Statutory corporation are public enterprises that came into existence by a Special, Act of the Parliament. The Act defines the powers and functions, rules and regulations governing the employees and the relationship of the corporation with government departments.

(iii) Government-owned companies : Government-owned or controlled companies refer to companies in which 51% or more of the paid up capital is held by the Central or any state Government (partly or wholly by both). It is registered under the Indian Companies Act and is fully governed by the provisions of this Act.

(iv) Autonomous bodies : Autonomous bodies are set-up whenever it is felt that certain functions need to be discharged outside the governmental set-up with some amount of independence and flexibility without day-to-day interference from the governmental machinery. These bodies are set-up by the concerned ministries or their departments and are funded through grants-in-aid either fully or partially, depending on the extent which such institutes generate internal resources of their own. These grants are regulated by the Ministry of Finance (MOF) through their instructions. They are mostly registered as societies under the 'Societies Registration Act' and in certain cases they have been set up as statutory institutions under the provisions contained in various Acts.

Disinvestment

- The New Industrial Policy, 1991, envisaged disinvestment of a part of government shareholdings in selected PSUs as an important element of public sector reforms. In pursuit of hits, the process of disinvestment began in 1991-92, with the sale of minority stakes in some PSUs.
- The primary of disinvestment in this phase was to raise non-inflationary finance to plug budgetary deficit. But, the focus of disinvestment shifted to strategic sale since 1999, in which substantial chunk of government equity is sold to private sector enterprises with an objective to improve the performance of the PSUs and to reorient public investment.

Objectives of Disinvestment

- To transfer the resources from non-strategic sector, which is much higher on social priority such as basic health, family welfare, primary education, etc.
- To raise funds to cover up the fiscal deficit of the government.
- To improve efficiency of the public sector by including private imitative and competition.
- To enhance accountability of the PSUs by exposing them to the capital market.
- To reduce political interference by imparting market orientation to the enterprise.
- Bring down government equity in all non-strategic PSU to 26% or lower.
- Restructure and revive potentially viable PSUs.
- Close down PSUs, which cannot be revived.
- Fully protect the interest of workers.

National Investment Fund

- In pursuance of the policy laid down in NCMP, the Central government set-up the National Investment Fund in November 2005. The proceeds from disinvestment of CPSUs will be channelised into NIF, which is to be maintained outside the Consolidated Fund of India.
- NIF will be professionally managed to provide sustainable returns to the government, without depleting the corpus. Selected public sector mutual fund will be entrusted with the management of corpus of NIF. 75% of the Annual Income of NIF will be used to finance selected social sector schemes, which promotes education, health and employment.
- The residual 25% of the annual income of the fund will be used to meet the capital investment requirements of profitable and revivable CPSUs that yield adequate returns or in order to enlarge their capital base to finance expansion diversification.
- The following Public sector Mutual Funds have been appointed initially as Fund Managers to manage the funds of NIF.
  * UTI Assets Management Company Limited.
  * SBI Funds Management Company (Private) Limited.
  * Life Insurance Corporation, Asset Managementss Company Limited.

Chapter 6

Agriculture

General Introduction

- Agriculture is an important sector of the economy. It is the source of supply of basic wage goods, that is, food items to the industry as well as to the people on the whole.
- It provides raw materials to various industries and other agro-based industries.
- It is also a great source of foreign exchange for the economy, specially for under-developed or poor countries where industry is not properly developed and is at an infancy. Further, it also provides market for industrial products.
- Therefore, agricultural progress is normally regarded as a pre-requisite for economic development.
- It is true that economic development in modern times has come to be associated with industrialisation; nevertheless it is generally accepted that industrialisation can follow only on the sound heels of agriculture.
- Agriculture sector in India employs about 50 (Economic Survey 2017-18) per cent of the work force, contributes 18 (Economic Survey 2017-18) per cent of the GDP and accounts for about 12 per cent share of the value of the country's exports. Comparison between the position of agriculture in India vis-a-vis other countries with respect to the share of agriculture in national income can be made.
- In the United Kingdom, agriculture contributes only two per cent of national income; in USA it is three per cent; in Canada it is four per cent; while in Australia, it is five per cent.
- The more developed a country is, smaller is the share of agriculture in the national output. India, having not yet reached the stage of an advanced economy, has an agriculture sector that is the most dominant sector of its economy.

Features of Indian Agriculture

- Indian agriculture is characterised by feudal relations of production, inadequate credit facilities, outdated farming techniques, heavy dependence on uncertain monsoons, predominance of small farmers, inequalities of land distributions, low levels of productivity and seasonal and disguised unemployment.
- All these factors add up to an agriculture sector, which has not been able to realise its full potential.
- Factors responsible for backwardness of Indian agriculture are given below:

1. General Factors

(i) Over-crowding in agriculture.

(ii) Poor finance and marketing facilities.

(iii) Socially and economically backward rural environment.

2. Institutional Factors

(i) Small and scattered land holdings due to subdivisions and fragmentation.

(ii) Defective tenurial system, which forces the tiller to pay heavy rent and provides very little security of tenancy.

3. Technological Factors

(i) Poor techniques of production.

(ii) Inadequate availability of inputs.

(iii) Poor quality of available inputs.

(iv) Regional disparities in quality and extent of irrigation facilities.

- **Analysis of Agriculture Production in India:** 4th Advance Estimates of production of major crops for 2017-18 have been released by the Department of Agriculture, Cooperation and Former's Welfare on 28th August, 2018.
- As a result of near normal rainfall during monsoon 2017 and various policy initiatives taken by the government, the country has witnessed record Foodgrain, Rice, Wheat, Sugarcane, Pulses production in 2017-18.

Major Crops	Production (in million tonnes)	Production (in million tonnes) 4th AE 2017-18	Analysis
(A) Food Grains	275.11	284.83	Production of food grains has increased by 9.72 million tonnes than the production of 275.11 million tonnes during 2016-17
(i) Rice	109.70	112.92	Production of Rice has increased by 3.22 million tonnes than the production of 109.70 million tonnes during 2016-17
(ii) Wheat	98.51	99.70	Production of wheat has increased by 1.19 million tonnes than the prodcution of 98.51 million tonnes during 2016-17.
(B) Nutri/Coarse Cereals	43.77	46.99	Production of Nutri cereals has increased by 3.22 million tonnes than the production of 43.77 million tonnes during 2016-17.
(i) Maize	25.90	28.72	Production of Maize has increased by 2.32 million tonnes than the production by 25.90 million tonnes during 2016-17.
(C) Pulses	23.13	25.23	Production of Pulses has increased by 2.10 million tonnes than the production by 23.13 million tonnes during 2016-17.
(D) Oilseed	31.28	31.31	Production of Oilseed has increased by 0.03 million tonnes the production by 31.28 million tonnes during 2016-17.
(i) Groundnut	7.46	9.18	Production of Groundnut has increased by 1.72 million tonnes than the production by 7.46 million tonnes during 2016-17.
(ii) Rapeseeds and Mustard	7.92	8.32	Production of Rapeseeds and Mustard has increased by 0.40 million tonnes than the production by 7.92 million tonnes during 2016-17.
(E) Sugarcane	306.07	376.91	Production of Sugarcane has increased by 70.84 million tonnes than the production by 306.07 million tonnes during 2016-17.
(F) Cotton	32.58	34.89	Production of Cotton has increased by 2.31 million tonnes than the production by 32.88 million tonnes during 2016-17.

Horticulture:

- The diversity of physiographic climate and soil characteristics enables India to grow a large variety of horticultural crops - fruits, vegetables, flowers, spices, cashew nut, coconut, cocoa, areca nut, root and tuber crops, medicinal and aromatic plants, etc. India is the largest producer of fruits in the world and the second largest producer of vegetables.
- India enjoys the unique distinction of being the single largest producer, consumer and exporter of spices in the world. India is also the leading producer and exporter of cashew in the world.
- Horticulture produce such as fruits, vegetables and flowers are highly perishable and suffer heavy damage or deterioration in quality during post harvest handling.
- According to the Planning Commission estimate, post harvest handling accounts for 37 per cent of the losses at different stages of storage, grading, packaging, etc.
- The National Horticulture Board is the nodal agency for establishing the post-harvest infrastructure, an essential aspect of which should be the creation of frozen storage capacity and, frozen transportation of perishable fruits and vegetables. Special efforts at creating new storage capacity through concessional finance are being pursued actively.
- The Department of Agriculture, Cooperation and Farmers Welfare has released the 2017-18 (3rd Advance Estimates) of area and production of horticulture crops. These estimates are based on the information received from different State/ UTs in the country.
- The total horticulture production of the country is estimated to be 306.8 million tonnes during 2017-18, which is 2.05% higher than the previous year and 8.5% higher than the past 5 year's average production.
- The total horticulture crops area of the country is estimated to be 25.7 million hectares during 2017-18 which is 3..26% higher than the previous year area.

- Indian economy is among the largest agriculture–based economies in the world.
- Agriculture in our country provides livelihood to about 60% of the population.
- According to census 2011, agriculture sector provides employment to 58.2% of the country's work force and is the single largest private sector occupation.
- The share of agriculture and allied sector in the gross domestic product has registered a steady decline from 36.4% in 1982–83 to 17% in 2017–18.
- Food grains Production (Million Tonnes)

2014-15	252.0
2015-16	251.6
2016-17	275.7
2017-18	284.83

(4th Advance Estimates 2017-18)

Source by: Economic survey 2017–18.

- During the 11th Five Year Plan, an average annual growth of 3.6% in the GDP came from agricultural and allied sector against a target of 4.0%.
- The 12th Five Year Plan targets an average annual growth of 4% in agriculture.
- The main food crop of India is rice.
- Every year in India from 1 July to 30 June, agriculture year is celebrated.

Land Reforms in India

- Productivity in agriculture is mainly dependent upon two sets of factors- Technological and Institutional.
- Among the technological factors are the use of agriculture inputs and methods such as improved seeds, fertilisers, improved ploughs, tractors, harvesters, irrigation, etc, that help in raising productivity, even if no land reforms are introduced.
- The institutional reforms include the re-distribution of land ownership in favour of the cultivating classes so as to provide them a sense of participation in rural life, improve the size of farms, provide security of tenure, regulation of rents, etc.
- In other words, the institutional factors such as the existence of feudal relations, small size of farms, subdivision and fragmentation, insecurity of tenancy rights, high rents, etc, act as disincentives to the peasantry to raise production.
- They weaken the capacity of the farmers to save and invest in agriculture, as also to enjoy the fruits of their labour.
- In a broad sense, land reforms refer to all kinds of policy-induced changes relating to ownership, tenancy and management of land.
- These may encompass the whole agrarian structure within which a farmer operates.
- Although the primary objective of land reforms may be to bring about a system of land ownership which is socially just and economically efficient, that is, a system in which land belongs to the tiller, these may include other measures also, that have a bearing on the conditions in which the tenants work or the size of holdings, etc.

Land Reform

- During British period there were three land systems, which are as follows:

Land System	Started in	Governor	Work
Zamindari system	**1793**	Lord Corn wallis	The owners of land zamindars used to collect revenue from farmers and hand it over to the state.
Mahalwari system	**1833**	Lord William	This system consisted of landlords or zamindars claiming to represent entire villages or even groups of villages. Along with the village communities, the landlords were jointly responsible for the payment of revenues.
Ryotwari system	**1892**	Thomas Munro	The owner of the land, the state directly collected revenues from the Rayats.

- Land reforms in India had three objectives similar to the other economies, which opted for it in the past:
  (i) Removing institutional discrepancies.
  (ii) Removing socio-economic inequality.
  (iii) Increasing agricultural production.
- To realise the objectives of the land reform, the government took three main steps, which had many internal sub-steps:
  1. **Abolition of Intermediaries:** Under this step, the age-old exploitative land tenure systems of the Zamindari, Mahalwari and Ryotwari were fully abolished.
  2. **Tenancy Reform:** Under this broader step, three inter-related reforms protecting the land tenants were effected;
     (i) Regulation of rent so, that a fixed and rational rate of rent could be paid by the share-croppers to the land owners.

(ii) Security of tenure, so that a share-cropper could be feet secure about his future income and his economic security.

(iii) Ownership rights to tenants than that of the landless masses.

3. **Reorganisation of Agriculture:** This step again has many inter-related and highly logical provisions in the direction of rational reforms.

(i) Redistribution of land among the landless poor masses after promulgating timely ceiling laws – the move failed with a few exception such as West Bengal, Kerala and partially in Andhra Pradesh.

(ii) Consolidation of land could only succeed in the regions of the Green Revolution (Haryana, Punjab and Western Uttar Pradesh) and remained marred with many loopholes and corruption.

(iii) Cooperative farming, which has a high socio–economic moral base, was only used by the big farmers to save their land from the draconian ceiling laws.

Classification of Major Crops in India:

1. **Crop: Kharif**

Month: This crop is sown in the months of July and harvested in October every year.

Major crops: Rice (Paddy), jowar, bajra, maize, cotton, sugarcane, sesamum, soyabean, groundnut.

2. **Crop: Rabi**

Month: This crop is sown in October last and is harvested in March/April every year.

Major crops: Wheat, Barley, Gram, Rapeseed, Mustard.

3. **Crop: Zaid**

Month: In some parts of the country, known as Zaid, crop is grown during March to June every year.

Major crops: Muskmelon, watermelon, vegetables, cucumber, moong, urad, etc.

- The Indian crops can be divided into two major groups.

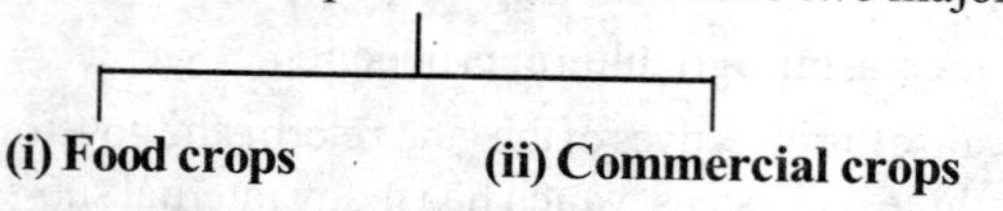

(i) **Food crops:** Food crops are those crops which are produced for daily consumption purpose, like– rice, wheat, gram, jowar, bajra.

(ii) **Commercial crops:** Commercial crops are those crops that are produced for trade purpose and earning money and not for self-consumption by the farmers. These commercial crops include:

1. **Oilseed crops:** Groundnut, mustard, sesamum, rapeseed, linseed, castor, sunflower, nigerseed and soyabean.
2. **Sugar crops:** Sugarcane and beat.
3. **Fiber crops:** Jute, mesta, sunhemp and cotton
4. **Narcotic crops:** Tobacco
5. **Beverage crops:** Tea, coffee

Green Revolution in India

- The entire concept of the green revolution is based on use of HYVs or High yield variety seeds, chemical fertilisers and irrigation facilities. It led to sharp rise in agriculture production during 60s. And as a result, India become self-sufficient in food grains.

Drawbacks of the Green Revolution:

- Limited benefit was received in few crops as wheat but for other crops, it remained ineffective.
- Only a few states like Punjab, Haryana and Western UP experienced success.
- Degradation of soil fertility due to excessive use of chemical fertilisers.
- Brought personal inequality and created regional disparity.

Second Green Revolution:

- In agriculture sector 4% of growth rate is needed. These reforms must focus on efficient use of resources, conservation of soil, water and ecology. Following this, a strategy web incorporated in the fifth five year plan which laid foundation for the second Green Revolution.

(a) Doubling the rate of growth of the irrigated area.

(b) Improving water management, rain water harvesting and watershed development.

(c) Reclaiming degraded land and focussing on soil quality.

(d) Bridging the knowledge gap through effective extension.

(e) Diversifying into high value outputs, fruits, vegetables, flowers, herbs and species, medicinal plants, bamboo, bio-diesel, but with adequate measures to ensure food security.

(f) Promoting animal husbandry and fishery.

(g) Providing easy access to credit at affordable rates.

(h) Improving the incentive structure and functioning of markets.

(i) Refocusing on land reforms issues.

- National Commission on Farmers has already laid the foundation for such framework.
- Programme formulation as well as their implementation in the states must be based on unique regional contexts incorporating agro-climatic conditions and availability of appropriate research and development (R&D), backed by timely and adequate extension and finance.

Call for Evergreen Revolution

- The concept of Evergreen Revolution was pioneered by Dr. M.S. Swaminathan in India. He highlighted to double the production level of food grains form 210 million tones to 420 million tones, and for making it a success, he emphasised an adopting best scientific techniques and promoting organised farming.
  - (i) Promoting soil health
  - (ii) Promoting lab to land exhibitions
  - (iii) Making rainwater harvesting compulsory
  - (iv) Providing credit to farmers on suitable conditions

Revolution in Indian Economy

Revolution		Area
Green Revolution	:	Agricultural development
Yellow revolution	:	Increasing oilseed production
White revolution	:	Milk production and dairy development
Blue revolution	:	Fishing production
Pink revolution	:	Prawn production
Brown revolution	:	Increased spices production and its export
Red revolution	:	Meat/tomato production
Golden revolution	:	Fruits production
Grey revolution	:	Increased fertilisers
Silver revolution	:	For the production of egg
Communication revolution	:	Development of communication technology and commu- nication services
Black revolution	:	Ethanol and biodiesel
Rainbow revolution	:	Refers to agriculture revolution in all relevant fields

Note: *To increase white revolution, "Operation Flood" was started.*

New National Agricultural Policy

- The Union government had announced new National Agricultural Policy in the Parliament on July 28, 2000. This policy had been planned under the provisions of the World Trade Organisation, so as to face the challenges of agriculture sector. This policy lays emphasis on promoting agricultural exports after fulfilling domestic demands.
- **The salient features of this policy are :**
  - ➤ 4% growth rate per annum for the next two decades.
  - ➤ Land reforms to provide land to poor farmers.
  - ➤ Consolidation of holding in all states of the nation.
  - ➤ Promoting private investments in agriculture.
  - ➤ To provide insurance umbrella for crops to farmers.
  - ➤ To promote biotechnology.
  - ➤ To promote research for developing new varieties and ensuring protection to the developed varieties.
- New Agriculture Policy has been described as "Rainbow Revolution", which includes the followings revolutions:
  - ➤ Green (food grain production)
  - ➤ White (milk)
  - ➤ Yellow (oil seeds)
  - ➤ Blue (fisheries)
  - ➤ Red (meat/tomato)
  - ➤ Golden (fruits–apple)
  - ➤ Grey (fertilizer)
  - ➤ Black/brown (non-conventional energy sources)
  - ➤ Silver (eggs)
  - ➤ Round (potato)
- The above Rainbow Revolution also includes "food chain revolution" to put a check on destroying food grains, vegetables and fruits.
- **Largest Crops Producing States of India**

Crops/Groups of Crops		States
I. Food grains		
Rice	:	West Bengal, Uttar Pradesh, Andhra Pradesh
Wheat	:	Uttar Pradesh, Punjab, Haryana
Maize	:	Karnataka, Andhra Pradesh, Maharashtra
Total coarse cereals	:	Rajasthan, Karnataka, Maharashtra
Total pulses	:	Madhya Pradesh, Uttar Pradesh, Rajasthan
Total food grains	:	Uttar Pradesh, Punjab, Madhya Pradesh
II. Oilseeds		
Groundnut	:	Gujarat, Tamil Nadu, Andhra Pradesh
Rapeseed & Mustard	:	Rajasthan, Madhya Pradesh, Haryana
Soyabean	:	Madhya Pradesh, Maharashtra, Rajasthan
Sunflower	:	Karnataka, Andhra Pradesh, Maharashtra
Total Oilseeds	:	Madhya Pradesh, Rajasthan, Gujarat
III. Other Cash Crops		
Sugarcane	:	Uttar Pradesh, Maharashtra, Tamil Nadu
Cotton	:	Gujarat, Maharashtra, Andhra Pradesh
Jute and mesta	:	West Bengal, Bihar, Assam
Potato	:	West Bengal, Uttar Pradesh, Bihar
Onion	:	Maharashtra, Karnataka, Gujarat

• **Important Agricultural Committees, Fund and Organisation**

	Committee/Fund/ Organisation	Year of Establishment	Purpose
1.	NABARD		12 July, 1982 for agriculture and rural branch
2.	National Forest Committee	7 Feb, 2003	–
3.	Indian Council of Agricultural Research	16 July, 1929	Major organisation of agricultural research
4.	National Farmer Commission	18 Nov, 2004	–
5.	Commission for Agricultural Costs and Prices (CACP)	1985	Earlier named as Agricultural Prices Commission (1965), which changed in 1985 and was named as (ACP).
6.	Price Stabilisation Fund	Feb, 2003	This fund is to control the prices of tea, coffee, rubber and tobacco.
7.	TRIFER (Tribal Cooperative Marketing Development Federation of India Ltd.)	August, 1987	This was formed with an objective to benefit tribal people by providing a better cost of their hand-made products and to prevent their products from being exploited by private traders.
8.	NAFED (National Agricultural Co-operative Marketing Federation of India Ltd.)	2 Oct, 1985	It is an open organisation which was set-up to promote cooperative marketing of agricultural produce to benefit the farmers.

Major Schemes of Agriculture

1. **National Agriculture Insurance Schemes (NAIS) :** It is a central sector crop insurance scheme launched in 1999-2000. It aims to provide financial support to farmers in the event of crop failure.
2. **Modified NAIS :** Some major improvements made under it:
   (a) Unit area of insurance reduced to village panchayat level for major crops
   (b) Indemnity for prevented / sowing risk and for post harvest losses
   (c) On accounts payments upto 25%
   (d) Only up front premium subsidy by gout
   (e) Claims are the liability of the insurance Companies
3. **Mega Food Parks :** Mega Food Park scheme was launched in 2008, in order to create excellent infrastructure. Currently, 13 Mega Food Parks are under implemention. The 12th FYP targeted to set up 50 MFPs during the plan period.

   National Mission on Food Processing (NMFP):

   • NMFP has been launched under the 12th Plan for a decentralised implementation of various schemes under the Ministry of Food Processing with the help of state governments.

   • It consists of the following main schemes- technology upgradation of food processing industries, cold chain facilities for non–horticultural produces, modernisation of abattoirs, primary processing center/collection center in rural areas, upgradation of quality of street food, etc.
4. **National Food Processing Development Council (NFPDC) :** NFPDC has been set–up to provide guidance to all schemes comprising the Agriculture Minister as, Chairman, representatives of state government, industry associations and related government officials.

National Food Security Mission, 2007

• The mission was launched to increase production through area expansion and productivity. It also aimed to create employment opportunities to enhance the farmer's income and reinstate the confidence of famers.

• Later, two additional programmes regarding to pulse production were adopted under NFSM in 2011.

1. Integrated scheme concerning oilseeds, pulses, oil, palm, and maize was merged with NFSM, Jharkhand and Assam were included under the program also with other states.
2. Accelerated Pulse Production Program was initiated to boost production of pulses. After all, NFSM had been a success, as it had already achieved the targeted food grain production.

Rashtriya Krishi Vikas Yojana (RKVY):

• The RKVY was launched in 2007-08 in order to achieve a 9% growth rate in agriculture and allied sectors. Under the 11th plan, an outlay of INR 25,000 crores was provided for incentivising states to enhance public investment.

• **The sub-scheme under RKVY are:**

➤ Bringing Green Revolution to eastern regions—Uttar Pradesh, Jharkhand, Bihar, Paschim Bangal, Assam, Odisha and Chhattisgarh. It was introduced in 2010-11.

➤ Integrated development of 60,000 pulses and oilseeds. Villages in rainfed areas introduced in 2010-11.

➤ Promotion of oil palm

➤ Initiative on village clusters

➤ Nutri-cereals

➤ National mission for protein supplements

➤ Accelerated fodder development programme

➤ Rainfed area development programme

➤ National Mission on Saffron–economic revival of Jammu and Kashmir. Saffron was introduced in 2010–11.

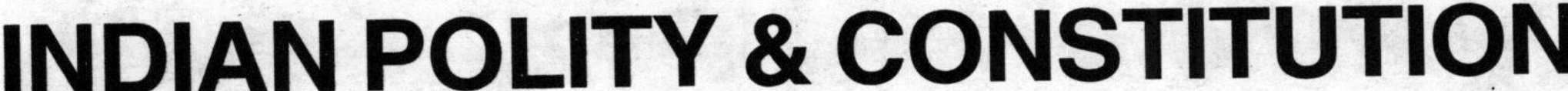

INDIAN POLITY & CONSTITUTION

1 Chapter Constitutional Developments and Drafting of The Indian Constitution

General Introduction

- Constitution is a legal document which has the basic governing principles of state.
- The Constitution provides guidance about the basic structure of the political system under which the people of the country are to be governed.
- The thought of Constitutionalism suggests ways and methods to work out a from of government with access to power, and ensures the freedom of an individual and their liberty.
- Constitutionalism denotes the way to reunite the power of the State with a person's liberty by prescribring the principles of organising the State.
- It explores the powers of the State, defines their responsibilites and regulates their relationships with each other and with the people of the country.
- The Constitution works as the "Fundamental Law" of a country and any other laws made should be in compliance with it in order to be legally endorsed.

Significance of the Constitution:

- Constitution determines the philosophy of the nation, and the kind of Government present there.
- The Constitution draws the outline for functioning of the State and it is the only document on which it must have faith.
- The Constitution provides the certain rights to the citizens of the country and it also defines their duties.
- The Constitution is a document which ensures the people of the country that they can have faith and hopes for their prosperity and better future in under the provision of it.
- The Constitution is the philosphical and organisational framework for the future. All the state of the country face challenges of changing the social, economic and political conditions in society, for this purpose, the Constitution provides the procedures of changes by means of amendments; so by this way, we can say that the Constitution is not static and can be **modified** as per the conditional changes.

There are two kinds of Constitutions:

- Written Constitution
- Unwritten Constitution

- Written Constitution is a document which involves provisions for guidance and it also presents the idea of the governance in the country. It provides the constitutional arrangements and procedures. In the Written Constitutional system, power is vested equally in the Legislative in Executive and in the Judiciary but above all, the Constitution is supreme.
- Unwritten Constitution is the document which has the provisions and procedures not codified in a legal format, for instance, the British Constitution is an Unwritten Constitution. It has Constitutional conventions that act as paradigm for the working of institutions and other documents such as the statutes and Acts. Here, the Parliament is supreme, but in the written Constitution, amendment process is not so easy. In the unwritten Constitution, every enactment passed by Parliament becomes a part of the Constitution.

India IndependenceAct. of 1947:

- By the act, the Executive Council provided by the Government of India Act, 1919 continued to advices the Governor General till 1947.
- It established India as an independent and sovereign state and responsible government at both levels (Centre and State).
- By the provision of this act, the Governor General of India and the provincial Governors became the Constitutional heads.
- The act made the provision of dual functions (one was constituent and another was the Legislative) to the Constituent Assembly, it proclaimed this dominion legislature as a sovereign body.

Institutions in India Established by British Government

- 1687 First Municipal Corporation was established in India.
- 1772 Lord Warren Hastings set-up the office of District Collector.
- 1829 Divisional Commissioner established by Lord William Bentick.
- 1859 Portfolio system introduced by Lord Canning.
- 1860 India's First Budget system was introduced.
- 1870 Lord Mayo's proposal of local self government institution in India.
- 1872 First census of India was conducted.
- 1881 Regular census started in the duration of Lord Ripan.
- 1882 Lord Ripon's proposal of local self government resolution of India.
- 1905 The tenure system came into existance by Lord Curzon.
- 1905 The Railway Board was set up.
- 1921 Public Accounts Committee was established at the Centre.
- 1921 Railway and General Budget was divided, they were separated.
- 1935 Reserve Bank of India was established by an Act of the Central Legislature.

Forming of the Constitution of India

- The Constitution of India was framed and adopted by the Constitutent Assembly which was set up in November 1946 and as per the Cabinet Mission Plan of 1946.
- In 1935, the Congress Party demanded for the Constitutent Assembly to draft the Constitution of India.
- It was accepted by the British Government in August Offer of 1940.
- The members for the Constituent Assembly were elected indirectly by the Provincial Assemblies according to the preparation of one member per one million population (except Muslims and Sikhs), the seats were allocated to mainly three communities Muslims, Sikhs and General.
- There were 389 members in the Assembly from which 296 were elected by members of Provincial Assemblies and others were nominated by Princely States.
- The Mountbatten Plan of June 3, 1947 announced the partition of the country and a separate Constituent Assembly for the proposed State of Pakistan.
- North-West Frontier Province and Sylhet decided through a referendum to remain with Pakistan.
- Therefore, the membership of the Constituent Assembly for India was reduced to 299 after partition.
- First meeting was held on 9th December 1946, Sachhidanand Sinha was the temparary President.
- The second meeting of the Constituent Assembly was held on 11th December 1946; Dr. Rajendra Prasad was the President.
- The 'Objective Resolution' was passed in the Constituent Assembly by Pt. Jawahar Lal Nehru on 13th December, 1946.
- Muslim League boycotted the first meeting of the Constituent Assembly.
- Mr. B.N. Rau was designated as Legal Advisor of the Constituent Assembly.
- Dr. B.R. Ambedkar is regarded as the 'Father of the Constitution of India.'
- The Constituent Assembly formed total 13 committees for drafting the Constitution.
- The Drafting Committee was appointed on 29 August 1947, in which Dr. B.R. Ambedkar was appointed as the Chariman.
- Its first draft was prepared in October 1947 by the Drafting Committee and submitted to the President of the Assembly on 21 February, 1948.
- The discussion on the Draft of the Constitution was held between 15 November, 1948 to 17 October, 1949. On 26 November 1949, the people of India through the Constituent Assembly adopted, enacted and gave to themselves the Constitution of India.
- The Constitution was finalised by the signature of the Constituent Assembly on 24 January 1950, which was the last day of the Assembly.
- The Consitution came into existance with effect from 26 January,1950.
- Meanwhile the Constituent Assembly acted as an 'Interim Parliament' [15 August 1947, 26 November, 1949].
- The Constitution was approved and signed in by 284 members of the Constituent Assembly.
- It was considered as the lengthiest Constitution of the world.
- The Constitution had 22 Parts, 395 Articles and 8 Schedules.
- It took 2 years, 11 months and 18 days to frame the Constitution and the expenditure cost was Rs. 6.4 crore.
- The National Flag was adopted by the Constituent Assembly on July 22, 1947 and on January 24, 1950.
- The National Anthem was adopted.
- The Constituent Assembly of India became the provisional Parliament of India from November 26, 1949.
- Only Jammu & Kashmir has its own Constitution.

- The first Parliament election was held in 1952 and first amendment to came into the Constitution in 1951.
- According to Article 394, provisions relating to the citizenship, elections, provisional Parliament and temporary and transitional provisions were contained in Articles 5, 6, 7, 8, 9, 60, 324, 366, 367, 379, 380, 388, 391, 392 and 393 that came into force on the day of adoption of the Constitution and the rest of provisions on the day of the commencement (i.e. 26 January 1950) of the Constitution.
- The Article 395 says that the Government of India Act of 1935 and the Indian Independence Act of 1947 got replaced with the commencement of the Constitution of India.
- January 26 was decided as the date of commencement of the Constitution of India because in 1930, Indians observed 'Independence day' on this date, following the resolution of 'Purna Swaraj' of the Congress session which was held in the midnight of December 31, 1929 at Lahore.

It is thus clear that **the Constituent Assembly was to be a partly-elected and partly-nominated body.**

Moreover, **the members were to be indirectly elected by the members of the provincial assemblies, who themselves were elected on a limited franchise.**

The elections to the Constituent Assembly (for 296 seats allotted to the British Indian Provinces) were held in July-August 1946. The Indian National Congress won 208 seats, the Muslim League 73 seats, and the small groups and independents got the remaining 15 seats. However, the **93 seats allotted to the Princely States were not filled as they decided to stay away from the Constituent Assembly.**

Although the Constituent Assembly was not directly elected by the people of India on the basis of adult franchise, the Assembly comprised representatives of all sections of Indian Society-Hindus, Muslims, Sikhs, Paris, Anglo-Indians, Indian Christians, SCs, STs including women of all these sections. **The Assembly included all important personalities of India at that time, with the exception of Mahatma Gandhi and M.A. Jinnah.**

Member list of the Drafting Committee Chairman : Dr. B.R. Ambedkar

Members

1. N Gopalaswami Ayyangar
2. Alladi Krishnaswami Iyer
3. KM Munshi
4. Mohammed Sadullah
5. BL Mittar (replaced by N Madhav Rao)
6. DP Khaitan (who died in 1948 and was replaced by TT Krishnamachari)

Phases of the Constituent Assembly

(i) *1st Phase:* In the first phase of Constituent Assembly was under the limitation if Cabinet Mission Plan from 6th December 1946 to 14th August 1947.

(ii) *2nd Phase:* In the second phase of Constituent Assembly was constituted with Sovereign Body+Provisional Parliament.

(iii) *3rd Phase:* As a Provisional Parliament from 27th November 1949 to March 1952.

Number of Committees of the Constituent Assembly

The Constituent Assembly appointed 22 committees to deal with different tasks of Constitution-formation. Out of these, 10 were on procedural affairs and 12 on substantive affairs. These were as follows:

Procedural Affairs Committees

1. Steering Committee (Chairman: Dr K M Munshi)
2. Rules of Procedure Committee (Chairman: Dr Rajendra Prasad)
3. House Committee
4. Hindi Translation Committee
5. Urdu Translation Committee
6. Finance and Staff Committee
7. Press Gallery Committee
8. Committee on the effect of Indian Independence Act of 1947
9. Orders of Business Committee
10. Credentials Committee

Substantive Affairs Committees

1. Drafting Committee *(Chairman:* Dr B R Ambedkar)
2. Committee for Negotiating with States (*Chairman:* Dr Rajendra Prasad)
3. Committee on Chief Commissioners' Provinces
4. Union Constitution Committee (*Chairman:* Jawaharlal Nehru)
5. Provincial Constitution Committee (*Chairman:* Sardar Patel)
6. Special Committee to Examine the Draft Constitution (*Chairman:* Sir Alladi Krishnaswamy Iyer)
7. Commission on Linguistic Provinces
8. Expert Committee on Financial Provisions
9. Ad-hoc Committee on National Flag

10. Union Powers Committee (*Chairman:* Jawaharlal Nehru)
11. Ad-hoc Committee on the Supreme Court
12. Committee on Fundamental Rights and Minorities (*Chairman:* Sardar Patel)

Borrowed Features of the Constitution:

Following are the borrowed features of Constitution from different countries:

From U.K.	• Nominal Head-President (like Queen) • Cabinet System of Ministers • Post of the Prime Minister • Parliamentary Type of Government • Bicameral Parliament • Lower House more powerful • Council of Minister responsible to Lower House • Speaker in Lok Sabha
From U.S.	• Written Constitution • Executive head of state known as the President and his being the Supreme Commander of the Armed Forces. • Vice-President as the ex-officio Chairman of the Rajya Sabha • Fundamental Rights • Supreme Colurt • Provision of States • Independence of Judiciary and Judicial Review • Preamble • Removal of Supreme Court and High Court Judges
From USSR	• Fundamental Duties • Five-year Plan
From AUSTRALIA	• Concurrent list • Language of the Preamble • Provision regarding trade, commerce and intercourse
From JAPAN	• Law on which the Supreme Court functions
From WEIMAR Constitution of GERMANY	• Suspension of Fundamental • Rights during the emergency
From CANADA	• Scheme of Federation with a strong centre • Distribution of powers between Centre and the States and placing Residuary Powers with the Centre
From IRELAND	• Concept of Directive Principles of States Policy (Ireland borrrowed it from SPAIN) • Method of election of President • Nomination of members in the Rajya Sabha by the President

Salient Features of the Indian Constitution

- The Indian Constitution is the lengthiest and most detailed of all constitutions in the world.
- Originally consisted of 395 articles divided into 22 parts and 9 schedules.
- There are 6 Fundamental Rights in the Constitution.
- India is a secular state (means state has no religion of its own)-Articles 25 to 28 give shape to this secularism.
- It provides for a single citizenship for the whole of India. There is no state citizenship.
- The Preamble of the Constitution declares India to be a Sovereign, Socialist, Secular, Democratic Republic.
- **Soverign:** Country is not dependent upon any outside authority.
- **Socialist:** Ownership of the means of production and distribution by the state-inserted by the 42nd Amendment Act.
- **Democratic:** It has a government which gets its authority from the will of the people.
- **Republic:** India does not have a hereditary monarch.
- The Indian democracy is based on adult suffrage. In other words, any person who is not less than 18 years of age, who is otherwise eligible, has a right to vote without any discrimination on gender and religion.

Chapter 2

Fundamental Rights

- In early 1895, Dr Annie Besant, founder of the Indian Home Rule League and a leader of the Indian National Congress, drafted a Constitution of India Bill.
- It envisaged a Constitution that makes provision to provide every citizen the freedom of expression, inviolability of one's house, right to property, equality before the law with regard to admission to public offices and the right to personal property.
- At a special session in 1918 at Bombay on the Montague-Chelmsford Report, the Congress demanded that the new Government of India Act contains a declaration of the rights of the Indians.
- In 1925, a sub-committee established by the All-Parties Conference chaired by M.K. Gandhi prepared a Commonwealth of India Bill.
- It asked for the rights to liberty, security and property, freedom of conscience and to profess and practice of any religion, freedom to express opinion, to assemble peacefully and without arms and to form associations or unions, free elementary education, use of roads, public places, courts of justice and the like, equality before the law-irrespective of nationality and freedom of the speech.
- The report of 1928 Motilal Nehru Committee incorporated all these demands and added the right of all citizens to the writ of *habeas corpus* protection in respect of punishment under *ex post facto* laws.
- It also asked for non-discrimination against any person on the basis of race, religion or creed in the matter of public employment, office of power or honour and in the exercise of any trade or calling, equal access of all citizens to public road, public wells and places of public resort.

Fundamental Rights:

- Right to Equality (Art. 14 – 18)
- Right to Freedom (Art. 19 – 22)
- Right against Exploitation (Art. 23 and 24)
- Right to Freedom of Religion (Art. 25 – 28)
- Cultural and Educational Rights (Art. 29 & 30)
- Right to Constitutional Remedies (Art. 32)

- Further, freedom of combination and association for the maintenance and improvement of labour and economic conditions and the right to keep arms in accordance with regulations were also demanded in this Act.

Article 13

- As per Art. 13(1) of the Constitution of India, all laws enforced in India immediately before the commencement of the Constitution, in so far as they are contradictory with any or all the fundamental rights, shall be void to the extent of such inconsistency. The Supreme Court in the case of Bikaji Narain vs the State of Madhya Pradesh (1955) it was propounded that the 'doctrine of eclipse' and clarified that any such law is not dead altogether. It is, in fact, overshadowed by the fundamental rights and remains dormant.

It is a good law when a question arises for the determination of rights and obligations incurred before the commencement of the Constitution, and also for the allocation of the rights of persons who have not been given fundamental rights under the Constitution. When the shadow cast by the fundamental rights are removed by a subsequent amendment, the eclipsed parts of such a law get revised and become effective once again.

Earlier, the Supreme Court ordered that the 'doctrine of eclipse' was applicable to pre-Constitutional laws only. However, in the State of Gujarat vs Shri Ambika Mills case (1974), the Court stated that the doctrine can be extended to the post-Constitutional laws as well.

The guarantee of Equality before Law is an aspect of what Lord Dicey calls the 'Rule of Law' which was originated in England. It means no man is above law and that every person, whatever be his rank or status is subject to the jurisdiction of ordinary courts. Also, it says that no person shall be subject to harsh, uncivilised or discriminatory treatment even for the sake of maintaining law and order.

There are three basic significance of 'Rule of Law':

- Absence of arbitrary power or supremacy of law a man can be punished for a breach of law, but he cannot be punished for anything else.
- Equality before law no one is above law.
- The Constitution is the Supreme law of the land and all laws passed by the legislature must be consistent with the provisions of the Constitution.

There are specific provisions in the Constitution which, under certain situation, limit the effectiveness of **Article 14.**

- Article 361 says that the President and the Governors are exempted from any criminal proceedings during the tenure of their offices.
- The scope of the Right to Equality under Article 14 has been considerably prohibited by the 42nd Amendment Act, 1976. The new Article 31-C added by the Amendment Act provides that laws made by the State for implementing the Directive Principles contained in clause (b) or clause (c) of Article 39 cannot be challenged on the ground that they are violative of Article 14. Such laws will be exceptions to Article 14 of the Constitution.
- Under the International Law, foreign sovereign, ambassadors and diplomats, enjoy full protection from any judicial process.
- Article 359 (1) makes the provision that where a proclamation of Emergency is in operation, the President may, by order, declare that the right to move any court for the enforcement of such rights conferred by Part III (except Articles 20 and 21) shall remain suspended. Thus, if the President of India issues an order, where a Proclamation of Emergency is in operation, enforcement of Art. 14 may be suspended for the period during which the Proclamation is in force.
- Part III of the Constitution includes a long list of the Fundamental Rights.
- The most striking difference between the Government of India Act, 1935 and the present Constitution is the presence of the Fundamental Rights in it.
- This portion of the Constitution has been described as the 'Magna Carta' of India.
- Part III of the Constitution is known as the 'Cornerstone' of the Constitution, and together with Part IV (Directive Principles), constitutes the 'conscience' of the Constitution.
- The Fundamental Rights were perceived essential to protect the rights and liberties of the people against the encroachment of the power delegated by them to their Government.
- There are the some limitations upon all the powers of the Government, legislative as well as executive.
- These rights are regarded as fundamental rights because they are essential for the attainment, by the individual of his/her full intellectual, moral and spiritual status.
- The declaration of the Fundamental Rights in the Constitution serves as the reminder to the rulling Government that definite liberties, assured to the people by the Constitution, are to be respected.
- The motive behind the inclusion of the chapter on the Fundamental Rights in the Indian Constitution is to establish 'a Government of law and not of a man'.
- The Fundamental Rights are the restricted rights, they do not give absolute powers to the only individual.
- Article 17 and Article 24 are the only absolute rights.
- But in certain case Right against discrimination [Art 15(2)], Right against untouchability (Art 17) and Right against exploitation [Art (23) and (24)] can be enforced against the private individuals also.
- Article 13 gives the provision for the Judicial Review of all the legislations in India.
- Judicial review means the power conferred on the High Courts and the Supreme Court of India to declare a law unconstitutional, if it is inconsistent with any of the provisions of Part III of the Constitution, to the extent of the contravention.
- The concept of the Judicial Review in the Constitution in Indian is taken from the Constitution of the US.
- The Supreme Court in many cases, from Shankari Prasad vs Union of India (1952) to Sajjan Singh vs State of Rajasthan (1965), held that by exercising its amending power under Article 368, the Parliament can amend even Part III of the Constitution.
- The Court in this case held that the Parliament can amend the provisions of the Constitution including Fundamental Rights by its amending power which has been given in Art 368, provided such amendments do not infringe the basic structure of the Constitution.
- The Constitution of India makes the provisions for automatic suspension of the Fundamental Rights under certain circumstances, as for e.g. during the National Emergency under Article 352 (i.e., war or external aggression).
- The Constitution of India empowers the President, under the Article 359, to suspend any or all the Fundamental Rights by issuing a separate Proclamation during a National Emergency.
- The 44th Amendment Act, 1978 prevents the suspension of Art. 20 and 21 (protection in respect of conviction for offences and protection of life and personal liberty respectively) even during a National Emergency.

Right to Equality (Art 14–18)

Article 14

- The State Government shall not deny to any person equality before the law or equal protection of the laws within the territory of India.
- The concept of Right to Equality before law is borrowed from the British Constitution.
- Equality before law means 'no man is above law' and every person, whatever be his/her social status, is subject to the jurisdiction of the courts.
- The rule of equality before law is, however, not an absolute rule and there are a many exceptions to it.
- Equal protection of law is a positive concept which is borrowed from the US Constitution.
- It means that all persons in similar situation/circumstances shall be treated alike.
- There can be a differentiation between the groups but not within the groups.
- Since the State stands for the welfare of all groups of the society, it can make certain discriminations in favour of those who are less privileged.
- The 'rule of law' described in Art. 14 is a "basic feature" of the Indian Constitution and hence, it cannot be destroyed even by an amendment of the Constitution under Article 368.
- The word 'any person' in Article 14 of the Constitution denotes that the guarantee of the equal protection of laws is available to everyone which includes any association, company or body of individuals.

Article 15

- Article 15 of the Constitution makes the provision for the prohibition of discrimination on the grounds of religion, race, caste, sex or place of birth.
- Article 15 directs the State not to discriminate against any citizen on the grounds **only** of race, caste, religion, sex or place of birth, etc.
- The word 'only' refers that the discrimination cannot be made merely on the ground that one belongs to a particular caste, religion, race, etc.
- If other credentials are equal, religion, race, caste, etc. should not be a disability.
- The guarantee under Article 15 is available to the citizens only and not to aliens whether 'citizen or non-citizen' as under Article14.
- The third clause of the constitution empowers the State to make special provisions for the protection of women and children.
- The fourth clause which was added by the 1st Constitutional Amendment Act 1951, empowers the State to make special provisions for the protection of the interests of the Backward Classes and is, despite, an exception to Article 15 and 29(2) of the Constitution.
- Art 29(2) states that no citizen shall be refused admission into any educational institution maintained by the State or receiving aid out of State funds on grounds only of religion, race, caste, language or any of them.

Article 16

- Equality of opportunity in all affairs of public employment.
- No citizen shall, on grounds only of religion, race, caste, sex, descent, place of birth or residence be unsuitable for, or discriminated against in respect of, any employment or office under the State.
- The State is free to specify the eligible. There cannot be any other ground for non-eligibility.
- The 81st amendment of the Constitution Act, 2000 added a new clause (4-B) in Article 16 of the Constitution which seeks to end the 50% limit for the SCs/STs and OBCs in backlog vacancies which could not be filled up due to the non- availability of eligible candidates of these categories in the previous years.

Note: *Under Article 16, the guarantee against discrimination is limited to 'employment' and 'appointment' under the State Government.*

- "Equal pay for equal work", although not explicitly declared to be a Fundamental Right, but it is clearly a Constitutional goal under Articles 14, 16 and 39 (c) of the Constitution and can be enforced by the Courts in the cases of unequal scales of pay based on irrational classification.

Exceptions

- Special favours can be provided to the Backward Classes which are not adequately represented.
- Religion may be a basis for discrimination in special cases. There are religious institutions taken over by the State, so, religious posts are reserved for the people of the same religious denomination.

Article 17

Abolition of untouchability

- Under Act. 17 'Untouchability' is abolished and its practice in any form is forbidden.
- The practice enforcement of any disability arising out of 'untouchability' shall be an offence, punishable in accordance with the law.
- The Constitution itself does not suggest any punishment under this Article.
- The Parliament validates the 'Untouchability (offences) Act, 1955' which prescribes the punishment for the practice of untouchability.
- The Constitution was amended by the 'Untouchability (offences) Amendment Act, 1976' in order to make the untouchability laws more stringent.
- The name of the actual Act was changed to 'Civil Rights (Protection) Act, 1976'.
- Later, when there was increase in physical violence against members of Scheduled Castes and Scheduled Tribes, leading to brutalities such as mass murder, rape, arson, grievous injuries, etc. The enactment of the special law for their protection was resorted to known as Scheduled Castes and Scheduled Tribes which specially for the (Prevention of Atrocities) Act, 1989 to provide for strong punitive measures which could serve as a deterrence.
- This Act does not define 'untouchability'.
- According to an order of the Supreme Court, 'untouchability' should not be understood in its literal or grammatical sense. It is to be understood as the 'practice as it had developed historically'.
- Article 17 also imposes an accountability on the public servants to investigate such offences.

Article 18

Abolition of Titles

- No title, not being a military or academic distinction, shall be awarded by the State.
- No citizen of India shall accept any title from any foreign State.
- Article 18 also prohibits a foreign national under the employment of the State to receive any title from any foreign State without the consent of the President.

Right to Freedom (Art 19–22)

- The Article 19 to 22 is related to personal liberty which are the most important among all the Fundamental Rights.
- Taken together, these four Articles from 19 to 22 form a chapter on personal liberties which gives the backbone of the chapter on the Fundamental Rights.

Article 19

- The Article of the Constitution guarantees to the citizens of India the six fundamental rights or freedoms which are as given below:
  - (i) Freedom of speech and expression,
  - (ii) To assemble peacefully and without arms,
  - (iii) To form associations or unions,
  - (iv) To move freely throughout the territory of India,
  - (v) To reside and settle in any part of the territory of India,
  - (vi) To practice any profession, or to carry on any occupation, trade or business.
- The Right to property, was a Fundamental Right, and was removed by the 44th Constitutional Amendment, 1978 and transferred to Art 300A.
- The six basic freedoms which have been prescribed in Article 19 are not absolute. The State can impose few restrictions on the basis of security of the State, friendly relations with the foreign States, public order, decency, morality, contempt of court, defamation, etc.
- The right to form associations, unions, and other group, etc. does not give the right to strike.
- Constitution does not provide for the freedom of press separately. It is implicit in Article 19, which grants freedom of speech and expression.

Right to Information

- A proper freedom of information regime is a important aspect of open government and a fundamental underpinning of democracy.
- It is effective only where there is a free flow of information that accountability can be ensured, corruption avoided and public's right to know is satisfied.
- Freedom of information is also a crucial prerequisite for sustainable development of the country.
- Resource management, social initiatives and economic strategies can only be effective if the public is well-informed and has confidence in the government.
- As an aspect of the international guarantee of freedom of expression, freedom of information is commonly known as comprising a number of different elements.

Article 19

Protection of conviction for offences-

This protection is available against the three types of convictions which are given below:

(a) *Ex-post facto legislation*

- It refers to enacting a law and giving it a retrospective (i.e. from a previous date /year) effect.
- The power has been conferred to the Parliament by the Constitution.
- It is applicable only for civil legislations while criminal legislations cannot be given contemplative effect.

Freedom of Press

- The Constitution does not grant for the freedom of press separately.
- It is ingrained in Art. 19, which grants freedom of speech and expression.
- Freedom of expression involves not only expression of one's own views but of others' as well.
- The restrictions that restrict the freedoms in the case of individuals apply to the press also.
- The laws that apply to the press include the following:
    * taxation;
    * laws regulating industrial relations;
    * regulations of the conditions of service of the employees;
    * defamation, contempt of House and Court , etc.
- In elucidation of Art. 19 in the 'airways case' February, 1995, the Supreme Court reiterated that the press would be bound by the rules of the Government, expressed through an autonomous body.

(b) *Double Jeopardy*

- It means that an individual can be punished for a crime only once and also not beyond the period prescribed by the authority.
- If a civil servant is dismissed on criminal charges his dismissal does not come under Double Jeopardy and he could be well prosecuted further in the Court.

(c) *Prohibition against self-incrimination*

- No person, accused of an offence, shall be compelled to be a witness against himself.
- The cardinal principle of criminal law is, an accused should be presumed to be innocent till the contrary is proved.
- It is the duty of the prosecution to prove the offence.

Article 20

Protection of Life and Personal Liberty

- No person shall be deprived of his/her life and personal liberty except according to the procedure established by law.
- Over the period, this Article has undergone a sea change and has become the most important Fundamental Right.
- The Supreme Court, through a liberal interpretation of the Article, has derived a number of inferred rights.
- The Article stands not merely for the right to life and personal liberty, but also for the right to dignity and all other attributes of human personality that are essential for the full development of a person.

Inferred Rights

The composite or inferred rights are those rights, which are not explicitly provided by the Constitution but have been derived by liberal interpretation of the various provisions of the Constitution. Some of the inferred rights are:

1. Right to health of the workers
2. Right to shelter
3. Right against cruel punishment
4. Right to live with dignity
5. Right to privacy
6. Right to speedy trials
7. Right against denial of wages and arbitrary dismissal of workers.

Article 21

- Article 21 has become the 'Foundation Stone of Part III' of the Constitution.
- In few judgements, the Supreme Court held that the right to clean and hygienic conditions of life is a part of Right to Life.
- Article 21 protects an individual both against legislative and executive actions.
- Domiciliary visit by police during night is an invasion of personal liberty and hence, Art 21.
- Right to travel abroad: Part of personal liberty- hence part of Art 21.
- Right to have primary education is a fundamental right under Art 21.
- Art 21 includes the principles of Natural Justice.
- Right to health and medical assistance: It is the professional obligation of all doctors, whether government or private, to extend medical aid to the injured immediately, to preserve life without waiting for legal formalities.

- Right to get pollution free water and air: Protection of ecology and environment come under Art 21.
- A minor girl's right to bear a child: Bearing child is a natural right of a woman.
- Right to free legal aid and speedy trial are guaranteed under Art 21. According to Supreme Court- "This is the State's duty and not Government charity".
- Rights against hand-cuffing: There should be clear and present danger of escape—breaking out of police control—and for this there must be clear material evidence.
- In the case of Chakma migrants, Supreme Court declared that even non-citizens are entitled for the right to life.
- Right against inhuman treatment. According to Art 21, use of "third degree" method by police is violative of Art 21.
- Telephone tapping is an invasion on right to privacy, hence violates Art 21.

Article 21A

Right to Education

The State shall give free and compulsory education to all children of the age of six to fourteen years in such manner as the State may, by law, determine.

- The Constitution (86th Amendment) Act 2002, seeks to make free and compulsory education a Fundamental Right for all children in the age-group 6-14 years by inserting a new Article 21A in Part III of the Constitution.
- The new Article 21A reads as follows: The State shall provide free and compulsory education to all children of the age of six to fourteen years in such manner as the State may, by law, determine.
- The aim of it is to benefit India's 190 million 6 to 14-year-olds, especially some 35 million, currently not attending school.
- The government is trying to target the children through a Sarva Shiksha Abhiyan and a series of measures and facilities — such as free mid-day meals, uniforms and textbooks.
- These steps are being taken to provide mobile schools to help certain students who are not staying long enough at one address — construction workers' children, for instance — or giving examination on demand to kids unable to meet regular schedules.
- Also, as per the Act, "the State shall endeavour to provide early childhood care and education for all children until they complete the age of six years".
- Further, the Act makes it the fundamental duty of parents and guardians to provide opportunities for education to their children/wards in the 6 to 14 age group.

Article 22

Protection against arrest and detention in certain cases

- The Authority cannot arrest or detain a person without properly informing him/her of the grounds for such arrests/ detention.
- The arrested person must be present before the nearest Magistrate within 24 hours of arrest (excluding the holidays and time taken during the journey).
- The period of the detention cannot be extended beyond what is authorized by the Magistrate.

Right against Exploitation (Art 23 and 24)

Article 23

Prohibition of traffic in human beings and forced labour

- Traffic in human beings and beggar and other similar forms of forced labour are prohibited.
- Any contravention of this provision shall be an offence punishable in accordance with law.
- Traffic in human beings means selling and buying being like goods and includes immoral traffic in women and children for immoral and other purposes.
- One shall not be forced to provide labour or services against his will even if remuneration is paid.
- If remuneration is less than minimum wages, it amounts to forced labour under Article 23.

Article 24

Prohibition of employment of children in factories, etc

- The essence of Article 24 is the prohibition of employment of children below 14 years of age in hazardous jobs.
- This provision is in the interest of public health and safety of children.
- In M.C. Mehta vs State of Tamil Nadu case, the Supreme Court held that the State authorities should protect economic, social and humanitarian rights of children, working illegally in the public and private sectors.

Right to Freedom of Religion (Art 25-28)

- India is a secular State, not an irreligious or an atheist State.
- The State protects all the religions; but interferes with none. It believes in the ancient Indian doctrine of 'Sarva Dharma Sambhava'.

- The State is concerned with the relations between man and woman and not with those of man and supernatural power.
- India is a home of various religions, thus, freedom of religion is the essence or an important element of freedom in India.

Article 25

Freedom of conscience, profession, practise and propagation of religion

- Subject to public order, morality and health and to the other provisions of this part, all the citizens are equally entitled to the freedom of conscience and the right to profess, practise and propagate religion.
- Right to propagate does not mean alluring a person to join any religion.
- A Constitution Bench of the Supreme Court, in a group of related cases in 1977 called the Rev. Stainislau vs State of Madhya Pradesh and Others case, ruled that Article 25(1) does not provide the right to convert but only the right to spread the tenets of one's own religion.
- Supreme Court was delivering the verdict about the legislation made in Madhya Pradesh and Orissa to outlaw conversions based on force, fraud and allurement in 1968.

Article 26

Freedom to manage religious affairs

The subject to public order, morality and health, every religious denomination or any section thereof shall have the following right:

1. Right to establish and maintain institutions for religious and charitable purposes.
2. Right to manage its own affairs in the matters of religion.
3. Right to own and acquire movable and immovable property and
5. Right to administer such property in accordance with law.

Article 27

Freedom as to payment of taxes for promotion of any particular religion.

- No any person shall be compelled to pay any tax for religious purposes.
- If the Government did any service for a particular religious denomination, the Government is free to charge fees from the devotees.

Article 28

Freedom as to the attendance at religious instruction or religious worship in certain educational institutions.

- Articles 28 divides educational institutions into four categories:
  1. Wholly maintained by the State
  2. Recognised by the State
  3. Receiving aids out of the State funds
  4. Administered by the State, but established under a religious endowment
- In the first case, there can be no religious instructions whatsoever.
- In the second and third case, religious instructions can be imparted, but the people cannot be compelled to attend such instructions.
- In the fourth case, there is no restriction whatever, as far as religious instructions are concerned.

Cultural and Educational Rights (Art 29–30)

Article 29

Protection of interests of minorities

- Any section of the citizens, dwelling in the territory of India or any part thereof, having a distinct language, script or culture of its own, shall have the right to conserve the same.

Article 30

The Right of minorities to establish and administer educational institutions.

- All minorities, whether based on religion or language, shall have the right to establish and administer their choice of educational institutions.
- It provides to religious, educational and cultural institutions, the right to own, possess and dispose immovable property.
- The State shall provide due compensation in case of acquisition of such property.
- The right to preserve language, culture or script can be implemented through educational institutions.
- The meaning of administer refers to the management of affairs of the institution.
- The State can regulate the working of such institutions.
- The Supreme Court observed that the Right to Administration does not explain the Right to Maladministration.
- The university can put basic qualifications for the selection of teachers.

Right to Constitutional Remedies (Art 32)

Article 32

- Article 32 provides institutional framework for the enforcement of the Fundamental Rights by the Supreme Court.
- Dr. B.R. Ambedkar has called this Article as "the fundamental of the Fundamental Right" and "the heart and soul of the Constitution."
- To enforce these Fundamental Rights, the Supreme Court is empowered under Art. 32, to issue writs of various forms.
- The concept of issuing writs has been taken from the UK.
- The five forms of writs are as given below:

1. **The Habeas Corpus** – The literal meaning is 'to have a body' i.e., to be produced before the Court.
    - This type of writ is issued to protect personal liberty of an individual against the arbitrary action of both the State and private individuals.
    - The aggrieved person can even claim for compensation against such action.
2. **Mandamus** – It means to 'Command'.
    - This kind of writ is issued against a public authority or an officer and inferior Courts for purpose of enforcing legal rights only.
    - This writ cannot be issued against the President and the Governors.
    - Private rights cannot be enforced by the writ of the Mandamus.
3. **Prohibition** – "to restrain".
    - This type of writ is issued by the higher courts to the lower courts or the quasi-judicial bodies when the latter exceed their judicial authority.
    - The aim of this writ is to keep the inferior courts or the quasi-judicial bodies within the limits of their respective jurisdiction.
    - The difference between 'Mandamus' and 'Prohibition' is that while the former can be issued against judicial as well as administrative authorities, the latter is issued only against the judicial or quasi-judicial authorities.
4. **Certiorari** – This writ is similar to the writ of "Prohibition".
    - The writ is issued to quash the order of a lower court or the decision of a tribunal in excess of its jurisdiction.
    - The aim of this writ is to secure that jurisdiction of an inferior court or tribunal is properly exercised and that it does not usurp the jurisdiction it does not possess.
5. **Quo Warranto**
    - It actually refers to "what is your authority".
    - This type of writ is issued to ensure that the person holding a public office is qualified to hold the office.

Note: *No time-limit is prescribed for issuing the writs in the Constitution, and has been left to the courts to decide.*

Chapter 3 Directive Principles of State Policy

General Introductions

- Articles 36 to 51 have the provisions of the Directive Principles which are included in Part IV of the Constitution.
- This feature of the Constitution has been adopted from the Constitution of Ireland.
- The concept of development in the Constitutional Governments throughout the world, is arising with the acceptance of a 'Welfare State'.
- The Directive Principles of the Constitution of India are a sole combination of Socialism, Gandhism, Western liberalism, and the ideals of the Indian freedom movement.
- These principles form the of directions or instructions to the State.
- Article 36 clearly directs the State to secure and protect a social order which stands for the welfare of the people.
- Article 37 says that Directive Principles are not justiciable but are fundamental to the Governance of the country, and the State has the duty in applying the Directive Principles of State Policies (DPSPs).
- In the condition not performed by the State, no one can move the Courts.
- The reason behind making the DPSPs explicitly non-justiciable are that they require resources which the State may not have at present.
- These principles can be described under the following categories:

The Socialist Principles

- *Article 38:* To secure a social order for the promotion of welfare of the people.
- *Article 39:* To strive to minimise inequalities of income.

PART IV: Directive Principles Of State Policy

Art 36	Definition.
Art 37	Application of the principles contained in this Part.
Art 38	State to secure a social order for the promotion of welfare of the people.
Art 39	Certain principles of policy to be followed by the State.
Art39A	Equal justice and free legal aid.
Art 40	Organisation of village panchayats.
Art 41	Right to work, to education and to public assistance in certain cases.
Art 42	Provision for just and humane conditions of work and maternity relief.
Art 43	Living wage, etc., for workers.
Art 43A	Participation of workers in management of industries.
Art 44	Uniform civil code for the citizens.
Art 45	Provision for free and compulsory education for children.
Art 46	Promotion of educational and economic interests of Scheduled Castes, Scheduled Tribes and other weaker sections.
Art 47	Duty of the State to raise the level of nutrition and the standard of living and to improve public health.
Art 48	Organisation of agriculture and animal husbandry.
Art 48A	Protection and improvement of environment and safeguarding of forests and wildlife.
Art 49	Protection of monuments and places and objects of national importance.
Art 50	Separation of judiciary from the executive.
Art 51	Promotion of international peace and security.

- *Article 39 (b):* Ownership and control of material resources of the community shall be so distributed so as to subserve the common good.
- *Article 39 (d):* Equal pay for equal work.
- *Article 39 (e):* Health and strength of workers, and the tender age of children must not be abused.
- *Article 39A:* Equal justice and free legal aid.
- *Article 42:* Provision of just and humane conditions for work and maternity relief.
- *Article 43 A:* Participation of workers in the management of the industries.

The Gandhian Principles

- *Article 40:* Organisation of Village Panchayats.
- *Article 46:* Promotion of educational and economic interests of the SCs, the STs and the other weaker sections of the society.

- *Article 48:* Organisation of agriculture and animal husbandry on modern and scientific lines to prohibit the slaughter of cows, calves and other milch and draught animals.
- *Article 43:* To promote cottage industry.
- *Article 47:* To bring about the prohibition of intoxicating drinks and drugs that are injurious to health.

The Western Liberal Principles

- *Article 44:* Uniform Civil Code for the citizens.
- *Article 45:* Provision for early childhood, care and education to children below the age of six years.

The State shall endeavour to provide early childhood care and education for all children until they complete the age of six years.

- *Article 50:* Separation of Judiciary from Executive.
- *Article 51:* To promote international peace and amity.
- Since the commencement of the Constitution, there have been a number of legislations to implement the DPSPs.
- In fact, the very first Amendment Act was for implementing land reforms.
- It was followed by the 4th, 17th, 25th, 42nd and 44th Amendment Acts.
- The 73rd Constitution Amendment Act (1992) is in pursuit of implementing Art. 40.
- National Rural Employment Guarantee Act is in the directions of implementing Right to work (Article 41).
- There have been several factory legislations to provide the conditions of work humane for the workers.
- The promotion of small industries has been one of the main aspects of the economic policy of the government and there exists the Khadi and Village Industries Commission for the purpose.
- Apart from this, Silk Board, Handloom Board, SSI Board, NABARD, etc, have been created.
- The government's position as regards the uniform civil code (UCC) is that the matter being sensitive in India unless the religious groups concerned come forward and voluntarily seek the enforcement of the UCC, it is not desirable to implement the code.
- The Supreme Court, in 1995, held that the UCC must be implemented, and 'directed' the Union Government to report to it on the progress made in the implementation of the UCC.
- Right to Education has been made a fundamental right for the age group of 6-14. (Article 21A) in Pursuance of Article 45.
- The policy of preferential treatment in education, administration and economy for the weaker sections including women, SCs, STs and OBCs has been a consistent plank of the government's welfare policy, the most recent being the implementation of the Mandal Commission Report, for which judicial clearance was given by the Supreme Court in 1992.

Do You Know?

- 42nd Amendment of 1976: Article 39A was inserted to provide free legal aid to the poor to ensure social justice. With this amendment, Article 43A was also inserted to direct the State to ensure participation of workers in the management of industry.
- 86th Amendment of 2002: All children between 6 and 14 years of age were given the right to free and compulsory education, making education a part of the Fundamental Rights.
- 97th Amendment of 2011 : Article 43B was introduced through this amendment. It promoted voluntary participation of co-operative societies.

- Many schemes like the Integrated Child Development Services, mid-day meal scheme and the policy of prohibition followed by some states are in pursuance of Art. 47.
- National Rural Health Mission is directly helping in improving public health conditions of the rural poor (Article 47).
- In pursuit of Art. 48, the Green Revolution and the research in biotechnology are aimed at modernising agriculture and animal husbandry, among other things.
- The Environment Protection Act, 1986; the Wild Life Act; the National Forest Policy, 1988 are some of the steps taken for the implementation of Art. 48A.
- In 1995, the Union Government established the National Environment Tribunal.

- The Archaeological Survey of India (ASI) is entrusted with the work of protection of monuments like the Taj Mahal.
- The ASI took up the work of protecting the Puri temple from dilapidation in late 1992.
- The National Mission on Monuments and Antiquities has been proposed with a view to document the antiquarian and monumental wealth of the country.
- The proposed National Mission is for a period of five years starting from 2006-07 to 2010-11 with a total budgetary outlay of Rs. 90 crore.
- Recently, the Government has decided to set up a National Heritage Sites Commission to monitor and issue directions on monuments and archaeological sites which are not under the Ancient Monument and Sites Remains Act (AMASR), 1958.
- As a quasi-judicial body, the Commission will have the power to intervene to ensure that the country's heritage is not tampered with and all sites of importance are treated uniformly, irrespective of whether they are under the Archaeological Survey of India (ASI) or any other agency.
- The functions of the Heritage Sites Commission would include advising the Government on short and long, term policies in respect of heritage conservation, preparing guidelines for conservation and management of heritage sites, suggesting necessary amendments to heritage legislations, commissioning studies, investigation, etc. leading to the identification, determination and categorisation of heritage sites and providing advice to Government on any matter pertaining to heritage.
- The amendments made to the Criminal Procedure Code to divest the executive of certain judicial powers at the district level are in pursuit of Art. 50.
- The efforts of India to secure international peace are many, like participating in the peace keeping operations of the UN (Somalia in 1992-93; Sierra Leone in 2000); pioneering and leading the Non-Aligned Movement and so on.

Importance of the DPSP

- Article 37 declares Directive Principles as fundamental in the governance of the Country.
- Since the Government is answerable to the people, the Directive Principles act as a sign post to all succeeding governments.
- The Directive Principles provide the yardstick for assessing the successes or failures of these governments.
- By uniform civil code, it is meant that all sections of society irrespective of their religion shall be treated equally according to a national civil code, which shall be uniformly applicable to all.
- Civil code covers areas like marriage, divorce, maintenance, inheritance, succession of property and adoption.
- Uniform civil code (UCC) has been provided under Art 44 of the Constitution as a directive principle.
- It will enhance the status of women and therefore, it is vitally desired to achieve the empowerment of women.
- Articles 25 and 26 guarantee right to freedom of religion and UCC is not opposed to secularism or will not violate these articles.
- Article 44 is based on the concept that there is no necessary connection between religion and personal law in a civilised society.

Do You Know?

Programme launched on the basis of Directive Principles of State Policy (DPSP)

1. Establishment of Planning Commission in 1950
2. Land Reform Law
3. Minimum Wages Act, 1948
4. Factory Act, 1948
5. Workman Compensation Act, 1923
6. Act for Maternity Relief, 1961
7. Equal Wagves Act, 1976
8. Legal Services Tribunal Act, 1987
9. Establishment of Khadi Gram Udyog Board and Commission of cottage industries in rural areas.
10. Community Development Programme 1952, Integrated Rural Development Plan 1978, Swarnjayanti Gram |Swarojgar Yojna 1999, Overall Rural Employment Planning 2001, **MGNREGA 2006.**
11. Forest and Wildlife Conservation/Protection Act, 1972, 1980.
12. Untouchability Act, 1955 that has been amended as Civil Right Protection Act, 1976.

- Marriage, succession and like matters are of secular nature and, therefore, law can regulate them.
- The UCC will not and shall not result in interference of one's religious beliefs relating, mainly to maintenance, succession and inheritance. But in matters of inheritance, right to property, maintenance and succession, there will be a common law.
- Article 25 confers right to practice and profess religion, while Article 44 divests religion from social relations and personal law.
- According to Justice R.M. Sahai " Freedom of religion is the core of our culture. But religious practices, violative of human rights and dignity and sacerdotal suffocation of essentially civil and material freedoms are not autonomy but oppression. "

Chapter 4 Fundamental Duties

General Introductions

- These are included in the Indian Constitution by the 42nd Amendment Act, 1976.
- It is based on the Japanese model.
- 11 duties of the citizens towards the State have been enumerated by inserting Article 51-A in Part IV A of our Constitution.
- With the 86th Amendment Act, 2002, one more duty was added to the list.
- Rights and duties are correlative. These serve as constant reminder to every citizen that, while the Constitution specifically confers on them certain Fundamental Rights, it also requires them to observe certain basic norms of democratic conduct and behaviour.

Eleven Fundamental Duties for citizens

1. To abide by and respect the Constitution, the National Flag and the National Anthem.
2. To cherish and follow the noble ideals of the freedom struggle.
3. To uphold and protect the sovereignty, unity and integrity of India.
4. To defend the country and render national service when required.
5. To promote common brotherhood and establish dignity of women.
6. To preserve the rich heritage of the nation's composite culture.
7. To protect and improve natural environment.
8. To develop scientific temper, humanism and spirit of inquiry.
9. To safeguard public property and abjure violence.
10. To strive for excellence in all spheres of individual and collective activity.
11. It shall be duty of every citizen of India who is a parent or guardian to provide opportunities for education to his child or as the case may be, ward, between the age of 6 and 14 years. (*Added by 86th Amendment 2002)*

Fundamental Duties in other countries

- None of the major democracies in the world has Fundamental Duties.
- Only Japan has made some mention of them.
- France has a passing reference only.
- It does not mean that people of these countries behave in an irresponsible manner.
- In all these countries, citizens have a high sense of patriotism as a result of education and training in the elementary duties and obligations of citizenship.
- But in socialist countries, there are specific Fundamental Duties.

Enforcement of duties

- The duties incorporated in the Constitution by the 42nd Amendment are statutory duties and shall be enforceable by law.
- Parliament, by law, will provide penalties to be imposed for failure to fulfil those duties and obligations.

The New Flag Code

- One can hoist the flag only from sunrise to sunset.
- The ratio of width to length of the flag should be 2:3.
- Don't print it on a costume, cushion or napkin either.
- Don't use as a shroud for funerals.
- Don't drape the flag on vehicles.
- Don't hoist it upside down. Must not touch the ground.
- Must fly higher than all other flags except that of the UN or other nations.
- Don't fly a damaged flag.
- The amended code came into effect from January 26, 2003.

- The success of this provision would, however, depend much upon the manner in which and the person against whom these duties would be enforced.

Flag Controversy and the New Flag Code

- The earlier Flag Code, which contained a long string of archaic provisions, made the right of flying the flag that of a privileged few.
- It was seven years ago that Navin Jindal, the vice-Chairman of Jindal Group, who filed a PIL in the Delhi High Court challenging the restraint on his right to fly the flag.
- With the Delhi High Court ruling that flying the tricolour is a Fundamental Right and the Supreme Court subsequently recommending the setting up of a committee to examine the question of liberalising the Flag Code.

- Subsequently, the Government set up a committee, and based on the committee's recommendations, the Union Cabinet has decided to relax the unduly stringent rules about flying the tricolour.

Fundamental Duties : Indian Citizens of the 21st Century

DUTY TO VOTE

Article 326 of the Constitution read with Section 62 of the Representation of People' Act, 1951confers the right to vote. Voting is considered as our civic duty determining our future and hence the citizens need to play a part in shaping it. In the last general elections in 2014, the votes polled amounted about sixty-seven per cent of the total vote population. As per our Constitution, voting is a civic right and not a civic duty and it under the chairmanship of Justice J.S. Verma recommended that *"duty to vote at elections, actively participate in the democratic process of governance and to pay taxes should be included in Article 51A of the Constitution "*.

Duty to Pay Taxes

The Indian Constitution does not recognise the duty to pay taxes as a Fundamental Duty, although the Swaran Singh Committee had recommended the addition of the same as part of the 42nd Constitutional Amendment. Research has found that tax evasion is a direct result of lack of trust among the people, in general, and the government, in particular. Citizens must believe that their taxes are bound to be used for public good. The right to pay taxes as part of Fundamental Duties in the Constitution will shift the onus onto the taxpayer to pay taxes rather than the tax department to collect them.

Duty to Help Accident Victims

According to the Law Commission of India, at least 50% of fatalities can be prevented if road accident victims receive medical attention within the critical first hour after the accident. The Ministry of Road Transport and Highways in 2013, released the data that around 1,37,572 people lost their lives in road accidents. With the increase in the number of accidents, it has become pertinent for India to recognise this duty as one owed by its citizens towards each other.

Duty to Keep the Premises Clean

The Supreme Court has held that the Right to Life under Article 21 also includes the Right to a Clean Environment. Hon'ble Prime Minister Shri Narendra Modi had launched a very thoughtful and an excellent project the Swachh Bharat Mission on 2 nd October 2014. The Union Government to enact a legislation directly dealing with sanitation and cleanliness, since 'public health' and 'sanitation' fall within the State List. The need to keep one's own premises clean has been recognised under the Factories Act,1948. In *M.C.Mehta v.U nion of India & Ors .*, the Supreme Court recognised the need for behavioural change and stressed upon the need for awareness.

Duty to Prevent Civil Wrongs

A responsible citizenry is actually the back bone of State. It is not enough that a citizen refrains from committing wrong he has a duty to see that fellow citizens do not indulge in the commission of wrongs. We have inherited the rich legacy of Mahatma Gandhi who always believed and preached the strength of *ahimsa* to dissuade wrongdoers. So, as a well-educated citizens of the country we should actively participate to fullfill our duty.

People seem to have stopped reacting to atrocities, they neither report crimes nor volunteer to testify in a court. Reasons such as the fear of getting stigmatised, the fear of danger to life or to avoid suffering inconvenience. As per the International Victimisation Survey, thirty per cent of people in India fail to report a crime. A victim or a witness' role in reporting a crime is very significant as they are aware of the details of the events and are in a position to provide first hand report of the offence. A victim or a witness, therefore, has a moral duty to aid the efforts of the state to punish the offender.

Duty to Protect Whistleblowers

A whistleblower plays a critical role in maintaining the moral solvency of the society, in as much as he typically exposes information about corruption and other related illegalities, human rights abuses, corporate frauds, etc. and guides public discourse on issues which were hitherto kept from the public. The role of a whistleblower was traditionally associated only with an insider who was privy to the 'secrets' of an organisation but now with the coming into force of The RTI Act, 2005, every citizen has become a potential whistleblower" and is similarly susceptible to reprisal.

Duty to Support Bonafide Civil Society Movements

In India also, there existed a culture of an organised and effective civil society from medieval times, back then, there existed collective institutions such as trade guilds, village and caste Panchayats which were outside the control of the State and can be regarded as the oldest manifestations of the Civil Society. The number of Non governmental Organisations working in different sectors such as human rights, health, education, etc. land have from time to time played an important role in preserving the cherished ideals of our founding fathers by acting as a conduit between the State and the Citizens. It is proposed that there must be an addition to Part IV A of the Constitution of India on this account. Every citizen of the country must have a duty to support the endeavours of civil society or well meaning citizens in their quest for change.

The Union Legislature

General Introductions

- According to Article of the 79 Constitution of India there shall be a Parliament for the Union which shall consist of the President and the two Houses to be known respectively as the Council of States (the Rajya Sabha) and the House of the People (the Lok Sabha).
- Though the President is not a member of either House of the Parliament, yet like the British crown, he is an integral part of the Parliament and performs certain functions related to its proceedings.

Functions of the Parliament

- The significant function of the Parliament is to legislate, i.e. make legislations for the development which benefits the society.
- The second important function is to exercise control over the Executive.
- It has financial control over the Executive. The Parliament is the sole authority to raise taxes.
- It gives an opportunity to deliberate on various policies and measures before their implementation. Thus, the Parliament is also an authoritative source of information, collected and disseminated through the debates and through the specific medium of 'Questions' to the Ministers.

The Rajya Sabha

- The Rajya Sabha consists of two categories of members—elected and nominated—who are members for a period of six years. They are indirectly elected by the members of the State legislatures.
- The election is scheduled in such a way that one-third of its members retire every two years.
- The Rajya Sabha represents the federal character of the Constitution in the Parliament.

Article 80: The Council of States shall consist of

(a) Twelve members to be nominated by the President in accordance with the provisions, and

(b) Not more than two hundred and thirty-eight representatives of the States and, of the Union Territories.

(Only Union Territories of Delhi and Puducherry have representation in the Rajya Sabha).

At present, the strength of the Rajya Sabha is 245, of which 233 are elected and 12 are nominated.

Criteria for nomination

The members to be nominated by the President are persons having special knowledge or practical experience in respect of such matters as the following: Literature, Science, Arts and Social Service.

Federal Features of the Rajya Sabha

- Under Art. 249, the Council of States or the Rajya Sabha is empowered to declare by a resolution, supported by not less than two-thirds of the members present and voting (a special majority) that Parliament should make laws with respect to any matter enumerated in the State List. Such a resolution remains in force for a specified period, not exceeding one year. (The resolution can be initiated only in the Rajya Sabha).
- Art. 312 empowers the Rajya Sabha to declare by a resolution, supported by not less than two-thirds of the members present and voting, that it is necessary or expedient in the national interest, that the Parliament should create one or more All India Services, including All-India Judicial Services (42nd Amendment, 1976), common to the Union and the States, and also to regulate the recruitment and conditions of the service of persons appointed to such services (the Lok Sabha cannot initiate the process).
- In case of the Constitutional Amendment Bill, it must be passed by the Rajya Sabha separately. There is no provision for a joint-sitting to pass such Bills.
- The Ordinary and Financial Bills should have the approval of the Rajya Sabha. There are provisions for joint-sittings in these cases.

- The members of the Council of Ministers could also be taken from the Rajya Sabha. Thus, states indirectly have a say in policy-making.
- The members of the Rajya Sabha participate in the election of the President. For the impeachment of the President, a resolution to this effect must have the approval of not less than two-third members of the Rajya Sabha separately.
- In cases of declaration of emergencies under Article 352 and Article 356 by the President (who, infact, proclaims them on the advice of the Council of Ministers), such declarations must be approved by the Rajya Sabha within a period of one month and two months respectively after such declarations.

Qualifications for the Membership of Rajya Sabha

Following are the qualifications needed to be elected to the Rajya Sabha:

- The person must be a citizen of India;
- The person must not be below the age of 30 years;
- He must be an ordinary citizen/registered voter in the State or Union Territory from where he is intended to be chosen;
- He should not hold any office of profit.

Utility of the Rajya Sabha

It is said that in a Federal Constitution, the second chamber is a necessity. It plays an important role in the matters of legislation and therefore, it should be retained. The Rajya Sabha is desirable because it fulfils the following purposes:

1. It is considered useful because the senior politicians and the statesmen might get an easy access to it without undergoing the ordeal of contesting general elections. So, the experience and the talent is not lost to the country and their services are utilised.
2. The Rajya Sabha acts as a revising House over the Lok Sabha, which, being a popular House, may be tempted to act rather hastily keeping in view the public opinion.
3. The Rajya Sabha is a House where the States are represented, keeping with the federal principles.

Officers of the Rajya Sabha

- ***Chairman:*** The Vice-President of India is the *ex-officio* chairman of the Rajya Sabha. He presides over the proceedings of the Rajya Sabha as long as he does not act as the President of India during a vacancy in the office of the President.
- ***Deputy Chairman:*** The Deputy Chairman is elected by the Rajya Sabha from amongst its members. In the absence of the Chairman, Deputy Chairman presides over the functions and proceedings of the House.

The Lok Sabha

- The Lok Sabha is the popular House of the Parliament because its members are directly elected by the citizens of India.
- All the members of the Parliament are popularly elected, except not more than two members of the Anglo-Indian community, who are nominated by the President.
- This is basically due to the fact that they are not concentrated in a particular constituency and hence the Anglo-Indian community, in the opinion of the President, is not adequately represented in the Lok Sabha.
- In the Constitution, the strength of the Lok Sabha was provisioned to be not more than 552-530 from the States, 20 from the Union Territories and 2 nominated from the Anglo-Indian community. But, the Constitution empowers the Lok Sabha to readjust the strength.
- The Parliament has fixed the strength of the Lok Sabha as 545 (530+13+2 respectively) at present.
- Also, regarding the revision of the representation after every Census, the Parliament, by the 42nd Amendment, has frozen the representation of the States and the Union Territories at 543 till the year 2001 A.D.
- The Vajpayee government also took a decisive step to freeze the strength of the Lok Sabha till 2026 A.D.

Tenure of the Lok Sabha

- The normal tenure of the Lok Sabha is five years. But the Houses can be dissolved by the President before the end of the normal tenure.
- The life of the Lok Sabha can be extended by the Parliament beyond the five-year term during the period of the National Emergency, proclaimed under Art. 352. But this extension is for a period of not more than one year at a time (no limit on the number of times in the Constitution).

- However, such extension shall remain in force for not more than six months after the emergency has been revoked.
- The original Constitution, under Art. 83, envisaged the normal tenure of the Lok Sabha to be 5 years. However, Parliament by 42nd Amendment extended it to 6 years, but the 44th Amendment Act again fixed the original normal tenure of five years.

Qualifications for the membership of the Lok Sabha

To become a member of the Lok Sabha, the person must

- Be a citizen of India.
- Be not less than 25 years of age.
- Be a registered voter in any of the Parliamentary constituencies in India.
- Should not hold any office of profit

Vacation of Seats

Provisions for vacation of the seats in the Parliament are enumerated in Art. 101. These are:

- No person shall be a member of both the Houses of the Parliament. If a person is chosen for both the Houses, he/she shall have to vacate membership of either House.
- If a member of either House is disqualified under Art. 102 (1) and (2), he must vacate his seat.
- If a member resigns in writing addressed to the Chairman (the Council of States) or the Speaker (the House of People) as the case may be, and if his resignation is accepted by the Chairman or the Speaker, as the case may be.
- If a member of either House absents himself from the House without its permission for a period of more than sixty days, the House may declare his seat vacant.

The Speaker and the Deputy Speaker of the Lok Sabha

- The Speaker is the Chief Presiding Officer of the Lok Sabha.
- The two officers are elected from amongst the Members of the Lok Sabha after a new Lok Sabha is constituted.
- The Speaker presides over the meetings of the House and his rulings on the proceedings of the House are final.
- He has the responsibility to uphold the dignity and the privileges of the House.
- In the absence of the Speaker, the Deputy Speaker performs the Speaker's duties.
- The Speaker continues to hold office even after the Lok Sabha is dissolved till the newly-elected Lok Sabha is constituted.
- The Speaker and the Deputy Speaker may be removed from their offices by a resolution passed by the House with an effective majority of the House after a prior notice of 14 days to them.
- The Speaker, to maintain impartiality of his office, votes only in the case of a tie, i.e to remove a deadlock arising from equality of votes.

Penalty for sitting and voting when not qualified

- If a person sits or votes as a member of either House of the Parliament before he has complied with the requirements of Art. 99 (Oath), or when he knows that he is not qualified or that he is disqualified for membership thereof, he shall be liable in respect of each day on which he so sits or votes to a penalty of five hundred rupees to be recovered as a debt due to the Union.

Prerogatives of the Parliament

The Members of Parliament enjoy certain prerogatives and privileges, not enjoyed by other citizens. The intention behind this is to enable them to discharge their functions efficiently and fearlessly. These are enjoyed in two forms.

1. ***Individually.*** These are the prerogatives enjoyed by the parliamentarians in an individual capacity.
   - *Freedom of Speech.* The extent of the freedom of speech enjoyed by the Members of Parliament is far wider than that of an ordinary citizen under Art. 19 (1). Not only does he enjoy absolute immunity from any action in the Court of law for anything he says within the House, but even in public speeches if he is so authorised by the Parliament. However, such freedom has two limitations:
     (a) It must conform to the rules and the procedures of the House; and
     (b) The Members cannot discuss the conduct of a Judge of the Supreme Court, or the High Courts, except on the resolution for the removal of the Judges.

- *Freedom from arrest.* A Member of the Parliament enjoys immunity from arrest, 40 days before the commencement and 40 days after the prorogation of a session of the House. This immunity is only in civil cases and does not extend to criminal proceedings, or the contempt of the Court or preventive detention.
- *Freedom from the jury service.* A Member of the Parliament cannot be compelled to give witness in the case pending in the Court of law when the Parliament is in session. This is because the parliamentary business is above all the other businesses.

2. ***Collectively.*** There are certain privileges, which the members of the Parliament enjoy as a collective body, there are:
   - right to publish or not to publish the parliamentary proceedings including the right to punish individuals for publishing such reports.
   - right to exclude civilians from the House.
   - right to regulate the internal affairs of the House.
   - right to decide about its business.
   - right to punish for the contempt of the House.
   - right to punish Members and the outsiders for breach of its privileges.

Categories and Passage of the Bills

The most important function of the Parliament is making laws. The legislative procedure is initiated in the form of a Bill.

- A Bill is a proposed legislation. It becomes a law when it is assented to by the President.
- These Bills are classified as— Ordinary, Financial, Money and the Constitutional Amendment Bills. The Bills are of two types–the Government Bills and the Private Member's Bills. Money, Financial and an Ordinary Bill under Art. 3 are essentially the Government Bills, because these can only be introduced on the recommendation of the President. Other Bills can be introduced by private members also (any Member other than a Minister is a private member). The procedure for the passage of both types of Bills is the same.

Ordinary Bills

- All the bills, other than Financial Bills, Money Bills and the Constitutional Amendment Bills are Ordinary Bills.
- Such bills can be introduced in either House of the Parliament (in Lok Sabha or the Rajya Sabha) without the recommendation of the President, except those bills under Article 3 (i.e. Bills related to reorganisation of the territory of a State).
- These Bills are passed by a simple majority by both the Houses. Both the Houses enjoy equal jurisdiction over such Bills and in case of a deadlock due to any reason, the tie is resolved by a joint sitting.
- The President has the right to return such Bills for reconsideration to the Parliament once.
- Each House has laid down a procedure for the passage of a Bill. According to the procedure of the House, a Bill has to pass through three stages commonly known as **Readings**.
- *First Reading:* The Bill is introduced in the House. At this stage, no discussion takes place.
- *Second Reading:* This is the consideration stage when the Bill is discussed clause by clause.
- *Third Reading:* During this stage, a brief general discussion of the Bill takes place and the Bill is finally passed.
- When the Bill is passed by one House, it is sent to the other House for its consideration.

Money Bills

Money Bill is defined in Art. 110 of the Constitution. As per the Article, any Bill dealing with all or any of the matters enumerated from (a) to (g) of the same Article shall be a Money Bill. These are:

a. Imposition, abolition, remission, alteration or regulation of any tax.

b. Regulation of the borrowings of money or giving of guarantee by the Government of India.

c. Custody of the Consolidated or Contingency Fund of India, payment into or withdrawal of money from any such fund.

d. Appropriation of money out of the Consolidated Fund of India (CFI).

e. Declaring any expenditure as 'Charged' on the CFI.

f. Receipt or issue of money from the CFI and audit of the accounts of the Union or the States.

g. Any matter incidental to any of the matter specified in the sub-clauses (a) to (f).

- If there arises any question over the validity of the Money Bill, the decision of the Speaker of the Lok Sabha is final. The Speaker duly certifies the Bill as Money Bill because this Bill passes through special procedures (Art. 109).
- A Money Bill can only originate in the Lok Sabha after the recommendation of the President.
- After being passed by the Lok Sabha, the Money Bill passes on to the Rajya Sabha which has four options:

  a) Pass the Bill in the original form;

  b) Reject the Bill;

  c) Take no action for 14 days;

  d) Send the Bill with suggestive amendments to the Lok Sabha.

If the case is either (b) or (c), the Bill shall be automatically deemed to have been passed by the Rajya Sabha. In case of (d), the Lok Sabha has sole authority to accept or reject one or all of the recommendation(s) and in this case also the Bill shall be deemed as passed with or without recommendations.

- There is no provision for a joint-sitting of the Parliament to pass a Money Bills
- After the Money Bill is passed by the Lok Sabha and the Rajya Sabha, it is presented to the President who unlike in the case of other Bills, has no right to withhold it (Art. 111).
- The 'Appropriation Bill' and the 'Annual Financial Bill' are Money Bills.

Financial Bills

Any Bill dealing with revenue or expenditure, but not certified as a Money Bill by the Speaker, is a Financial Bill. These Financial Bills are of two classes:

a) A Bill containing any of the matters specified in Art. 110, but not exclusively dealing with those matters. For example, a Bill containing taxation clause, but not solely dealing with taxation. This is called the Financial Bill of First Class.

b) An Ordinary Bill contains provisions involving expenditure from the Consolidated Fund of India. This is called the Financial Bill of Second Class.

As regards the procedure for its passage, a Financial Bill is as good as an Ordinary Bill except that a Financial Bill cannot be introduced without the President's recommendation, and it can only be introduced in the Lok Sabha. Thus, a Financial Bill is passed according to the ordinary procedure provided for passing of an Ordinary Bill.

Constitutional Amendment Bills

- Art. 368 deals with the power of the Parliament to amend the Constitution, and the procedure thereof.
- A Bill for this can be introduced in either House (the Lok Sabha or the Rajya Sabha) of the Parliament and there is no need of the President's recommendation for this.
- Such a Bill must be passed by each House separately with a special majority required under Art. 368, i.e. not less than two-third of the Members of the House present and voting.
- This majority should be more than the absolute majority of the House.
- The joint-sitting of Parliament is not possible for passing such a Bill (Art. 108).
- If the Bill is passed by both the Houses, it goes for the President's assent.
- By the 24th Constitutional Amendment Act, it is obligatory for the President to give his assent to the Bill amending the Constitution.
- But the constitutional amending power of the Parliament is subject to the 'Basic structure of the Constitution'. Thus, the amending power is limited.
- The Supreme Court can strike down any such amendment, if it is not in concurrence with the basic structure of the Constitution.
- The Government should not take the decision of the Court as a challenge against it, but in the spirit of the compromise and cooperation between the two important organs of the State.

The Budget

- According to Article 112, the President shall in respect of every financial year, cause to be laid before both the Houses of the Parliament, an annual financial statement commonly known as the Budget.
- This statement gives out the estimated income and expenditure for that year.

The estimated expenditure is shown separately under two heads–

a) The sums *charged* upon the Consolidated Fund of India, and

b) The sums required to meet other expenditure out of the Consolidated Fund of India.

- The Budget provides an opportunity to review and explain financial and economic policies and programmes of the Government.
- After introduction of the Budget, the Lok Sabha discusses the proposed expenditures (Demands for Grants) of various Ministries and Departments, and approve it one by one.
- All the expenditures approved through various Demands for Grants and expenses charged on the Consolidated Fund of India are then presented in the form of a single Bill called the 'Appropriation Bill'.
- The proposal for taxation to raise revenue are separately presented in the form of a 'Financial Bill'. Both these Bills are Money Bills and are passed accordingly.

Parliamentary Control over Financial System

- In financial matters, the Parliament has effective control over the Executive.
- The Annual Budget is presented to the Parliament and is passed by it.
- The Appropriation and the Financial Bills are also passed by the Parliament.
- Unless the Appropriation Bill is passed, no money can be withdrawn by the Government from the Consolidated Fund of India.
- It also exercises control over financial matters through the Public Accounts Committee and the Estimates Committee.
- The Public Accounts Committee considers the Appropriation accounts.
- It also considers the report of the Comptroller and Auditor General. The report is submitted to the House.
- The Estimates Committee examines such estimates (presented to the Lok Sabha) of the Budget as may seem fit to the Committee, suggests economy in the expenditure and other steps for increasing efficiency, finds out whether the money is well laid out and also suggests the form in which the estimates should be presented to the Parliament.

Parliamentary Committees

- The Legislature has to perform complex and enormous quantity of work.
- Due to the paucity of time in the Legislature, the initial work is mostly done by the Committees, appointed or elected for specific purposes.
- These Committees essentially belong to the Lok Sabha and function under the Speaker to whom they submit their reports.
- These Parliamentary Committees are classified as– the Standing Committees and the *Ad-hoc* Committees. While the former are permanent in nature, the latter are constituted for specific purposes and they cease to exist after completion of the specific work.
- Presently, there are 24 standing committees of Parliament.
- The most important Committees, with their strength in brackets, are as follows:

  Business and Advisory Committee (15), Estimates Committee (30), Committee on Public Accounts (22), Committee on Petitions (15), Committee on the Welfare of the Schedule Castes and Scheduled Tribes (30).
- Members of the Rajya Sabha are also given representation, usually about one-third, except in the Estimates Committee.
- Members of the Committees are generally elected or nominated for a term of not more than one year. As far as possible, all the parties in the Parliament are represented in these Committees in proportion to their strength in the Parliament, so that they become a microcosm of the whole House of the Parliament.
- The Chairperson of all the Committees of Parliament are appointed by the Speaker, except that of the Joint Committee on Salaries and Allowances of the Members of the Parliament, who is elected by the Committee itself.
- Wherever the Speaker is a member of a Committee, he is the ex-officio Chairman of that (those) Committee(s).
- The Chairman of the Committee on Public Accounts is appointed by the Speaker from amongst the Members of the Lok Sabha, and is generally an opposition member.

Details of some of the important Committees are:

1. ***Committee on Estimates.*** This Committee consists of 30 members, all derived from the Lok Sabha. All the parties in the Parliament are given proportionate representation in this Committee. The Chairman is appointed by the Speaker from amongst its members. A Minister is not liable to be elected to the Committee and if its member is appointed a Minister, he ceases to be a member of the Committee. The term of the office is for not more than one year. The functions of the Committee are:
   - To report on the efficiency of the policy underlying the estimates;
   - To examine whether the money is well laid out within the limits of the policy implied in the estimates;
   - To suggest the form in which the estimates are to be presented in the Parliament.

   The Committee works well within the limits of the policy approved by the Parliament, but it may suggest a change if it thinks so.

2. ***Committee on Public Accounts.*** The twenty-two member Committee is elected through a single transferable vote, 15 from the Lok Sabha and 7 from the Rajya Sabha. Externally, the Committee belongs to the Lok Sabha and its Chairman is appointed by the Speaker and is from the Lok Sabha. *By convention, the Speaker appoints a member of the Opposition to chair the Committee.* A Minister is not eligible for election to the Committee and when its member is given the portfolio of a Ministry, he ceases to be a member of that Committee. The term of the office, is one year.

Ancillary Information

- The Union List has 97 items on which Parliament has exclusive power to legislate, e.g., defence and armed forces. The State List consists of 66 items, and individual states have exclusive authority to legislate on items included in this list (e.g. public order, police, administration of justice). Though states have exclusive powers to legislation with regard to items on the states list, Articles 249, 250, 252 and 253 mention situations in which the Union government can legislate on these items. The Concurrent List consists of 47 items on which both the states and the Union can legislate. Residuary powers are vested in the Parliament. They include the power to make any law that seeks to impose a tax not mentioned in either the Concurrent List or the State List.

The functions of the Committee include:

a. To examine the accounts showing the appropriation granted by the Parliament to meet the expenditure of the Government of India.

b. To examine the Annual Finance Accounts of the Government of India and other accounts laid before the House.

c. To examine the reports of the Comptroller and Auditor General (CAG) of India on revenue receipts.

3. ***Committee on Public Undertakings.*** This Committee consists of 15 members of the Lok Sabha and 7 associated members of the Rajya Sabha, elected by means of a single transferable vote in both the Houses. The Chairman of the Committee is appointed from amongst the members of the Lok Sabha by the Speaker. A Minister is not eligible to be elected as a member of the Committee. The functions of the Committee are:

   a. To examine the reports and the Accounts of the Public Undertakings specified in the Fourth Schedule of the Rules of Procedure and Conduct of Business of the Lok Sabha and also the report of the CAG, if any.

   b. To examine the efficiency and autonomy of the Public Undertakings.

   c. To examine other specific subjects or matters referred to it by the House or the Speaker.

4. ***Committee on Welfare of the Scheduled Castes and Scheduled Tribes.*** This Committee consists of 20 members from the Lok Sabha and 10 members from the Rajya Sabha. The members are elected by means of a single transferable vote through the principle of proportional representation. The Chairman is one of the members of the Committee and is appointed by the Speaker. A Minister is not eligible to become member of the Committee. The functions include:

   a. To consider the reports submitted by the Commissioner for the Schedule Castes and the Scheduled Tribes.

   b. To examine the representation of the Scheduled Castes and the Scheduled Tribes in services of the Central Government Departments, Central Public Undertakings, Nationalised Banks, and so on.

   c. To review the working of the welfare programmes of the Central Government for the Scheduled Castes and the Scheduled Tribes and to examine such other matters referred to it by the House or the Speaker.

d. May examine implementation of the welfare programme for the SCs and the STs by the State Government, provided the funds for this, made available partly or wholly by the Central Government.

- By President on advice of PM.
- Bills pending in Rajya Sabha, passed by Lok Sabha also lapse unless President calls a joint sitting of the 2 houses.
- Bills pending in Rajya Sabha, not passed by Lok Sabha don't lapse.
- The Contingency Fund of India was established through an Act of Parliment in 1950 in exercise of the power vested in it by Article 267 of the Constitution.
- The Fund has been placed at the disposal of the President to make advances out of this fund to meet unforeseen expenditure.
- However, these expenses must be subsequently authorised by Parliament and recovered through supplementary, additional or excess grants.

Chapter 6 Panchayati Raj & Local Urban Government in India

- The panchayati Raj is a South Asian political system in India, Pakistan, and Nepal. "Panchayat" literally means assembly (yet) of five (panch) wise and respected elders elected and accepted by the village community. Traditionally, these assemblies settled disputes between individuals and villages. After Independence, the modern Indian government has decentralised several administrative functions to the village level, empowering elected Gram panchayats. Gram panchayats are not to be confused with the unelected khap panchayats (or caste panchayats) found in some parts of India.
- Panchayati Raj translates literally to `Governance by five individuals'. The idea is to ensure at the village or grass root level a functioning and vibrant democracy. While the idea of grass roots democracy is not imported to our country, in a society where there are sharp inequalities, democratic participation is hindered on grounds of gender, caste and class. Therefore, traditionally there have been caste panchayats in villages. But they have usually represented dominant groups.
- Panchayat or Panchayati Raj is a system of governance in which gram panchayats are the basic units of administration. It has 3 levels : village, block and district. The term `panchayat raj' is relatively new, having originated during the British administartion `Raj' explains the governance or government. Mahatma Gandhi advocated Panchayati Raj, a decentralised form of Government where each village is responsible for its own affairs, as the foundation of India's political system. His term for such a vision was "Gram Swaraj" (Village Self-governance).
- Panchayats played an important role in India and have been the backbone of the Indian citizens. It was adopted by state governments during the 1950s and 60s as laws were passed to setup Panchayats in various states. It also found backing in the Indian Constitution, with the 73rd amendment in 1992 to accommodate the idea. The Amendment Act of 1992 contains procedures for devolution of powers and responsibilities to the panchayats to both for preparation of plans for economic development and social justice and for implementation with relation to twenty-nine subjects listed in the eleventh schedule of the Constitution.
- The Panchayats receive funds from three sources -
  1. The local body grants, as suggested by the Central Finance Commission.
  2. The funds for implementation of centrally-sponsored schemes, and
  3. The funds released by the state governments on the recommendations of the State Finance Commissions.
- In the history of Panchayati Raj in India on 24 April 1993, the Constutional (73rd Amendment) Act, 1992 came into force to provide constitutional status to the Panchayati Raj institutions.
- The main objective of this act is to provide 3-tier system of Panchayati Raj for all states having population of over 2 million, to hold Panchayat elections regularly every 5 years, to provide reservation of seats for Scheduled Castes, Scheduled Tribes and Women, to appoint State Finance Commission to make recommendations as regards the financial powers of the Panchayats and to constitute District Planning Committee prepare draft development plan for the district.
- The 73rd and 74th amendments to the Constitution ensured the reservation of one-third of the total seats for women in all elected offices of local bodies in both the rural and urban areas. Out of this, 17 percent seats are reserved for women belonging to the scheduled castes and tribes. It is a significant amendment as for the first time it brought women into elected bodies which also empower them to take decision.
- One-third of the seats in local bodies, gram panchayats, village panchayats, municipalities, city coropration and district boards are reserved for women. The 1993-94 elections, soon after the 73rd amendment brought in 800,000 women into the political processes in a single election. A constitutional amendment prescribed a three-tier system of local self-governance for the entire country, effective since 1992-93.
- The three-tier system of Panchayati Raj Institution. The structure is like a pyramid. At the base of the structure stands the unit of democracy or Gram Sabha. This consists of the entire body of citizens in a village or gram.
- This is general body that elects the local government and charges it with specific roles and responsibilities. The Gram Sabhas ideally ought to provide an open forum for discussion and village-level development activities and play a crucial role in ensuring inclusion of the weaker sections in the decision-making processes.

Functioning of Panchayats

- According to the Constitution, Panchayats in respective areas would prepare plans for economic development and social justice and also execute them. To promote this, states are supposed to devolve functions to Panchayats (29 subjects as mandated) and also make funds available for doing these (as per State Finance Commissions recommendations).
- The works of Panchayats are divided among different Committees (as ministries are formed in state and union government), which are called Standing Committee/ Sthayee Samitis/Upa Samitis, etc. One of the members remains in charge of each of such committees while the over-all charge rests with the chairperson of the Panchayat. Panchayats are assisted by a host of other of officials, the number of which varies from state to state.
- Apart from grants received from the government under the Suggestion of the Finance Commission, Panchayats receive schematic funds for execution of schemes (MGNREGS, BRGF, IAY, etc.). They can also raise revenue by imposing taxes, fees, penalties, etc. as per rule of the state.
- The concept of Panchayti Raj was dreamt by Mahatma Gandhi, the father of the nation, its need was stressed by Pandit Nehru, and it was repeatedly and forcefully advocated by Late Shri Jai Prakash Narayan. But, unfortunately, for various reasons, not much headway could be made for the realisation of this ideal. Ever since Late Shri Rajiv Gandhi came to the helm of affairs in the country, he repeatedly stressed the importance of Panchayati Raj.
- He formed his views on the subject by undertaking whirlwind tours of rural India to familiarise himself with the realities of rural life, by holding frequent workshops of District magistrate all over the country, and thus assessing their views and understanding their difficulties.
- As a result of this interaction with the people and the administrators, his views on Panchayati Raj gradually evolved, his thoughts were clarified and he could from his own plan of Panchayati Raj and place it before the parliament with perfect self-confidence. He also sought to give it constitutional sanction by proposing to add a fresh chapter to the Indian constitution in the form of the 64th amendment, through the Bill which he moved in the parliament on the 15th of May, 1989. As a result of his clarity of thought and powerful advocacy, the bill was passed with near unanimity, with only five M.P.S voting against it.
- Panditji established the institution of Panchayati Raj as the primary instrument for bringing development to the doorstep of rural India. Indiraji stressed the need for the people's participation in the processes of economic and social transformation."
- The Act has provision for regular periodic elections of Panchayati Raj Institutions. In the absence of any compelling provision to reconstitute Panchayats within a reasonable period of time, by democratic elections, suspended Panchayats have remained dissolved for up to a decade or even more. Their existence depended less on the mandate of the people than on the whim of state governments.

Panchayati Raj Committees

S.No.	Chairman	Committee	Year
1.	V.R. Rao	Committee on Rationalisation of Panchayat Statistics	1960
2.	S.D. Mishra	Working Group on Panchayats & Co-operatives	1961
1.	V. Ishwaran	Study Team on Panchayati Raj Administration	
2.	G.R. Rajgopal	Study Team on Nyaya Panchayats	1962
3.	R.R. Diwakar	Study Team on the Position of Gram Sabha in Panchayati Raj Movement	1963
4.	M. Rama Krishnayya	Study Team on Budgeting and Accounting Procedure of Panchayati Raj Institutions	
5.	K. Santhanam	Study Team on Panchayati Raj Finances	1963
6.	K. Santhanam	Committee on Panchayati Raj Elections	1965
7.	R.K. Khanna	Study Team on the Audit and Accounts of Panchayati Raj Bodies.	1965
8.	G. Ram Chandran	Committee on Panchayati Raj Training Centres	1966
9.	Smt. Daya Chaube	Committee on Community Development and Panchayati Raj	1976

Ashok Mehta Committee:

In **December 1977,** the **Janta Party Government** appointed a committee on **Panchayati Raj institutions** under the **Chairmanship** of **Ashok Mehta.** The Committee submitted its report in **November, 1978** and 132 recommendations to revive and strengthen the Panchayati Raj system in the country.

Its main recommendations are as following :

The **three-tier system of Panchayati Raj should be replaced by the two-tier system,** that is, **ZilaParishad, at the district** level, and below it, the **Mandal Panchayat** consisting of a **group of villages** with a total population of 15000-20000.

There should be an official participation of political parties at all levels of Panchayat elections.

The Panchayati Raj institutions should have **power of leving taxes.**

The **Nyaya Panchayats** should be kept as separate bodies from the development Panchayats.

Seats for SC's and ST's should be reserved on the basis of **their population.**

The state government should not supersede the Panchayati Raj institutions. In case of an imperative super sessions, **elections should be held within six months from the date of super session.**

G.V.K. Rao Committee :

This committee was constituted in **1985** by the **Planning Commission of India.**

Its recommendations are as follows :

The district level body, that is, **Zila Parishad** should be of pivotal importance in the scheme of democratic decentralisation.

A post of **District Development Commissioner should** be created.

Elections of Panchayati Raj Institutions should be held **regularly.**

L.M. Singhvi Committee :

In 1986, Rajiv Gandhi government appointed a Committee on **'Revitalisation of Panchayati Raj Institutions for Democracy and Development'** under the **Chairmanship** of **L. M. Singhvi.**

Its recommendation are as follows :

The Panchayati Raj Institutions should be constitutionally recognised, protected and preserved. **For this purpose, a new chapter should be added to the Constitution of India.**

Nyaya Panchayats should be **established.**

·The **Villages Panchayats** should have more **financial resources.**

·**The judicial tribunals should be established.**

After approving L.M.Singhvi Committee report, the Rajiv Gandhi government introduced the **64th Constitutional Amendment Bill in the Lok Sabha in July 1989** to constitutionalise the **Panchayati Raj institutions** and make them more powerful and broad-based. Apart from it, the government also introduced **65th Constitutional Amendment Bill** related to **Municipalities** in the **Lok Sabha,** but this could not be passed. Soon after, the **V.P. Singh** government introduced a constitutional amendment bill in **September, 1990 in the LokSabha** related to the strengthening of the Panchayati Raj bodies, but it too, did **not pass due to the falling of the government introduced 73rd Constitutional Bill for** the **Panchayati Raj Systems** and **74th Constitutional Amendment Bill for the Municipalities in the LokSabha.** This **bill finally emerged as the 73rd and 74th Constitutional Amendment Act** respectively and provided a strong constitutional base to the **Panchayats and Municipalites.**

- The bill empowers to the state to decide the grounds and conditions on which Panchayats may be suspended or dissolved. The State Legislatures are to specify the grounds on which the Governor may suspend or dissolve a Panchayat. That is a matter for the Governor, acting in accordance with the constitution on the advice of the state Government.
- But dissolved Panchayats must be reconstructed within a reasonable period of time. It is the people who will determine, within a matter of months, the shape of the reconstituted Panchayat. The Bill will ensure that Panchayati Raj has a democratic character similar to the Lok Sabha and the state Assemblies and Constitutional protection for their functioning as representative institutions of the people.
- Once the people have their own elected representatives from electorates as small as a hundred persons, the source of power will lie only as far away as the Panchayat Ghar, not in some distant state capital or even the more distant capital of the country.
- There will be direct elections to Panchayats at all levels. Every voter has power to the Gram Panchayat, the mid-level Panchayat. The representative will be responsible to small and recognised electorate. if the elected panchayats does not work for the people's need, then people can reject them in next term elections or by not giving vote to them for next term elections. It is the Power of Vote.

- In establishing the institutions of democracy in Parliament and in the State Legislature, our founding fathers gave particular recognition to the disabilities suffered by the Scheduled Castes and tribes. The procedures was made for the reservation of seats for the total electorate. This is a principle which has not been incorporated in most of the Panchayat Raj legislations enacted by the state Legislatures.
- The democratic rights of the Scheduled Castes and Scheduled Tribes cannot be secured by good intentions alone. It has to be secured in the first instance, by reservation in Panchayati Raj Institutions on the same basis as reservations are given in the Lok Sabha and the state Assemblies. The Bill makes it mandatory for the state legislatures to ensure reservation for the Scheduled Castes and the Scheduled Tribes in proportion to their population in the relevant Panchayat area.
- The Panchayats will have the power and authority to draw of plans within the framework of guidelines and conditions to be laid draw by the state Government. These plans will constitute the basic inputs for the planning process of higher levels. This will ensure that the voice of the people, their needs, their aspirations, their priorities become the building blocks of the edifice of planning. The second major responsibility of the Panchayat will be the impelementation of development schemes assigned to them by the state governments.

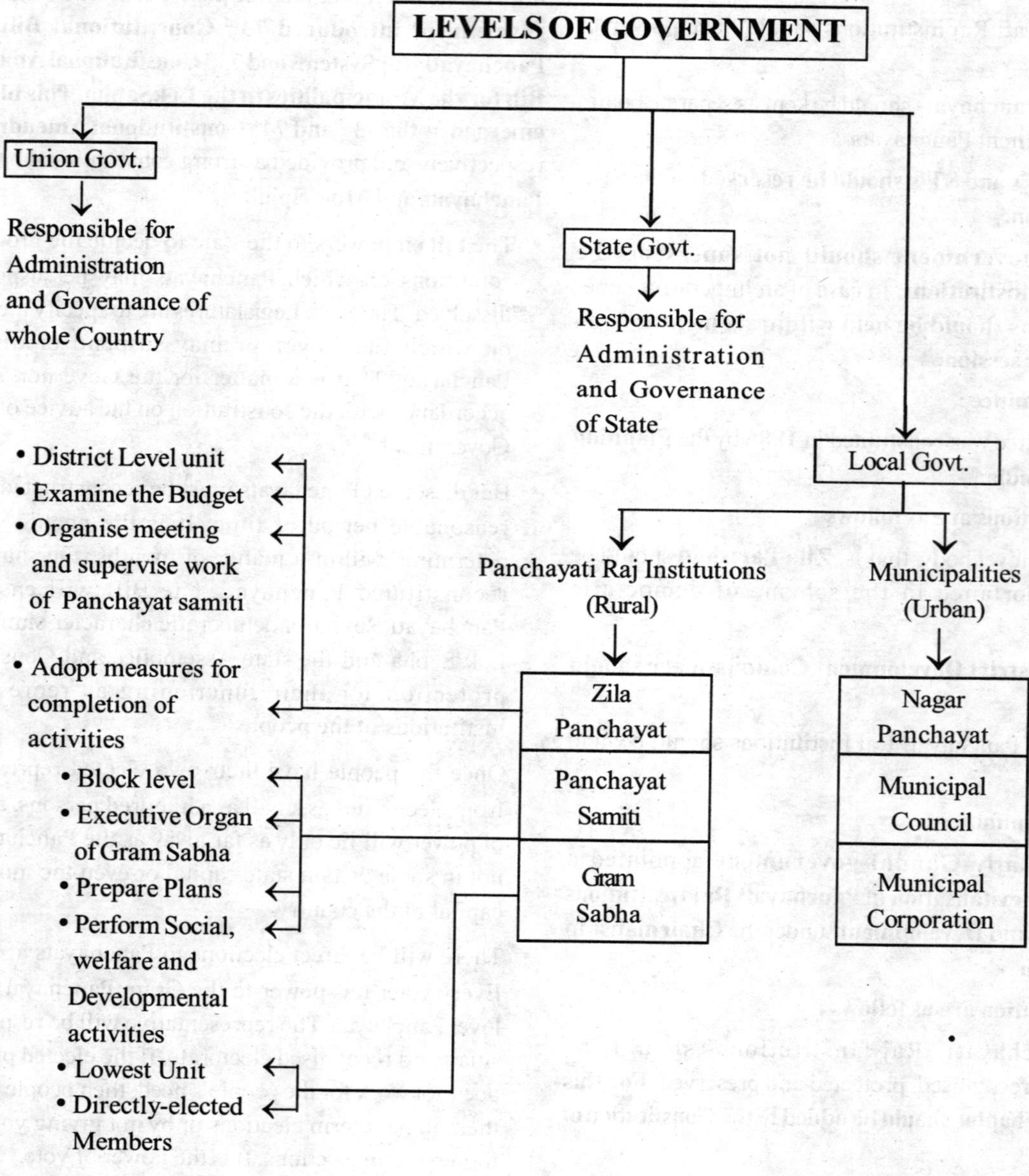

- In this way, development will be taken to the grassroots in rural India. The same concern must be extended to the growing urban and semi-urban population of the country. To this end, a new chapter has been added to the Constitution. Urban municipalities and corporations have been brought within the two major questions have been raised repeatedly.
- Our democracy has reached the stage where the full participation of the people seeks no further delay. Those who decry Panchayati Raj as an election stunt are only those whose feudal interest will be overthrown by the power reaching the people. The late Prime Minister Rajiv Gandhi said, "We trust the people. We have faith in the people. It is the people who must determine their own destinies and the destiny of the nation. To the people of India let us ensure maximum democracy and maximum devolution of power. Let there be by the States to Panchayats.

'Urban Local Government'

The term **'Urban Local Government'** in India signifies the governance of an **urban area by the people** through their **elected representatives.** Urban local government was introduced by **Rajiv Gandhi Government** at first through the **65th Constitutional Amendment Bill** in the **Lok Sabha in 1989.** The bill aimed at strengthening the municipal bodies by conferring a constitutional status on them. However, the **bill could not be passed due to some reason.** Further, **P.V. Narasimha Rao's Government** introduced the modified **Municipalities Bill in the Lok-Sabha** in**September 1991.** It finally emerged as **the 74th Constitutional Amendment Act-1992** approved by **the President in April-1993 and came** into force on **June 1, 1993.** This Act added a **new part-IX A** to the **Constitution of India** and entitled as **'the Municipalities'.** It consists of **Provisions from Article-243-P to 243-ZG.** In addition, the Act also added a new **Twelfth Schedule** to the **Constitution,** containing **eighteen (18) functional items of Municipalities.**

There are three types of Municipalities mentioned in the Constitution :

1. **Nagar Panchayat** – Its a transitional form of rural and urban area.
2. **Nagar Palika/Municipal Council** – It consists of **20,000 to 3 lakhs of population.**
3. **Nagar Nigam/Municipal Corporation** – It consists of **more than 3 lakhs of population.**

All the members of a municipality are **elected directly by the people** of the municipal area. For this purpose, each municipal area is divided into **Wards.** The **State Legislature decides the manner in which election of the Chair-person of a municipality is held.** The members of the **Lok-Sabha and the State Legislative Council** is registered as **electors within the municipal area. The act provides for the reservation of seats on the basis of total population in a Municipal area.** Further, it provides for the **reservation of not less than one-third of the population in the municipal area.** The state legislature may provide for the manner of reservation of offices of chair-persons in the municipalities. **The term of a Municipality is fixed for 5 years.** However, it may dissolve before the completion of its term, the **fresh election must be completed within six months from the date of its dissolution. Anyone can be elected as or for** being a **member of a municipality he is 21 yrs. of age.** The municipality works on the subjects given in the **Twelvth Schedule** of the **Constitution.**

1. **Urban planning including town planning;**
2. **Regulation of land use and construction of building;**
3. **Economical and social development planning;**
4. **Roads and bridges;**
5. **Water supply for domestic, industrial and commercial purposes;**
6. **Public health, sanitation, conservancy and solid waste management;**
7. **Fire sevices**
8. **Urban forestry protection of the environment and promotion of ecological aspects;**
9. **Safeguarding of interests of weaker sections of society including the handicapped and mentally retarded;**
10. **Slum improvement and upgradation;**
11. **Urban poverty allevation;**
12. **Provisions of urban amenities and facilities such as park, garden and play-grounds;**
13. **Promotion of cultured, educational craesthetic aspects;**
14. **Burial and burial grounds, cremation and cremation grounds and electrical crematoriums.**
15. **Cattle ponds, prevention of cruelty to animals**
16. **Vital statistics including registration of births and deaths;**
17. **Public amenities including street lighting, parking lots, bus stop and public conveniences, and**
18. **Regulation of slaughter houses and tanneries.**

District Planning Commission

This committee has been constituted under Article-243(ZD) of the Constitution. It consolidates the plans prepared by panchayats and municipalities in the district and prepares a draft of development plan for the district as a whole. The four-fifth of the members of a district planning committee should be elected by the elected members of the district panchayat and municipalities in the district from the amongst themselves. The Chairman of the Committee shall forward the plan to the State Government.

Metropolitan Planning Commission

This committee has been constituted under Article-243(ZE) of the Constitution. Its main function is to prepare a draft of Metropolitan Development Plan and forward it to the State Government. Two-thirds member of the Committee are elected by the elected members of the municipalities and the chairpersons of the panchayats in the metropolitan area from amongst themselves.

Types of Urban Government

There are eight types of urban local bodies are created in India for the administration of urban areas –

1. Municipal Corporation
2. Municipality
3. Notified Area Committee
4. Cantonment Board
5. Township
6. Port Trust
7. Special Purpose Agency
8. Town Area Committee

Provisions of the Panchayats (Extention to the Scheduled Areas) Act, 1996 (PESA)

The Provisions of Part-IX under Article-244 of the Constitution relating to the panchayats are not applicable to the fifth scheduled areas. The main objects of this act are to provide self rule for the bulk of the tribal population, to evolve a suitable administrative framework consistent with traditional practices and to empower panchayats at the appropriate level with specific powers conducive to tribal requirement.

Features of the Act

1. Every Village shall have a Gram sabha consisting of persons whose names are included in the electral rolls for the Panchayat at the village level.
2. The Gram shall work to safeguard and preserve the traditions and customs of the people, their cultural identity, community resources and the customary made of dispute resolution.
3. A village shall ordinarily consist of a habitation or a group of habitations or a hamlet or a group of hamlets comprising a community and managing its affairs in accordance with traditions and customs.
4. The Gram Sabha shall approve the plans, programmes and projects for social and economical development before they are taken up for implementation by the Panchayat at the village level.
5. Every Panchayat at the village level shall be required to obtain a certification of utilisation of funds for the above plans, programmes and projects.
6. Planning and management of minor water bodies in the Scheduled Area shall be entrusted to Panchayats at the appropriate level.
7. The prior recommendation of the Gramm Sabha or the panchayats at the appropriate level shall be mandatory for grant of concession for the exploitation of minor minerals by a action.
8. The Panchayats in the scheduled area are being empowered with suitable powers and make them enable to function as institution.

7 Chapter
Centre-State Relations

General Introduction

- The Centre and the States are the important feature of federalism. A federal Constitution establishes dual polity with the Union at the Centre and the States at the periphery, each endowed with sovereign powers to be exercised in the field assigned to them respectively by the Constitution.
- The one is not subordinate to the other in its own field, the authority of one is concurrent with that of the other.
- The basic principle of federation is that the legislative, executive and financial authority is divided between the Centre and the States, not by any law passed by the Centre, but by the Constitution itself.

A. The Legislative Relations

- Our Constitution-makers followed the Canadian scheme, opting for a strong Centre. However, they added one more List—the Concurrent List.
- The present Constitution adopts the method followed by the Government of India Act, 1935, and divides the powers between the Union and the States in three Lists—the Union List, the State List and the Concurrent List.
- The Union List has the of 99 subjects. The subjects mentioned in the Union List are of national importance, i.e. defence, foreign affairs, banking, currency, coinage, citizenship, post and telegraphs, etc.
- The State List consists of 66 subjects. These are of local importance, such as, public order and police, local government, public health and sanitation, agriculture, justice, irrigation, etc.
- The Concurrent List has 46 subjects. Both the Centre and the States can make laws on the subjects mentioned in the Concurrent List. But in the case of any conflict between the Central and the State laws on the Concurrent subjects, the Central law will prevail.

Residuary Powers: Article 248 vests the residuary powers in the Parliament. It explains that the Parliament has exclusive power to make any law with respect to any matter not enumerated in the Concurrent List or the State List.

Parliament's power to Legislate on State Subjects. Though in general the division of powers must be strictly maintained and neither the States nor the Centre can encroach upon the sphere allotted to the other by the Constitution, but in certain exceptional circumstances, the above system of distribution is either suspended or the powers of the Union Parliament are extended over the subjects mentioned in the State List. The exceptional circumstances are:

1. ***Parliament is authenticated to legislate in the national interests:***
   - According to Article 249, if the Rajya Sabha passes a resolution, supported by 2/3rd of the members present and voting, that it is essential or expedient in the national interest that the Parliament should make laws with respect to any matter enumerated in the State List, specified in the resolution.
   - It shall be according to law for the Parliament to make rules for the whole or any part of the territory of India with respect to that matter while the resolution remains in force.
   - Such a resolution normally lasts for a year; it may be renewed as many times as necessary but not exceeding for a year at a time.
2. ***During a Proclamation of Emergency:***
   - According to Article 250, while the Emergency is in operation, the Parliament shall have power to make laws for the whole or any part of the territory of India with respect to all matters in the State List.

3. ***Parliament's power to legislate with the consent of the States:***

- According to Article 252, if the Legislatures of two or more States pass a resolution to the effect that it is desirable to have a law passed by the Parliament on any matter in the State List, it shall be legitimate for the Parliament to make laws regulating that matter.
- Any other State may adopt such a law by passing a resolution to that effect. Such type of rules can only be amended or repealed by an Act of the Parliament and not by an Act of the Legislature of that State.

4. ***Parliament's power to legislate for giving effect to the treaties and international agreements:***

- Article 253 gives power to the Parliament to make any law for the whole or any part of the territory of India for implementing the treaties and international agreements and convention, even if the subjects covered by such treaties and agreements fall within the State List.
- In another words, the general distribution of the powers will not stand in the way of the Parliament to pass a law for giving effect to an international obligation even though such law relates to any of the subject in the State List.

5. ***In case of incapability of the Constitutional function in a State:***

- Under Article 356, the Parliament is empowered to make laws with respect to all the matters in the State List when the Parliament announces that the State Government cannot be carried on in accordance with the provisions of the Constitution and the Parliament assumes all the Legislative functions of the States.

  Thus, from the scheme of division of legislative powers between the Union and the States, it is quite evident that the framers have given more powers to the Union Parliament as against the State Legislatures.

Centre's control over the State Legislation

In addition to the Parliament's power to legislate directly on the State subjects, the Constitution also has the provision for the Centre's consent before a Bill passed by a State Legislature can become a law.

(a) Although the State enjoys authority to legislate on the subjects of the State List, the Centre is authenticated to direct the State Legislature to have conformity with the Union Laws.

(b) Any legislation approved by the State Legislature for acquisition of private property for public purposes will not become a law unless it has the assent of the President (Art. 31A).

(c) Under Art. 200, the Governor has power to reserve a Bill for the President's consideration. Further, under the same Article, the Governor has been directed to reserve any Bill affecting the dignity and functioning of the High Court for the President's consideration.

(d) Under Art. 288(2), a State is authorised to apply taxes on water, electricity – stored, generated, consumed or distributed by the Central authority, e.g. National Thermal Power Corporation (NTPC), National Hydel Power Corporation (NHPC), etc. however this kind of regulations are effective only after the President's assent.

(e) Under Art. 304(b), the State Legislature is authorised to pass Bills related to the imposition of reasonable restrictions on the freedom of trade, commerce, and intercourse within the State in public interest. But any such Bill requires the President's prior approval for its introduction in the House.

(f) The Parliament may authorise the Central Government to delegate its functions or duties to a State Government or its officials even without the consent of the concerned State (Art. 258).

B. Administrative Relations

- The success and strength of a federal polity depends upon the *maxim* of co-operation and co-ordination between the Governments.
- In fact, the adjustment of the administrative relations between the Union and the States is one of the complicated problems in a federal system of Government.
- The framers of the Indian Constitution, therefore, decided to include detailed provisions to avoid clashes between the Centre and the States in the administrative domain.

- The Indian Constitution has a strong bias towards the Centre to make it strong. The Central administration prevails over the State administration.
- The executive powers of the State should be so exercised as to ensure compliance with the laws of the Union Parliament (Art. 256) and not impede or prejudice the executive power of the Union (Art. 257).
- If the State does not comply with the directives of the Centre, the latter may invoke Art. 356 and take-over the administration of the State to itself (President's rule).
- Under Art.258(2), the Parliament is given power to use the State machinery to enforce the Union laws.
- In case of any untoward happenings, officials of the All-India Services [e.g. IAS, IPS and IFS (Forest)] can only be suspended by the State. The State cannot take disciplinary action.
- The Centre can deploy military and para-military forces in a State even against the wishes of the State Government.
- In case of disputes related to the waters of the inter-State rivers or river valleys, the Parliament has the power to adjudicate. Under this power, the Parliament has constituted a 3-member River Water Tribunal whose award, if published by the Union Government in the Gazette, is binding on the concerned States (Art. 262).
- For co-ordination between the States, the President is empowered under Art. 263 to constitute a Council to resolve the disputes and or to discuss subjects of common interest between the States *inter se* and between the States and the Union. Exercising this power, the President has so far constituted three such Councils— (i) Central Council of Health; (ii) Central Council of Local Self-government; and (iii) Transport Development Council.

C. Financial Relations

- The procedure for the financial relations between the Union and the States is heavily derived from the Government of India Act, 1935.
- The Constitution makes a distinction between the legislative power to impose a tax and the financial power to appropriate the process of the tax. But this division is not water-tight.
- The residuary power about the taxes belongs to the Parliament.
- In general, the States have little power in taxation and are heavily dependent on the Centre for financial resources. For this reason, they are often called 'Glorified Municipalities'.
- The main source of the finance for the States is the Grants-in-aid from the Centre. Thus, the Centre has an overwhelming control upon the finances of the States.
- The Constitution classifies the Union taxes into four categories on the basis of their collection and appropriation between the Union and the States. These are:

(a) Taxes levied by the Union but collected and wholly appropriated by the State (Art. 270). These are stamp duties and duties of excise on medicinal and toilet preparations.

(b) Taxes imposed and collected by the Centre, but wholly assigned to the States (Art.269). These are:

(i) Duties on the succession to the property other than the agricultural land;

(ii) Estate duty on property other than the agricultural land;

(iii) Terminal taxes on the goods and the passengers (railway, sea or air);

(iv) Taxes on railway fares and freights;

(v) Taxes on stock exchange other than the stamp duties;

(vi) Taxes on inter-state consignment of goods; and

(vii) Taxes on the sale or purchase of the newspapers and on advertisements therein.

(c) Taxes levied and collected by the Union and disseminated between the Union and the States (Art. 270). This includes taxes on income other than the agricultural income. The ratio of the division, decided by the Finance Commission appointed by the President every five year, is 78:22.

(d) Taxes levied and collected by the Union but may be shared with the States. This includes the customs and excise duties (other than those on medicinal and toilet preparations), if the Parliament by law so provides.

- Apart from these, the Centre is also authenticated to grant loans and provide Grants-in-aid (Art. 275) to the States especially for the purposes of promoting the welfare of the Scheduled Tribes and raising the level of administration of the Scheduled Areas. This is, in fact, the most important source of income for the States.
- The Union Government can borrow money on the security of the Consolidated Fund of India, but to raise loans, the States are required to take prior permission of the Parliament.
- The Comptroller and Auditor General (CAG) of India is empowered to determine the manner of maintenance of the accounts of the States and also audit those accounts. After the 73rd and 74th Amendments, the CAG can audit accounts of the Panchayats and the Municipal Corporations.
- In the duration of Financial Emergency (Art. 360), the President can require the States to decrease the salaries of their servants and direct the Governors to reserve all the Money Bills for his approval.
- It is obvious from the above details of the legislative, administrative and financial relations between the Union and the States that, the former has been provided with a predominant role in the Constitution. The States are, in many cases, given a subordinate role and in almost all aspects are heavily dependent on the Union.

Inter-State Council

- In a dual polity within the federal framework, co-ordination of the national and the state policies and their implementation becomes crucial, especially in view of the large areas of common interest and shared action. A federal forum that assists in the co-operation and co-ordination is provided in Art. 263 to bring together the federal units.

Article 263 states, if at any time it appears to the President that the public interest would be served by the establishment of a Council charged with the duty of:

- inquiring into and advising upon the conflicts which may have increased between the States;
- investigating and discussing the issue in which some or all of the States, or the Union and one or more of the States, have a common interest; or
- giving suggestion on any such subject and, in particular, recommendations for the better co-ordination of the policy and action with respect to that subject, he may establish such a Council.

The duty of any such Council is to inquire into and advise upon the relevant matters and not one of adjudicating. The President set up the Inter-State Council in 1990 with the following composition:

1. The Prime Minister as the Chairman
2. Chief Ministers of the States and those of the UTs with a Legislative Assembly, and
3. Six Union Cabinet Ministers as the members.

- The Ministers of State in the Union Council may be invited to the meetings if the agenda has any relevance for them.
- The proceedings of the Council are to be held in camera and decisions are to be taken by consensus.
- Previously, the President set up Central Council of Local Self-Government, Transport Development Council, etc.
- The Sarkaria Commission recommended that in order to differentiate the Inter-State Council from other bodies set up under the Article, it must be called the Inter-Governmental Council.
- In July 1997, the Inter-State Council meeting resolved to implement the Alternative Devolution Scheme of the Tenth Finance Commission and also recommended significant steps for making the use of Art. 356 difficult.

Zonal Councils

- The idea of development of Zonal Councils was raised by the first Prime Minister of India, Pandit Jawahar Lal Nehru in 1956 when during the course of debate on the report of the States Re-organisation Commission, he recomended that the States proposed to be reorganised may be grouped into four or five zones having an Advisory Council "to develop the habit of cooperative working" among these States.

- It was suggested by Pandit Nehru at a time when linguistic hostilities and bitterness as a result of re-organisation of the States on linguistic pattern were threatening the very fabric of our nation.
- As an antidote to such critical circumstances, it was suggested that a high level advisory forum should be set up to minimise the impact of these hostilities and to develop healthy inter-state and Centre-State environment with a view to solving inter-State problems and fostering balanced socio-economic development of the respective zones.
- India is a federal country. The distribution of functions between the Union and the State enshrined in the Constitution is such that the States enjoy autonomy within the spheres allotted to them.
- However, the economic development does not respect boundaries of the States since it is the region and the nation as a whole which constitute appropriate units of development.
- A federation, despite a clear-cut division of functions between it and its units, is therefore obliged to evolve institutions to smooth over the rigidities inherent in federalism.
- Zonal Council is one such institution, which plays a very significant role in improving the Centre-States relations.
- There are five Zonal Councils which cover between them all the States and the Union Territories except Goa, Daman and Diu, the Andaman and Nicobar Islands, and the Lakshdweep Islands. They are as follows:
    1. **Northern Zonal Council.** Includes the States of Haryana, Himachal Pradesh, Punjab, Rajasthan, National Capital Territory of Delhi and the UT of Chandigarh. Its headquarters is in New Delhi.
    2. **Central Zonal Council.** Includes the states of Uttar Pradesh and Madhya Pradesh. Its headquarters is in Allahabad.
    3. **Eastern Zonal Council.** Includes the States of Bihar, West Bengal, Orissa and Sikkim. Its headquarters is in Kolkata.
    4. **Western Zonal Council.** Includes the States of Maharashtra, Gujarat, Goa and the UTs of Dadar and Nagar Haveli and Daman and Diu. Its headquarters is in Mumbai.
    5. **Southern Zonal Council.** Includes the States of Andhra Pradesh, Karnataka, Kerala, Tamil Nadu and the UT of Puducherry. Its headquarters is in Chennai.
- The seven North Eastern States, i.e. (i) Assam (ii) Arunachal Pradesh (iii) Manipur (iv) Tripura (v) Mizoram (vi) Meghalaya and (vii) Nagaland not part in the Zonal Councils and their special problems are looked after by the **North Eastern Council**, set up under the North Eastern Council Act, 1972.

Composition

- A Zonal Council has the Union Home Minister as the Chairman of all the Councils, and the Chief Ministers of different States covered by a particular Council.
- The Chief Ministers act as the Vice-Chairman of the Council by rotation, each holding office for a period of one year at a time.
- The Councils may also be related with the following as 'advisors' for the assistance in the performance of its duties:
    (i) One person nominated by the Planning Commission,
    (ii) The Chief Secretary of each of the States in the Zone, and
    (iii) The Development Commissioner of each of the States.

Finance Commission

Article-280 of the Constitution of India provides for a Finance Commission, which is a quasi- judicial body. It is constituted by the President of India at such earlier time as he considers necessary.

The Finance Commission consists of a Chairman and four other members to be appointed by the President. The Chairman must have experience in public affairs and the four other members should be selected from amongst, the following:

1. The Judge of High Court or one who is qualified to be appointed as the same.
2. A person having specialised knowledge of finance and accounts of the government.
3. A person having wide experience in financial matter and in administration.
4. A person who has special knowledge of economics.

The Constitution authorises the parliament to determine the qualifications of members of the Commission and the manner in which they should be selected. The commission submits its report to the President, who lays it before both the Houses of Parliament. The recommendations made by the Finance Commission are only of advisory nature, not bounding. Thus, the President is not bound by them.

Functions of the Commission

1. The distribution of the net proceeds of taxes to be shared between the Centre and the States.
2. The principles that should govern the grants-in-aid to the States by the Centre (out of the Consolidated fund of India).
3. The measures needed to augment the Consolidated Fund of State to supplement the resources of the Panchayats and Municipalities in the State on the basis of the recommendations made by the State Finance Commission.
4. Any other matter referred to it by the President in the interest of sound finance.

GENERAL SCIENCE

1 Chapter

Reflection of Light

- A ray of light, the incident ray, travels in a medium.
- When it encounters a boundary with a second medium, part of the incident ray is reflected back into the first medium.
- This means it is directed backward into the first medium.

Laws of Reflection of light

- The angle of incidence and angle of reflection is equal.
- The incident ray, reflected ray and normal to the point of reflection, lie in the same plane.

Reflection of Light in a Plane Mirror

- The image formed by a plane mirror is always virtual, upright, and of the same shape and size as the object it is reflecting.

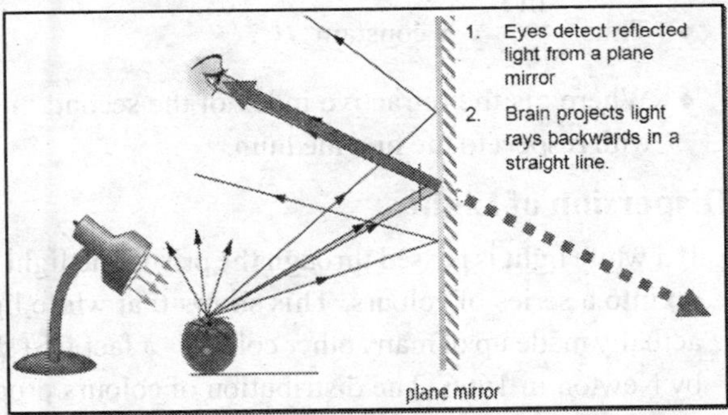

- When an object is placed in front of a plane-mirror, an image is formed behind the mirror at a distance equal to the distance of the object from the mirror.
- The focal length of plane mirror is infinity because there is no divergence or convergence and runs parallel forever. The focal length of plane mirror does not exist.
- Emergency vehicles are usually reverse-lettered, so the lettering appears normal in the rear view mirror of a car.
- The minimum mirror height necessary to see one's full image is a half-length mirror.
- The point on the mirror surface, where the incident ray strikes is called the point of incidence.
- The ray which is directed towards the reflecting surface is called the incident ray.
- The ray which is sent back into the medium is called the reflected ray.
- The perpendicular drawn at the point of incidence to the surface of mirror is called normal.
- Angle between the incident ray and normal is called the angle of incident.
- Angle between the reflected ray and normal is called the angle of reflection.

Spherical Mirror

- A spherical mirrors is actually a mirror whose surface forms a part of a hollow sphere. The sphere can be made from any type of polished metal surface, like glass.

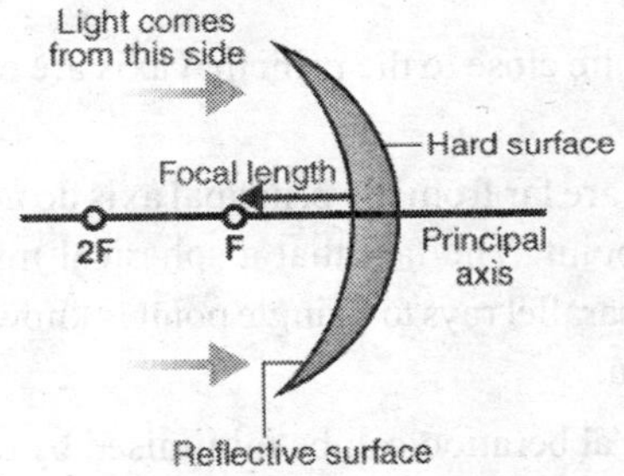

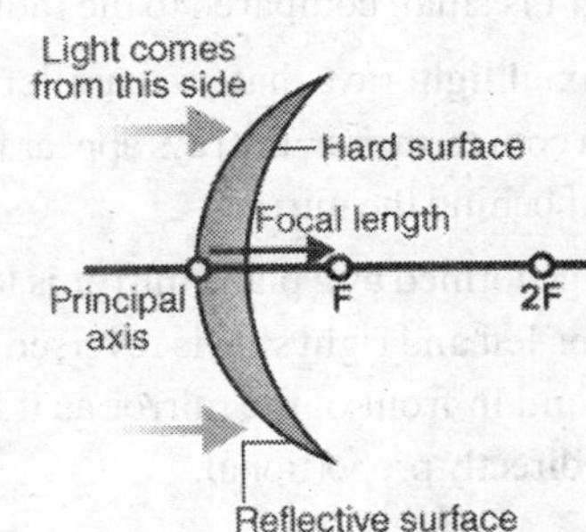

- **Convex Mirror:** A mirror with a spherical surface and reflecting from the exterior of the curvature is called a convex mirror. A convex mirror is also known as Diverging Mirror as it diverges the incident rays after reflection.
- **Concave Mirror:** A mirror with a spherical surface and reflecting from the interior of the curvature is called a concave mirror. A concave mirror is also known as Converging Mirror as it converges the incident rays after reflection.

Reflection at Spherical Surface

- The geometric centre of a spherical mirror is called its pole.

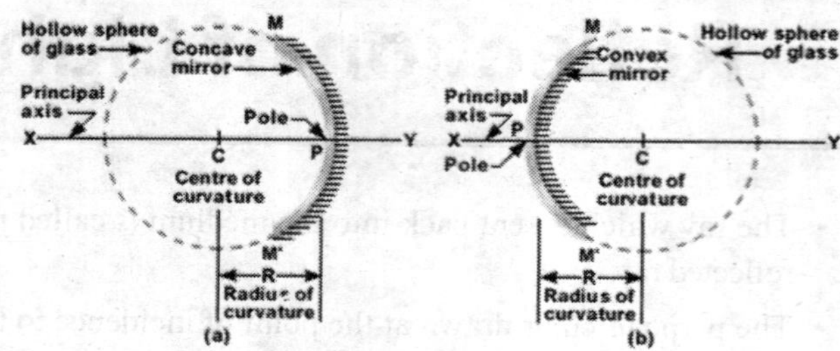

- The centre of the hollow sphere for which the mirror is a part, is called the centre of curvature.
- The line joining the centre of curvature and the pole is the principle axis.
- A light ray incident on spherical mirror, after reflection appears to pass through the principal focus in the case of a convex mirror and passes through the focus in the case of concave mirror.
- The diameter of the spherical mirror gives the measure of its aperture.
- Rays that lie close to the principal axis are called paraxial rays.
- Rays that are far from the principal axis do not converge to a single point. The fact that a spherical mirror does not bring all parallel rays to a single point is known as spherical abberation.
- Spherical abberation can be minimised by using a mirror whose height is small compared to the radius of curvature.
- When paraxial light rays that are parallel to the principal axis strike a convex mirror, the rays appear to originate from a focal point behind the mirror.
- Virtual image formed by a plane mirror is laterally inverted which means left and right side is reversed and same as the object size and in front of the mirror as it is kept from the mirror, it is directly proportional.
- Whereas image formed by convex mirror is virtual, diminished and covers larger area is and used as a rear view mirror.

Laws of Refraction

- When a ray of light travelling through a transparent medium encounters a boundary leading into another transparent medium, part of the ray is reflected and part of the ray enters the second medium.

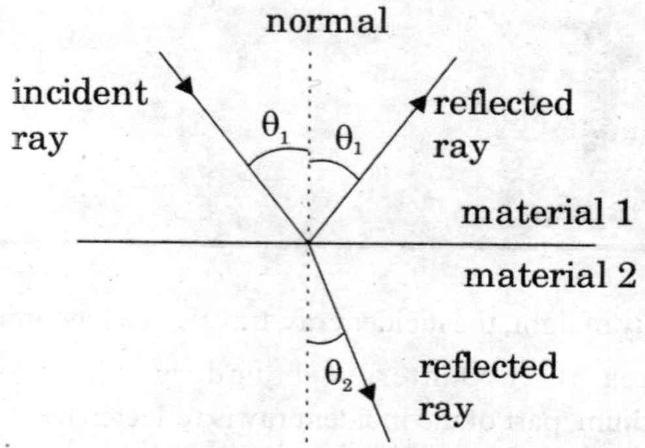

- The ray that enters the second medium is bent at the boundary.
- This bending of the rays is called refraction.
  - The incident ray, the refracted ray and the normal to the surface at the point of incidence, all lie in one plane.
  - For any two given pair of media, the ratio of the sine of the angle of incidence to the sine of the angle of refraction is a constant.
  - The above law is called Snell's law after the scientist Willebrod Snellius who first formulated it.
  - Thus $\dfrac{\sin i}{\sin r}$ = a constant μ .
  - Where is the refractive index of the second medium with respect to the first medium.

Dispersion of Light

- If a white light is passed through the prism, the light splits up into a series of colours. This shows that white light is actually made up of many other colours - a fact first shown by Newton in 1666. The distribution of colours produced when white light is dispersed by a prism the is spectrum.

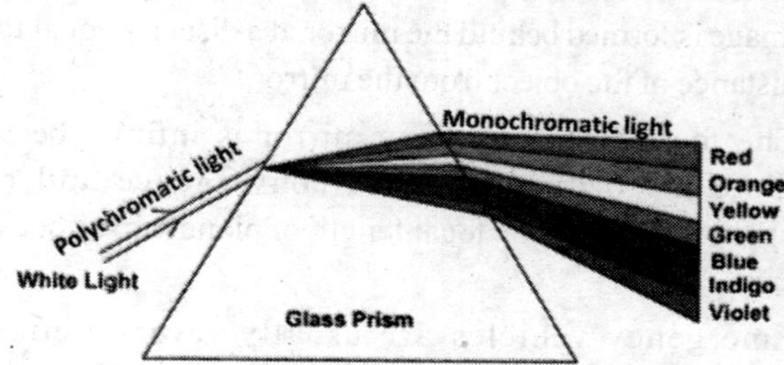

- White light is dispersed because different colours are affected differently by the passage into glass. Specifically, the different colours travel at different speeds through the glass (Because of this, each colour has its own index of refraction).

- Red light is refracted the least when it enters the block, and violet light is refracted the most. This effect is called dispersion. However, this difference is corrected when the light leaves the block, so the effect is not noticeable.
- Refraction of white light through a glass prism, which has sides that are not parallel, causes this difference in refraction of different colours of light to be exaggerated - so we see a spectrum of light emerging from the prism.
- The speed is related to the wavelength as ($V = \mu\lambda$) where V = velocity of light, n = frequency and λ = wavelength of light wave. This indicates that the colour with the highest speed (red) has the longest wavelength, while the colour with the slowest speed (violet) has the shortest wavelength.
- Because frequency is inversely proportional to wavelength, we can also determine the relative frequencies. Red would have the lowest, while violet has the highest.
- **The primary colours** are red, blue and green.
- **Additive colour** mixing involves multiple sources of light with different colours in each source. Three additive primary colours are red, green and blue (RGB).
- **Subtractive colur** mixing involves a single source of light with different colours absorbing various wavelengths of the colour spectrum. The subtractive primary colours are cyan blue, magenta red, and yellow (CMYK).

Total Internal Reflection

- When light travels from one medium to another it changes speed and is refracted.

Reflection and Refraction

Air $\theta_r = 90°$

Water

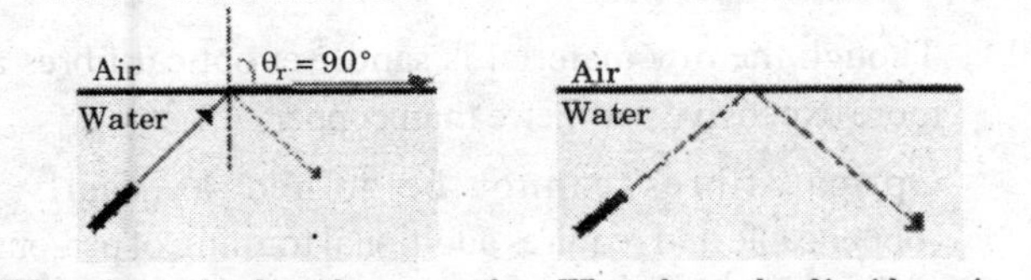

When the angle of incidence equal the critical angle, the angle of refraction is 90 degrees.

Total Internal Reflection

Air

Water

When the angle of incidence is greater than the critical angle, all the light undergoes reflection.

- If the light rays are travelling from a less dense material to a dense medium, they are refracted towards the normal and if they are travelling from a dense to less dense medium, they are refracted away from the normal.
- For total internal reflection to occur, the light must travel from a dense medium to a less dense medium (e.g. glass to air or water to air).
- As the angle of incidence increases, so does the angle of refraction.
- The critical angle is the angle of incidence above which total internal reflection occurs. When the angle of incidence reaches a value known as the critical angle, the refracted rays travel along the surface of the medium, or in other words, are refracted to an angle of 90^0. The critical angle for the angle of incidence in glass is 42^0.
- Total internal reflection also explains why diamonds are so bright. Diamond has a very large index of refraction (around 2.4), so light entering the diamond has a hard time getting out. Diamonds are cut in such a way that most of the light entering the bottom and the sides goes out through the top.
- The formation of a rainbow involves a series of physical phenomena - relfection, refraction, dispersion and total internal reflection.

For total internal reflection to take place, two conditions are required :

- The rays of light must travel from a dense medium to a less dense medium.
- The angle of incidence must be greater than the critical angle.

Opticalibre

Fibre optics is a transmission system based on the concept of Total Internal Reflection (TIR) of light and employs transmission of data in the form of pulses of light. It employes glass fibres, usually 120 micrometers in diameter. Each fibre consists of a glass core, about 50 micrometers in diameter surrounded by a glass optical cladding. They make use of TIR to confine light within the core. The core has a high refractive index than the cladding. Even if the cladding does not carry light, it is nevertheless an essential part of the fibre. The cladding keeps the value of the critical angle constant throughout the whole length of the fibre. As early as in 1960, when lasers were used as a source of coherent light, interest was generated for using light as a carrier of information. To use optical fibres as a practical transmission distances were very short, but in 1970 it became feasible to use optical fibres as a practical transmission medium.

Essentially, there are two types of fibres:

1. Step Index fibre (multimode, singlemode).
2. Graded Index fibre.

Step Index Fibre

Multi-mode Fibre

Such fibres are suitable for local area networks (LANs) because it can carry enough energy to support all the subscribers to the network. In a LAN, the distances invloved, however, are small. Little pulse spreading can take place and so, the effects of dispersion are unimportant. Any ray of light can travel down the fibre. In fact, because of the wave nature of light, only certain ray directions can actually travel down the fibre. These are called the 'Fibre Mode". In a multimode fibre, many different modes are supported by the fibre.

Single Mode Fibre

Since the core in very small single mode fibre can support only one mode, this is called the 'Lowest Order Mode'. The energy carried by a single mode fibre is much less than that carried by a multi-mode fibre.

Graded Index Fibre

In these fibres, rays of light follow sinusoidal paths. This means that low order modes, i.e., oblique rays, stay close to the centre of the fibre, high order modes spend more time near the edge of the core. Low order modes travel in the high index part of the core and so travel faster, whereas high order modes spend predominantly more time in the low index part of the core and so travel faster. This way, although the paths are of different lengths, all the modes travel the length of the fibre in tandem, they all reach the end of the fibre at some time. This eliminates multi-mode dispersion and reduces pulse spreading.

In addition to glass optical fibres, plastic can also be used for making fibres. Plastic fibres are usually made of polymethyl methacrylate, polystyrene or polycarbonate. These fibres are cheaper to produce and are found to be more flexible than glass fibres, but their greater attenuation of light restricts their use to much shorter distance.

Pulse Spreading

The data which is carried in an optical fibre consists of pulses of light energy following each other rapidly. There is a limit to the highest frequency. In other words, it is pertinent to know the quantity of pulses per second which can be sent into a fibre and be expected to emerge intact at the other end. This is because of a phenomenon known as pulse spreading which limits the band width of the fibre.

Types of pulse spreading

Pulse spreading is caused due to dispersion which may be of two types, namely chromatic dispersion and modal dispersion. Chromatic dispersion, in fact, is the variation of refractive index with the wavelength or the frequency of light. Like in prism, light rays of varying wavelengths travel through optical fibres at different speeds. On the other hand, modal dispersion is a phenomenon in which rays travel almost parallel to the centre line of the fibre and reach the end of the fibre sooner. The more zig-zag rays take a longer route as they pass along the fibre and so, reach the end of the fibre later. Thus, Total Dispersion = Chromatic Dispersion + Multi-mode (Modal) Dispersion.

Therefore, a pulse which starts off as a narrow burst of light gets wider because some components race ahead, while the others lag behind. Pulse spreading limits the maximum frequency (bandwidth) of signal which can be sent along a fibre.

Advantages and Disadvantages of Optical Fibres

Advantages

1. Optical fibres are able to carry signals with much less energy loss than copper cables and with a much higher bandwidth.
2. Optical fibres are lighter and thinner than copper or conventional cables.
3. Optical fibres are immune to electromagnetic interference from radio signals, car ignition systems, lightning, etc.
4. Optical fibres can be routed safely through explosive or flammable atmospheres.
5. It is nearly impossible to eavesdrop on fibre optic system without being easily detected. Because of the absence of current flow through the fibre, intrusion into the system is also prevented. Secret information cannot be routed to unwanted receivers, nor can false information be fed into the data system.
6. There is no chance of spark flash.
7. Optical fibre networks consume much less energy than copper cable networks.
8. Optical fibres avoid cross-talk or noise.

Disadvantages

1. Though the raw material is sand, yet optical fibres are more expensive per metre than copper.
2. Optical fibres cannot be joined as easily as copper cable and requires additional training of personnel and expensive precision splicing and measurement equipment.
3. Popular light-emitting sources are restricted to very low power devices.
4. The ways in which light source can be modulated are limited.
5. Because of low power sources, the distance between repeater amplifiers must be relatively short for high data rates demanded in some system.

Major Projects Related to Optical Fibres

1. **Fibre Optics Link Around the Globe (FLAG)**

   The project was completed in 1997, linking the UK to Japan by complex underwater optical fibre cable system. It spans over 28,800 kms. FLAG is able to carry 1,20,000 circuits as 64-kb/s chanels on two fibre pairs. The FLAG Network Operation Centre (FNOC) is located at Fujairah in UAE. It provides round the clock network surveillance. The project involved $ 1.5 billion.

2. **South Africa Far East (SAFE)**

   The SAFE optical fibre submarine cable system connects India with the African continent and the Far East. Stretching a total distance of 28,800 km, the SAFE cable system has a total capacity of 80 gigabytes and provides a great boost to the international telecom traffic throughout the African and South East Asian region. With its only landing point on the Indian subcontinent at Kochi, SAFE cable has other landing points at Cape Town in South Africa, Bay Jacote in Mauritius and Penang in Malaysia. One of the major benefits of the project is that it is controlled and maintained by the individual operators, such as BSNL in India. The $600 million project consists of two parts. One is a 15,000 km link between South Africa and Europe with landings at 10 western and southern African countries. The second is a 13,800 km link from South Africa to Malaysisa.

Fibre Optic Sensors

Sensing devices are tiny in structure, but need ultra pure materials and very sophisticated manufacturing facilities. Semi-conductors, certain gase, microbes, chain polymers and other selected materials are deployed in the tiny gadgets to act as sensors. The Chandigarh-based Central Scientific Instruments Organisation (CSIO) has developed a variety of sensors based on the fibre optic technology. In fact, fibre optic sensors are highly sensitive, have high bandwidth and can work over a wide temperature range. They are immune to electromagnetic interference (EMI), radio fequency interference (RFI) and toxic and hazardous environment. Moreover, these sensors can be interfaced with fibre optic data links, facilitating the dual purpose of effective communication and in-situ sensing.

Fibre Amplifiers

Fibre amplifiers are optical amplifiers based on optical fibres as gain media. In most cases, the gain medium is a glass fibre doped with rare earth ions, such as erbium (EDFA = erbium-doped fibre amplifier), neodymium, ytterbium (YDFA), praseodymium, or thulium. This active dopant is pumped (provided with energy) with light from a laser, such as a fibre-coupled diode laser; in almost all cases, the pump light propagates through the fiber core together with the signal to be amplified.

Neodymium and Ytterbium Fibre Amplifiers

Fibre amplifiers based on ytterbium- or neodymium-doped double-clad fibres can be used to boost the output power of 1um laser sources to very high levels of up to several kilowatts.

Neodymium-based amplifiers can also be used in the 1.3-um spectral region, but with less favorable performance.

Erbium Fibre Amplifiers

Fibre amplifiers based on erbium-doped single-mode fibres (EDFAs) are widely used in long-range optical fibre communication systems for compensating the loss of long fibre spans.

Thuium Fibre Amplifiers

Thulium-doped fluoride fibres (TDFA = thulium-doped amplifier) pumped around 1047 or 1400 nm, can be used for amplification in the telecom S band around 1460-1530 nm, or even around 1.65um. Combined thulium-erbium amplifiers can thus provide optical amplification in a very wide wavelength range.

Praseodymium Fibre Amplifiers

Fibre amplifiers have a lower performance compared with t hat of erbium-doped amplifiers. They can be based on praseodymium-doped fluoride fibres (PDFA = praseodymium-doped amplifier), which are pumped around 1020 nm (a relatively inconvenient pump wavelength) or at 1047 nm.

2 Chapter Electricity

Charge

- Charge is the fundamental quantity of electricity.
- The classical study of electricity is generally divided into many areas:
  * **Electrostatics:** It deals with phenomena due to attractions or repulsions of electric charges, but not dependent upon their motion.
  * **Electric Current:** The study of the forms of energy associated with the flow of electric charge.
  * **Electromagnetism:** The study of the forces acting between electrically-charged praticles in motion.
  * **Electric Charge:** (Often just called charge) comes in two and only tow types, i.e., positive (+) and negative (-) charges.
- The term neutral does not refer to the third type of charge, but to the presence in a region of positive and negative charges in equal amount.

Methods of Charging

- **Friction:** The frictional charging process results in a transfer of electrons between the two objects that are rubbed together.
- **Conduction:** It involves touching a negatively- charged object to a neutral object. Upon contact, electrons move from the negatively-charged object to the netural object.
- **Induction:** If a negatively-charged object is used to change a netural object by production, then the netural object will acquire a positive charge and vice-versa.

Electrical Properties of Materials

- **Conductors:** Charge moves easily in.
  * Metals
  * Electrolytes (ionised liquids)
  * Plasmas (ionised gases)
- **Insulators:** Charge does not move easily in.
  * Non-metals (pure water, organics, gases)
  * **Semi-conductors:** Sometimes behave as a conductor and sometimes as insulator.
  * Metalloids (silicon, germanium, doped materials,)
- **Super-conductors:** The perfect conductor, offers no resistance below critical temperature.
- Many substances are super-conductors below some critical temperature.
- The SI unit of charge is the coulomb (C).

Coulomb's Law

The force between two point charges is : Directly proportional to the product of magnitude of each charge (q_1, q_2) inversely proportional to square of the separation between their centres (r), and directed along the line connecting their centres (r). This relationship is known as the Coulomb's Law.

Electric Current

- Electric current is the rate at which charge flows through a surface.
- As a scalar quantity, it has magnitude only.
- The symbol for current is I.
- The SI unit of current is the ampere (A) which is named after the French scientist Andre-Marie Ampere.
- Since charge is measured in coulombs and time is measured in seconds, an ampere is the same as a coulomb per second.

$$\left[A = \frac{C}{S}\right]$$

Resistance

- Resistance is the property of a conductor to resist the flow of charges through it. Its SI unit is ohm (Ω).
- Resistivity is a characteristic property of the material. It is a measure of material's ability to oppose electric current. It s SI unit is W Ω -m (ohm-metre).

  resistivity depends on the nature of the material not on its dimensions as resistance.

$$\text{Resistance (R)} = p\frac{\text{length(l)}}{\text{area(A)}}$$

where, p = resistivity of cross section

Ohm's Law

- The resistor's current *I* in amps (A) is equal to the resistor's voltage V in volts (V) divided by the resistance R in ohms (Ω):

$$I = \frac{V}{R}$$

- The resistance of a given conductor depends on the material it is made of, and on its dimensions. For a given material, the resistance is inversely proportional to the cross-sectional area, for example, a thick copper wire has lower resistance than an otherwise-identical thin copper wire. Also, for a given material, the resistance is proportional to the length, for example, a long copper wire has higher resistance than an otherwise-identical short copper wire.
- Conductors have positive temperature coefficient of resistance, that is, their resistance increases with increase in temperature.
- While for insulators and semi-conductors, the resistance decreases with increase in temperature, i.e., they have negative temperature coefficient of resistance.
- The electrical resistance of a metal or alloy is a function of temperature.
- It decreases with decrease in temperature.
- When temperature reaches 'absolute zero' for certain metals/ alloys, the resistance becomes almost zero.
- But keeping this temperature is an extremely costly affair.

Super-conductivity is a phenomenon occurring in certain materials at extremely low temperatures, characterized by exactly zero electrical resistance and the exclusion of the interior magnetic field (the Meissner effect).

The electrical resistivity of a metallic conductor decreases gradually as the temperature is lowered. However, in ordinary conductors such as copper and silver, impurities and other defects impose a lower limit. Even near absolute zero, a real sample of copper shows a non-zero resistance. The resistance of a super-conductor, on the other hand, drops abruptly to zero when the material is cooled below its "critical temperature". An electrical current flowing in a loop of super-conducting wire can persist indefinitely with no power source. Like ferromagnetism and atomic spectral lines, superconductivity is a quantum mechanical phenomenon. It cannot be understood simply as the idealisation of "perfect conductivity" in classical physics.

Superconductivity occurs in a wide variety of materials, including simple elements like tin and aluminium, various metallic alloys and some heavily-doped semiconductors. Super- conductivity does not occur in noble metals like gold and silver, nor in most ferromagnetic metals.

In 1986, the discovery of a family of cuprate-perovskite ceramic materials known as high-temperature super-conductors, with critical temperatures in excess of 90 kelvin, spurred renewed interest and research in super-conductivity for several reasons. As a topic of pure research, these materials represented a new phenomenon not explained by the current theory. And, because the super-conducting state persists up to more manageable temperatures, more commercial applications are feasible, especially if materials with even higher critical temperatures could be discovered.

As of 2001, the highest critical temperature found for a conventional superconductor is 39 K for magnesium diboride (MgB2).

Applications

- For transmission of power. It can save upto 30% power.
- Store energy in large solinoids without loss of power.
- Super conductor magnets can be used in MHD power generation.
- Super conductor magnets are used in fusion experiments.
- They can make trains run – 500 km/hr cheaper and easier than flights.
- Super conductor antennas-very miniature–very sensitive, can detect very weak signals.
- Thin films of super conductor can be used in Geo-physics – meteorology etc.

Super conductor in India

1987 – Programme Management Board was constituted for development of super -conductors.

1991 – National Super-Conductivity Science and Technology Board constituted.

- Around 65 projects started.
- CSIR, IIT, DAE, IIS, etc, conduct research.

Static electricity

- Static electricity is the result of an imbalance between negative and positive charges in an object.
- The charge remains until it is able to move away by means of an electric or electrical discharge. Static electricity is named in contrast with current electricity which flows through wires or other conductors and transmits energy.
- The rubbing of certain materials against one another can transfer negative charges, or electrons. For example, if a person rubs his shoe on the carpet, his body collects extra electrons. The electrons cling to his body until they can be released. As he reaches and touches his furry dog, he will get a shock. It is only the surplus electrons being released from you to your unsuspecting pet.

Current Electricity

- Current electricity is the form of electricity which makes all of our electronic gizmos possible. This form of electricity exists when charges are able to constantly flow. As opposed to static electricity where charges gather and remain at rest, current electricity is dynamic, charges are always on the move. We'll be focusing on this form of electricity throughout the rest of the tutorial.

Circuits

- In order to flow, current electricity requires a circuit: a closed, never-ending loop of conductive material. A circuit could be as simple as a conductive wire connected end-to-end, but useful circuits usually contain a mix of wire and other components which control the flow of electricity. The only rule when it comes to making circuits is they can't have any insulating gaps in them.
- If you have a wire full of copper atoms and want to induce a flow of electrons through it, all free electrons need somewhere to flow in the same general direction. Copper is a great conductor, perfect for making charges flow. If a circuit of copper wire is broken, the charges can't flow through the air, which will also prevent any of the charges towards the middle from going anywhere.

Electric Power

- Power is the rate at which work is done. It is the work/time ratio. Mathematically, it is computed using the following equation.

Power = Work / time

- Like current, power is a rate quantity. Its mathematical formula is expressed on a per time basis.

$$\text{Power} = \frac{\text{Work Doneon Charge}}{\text{Time}}$$

$$= \frac{\text{Energy Consumed by Load}}{\text{Time}}$$

- **Mechanical Power** is commonly measured in "horsepower." One horsepower is equivalent to approximately 746 Watts.
- **Electrical Power** is almost always measured in "watts" and it can be calculated by the formula P = VI

  Where, V= Potential difference and I = amount of electricity
- The standard unit of voltage is. therefore, the joule per coulomb, a unit that has its own name, the volt (V):
- 1 volt = 1 joule coulomb
- Watts = Joules . second
- 1 KWH = 3.6 mega joules
- Volt is the unit of measurement for potential difference, while watt is a unit of measurement for power.
- An ampere, or amp (A or I, for current), is the amount of current in a circuit, while voltages (V) is the strength of the current as it flows through the circuit and watts (W) are the total electrical power released by circuit per second. One watt is equal to one volt multiplied by one amp, which can also be expressed as.

  1 W = 1 V x 1 A
- Power is the rate at which energy is added to or removed from a circuit by a battery or a load. Current is the rate at which charge moves past a point on a circuit. The electric potential difference across the two ends of a circuit is the potential energy difference per charge between those two points. In equation form, these definitions can be stated as:

$$I = \frac{Q}{T}$$

Where,

I = electric current

Q = electric charge

T = Time

Transformer

- A transformer is a device that changes (transforms) an alternating potential difference (voltage) from one value to another value, be it smaller or greater using the principle of electromagnetic induction.

- Michael Faraday built the first transformer, although he used it only to demonstrate the principle of electromagnetic induction and did not foresee the use to which it would eventually be put.
- The transformer is based on two principles: first, that an electric current can produce a magnetic field (electromagnetism), and second that a changing magnetic field within a coil of wire induces a voltage across the ends of the coil (electromagnetic induction).
- Changing the current in the primary coil changes the magnetic flux that is developed.
- The changing magnetic flux induces a voltage in the secondary coil.
- Transformers require a varying flux to work. They are, therefore, perfect for AC power, but do not work at all for DC power, which would keep the flux constant.

3 Chapter Magnetism

- A magnet is an object or a device that gives off external magnetic field.
- Basically, it applies a force over a distance on other magnets, electrical currents, beams of charge, circuits, or magnetic materials.
- The magnetic field of an object can create a magnetic force on other objects with magnetic fields. That force is what we call magnetism.
- When a magnetic field is applied to a moving electric charge, such as a moving proton or the electrical current in a wire, the force on the charge is called Lorentz force.
- Magnets have two poles, called the north (N) and south (S) poles. Two magnets will be attracted by their opposite poles, and each will repel the like pole of the other magnet.
- **Repulsion:** When two magnetic objects have like poles facing each other, the magnetic force pushes them apart.
- A magnetic field consists of imaginary lines of flux coming from moving or spinning electric circuit.
- **Examples:** include the spin of a proton and the motion of electrons through a wire in an electric circuit.
- Magnets also strongly attract ferro-magnetic materials such as iron, nickel and cobalt.

Magnetism

- A magnetic field consists of imaginary lines of flux coming from moving or spinning electrically- charged particles. Examples include the spin of a proton and the motion of electrons through a wire in an electric circuit.
- Magnetism is the force exerted by magnets when they attract or repel each other. Magnetism is caused by the motion of electric charges.
- In most substances, equal numbers of electrons spin in opposite directions, which cancels out their magnetism. That is why, materials such as cloth or paper are said to be weakly magnetic. In substances such as iron, cobalt and nickel, most of the electrons spin in the same direction. This makes the atoms in these substances strongly magnetic-but they are not yet magnets.
- A magnet is an object that exhibits a strong magnetic field and will attract materials like iron to it. Magnets have two poles, called the north (N) and south (S) poles. Two magnets will be attracted by their opposite poles and each will repel the like pole of the other magnet.

Magnetic field

- A magnetic field consists of imaginary lines of flux comming from moving or spinning electrically- charged particles. Examples include the spin of a proton and the motion of electrons through a wire in a electric circuit.

Chapter 4

Pressure

- Pressure is defined as the force acting normally per unit area.
- Pressure on an area, A is the area of the surface on contact and F is the normal force applied.
- Pressure is a scalar quantity.

$$P = (F/A)$$

- If the force is due to the weight (W) of the object, the equation is then:

$$P = W / A$$

- Hydrostatice pressure is the pressure that is excuted by a fluid at equilibrium at a given point within the fluid, due to the force of gravity.
- Hydrostatic pressure equations is:

$$P = hdg$$

where; p = pressure (N/M^2 of Pa) h = height (m) d = density (kg/m^3) g = acceleration due to gravity (9.81 m/s^2)

- The SI unit for pressure is the pascal, Pa, where 1 Pa = 1 N/m^2.
- The standard atmospheric pressure is measured in various units:

1 Atmosphere = 760 mmHg = 101.3 kpa

- The mercury barometer and other manometer devices are reliable pressure measurment devices. A "rising" barometer indicates increasing air pressure, i.e., calm weather, a "falling" barometer indicates decreasing air pressure, i.e., inclement weather or harsh weather.
- **Factors Affecting the Magnitude of Pressure**
  - ♦ **Magnitude of the force:** The larger the force, the higher the pressure.
  - ♦ **Contact area:** The larger the contact area, the lower the pressure.
- The pressure at any level in the atmosphere may be interpreted as the total weight of the air above a unit area at any elevation.

Pascal's Principle

- Pascal's Principle is used to quantitatively relate the pressure at two points in an incompressible static fluid.
- It states that pressure is transmitted, undiminished, in a closed static fluid.
- The total pressure at any point within an incompressible, static fluid is equal to the sum of the applied pressure at any point in that fluid and the hydrostatic pressure changes due to a difference in height within that fluid.

Applications:

- The underlying principle of the hydraulic pressure.
- Used for amplifying the force of the driver's foot in the braking system of most cars and trucks.
- Used in artesian wells, water towers, and dams.
- Scuba divers must understand this principle. At a depth of 10 metres under water, pressure is twice the atmospheric pressure at sea level, and increases by about 105 kPa for each increase of 10m depth.

Surface Tension (T)

- **Surface Tension (T):** It is the property of a liquid by virtue of which it behaves like an elastically stretched membrane with a tendency to contract, so as to occupy a minimum surface area.
  - ♦ Mathematically T = F/I
  - ♦ S.I. Unit is : Nm^{-1} and Dimensional formula is : $M^1L^0T^{-2}$

Surface Energy

- The energy responsible for the phenomenon of surface tension may be thought of as approximately equivalent to the work or energy required to remove the surface layer of molecules in an unit area. The potential energy per unit area of the surface film is called the surface energy.
- Surface tension is numerically equal to surface energy. **Its unit is N/m**
- An increase in temperature lowers the net force of attraction among molecules and hence, decreases surface tension.
- **The Surface of Water:** Surface tension creates a thin elastic film on the surface of water.
- **Surface Tension at the Molecular Level:** A water molecule has one oxygen atom (O) and two hydrogen atoms (H). The negative end of the water molecule is attracted to the positive end of other water molecules. Under the surface of water these attractions balance out, but on the surface they are unbalanced. This is because the molecules on the surface have one surface exposed to the air and no other water molecules are there to balance out the charges. So, the surface molecules are pulled inward and surface tension is created.

- **Breaking Up Surface Tension:** Surface tension can be broken by adding soap to water. Soap disrupts the surface tension causing the thin film to split and fly apart.
- **Adhesive Forces:** Forces of attraction between a liquide and a solid surface are called adhesive forces. Force of attraction between like molecules of surface are called the cohesive forces. The difference in strength between cohesive forces and adhesive forces determines the behaviour of a liquid in contact with a solid surface.
  - ♦ Water does not wet waxed surfaces because the cohesive forces within the drops are stronger than the adhesive forces between the drops and the wax.
  - ♦ Water wets glass and spreads out on it because the adhesive forces between the liquid and the glass are stronger than the cohesive forces within the water.

Capillary Action

- **Capillary Action** can be defined as the ability of liquid to flow through slim tube, cylinder or permeable substance due to adhesive and cohesive forces interacting between the liquid and surface.
- The liquid creeps up the inside of the tube (as a result of adhesive forces between the liquid and the inner walls of the tube) until the adhesive and cohesive forces of the liquid are balanced by the weight of the liquid.
- The smaller the diameter of the tube, the higher the liquid rises.

Buoyancy

- It is an upward force exerted by a fluid that opposes the weight of an immersed object.

Archimedes' Principle

- It states that when a body is immersed completely or partly in a fluid, it loses weight equal to the weight of the fluid displaced by it.
- Apparent weight of body,

  = Actual Weight of Body - Upthrust
- Buoyant force depends on the density of the fluid and not on the density of body acting on the centre of gravity of fluid.

Archimedes' Law of Floatation

- When a body is immersed in a fluid, then if :
  - ♦ The weight W of body is more than the upthrust W' (W>W'), the body will sink.
  - ♦ The weight W of the body is equal to upthrust W' (W' = W), the body floats with whole of its volume inside the liquid.
  - ♦ The weight (W<W'), the body will float with some of its part outside the liquid.
- When a block of ice floats in a liquid having density greater than that of water, the liquid level rises when all the ice melts into water.
- When an ice block floats in a liquid of density less than that of water, the liquid level falls when all the ice melts into water.
- When an ice block floats in water, the water level will remain the same when all the ice melts into water.

Equilibrium of Floating Body

1. Stable equilibrium
2. Unstable equilibrium
3. Neutral equilibrium

Stable equilibrium: When a body is given a small angular displacement, i.e., it is tilted slightly by some external force and then it returns back to original position due to internal forces, such equilibrium is called stable equilibrium.

Unstable equilibrium: If a body does not return to its original position from the slightly displaced angular position and moves father away when given a small angular displacement, such equilibrium is called an unstable equilibrium.

Netural equilibrium: The body remains at rest in any position to which it may be displaced, no net force tends to return the body to its original state or to drive it further away from the original position, is called neutral equilibrium.

Meta-centre: When a small angular displacement is given to a body floating in a liquid, it starts oscillation about some point M. This point about which the body starts oscillating is called the meta-centre.

Meta-centric height: The distance between the centre of gravity of a floating body and the meta-centre, i.e., distance GM is called meta-centric height. Relation between centre of gravity and meta-centre in different three types of equilibrium:

- **Stable equilibrium:** In this, position of meta-centre (M) remains higher than the centre of gravity of the body.
- **Unstable equilibrium:** In this position, meta-centre (M) remains lower than the centre of gravity of body.
- **Netural equilibrium:** The position of meta-centre (M) coincides with the centre of gravity of body.

Chapter 5 Elements

- An elements is a substance which can neither be broken nor built from two or more simple substances by any physical or chemical method. Or in other words, an element is a pure substance which contains only on kind of atom, e.g., Fe (Iron), Na (Sodium), etc.

Types of Elements

(a) Metals (b) Non-metals

(c) Metalloids

Compounds

- A compound is a pure substance which ontains more than one kind of elements or atom in fixed proportion by weight, e.g., NaCl (Sodium chloride), SO_2 (Sulphur dioxide), etc.

Types of Compounds

(a) Organic compounds

(b) Inorganic compounds

- The properties of a compound are completely different from those of its constituents.

Mixtures

- A material containing two or more elements or compounds in any proportion is a mixture. It can be seperated into constituents, e.g., air, milk, paints, cements, etc.

Types of Mixture

(a) Homogeneous

(b) Heterogeneous

(a) A mixture is said to be homogeneous if its composition is uniform throughout.

(b) A mixture is said to be heterogeneous if its composition is not uniform.

- The properties of a mixture are the properties of its constituents.
- A mixture with definite boiling point is known as azeotropic mixutre.

Seperation of Mixtures

(a) **Sublimation** : In this process, a solid substance passes directly into its vapours on application of heat, and when vapours are cooled, they given back the original substance, e.g., iodine, napthalene, benzoic acid, etc.

(b) **Sedimentation and decantation** : This method is used when one component is liquid and the other is insoluble solid.

(c) **Crystallisation** : This method is based on the difference in solubility of the various compounds in a solvent, e.g., mixture of KNO_3 and Nacl can be separated by this process.

(d) **Filtration** : It is used for quick and complete removal of solid suspended particles from a liquid (or gas) by passing the suspension through a filter.

(e) **Evaporation** : It this method the solution is heated so that the solvent vaporises to give the solute (solid substance) e.g., salt can be obtained from salt solution.

(f) **Distillation** : A mixture of two substances, only one of which is volatile, can be separated by this process, e.g., NaCl can be separated from water by distillation.

(g) **Fractional distillation** : This process is used if both the components of a mixture are volatile. It is based on the difference of boiling points. e.g., the various fractions of crude petroleum can be separated by this process.

(h) **Steam distillation** : It is used to separate a liquid (should be immiscible with water) from a mixture by heating with steam, e.g., lemon oil, toluene, nitrobenzene, etc.

(i) **Mechanical separation** : Two immiscible liquids can be separated by using a seperatory funnel, e.g., oil and water.

(j) **Magnetic separation** : Two solids, one of which is magnetic substance can be separated by this method.

(k) **Atmolysis** : In this process, a mixture of gases can be separated based on their rates of diffusion, e.g., Isotopes of uranium (U_{235} and U_{238}) are separated by converting them into gaseous UF_6.

(l) Chromatography : This is the most versatile separation method which can be applied to solid, liquid or gas. In this method, the components of a mixture are adsorbed on a suitable adsorbent at different rates and thus get separated. e.g. to separate coloured materials from dyes, green vegetables, ink, etc.

Atom

- It is the smallest particle of an element which does not always exist independently. for example, atoms of hydrogen do not exist independently but instead, always occur in pairs. Two atoms of hydrogen form a molecule of hydrogen which exists independently. Atom is the smallest particle of an element that can take part in a chemical change.

Atomicity

- It is the number of atoms present in a molecule of an element. Atomicity of hydrogen, oxygen, nitrogen and chlorine is 2, for ozone it is 3 and for phosphorus it is 4.

Molecule

- It is the smallest part of an elements or compound that can normally exist separately.

Atomic Weight (or Atomic Mass)

- The atomic mass of an elements is the number of times its atom is heavier the 1/12th of the mass of carbon atom. The unit used to measure atomic mass is called atomic mass unit, i.e., amu. In this unit, atomic mass of hydrogen is 1 amu, and that of oxygen is 16 amu.

∴ Atomic wt. of an elements

= Average wt. of one atom of the element

wt. of one atom of C^{x12}_{12}

Atomic Mass of Some Common Elements

Elements	Atomic Mass	Element	Atomic Mass
Hydrogen	1	Sulphur	32
Helium	4	Potassium	39
Carbon	12	Iron	56
Nitrogen	14	Copper	64
Oxygen	16	Zinc	65
Sodium	23	Mercury	201
Phosphorous	31	Uranium	238

Molecular Weight

- The molecular weight of an element or compound is the number of times its molecule is heavier than 1/12th of mass of carbon atom.

∴ Mol. wt. of an element or compound

(average wt.of one atom of the element or compount)

=x12

wt. of one atom of C_{12}

Mole

- (Or Mol) One mole is equal to the number of atoms present in 12 gram C_{12} i.e.,

1 mole = 6.022×10^{23} amu,

Here 6.022×10^{23} is known as avogadro's number

- Relation between gram and amu

=1 gram = 6.022×10^{23} amu.

Equivalent Weight

- It is the number of the parts of a substance by weight, which combines with or displaces directly or indirectly1.008 part by weight of H, 8 parts of weight of O or 35.5 parts by weight of Cl.

Chapter 6

Metals - Physical Properties

(a) **Physical Change** : A physical change is a change of state only and is not accompanied by an alteration in the chemical composition, weight or chemical properties of any substance e.g., melting of ice, magnetising a needle, etc.

(b) **Chemical Change** : A chemical change gives rise to a new substance having composition and properties altogether different from those of the original substance, e.g., radioactive decay, rusting of iron, photosynthesis, etc. Energy is absorbed or released during a chemical change.

Physical and Chemical Properties

(a) **Physical Properties** : The properties which do not depend on reaction with any other substance, e.g., colour, melting point, boiling point, density, etc.

(b) **Chemical Properties** : The chemical properties of a substance are those that describe its reactions with other substances.

Empirical Formula

- The emperical formula gives the simple whole number ration between the number of atoms of the different elements forming the compound, e.g., H_2O tells that there are twice as many H atoms as O atoms.

Molecular Formula

- It indicates the number of atoms in a molecule of a molecular substance. Elements as well as compounds can be represented by a molecular formula, e.g., H_2,O_2,N_2, etc.

Colloids

- Colloidal particles may be cristalline or non-crystalline. When these are dispersed in a liquid, solid or gas, they result in formation of a coloidal system, e.g., top soil of earth, protoplasm, etc.

  (a) **Sol** : When a solid is dispersed in a liquid. the particles of a sol will not settle out.

  (b) **Gel** : In a gel, the liquid contains a colloidal solid dispersed throughout the system but set in a structure which does not flow, e.g., gelatin, jellies, etc.

  (c) **Aerosol** : The dispersion of either a solid or a liquid in a gas. When teh dispersed colloidal particle is solid, the result is **smoke** and when it is liquid, the result is fog.

  (d) **Emulsion** : When one liquid is dispersed into another in which it is not soluble e.g., milk, paint, etc.

Properties of Colloids

- When the beam of light is passed through a true solution the path of the beam is not visible but when it is passed through a solution its path is visible. This effect is known as **Tyndall Effect**.

Metallurgy

- It comprises the various processes involved in the production of metal from the ore which generally contains a large percentage of rocky materials, called gangue or matrise.

Rusting

- It is caused in iron due to the presence of moisture, oxygen, CO_2 in the air. Rusting is prevented by surface coating with film of oil, paint or metal coating such as chromium coating, nickel plating, tin plating and copper plating.

Alloy

- It is a mixture of two or more metals, and small amount of non-metals also.

Ores

- These are mineals from which metals are produced.

Minerals

- These are the natural materials extracted from the earth that are formed through geological processes. Minerals range in composition from pure elements and simple salts to very complex silicates with thousands of known forms.

7

Chapter

Supplementary Facts

Some Important Fish

(Fishes : True, means belonging to class fishes of vertebrates)

1. Dog Fish	Scolidon
2. Tiger fish	Stegostoma
3. Electric Fish	Topedo
4. Saw fish	Pristis
5. Rat fish	Chimaera (Rabbitfish)
6. Flute fish	Fistularia
7. Scorpion fish	Pterois
8. Cat fish	Clarias
9. Pipe fish	Syngnathus
10. Climbing	Anabas
11. Sucker fish	Echenies Remora
12. Horse fish	Hippocampus
13. Flying fish	Exocoetus
14. Mosquito fish	Gambusia
15. Angel fish	Cryptopsarus
16. Porcupine fish	Diodon
17. Guitar fish	Rhinobates
18. Lizard fish	Synodus
19. Globe fish	Tetradon

Some Important Living Organism and their Class/ Phyum

Name	Class/Phylum
1. Sea Urchin	Echinodermata
2. Sea Pen	Cnidaria
3. Sea Anemones	Cnidaria
4. Sea Cow	Mammalia
5. Sea Cucumber	Echinodermata
6. Sea Fan	Cnidaria
7. Sea Hare	Mollusca
8. Sea Horse	Pisces
9. Sea Lily	Echinodermata
10. Sea Mouse	Annelida

Cranial Capacities

1. Chimpanzee	400 cm^3
2. Gorilla	510 cm^3
3. African Anthropoid Ape	450-650 cm^3
4. Java man	800-900 cm^3
5. Peking Man	1050-1300 cm^3
6. Neanderthal Man	1400-1600 cm^3
7. Cro-Magnon	1600-1750 cm^3
8. Modern Man	1600-1750 cm^3

Dental Formula

- Mammalian heterodonty is expressed by a dental formula.
- In mammals, number of teeth varies in different species. However, number of teeth is constant and characteristic for every species.
- The number and kind of teeth in a species of mammals can be represented by a short of equation, called dental formula.
- Since two halves of each jaw are identical, only the teeth of one side are recorded. Those of the upper and lower jaws are separated by a horizontal line.
- Kinds of teeth are denoted by their initial letters-i,c, pm and m representing incisors, canines, premolars and molars respectively.
- The teeth of the upper jaw are placed as numerators and those of the lower jaw as denominators.

True and False Worms

True worms : Belonging to Phylum Nemathel minthes

1. Round worm - Ascaris lumbricoides
2. Thread worm (Pin worm) - Enterobius vermicularies
3. Hook worm - Ancylostoma duodenale
4. Trichinea worm - Trichinella spiralis
5. Guinea worm - Dracunculus medinesis
6. Whip worm (Serpent worm) - Trichuris trichura
7. Eye worm - Loa loa
8. Gape worm - Syngamus
9. Filaria worm - Wuchereriabancrofti
10. Lung worm - Matastrongylus

False Worms : Means do not belong to Phylum Nem-athelminthes

1. Glass worm or Arrow worm-Sagitta chaetognatha
2. Earth worm - Pheratima posthuma : annelida
3. Spring headed worm - Acanthocephala
4. Ribbon worm - Nemertinea
5. Flat worm - Planaria, Fasciola heptatica : Platyhelminthes
6. Tape worm - Taenia solium, (pork tape worm) or T. Saginatum (Beef tape worm) : Platyhelminthes
7. Scale worm - Polynoe : Annelida
8. Sand worm or Rag worm or Clam worm - Nereis : Annelida
9. Lung worm - Arenicola : Annelida
10. Fire worm - Odontosyilis : Annelida
11. Polalo worm - Eunice : Annelida
12. Paddle worm - Chaetopterus : Annelida
13. Lac worm - Tachardia lacca : Arthropoda
14. Silk worm - Bombyx-mori : Arthropoda
15. Acron worm (Tongue worm) - balanoglossus : Hemichordata
16. Blind worm - Ichthyophis : Amphibia
17. walking worm - Peripatus : Onychophora
18. Ship worm - Teredo : Mollusca
19. Peacock worm - Sabella : Annelida
20. Peanut worm - Sipunculus : Sipunculida

Zoo and Museums

1. Largest Museum of India - Chennai
2. Largest Aquarium of India - Tarapur (Mumbai)
3. Largest Zoo of the World - Kruger (S. Africa)
4. Largest Zoo of India - Alipur (Kolkata)
5. Largest collection of animals - Zoological garden (West Berlin)
6. Famous and the largest desert of the World - Sahara (Africa)
7. Famous water bird sanctuary - Ghana, Bharatpur (Rajasthan)
8. National Carbett Park (Wild life) - Nainital (Uttarakhand)
9. Saddle Peak National park (Famous for birds) - Andman and Nicobar

Famous Research Institutes of India

1. Forest Research Institute (F.R.I.) - Dehradum (Uttarakhand)
2. Hoffkin's Research Institute of Pharmacology - Mumbai
3. Cattle Breeding Institute - Hissar (Haryana)
4. National Dairy Research Institute (N.D.R.I.) - Karnal (Haryana)
5. Central Drug Research Institute (C.D.R.I.) - Lucknow (U.P.)
6. Industrial Toxicology Research Centre (I.T.R.C.) - Lucknow (U.P.)
7. Central Food Technological Research Institute (C.F.T.R.I.) - Mysore (Karnataka)
8. Central Institute of Virology - Pune (Maharashtra)
9. Indian lac Research Institute - (Ranchi Jharkhand)
10. Indian agricultural Research Institute (IARI) - New Delhi
11. International Crop Research Institute for Semi-Arid Tropics (ICRISAT) - pattancheru Hyderabad (A.P.)

Some Important Facts About Human Body

1.	Average Body weight	70 kg.
2.	Average Age	53 years
3.	Average Alimentary canal length	8 metres
4.	B.M.R. (Basal metabolic	1600 k. cal/day Rate)
5.	Breathing Rate	16-20 per minute
6.	Blood Volume	5-6 litres in (70 kg body)
7.	Blood Platelets count	2,00,000-4,00,000 per cubic mm
8.	Blood Clotting time	2-5 minutes
9.	D.L.C. (Differential	(a) Basophils Leucocyte count) 0.5-1% (b) Eosinophils 1-3% (c) Monocytes 3-8% (d) Neutrophil 40-70% (e) Lymphocytes 20-25%
10.	Dental Formula	$\frac{2123}{2123} = 32$(adult) $\frac{2120}{2120} = 20$ (Child) Milkteeth
11.	E.S.R. (Erythrocyte)	4-10 minutes (Sedimentation Rate)
12.	Gestation Period	9 Month (253-266 days)
13.	Greatest Regeneration Power	In liver
14.	Haemoglobin percentage	In male - 14-18 gm/100 ml of blood in female - 12-16 gm/100 ml of blood
15.	Haemoglobin content of the body	500-700 gm
16.	Longest Bone	Femur of thigh bone
17.	Life Span of RBC	120 days
18.	Life Span of WBC	2-5 days
19.	Largest Endocrine Gland	Thyroid
20.	Largest Gland	Liver
21.	Largest Body Muscle	Gluteus maxi mum (Buttock Muscle)

Supplementary Facts

22. Largest Artery	Abdominal aorta
23. Largest Vein	Inferior vena cava
24. Largest WBC	Monocyte
25. Longest Nerve	Sciatic nerve
26. Longest Cell	Neuron or nerve cell
27. Largest organ of the body	Skin
28. Menstrual Cycle	28 days
29. Menopause Age	45-50 years
30. Minimum Regenerative	In Brain Cells Power
31. Minimum Regenerative	25 c.m. for Proper vision
32. Number of Cells in the body	75 trillion
33. Narmal Blood Pressure	120/80 mm of Mercury
34. Number of RBCs	In Male-5-5.5 million/cu.mm In Female-4.5-5 million/cu.mm
35 Normal WBC Count	5,000-11,000/cu.mm
36. Normal Body Temperature for 37°C	98.4°F
37. Number of Cranial	12 Pairs Nerves
38. Number of Spinal Nerves	31 pairs
39. Normal Hear Beat	72-75/ minute
40. Normal Sperm Count per ejaculation	200-350 million
41. Pulse Rate	72/minute
42. pH of gastric juice	1.4
43. pH of urine	6.0
44. pH of blood	7.35-7.45
45. pH of bile	7.5
46. pH of Pancreative Juice	8.5
47 Smallest bone	Stapes (Ear os sicles)
48. Smallest Muscle in the body	Stepedius
49. Smallest WBC	Lymphocytes
50. Types of Placenta (Chorioallantoic)	Haemochorial
51. Thinnest skin	Conjuctive
52. Total Number of Bones	206
53. Total Number of Muscles	639
54. Universal Blood Donor	O Rh+ve
55. Universal Blood recipient	AB
56. Volume of Semen	2-4ml/ejaculation
57. Weight of Brain	1400 gm
58. Bacterial Living on skin	(i) Corynebacte rium acnes (ii) Micrococci (iii) Steptococci (iv) Coliform bacteria
59. Intestinal Bacteria	(i) Escherichia Coli (ii) Bacteriocles (iii) Lactobacilli (iv) Clostridia (v) Streptococci
60. Yeast found on skin	(i) Malassezia furfur (ii) Candida ablicans (iii) Trichospora beigelli
61. Fungi found on skin	(i) Trichophyton (ii) Microsporum
61. Virus living in nerves	(i) Herpes simplex

Prominent Scientists

Albert Claude

A biologist, shared the 1974 Nobel Prize in Medicine. His field of research relates to causes and treatment of cancer.

Alexander Fleming

A British bacteriologist, whe discovered Lysozyme (1922), followed by penicillin (1929), an antibiotic drug. He lived between 1881 and 1955.

C.N.R. Rao

Professor C.N.R. Rao had been a renowned scientist of International Authority in solid State and Material Chemistry, and conferred Bharat Ratna of Feb. 4, 2014. He is the only Indian scientist with close to 50,000 citations.

Charles Darwin

British scientist who lived between 1809 and 1882. He discovered the principle of natural selection.

Daniel Rutherford

A Scottish scientist who lived betwen 1749 and 1819. He discovered nitrogen in 1772.

D.I. Mandeleev

A russian chemist who lived between 1834 and 1901. He was the founder of periodic table and the development of petroleum and other industries in Russia.

Edward Jenner

British scientist, born in 1749. He discovered the vaccination of small pox. He died in 1823.

Dr. Edward Teller

U.S. Nuclear scientist who developed the hydrogen bomb.

Sir Frederick Gowland Hopkins

An English biochemist who worked on proteins and vitamins. He received the Nobel Prize in medicine in 1929 for the discovery of vitamin D.

G. Henry Moseley

He was born in 1887 in Britain. He propunded 'Moseley law' and devised the series of atomic number. He died in 1915.

Dr. Gerhard Herzberg

A Canadian and the 1971 Nobel Prize winner in chemistry for his researches in atomic and molecular structures, particularly free radicals.

Dr. Gerald Maurice Edelman

Belongs to the U.S.A. and is the co-winner of the Noble Prize for Medicine, 1972. He found out the chemical structure of blood proteins or antibodies which shield the human body against infection.

Henri Becquerel

He was a French physicist who discovered Becquerel rays, the first indications of radioactivity; later named gamma rays. he shared Nobel Prize with the Curies in 1903 for the discovery of radioactivity of uranium. He lived between 1852 and 1908.

Sir Henry Bessemer

A British engineer who invented the process for the manufacture of steel. He lived between 1779 and 1898.

Henry Cavendish

Born in 1731 in Britain. He discovered hydrogen, determined the structure of water molecule and experimentally calulated the dinsity of earth. He died in 1810.

Sir Humphry Davy

A British chemist. He invented the safety lamp. He was the first to apply electric current for the isolation of metals. He lived between 1778 and 1829.

Joseph Lister

He was a british surgeon who used antiseptic treatment for wounds, introduced antiseptic surgery. He lived between 1827 and 1912.

Joseph Priestley

He was a British chemist.He discovered oxygen and methods of collecting gases. He lived between 1733 and 1804.

John Dalton

He was a British scientist. He is the founder of the 'Atomic Theory and Law of Multiple Proportions'. He lived between 1776 and 1844.

John Paul Flory

He was an American scientist. He worked in the field of artificial polymers. He physiochemically analysed the micro molecule, for this he received a Nobel Prize in 1974.

Pasteur Louis

A French chemist who discovered the causes of fermention in alcohol and milk and founded the Pasteur institute. He discovered the treatment of hydrophobia and also laid the foundation of stereo chemistry. He lived between 1822 and 1895.

Michael Faraday

He was a British scientist. He lived between 1791 and 1867. He discovered the laws of electrolysis. He is also called the 'father of alternating current'. He also discovered the laws of electromagnetic induction.

A.K. Lavoisier

He was a French chemist. He established the law of industructibility of matter, composition of water and air. He lived between 1743 and 1794.

Ronald Ross

He was a British physician. He discovered the cause of malaria and its treatment. He was awarded Nobel Prize for medicine in 1902. He lived between 1857 and 1932.

Paracelsus

A Swiss mystic and chemist. He was the first to employ laudanum and antimony in pharmacy. He lived between 1493 and 1541.

Prof. S.S. Joshi

A famous Indian chemist. His works on physical and chemical reaction under electrical discharge on active nitrogen, colloids and hydrogen peroxide are noteworthy.

William Ramsay

He was a British chemist. He lived between 1852 and 1916. He discovered the inert gases like helium, neion, argan, etc. He was awarded with Nobel Prize for this discovery in 1904.

Dr. Shanti Swaroop Bhatnagar

A great Indian scientist who lived between 1895 and 1955. He was the first Director General of Council of Scientific and Industrial Research. Under his directorship many research laboratories was established throughout India.

Dr. Hargobind Khurana

He was born in 1922. He was an American of Indian origin. He created an artificial gene and deciphered genetic code. He was awarded Nobel Prize for medicine in 1968.

Dr. B. D. Nag Choudhury

An eminent Indian Nuclear physicist known all over the world. He assisted Dr. Lawrence in the invention of cyclotron. He has also been the Director of Saha Nuclear Instt., Calcutta.

Acharya P.C. Roy (1861-1944)

Author of Hindu Chemistry. He founded the Indian Chemical Society and Bengal Chemical and Pharmaceuticals Ltd. He did good work on nitrous acid and its salts.

Nagarjuna

A great Buddhist philosopher and chemist. He mentioned about crucibles, sublimation; colouring process, etc. His works are still available in China and Tibet. His theorty on extraction of copper and metallic oxides are noteworthy.

Dr. Atmarama

A well-known Indian chemist. He greatly contributed in the establishment of chemical industry in India.

Dr. R.S. Paroda

He is the Indian Agricultural Scientist, former Director General (DG) of the Indian Council of Agricultural Research (ICAR) & Secretary DARE and had been elected to the high, level taskforce for the Global framework and Climate change (GFCC) by the World Meteorological Organisation (WMO), the only Indian among 16 member taskforce.

Dr. M.S. Swaminathan

The Father of the Green Revolution in India, he has been awarded World Food Prize; Ex-D.G.-ICAR, New Delhi, EX-DG.-IRRI (Internation Rice Research Institute) Manila (Philippines), founder of M.S. Swaminathan Research Foundation, Chennai (T.N.), Padma Vibhushan awarded, also known as the Father of Economic Ecology.

Dr. V. Kurien

Born in Kerala on 26 Nov., 1921 and died on September 9,2012 (90 years aged), he was the Father of White Revolution in milk production in India, founder of NDDB (National Dairy Development Board) Anand (Guj.), started Operation Flood (3 stages). Dr. Verghese Kurien was awarded Padma Vibhushan, World Food Prize and Magsaysay Award for Community Leadership and also called as the Milk Man of Indian and remained the Chairman of NDDB, Anand (Guj.), for 33 years (1965-1998).

Norman Earnest (NE) Borlaug

He was an American scientist, the Father of Green Revolution in agricultural foodgrains production in the World, died at 95 years age (2008) in Dalas city of Texas, developed HYVs of wheat, the only Naube laureate in agriculture in the world so far, developed Maxican wheat varieties-Lermarojo, Sonara-63 & 64, resulting high yielding and resistance capacity wheat varieties, the wheat production in India reached two times between 1965 to 1970.

General Physics Summary

1. Units of Measurement

Quantity	Unit (SI)	Quantity	Unit (SI)
Length	Metre	Viscosity	Poise
Time	Second	Surface Tension	Newton/Square metre
Mass	Kilogram	Heat	Joule
Area	Square metre	Temperature	Kelvin
Volume	Cubic metre	Absolute temperature	Kelvin
Velocity	Metre/second	Resistance	Ohm
Acceleration	Metre/second square	Electric current	Ampere
Density	Kilogram/metre cube	Electromotive force	Volt
Momentum	Kilogram metre/Second	Electrical conductivity	Ohm/metre
Work	Joule	Electric energy	Kilo watt hour
Energy	Joule	Electric power	Kilo watt or watt
Force	Newton	Magnetic intensity	Orsted
Pressure	Pascal or Newton/Sq.metre	Charge	Coulomb
Frequency	Hertz	Magnetic induction	Gauss
Power	Watt	Luminous flux	Candela
Weight	Newton or Kilogram	Intensity of sound	Decibel
Impulse	Newton-second	Power of lens	Dioptre
Angular Velocity	Radian/second	Depth of sea	Fathom

2. Important Scientific Instruments

Instrument		Use
Altimetre	:	It measures altitudes and is used in aircrafts.
Ammeter	:	It measures strength of electric current (in amperes).
Anemometer	:	It measures force and velocity of wind.
Audiometer	:	It measures intensity of sound.
Audiophone	:	It is used for improving imperfect sense of hearing.
Barograph	:	It is used for continuous recording of atmospheric pressure.
Barometer	:	It measures atmospheric pressure.
Binocular	:	It is used to view distant objects.
Bolometer	:	It measures heat radiation.
Calorimeter	:	It measures quantity of heat.
Carburetor	:	It is used in an internal combustion engine for charging air with petrol vapour.
Cardiogram	:	It traces movements of the heart, recorded on a cardiograph.
Chronometer	:	It determines longitude of a place kept onboard ship.
Cinematography	:	It is on instrument used in cinema making to throw on screen and enlarged image of photograph.
Crescograph	:	It measures the growth in plants.
Cyclotron	:	A charged particle accelerator which can accelerate charged particles to high energies.
Dynamo	:	It converts mechanical energy into electrical energy.
Dynamometer	:	It measures electrical power.
Electrometer	:	It measures electricity.
Electroscope	:	It detects presence of an electric charge.
Endoscope	:	It examines internal parts of the body.
Eudiometer	:	A glass tube for measuring volume changes in chemical reactions between gases.
Fathometer	:	It measures the depth of the ocean.
Galvanometer	:	It measures the electric current of low magnitude.
Hydrometer	:	It measures the specific gravity of liquids.
Hygrometer	:	It measures humidity in air.
Hydrophone	:	It measures sound under water.
Kymograph	:	It graphically records physiological movements (Blood pressure and heart beat.
Lactometer	:	It determines the purity of milk.
Manometer	:	It measures the pressure of gases.
Mariner's compass	:	It is an instrument used by the sailors to determine the direction.
Microphone	:	It converts the sound waves into electrical vibrations and to magnify the sound.
Mocroscope	:	It is used to obtain magnified view of small objects.
Odometer	:	An instrument by which the distance covered by wheeled vehicles is measured.
Phonograph	:	An instrument for producing sound.
Photometer	:	The instrument compares the luminous intensity of the source of light.
Periscope	:	It is used to view objects above sea level (used in sub-marines).
Potentiometer	:	It is used for comparing electromotive force of cells.
Pyrometer	:	It measures very high temperature.
Radar	:	It is used for detecting the direction and range of an approaching plane by means of radio microwaves.
Rain Guage	:	An apparatus for recording rainfall of a particular place.

Supplementary Facts

Radiometer : It measures the emission of radiant energy.

Refractometer : It measures refractive indes.

Saccharimeter : It measures the amount of sugar in the solution.

Seismograph : It measures the intensity of earthquake shocks.

Salinometer : It determines salinity of solution.

Sextent : This is used by navigators to find the latitude of a place by measuring the elevation above the horizon of the sun or another star.

Spectrometer : It is an instrument for measuring the energy distribution of a particular type of radiation.

Speedometer : It is an instrument placed in a vehicle to record its speed.

Sphygmomanometer : It measures blood pressure.

Spherometer : It measures the curvatures of surfaces.

Stereoscope : It used to view to dimensional pictures.

Stethoscope : An instrument which is used by the doctors to hear and analyse heart and lung sounds.

Straboscope : It is used to view rapidly moving objects.

Tachometer : An instrument used in measuring the speed of aeroplanes and motor boats.

Teleprinter : This instrument receives and sends typed messages from one place to another.

Telescope : It views distant objects in space.

Theodolite : It measures horizontal and vertical angles.

Thermometer : This instrument is used for the measurement of temperatures.

Thermostat : It regulates the temperature at a particular point.

Viscometer : It measures the viscosity of liquids.

Voltmeter : It measures the electric potential difference between two points.

3. Inventions and Discoveries

Invention	Year	Inventor	Country
Acetylene gas	1862	Berthelot	France
Adding machine	1642	Pascal	France
Adhesive tape, (Scotch)	1930	Richard Drew	U.S.A.
Aeroplane	1903	Orville & Wilbur Wright	U.S.A.
Air conditioning	1902	Carrier	U.S.A.
Airplane, (Jet engine)	1939	Ohain	Germany
Airship (Non-rigid)	1852	Henri Giffard	France
Aerosol spray	1926	Erik Rotheim	Norway
Artificial heart	1957	Willem Kolff	Netherlands
Automic bomb	1945	J.Robert Oppenheimer	U.S.A.
Automic numbers	1913	Moseley	Britain
Automic theory	1803	Dalton	Britain
Automic rifle	1918	John Browning	U.S.A.
Bakelite	1907	Leo H.Baekeland	Belgium
Ballistic missile	1944	Wernher von Braun	Germany
Balloon	1783	Jacques & Joseph Montgolfier	France
Ball-point pen	1888	John. J.Loud	U.S.A.
Barometer	1644	Evangelista Torricelli	Italy
Battery (Electric)	1800	Alessandro Volta	Italy

Bicycle	1839-40	Kirkpatrick Macmillan	Britain
Bicycle	1888	John Boyd Dunlop	Britain
Bifocal lens	1780	Benjamin Franklin	U.S.A.
Bleaching powder	1798	Tennant	Britain
Bunsen burner	1855	R. Willhelm von Bunsen	Germany
Burglar alarm	1858	Edwin T.Holmes	U.S.A.
Calculas	1670	Newton	Britain
Camera, (Kodak)	1888	Walker Eastman	U.S.A.
Canned food	1804	Appert	France
Car (Steam)	1769	Necolas Gugnot	France
Car (Petrol)	1888	Karl Benz	Germany
Carburator	1867	Gottlieb Daimler	Germany
Cassette (Audio)	1963	Philips Co.	Holland
Cassette, (Videotape)	1969	Sony	Japan
Celluloid	1861	Alexander Parkes	Britain
Cement (Portland)	1824	Joseph Aspdin	Britain
Ehemotherapy	1909	Ehrlich	Germany
Chronometer	1735	John Harrison	Britain
Cinema	1895	Nicolas & Jean Lumiere	France
Clock (Mechanical)	1725	I-Hsing & Liang Ling-Tsan	China
Clock (Pendulum)	1656	Christian Huygens	Netherlands
Cloning, (DNA)	1973	Boyer, Cohen	U.S.A.
Cloning (Mammal)	1996	Wilmut et al	U.K.
Compact disc	1972	RCA	U.S.A.
Compact disc player	1979	Sony, Philips	Japan. Netherlands
Computer (Laptop)	1987	Sinclair	Britain
Computer (Mini)	1960	Digital Corp.	U.S.A.
Crossword puzzle	1913	Author Wynne	U.S.A.
CT scan	1973	Hounsfield	Britain
Diesel engine	1895	Rudoff Diesel	Germany
Disc brake	1902	Dr. F.Lancherster	Britain
Disc. (Video)	1972	Philips Co.	Holland
DNA(Structure)	1951	Crick-UK, Watson-US Wilking-UK	U.K./U.S.
Dynamo	1832	Hypolite Pixii	France
Electric flat iron	1882	H.W. Seeley	U.S.A.
Electric lamp	1879	Thomas Alva Edison	U.S.A.
Electric motor (DC)	1873	Zenobe Gramme	Belgium
Electric motor (AC)	1888	Nilola Tesla	U.S.A.
Electric iron	1882	Henry W. Seely	U.S.A.
Electric washing machine	1906	Alva J.Fisher	U.S.A.
Electro-magnet	1824	William Sturgeon	Britain
Electron	1897	Thomson J.	Britain
Electroplatina	1805	Luigi Brugnatelli	Italy

Electric computer	1824	Dr. Alan M. Turing	Britain
Facsimile machine	1843	Alexander Bain	Britain
Fibre optics	1955	Kepany	Britain
Film (Moving outlines)	1885	Louis Prince	France
Film (Talking)	1922	J. Engl, J.Mussolle & H.Vogt	Germany
Film (Musical sound)	1923	Dr. Le de Forest	U.S.A.
Floppy disk	1970	IBM	U.S.A.
Frequency Modulation (FM)	1933	E.H. Armstrong	U.S.A.
Frisbee	1948	Fred Morrisson	U.S.A.
Fountain pen	1884	Lewis E. Waterman	U.S.A.
Galvanometer	1834	Andre-Marie Ampere	France
Glider	1853	Sir George Cayley	Britain
Gramophone	1878	Thomos Alvo Edison	U.S.A.
Helicopter	1924	Etinne Oehmichen	France
HIV	1984	Martagnier	French
Holography	1947	Denis Gason	Britain
Hydrogen bomb	1952	Edward Teller	U.S.A.
Intelligence testing	1905	Simon Binet	French
Jet Engine	1937	Sir Frank Whittle	Britain
Laser	1960	Theodore	U.S.A.
Lounderatte	1934	J.F. Cantrell	U.S.A
Lift (Mechanical)	1852	Elisha G. Otis	U.S.A
Lighting conductor	1752	Benjamin Franklin	U.S.A.
Locomitive	1804	Richard Trevithick	Britain
Logarithms	1614	Napier	Britain
Loom, (Power)	1785	F. Cartwright	Britain
Loudspeaker	1900	Horace Short	Britain
Machine gun	1718	Richard Gatling	Britain
Magnetic recording Tape	1928	Fritz Pfleumer	Germany
Match, (Safely)	1826	John Walker	Britain
Microphone	1876	Alexander Graham Bell	U.S.A.
Microprocessor	1971	Rebert Noyce & Gardon More	U.S.A.
Microscope(Comp)	1590	Z. Janssen	Netherlands
Microscope (Elect.)	1931	Ruska Knoll	Germany
Microware oven	1947	Percy LeBaron Spencer	U.S.A.
Motor cycle	1885	G Daimler	Germany
Movie projector	1893	Thomas Edison	U.S.A.
MRI	1971	Damadian	U.S.A.
Neon lamp	1910	Georges Claude	France
Neutron	1932	Chadwick	Britain
Neutron bomb	1958	Samuel Cohen	U.S.A.
Nylon	1937	Dr. Wallace H.Carothers	U.S.A.
Optical fibre	1955	Narinder Kapany	Germany

Paper	A.D. 105	China	
Pace-maker	1952	Zoll	U.S.A.
Pasteurisation	1867	Louis Pasteur	France
Pencil	1792	Lacques-Nicolas Conte	France
Periodic table	1869	Mendeleyev	Russia
Photocopier	1938	Carlson	U.S.A.
Photoelectric cell	1893	Julius Elster, Hans F.Geitel	Germany
Photo film(Celluloid)	1893	Reichenbach	U.S.A.
Photo film (Transparent)	1884	Goodwin Eastman	U.S.A.
Photography (On metal)	1826	J.N. Niepce	France
Photography (On paper)	1835	W.H.Fox Talbot	Britain
Photography (On film)	1888	John Carbutt	U.S.A.
Piano	1709	Cristofori	Italy
Pistol, Revolver	1836	Colt	U.S.A.
Plutonium fission	1940	Kennedy,Whal,Seaborg Segre	U.S.A.
Pop-up toaster	1927	Charles Strite	U.S.A.
Printing press	1455	Johann Gutenberg	Germany
Printing(Rotary)	1846	Richard Hoe	U.S.A.
Printing(Web)	1865	William Bullock	U.S.A.
Proton	1919	Rutherford	N.Zealand
Quantum theory	1900	Plank	Germany
Radar	1922	A.H.Taylor & Leo C.Young	U.S.A.
Radiocarbon dating	1947	Libby	U.S.A.
Radio telegraphy	1864	Dr. Mohlon Loomis	U.S.A.
Radio telegraphy (Trans Atlantic	1901	G.Marconi	Italy
Rayon	1883	Sir Joseph Swan	Britain
Razor(Electric)	1931	Col. Jacob Schick	U.S.A.
Refrigerator	1850	James Horrison Alexander Catlin	U.S.A.
Relativity theory	1905	Einstein	Germany
Rubber (Latex foam)	1928	Dunlop Rubber Co.	Britain
Rubber (Tyres)	1846	Thomas Hancock	Britain
Rubber (Vulcanised)	1841	Charles Goodvear	U.S.A.
Rubber(Waterproof)	1823	Charles Macintosh	Britain
Safety pin	1849	Walter Hunt	U.S.A.
Seat belt	1959	Volvo	Sweden
Self-starter	1911	Charles F. Kettering	U.S.A.
Ship (Steam)	1775	I.C. Perier	France
Ship (Turbine)	1894	Hon. Sir C. Parsons	Britain

REASONING

1 Chapter Logical Reasoning

Coding & Decoding

In this type of question a word is coded in a particular way and the candidate is as per to code other word in same way.

In each question a word changes in certain logic.

All questions is a process of encrypt or decrypt any word, letter or sentence in a set pattern or code based.

To solve these questions a candidate must know the place value of English alphabet.

A	Z
1	26

We count place value of letters always from left like

D = 4

But if we count D from right it should be subtracted from

27 − 4 = 23

Means	D	
	4	from left
	D	
	23	from Right

Coding & decoding is divided in 3 Parts

Type I :

In this coding letter are changed in numbers

Example : In certain code L I O N is written as 21 90 51 41 than in same way what is the code of ROA D.

Solve :	L	I	O	N
	12	09	15	14
	21	90	51	41

Place value is in reverse

	R	O	A	D
	18	15	01	04
Reverse				
	81	51	10	40

Answer is - 81511040

Type-II :

In this type of coding letters of words change their position.

Example: in a certain code language FAMOUS is written as SMAUOF then is same way what is the code of PERSON

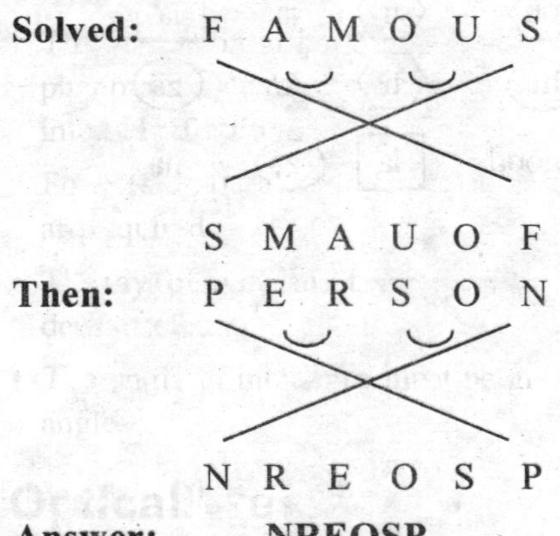

Answer: **NREOSP**

Type-III:

In this type of coding place value of letters changes in addition and substraction.

Example: In a certain code language REASONING is written as SFBTPOJOH then what will be UNIVERSAL in same way.

R	E	A	S	O	N	I	N	G
18	5	1	19	15	14	9	14	7
+1	+1	+1	+1	+1	+1	+1	+1	+1
19	6	2	20	16	15	10	15	8
S	F	B	T	P	O	J	O	H

Then:

U	N	I	V	E	R	S	A	L
21	14	9	22	5	18	19	1	12
+1	+1	+1	+1	+1	+1	+1	+1	+1
20	15	10	23	6	19	20	2	13
T	O	J	W	F	S	T	B	M

Answer: **TOJWFSTBM**

Type-IV:

In this type of question based on sentences and words of sentences change in certain codes.

Example: In a certain code language **"time is on"** means **"ti ja la"** and **"go on he"** means **"ti ka za"** and **"is he good"** means **"la za na"** then what is the code of **"Time"**

Solved:

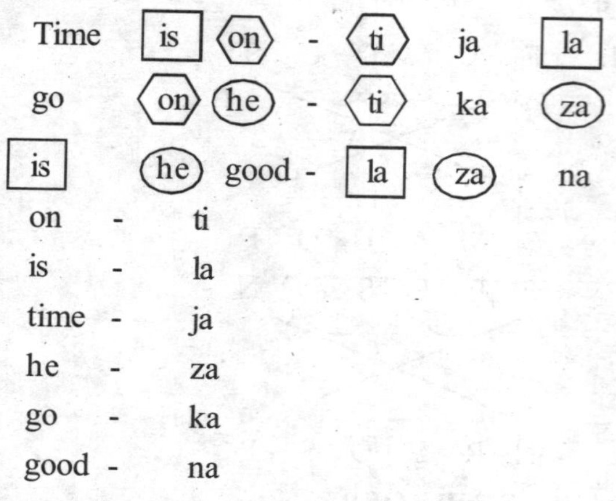

Answer is - ja

Segregate

Classification means to assort the items of a given group on the basis of a certain common quality.

In this type of question you are given a group of certain items, out of which all excepts one similar to one another in same manner the candidate is revised to choose which one item which does not fit the that group.

Type of question based on classification here.

Type-1: Choose the odd word: In this type of question General Knowledge of a student's is checked.

Example: Choose the word which is least like the other words in the group.

(i) Jaipur (ii) Lucknow

(iii) Ptna (iv) Indore

Answer is (iv) : Indore because others are Capital of Indian States

Type-2: Choose the odd letters: In this type of question based on latter of English Alphabet.

Example: choose the word which is least like the other words in the group.

(i) XC (ii) SH

(iii) LP (iv) DW

Answer is (iii): LP because others are revers of alphabet

Type-3: Choose the odd number: In this type of question based on numbers.

Example: Choose the word which is least like the other words in the group.

(i) 36

(ii) 100

(iii) 25

(iv) 72

Answer is (iv) : 72 because others are perfect squire of numbers.

Type-4: Choose the odd pairs: In this type of question option is based on pairs of words which is related to each other in a certain logic.

Example: choose the word which is least like the other words in the group.

(i) Painter - Brush

(ii) Sculptor – Stone

(iii) Potter – Utensil

(iv) Dancer – Shoes

Answer is (iii): Here is the answer Potter – Utensil why other are not because Potter makes Utensil

Large & Small

In this type of question a set of different aliments are given using by symbols. Here's some statements will be provided with conclusions. In the statements some characters are given and students solve comparisons in those characters and find out conclusions.

There are five times of inquality signs which used

Signs	Meaning
$<$	Less than
$>$	Greater than
$\leq$	Less than or equal to
$\geq$	Greater than or equal to
$=$	Equal to

Let us consider two variables P and Q, then inequalities can be shown as follows:

Signs	Meaning
$P < Q$	P is less than B
$P > Q$	P Greater than B
$P \leq Q$	A is Less than or equal to B
$P \geq Q$	A is Greater than or equal to B
$P = Q$	A is Equal to B

Type-1: In these types of equation all signs are in same direction conclusions will come 100% true.

1. $> \geq =$ (First priority should go to $>$, Next $\geq$ Last $=$)

   Example: If $T > P \geq Q = R$

   then. $T > Q$ and $T > R$

2. $< \leq =$ (First priority should go to $<$, Next $\leq$ Last $=$)

   Example: If $W < X \leq V = Y$

   then. $W < Y$ and $W < V$

Type-2: In these types of equation all signs are in opposit direction conclusions will not come 100%.

1. $><$ (No relation)

   Example: If $Q > K < L$

   Then, there will be no relation between Q and L

2. $<>$ (No relation)

   Example: If $F < H > D$

   Then, there will be no relation between F and D

Example: (1 and 2)

(a) If only conclusion I follows.

(b) If only conclusion II follows.

(c) If either conclusion I or II follows.

(d) If neither conclusion I nor II follows.

(e) If both conclusion I and II follows.

1. Statement: $U \leq V < W = X < Y$

   Conclusion:

   I. $Y > V$ II. $W > U$

   Solved: $U \leq V < W = X < Y$

   This is fix all signs are in same direction then answer will be 100%.

   then both are 100% ture.

   answer (e)

2. Statements: $P > L \leq M < N > Q$

   Conclusion:

   I. $P > Q$

   II. $Q > M$

   Solved: $P > L \leq M < N > Q$

   This is fix all signs are not in same direction then answer will not be 100%.

   then both are not 100% ture.

   answer (d)

3. Which of the following symbols shoud replace the question mark in the given expression in order to make the expressions. 'I > L' as well as 'M K' definitely ture?

   $I > J \geq K ? L \leq N = M$

   (a) $>$ (b) $<$

   (c) $\leq$ (d) $=$

   (e) $\geq$

   Solved-(d): On putting sign (=) in place of question mark (?)

   $I > J \geq K ? L \leq N = M$

   $\Rightarrow$ **Means I > L and M K**

Causes & Effect

Cause and effect questions are one of the most important questions that forms a part of the logical reasoning section in entrance exams. Even though cause and effect questions might seem easier for some, there are chances that what you think of as the answer, does not turn out to be the answer in reality. Hence, it is imperative to understand what all is there in such types of questions and how to prepare for them.

Some important Definitions

1. **Cause :** Condition under which the event or situation occurs.
2. **Effect :** The repercussion or consequences of the situation occurred.
3. **Sufficient condition :** The statement explaining the cause of the situation is known as the sufficient condition.
4. **Necessary condition :** The necessary condition is the one that has to be satisfied for the event to occur. This condition is mandatory for the event to cause.

Rules to keep in mind while solving cause and effect questions

- You must be able to make out whether one statement is the cause of the other statement and vice versa.
- Cause occurs before the effect. Both the statements must lead to a sort of relationship with each other.
- It might be possible that which reading the sentences, you may come across a third event that is responsible for creating the effect or acts as a common cause for both the events. But for analysing that event, you need to read the statements properly.
- If no relationship seems to be established, both the statements are independent situatio.

The typical format that a cause and effect problem follows is shown below, this is in no way an exhaustive list of the format. There may be cause and effect relationship between the two statement. These two statement may be the effect of the same cause or independent cause, these statement may be independent. Causes without having any relationship. Read both the statement in each question and mark answer as:-

(a) If statement I is cause & II is its effect

(b) If statement II is cause & I is its effect

(c) If Both the statement I & II are effects of independent causes.

(d) If Both the statement I and II are effects of common Causes.

Ex.- **(i):** The trian services in the city were disrupted for almost a day.

(ii) Due to derse fog the visibility was almost nil on the train routs. answer (b) - Train services yot disrupted because of dense fog an train routes leading to Zero visibility.

Blood Relation

Problems based on blood relations are very important segment of analytical reasoning. The question papers of almost every competitive exams of objective type include 4-5 questions based on blood relation. Particularly for getting jobs in banking sectors, one has a good skill of solving such questions. In this chapter, we are giving quicker approach to crack problems based on blood relation.

- Here, we are providing a complete Blood Relation Chart that can help you to know about all types of blood relations in a family:

Father of Grand-father or Grand-mother	Great Grand-father
Father of Grand-father or Grand-mother	Great Grand-father
Mother of Grand-father or Grand-mother	Great Garand-mother
Father of father or mother	Grand father
Mother of father or mother	Grand mother
Husband of Mother	Father
Wife of Father	Mother
Brother of Father	Uncle
Brother of Mother	Maternal Uncle
Sister of Father	Aunt
Sister of Mother	Maternal Aunt
Husband of Aunt	Uncle
Wife of Uncle	Aunt
Son of Grand-father/ Grant-mother	Father/Uncle
Daughter of father-in-law/ Mother in-law of father	Mother/Aunt
Son of Father or Mother	Brother
Daughter of Father of Mother	Sister
Son/Daughter of Uncle/Aunt	Cousin
Sister of Husband or Wife	Sister-in-law
Brother of Husband or Wife	Brother-in-law
Wife of brother	Sister-in-law
Husband of Sister	Brother-in-law
Son of Brother or Sister	Nephew
Daughter of Brother/Sister	Niece
Husband of Daughter	Son-in-law
Wife of Son	Daughter-in-law
Son of Son/Daughter	Grandson
Daughter of Son/Daughter	Grand Daughter

Type-1: Indication Based:

The question on this type are generally a dialogue/ conversation between people and followed up with a question on the basis of information provided in the conversation.

Example: Pointing to a man a man said he is the son of my grand father's only doughter in laws, then how is that man related to the man.

(a) Brother (b) Son

(c) Father (d) Grand Father

Solved:

Grand Father

Daughter in law

Father Wife

Man Man

Brother

Answer: Brother

Type-2: Contant Based:

In this type of questions, latters of alphabet used in the question as a relations

Example: K is the father of L who is the husband of M, M is mother of Z, Z is brother P than how is K related to P.

(a) Brother (b) Son

(c) Father (d) Grand Father

Solved:

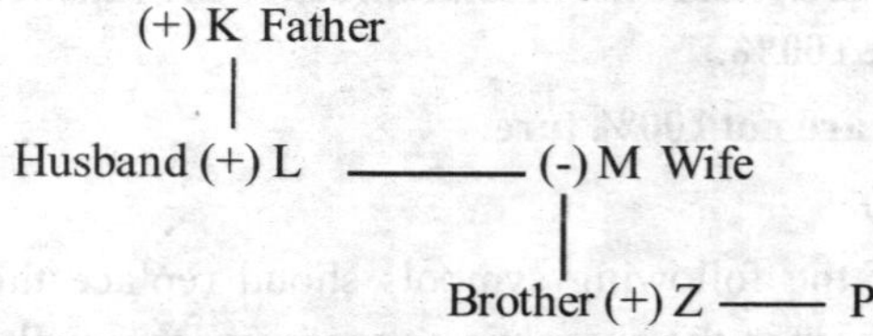

Answer-(d): Grand father

Type-3: Symbol Based:

In this type of questions, the relationships among the members of the family are represented by certain specific codes or symbols such as +, -, *, #, @ ! etc. The answer are obtained by decoded the relationships hidden in the symbols.

Example: A + B means A is father of B

A % B means A is brother of B

A * B means A is Doughter of B

Which of the following shows that K is Uncle of C.

(a) C + K % J (b) J + K % C

(c) C + J % K (d) K % J + C

Solved:

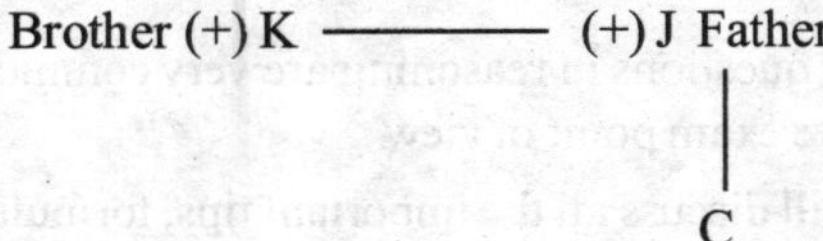

Answer-(d): K is Uncle of C

Type-4: Family :

(i) A family consists of 6 members P, Q, R, X, Y, Z.

(ii) Q is the son of R but R is not mother of Q.

(iii) P and R are married couple.

(iv) Y is the brother of R, X is the daughter of P.

(v) Z is the brother of P.

1. How is Q related to X ?
2. How is Y related to P ?

Solved:

Y^{+} - R^{+} - P^{-} Z^{+}

Q^{+} - X^{-}

Answer-1: Q is the brother of X

Answer-2: Y is the brother in law of P

Calendars

The year consists of 365 days, 5 hours, 48 minutes (52 weeks and 1 odd day). An extra day is added once in every fourth year which was called the leap year, which has 366 days (52 weeks and 2 odd days).

To find the day of any given date of the year, you need to understand the calendar calculations:

1. The day gets repeated after every seventh day (concept of a week), if today is Monday, then 28th day from now will also be Monday as it a multiple of 7 (28/7 = 4, so four weeks). Here the 30 day will be calculated by 30/7, which is 4 weeks and 2 days, these two days are called odd days. With starting day as Monday and two odd days, the day will be Wednesday, this point is the most critical in calendars. The other of looking at it is since the 28th day is Monday, so the 30th day will be Wednesday. But you have to understand and use the concept of odd days as the question may be about thousands of years.
2. First thing to remember, first January 1 AD was Monday therefore, we must count days from Sunday. This means the 0th day was Sunday, so the 7th day was Sunday again and so on and so forth.
3. In 100 years there are 24 leap years and 76 normal years, so the number of odd days are 24(2) + 76 = 124, which is 17 weeks + 5 odd days, so 100 years have 5 odd days.
4. In a normal year there are 365 days so 52 weeks and 1 odd day, in a leap year there are 366 days so 52 weeks and 2 odd days.
5. 400 year is a leap year, similarly the multiples of 400 are also leap years.
6. In 400 years, the number of odd days become 20+1 (from the leap year), so total days are 21, which is three weeks and 0 odd days. In 400 years there are 0 odd days.

Example:

1. If today is Monday, what will be the day 350 days from now?

Ans.: 350 days, 350/7 = 50, no odd days, so it will be a Monday.

2. What day of the week was 15th August 1949?

Solution:

15th August, 1949 means

1948 complete years + first 7 months of the year 1949 + 15 days of August.

1600 years give no odd days.

300 years give 1 odd day.

48 years give [18 + 12] = 60 = 4 odd days.

{∵ For ordinary years → 18 odd days and for leap year 1 more day (48 ÷ 4) = 12 odd days, 60 = 7 x 8 4}

From 1st January to 15th August 1949

Odd days:

January - 3

Feburary - 0

March - 3

April - 2

May - 3

June - 2

July - 3

August - 1

17 ⇒ 3 odd days.

∴ 15th August 1949 → 1 + 4 + 3 = 8 = 1 odd day.

This means that 15th Aug. fell on 1st day. Therefore, the required day was Monday.

Clock

1. Angle traced by hour hand in 12 hours = 360^0.
2. Angle traced by minute hand in 60 minutes are 360^0.
3. When both hour and minute hands are at right angle they are 15 minutes space apart.
4. A clock has two hands, smaller hand is called short hand or short hand or bour hand. While larger hand is called long hand or minute hand.
5. Both hands of clock coincides in one hour.
6. When both the hands are at right angle, they are 15 minutes space apart.
7. Both hands are in straight line when they are opposite to each other or coincident to each other.
8. In each 60 minutes, the minute hand gains 55 minutes on the hour hand.

Some important points:

1. In 12 hours both hands are at right angled 22 times and 44 times in a day.
2. In 12 hours both hands are in opposite direction 11 times, between 5 to 7, they are opposite at 6 o'clock only. So in a day 22 times in opposite directions.
3. Clock hands coincide 11 times in every 12 hours, as they coincide only one time between 11 and 1, at 12 o'clock.
3. In 12 hours both hands are in straight line (either coincides or in opposite direction)
4. So, both hands coincide 22 times in 24 hours or in a day.
5. So, in 24 hours both hands are in straight line (either coincides or in opposite direction) 44 times.

Example : Find the angle between the hour hand and the minute hand of a clock when the time 2.45.

Solved:

Angle traced by the hour hand in 12 hours = 360

Angle traced in 2 hours 45 minutes by hour hand

$$= \left(\frac{360}{12} \times \frac{11}{4}\right)0 = \left(\frac{165}{2}\right)0$$

Angle traced by minute hand in 60 minutes = 360^0.

Angle traced in 45 minutes by min. hand

$$= \left(\frac{360}{60} \times 45\right)0 = (270)0$$

Angle between hour and min. hand

$$= \left(270 - \frac{165}{2}\right)0 = (187.5)0$$

Example : Clock is set right at 8 a.m. The clock loses 1 minute in 24 hours. What will be true time when clock indicates 8 p.m. on the third day?

Solved:

Time from 8 a.m. on first day to 8 p.m. of third day = 60 hrs.

Aslo 23 hrs and 45 min. = 95 / 4 hrs.

95 / 4 hrs of this clock = 24 hrs of correct clock. So 60 hrs of this clock

$$= \left(24 \times \frac{4}{95} \times 60\right) = 60 = \frac{96}{95} = 61 \text{ hrs approx.}$$

= 61 hrs of correct clock. So, the correct time will be 9 p.m.

Ranking

Order and Ra nking questions in reasoning are very common from any competitive exam point of view.

In this chapter we will discuss all the important tips, formulas and patterns of the question that can be asked in the exam. Below are the forms of questions that can be asked form this chapter.

- The rank of a person from the left or right side.
- Total number of persons based an the given data.
- Number of persons in between two persons.
- Minimum/Maximum number of persons in a row.
- Number of persons on either side of a particular person.
- Rank of persons after interehanging the position.
- Ascending/Descending order of persons according to their categories (age, height, ranking, marks etc.)

Type-I:

(i) To find the total number of persons, when position of one person is given from both sides of the row.

Total number of persons = (Sum of position of the persons from both sides i.e., left and right side or top and bottom)-1

Example:

In a row of 52 persons, position of Ranjan from the right side of the row is 32nd. What is the position of Ranjan from the left side of the row?

Solved:

Position of Ranjan from left = (Total number of persons - position Ranjan from the right side) +1

= (52 - 32) + 1

= 20 + 1

= 21

Hence, Position of Ranjan from left side row is 21st.

Type-II:

When there is a specific number of persons after or before of a person and we have the position of that person from the other side.

Using this formula we find.

Total number of persons = Number of persons after or before the given persons in a row + position of the same person from the other side.

Example:

In a row of 16 persons, position of P form the right side of the row is 6th. Find the number of persons before P in the row?

Solved:

Number of persons before P = Total number of persons - position of P from the right side number of persons before P = 16 - 6 = 10

Type-III

To find the total number of persons in row, when ranks of two persons and number of the persons who are sitting between these two persons are given.

Such types of problem two possible cases arise when trying to determine the number of persons in between the two persons.

(i) Not Overlapping Case: When total number of students > (Left position of one persons + right position of another person).

Total number of persons = (Sum of the position of two different persons from both sides) + number of persons between two persons.

Example:

In a row of 70 persons. Janvi is 28th from the right side of row and Rupesh is 33th from the left side of row. Find out the number of persons sitting between them?

Solved:

Number of persons between Janvi and Rupesh

$$= 70 - (28 + 33)$$

$$= 70 - 61 = 9$$

Type-IV:

When in a row, the positions of two persons is given and their positions are interchanged and after interchanging the position of 1st person is given from the same side as before interchanging.

New position of the 2nd person from the same side as before interchanging = position of 2nd person from the same side before interchanging + (Position of the 1st person after interchanging - position of the 1st person before interchanging from the same side).

Total number of persons = sum of the position of person (same perosn) from both sides -1.

Number of persons between two persons = Difference in the positions of a person (same person) whose position from same side before and after interchanging is given -1.

Example:

Raju and Rama are standing in a row of persons. Raju is 12th from the left side and Rima is 18th from the right side of the row. If they interchanged their position, Raju become 25th from left. Find these-

1. Total number of persons.

   Ans: In this questions, Raju position changes from 12 to 25 from left. That means 24 persons are standing from his left side. Now, Raju is at Rima's position which is 18th from the right side. That means 17 persons are standing from his right.

   So, Total number of persons = 24 + 17 + 1 (Raju's own position) = 42

Type-VI:

If the position of two different persons are given from opposite sides of the row and third persons is sitting exactly in the middle of the two. If total number of persons is to be calculated, then there are two conditions:

Example:

In a row of boys, position of R from the right side of the row is 11th, S from the left side of row is 19th. If T is sitting in middle of R and S and position of T from R is 7th. Find the total number of the boys in the row?

Solved:

Position of T from the right = Position of R from right + positions of T from R

$$= 11 + 7 = 18\text{th}$$

Accoreding to question.

T is 7th from R and T is sitting in middle of R and S then also T is at 7th position away from S.

Position of T from Left = Position of S from left + position of T from S

$$= 19 + 7 = 26\text{th}$$

Total number of boys

$$= (\text{sum of position of T from both side} - 1)$$

$$= (18 + 26) - 1$$

$$= 44 - 1 = 43$$

2 Elementary Arithmetic

Chapter

Whole Numbers, Fractions and Decimals

Digits

The ten symbols 0, 1, 2, 3, 4, 5, 6, 7, 8, 9 are called digits, which can represent any number.

Face Value and Place Value

Face value is absolute value of a digit. Place value is value of a digit in relation to its position in the number. For example, face value and place value of 9 in 14921 are 9 and 900 respectively. Note that to find the place value of a digit in a number, we put as many zero (0) after the digit as the number of digits after the digit whose place value is to be find in the given number.

The Number Line

The number line is a straight line between negative infinity on the left to positive infinity on the right.

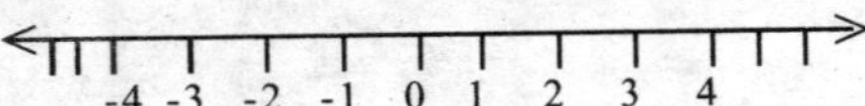

Each point on the number line represents a unique number on the number line.

Numbers

Natural Numbers

These are the numbers (1, 2, 3, etc.) that are used for counting. It is denoted by N.

There are infinite natural numbers and the smallest natural number is 1 (one).

Whole Numbers

The natural numbers along with zero (o), form the system of whole numbers.

It is denoted by W.

There is no largest whole number and the smallest whole number is 0.

Integers

The number system consisting of natural numbers, their negative and zero is called integers.

It is denoted by Z or I.

The smallest and the largest integers cannot be determined.

Even Numbers

An integers which are divisible by 2 are even numbers. It is denoted by E.

E = - 24, - 4, - 2, 4, 6, 8, ...

Smallest even natural number is 2. There is no largest even number.

Odd Numbers

Integers which are not divisible by 2 are odd numbers. It is denoted by 0.

0 = 1, 3, 5, 7, ...

Smallest odd natural number is 1.

There is no largest odd number.

Prime Numbers

Natural numbers which have exactly two factors, I and the number itself are called prime numbers.

The lowest prime number is 2.

2 is also the only even prime number.

All prime number (Except 2 and 3) can be expressed in the form of $6N \pm 1$, where N = 1, 2, 3, ...

All prime numbers less than 100 are 2, 3, 5, 7, 11, 13, 17, 19, 23, 29, 31, 37, 41, 43, 47, 59, 61, 67, 71, 73, 79, 83, 89, 97

Composite Numbers

It is a natural number that has atleast one divisor different from unity and itself.

Every composite number can be factorised into its prime factors.

For Example: 24 = 2 x 2 x 2 x 3. Here, 24 is a composite number and 2, 3 are prime numbers.

The smallest composite number is 4.

Co-prime Numbers

Those numbers are said to be co-prime if they do not have any common factors other than 1.

For Example: 14 and 15 are co-prime numbers, 14 and 15 have only common factor as 1.

Remember

- 1 is neither prime nor composite.
- 1 is an odd integer.
- 0 is neither positive nor negative.
- 0 is an even integer.
- 2 is prime & even both.
- All prime numbers (except 2) are odd.

Real Numbers

All numbers that can be represented on the number line by the points on it are called real numbers.

It is denoted by R.

R^+ : Positive real numbers and

R : Negative real numbers.

Real numbers = Rational numbers + Irrational numbers.

(i) Rational Numbers

Any number that can be put in the form of $\frac{p}{q}$, where p and q are integers and q # 0, is called a rational number.

It is denoted by Q.

Every integer is a rational number.

Zero (0) also a rational number. The smallest and largest rational numbers cannot be determined.

Note that every integer is a rational number. Average of any two rational numbers is also a ration number. There are infinite number of rational number between any two rational numbers, Decimal representational of any rational number is either terminating decimal number or non-terminating recurring (repeating) decimal number. So, all terminating decimal numbers (2.348, 0.07315, etc.) and all non-terminating repeating (recurring) decimal numbers (54.342, 0.063, 5.2, etc.) are also rational numbers.

Remember

- If x and y are two rational numbers, then $\frac{x+y}{2}$ is also a rational number and its value lies between the given two rational numbers x and y.
- An infinite number of rational numbers can be determined between any two rational numbers.

(ii) Irrational Numbers

The numbers which are not rational or which cannot be put in the form of $\frac{p}{q}$, where p and q are integers and q # 0, is called irrational number.

It is denoted by Q' or Q^0.

$\sqrt{2}, \sqrt{3}, \sqrt{5}, 2+\sqrt{3}, 3-\sqrt{5}, 3\sqrt{3}$ are irrational numbers.

Conversion of Recurring Decimal into the Rational Number of the Form $\frac{p}{q}$

First, write the non-terminating repeating decimal number in recurring form i.e., write

64.20132132132..... as $64.20\overline{132}$

In short; $0.\bar{a} = \frac{a}{9}, 0.\overline{ab} = \frac{ab}{99}, 0.\overline{abc} = \frac{abc}{999}$, ect.

and

$$0.a\bar{b} = \frac{ab-a}{90}, .a\overline{bc} = \frac{abc-a}{990}, .ab\bar{c} = \frac{abc-ab}{900}$$

$$0.ab\overline{cd} = \frac{abcd-ab}{9900}, 0.abcde = \frac{abcde-abc}{990}, etc.$$

Example-1:

1. Convert $2.\overline{46102}$ in the $\frac{p}{q}$ form of rational number.

Sol.: Required $\frac{p}{q}$ form $= \frac{246102-2}{99999} = \frac{246100}{99999}$

Fractions

A number which can be expressed in the form of $\frac{p}{q}$, where p and q are both integer but q # 0. In the fraction, p is called numerator and q is called denominator.

For example:

$\frac{5}{7}, \frac{1}{8}, \frac{-3}{4}, \frac{5}{-7}, -\frac{3}{19}, -\frac{5}{9}, \frac{9}{4}, \frac{-12}{7}$, *etc.*

An integer such as 5 can be thought as having the denominator 1. Thus 7 can be also written as $\frac{7}{1}$. So each integer is also a fraction. In the fraction $\frac{5}{7}$, 5 is numerator and 7 is denominator. The fraction bar may be horizontal $\left(as\ in\ \frac{2}{7}\right)$ *or diagonal* $\left(as\ in\ \frac{2}{9}\right)$

Note: The fraction $\frac{a}{b}$ is also used to represent the ratio a : b and the division $a \div b$.

Note that

(i) If the numerator of a fraction is zero and denominator is not equal to zero, then the value of fraction is zero.

(ii) If the numerator of a fraction is non-zero and denominator is zero, then the value of the fraction is infinity.

(iii) If the numerator and denominator of any fractions is either multiplied or divided by the same number, then the value of the fraction remains unchanged.

Decimal Fractions

Fractions whose denominators are powers of 10 are known as decimal fractions, e.g. $\frac{2}{10}, \frac{7}{100}, \frac{999}{1000}$, etc. are deco,a; fractopms/ Amu fraction with denominator in power of 10 can be expressed as decimal number e.g.:

$$\frac{2}{10} = 0.2 \quad \frac{7}{100} = 0.07, \quad \frac{999}{1000} = 0.999, etc.$$

Changing Fraction into Decimal Number: A fraction can be converted to decimal by dividing the numerator by its denominator,

For example: $\frac{3}{4} = 0.75, \frac{1}{100} = 0.01$

Changing Decimal Number into Fraction: To convert a given decimal number into fraction, take the given number without decimal as numerator and take the denominator as 10^n, where n is a natural number, which is equal to the number of digits after decimal in the given decimal number.

For example:

$$2.56 = \frac{256}{10^2} = \frac{256}{100} = \frac{64}{25} \; (Simplest\ form)$$

$$0.069 = \frac{0069}{10^3} = \frac{69}{1000} \; (Simplest\ form)$$

$$25.2016 = \frac{252016}{10^4} = \frac{252016}{10000} = \frac{15751}{625}$$

(*Simplest form*)

Addition and Subtraction of Decimal Numbers: To add or subtract given decimal fractions, the numbers must be arranged one below the other in such a way that decimal point must lie in the same column. Now they can be added or subtracted in usual way.

Note that if we add any number of zeros to the right of a decimal number, its value does not changed.

For example: 2.3 = 2.300, 0.06 = 0.06000 etc.

Example-2:

Find the sum of 54.6032, 0.532 and 2.50024

Solutions:

```
  54.6032
   0.532
+2.50024
 57.63544
```

Rounding off (Approximation) of Decimal Numbers

In some decimal numbers, there are large number of digits after decimal place.

For example: 4.5073291307856.

Many time is such cases, we what to consider the decimal number only upto a certain place after decimal. For this

- We will take the number upto the required place without any change, if the next digit of the required place is less than 5 (this is called **rounding down).**
- We will take the number upto the required place by increasing the required place digit by 1, if the next digit of the required place is 5 or greater than 5 (this is called **rounding up).**

Example-3:

Rounding off the following numbers upto 3 decimal places:

(i) 5.67325698 (ii) 0.0045286

(iii) 62.586631

Solutions:

(i) 5.673 [as the fourth place digit (2) after decimal is less than 5].

(ii) 0.005 [as the fourth place digit (5) after decimal is 5]

(iii) 62.587 [as the fourth place digit (6) after decimal is greater than 5]

Percentage

The word "per cent" is derived from the latin words "per-centum", which means "Per hundred".

It is denoted by the symbol %.

Thus 25 per cent is written as 25% and it means 25 out of 100.

This is written in the ratio form as $\frac{25}{100}$.

Value of Percentage

Value of percentage always depends on the quantity to which it refers.

Consider the statement, "65% of the students in the class are boys". From the context, it is understood that boys form 65% of the total number of students in the class. To know the value of 65% of the students, the value of the total number of students in the class should be known.

If the total number of students in the class is 200, then, the

number of boys = 65% of 200 = $\frac{200\times 65}{100}=130$

It can also be written as (200) x (0.65) = 130.

Note that the expressions 6%, 63%, 72%, 155% etc. do not have any value. Their values depend on the quantities to which they refer.

To express the fraction equivalent to %:

Express the fraction with the denominator 100, then its numberator is the required equivalent percentage.

For example, to express the fraction $\frac{5}{20}$ to equivalent %, we have to write $\frac{5}{20}$ as $\frac{5}{20}\times\frac{5}{5}=\frac{25}{100}$, whose denominator is 100. Then the fraction is equivalent to 25%.

To express % equivalent to fraction : $a\,\% = \frac{a}{100}$

Fractional Equivalents of %

(i) $2\% = \frac{2}{100} = \frac{1}{50}$

(ii) $50\% = \frac{50}{100} = \frac{1}{2}$

(iii) $100\% = \frac{100}{100} = 1$

(iv) $1\% = \frac{1}{100}$

(v) $40\% = \frac{40}{100} = \frac{2}{5}$

(vi) $24.31\% = \frac{24.31}{100} = 0.2431$

(vii) $33\frac{1}{3}\% = \frac{33\frac{1}{3}}{100} = \frac{1}{3}$

(viii) $4\% = \frac{4}{100} = \frac{1}{25}$

Percentage Increase, Decrease or Error

$$\text{Increase \% or percentage increase} = \frac{\text{Increase value}}{\text{Original value}}\times 100\%$$

$$\text{Decrease \% or percentage decrease} = \frac{\text{Decrease value}}{\text{Original value}}\times 100\%$$

$$\text{Error percent} = \frac{\text{Error}}{\text{Correct value}}\times 100\%$$

Note

If the value of any thing increases, then percentage change is the percentage increase and if the value of any thing decreases, then percentage change is the percentage decrease. Thus, Percentage change = Percentage increase, if value of the thing increases and Percentage change = Percentage decrease, if value of the thing decreases.

Changing a Quantity by a Given Percent

(i) If any quantity x increased by a %, then final value of

$$x = \left(\frac{100-a}{100}\right)x$$

(ii) If any quantity x decreased by a %, then final value of

$$= \left(\frac{100-a}{100}\right)x$$

Successive change in a quantity by different given percent

If any quantity x increased by a %, then increased by b %, then decreased by c %, then increased by d %, ..., then final value of x

$$= x\left(\frac{100+a}{100}\right)\times\left(\frac{100+b}{100}\right)\times\left(\frac{100-c}{100}\right)\times\left(\frac{100+d}{100}\right)\times\ldots$$

Population Formula

If the original population of a town is p, and the annual increase is r %, then the population after n years is

$p\left(1+\frac{r}{100}\right)^n$ and population before n years

$$= \frac{p}{\left(1+\frac{r}{100}\right)^n}.$$

If the annual decrease by r %, then the population after n years is $p\left(1-\frac{r}{100}\right)^n$ and population before n years

$$\frac{p}{\left(1-\frac{r}{100}\right)^n}$$

Student and Marks

The percentage of passing marks in an examination is x%. If a candidate who scores y marks fails by z marks, then the maximum marks, $M = \frac{100(y+z)}{x}$.

A candidate scoring x% in an examination fails by 'a' marks, while another candidate who scores y% marks gets 'b' marks more than the minimum required passing marks. Thent maximum marks, $M = \frac{100(a-b)}{y-x}$

In an examination x% and y% students respectively fail in two different subjects while z% students fail in both subjects. Then the % of student who pass in both the subjects will be {100-(x+y-z)}%.

Dimensional Figure and Area

If the sides of a triangle, square, rectangle, rhombus or radius of a circle is increased by a%, its area is increased by $\frac{a(200+a)}{100}$%.

If the side of a triangle, square, rectangle, rhombus or radius of a circle are decreased by a% then its area is decreased by $\frac{a(200-a)}{100}$%.

If length and breadth of a rectangle are changed by x% and y% respectively, then % change in area

$= x + y + \frac{xy}{100}$ (+/- according to increase or decrease).

Shortcuts

Shortcut Approach-1:

If the price of a commodity increases by r%, then the reduction in consumption so as not to increase the expenditure, is

$$\left(\frac{r}{100+r}\times 100\right)\%$$

Examples:

1. The price of sugar is increased by 25%. If a family wants to keep its expenses on sugar unaltered, then the family will have to reduce the consumption of sugar by

(a) 20% (b) 21%

(c) 22% (d) 25%

Ans-(a): Required percentage

$$=\left(\frac{r}{100+r}\times 100\right)\% = \left(\frac{25}{100+25}\times 100\right)\% = 20\%$$

Shortcut Approach-2:

If the price of a commodity decreases by r%, then, increase in consumption, so as not to decrease expenditure on this item is $\left[\frac{r}{100-r}\times 100\right]\%$

2. If the price of tea falls down by 6% then by how much percent must a householder increase its consumption, so as not t odecrease expenditure?

(a) $5\frac{16}{47}\%$ (b) $4\frac{18}{67}\%$

(c) $6\frac{18}{47}\%$ (d) $6\frac{17}{47}\%$

Ans. (c): Required percentage

$$=\left(\frac{r}{100-r}\times 100\right)\% = \left(\frac{6}{100-6}\times 100\right)\% = 6\frac{18}{47}\%$$

Simple Arithmatic Equations

Equation

When an algebraic expression equated to any number or two algebraic expressions are connceted by the sign of equality (=), they form an equation.

For example:

$2x^3 - 5x = 6$, $2p^2 + 3p = 3p^3 - 5$, etc.

Linear Equations

A polynomial of any variable of degree one is called a linear polynomial.

Standard form of a linear polynomial in one variable (say x) is as + b, where a and b are some real numbers but a # 0. When a linear polynomial is equated to zero (0), they form a linear equation.

Hence standard form of a linear equation in any one variable x is ax + b = 0 and standard form of linear equation in any two variable x and y is ax + by + c = 0.

For example:

2x + 3 = 0 (Linear equation in one variable),

3x - 2y + 6 = 0 (Linear equation in two variables) etc.

Solution of a Linear Equation of One Variable

The value of variable which satisfy a given equation is called solution of the equation. The solution is also known as root of the equation.

For example, for a linear equation: 2x - 8 = 0, x = 4 is a solution or root, because by putting x = 4 in the equation, both sides of the equation become equal. In other words, x = 2 satisfies equation 2x - 8 = 0.

Example-1:

Verify that x = 3 is a solution of equation 3x + 5 = 14

Solutions:

If x = 3 is a solution of the given equation, then by putting x = 3 in the given equation will make both sides of equation equal.

∴ put x = 3 in the equation, we get

L. H. S. = 3 x3 + 5 = 9 + 5 = 14 = RHS

Hence x = 3 is a solution of 3x + 5 = 14

Example-2

Verify that x = 2 is a solution of 2x + 3 = 5x - 6.

Solutions:

By putting x = 2, we get

L. H. S. = 2x + 3 = 2 x 2 + 3 = 7

R. H. S. = 5x - 6 = 5 x 2 - 6 = 4

So x = 2 is not a solution of 2x + 3 = 5 x - 6

Rules for Solving a Linear Equation in One Variable

While solving a linear equation, following rules are to be remembered.

(a) Addition/Subtraction of same quantity to/from both sides of an equation does not change the equality.

(b) Multiplication by a same number on both sides of an equation does not change the equality.

(c) Division by a same non-zero number on both sides of an equation does not change the equality.

(d) Any term may be transposed from one side of equality to another side by changing the sign of the term (from + to –, or from – to +),

(e) A multiplier may be removed from one side of an equation by making it a divisor on the other side.

(f) A divisor may be removed from one side of an equation by making it a multiplier on the other side.

Example-3:

Solve: $\frac{1}{3}x - \frac{5}{2} = 6$

Solutions:

We have, $\frac{1}{3}x - \frac{5}{2} = 6$

$$\Rightarrow \frac{1}{3}x - \frac{5}{2} + \frac{5}{2} = 6 + \frac{5}{2}\left(\text{Adding } \frac{5}{2} \text{ onbothsides}\right)$$

$$\Rightarrow \frac{1}{3}x = 6 + \frac{5}{2} \Rightarrow \frac{1}{3}x = \frac{12+5}{2}$$

$$\Rightarrow \frac{1}{3}x = \frac{17}{2} \Rightarrow 3\times\frac{1}{3}x = 3\times\frac{17}{2} \Rightarrow x = \frac{51}{2}$$

(∵ Multiplying both sides by 3)

To Find the Solution(s) or Root (s) of a Linear Equation in Two Variables

Standard from of a linear equation in two variables:

ax + by + c = 0 (a, b # o)

Express any one variable y in terms of other variable say x as

$$y = -\frac{ax+c}{b} \quad ...(i)$$

Now by putting any real value of x in above equation (i), you will get the corresponding real value of y. The value of x and its corresponding value of y is one set of solution of the given linear equation in two variables. In the same way by putting another real value of x in the above equation (i), you will get another value of y. Thus you will get another set of solution. In this way, you will get infinite sets of solution.

Example-4:

Find any three sets of solution of -x + 2y = 4

Solutions:

Consider - x + 2y = 4

⇒ x = 2y - 4 .... (i)

Put y = 0 in equation (i), then x = 2 x 0 - 4 = - 4

Hence, one set of solution : x = - 4, y = 0

Put y = 1 in equation (i), then x = 2 x 1 - 4 = 2 - 4 = - 2

Hence, second set of solution : x = - 2, y = 1

Put y = 2 in equation (i), then x = 2 x 2 - 4 = 0

Hence, third set of solution : x = o, y = 2

Thus, three sets of solution are (-4, 0), (-2, 1) and (0, 2)

A Pair of Linear Equations in Two Variables

Standard form of a pair of linear equations in two variables (say x and y) is

$a_1x + b_1y + c_1 = 0$

$a_2x + b_2y + c_2 = 0$

Here a_1, b_1, c_1, a_2, b_2 and c_2 are some real numbers.

We know that a linear equation is two variables has always infinite sets of solution. But number of solution of a pair of linear equations in two variables depends upon the different conditions. These are.

Condition-I:

If $\frac{a_1}{a_2} \# \frac{b_1}{b_2}$, then there is a unique (i.e. one) solution.

Condition-II:

If $\frac{a_1}{a_2} \# \frac{b_1}{b_2} = \frac{c_1}{c_2}$, then there are infinite set of solution.

Condition-III:

If, $\frac{a_1}{a_2} = \frac{b_1}{b_2} \# \frac{c_1}{c_2}$, then there is no solution.

There are three methods to solve a pair of linear equations in two variables.

Substitution Method

Algorithm to find the solution:

A system of a pair of linear equations in two variables:

$a_1x + b_1y + c_1 = 0$ ...(1)

$a_2x + b_2y + c_2 = 0$ ...(2)

Step-1: Find the value of one variable, say y in terms of the other variable, i.e., x from either equation (1) or (2), whichever is convenient. Consider this equation as equation (3).

Step-2: Substitute this value of y in the other equation, which reduce it to an equation in one variable, i.e., in terms of x, which can be solved. Sometimes, on solving you can get an equation with no variable. If this statement is true, you can conclude that the pair of linear equations has in finite set of solutions. If the statement is false, then the pair of linear equations has no solution.

Step 3: Substitute the value of x (or y) obtained in Step 2 in the equation (3) to obtain the value of the other variable.

Let us understand this method through the following illustration.

Example-5:

Find the solution of the following system by substitution method:

$4x + y = 11$ ...(1)

$x + 2y = 8$ ...(2)

Solutions:

It is easy to solve for either y from the first equation or x from the second equation. Let us solve for y from the equation (1)

The result is $y = 11 - 4x$ ...(3)

Non substitute the above value of y in the equation (2).

We get, $x + 2(11 - 4x) = 8$

Hence, solution is $x = 2$ and $y = 3$.

Square

When a number is multiplied by itself, then we get the square of the number.

For example: Square of $5 = 5 \times 5 = (5^2) = 25$.

Square of 2 and 3 digits numbers are very useful for calculations. For this it is advised to learn the square of 1 to 30 as given in the table.

Number	Square	Number	Square
1	1	16	256
2	4	17	289
3	9	18	324
4	16	19	361
5	25	20	400
6	36	21	441
7	49	22	484
8	64	23	529
9	81	24	576
10	100	25	625
11	121	26	676
12	144	27	729
13	169	28	784
14	196	29	841
15	225	30	900

Properties of Square of a Number

(i) No square number ends in 2, 3, 7 or 8 i.e. unit place digit in a square number can bever be 2, 3, 7 or 8.

(ii) If a number is even then its square is also even. If a number is odd then its square is also odd.

(iii) Number of zeroes at the end of a perfect square number is always even. In other words we can say that numbers ending with odd numbers of zeroes are never perfect squares.

(iv) The difference of squares of two consecutive numbers will always be equal to the sum of the numbers i.e.

$a^2 - b^2 = a + b$, where a and b are natural numbers and a is greater than b.

For example: $16^2 - 15^2 = 16 + 15 = 31$

(v) Square of any number is always a positive number.

I : Multiplication Method:

Using this method, the square of any 2-digits number can be calculated. You can understand this method very easily through the following examples:

(i) $(87)^2 = (7)^2 = (4)(9)$ $2 \times 8 \times 7 + 4 = (11)(6)$ $(8)^2 + 11 = (75) = 75\ 6\ 9$

Carry Carry

(ii) $(79)^2 = (9)^2 = (8)(1)$ $2 \times 8 \times 9 + 8 = (13)(4)$ $(7)^2 + 13 = (62) = 62\ 4\ 1$

Carry Carry

(iii) $(79)^2 = (9)^2 = 8\ (1)$ $2 \times 7 \times 9 + 8 = (13)(4)$ $(7)^2 + 13 = (62) = 62\ 4\ 1$

This can be also written in one short as:

$(79)^2 = 8\ (1)\ 13\ (4)(62) = 62\ 4\ 1$

II : Algebraic Method

This method is used to find the square of any two digits number. In this method, we use the following identity of algebra:

$(a + b)^2 = a^2 + 2\,ab + b^2$ and $(a - b)^2 = a^2 - 2ab + b^2$

This method can be easily understand using the following examples:

(i) $(64)^2 = (60 + 4)^2 = (60)^2 + 2 \times 60 \times 4 + (4)^2$

$= 3600 + 480 + 16 = 4096$

(ii) $(87)^2 = (90 - 3)^2 = (90)^2 - 2 \times 90 \times 3 + (3)^2$

$= 8100 - 540 + 9 = 7569$

Note that in the above examples 'a' is the multiple of 10 nearest to the given number and 'b' is the number required to be added or subtracted from 'a' so that sum or difference of 'a' and 'b' respectively will be the given number.

III : Square of Decimal Numbers

To find the square of any decimal number, write the square of the number ignoring the decimal number and then place the decimal number after twice the place of the original number starting from right side. Let us understand through the following examples:

(i) $(4.7)^2 = ?$

$(47)^2 = 2209$

Here decimal in 4.7 after one digit from right. Therefore, the decimal in the value of the square of 47 will be after two digits from right.

$\therefore (4.7)^2 = 22.09$

(ii) $(6.21)^2 = ?$

$(621)^2 = 385641$

$\therefore (6.21)^2 = 38.5641$

Pythagorean Triplets

If in a triplet of three numbers, sum of square of the two smaller numbers is equal to square of the third number, then the triplet of three numbers is called Pythagorean triplets.

For exampe: 3, 4, 5 because $3^2 + 4^2 = 5^2$

Some other Pythagorean triplets are

(i) 5, 12, 13 (ii) 8, 15, 17

(iii) 7, 24, 25 (iv) 6, 8, 10

(v) 10, 24, 26 (vi) 16, 30, 34

(vii) 20, 21, 29 (viii) 9, 12, 15

(ix) 9, 40, 41 (x) 11, 60, 61

Square Rotts

Square root of a number is that number, the square of which is equal to the given number. There are two types of square roots of a number, positive and negative. Square root is also known as under-root or 2nd root.

Symbolically, square root of a positive number 'n' is written as

$$\sqrt{n},\ \sqrt[2]{n} \text{ or } (n)^{\frac{1}{2}}$$

We know that $4 \times 4 = 16$ [or $(+4) \times (+4) = 16$] and $(-4) \times (-4) = 16$.

$$\therefore \sqrt{16} = \pm 4,\ \sqrt[2]{16} = \pm 4 \text{ and } (16)^{\frac{1}{2}} = \pm 4$$

Here + 4 (i.e. 4) is called positive square root of 16 and - 4 is called negative square root of 16.

Aslo $\sqrt{a} \times \sqrt{a} = a$

Note that normally, we consider only positive square root of a number.

If the number whose square root is to be find out is a perfect square, then its square root is an integer otherwise square root is not an integer.

Properties of Square Roots

(i) If a number has a natural number square root, then its unit digit must be 0, 1, 4, 5, 6 or 9.

Unit digit of square number	0	1	4	5	6	9
Unit digit of square root	0	1 or 9	2 or 8	5	4 or 6	3 or 7

(ii) If unit digit of a number be 2, 3, 7 or 8; then it does not have a natural number square root.

(iii) If a number ends in odd number of zeros, then it does an even number of zeros, it has a square root in which the number of zeros in at the end is falf the number of zeros in the number.

(iv) Negative number has no square root.

Methods to find Square Root of a Perfect Square Number

Method-I: Prime Factorisation Method

(i) Express the given number into prime factors by successive division.

(ii) Make pairs of prime factors such that both the factors in each pair are equal.

(iii) Take one factor from each pair.

(iv) Find the product of factors obtained in step (iii).

The product thus obtained is the required square root.

Example:

Show that 63504 is a perfect square. Aslo, we obtain

$63504 = 2 \times 2 \times 2 \times 2 \times 3 \times 3 \times 3 \times 337 \times 7$

Grouping the factors in pairs of equal factors, we obtain

$63504 = (2 \times 2) \times (2 \times 2) \times (3 \times 3) \times (3 \times 3) \times (7 \times 7)$

Clearly, no factor is left over in grouping the factors in pairs of equal factors, So, 63504 is a perfect square.

Again, $63504 = (2 \times 2 \times 3 \times 3 \times 7) \times (2 \times 2 \times 3 \times 3 \times 7)$

[Grouping first factors in each group

$= 252 \times 252 = 252^2$

Thus, 63504 is the square of 252

Method-II : Division Method

This method can be easily understood with the help of the following example:

Example:

Find the square root of 24336.

(a) 144 (b) 154

(c) 156 (d) 166

Solution-(c):

	1 5 6
1	$\overline{2}\ \overline{43}\ \overline{36}$
	1
25	1 43
	1 25
306	18 36
	18 36
	0

$\sqrt{24336} = 156$

Square Root of Numbers Which are not Perfect Squares.

Division method can also be applied for finding square root of numbers which are not perfect square numbers. Method is explained with the following illustrative examples.

Example:

Find square root of 3 upto 3 decimal places.

Solution:

	1.732
1	$\overline{3}.\overline{00}\ \overline{00}\ \overline{00}$
	1
27	2 00
	1 89
343	11 00
	10 29
3462	71 00
	69 24
	1 76

Here we have added 3 pairs of zeros after decimal. One pair each for 1 digit after decimal point.

$\therefore \sqrt{3} = 1.732$ upto three decimal places.

Square Root of Decimal Numbers.......

to find the square root of a decimal number, first count the number of digits after decimal in the given number, if it is not even, then put a 0 (zero) at the extreme right, so that there will be an even number of digits after decimal point.

Now, periods are marked by putting the bar over it as marked for finding the square root of a perfect square number starting from right hand side before the decimal and from the let hand side after the decimal points.

For example: 1 46 96 71 29

Direction of marking periods

After marking the periods, follow the same steps as for finding the square root of a perfect square number without considering the decimal point. In the final answer, put decimal point after as many number of digits from right as the number of periods after point in the given number.

	1 2 1 . 2 3
1	$\overline{1}\ \overline{46}\ \overline{96}\ .\ \overline{71}\ \overline{29}$
	1
25	46
	44
306	2 96
	2 41
2422	55 71
	48 44
24243	7 27 29
	7 27 29
	0

$\sqrt{14696.7129} = 121.23$

Square Root of a Fraction

To find the square root of a fraction, we find the square root of numerator and denominator both separately.

For example : $\sqrt{\frac{1369}{1521}} = \frac{\sqrt{1369}}{\sqrt{1521}} = \frac{37}{39}$

To Find Smallest and Largest n-digit Number Which is a Perfect Square

This can be understnd through the following illustrations.

Solution:

Smallest 6 digit number = 100000.

```
         3 1 7
    ------------------
  3 |  10 00 00
    |   1
    ------------------
 61 |  1 0 0
    |    6 1
    ------------------
627 |    3 9 0 0
    |    4 3 8 9
    ------------------
    |    - 4 8 9
```

Since 626 × 6 = 3756

627 × 7 = 4389

Now, 3756 < 3900 < 4389

⇒ 626 × 6 < 3900 < 627 × 7

Clearly smallest 6-digit number which is perfect square will be 489 greater than 100000.

Therefore, required number = 100000 + 489 = 100489.

Cubes

If a number is multiplied itself two time, then the result of this multiplication is called the cube of that number.

For examples :

Cube of 3 = 3 × 3 × 3 = 27

Cube of 4 = 4 × 4 × 4 = 64

Cube of any number a is denoted by $(a)^3$ or a^3.

∴ $(3)^3 = 27$, $(4)^3 = 64$.

Test of Perfect Cube

In a prime factorisation of a perfect cube, every number occurs three times or multiple of three times.

For example:

(i) $64 = 2 \times 2 \times 2 \times 2 \times 2 \times 2 = (2)^6$

64 is a perfect cube.

(ii) $729 = 3 \times 3 \times 3 \times 3 \times 3 \times 6 = (3)^6$

729 is a perfect cube.

Example:

Examine (i) 243 (ii) 26136 are perefect cubes.

Solutions:

(i) $243 = (3 \times 3) \times 3 \times 3$

Here occurrence of 3 is not in multiple of '3' so 243 in not a perfect cube number.

(ii) $21636 = (2 \times 2) \times (3 \times 3) \times 11 \times 11$

In 21636, prime number 11 does not occur in group of three, so 21636 is not a perfect cube number.

Properties of Cube of a Number

(i) If a number is negative then its cube is also negative.

Example: (i) $(-2)^3 = (-2) \times (-2) \times (-2) = -8$

(ii) $(-5)^3 = (-5) \times (-5) \times (-5) = -125$

This shows that negative numbers can also be perfect cubes.

(ii) Cube of an even number is also even.

Example: (i) $(2)^3 = 2 \times 2 \times 2 = 8$

(ii) $(7)^3 = 6 \times 6 \times 6 = 216$

(iii) Cube of an odd number is also odd.

Example: (i) $(3)^3 = 3 \times 3 \times 3 = 27$

(ii) $(7)^3 = 7 \times 7 \times 7 = 343$

Relation between Unit Digit of a Number and its Perfect Cube

Observe the following table

x	1	2	3	4	5	6	7	8	9
x^3	1	8	27	64	125	216	243	512	729

In can be observed from the table that if the unit digit of a number is 1, 4, 5, 6, 9 then unit digit of cube is also 1, 4, 5, 6, 9. If the unit digit of number is 2 or 8 then the unit digit in cube is 8 or

2 respectively.

3 and 7 form similar pair as 2 and 8.

Example:

(i) Unit place digit of cube of 41 is 1 because unit place digit of 41 is 1.

(ii) Unit place digit of cube of 76 is 6 because uunit place digit of 76 is 6.

(iii) Unit place digit of cube of 92 is 8 because unit place digit of 92 is 2.

Cube Roots

If x is a perfect cube such that $x = y^3$, then y is called cube root of x and it is denoted by $\sqrt[3]{x} = y$

For example, $216 = (6)^3$ ∴ $\sqrt[3]{216} = 6$

Method to Find Root of a perefect Cube Number

Cube root of a perfect cube number is find out by its prime factorisation. For this follow the steps:

(i) Find prime factors of the given number.

(ii) Group the factors in triplets such that all three factors in each triplet are same.

(iii) Choose one factor from each group and take the product. The product is the cube root of the given number.

Indices

When a number is multiplied by itself, it given the square of the number i.e. $a \times a = a^2$

(Example $5 \times 5 = 5^2$)

If the same number is multiplied by itself twice we got the cube of the number i.e., $a \times a \times a = a^3$

(Example $4 \times 4 \times 4 = 4^3$)

In the same way $a \times a \times a \times a \times a = a^5$ and $a \times a \times a \times$ ..... upto n time $= a^n$

In a^n, 'n' is called power, index or exponent and 'a' is called base. a^n is known as n^{th} power of 'a' and is read as 'a' raised to the power 'n' or 'a' to the power 'n'.

Basic Rule of Indices (or Power)

(i) $a^m \times a^n = a^{m+n}$

$$\left(Example: 5^3 \times 5^4 = 5^{3+4} = 5^7\right)$$

(ii) $\dfrac{a^m}{a^n} = a^{m-n}$, if $m > n$

$$\left(Example: \frac{6^5}{6^2} = 6^{5-2} = 6^3\right)$$

$\dfrac{a^m}{a^n} = \dfrac{1}{a^{n-m}}$, if $m < n$

$$\left(Example: \frac{4^3}{4^8} = \frac{1}{4^{8-3}} = \frac{1}{4^5}\right)$$

and $\dfrac{a^m}{a^n} = 1$ If $m = n$ $a^{m-m} = 9^0 = 1$

$$\left(Example: \frac{3^4}{3^4} = 3^{4-4} = 3^0 = 1\right)$$

(iii) $\left(a^m\right)^n = a^{mn} = \left(a^n\right)^m$

$$\left(Example: \left(6^2\right)^4 = 6^{2\times 4} = 6^8 = \left(6^4\right)^2\right)$$

(iv) $(ab)^n = a^n b^n = \left(Example\ (6\times 4)^3 = 6^3 \times 4^3\right)$

$$\left(\frac{a}{b}\right)^n = \frac{a^n}{b^n}, b \neq 0 \left(Exampl: \left(\frac{5}{3}\right)^4 = \frac{5^4}{3^4}\right)$$

and $\left(\dfrac{b}{a}\right)^n = \left(\dfrac{a}{b}\right)^n \left(Exampl \left(\dfrac{3}{5}\right)^{-4} = \left(\dfrac{5}{3}\right)^4\right)$

(v) $a^{-n} = \dfrac{1}{a^n}$ $\left(Example\ 5^{-3} = \dfrac{1}{5^3}\right)$

(vi) $\dfrac{1}{a^{-n}} = a^n$ $\left(Example: \dfrac{1}{5^{-3}} = 5^3\right)$

Surds

If $a^n = b$, where 'a' is a non-zero rational number and 'n' is a positive integer (i.e. natural number), then $a^n = b$ can be also written as $a = (b)^{1/n}$ or $\sqrt[a]{b}$.

For example : $2^5 = 32 \Rightarrow 2 = (32)^{1/5}$ or $\sqrt[5]{32}$.

Here $\sqrt[n]{32}$ is called n^{th} root of b. So, 5th root of 32 i.e. or $(32)^{1/5} = 2$.

If $\sqrt[n]{b}$ is an irrational number then it is called surd of order n.

Here, the sign $\left(\sqrt{\ }\right)$ is called radical sign, 'b' is called radicand. Note that in case of square root of a number, order of the surd is not shown. For example, sqaure root of 8 is written as $\sqrt{8}$. In the surd $\sqrt{8}$, order is not shown. In this case order of is always taken as 2.

Basic Rules of Surds

(i) $\sqrt[n]{a} = (a)^{1/n}$

(ii) $\left(\sqrt[n]{a}\right)^m = (a)^{m/n} = \sqrt[n]{a^m}$

Special case : $\left(\sqrt[n]{a}\right)^n = a$

(iii) $\sqrt[n]{ab} = \sqrt[n]{a}\,\sqrt[n]{b}$

(iv) $\sqrt[n]{\dfrac{a}{b}} = \dfrac{\sqrt[n]{a}}{\sqrt[n]{b}}$

(v) $\sqrt[m]{\sqrt[n]{a}} = \sqrt[mn]{a}$

(vi) $\sqrt[n]{a} = \sqrt[n \times m]{a^m}$

Example -17:

Find the value of :

(i) $\left(\sqrt[4]{5}\right)^{12}$

(ii) $\left(\sqrt[7]{21}\right)^{14}$

(iii) $\left(\sqrt[5]{27}\right)^{5}$

Solutions:

(i) $\left(\sqrt[4]{5}\right)^{12} = (5)^{12/4} = (5)^3 = 125$

(ii) $\left(\sqrt[4]{21}\right)^{14} = (21)^{14/7} = (21)^2 = 441$

(iii) $\left(\sqrt[5]{27}\right)^{5} = (27)^{5/5} = (27)^1 = 27$

Average

Average is a very simple and effective way of representing an entire group by a single value.

$$\text{Average of Means} = \frac{Sum\ of\ given\ quantities}{Number\ of\ quantities}$$

To calculate the sum of quantities, they should be in the same unit.

Note

If X is the average of $x_1, x_2, x_3 ....x_n$ then

- The average of $x_1 + a, x_2 + a, x_3 + a ...... x_n + a$ is $X + a$.
- The average of $x_1, - a, x_3 - a, x_3 - a .... x_n - a$ is $X - a$
- The average of $ax_1, ax_2 .. ax_n$ is aX, provide $a \neq 0$
- The average $\frac{x_1}{a}, \frac{x_2}{a}, \frac{x_3}{a}, ... \frac{x_n}{a}$ of is $\frac{X}{a}$, provided $a \neq 0$

Average of a Group Consisting Two Different Groups When Their Averages are Known

Let group A contains m quantities and their average is a and group B cantains n quantities and their average is b, then **average of group *C*** containing these $(m + n)$ quantities

$$= \frac{ma + nb}{m + n}$$

Weighted Average

If we have two or more groups of members whose individual average are known, then combined average of all the members of all the groups is known as weighted average. Thus if there are k groups having member of number $n_1, n_2, n_3 .... n_k$ with averages $A_1, A_2, A_3 .... A_k$ respectively then weighted average.

$$A_w = \frac{n_1 A_1 + n_2 A_2 + n_3 A_3 + ... + n_k A_k}{n_1 + n_2 + n_3 + ... + n_k}$$

Average Speed if Equal Distances are Travelled by Two Different Speeds

If a car travels at a speed S_1 from A to B and at a speed S_1 from B to A. Then

$$\text{Average speed} = \frac{2 S_1 - S_2}{S_1 + S_2}$$

The avove formula can be found out as follows:

If distance between A and B is d, then

$$\text{Average speed} = \frac{Total\ distance}{Total\ time} = \frac{2d}{\frac{d}{S_1} + \frac{d}{S_2}}$$

$$= \frac{2}{\frac{1}{S_1} + \frac{2}{S_2}} = \frac{2 S_1 . S_2}{S_1 + S_2}$$

Ages and Averages

If the average age of a group of persons is x years today then after n years their average age will be $(x + n)$ years because for a group of people, 1 year is added to each person's age every year.

Similary, n years ago their average age would have been $(x - n)$ years, because 1 year is subtracted from each person's age before every year.

Shortcuts

Shortcut Approach-3:

If the average if n numbers is A and on rechecking, it is noticed that some of the numbers n (i.e. $x_1, x_2, x_3, .., x_n$) are wrongly taken as $(x'_1, x'_2, x'_3, ... x'_n)$, then their correct average

$$= A + \frac{(x_1 + x_2 + x_3 + ... + x_n) - (x'_1 + x'_2 + x'_3 + ...+ x'_n)}{n}$$

Example-18:

1. **The means of 50 observations was 36. It was found later that an observation 48 was wrongly taken as 23. The corrected (new) mean is:**

(a) 35.2 (b) 36.1

(c) 36.5 (d) 39.1

Solution : (c) Correct average

$$= 36 + \frac{48-23}{50} = 36+\frac{25}{50}=36.5$$

Shortcut Approach-4:

The average of marks obtained by n candidates in a certains examination is *T*. If the average marks of passed candidates is *P* and that of the failed candidates is *F*. Then the number of candidates who passed the examination

$$= \frac{Total\ candidates\ (Total\ Average - Failed\ Average)}{Passed\ Average - Failed\ Average}$$

$$= \frac{n(T-F)}{P-F}$$

Example-19:

The average of marks obtained by 120 candidates in a certain examination is 35. If the average mark of passed candidates is 39 and that of the failed candidates is 15, what is the number of candidates who passed the examination?

(a) 90 (b) 85

(c) 100 (d) 120

Solution : (c) No. of passed students

$$= \frac{n(T-F)}{P-F} = \frac{120(35-15)}{(39-15)} = 100$$

Shortcut Approach-5:

The average of weight of *n* persons is increased by *x kg.* when some of them whose weight ($y_1 + y_2 + ...$ *where,* $y_1 + y_2 + ... = y$ *kg)* are replaced by the same number of persons. Then the weight of the new persons.

= Weight of removed person(s) + (No. of persons) (Increase in average)

$= y + nx.$

Example-20:

The average age of 8 persons is increased by 2 years, when one of them, whose age is 24 years, is replaced by a new person. The age of the new person is:

(a) 42 yrs (b) 40 yrs

(c) 38 yrs (d) 45 yrs

Solution : (b) The age of the new man - $y + nx$

$= 24 + 8 \times 2 = 40$ years

Chapter 3 Graphs

Graph:

Graphs are a convenient way to represent information. the graphs should be labelled properly to show what part of the graphs shows what a value.

Bar Graph:

Bar diagram consists of a number of equidistant rectangles. One for each category of the data in which the magnitudes are represented by the length or height of rectangle, whereas width of rectangles are immaterial. Thus, a bar is just one dimensional as only the length of the bas is to be considered and not the width. All the bars drawn in a diagram are generally of uniform width which depends on the number of bars to be constructed and the availability of the spact.

Types of Bar Graph are :-

(i) Simple Bar Graph: It is used to represent only one dependent variable.

For Example:

Percentage of Students passed in an examination from states A, B, C, D, E and F of a country in 2019.

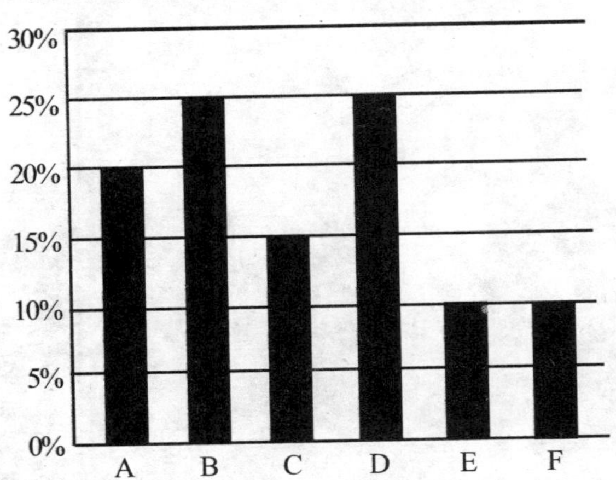

(ii) Sub-divided Bar Graph: These are used to represent the breakdown of a total into its component bars. A bar is divided into different segments, each segment represents a given component. Different shades, colours, designs etc. are used to distinguish the various components. An index is given to represent the various components. in the different bars is same. Generally this type of graphs asked in Bank Exams.

For Example:

Percentage of five different types of ers produced by a company during two year.

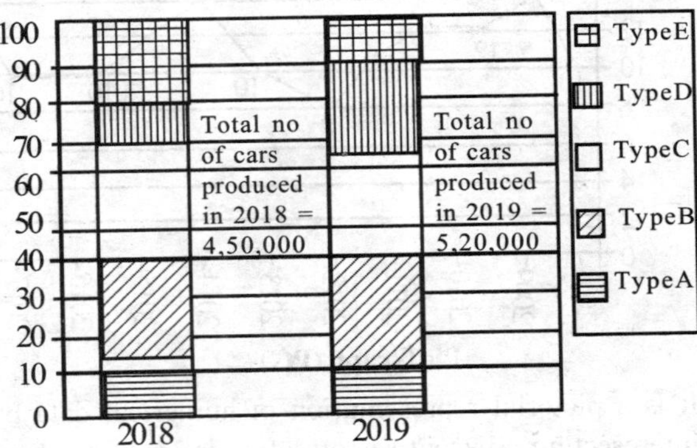

(iii) Multiple Bar Graph (MBG): When a combination of inter-related variables are to be represented graphically, multiple bar diagrams are used. These are extended form of simple bar diagrams. In MBG many aspects of the data are presented simultneously with separatd bars of various shades of colours. An index is given to explain the shades or colours used

For Example:

Export and Production of Tea (in million kg) in India during (2013-2018)

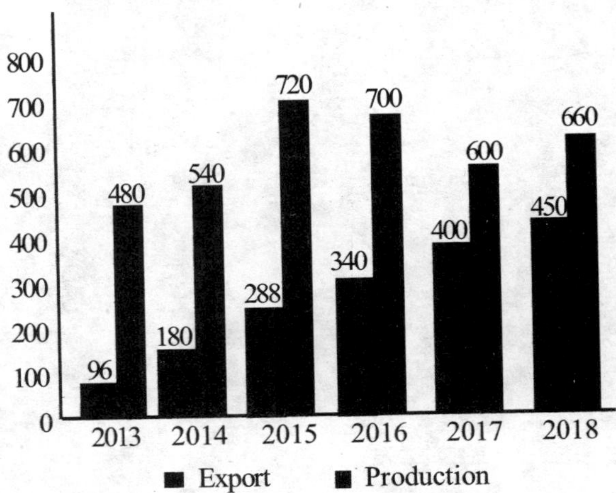

Line Graph (LG)

Very often the quantity is measured as time changes. LG are used to show how a quantity changes. If the line goes up, the quantity is increasing and the line goes down, the quantity is decreasing. If the line is horizontal, the quantity is not changing.

For Example:

Price per unit in different years

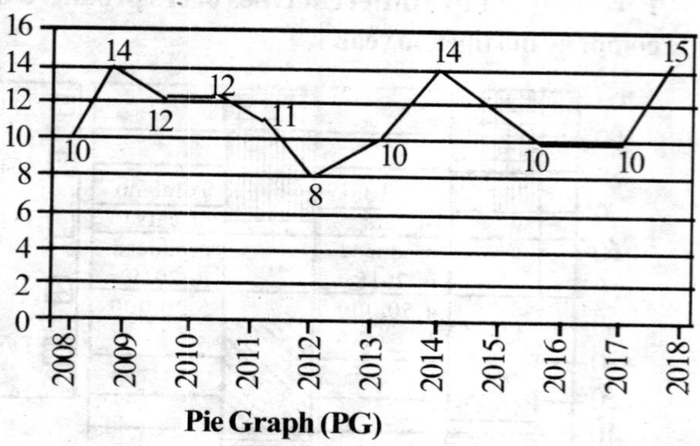

Pie Graph (PG)

It is a pictorial representation of numerical data by non-interesecting adjacent sectors of a circle. Central angle of each sector is proportional to the magnitude of the data represented by the sector.

Valué of central angle of the sector representing 1% of total value of the data =

The % of components parts can be converted to central angle in degree of the sector repersenting this components part by multiplying 3.6⁰.

For Example:

Percentage wise distribution of the number of mobile phones sold by a shopkeeper during six months.

Total number of mobile phone sold =45,000

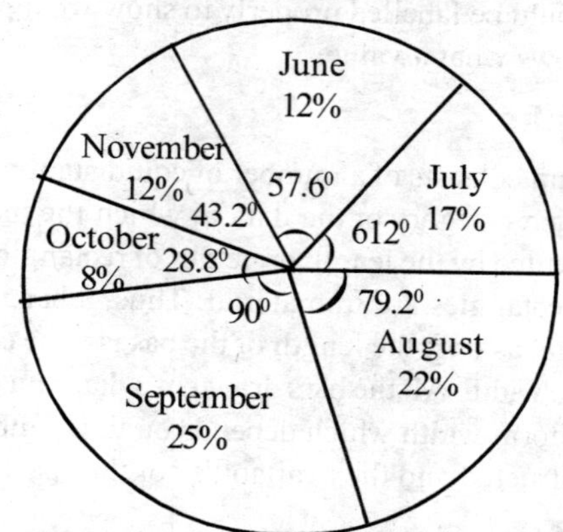

Data Interpretation & Analysis

Introduction

Data Interpretation questions are based on the information given in the tables and graphs

Classification of Data Interpretation

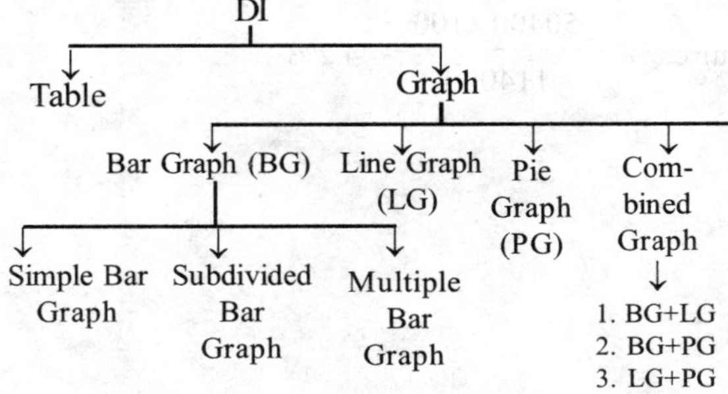

Table

A table is one of the easiest way for summarising data.

A statistical table is the logical listing of related quantitative data in vertical columns and horizontal rows of numbers with sufficient explanatory and qualifying words, pharases and statements in the form of heading and notes to make clear the meaning of data.

For example:

Monthly rent (in ₹ thousand) at five different places in six different years.

Place

	Churchgate	Dadar	Kandivali	Borivali	Virar
2014	5.3	3.8	1.5	2.7	1.1
2015	12.5	8.3	3.4	4.8	2.1
2016	16.7	11.7	5.5	6.6	1.8
2017	20.9	13.6	9.8	12.7	3.6
2018	25.8	14.5	11.5	14.1	5.5
2019	30.3	20.9	15.6	15.9	7.8

Remember

$$\text{Average} = \frac{\text{Sum of all items}}{\text{Total number of items}}$$

$$\%\text{ change} = \frac{\text{Final value - Initial value}}{\text{Initial value}} \times 100$$

$$\%\text{ increase} = \frac{\text{Final value - Initial value}}{\text{Initial value}} \times 100$$

$$\%\text{ decrease} = \frac{\text{Initial value - Final value}}{\text{Initial value}}$$

Missing Data Tabulation

In these types of tabulation questions, we need to find out some hidden values of the table for the answer of given questions. In these days these type of questions are most important for the competitive exams

For example:

Items	Cost Price	Selling Price	Market Price	Profit%	Loss %	Discount %	Profit Amount	Loss Amount	Discount Amount
TV	-	-	-	20%	-	25%	1800	-	-
AC	-	-	40,000	-	25%	25%	-	-	-
Laptop	-	50,000	-	25%	-	-	-	-	10,000
PC	25000	-	-	-	-	40%	5,000	-	-

Example: What is profit of shopkeeper if he sells all items at marked prices?

(a) 44.2%

(b) 42.8%

(c) 41.1%

(d) 47.6%

(e) None of these

Sol. (a)

Cost price of TV=1800 100 20=9000

Market price of TV = 9000 120 75=14400

Cost price of AC=40000 75 75=40000

Market Price of AC = 40000

Cost price of Laptop = 50000 100 125=40000

Market price of Laptop = 50000+10000=60000

Cost price of PC = 25000

Market price of PC = $(25000+5000)\dfrac{100}{60} = 50000$

Total cost price of all items together

=9000+40000+40000+25000=114000

Total market price of all items together

=14400+40000+60000+50000=164400

Profit=164400-114000=50400

Required % = $\dfrac{50400 \times 100}{114000} = 44.2\%$

GENERAL HINDI

1 Chapter संधि

परिभाषा- दो अक्षरों के आपस में मिलने से उनके आकार और ध्वनि में जब विकार पैदा होता है, उसे संधि कहते हैं।

सन्धि और संयोग में अंतर है। **स्वरों से रहित व्यंजन आपस में मिलें, तो वह संयोग कहलाता है।** जैसे, क्य- यहाँ 'क्' और 'य' के बीच कोई स्वर नहीं है। ये दोनों अक्षर बाद वाले ('य' में मिले हुए 'अ') स्वर के सहारे खड़े हैं। दूध शब्द में चार वर्ण हैं- द्, ऊ, ध्, अ। इन चारों का संयोग होने पर 'दूध' शब्द बना है। यहाँ इन वर्णों के संयोग से इनमें कोई अन्तर नहीं आया है।

सन्धि में अक्षर बदल जाते हैं, उनके उच्चारण में अन्तर पड़ जाता है। 'जगत्' और 'नाथ' शब्द की सन्धि करने पर 'जगन्नाथ' शब्द बनता है। यहाँ 'जगत्' शब्द के 'त्' का सन्धि के कारण 'न्' हो गया है।

जिन अक्षरों के बीच संधि हुई हो, उन्हें संधि के पहले के रूप में अलग-अलग करके रखना संधि-विच्छेद कहलाता है; जैसे, 'जगन्नाथ' का सन्धि विच्छेद 'जगत्+नाथ' होगा और 'रमेश' का 'रमा+ईश'। जिन अक्षरों की संधि की जाती है उनके बीच '+' का चिह्न देने की परिपाटी है।

भेद- सन्धि तीन प्रकार की होती है-(क) स्वर-सन्धि, (ख) व्यंजन-सन्धि और (ग) विसर्ग सन्धि।

(क) स्वर-सन्धि

दो स्वरों के पास-पास आने से जो सन्धि या वर्ण-परिवर्तन होता है, उसे 'स्वर-सन्धि' कहते हैं; जैसे- रमा+ईश = रमेश। यहाँ 'रमा' शब्द का 'आ' तथा 'ईश' शब्द का 'ई' दोनों पास-पास हैं, अत: इनकी संधि हो जाती है और 'आ' एवं 'ई' मिलकर 'ए' हो जाता है। 'आ' और 'ई' का मिलकर 'ए' होना ही यहाँ सन्धि है।

स्वर-सन्धि के पाँच भेद हैं-

1. दीर्घ सन्धि
2. गुण सन्धि
3. वृद्धि सन्धि
4. यण् सन्धि
5. अयादि-सन्धि

1. **दीर्घ सन्धि**- ह्रस्व या दीर्घ अ, इ, उ के बाद यदि ह्रस्व या दीर्घ क्रमश: अ, इ, उ हों तो दोनों के स्थान पर एक सवर्ण दीर्घ वर्ण होना 'दीर्घ संधि' है; जैसे-

ह्रस्व एवं दीर्घ अकार की सन्धि

अ + अ = आ   ज्ञान + अभाव = ज्ञानाभाव
आ + आ = आ   धर्म + आत्मा = धर्मात्मा
आ + अ = आ   तथा + अपि = तथापि
आ + आ = आ   विद्या + आलय = विद्यालय

ह्रस्व एवं दीर्घ इकार की सन्धि

इ + इ = ई   रवि + इन्द्र = रवीन्द्र
इ + ई = ई   गिरि + ईश = गिरीश
ई + इ = ई   मही + इन्द्र = महीन्द्र
ई + ई = ई   मही + ईश्वर = महीश्वर

ह्रस्व तथा दीर्घ उकार की सन्धि

उ + उ = ऊ   गुरू + उपदेश = गुरूपदेश
उ + ऊ = ऊ   लघु + ऊर्मि = लघूर्मि
ऊ + उ = ऊ   वधू + उत्सव = वधूत्सव
ऊ + ऊ = ऊ   भू + ऊर्ध्व = भूर्ध्व

2. **गुण सन्धि**- अकार या आकार के बाद यदि ह्रस्व या दीर्घ इ, उ या ऋ रहे तो अ + इ =ए, अ + उ = ओ और अ + ऋ = अर् होता है। इसी को 'गुण सन्धि' कहते हैं; जैसे-

अ या आ + इ या ई = ए

अ + इ = ए   देव + इन्द्र = देवेन्द्र
अ + ई = ए   गण + ईश = गणेश
आ + इ = ए   महा + इन्द्र = महेन्द्र
आ + ई = ए   रमा + ईश = रमेश

अ या आ + उ या ऊ = ओ

अ + उ = ओ   वीर + उचित = वीरोचित
अ + ऊ = ओ   नव + ऊढ़ा = नवोढ़ा
आ + उ = ओ   महा + उत्सव = महोत्सव
आ + ऊ = ओ   महा + ऊरू = महोरू

अ या आ + ऋ = अर्

आ + ऋ = अर्   सप्त + ऋषि = सप्तर्षि
आ + ऋ = अर्   महा + ऋषि = महर्षि

3. **वृद्धि सन्धि**- जब अ या आ के बाद ए अथवा ऐ रहे, तब दोनों का ऐ और जब अ या आ के बाद ओ या औ रहे, तब दोनों का औ होता है। यही 'वृद्धि सन्धि' है; जैसे-

अ + ए = ऐ   एक + एकश: = एकैकश:
आ + ए = ऐ   सदा + एव = सदैव
अ + ओ = औ   जल + ओघ = जलौघ
आ + औ = औ   महा + औदार्य = महौदर्य

4. **यण् सन्धि**– ह्रस्व या दीर्घ इकार, उकार या ऋकार के बाद यदि असवर्ण अर्थात् इ, उ, ऋ को छोड़कर अन्य कोई स्वर आये, तो इकार का य्, उकार का व् तथा ऋकार का र् होता है। इसे ही 'यण्-सन्धि' कहते हैं; जैसे-

इ + अ = य	यदि + अपि = यद्यपि
इ + आ = या	इति + आदि = इत्यादि
इ + उ = यु	प्रति + उपकार = प्रत्युपकार
इ + ऊ = यू	नि + ऊन = न्यून
इ + ए = ये	प्रति + एक = प्रत्येक
उ + अ = व	अनु + अय = अन्वय
उ + ए = वे	अनु + एषण = अन्वेषण
ऋ + आ = रा	पितृ + आदेश = पित्रादेश

5. **अयादि सन्धि**– ए, ओ, ऐ तथा औ के बाद यदि स्वर हो, तो ए का अय्, ओ का अव्, ऐ का आय् तथा औ का आव् होता है। यह 'अयादि सन्धि' है; जैसे-

ए + अ = अय	ने + अन = नयन
ऐ + अ = आय	नै + अक = नायक
ओ + इ = अवि	पो + इत्र = पवित्र
औ + अ = आव	पौ + अक = पावक

(ख) व्यंजन-सन्धि

जिन दो वर्णों में सन्धि होती है, उनमें से यदि पहला वर्ण व्यंजन हो और दूसरा वर्ण स्वर या व्यंजन हो, तो 'व्यंजन सन्धि' होती है; जैसे-

जगत् + ईश = जगदीश। सत् + जन = सज्जन।

1. **क्, च्, द्, त्, प्** व्यंजनों के बाद यदि कोई स्वर हो, किसी वर्ग का तृतीय या चतुर्थ वर्ण हो अथवा **य, र, व** में से कोई एक हो तो **क्** का **ग्**, **च्** का **ज्**, **ट्** का **ड्**, **त्** का **द्** और **प्** का **ब** होता है; जैसे-

   वाक् + ईश = वागीश। अच् + अन्त = अजन्त। उत् + वेग = उद्वेग। दिक् + गज = दिग्गज। षट् + दर्शन = षड्दर्शन। सत् + गति = सद्गति। सत् + धर्म = सद्धर्म। भगवत् + भक्ति = भगवद्भक्ति। तत् + रूप = तद्रूप। उत् + घाटन = उद्घाटन। अप् + ज = अब्ज। सत् + रत्न = सद्रत्न।

2. यदि किसी वर्ग के प्रथम वर्ण **(क्, च्, ट्, त्, प्)** के बाद किसी वर्ग का पंचम वर्ण **(ङ्, ञ्, ण्, न्, म्,)** हो तो पहले वर्ण के स्थान में उसी वर्ग का पंचम हलन्त वर्ण हो जाता है; जैसे-

   वाक् + मय = वाङ्.मय। षट् + मास = षण्मास। तत् + मय = तन्मय। जगत् + नाथ = जगन्नाथ। अप् + मय = अम्मय।

3. **'छ'** के पहले यदि कोई स्वर हो, तो **'छ'** के स्थान पर 'च्छ' हो जाता है; जैसे-

   वि + छेद = विच्छेद। छत्र + छाया = छत्रच्छाया। आ + छादन = आच्छादन

4. त् या द् के बाद यदि च् अथवा छ् हो, तो त् या द् के स्थान में च् होता है, ज् या झ् हो तो ज्, ट् या ठ् हो, तो ट्, ड् या ढ् हो तो ड् और ल् हो तो ल् होता है; जैसे-

   उत् + चारण = उच्चारण। शरद् + चन्द्र = शरच्चन्द्र। सत् + छत्र = सच्छत्र। सत् + जन = सज्जन। विपद् + जाल = विपज्जाल। तत् + टीका = तट्टीका। उत् + डयन = उड्डयन। उत् + लेख = उल्लेख। उत् + लास = उल्लास।

5. यदि त् या द् के बाद ह् रहे तो त् या द् के स्थान में द् होता है और ह् के स्थान में ध; जैसे-

   तत् + हित = तद्धित। उद् + हरण = उद्धरण।

6. यदि त् या द् के बाद श् हो तो त् या द् का च् होता है और श् का छ; जैसे-

   उत् + शिष्ट = उच्छिष्ट। सत् + शास्त्र = सच्छास्त्र

7. ष् के बाद यदि त हो तो त् का ट होता है और थ हो तो थ का ठ होता है; जैसे-

   आकृष् + त = आकृष्ट। उत्कृष् + त = उत्कृष्ट। पृष् + त = पृष्ट। षष् + थ = षष्ठ।

8. म् के बाद यदि अन्तःस्थ **(य, र, ल, व)** या ऊष्म **(श, ष, स, ह)** वर्ण हो तो म् का अनुस्वर हो जाता है; जैसे-

   किम् + वा = किंवा। सम् + हार = संहार। सम् + योग = संयोग। सम् + वाद = संवाद। सम् + शय = संशय। सम् + सार = संसार।

9. म् के बाद यदि स्पर्श वर्ण हो, तो म् के बदले अनुस्वार अथवा अगले वर्ण के वर्ग का पंचम हलन्त वर्ण आता है; जैसे-

   सम् + कल्प = संकल्प, सङ्.कल्प। सम + तोष = संतोष, सन्तोष। सम् + चय = संचय, सञ्चय।

णत्व एवं षत्व विधान

1. यदि ऋ, र, या व् के सीधे बाद न् हो अथवा दोनों के बीच कोई भी स्वर वर्ण, कवर्ग, पवर्ग अथवा य्, व्, र् में से कोई हो, तो भी 'न्' के स्थान में 'ण्' हो जाता है; जैसे-

   ऋ + न = ऋण। कृष् + न = कृष्ण। उष् + न = उष्ण। भर् + अन = भरण। राम + अयन = रामायण। प्र + मान = प्रमाण। भूष् + अन = भूषण। तृष् + ना = तृष्णा।

2. यदि अकार और आकार को छोड़कर किसी स्वर के बाद स या स् हो, तो स या स् का ष हो जाता है।

अभि + सेक = अभिषेक। नि + सिद्ध = निषिद्ध। वि + सम = विषम। नि + संग = निषंग। सु + सुप्ति = सुषुप्ति। प्रति + स्थान = प्रतिष्ठान।

हिन्दी व्याकरणों में णत्व (न का ण हो जाना) तथा षत्व (स का ष हो जाना) को सन्धि प्रकरण में रखा गया है, जो उचित नहीं है।

लोप और निपात

1. संस्कृत के यौगिक शब्दों में प्रथम आने वाले शब्द के अन्त में यदि न् हो, तो उसका लोप हो जाता है; जैसे–

प्राणिन् + मात्र = प्राणिमात्र। मंत्रिन् + मण्डल = मंडिमण्डल। हस्तिन् + दन्त = हस्तिदन्त। ब्रह्मन् + वाक्य = ब्रह्मवाक्य।

2. 'अहन्' शब्द के बाद यदि कोई शब्द आये, तो अहन् के 'न्' का 'र्' हो जाता है, परंतु 'रात्रि' और 'रूप' शब्द आने पर 'न्' का 'ओ' हो जाता है। इस तरह बदल जाने को 'निपात' कहते हैं; जैसे–

अहन् + निश = अहर्निश। अहन् + मुख = अहर्मुख। अहन् + रात्र = अहोरात्र। अहन् + रूप = अहोरूप।

हिन्दी व्याकरणों में इन्हें सन्धि के अन्तर्गत रखा गया है, किन्तु यह लोप या निपात का विषय है।

(ग) विसर्ग-सन्धि

विसर्ग के साथ स्वर या व्यंजन की सन्धि को 'विसर्ग सन्धि' कहते हैं; जैसे–

तपः + वन = तपोवन। निः + अन्तर = निरन्तर। दुः + आचार = दुराचार।

1. यदि विसर्ग के बाद च् या छ् हो, तो विसर्ग का श् हो जाता है, ट् या ठ् हो तो ष् और त् अथवा थ् हो तो स् हो जाता है; जैसे–

मनः + चांचल्य = मनश्चांचल्य। निः + छिद्र = निश्छिद्र। धनुः + टंकार = धनुष्टंकार। मनः + ताप = मनस्ताप।

2. विसर्ग के बाद श्, ष् या स् हो, तो विसर्ग ही रह जाता है अथवा उसके स्थान में आगे का हलन्त वर्ण हो जाता है; जैसे–

दुः + शासन = दुःशासन, दुश्शासन। निः + संदेह = निःसंदेह, निस्सन्देह।

3. यदि विसर्ग के पहले इ या उ हो, तो क्, ख् या प्, फ के पहले के विसर्ग का 'ष्' हो जाता है; जैसे–

निः + कपट = निष्कपट। दुः + कर्म = दुष्कर्म। निः + फल = निष्फल। दुः + प्रकृति = दुष्प्रकृति।

4. यदि अ या आ के बाद विसर्ग हो और उसके बाद क, ख या प, फ आये तो–

(क) विसर्ग का विसर्ग ही रह जाता है; जैसे– रजः + कण = रजःकण। पयः + पान = पयःपान।

(ख) कुछ शब्दों में विसर्ग का 'स्' भी होता है; जैसे– नमः + कार = नमस्कार। भाः + कर = भास्कर। पुरः + कार = पुरस्कार। भाः + पति = भास्पति।

5. यदि विसर्ग के पहले 'अ' हो और बाद में स्पर्श वर्णों के किसी भी वर्ग के तृतीय, चतुर्थ, पंचम अथवा य, र, ल, व या ह में से कोई एक हो, तो अकार और विसर्ग (अः) के स्थान पर 'ओ' हो जाता है; जैसे–

अधः : गति = अधोगति। मनः + योग = मनोयोग। तेजः + राशि = तेजोराशि। वयः + वृद्ध = वयोवृद्ध।

6. यदि विसर्ग के पहले 'अ' हो और बाद में भी 'अ' हो तो पहले अकार और विसर्ग के स्थान पर 'ओ' हो जाता है तथा बाद वाले अकार का लोप हो जाता है; जैसे–

मनः + अनुकूल = मनोनुकूल। मनः + अनुसार = मनोनुसार।

7. यदि र् (रेफ) के आगे र हो, तो पहले र् का लोप हो जाता है और उसके पूर्व का ह्रस्व स्वर दीर्घ कर दिया जाता है; जैसे–

निर् + रस = नीरस। निर् + रोग = नीरोग। निर् + रन्ध्र = नीरन्ध्र। निर् + रव = नीरव। निर् + रूज = नीरूज।

[निर् के र् के स्थान पर (:) भी लिखा जाता है; जैसे– निः + रूज = नीरूज आदि।]

सन्धि-कोश

1. अन्वय = अनु + अय
2. अन्यान्य = अन्य + अन्य
3. अधिकांश = अधिक + अंश
4. अत्यधिक = अति + अधिक
5. अतएव = अतः + एव
6. अब्ज = अप् + ज
8. आशीर्वाद = आशीः + वाद
9. इत्यादि = इति + आदि
10. उद्धृत = उत् + हृत
11. उद्धार = उत् + हार
12. उच्चारण = उत् + चारण
13. उन्नति = उत् + नति
14. उल्लास = उत् + लास
15. उद्भव = उत् + भव
16. उज्जवल = उत् + ज्वल
17. उन्मत्त = उत् + मत्त
18. एकैक = एक + एक
19. कपीस = कपि + ईश
20. खरारि = खर + अरि
21. गोष्पद = गोः + पद
22. जनार्दन = जन + अर्दन
23. तल्लीला = तत् + लीला
24. तद्धित = तत् + हित

25. दिग्गज = दिक् + गज
26. दिगम्बर = दिक् + अम्बर
27. देवर्षि = देव + ऋषि
28. निर्दय = नि: + दय
29. निष्फल = नि: + फल
30. नीरज = नि: + रज
31. निश्छल = नि: + छल
32. नयन = ने + अन
33. नाविक = नौ + इक
34. नायक = नै + अक
35. नरेश = नर + ईश
36. नीरस = निर् + रस
37. पीताम्बर = पीत + अम्बर
38. परमेश्वर = परम + ईश्वर
39. प्रत्येक = प्रति + एक
40. पित्रर्थ = पितृ + अर्थ
41. पितृण = पितृ + ऋण
42. पवन = पो + अन
43. पवित = पो + इत्र
44. पुस्तकालय = पुस्तक + आलय
45. प्रात:काल = प्रात: + काल
46. पृष्ठ = पृष् + थ
47. भवन = भो + अन
48. भूषण = भूष् + अन
49. भावुक = भौ + अक
50. मनोहर = मन: + हर
51. महर्षि = महा + ऋषि
52. महेन्द्र = महा + इन्द्र
53. मनोज = मन: + ज
54. मात्रानंद = मातृ + आनन्द
55. यद्यपि = यदि + अपि
56. यथेष्ट = यथा + इष्ट
57. रामायण = राम + अयन
58. रामेश्वर = राम + ईश्वर
59. रवीन्द्र = रवि + इन्द्र
60. विद्यालय = विद्या + आलय
61. विपज्जाल = विपद् + जाल
62. वाचनालय = वाचन + आलय
63. विद्यार्थी = विद्या + अर्थी
64. स्वागत = सु + आगत
65. सज्जन = सत् + जन
66. संसार = सम् + सार
67. सोदाहरण = स + उदाहरण
68. संवाद = सम् + वाद
69. समाचार = सम् + आचार
70. सतीश = सती + ईश
71. सच्चरित्र = सत् + चरित्र
72. सदैव = सदा + एव
73. सरोज = सर: + ज
74. सन्धि = सम् + धि
75. संकल्प = सम् + कल्प

पुनरूक्ति

परिभाषा- पुनरूक्ति का अर्थ है- आवृत्ति (पुन: + उक्ति) अथवा दुहराना। एक ही शब्द की जब दो बार आवृत्ति की जाती है, तो उसे पुनरूक्ति कहते हैं। इनकी सहायता से हिन्दी में शब्दों का निर्माण बहुत बड़ी संख्या में हुआ है। इनकी रचना सार्थक शब्दों की आवृत्ति से ही होती है; जैसे-

1. **संज्ञा शब्द की पुनरूक्ति**- पानी-पानी, घर-घर, कौड़ी-कौड़ी, हँसी-हँसी, द्वार-द्वार आदि।
2. **सर्वनाम शब्द की पुनरूक्ति**- अपना-पना, कुछ-कुछ, कोई-कोई, क्या-क्या, जो-जो आदि।
3. **विशेषण शब्द की पुनरूक्ति**- पीला-पीला, मोटे-मोटे, छोटे-छोटे, लाल-लाल, गोल-गोल आदि।
4. **क्रिया शब्द की पुनरूक्ति**- छपते-छपते, रोते-रोते, खाते-खाते, पढ़ते-पढ़ते, आइए-आइए आदि।
5. **क्रिया-विशेषण शब्द की पुनरूक्ति**- धीरे-धीरे, जल्दी-जल्दी, ऊपर-ऊपर, नीचे-नीचे, पास-पास आदि।
6. **विस्मयादिबोधक शब्द की पुनरूक्ति**- राम-राम, हाय-हाय, छि:-छि:, अरे-अरे, हरे-हरे आदि।
7. **विभक्तियुक्त शब्द की पुनरूक्ति**- पास ही पास, घर का घर, गाँव का गाँव, झुण्ड का झुण्ड आदि।

सरल शब्द

परिभाषा- जिन शब्दों का निर्माण दूसरे शब्दों के मेल के बिना ही हुआ हो, उसे सरल शब्द कहते हैं। ऐसे शब्दों के खंड भी नहीं होते तथा इनके उच्चारण और अर्थ बिल्कुल ही सहज हुआ करते हैं। यानी इनके अर्थ के लिए कोश देखने की आवश्यकता नहीं पड़ती; जैसे- गाय, घोड़ा, नाक, कान, आँख आदि।

तिग्म, नक्र, कृत्स्न- इन शब्दों के भी खंड नहीं हो सकते। किंतु, इनके उच्चारण और अर्थ सुकर नहीं हैं। अत: इन्हें हम सरल शब्द नहीं कह सकते हैं।

Chapter 2

विलोम शब्द

परिभाषा- किसी शब्द का विलोम बतलाने वाले शब्द को विलोमार्थक शब्द कहते हैं; जैसे- अच्छा-बुरा, ज्ञान-अज्ञान आदि। उपर्युक्त उदाहरणों में 'अच्छा' और 'ज्ञान' के विलोम अर्थ देने वाले क्रमश: 'बुरा' और 'अज्ञान' शब्द हैं।

विलोमार्थक शब्द को ही **विपरीतार्थक शब्द** कहते हैं। विलोमार्थक शब्द मुख्यत: तीन प्रकार के होते हैं-

(क) वे शब्द जो अ, अन्, वि, अनु, प्रति, अव, अप आदि अनुकूल-प्रतिकूल उपसर्ग जोड़ने से एक-दूसरे के विलोम या विपरीत अर्थ देते हैं; जैसे-

1. अभिज्ञ - अनभिज्ञ
2. खाद्य - अखाद्य
3. अर्थ - अनर्थ
4. गुण - अवगुण
5. अनुरक्त - विरक्त
6. ज्ञान - अज्ञान
7. अनुराग - विराग
8. घात - प्रतिघात
9. आगत - अनागत
10. चल - अचल
11. आचार - अनाचार
12. चिन्मय - अचिन्मय
13. आदर - अनादर
14. चेतन - अचेतन
15. आवश्यक - अनावश्यक
16. जाति - विजाति
17. आकर्षण - विकर्षण
18. धर्म- अधर्म
19. आरोह - अवरोह
20. धार्मिक - अधार्मिक
21. आस्था - अनास्था
22. नश्वर - अनश्वर
23. आहार - अनाहार
24. नित्य - अनित्य
25. इच्छा - अनिच्छा
26. परिमित - अपरिमित
27. इष्ट - अनिष्ट
28. पूर्ण- अपूर्ण
29. उदार - अनुदार
30. प्रत्यक्ष - अप्रत्यक्ष
31. उचित - अनुचित
32. प्रसन्न - अप्रसन्न
33. उत्तीर्ण - अनुत्तीर्ण
34. योग - वियोग
35. उदात्त - अनुदात्त
36. योग्य - अयोग्य
37. उपयुक्त - अनुपयुक्त
38. रत - विरत
39. उपस्थित - अनुपस्थित
40. राग - विराग
41. उन्नति - अवनति
42. लौकिक - अलौकिक
43. एक- अनेक
44. वाद - प्रतिवाद
45. एकता - अनेकता
46. विश्वास - अविश्वास
47. औचित्य - अनौचित्य
48. शकुन - अपशुकन
49. ऋत - अनृत
50. शान्ति - अशान्ति
51. औदात्य - अनौदात्य
52. शुभ - अशुभ
53. कीर्ति - अपकीर्ति
54. श्लील - अश्लील
55. कृतज्ञ - अकृतज्ञ
56. संघटन - विघटन
57. संतोष - असंतोष
58. सभ्य - असभ्य
59. सक्षम - असक्षम
60. सुर - असुर
61. सत्य - असत्य
62. स्पष्ट - अस्पष्ट
63. सफलता - असफलता
64. स्वस्थ - अस्वस्थ

(ख) वे शब्द जो अन्यान्य उपसर्ग बदलने या सामासिक प्रथम पद के समासगत रूप के कारण एक-दूसरे के विलोम या विपरीत अर्थ देते हैं; जैसे-

1. अज्ञ - विज्ञ
2. मान - अपमान
3. अतिवृष्टि - अनवृष्टि
4. यश - अपयश
5. अनुराग - विराग
6. विधवा - सधवा
7. अनुकूल - प्रतिकूल
8. विपत्ति - संपत्ति
9. अपमान - सम्मान
10. विपन्न - सम्पन्न
11. अवनति - उन्नति
12. वैमनस्य - सौमनस्य
13. आगत - अनागत
14. संकल्प - विकल्प
15. आदान - प्रदान
16. संघटन - विघटन
17. सामिष - निरामिष
18. संयोग - वियोग
19. आहार - अनाहार
20. सच्चरित्र - दुश्चरित्र
21. उत्कर्ष - अपकर्ष
22. सजीव - निर्जीव
23. उत्कृष्ट - निकृष्ट
24. सज्जन - दुर्जन
25. उन्मीलन - निमीलन
26. सदाचार - दुराचार
27. उपकार - अपकार
28. सपूत - कपूत
29. कुप्रबंध - सुप्रबंध
30. सबल - निर्बल
31. कृतज्ञ - कृतघ्न
32. सरस - नीरस
33. खंडन - मंडन
34. सहयोगी - प्रतियोगी

35. नास्तिक - आस्तिक
36. साकार - निराकार
37. निरर्थक - सार्थक
38. सुकाल - दुष्काल
39. निरामिष - सामिष
40. सुगन्धि - दुर्गन्धि
41. निश्चेष्ट - सचेष्ट
42. सुबोध - दुर्बोध
43. निष्काम - सकाम
44. सुभग - दुर्भग
45. परतंत्र - स्वतंत्र
46. सुमार्ग - कुमार्ग
47. प्रवृत्ति - निवृत्ति
48. सुलभ - दुर्लभ
49. प्राचीन - अर्वाचीन
50. सौभाग्य - दुर्भाग्य

(ग) वे शब्द जो भिन्न शब्द युग्मों में ही एक-दूसरे के विलोम या विपरीत अर्थ देते हैं। रचना की दृष्टि से इनमें संबंध नहीं होता है; जैसे-

1. अंत - आदि
2. आकाश - पाताल
3. अंतरंग - बहिरंग
4. आजाद - गुलाम
5. अंधकार - प्रकाश
6. आलोक - अंधकार
7. अच्छा - बुरा
8. उत्तम - अधम
9. अधिक-कम
10. उत्थान - पतन

3 Chapter

वाक्यांश के लिए एक शब्द

संक्षिप्तीकरण करना मानव की प्रकृति है। प्राचीन काल से ही स्मृति के लिए सूत्र शैली अपनायी जा रही है। वाक्य में संक्षिप्ता भावगाम्भीर्य लाने व लम्बे वाक्यों को सामसिक पद के रूप में अपनाने का प्रचलन चलता रहा है। इसके लिए सबसे उत्तम साधन है वाक्यांश के लिए एक शब्द है। जैसे-विश्व का भरण पोषण करने वाला विश्वंभर।

वाक्यांश	शब्द
जिसकी सीमा न हो	असीम
जिसे जीता न जा सके	अजेय
जो कहा न जा सके	अकथनीय
गोद में सोने वाली स्त्री	अंकषायिनी
जिसके समान कोई दूसरा न हो	अद्वितीय
सबके हृदय की बात जानने वाला	अंतर्यामी
जो बीत चुका है	अतीत
जिसकी गहराई का पता न चले	अथाह
पृथ्वी और सूर्यादि लोकों के मध्य का स्थान	अंतरिक्ष
गुरू के समीप रहने वाला विद्यार्थी	अंतेवासी
महल के अन्दर का हिस्सा	अंत:पुर
अंडे से जन्म लेने वाला	अंडज
जिसको गोद में स्थान मिला हो	अंकस्थ
जो छः माह में एक बार हो	अर्द्धवार्षिक
जिसकी तुलना न की जा सके	अतुलनीय
जो दिखाई न देता हो	अदृश्य
जिसे पढ़ा न जा सके	अपठनीय
जो पढ़ा न गया हो	अपठित
जो अनुकरण करने योग्य हो	अनुकरणीय
वह कार्य जो बिना वेतन के सम्हाला जाए	अवैतनिक
वह बात जो न सुनी गई हो	अनसुनी
वह वस्तु जिसके आर-पार न देखा जा सके	अपारदर्शी
दोपहर के बाद का समय	अपरान्ह
जो नया न हो	अनूतन
जिसका कभी जन्म न हो	अजन्मा
जिसके आने की तिथि ज्ञात न हो	अतिथि
जो कहा न गया हो	अकथित
जो गिना न जा सके	अगणित
जिसका कोई शत्रु न उत्पन्न हुआ हो	अजातशत्रु
जो घटित न हुआ हो	अघटित
जो न जाना गया हो	अनवगत
किसी कथा, बात या प्रसंग के अन्तर्गत आने वाली कोई दूसरी कथा या प्रसंग	अन्तर्कथा
जिसका कोई नाथ न हो	अनाथ
जिसके बिना काम न चल सके	अनिवार्य
जिसका जन्म पीछे हुआ हो	अनुज
जिसका जन्म पहले हुआ हो	अग्रज
जो रूका हुआ न हो	अनिरूद्ध
पर्वत के ऊपर की समतल भूमि	अधित्यका
जिसे त्यागा न जा सके, जिका परिहार न हो सके	अपरिहार्य
वह (रोग) जिसका ठीक होना कठिन हो	असाध्य
जिसमें विवेक का अभाव हो	अविवेकी
जिसका विवाह न हुआ हो	अविवाहित
हिसाब-किताब की जॉच करने वाला	अंकेक्षक
एक से अधिक मताओं से पैदा हुआ भाई	अन्योदर
जिसे अन्य का बल या सहारा हो	अपरबल
बिगड़ा हुआ शब्द	अपभ्रंश
जसके सब अंग दुरूस्त न हो	अपांग
जिसकी परिभाषा देना संभव न हो	अपरिभाष्य
जिस पर आक्रमण न किया गया हो	अनाक्रान्त
जो अभी तक न आया हो	अनागत
प्रत्येक पदार्थ को क्षणि और नश्वर मानने वाला	अनित्यवादी
जो नियमानुकूल न हो	अनियमित
जिस पर कोई रोक-टोक न हो	अनियन्त्रित
जिसका वर्णन न हो सके	अवर्णनीय, अनिर्वचनीय
जो किसी चीज पर आसक्त न हो	अनुरक्त
जिसका जवाब न दिया गया हो	अनिस्तीर्ण
जिस पर अनुग्रह किया गया हो	अनुगृहीत
किसी पुरूष से प्रेम करने वाली अविवाहित स्त्री	अनूढ़ा
जो (जानवर) किसी की देख-रेख में न हो	अनेर
जिसके पान करने का निषेध हो	अज्ञ

जिसका खण्डन न किया जा सके	अखण्डनीय	जिस पर मद दे दिया गया हो	अभिमत
जो खाने योग्य न हा	`अखाद्य	जो भेदा या छेदा न जा सके, जो टूट न सके	अभेद्य
जो सबके आगे रहता हो	अग्रणी	जो नीचे लिखा गया है	अधोलिखित
जिसका ज्ञान इन्द्रियों द्वारा न हो	अगोचर	जो शोक करने योग्य न हो	अशोच्य
वह स्त्री जिसका पति दूसरा विवाह कर ले	अध्यूढ़ा	जो दूर की बात न सोच सके	अडिग
जो बकवादी न हो	अप्रगल्भ	जो (अपने निश्चय पर) डिग न सके	अडिग
जो किसी समय निश्चित अवधि तक लागू हो	अध्यादेश	सबसे पहले गिना जाने वाला	अग्रगण्य
अधिकार में आया हुआ, अधिकार प्राप्त	अधिकृत	जो बराबर न हो	असम
जिसमें प्रतिभा का अभाव हो	अप्रतिभ	जो आगे की बात सोचता हो	अग्रशोची
जो व्यवहार में न लाया गया हो	अव्यवहृत	जो जाना न जा सके	अज्ञेय
किसी कथन को बढ़ा-चढ़ा कर कहना	अतिशयोक्ति	अन्य से सम्बन्ध न रखने वाला	अव्याप्ति
जो चिन्तन करने योग्य न हो	अचिंत्य	सम्पूर्ण लक्ष्य पर लक्षण का न घटित होना	अतीन्द्रिय
परम्परा से कही हुई बात या उक्ति	अनुश्रुत	जो किसी अन्य के भरोसे अथवा संरक्षण में न हो	अनन्याश्रित
जिसकी उपमा न दी जा सके	अनुपम	बना पलक गिराए	अनिमेष
पुरूष जो अभिनय करता हो	अभिनेता	जो कम जानता हो	अल्पज्ञ
जिसे भुलाया न जा सके	अविस्मरणीय	एक-एक अक्षर तक	अक्षरशः
जो अभियोग लगाये या शिकायत करे	अभियोगी	अग्रज के विवाह के पूर्व अनुज का विवाह	अनुवेश
जिसे भुलाया न गया हो	अनाहूत	जो न मरे	अमर्त्य, अमर
जो ढंका हुआ न हो	अनावृत्त	जो इस लोक से परे हो	अलौकिक
जिस पर अभियोग लगाया गया हो	अभियुक्त	अवश्य होने वाला	अवश्यम्भावी
जो पहले न घटित हुआ हो	अभूतपूर्व	जो धर्म और ईश्वर में विश्वास करता हो	आस्तिक
जिसका उपकार किया गया हो	अपकृत	जिसका अनुभव इन्द्रियों द्वारा न हो	अतीन्द्रिय
आवश्यकता से अधिक धन का त्याग	अपरिग्रह	आदर्शमूलक भावना को प्रश्रय देने वाला मत	आदर्शवाद
जिसकी नाप तौल न हो सके	अपरिमेय	आत्मा से सम्बन्ध रखनेवाला	आध्यात्मिक
जो ढंका हुआ न हो	अपरिच्छिन	एक देश द्वारा दूसरे देशों से वस्तुओं का मंगाया जाना	आयात
साधारण या व्यापक नियम से विरूद्व चीजें	अपवाद	जो सूघंने योग्य हो	आघ्रेय
व्यर्थ ही अधिक खर्च करने वाला	अपव्ययी	जिस पर आक्रमण हो	आक्रान्त
जो पहले न रहा हो	अपूर्व	अपने मत का अनुयायी	आत्माभिमत
जो सर्व साधारण के सामने न रखा गया हो	अप्रकाशित	दूसरों के सुख के लिए आत्म सुख का त्यागना	आत्मोत्सर्ग
जिसका निश्चय न हो सके	अप्रतीयमान	धन से सम्बन्ध रखने वाला	आर्थिक
जिसकी आशा न रही हो	अप्रत्याशित	जिसका अहंकार चूर्ण हो गया हो	आत्तगर्व
जो प्रशंसा के योग्य न हो	अप्रशस्त	आशा से अधिक	आशातीत
जो प्रमाण से सिद्व हो सके	अप्रमेय	जिसका साधन किसी दूसरे प्रधान कार्य के करते समय थोड़े प्रयास से ही हो जाए	आनुषांगिक
जो कपड़ा न पहना हो	अप्रामाण्य	जो आदर करने योग्य हो	आदरणीय
जिसे मारना उचित न हो	अवध्य	प्रारम्भ से लेकर अनत तक	अद्योपान्त
जो समझाने के अयोग्य हो अथवा जो समझाया न जा सके	अबोध	वह नायिका जिसका पति परदेश से लौटा हो	आगतपतिका
जो बांटा न गया हो	अविभक्त	देवता अथवा भूतादि के द्वारा होने वाला दु:ख	आधिदैविक

वाक्यांश के लिए एक शब्द

जीवों या शरीरधारियों के द्वारा प्राप्त दु:ख	आधिभौतिक
पैर से सिर तक	आपादमस्तक
अतिथि की सेवा करने वाला	आतिथेय
जो इधर-उधर से घूमता फिरता आ जाए	आगन्तुक
जिसकी समस्त कामनायें पूरी हो गयी हों	आप्तकाम
किसी के गुण दोष की विवेचना करने वाला	आलोचक
नवीन बनाने की क्रिया	आधुनिकीकरण
किसी मत का सर्वप्रथम प्रवर्तन करने वाला	आदि प्रवर्तक
परम्परा से सुना हुआ	आनुश्राविक
जो किसी वंश में बराबर होता आया है	आनुवंशिक
वह कवि जो तत्काल कविता कर सके	आशुकवि
वह स्त्री जिसका पति आने वाला है	आगमिस्यत्पतिका
इन्द्र को जीतने वाला	इन्द्रजित
जिस (वस्तु) की आकाश हो	ईप्सित
इतिहास को जानने वाला	इतिहासज्ञ
इन्द्रियों को वाश में रखने वाला	इन्द्रियजित
जो इन्द्रियों की पहुँच के बाहर हो	इन्द्रियातीत
जिसकी आकाश हो	इष्ट
जो दूसरों की उन्नति देख कर जलता हो	ईर्ष्यालु
पर्वत के पास की भूमि	अपत्यका
उपकार करने वाला	उपकारी
सूर्योदय से पहले का समय	उषाकाल
जिसका उपकार किया गया हो	उपकृत
किसी के बाद उसकी सम्पत्ति पाने वाला	उत्तराधिकारी
जिसने ऋण चुका दिया हो	ऊऋण
जल-थल दोनों जगह रहने वाला जीव	अभयचर
सूर्य जिस स्थान से निकलता है	उदयाचल
जिसका उल्लख करना आवश्यक हो	उल्लेखनीय
ऊपर कहा हुआ	उपर्युक्त
जिसके दांत न में हों	उदन्त
जो भूमि उपजाऊ हो	उर्वरा
जिसका ऊपर उल्लेख किया जा चुका है	उपर्युल्लिखित
ऊपर की ओर जाने वाला	ऊर्ध्वगामी
जिस भूमि में कुछ उत्पन्न न हो	ऊसर
जो अपने वीर्य को न गिरने दे	ऊर्ध्वरेता
एक या अकेले आदमी का अधिकार	एकाधिकार
जिसकी एक ही आँख हो	एकाक्ष
जिसका चित्त स्थिर हो	एकाग्रचित
जो अपनी इच्दा पर निर्भर हो	ऐच्छिक
किसी वस्तु के क्रय-विक्रय का एकछत्र	अधिकार
	एकाधिकार
इस लोक से सम्बन्ध रखने वाला	ऐहलौकिक
उपनिवेश सम्बन्धी	औपनिवेशिक
उपन्यास सम्बन्धी	औपन्यासिक
जो केवल कहने-सुनने के लिए हो	औपचारिक
विवाहित स्त्री से उत्पन्न पुत्र	औरस
उपनिषद सम्बन्धी	औपनिषदिक
जो फूल अभी नहीं खिला है	कली
वह कथा जो जन-साधारण मे प्रचलित हो	किम्वदंती
जिसकी उत्पत्ति स्वभावगत न हो	कृत्रिम
किए हुए उपकार को न मानने वाला, एहसान भूल जाने वाला	कृतघ्न
राजनीतिज्ञों एवं राजदूतों की कला	कूटनीति
अपना स्थान छोड़ कर बाहर न जाने वाला	बाह्य
जगत के सम्बन्ध में ज्ञान न रखने वाला	कूप मण्डूक
किए हुए उपकार को मानने वाला	कृतज्ञ
केन्द्र से दूर जाने की प्रवृत्ति रखने वाला	केन्द्रापसारी
जो कर्तव्य से च्युत हो गया हो	कर्तव्यच्युत
कर्म करने वाला	कर्मठ
केन्द्र की ओर उन्मुख होने वाला	केन्द्राभिमुख
किसी की कृपा से अति सन्तुष्ट	कृतार्थ
जो अपने काम से जी चुराता हो	कामचोर
जो कल्पना से परे हो	कल्पनातीत
जिसके पास करोड़ों रूपये हों	करोड़पति
सुन्दर बड़े बालों वाली स्त्री	केशिनी
जो पाप-पुण्य से रहित हो	केवलात्मा
जिस लड़की का विवाह न हुआ हो	कुमारी
जिसे अपने कर्तव्य का ज्ञान न हा	किंकर्तव्यविमूढ़
जो अच्छे कुल में उत्पन्न हुआ हो	कुलीन
दूसरों की बात व्यर्थ ही काटने वाला	किन्तुवादी
जो कहा गया है	कथित
कुश की नोक सी तीखी जिसकी बुद्वि हो	कुशाग्रबुद्धि
क्षण भर में नष्ट होने वाला	क्षणभंगुर
शीघ्र काम करने वाला	क्षिप्रहस्त
क्षमा करने योग्य	क्षम्य
जहाँ पृथ्वी और आकाश मिले दिखें	क्षितिज

वाक्यांश	शब्द
वह नायिका जिसका पति रात को किसी अन्य स्त्री के पास रहकर सबेरे आये	खण्डिता
सूर्य या चन्द्र के समस्त मण्डल के ढंक जाने वाला ग्रह	खग्रास
खाने योग्य वस्तु	खाद्य
छोटा कथात्मक प्रबन्ध काव्य जिसमें काव्य के समस्त लक्षण न हों	खण्ड काव्य
शाम का वह समय जब पशु चरकर लौटते हैं	गोधूलि
बिना सोच विचार के अन्धावत् अनुकरण करने वाला	गतानुगतिक
जिसमें गीत अधिक हो वह नाटक	गीतिरूपक
जो शीघ्र न पचे	गरिष्ट
गणित को जानने वाला	गणितज्ञ
जो छिपाने के योग्य हो	गोपनीय
गायों के रहने का स्थान	गोशाला, गोष्ठ
गाँव में रहने वाला	ग्रामीण
गायों के चराने का स्थान	गोचर
इन्द्रियों से न जानने योग्य	गोतीत
जो पहाड़ को धारण करता हो	गिरिधर
जिसकी घोषणा की गई हो	घोषित
घृणा करने योग्य	धृण्य
जिसे देख या सुनकर घृणा उत्पन्न हों	घृणित
अपने स्थान से हटा हुआ	च्युत
जिसके चार भुजाएं हों	चतुर्भुज
जिसके हाथ में चक्र हो	चक्रपाणि
जिसके सिर पर चन्द्रमा है	चन्द्रशेखर
जो चक्र धारण करता है	चक्रचर
चलने वाली वस्तु	चलायमान
गद्य और पद्य युक्त काव्य	चम्पू
आँख से सम्बन्ध रखने वाला	चाक्षुष
चन्द्र है चूड़ा पर जिसके	चन्द्रचूड़
जिसके चार पैर हों	चतुष्पद
बहुत समय तक जीने वाला	चिरंजीवी
ब्रह्रूप में समाहित होने की रमणीक स्थिति	चिद्विलास
बहुत दिनों तक रहने वाला	चिरस्थायी
जिस पर चिन्ह लगाया गया हो	चिन्हित
फटा पुराना कपड़ा	चिरकुट
जहाँ से अनेक मार्ग चारों ओर जाते हों	चौरास्ता
कर्मचारी आदि को हटाने की क्रिया	छंटनी
बनावटी वेश धारण करने वाला	छिद्रान्वेषी
अकस्मात बिना सूचना के छापा मारने वाला	छापामार
सेना के ठहरने का स्थान	छावनी
रात्रि में बेखबर लोगों पर आक्रमण	छापा
जल-स्थल दोनों जगह रह सकने वाला प्राणी	जलभूमिया
जिसकी इन्द्रियां वश में हो	जितेन्द्रिया
जानने या ज्ञान प्राप्त करने की इच्छा	जिज्ञासा
जीतने की इच्छा	जिजीविषा
जानने या ज्ञान प्राप्त करने की इच्छा	जिज्ञासु
जीतने की इच्छा वाला	जिगीषु
भोजन की इच्छा वाला	जिघत्सु
जानने योग्य	ज्ञेय, ज्ञातव्य
किसानों की सहायता के लिए सरकार द्वारा दिया गया धन	तकावी
रात्रि का तीसरा पहर	त्रिमाया
भूत भविष्य और वर्तमान को देखने वाला	त्रिकालदर्शी
दोनों भौहों का मध्यवर्ती स्थान	त्रिकुटी
छुटकारा दिलाने वाला	त्राता
त्याग करने योग्य	त्याज्य
चारी छिपे माल का एक स्थान से दूसरे स्थान को ले जाने वाला	तस्कर
तैरने, तरने या पार होने की इच्छा रखने वाला	तितीर्षु
गुटों से अलग रहने वाला	तटस्थ
तैरने, तरने या पार होने की इच्छा	तितीर्षा
तत्व को जानने वाला	तत्वज्ञ
जिसकी बुद्धि तत्काल क्रियाशील हो सके	तत्वी
जो तीन माह में एक बार हो	त्रैमासिक
वह व्यक्ति जो दूर की बातों को सोच लेता हो	दूरदर्शी
गोद लिया हुआ पुत्र	दत्तक
स्त्री और पुरूष का जोड़ा	दम्पत्ति
वह व्यक्ति जो अपने ऋणों को चुकता करने में असमर्थ हो	दिवालिया
जंगल की आग	दावानल
बुरे भाव से मेल या एका करना	दुरभिसन्धि
जो काफी दिक्कत से काबू में आ सके या पकड़ा जा सक	दुरभिग्रह
जिसे प्रसन्न करना या आराधना करना कठिन हो	दुराराध्य
जो फांदने या लांघन योग्य न हो	दुर्लंध्य
जिसक जीतना कठिन हो	दुर्जेय
जो कठिनता से जाना जाए	दुर्ज्ञेय

दमन करने में कठिन, जिसका दमन करना बहुत कठिन हो	दुर्दम्य
जहाँ जाना कठिन हो	दुर्गम
कठिनाई से जो समझ में आवे	दुर्बोध
जिसको सिद्व करना कठिन हो	दुःसाध्य
जिसे खाना मुश्किल हो	दुर्भक्ष
वह स्त्री जिस पर स्वामी का प्रेम न हो सके	दुर्भगा
जिसमें जल्दी छेद न हो, शीघ्र पार न हो सके	दुर्भेद्य
धारण करने में कठिन	दुर्वह
जिसके बारे में सोचा तक न जा सके, जिसकी कल्पना तक न हो सके	दुर्विभाव्य
बुरा स्वभव या टेव वाला	दुर्व्यसनी
जो बहुत कठिनाई से प्राप्त हो	दुर्लभ
अनुचित बात के लिए आग्रह	दुराग्रह
जिसका होना या करना कठिन हो	दुस्कर
जिसका ठीक तौर से कथन सम्भव न हो	दुष्परिमेय
जिसका रोकना या निवारण करना कठिन हो	दुर्निवार्य
जिसे दबाया या सताया गया हो	दलित
दो बार जन्म लेने वाला	द्विज
वह रोग जिसमें सूर्य की तेज किरणों के कारण दिन में बहुत कम दिखाई देता हो	दिनौंधी
किसी काम में पूर्ण रूप से मन लेने वाला	दत्तचित्त
जिसको अपने देश से प्रेम हो	देशभक्त
शीघ्र जानेवाला	द्रुतगामी
अपने देश के साथ विश्वासघात करने वाला	देशद्रोही
ध्यान या विचार करने वाला	ध्याता
धर्म में आस्था रखने वाला	धर्मात्मा
जो स्पष्ट न दिखाई दे	घूमिल
धन देने वाला	धनद
धारण करने या रोकने वाला	धारक
धारण करने वाली	धारयित्री
जो धर्म और ईश्वर में विश्वास न करता हो	नास्तिक
जिसका कोई आकार न हो	निराकार
हाल की व्याही, समान लज्जा और शील वाली नायिका	नवोढ़ा
वह (कार्य) जिसके बदले में कुछ देना न पड़े	निःशुल्क
एक देश से दूसरे देश को वस्तुओं को भेजा जाना	निर्यात
रात्रि का दूसरा पहर	निशीथ
जिसे त्याग अथवा हटा दिया गया है	निरस्त
निर्णय करने वाला	निर्णायक
जिसके कोई सन्तान न हो	निस्सन्तान
नीति का ज्ञान रखने वाला	नितिज्ञ
जिसकी जड़ अथवा उत्पत्ति का ज्ञान न हो	निर्मूल
नया उत्पन्न हुआ	नवजात
नया आया हुआ	नवागन्तुक
आकाश में विचरण करने वाला	नभचर
जो निन्दा के योग्य हो	निन्दनीय
जिसके विषय में विवाद न हो	निर्विवाद
नगर में रहने वाला	नागरिक
नगर से सम्बन्धित, अत्यन्त निष्कृष्ट	नारकीय
रात को चलने फिरने वाला	निशाचर
जो नष्ट होने वाला हो	नश्वर
जिसक कोई इच्छा न हो	निस्पृह
जिसमें दया का अभाव हो	निर्दय, निष्ठुर
बिना पलक गिराए	निर्निमेष
जिसको लिखने पढ़ने का ज्ञान न हो	निरक्षर
जिसमें ममता का अभाव हो	निर्मम
जिसके मन में पान न हो	निष्पाप
जिस पर कोई कलंक न लगा हो	निष्कलंक
जो मांस न खाता हो, मांस रहित	निरामिष
पूर्ण रूप से फूला, पका या पचा हुआ	परिपक्व
जो दूसरों की भलाई करता हो	परोपकारी
जैसा कि साधारण रूप में मालूम पड़ता है	प्रतीयमानतः
जाकर लौटा हुआ	प्रत्यागत
जो दूसरों का भला चाहता हो	परार्थी
पुस्तक की हाथ से लिखी हुई प्रति	पांडुलिपि
किसी व्यक्ति को उसके श्रम के लिए दी जाने वाली रकम	परिश्रमिक
जिसमें बहुतो का भला हो	परमार्थी
रात्रि का प्रथम पहर	प्रदोष
दोपहर के पहले का समय	पूर्वाह
जो तौला या मापा जा सके	परिमेय
बिना अधिकार के भी दूसरों की वस्तु का उपयोग करने वाला	परिभोक्ता
वह (वस्तु) जिसके आर-पार देखा जा सके	पारदर्शी
जो भली भाँति पाला पोषा गया हो	परिपुष्ट
जो दूसरों के अधीन हो	पराधीन
जो प्रमाण से सिद्व हो सके	प्रमेय
पत्ते की बनी हुई कुटी	पर्णकुटी

वाक्यांश	शब्द
शीघ्र आग पकड़ने वाला	प्रज्जवलनशील
पखवारे में क बार होने वाला	पाक्षिक
उत्तर द्वारा जिसका खण्डन किया जाए	पत्युक्त
वह स्थान जहाँ लोगों को दिखने हेतु भाँति भाँति की वस्तुएँ रखी जावें	प्रदर्शनी
जिसका पति परदेश गया हो	प्रोषितपतिका
जो फिर से या ठीक समय पर उत्पन्न हो	प्रत्युत्पन्न
जिसका स्पष्टीकरण किया जाए	प्रतिपाद्य
परपुरूष से प्रेम करने वाली नायिका	परकीया
बच्चा जनने वाली स्त्री	प्रसूता
जो देखने में प्रिय लगे	प्रियदर्शी
जो पृथ्वी से सम्बन्धित हो	पार्थिव
रास्ता दिखाने वाला	पथप्रदर्शक
पहनने के योग्य	परिमेय
जो देखा न गया हो	परोक्ष
जिस स्त्री को उसके पति ने छोड़ दिया	परित्यक्ता
एक बार कहे शब्द या वाक्य को फिर कहना	पिष्टपेषण
प्रतिकार करने या बदला चुकाने की इच्छा	प्रतिचिकीर्षा
इतिहास के पूर्व काल से सम्बन्धित	प्रागैतिहासिक
दूसरों को शिक्षा देने वाला	परोपदेशक
इन्द्रियों से प्राप्त निश्चयात्मक ज्ञान	प्रत्यक्ष
सूक्ष्मता से देखने वाला	प्रेक्षक
पहर-पहर पर घण्टा बजाने वाला, पहरा देने वाला	प्रहरी
दोष या पाप मिटाने के लिए शास्त्रनुकूल कर्म या कृत्य	प्रायश्चित
प्राण रक्षा करने वाला	प्राणद
श्वास-प्रश्वास की गति का क्रमशः दमन	प्राणायाम
जो पढ़ने योग्य हो	पठनीय
पशु के ढंग का	पाशविक
राह या मार्ग का भोजन	पाथेय
खंडन या प्रतिवाद करने वाला, जिस पर मुकदमा चलाया गया हो	प्रतिवादी
जिसकी कामना पूरी हो गयी हो	पूर्णकाम
पीने की इच्छा वाला	पिपासु
तुरन्त उपयुक्त बात या हल सोचने वाला	प्रत्युत्पन्नमति
दूसरे देश में रहने वाला	प्रवासी
उत्तर पाने पर दिया हुआ उत्तर	प्रत्युत्तर
प्रार्थना करने वाला	प्रार्थी
कठिनाइयों से भागने की प्रवृत्ति	पलायनवाद

वाक्यांश	शब्द
दूध, दही, घृत, शर्करा और मधु मिश्रित वह पदार्थ जो देवताओं के स्थान हेतु बनाया जाता है	पंचामृत
जिसका उत्तर खोजना पड़े, ऐसा कथन	प्रहेलिका
किसी विषय या क्षेत्र का पूरा ज्ञान रखने वाला	पारंगत
पीने योग्य	पेय
प्रकृति सम्बन्धी	प्राकृतिक
परलोक सम्बन्धी	पारलौकिक
हास्यरस प्रधान कहानी या लेख	प्रहसन
पूछने के योग्य	प्रष्टव्य
जो प्रतिकूल पक्ष का हो	प्रतिपक्षी
व्यर्थ व्यय करने वाला	फिजूलखर्च
फल देने वाला	फलदायी
केवल फल खाकर रहने वाला	फलाहारी
समुद्र की आग	बड़वानल
रात्रि के चार बजे का समय	ब्रह्मभाषाविद्
जिसे समाज, जाति अथवा देश से निकाल दिया गया हो	बहिष्कृत
बाहर आया या निकला हुआ	बहिर्गत
अनेक धन्धों से सम्बन्ध रखने वाला	बहुधन्धी
बहुत से लागों की मिलकर एक राय	बहुमत
बड़े दाम का	बहुमूल्य
खाने की इच्छा	बुभुक्षा
भय से घबराया हुआ	भयाकुल
वर्तमान से पूर्व का	भूतपूर्व
वह प्रभाव जो भूतकाल की तिथि से लागू हुआ हो	भूतप्रभावी
भूगोल सम्बन्धी	भौगोलिक
आगे होने वाला	भावी
टूटे-फूटे पदार्थ के बचे टुकड़े	भग्नावशेष
भारत और यूरोप से सम्बन्ध	भारोपीय
गर्भस्थ शिशु की हत्या	भ्रूणहत्या
जो भूमि को धारण करता है	भूधर
जिसका भोग करना उचित हो	भोग्य
जो जमीन के भीतर की वस्तुओं का ध्यान रखता हो	भूगर्भवेत्ता
जो भविष्य के अवश्य होने वाला है	भवितव्य
जो व्यक्ति भाग्य पर विश्वास करे	भाग्यवादी
जो भारत में रहता हा	भारतवासी, भारतीय
किसी गूढ़ विषय की वृहत् टीका	भाष्य
दोपहर का समय	मध्याह्न
भाषा विज्ञान का विद्वान्	भाषाविद्

तत्व या भेद जानने वाला	मर्मज्ञ	उत्तराधिकारी में मिली जाएदाद	रिक्थ
मद्यपान करने का आदी	मद्यप	लालिमा ये युक्त	रक्तिम
जो मृत्यु की समीप हो	मरणासन्न	रोंगटों के उभार से युक्त	रोमानिचत
जो फूल आधा खिला हो	मुकुल	राष्ट्र का प्रधान	राष्ट्रपति
वह स्थिति जब मुद्रा का चलन अधिक हो	मुद्रास्फीति	बच्चों को सुलान का गीत और थपकी	लोरी
कम या मर्यादित खर्च करने वाला	मितव्ययी	जो लेखा-जोखा रखता हो	लेखाकार
कम बोलने वाला	मितभाषी	जो भूमि का लेखा-जोखा रखता हो	लेखपाल
सूक्ष्म भोजन करने वाला	मिताहारी	इस लोक से सम्बन्धित	लौकिक
मृत्यु को जीतने वाला	मृंत्युजय	जो लोक या संसार में न हो	लोकोत्तर
मोक्ष की इच्छा रखने वाला	मुमुक्षु	चाटने योग्य वस्तु	लोह्य
वह दानी जो खुले हाथ दान करे	मुक्तहस्त	लुभाया या ललचाया हुआ	लुब्ध
झूठ बोलने वाला	मिथ्यावादी	किसी वस्तु के बदले कोई वस्तु बेचने की क्रिया	वस्तु निनियम
मन बचन और कर्म से	मनसा-वाचा	वे वस्तुयें जो विरोधी प्रकृत्ति की हों	विजातीय
	-कर्मणा	जो वर्ष में एक बार हो	वार्षिक
किसी विषय की मीमांसा करने वाला	मीमांसक	जिस स्त्री का पति मर गया हो	विधवा
मछली के समान जिसकी आँखे हों	मीनाक्षी	जो दूसरों में लीन या मिल गया हो	विलीन
हिरण की ऑख के समान आँखें वाली	मृगनयनी	जिस पुरूष की स्त्री मर गयी हो	विधूर
मांस भक्षण करने वाला	मांसाहारी	हिलोरें उत्पन्न करने वाला	बिलोडक
जो मूल से सम्बन्धित हो	मौलिक	जो जीत लिया गया हो	विजित
मरने की इच्छा या कामना	मुमूर्षा	भले बुरे की पहचान का ज्ञान	विवेक
मृत्यु का इच्छुक	मुमुर्षु	जो पास-पास या घना न हो	विरल
युद्व करने या लड़ने की इच्छा	युयुत्सा	दो दिशाओं के बीच का कोना	विदिश
जिसने यश प्राप्त किया हो	यशस्वी	जिससे विकार उत्पन्न हो	विकारी
जो युद्व में स्थिर रहता है	युधिष्ठिर	जो दूसरे को वाणी से प्रसन्न कर दे	वाग्दत्त
जहाँ तक सम्भव हो	यथासम्भव	जो किसी विषय की विशेष जानकारी रखता हो	विशेषज्ञ
युद्व करने या लड़ने की इच्छा रखने वाला	युयुत्सु	विश्वास के योग्य	विश्वसनीय
यंत्र सम्बन्धी	यांत्रिक	एक से अधिक बातों में किसी को स्वीकार करना	विकल्प
शक्ति के अनुसार	यथाशक्ति	जो कनून के प्रतिकूल हो	विधिविरूद्व
क्रम के अनुसार	यथाक्रम	सौतेली माता	विमाता
जैसा उचित हो	यथोचित	जिसे अपने स्थान से हटा दिया गया है	विस्थापित
खून से रंगा हुआ या लथ-पथ	रक्तरंजित	विज्ञान का ज्ञाता	वैज्ञानिक
रात को दिखाई न देने वाला रोग	रतौंधी	व्याकरण का ज्ञाता	वैयाकरण
राजा या राज्य के प्रति किया गया विद्रोह	राजद्रोह	बचपन और जवानी के बीच का समय	वय:सन्धि
पुलिस या सेना का नया सिपाही	रंगरूट	जो अवश्यकता से अधिक बोलता हो	वाचाल
यज्ञ करने या कराने वाला	याज्ञिक	जो कानून के अनुसार हो	वैध
दूसरे देश में अपने राष्ट्र का प्रतिनिधित्व करने वाला	राजदूत	जिसका वर्णन न हो सके	वर्णनातीत
राज्य द्वारा आधिकारिक रूप से प्रकाशित होने वाला पत्र	राजपत्र	जिसकी पत्नी साथ में न हो	विपत्नीक
वह काव्य जिसका अभिनय हो सके	रूपक	जो सबमें व्याप्त है	विभु

अनुचित यौन सम्बन्ध करने वाला	व्यभिचारी
जो किसी विकार से ग्रस्त हो	विकृत
बिजली का चमकना	विद्युतद्युति
सर्वसाधारण को सूचित करने या जताने की क्रिया	विज्ञप्ति
जो वाद (मुकदमा) चलाए	वादी
जिसके हाथ में बज्र हो	बज्रपाणि
बहुत पढ़ी-लिखी महिला	विदुषी
जिसका कोई अंग टूट या बिगड़ गया हो	विकलांग
चौड़ा या फाड़ा हुआ	विदीर्ण
विदेश से सम्बन्धित	वैदेशिक
शत्रु का हनन करने वाला	शत्रुघ्न
जिस पर शासन किया जाए	शासित
शिव की उपासना करने वाला	शैव
तरकारी और फलों का भोजन करने वाला	शाकाहारी
हरा-भरा मैदान	शाद्वल
शरण में जो आया हो	शरणागत
शक्ति की आराधना करने वाला	शाक्त
शब्द से निशाना कारने वाला	शब्दवेधी
जो अपना ही हित चाहता हो	स्वार्थी
जो शरण का इच्छुक हो	शरणार्थी
जो सबको समान समझता अथवा देखता हो	समदर्शी
दो धाराओं या नदियों के बीच का स्थान	संगम
जो स्वयं उत्पन्न हुआ हो	स्वयम्भू
जिस स्त्री का पति जीवित हो	सधवा
जो स्मरण रखने योग्य हो	स्मरणीय
जो सदा से चला आ रहा हो	सनातन
एक समय में रहने वाला अथवा होने वाला	समकालीन
जो असत्य न बोले	सत्यवादी
अपनी इच्छानुसार आचरण करने वाला	स्वेच्छाचारी
मांस से कुक्त	सामिष
जिसकी ग्रीवा सुन्दर हो	सुग्रीव
जिसका कोई आकार हो	साकार
वे स्तुएं जो एक प्रकृति की हों	सजातीय
छूत या संसर्ग से फैलने वाला रोग	संक्रामक
जो दूसरे के अधीन हो	पराधीन
एक ही माँ से उत्पन्न भाई	सहोदर
जो सग कुछ जानता हो	सर्वज्ञ
अपने ही पति की अनुरागिनी स्त्री	स्वकीया
सेवा और आराधना करने योग्य	स्वावलम्बी
दूसरी वस्तु के सहारे रहने वाला	सापेक्षित
जो लिखना-पढ़ना जानता हो	साक्षर
जो स्त्री के वशीभूत या उसके स्वभाव का है	स्त्रैण
किसी सच्चे या न्याय-संगत पक्ष की स्थापना के हेतु सदा शन्ति पूर्वक अपने हठ का निर्वाह	सत्याग्रह
सम्पूर्ण पृथ्वी से सम्बन्धित	सार्वभौम
जिसकी पत्नी साथ में हो	सपत्नीक
दीनों को नित्य भोजन देना	सदावर्त
अच्छे आचरण वाला	सदाचारी
जिसका सम्बन्ध साहित्य से हो	साहित्यिक
सर्वसाधारण से सम्बन्ध रखने वाला	सार्वजनिक
यह बात जिसकी सिद्दि के हेतु प्रमाण अनावश्यक हो	स्वत:सिद्ब
स्वेच्छा से पुरस्कार के बिना ही किसी कार्य में योग देने वाला	स्वयंसेवक
पसीने से पेदा होने वाला	स्वयंवरा
किसी के स्थान पर आया हुआ	स्थानापन्न
गहरी नींद में सोया हुआ	सुषुपत
कई वस्तुओं का एक में मिला होना	संश्लेषण
जो एक जगह से दूसरी पर न लाया जा सके	स्थावर
शपथ पूर्वक दिया हुआ लिखित बयान	हलफनामा
जो होने को हो या होकर ही रहे	होनहार
हाथ की चतुराई	हस्तलाघव
हाथ की कारीगरी	हस्तकौशल
जिसका उत्साह समाप्त हो चुका हो	हतोत्साहित
हाथ में आया हुआ	हस्तगत
भलाई चाहने वाला	हितैषी
हँसी के योग्य	हास्यास्पद
हाथ का लिखा हुआ	हस्तलिखित

4 Chapter मुहावरे और लोकोक्तियाँ

मुहावरे एवं लोकोक्तियाँ देखने में जितने सरल दिखते हैं, वस्तुत: वे उतने सरल होते नहीं हैं। इनके अध्ययन के पहले इनके बारे में समझना आवश्यक है।

मुहावरा

विशिष्ट अर्थ की प्रतीति कराने वाले वाक्यांश को 'मुहावरा' कहते हैं। अरबी भाषा का 'मुहावर' शब्द हिन्दी में 'मुहावरा' हो गया है। उर्दू बोलने वाले 'मुहाविरा' बोलते हैं। मुहावरा का अर्थ एक प्रकार की बातचीत या अभ्यास है। मुहावरा कभी-कभी रोजमर्रा या 'वाग्धारा' से सम्बन्धित अर्थ में भी लिया जाता है। हिन्दी में मुहावरा एक पारिभाषिक शब्द बन गया है।

मुहावरे के प्रयोग से भाषा में सरलता, सरसता, चमत्कारिकता और प्रवाह उत्पन्न होता है। इसका कार्य है वार्ता एवं संप्रेषण के दौरान श्रोता को अर्थ बोध भी हो जाए और वह उसे प्रभावित भी करे।

मुहावरे के सम्बंध में निम्नलिखित बातों का ध्यान रखना चाहिए-

(1) मुहावरे लिंग, वचन, कारक, काल के अनुसार परिवर्तित होते हैं।

(2) मुहावरे अर्थ की दृष्टि से अधूरे होते हैं।

(3) मुहावरा लोकोक्ति की अपेक्षा व्याकरण की दृष्टि से अधिक परिष्कृत होता है।

(4) मुहावरे के अंत में ना का प्रयोग होता है परन्तु ये ना क्रिया के रूप में आता है और क्रिया में ना एक बार ही आना चाहिए।

(5) मुहावरे में लक्षणा शब्द शक्ति हेती है और लक्षणा में भी रूढ़ा लक्षणा शब्द शक्ति होती है।

(6) मुहावरे का वाक्य में प्रयोग आदि, मध्य और अंत तीनों ही स्थानों पर होता है।

(7) मुहवरा को वाक्यों में प्रयोग किया जाये तो मूल रूप ही प्रयुक्त होना चाहिए।

(8) मुहावरे अधिकांशत: शरीर के अंगों से संबंधित होते हैं।

(9) मुहावरे भाषा को प्रभावशाली संक्षिप्त बनाते हैं।

(10) मुहावरे सारगर्भित होते हैं, इनके द्वारा कम शब्दों में अधिक बात कही जा सकती है।

मुहावरे पहचानने का सूत्र = क्रिया + ना (एक बार ना आये)

टिप्पणी- यदि ना एक से अधिका बार आये तो उसे लोकोक्ति ही समझा जाए।

मुहावरों की विशेषताएँ-

(1) मुहावरों का प्रयोग वाक्य प्रयोग में होता है अलग से नहीं।

(2) मुहावरों का असली रूप कभी नहीं बदलता अर्थात उन्हें पर्यायवाची शब्दों में अनूदित नहीं किया जा सकता है, जैसे 'कमर टूटना' के स्थान पर 'कटिभंग' का प्रयोग नहीं होगा।

(3) मुहावरे का शब्दार्थ नहीं बल्कि उसका अवबोधक अर्थ ही ग्रहण किया जाता है, जैसे-'खिचड़ी पकाना' का अपना कोई अर्थ नहीं है, पर प्रयोग करने पर इसका अर्थ 'गुप्त रूप से सलाह करना' होगा।

(4) हिन्दी में मुहावरों का सीधा सम्बन्ध शरीर के भिन्न-भिन्न अंगों से है।

(5) समाज और देश के अनुरूप मुहावरे बनते और बिगड़ते हैं।

(6) मुहावरे भाषा की समृद्धि और विकास के मापक हैं।

(7) मुहावरे का अर्थ प्रसंग के अनुसार होता है जैसे 'लड़ाई में खेत होना' का अर्थ युद्ध में शहीद हो जाना, न कि लड़ाई के स्थान पर किसी खेत का होना है।

लोकोक्तियाँ

लोकोक्तियाँ किसी भाषा के भाषियों की पारस्परिक सांस्कृतिक विरासत होती हैं। वे इतिहास में किन्हीं विशिष्ट घटनाओं एवं स्थितियों से उपजती हैं और फिर भाषा के माध्यम से देश और काल में छा जाती हैं। लोकोक्तियाँ समाज का भाषाई इतिहास होती हैं इसलिए लोकोक्तियों के माध्यम से उस समाज का सांस्कृतिक, आर्थिक, राजनीतिक एवं व्यावहारिक अध्ययन किया जा सकता है।

मुहावरे और लोकोक्तियाँ में अंतर

	मुहावरे	लोकोक्तियाँ
1.	मुहावरे अपना शाब्दिक/कोशगत अर्थ छोड़कर नया अर्थ छोड़कर नया अर्थ देते हैं।	1. लोकोक्तियाँ विशेष अर्थ देती हैं, पर उनका कोशगत अर्थ भी बना रहता है।
2.	मुहावरे के अंत में क्रियापद अवश्य होता है।	2. लोकोक्तियों के अंत में क्रियापद का होना आवश्यक नहीं है।
3.	मुहावरा वाक्यांश होता है। उसका क्रियारूप, लिंग वचन, कारक के अनुसार बदल जाता है।	3. लोकोक्तियाँ स्वयं में एक स्वतंत्र वाक्य होती हैं तथा प्रयोग में आने पर उनमें कोई परिवर्तन नहीं होता है।
4.	मुहावरों के अंतमें बहुधा ना आ जाता है, जैसे- खाक छानना, चलता बनना, चाँदी काटना।	4. लोकोक्तियों के अंतमें ना आना आवश्यक नहीं।
5.	उद्देश्य, विधेय का पूर्ण विधान नहीं होता, वाक्य के प्रयोग के बिना अर्थ का कोई बोध नहीं।	5. उद्देश्य और विधेय दोनों का पूर्ण विधान होता है तथा अर्थ स्पष्ट होता है।

समानता

(1) दोनों की सार्थकता प्रयोग के बाद सिद्ध होती है।

(2) दोनों में प्रयुक्त शब्दों के स्थान पर पर्यायवाची या समानार्थी शब्दों का प्रयोग नहीं हो सकता है।

(3) दोनों ही गंभीर और व्यापक अनुभव की उपज हैं।

(4) दोनों ही विलक्षण अर्थ प्रकट करते हैं।

(5) दोनों ही भाषा शैली को सरस एवं प्रभावशाली बनाते हैं।

लाकोक्तियाँ (कहावतें)

अंक

1. **अंक भरना**– गोद में भर लेना, आलिंगन। माँ ने दौड़कर अपने इकलौते बेटे को अंक भर लिया।
2. **अंक लगाना**– आलिंगन करना। ज्योंही मोहन को परीक्षा में प्रथम श्रेणी में उत्तीर्ण होने की सूचना मिली, उसने अपने मित्र सोहन को अंक लगा लिया।

अंग

1. **अंग टूटना**– थकान की पीड़ा होना। काम करते–करते अंग टूटने लगे।
2. **अंग-अंग मुसकाना**– प्रसन्नता से रोम–रोम खिलना। युद्ध के पश्चात् विजयी वीरों का अंग–अंग मुसकाता है।
3. **अंग मोड़ना**– लज्जा से देह सिकोड़ना। किसी अपरिचित के सामने अंग मोड़ना स्त्रियों का स्वभाव है।

अँगूठा

1. **अँगूठा दिखाना**– मौके पर धोखा देना। चालबाजों से बचकर रहो, वे अँगूठा दिखाना खूब जानते हैं।
2. **अँगूठा चूमना**– खुशामद करना। साहित्यिक भी जब शासकों का अँगूठा चूमते हैं, तो बहुत दुःख होता है।
3. **अँगूठे पर मारना**– परवाह न करना। तुम्हारे–जैसे कितनों को मैं अँगूठे पर मारता हूँ।

आँखे

1. **आँखे अटकना**– प्रेम होना। शकुन्तला पर दुष्यन्त की आँखे अटक गयीं।
2. **आँख आना**– आँख में रोग होना। गर्मी की धूप में घूमने से आँख आ जाती है।
3. **आँख उठाकर न देखना**– ध्यान न देना। धनी गरीब की ओर आँख उठाकर भी नहीं देखते।
4. **आँख खुलना**– बोध होना। जिन्दगी में ज्यों–ज्यों ठोकर लगती है, त्यों–त्यों आँख खुलती है।
5. **आँख गड़ना**– लालच होना। मेरी घड़ी पर उसकी आँख गड़ गयी।
6. **आँखे चुराना**– लज्जित होना, कतरा जाना। तुम लाख आँखे चुराओ, मैं तुम्हें छोड़ने को नहीं।
7. **आँखे डबडबाना**– बेटी की विदाई के समय किसकी आँखे डबडबा नहीं जातीं।
8. **आँख दिखाना**– क्रोध करना। यदि दुश्मन आँखे दिखाये, तो उसकी आँखे निकाल लो।
9. **आँख मारना**– इशारा करना। आँख मत मारो, जो कुछ कहना है साफ–साफ कहो।
10. **आँख सेंकना**– दर्शन–सुख लूटना। जगदीश, मैं जानता हूँ, तुम आजकल कहाँ आँख सेंकने जाया करते हो।
11. **आँखे बिछाना**– बाट जोहना। प्रेमी तो प्रेमिका के लिए आँखें बिछाये रहता है।
12. **आँख में चढ़ना**– पसंद आना। दाम क्या पूछती हो, यदि यह साड़ी आँख में चढ़ गयी तो ले लो।
13. **आँखों का काँटा होना**– शत्रु होना। मैंने उसे वोट नहीं दिया कि उसकी आँखों का काँटा हो गया।
14. **आँख का काजल चुराना**– सफाई के साथ चोरी करना। रेलगाड़ी में ऐसे पाकेटमार घूमते हैं कि आँख का काजल तक चुरा लें।
15. **आँख की किरकिरी होना**– जिसे देखकर कष्ट हो। देशद्रोही आँख की किरकिरी नहीं तो और क्या है?
16. **आँख का तारा**– अत्यंत प्रिय। कैसा भी बेटा क्यों न हो, वह माँ–बाप की आँखों का तारा (आँख की पुतली) होता ही है।
17. **आँख की पुतली होना**– अत्यन्त प्यारा – हर बच्चा अपने माँ का आँख की पुतली होता है।
18. **आँखों के आगे अँधेरा छाना**– दुर्बलता के कारण मूर्छा आना, संसार सूना मालूम पड़ना। पिता की मृत्यु का समाचार पाते ही उसकी आँखों के आगे अँधेरा छा गया।
19. **आँखें नीली-पीली करना**– नाराज होना। नौकरों पर खामखाह आँखें नीली–पीली करोगे, तो वे काम बिगाड़ डालेंगे।
20. **आँख में पानी न होना**– लज्जा न होना। स्त्रियों की आँखों में पानी न होना दूषण ही है।
21. **आँखों पर चर्बी छाना**– घमण्ड से उपेक्षा करना। धनवानों की आँखों पर चर्बी छा ही जाती है।
22. **आँखों पर पर्दा पड़ना**– अज्ञान के अंधकार में रहना। अब तक आँखों पर पर्दा पड़ा था, महात्माजी ने आँखें खोल दीं।
23. **आँख में गड़ना**– अच्छा न लगना। बेढ़ंगापन आँख में गड़ता ही है।
24. **आँख में धूल झोंकना**– धोखा देना। परीक्षक की आँख में धूल झोंककर कुछ विद्यार्थी अच्छे अंक भले ही ले आयें, पर इससे क्या वे जीवन में भी अच्छे अंक ला पायेंगे?
25. **आँख से ओझल होना**– नजर से दूर होना। परदेशी प्रियतम आँख से ओझल हुआ कि बेचारी की आँखें भर आयीं।

26. **आँखों में रात काटना**– चिंता या व्यग्रता में रात बिताना। प्रेमी तो आँखों में ही रात काट देते हैं।

27. **आँख बदल जाना**– कृपादृष्टि न रखना। पता नहीं क्यों, उनकी आँख इन दिनों बदल गयी हैं।

28. **आँखें बैठना**– नेत्र-ज्योति समाप्त होना। किसी ऐरे-गेरे की बतायी दवा लगायी और उसकी आँखें बैठ गयी।

29. **आँखें चार होना**– देखादेखी होना। मित्र से आँखें चार होते ही मैं उसकी ओर तेजी से बढ़ा।

30. **एक आँख से देखना**– सम भाव से देखना। महापुरूष हर छोटे-बड़े को एक आँख से देखते हैं।

उँगली

1. **उँगली उठाना**– बदनाम करना। भले पर कौन उँगली उठा सकता है?
2. **उँगली पर नचाना**– अपने काबू में कर लेना। गोपियाँ श्रीकृष्ण को अपनी उँगलियों पर नचाती थीं।
3. **उँगली रखना**– दोष दिखाना। महापुरूषों पर उँगली रखना अनुचित है।
4. **उँगली पकड़कर पहुँचा पकड़ना**– थोड़ा पाकर अधिक पाने की इच्छा करना। लोभियों से सावधान रहो, वे उँगली पकड़कर पहुँचा पकड़ना जानते हैं।
5. **पाँचों उँगलियाँ घी में होना**– मौज-मस्ती में रहना। वह तिकड़मी मंत्री क्या हुआ कि अब उसकी पाँचों उँगलियाँ घी मे हैं।

कमर

1. **कमर कसना**– दृढ़ निश्चय करना। विजय चाहते हो तो युद्ध के लिए कमर कस लो।
2. **कमर सीधी करना**– विश्राम करना। अभी तो टेस्ट परीक्षा समाप्त हुई है, जरा कमर सीधी करने दो फिर पढ़ाई चलेगी।
3. **कमर टूटना**– निरूत्साह होना। परीक्षा में कई बार फेल होने से उसकी कमर टूट गयी।

कलेजा

1. **कलेजा काढ़ना**– प्रिय वस्तु का निकल जाना। उसने मेरी पांडुलिपि क्या खो दी, मेरा कलेजा काढ़ लिया।
2. **कलेजा फटना**– ईर्ष्या होना। मेरी उन्नति देखकर इन दिनों मेरे एक सहयोगी का कलेजा फट रहा है।
3. **कलेजा ठंडा होना**– डाह पूरा होने पर संतोष होना। सौत की हानि पर हर स्त्री का कलेजा ठंडा हो जाता है।
4. **कलेजा टूक-टूक होना**– हृदय पर गहरा आघात पहुँचना। नृप हरिश्चन्द्र की विपत्तियों को देखकर किसका कलेजा टूक-टूक नहीं होता?
5. **कलेजा थामकर रह जाना**– मन मसोसकर रह जाना। उस लड़के को तो मजा चखा देता, मगर मालिक का लड़का ठहरा, इसीलिए कलेजा थामकर रह गया।
6. **कलेजा निकालकर रख देना**– हृदय की बात कहना। उसने अपनी चिट्ठी में कलेजा निकालकर रख दिया।
7. **कलेजा मुँह को आना**– बहुत अफसोस होना। उसकी बीमारी देखकर कलेजा मुँह को आता है।
8. **कलेजे पर साँप लोटना**– किसी की उन्नति देख कर जलन होना। राम के राज्याभिषेक की खबर से कैकेयी की दासी मन्थरा के कलेजे पर साँप लोटने लगा।
9. **कलेजे पर पत्थर रखना**– दिल मजबूत करना। छोटे भाई विभीषण की दगाबाजी पर रावण ने कलेजे पर पत्थर रख लिया, इसके सिवा उसके पास चारा ही क्या था?
10. **कलेजा चीरकर दिखाना**– पूर्ण विश्वास दिलाना। तुम्हीं मेरे सब कुछ हो, यह मैं कलेजा चीरकर दिखा सकता हूँ।

कान

1. **कान काटना**– मात करना। इसे छोटा न समझो, भाषण देने में तो यह बड़ों के कान काटता है।
2. **कान देना**– ध्यान देना। गुरू के वचन पर कान दो।
3. **कान खड़े होना**– सावधान होना। अपनी ही टीका-टिप्पणी होते देख उसके कान खड़े हो गये।
4. **कान ऐंठना**– प्रतिज्ञा करना। मैं कान ऐंठता हूँ कि कभी ऐसी गुस्ताखी न करूँगा।
5. **कान पकड़ना**– अपनी भूल स्वीकार कर भविष्य में वैसी बात न करने की प्रतिज्ञा करना। राजू को जब डाँट पड़ी, तो उसने कान पकड़े।
6. **कान पर जूँ तक न रेंगना**– कुछ भी ध्यान न देना। उसे लाख समझाओ, फिर भी उसके कान पर जूँ तक नहीं रेंगती।
7. **कान फूँकना**– बहकाना। आजकल कान फूँकनेवालों की कमी नहीं है।
8. **कान भरना**– किसी के विपरीत कुछ कहना। भाई, मुझपर खफा क्यों हो। किसी न मेरे खिलाफ कान भर दिए हैं क्या?
9. **कान में तेल डालकर बैठना**– लापरवाह होना। मिल-मालिक तो कान में तेल डालकर बैठ गया, मजदूरों की हालत सुधरे कैसे?
10. **कान का पर्दा फटना**– बहुत हल्ला होना। सुबह आप मुसल्लहपुर हाट से गुजरें, तो कान के पर्दे फटन लगेंगे।

खून

1. **खून खौलना**– गुस्से से भर जाना। दुश्मन की हमलावर हरकतों से किसका खून नहीं खौलता?
2. **खून सूखना**– भय से पीला पड़ जाना। बाघ को देखकर मेरा खून सूख गया।
3. **खून की नदी बहाना**– बहुत मारकाट करना। अशोक ने कलिंग-युद्ध में खून की नदी बहा दी।

4. **खून ठंढा होना**– भयभीत होना। अंग्रेज समझते हैं कि भारत के लोग साँप से खेला करते हैं और इधर हम भारतीय हैं कि साँप देखा, तो खून ठंढा होने लगा।
5. **खून उतरना**– क्रोध से मुँह और आँख लाल होना। उसकी हरकत देख मेरे चेहरे पर खून उतर आया।

गला

1. **गले मढ़ना**– इच्छा के विरूद्ध कुछ सौंपना या सामान थोप देना। आखिर उसने अपना रद्दी रेडियो मेरे गले मढ़ ही दिया।
2. **गले लगाना**– प्रेम करना। दीनों को गले लगाओ।
3. **गले का हार**– अत्यन्त प्रिय या शोभा बढ़ानेवाला। विद्या के गले का हार विनय ही है।
4. **गाल फुलाना**– रूठना। कैकेयी ने गाल फुला लिया, तो दशरथ परेशान हो गये।
5. **गाल बजाना**– डींग हाँकना। यदि बहुत गाल बजाओगे, तो इज्जत चली जायेगी।

घुटना

1. **घुटने टेकना**– हार मानना। वीर घुटने टेकना नहीं जानते।

छाती

1. **छाती जुड़ाना**– इच्छा पूरी होना। अपने मित्र की उन्नति से मेरी छाती जुड़ा गयी।
2. **छाती (जी) जलना**– डाह होना। किसी की छाती जले, परवाह नहीं, मुझे तो आगे बढ़ते जाना है।
3. **छाती फुलाना**– अभिमान करना। रमेश पुलिस-अफसर क्या हुआ, हमेशा छाती फुलाये चलता है।
4. **छाती पीटना**– विलाप करना। बेटे को मरते देख माँ छाती पीटने लगी।
5. **छाती पर साँप लोटना**– ईर्ष्या होना। राम की सफलता देख श्याम की छाती पर साँप लोट गया।
6. **छाती पर कोदो दलना**– प्रतिशोधात्मक कष्ट पहुँचाना। अपना ध र्म मानना साम्प्रदायिकता नहीं है, साम्प्रदायिकता है दूसरे धर्मवालों की छाती पर कोदो दलना।

जबान

1. **जबान देना**– प्रतिज्ञा करना। मैंने उसे जबान दी है, अत: पीछे नहीं हटूँगा।
2. **जबान पर होना**– कण्ठस्थ होना। सारी रामायण तो उसकी जबान पर है।
3. **जबान खींचना**– उद्दण्ड बोली के लिए दंड देना। बकवास किया, तो जबान खींच लूँगा।
4. **जबान खोलना**– बोलना, माँगना। एक छोटी-सी चीज के लिए क्या जबान खोलूँ।
5. **जबान पर लगाम न होना**– वाणी पर नियंत्रण न होना। जिसकी जबान पर लगाम नहीं, उसे मुँह लगाना ठीक नहीं।
6. **जबान (बोलती) बन्द होना**– निरूत्तर होना। आज उसने ऐसी बहस की कि बड़े-बड़े वकीलों की जबान बंद हो गयी।
7. **जबान चलाना**– अनुचित शब्द निकालना। यदि जबान चलाओगे, तो जबान खींच लूँगा।

टाँग

1. **टाँग अड़ाना**– फिजूल दखल देना। तुम बात-बात में टाँग अड़ाते हो, यह ठीक नहीं।
2. **टाँग पसारकर सोना**– निश्चित होकर सोना। परीक्षा समाप्त होने पर विद्यार्थी टाँग पसारकर सोते हैं।

तलवा

1. **तलवा चाटना, तलवा धो-धोकर पीना, तलवा सहलाना**– खुशामद करना। चाटुकारों का काम तो तलवे चाटना (धो-धोकर पीना, सहलाना) ही है।
2. **तलवों में आग लगना**– बहुत क्रोध होना। तुम्हारी बेतुकी बातें तलवों में आग लगा देती हैं।

दाँत

1. **दाँत उखाड़ना**– कठिन दंड देना। यदि तुम अपनी दुष्टता से बाज न आये, तो दाँत उखाड़ डालूँगा।
2. **दाँत काढ़ना या निपोरना**– गिड़गिड़ाना, विवशता प्रकट करना। जब मंटू दाँत काढ़ने (निपोरने) लगा, तो मैंने उसे दस रूपए दे दिए।
3. **दाँत खट्टे करना**– परास्त करना। कर्ण ने महाभारत युद्ध में विपक्षियों के दाँत खट्टे कर दिए थे।
4. **दाँत जमाना**– कुछ हड़पने के लिए दृढ़ होना। मेरी बगिया पर तुम दाँत लगाये हो, मै फौजदारी तक देख लूँगा।
5. **दाँतों तले उँगलियाँ दबाना**– चकित होना। लव-कुश की वीरता देखकर राम दाँतों तले उँगलियाँ दबाने लगा।
6. **दाँत-काटी रोटी होना**– बहुत मित्रता होना। कृष्ण-सुदामा में दाँत-काटी रोटी थी।
7. **दाँत से दाँत बजना**– बहुत जाड़ा पड़ना। इस साल दिसम्बर में दाँत से दाँत बजने की नौबत आ गयी।

नाक

1. **नाक कटना**– प्रतिष्ठा जाना। इस मुकदमे में राय साहब की नाक कट गयी।
2. **नाक काटना**– प्रतिष्ठा नष्ट करना। तुमने तो इस प्रतियोगिता में मेरी नाक काट ली।
3. **नाक रगड़ना**– बहुत आरजू-मिन्नत करना। वह बड़ा संगदिल है, नाक रगड़ने से काम नहीं चलेगा।
4. **नाक में दम करना**– परेशान करना। उसने दो रूपए के लिए नाक में दम कर दिया है।

5. **नाक-भौं सिकोड़ना**- घृणा करना। वह तो मुझे देखते ही नाक-भौं सिकोड़ता है।
6. **नाक पर मक्खी बैठने न देना**- बहुत सतर्क रहना, खरी प्रकृतिक का होना। सेठजी तो नाक पर मक्खी बैठने ही नहीं देते।
7. **नाक का बाल होना**- खुशामद के कारण प्रिय होना। आजकल अफसर की नाक का बाल वह होता है जो करे-धरे कुछ नहीं, खाली चुगली खाना जाने।
8. **नाकों चने चबवाना**- बहुत परेशान करना। इस बार भारतीय सेना ने दुश्मनों के नाको चने चबवा दिए।
9. **नाक रखना**- प्रतिष्ठा रखना। क्रिकेट में जय न कॉमर्स कॉलेज की नाक रख ली।

पलक

1. **पलक लगना**- सो जाना। आदमी जो ठहरा, सारे दिन और सारी रात कैसे जागता, तीन बजे सुबह तो पलक लग ही गयी।
2. **पलक पाँवड़े बिछाना**- अत्यन्त आदर से स्वागत करना। शवरी राम के लिए न मालूम कबसे पलक-पाँवड़े बिछाए थी।
3. **पलक झपकते**- क्षण मात्र में। पलक झपकते चोर गठरी ले भागा।

पसीना

1. **पसीने-पसीने होना**- बिलकुल लज्जित होना। अब वह जब भी मुझे देखता है, पसीने-पसीने हो जाता है।
2. **पसीने की कमाई**- गाढ़ी मेहनत की कमाई। पसीने की कमाई व्यर्थ लुटाने में मोह होता ही है।
3. **पसीने की जगह खून बहाना**- कम के बदले अधिक देना। मैं वैसा आदमी हूँ, जो अपने मित्रों के लिए पसीना की जगह खून बहाने की तैयार रहता हूँ।

पाँव

1. **पाँव (टाँग) अड़ाना**- बाधा देना। हर काम में पाँव मत अड़ाओ।
2. **पाँव उखड़ जाना**- पराजित होना। थानेश्वर की लड़ाई में पृथ्वीराज की सेना के पाँव उखड़ गए।
3. **पाँव चूमना**- पूजा करना, खुशामद करना। आज यदि परमवीर अब्दुल हमीद होते, तो हम सभी उनके पाँव चूमते।
4. **पाँव भारी होना**- गर्भवती होना। जब राजा ने सुना कि उसकी रानी के पाँव भारी हुए, तो उसकी खुशी का ठिकाना न रहा।
5. **पाँव तले की मिट्टी (धरती) खिसकना**- स्तब्ध हो जाना। जब सट्टे में उसे एक लाख रूपये की चपत लगी, तो उसके पाँव तले की जमीन खिसक गयी।
6. **पाँव खींचना**- रूकावट डालना। आजकल पाँव बढ़ाने वाले दो-चार होते हैं, तो पाँव खींचनेवाले दस-बीस।
7. **पाँव फिसलना**- गलती होना। जवानी में तो बहुतों के पाँव फिसल जाते हैं।
8. **पाँवों में पर लगाना**- बहुत तेज चलना। मोहन की वंशी सुनकर गोपियों के पाँवों में पर लग जाते हैं।

पीठ

1. **पीठ दिखाना**- हारकर भाग जाना। बहादुर मैदाने-जंग में पीठ नहीं दिखाते।
2. **पीठ ठोकना**- प्रोत्साहन देना। छात्रों की बराबर पीठ ठोंके, वे कमाल कर दिखायेंगे।
3. **पीठ पर होना**- सहायक होना। जब आप मेरी पीठ पर हैं, तो फिर डर किस बात का?
4. **पीठ फेरना**- मुँह मोड़ना। गाढ़े समय में तुमने भी पीठ फेर ली।

पेट

1. **पेट काटना**- थोड़ा खाकर बचाना। सन्तान के लिए पेट काटना ही पड़ता है।
2. **पेट की आग बुझाना**- भूख मिटाना। आज गाँवों में अधिक व्यक्ति ऐसे हैं, जो दो-दो शाम तक पेट की आग बुझा नहीं पाते है।
3. **पेट में आग लगना**- बहुत भूख लगना। जब पेट में आग लगती है, तो कोई काम अच्छा नहीं लगता।
4. **पेट में चूहे दौड़ना (कूदना, डंड पेलना)**- उपरिवत्।
5. **पेट-पीठ एक होना**- भूख के मारे पेट भीतर धँस जाना। भिक्षुक के पेट-पीठ एक हो गए है।
6. **पेट का पानी न पचना**- बात न पचना। उनसे कुछ न कहो, क्योंकि उनके पेट का पानी नहीं पचता।
7. **पेट में दाढ़ी होना**- अल्पायु में ही बुद्धिमान होना। रामू है तो आठ साल का, लेकिन लगता है कि उसे पेट ही में दाढ़ी हो गयी है।

बाँह

1. **बाँह गहना या पकड़ना**- अपनाना। निश्वार्थ और ईमानदार व्यक्तित्व का अकसर लोग बाँह गहते रहते हैं।
2. **बाँह देना**- सहारा देना। निस्सहायों को सदा बाँह दो।
3. **बाँह टूटना**- आश्रयहीन होना। मालिक क्या गये, तेरी बाँह ही टूट गयी।

बाल

1. **बाल-बाल बचना**- साफ बच जाना। इस रेल दुर्घटना में वह बाल-बाल बच गया।
2. **बाल की खाल निकालना**- व्यर्थ टीका-टिप्पणी करना। कुछ लोग कुछ करते हैं, तो कुछ लोग केवल बाल की खाल निकालते हैं।

मन

1. **मन डोलना**- लालच होना। मेनका को देखकर विश्वामित्र का भी मन डोल गया था।
2. **मन चलना**- इच्छा होना। आज खिचड़ी खाने को मन चल गया।
3. **मन मारकर बैठ जाना**- निराश होना। वीर अपनी पराजय पर मन मारकर बैठते नहीं।

4. **मन की मन में रहना**- इच्छा पूरी न होना। एम. एल. ए. साहब मंत्री होना चाहते थे, किन्तु उनकी तो मन की मन में ही रह गयी।
5. **मन के लड्डु खाना**- काल्पनिक प्रसन्नता से प्रसन्न होना। व्यावहारिक लोग मन के लड्डू नहीं खाते।
6. **मन फटना**- विरक्त होना। उससे मेरा मन ही फट गया।
7. **मन मिलना**- प्रेम या मित्रता होना। जिससे मन नहीं मिला, उससे संबंध कैसा?

मुट्ठी

1. **मुट्ठी में करना**- वश में करना। उसने तो साहब को ही मुट्ठी में कर लिया है।
2. **मुट्ठी गरम करना**- रिश्वत देना। कचहरी में मुट्ठी गरम करो, तभी काम होगा।

मुँह

1. **मुँह लगाना**- गुस्ताख बना देना। ओछों को मुँह लगाना ठीक नहीं।
2. **मुँह की खाना**- आशा के विरूद्ध पराजय। यदि चीन हमपर आक्रमण करेगा, तो उसे मुँह की खानी पड़ेगी।
3. **मुँह आना**- मुख में छाले पड़ना। उसे मुँह आ गया है, अतः ठीक से खा नहीं सकता।
4. **मुँह चुराना**- लज्जावश सामने नहीं आना। तुम मुझसे मुँह क्यों चुराते हो?
5. **मुँह फुलाना**- गुस्से से न बोलना। जरा डाँटा कि मुँह फुला बैठे।
6. **मुँह धोना**- उम्मीद न करना। अब मुँह धो लो, यह पुस्तक तुम्हें नहीं मिलेगी।
7. **मुँह न दिखाना**- लज्जावश सामने न आना। उसने ऐसा काण्ड किया है कि मुँह न दिखा सका।
8. **मुँह न देखना**- घृणा करना। जो छात्र होकर भी असभ्य है, उनका मुँह न देखो।
9. **मुँह बनाना**- घृणा प्रकट करना। मोहन की फटकार पर रामू मुँह बनाकर बैठ गया।
10. **मुँह में कालिख लगाना**- कलंक लगना। तुमने ऐसा काम किया कि मुँह में कालिख लगा ली।
11. **मुँह में लगाम न होना**- बिना समझे बोलना। जिसके मुँह में लगाम नहीं, उससे सँभलकर बात करो।
12. **मुँह में पानी भर आना**- जी ललचना। अच्छे आम देखकर किसके मुँह में पानीं नहीं भर जाता।
13. **मुँह मीठा करना**- शकुनसूचक मिठाई खिलाना। भाई ! मुँह मीठा कराओ, तुम्हें लड़का हुआ है।
14. **मुँह बन्द कर देना**- निरूत्तर कर देना। उसने अपने प्रतिपक्षियों का मुँह बंद कर दिया।
15. **मुँह में खून लगना**- बुरी आदत पड़ जाना। घुसखोर अपने मुँह में खून लगा लेता है।
16. **मुँह से लार टपकना**- ललचना। पाण्डेयजी पेट-खराबी की बात करते हैं जरूर, पर भोज की चर्चा छिड़ी कि मुँह से लार टपकने लगी।
17. **मुँह (चेहरे) पर हवाई उड़ना**- डर से मुख विवर्ण हो जाना। मास्टर साहब की आहट पाते ही उसके मुँह पर हवाई उड़ने लगी।

मूँछ

1. **मूँछे उखाड़ना**- घमंड चूर कर देना। तुम्हारी क्या बात, उसने बड़े बीहड़ लोगों की मूँछें उखाड़ ली हैं।
2. **मूँछों पर ताव देना**- अभिमान प्रदर्शित करना, चिन्तामुक्त होना। कुश्ती में बाजी मारकर पहलवान मूँछों पर ताव दे रहा है।

सिर

1. **सिर उठाना**- विरोध करना। यदि सिर उठाओगे, तो बुरा नतीजा भुगतना पड़ेगा।
2. **सिर ऊँचा होना**- प्रतिष्ठा पाना। रमेश भारतीय शासन-सेवा की परीक्षा में प्रथम आया जिससे हमारे विद्यालय का सिर ऊँचा हुआ है।
3. **सिर पर सवार होना**- पीछे पड़े रहना। जब तक सिर पर सवार न रहोगे, तब तक वे काम ही न करेंगे।
4. **सिर खुजलाना**- बहाना करना। जब कभी रूपया माँगो, लालाजी सिर खुजलाने लगेंगे।
5. **सिर पड़ना**- जबर्दस्ती लाद देना। दोष किसका और सिर मेरे मढ़ते हो?
6. **सिर खाना**- परेशान करना। व्यर्थ सिर मत खाओ, तुम्हारी अक्ल पर तो पत्थर पड़ा है।
7. **सिर पर आ जाना**- बहुत नजदीक आना। परीक्षा सिर पर आ गयी है।
8. **सिर पर उठा लेना**- बहुत ऊधम मचाना। शंभु ने तो बिस्कुट के लिए सारा घर सिर पर उठा लिया।
9. **सिर फिरना**- बुद्धि नष्ट होना। इन दिनों तो उसका सिर ही फिर गया है, इसलिए उससे सँभलकर बात करो।
10. **सिर पर खेलना**- किसी के मत्थे कुछ करना। चालबाज लोग दूसरे के सिर पर खेलना खूब जानते हैं।
11. **सिर से कफन बाँधना**- वीरत्व के लिए प्राण की परवाह न करना। जो सिर से कफन बाँध चुका, वह पाँव हटाना क्या जाने?
12. **सिर पर भूत सवार होना**- धुन सवार होना। उसके सिर पर एक ही भूत सवार है- पैसा, हाय पैसा।
13. **सिर से पैर तक आग लग जाना**- अत्यंत क्रोध होना। लक्ष्मण की बात सुनकर परशुराम के सिर से पैर तक आग लग गयी।

मुहावरे

क्रम	मुहावरा	अर्थ	वाक्य प्रयोग
1.	अंग-अंग ढीला होना	शिथिल पड़ना	कड़ा परिश्रम करने पर अंग-अंग ढीला हो जाता है।
2.	अंग लगाना	गले लगाना	राम ने सुग्रीव को अंग लगाया।
3.	अन्धे केहथ बटेर लगना	बिना प्रास प्राप्ति होना	बिना तैयारी के ही राम परीक्षा में पास हो गया मानों अन्धे के हाथ बटेर लग गयी।
4.	अंकित होना	अच्छी तरह बैठ जाना	भारत-पाकिस्तान का युद्ध मेरे मस्तिष्क में अंकित हो गया।
5.	अंड-बंड बना	व्यर्थ बकना/गाली देना	राम श्याम पर क्रोधित होकर अंड-बंड बकने लगा।
6.	अंकुश न मानना	ढिठाई करना	आजकल के लड़के बड़ों का अंकुश नहीं मानते।
7.	अँधेरे में तीर चलाना	दिशा विहीन प्रयास करना	पूछे गये प्रश्न का उत्तर उसे आता नहीं था। साक्षात्कार के समय वह केवल अँधेरे में तीर चला रहा था।
8.	अंग फूले न समाना	अत्यधिक आनन्दित होना	लॉटरी में इनाम पाकर उसके अंग फूले न समाते थे।
9.	अन्त करना	खत्म करना	राम ने रावण का अन्त कर दिया।
10.	अँगूठा चूमना	खुशामद करना	पहले तो वह अधिकारी से लड़ पड़ा पर बाद में अपना अनिष्ट जान उसके अँगूठे चूमने लगा।
11.	अंगार उगलना	कड़ी बातें कहना	दादा जी ने परीक्षा में मेरी असफलता सुनते ही अंगार उगलना शुरू कर दिया।
12.	अंडे सेना	घर में बेकार बैठे रहना	कुछ काम करो घर में क्या अंडे सेते रहते हो।
13.	अंग टूटना/अंग-अंग टूटना	दर्द होना	दिनभर काम करते रहने से अंग टूट रहे हैं।
14.	अन्त पा लेना	रहस्य पा लेना	राम ने रावण को मारने का अन्त पा लिया।
15.	अंचल पकड़ना	सहारा देना	वह चाहती थी कि केई उसा अंचल पकड़ने वाला मिल जाये।
16.	अंगार बरसना	चिलचिलाती धूप होना	आजकल मई-जून के महीने में अंगार बरसता है।
17.	अक्ल का अन्धा	मूर्ख	तुमने वहाँ कुछ और का और कह दिया हो ही अक्ल के अन्धे।
18.	अंगार उगलना	क्रोध में बुरा भला कहना	जरा सी बात पर चिढ़कर सोहन अंगार उगलने लगता है।
19.	अँगूठा दिखाना	धोखा देना/चिढ़ाना	अपने दिए हुए रूपये वापस माँगने पर सोहन ने मोन को अँगूठा दिखा दिया।
20.	अन्धा होना	विवेकहीन होना	अत्यधिक क्रोध में वह अन्धा हो गया और अपने भाई को मार बैठा।
21.	अन्धे की लकड़ी लाठी	एकमात्र सहारा	राघव अपनी बूढ़ी दादी के लिए अन्धे की लकड़ी है।
22.	अँधेर नगरी	अत्यन्त अन्याय	भ्रष्टाचार के इस युग में मानों हम लोग अँधेर नगरी में जी रहे हैं।
23.	अन्धा बनना	धोखा देना/मूर्ख बनाना	इसकी मुझे पूर्ण जानकारी है, मुझे अन्धा मत बनाओं।
24.	अपनी नींद सोना	निश्चिंत रहना	जबसे लाल जी के बच्चों ने कार्यभार सम्भाल लिया है, वे अपन नींद सोते हैं।
25.	अक्ल पर पत्थर/परदा पड़ना	समझ न रहना	राम ने ऐसा क्यों किया, क्या उसके अक्ल पर पत्थर/परदा पड़ गया था।
26.	अँधेरे मुंह	प्रात: काल	सोहन नौकरी के लिए अंधेरे मुंह घर से निकल जाता है।
27.	अपना किया पाना	कर्म का पुल भोगना	रावण ने अधर्म को अपनाया जिसके कारण भगवान राम ने उसका सर्वनाश कर दिया, मानो रावण अपना किया पा गया।
28.	अँधेरा छाना	शोक छाना	इकलौते पुत्र की मृत्यु से शर्मा जी के घरमें अंधेरा छा गया।
29.	अनसुनी करना	परवाह न करना	आजकल के बच्चे बड़ो की बातों को अनसुनी कर देते हैं।
30.	अच्छी बीतना	आनन्द से समय गुजरना	जब से गुप्ता जी के बेटे की सरकारी नौकरी लगी है उनकी अच्छी बीत रही है।

31.	अगर-मगर करना	टाल-मटोल करना	सरकारी कार्यालयों में क्लर्क बिना पैसा लिए कार्य को अगर-मगर करते रहते हैं।
32.	अनबन रहना	झगड़ा/मनमुटाव होना	पिता की मृत्यु के बाद दोनों भाइयों में अनबन रहती है।
33.	अट-पट बोलना	बेकार की बातें/गाली देना	जब राम की सच्चाई पकड़ ली गयी तो वह मोहन को अट-पट बोलने लगा।
34.	अड़ंगा लगाना/डालना	बाधा डालना	आजकल अपने ही अच्छे कार्यो में अड़ंगा लगाते हैं।
35.	अकड़ जाना	जिद्द पर डटे रहना	पिता के लाख समझाने पर भी पुत्र अपनी गलत बात पर अकड़ गया।
36.	अन्न-जल उठना	किसी जगह से चले जाना	स्थानान्तरण हो जाने के साथ ही मेरा इस नगर से अन्न-जल उठ गया।
37.	अपनी खिचड़ी आप पकाना	सबसे अलग रहना	हम सभी को एक मत होकर कोई कदम उठाना है, सब लोग अपनी खिचड़ी अलग पकायेंगे तो सफलता कैसे मिलेगी।
38.	अँधेरे घर का उजाला	इकलौता पुत्र	श्याम अपने पिता के अँधेरे घर का उजाला है।
39.	अजान बनना	जानते हुए भी अनजान का स्वांग	राम को यद्यपि पता था कि सीता हरण रावण ने किया है फिर भी वह अनजान बने रहे।
40.	अठखेलियाँ करना	हँसी दिल्लगी करना	में फेल हो गया और तुम्हें अठखेलियाँ सूझ रही हैं।
41.	अपने पाँव आप कुल्हाड़ी मारना	अपना अनिष्ट स्वयं करना	शेयर मार्केट में पैसा लगाकर मैंने अपने पाँव पर कुल्हाड़ी मार ली।
42.	अपना उल्लू सीधा करना	अपना स्वार्थ साधना	आजकल सभी नेता और अधिकारी अपन उल्लू सीधा करने में लगे रहते हैं।
43.	अक्ल चकराना/ चक्कर खाना	चकित होना	राधे के अमेरिका जाने की खबर सुनकर मेरी अक्ल चकरा गयी।
44.	अछूता होना	बेदाग होना	आजकल कम ही अधिकारी ऐसे हैं, जो अछूते हैं।
45.	अपनी-अपनी पड़ना	सभी का स्वार्थी होना	आजकल सभी को अपनी-अपनी पड़ी रहती है।
46.	अपने सिर लेना	अपने ऊपर लेना/ स्वीकार करना	राम ने सोहन की मुसीबत अपने सिर ले ली।
47.	अक्ल का दुश्मन होना	महामूर्ख होना	अक्ल के दुश्मन ही बरसात में पहाडों का सफर करते हैं।
48.	अट्टहास करना	जोर से हँसना/व्यंग्य से हँसना	राम को सामने देखकर रावण अट्टहास करने लगा।
49.	अपना ठिकाना करना	रहने/जीविका का प्रबन्ध करना	एक छोटी सी नौकरी से ही प्रेमशंकर ने शहर में अपना ठिकाना कर लिया।
50.	अपना राग अलापना	केवल अपनी ही बात कहना	केशव किसी की बात न सुनकर अपना ही राग अलापता रहता है।
51.	अपना-सा मुँह लेकर रहजाना	लज्जित होना	चोरी पकड़ी जानेपर प्रेम अपना-सा मुँह लेकर रह गया।
52.	अरमान निकालना	इच्छा पूरी करना	नौकरी मिलते ही मेरे अरमान पूरे हो गये।
53.	अपने पाँव पर खड़ा होना	स्वावलम्बी होना	रोहन अब काफी कमा लेता है, कम से कम अपने पाँव पर खड़ा हो गया है।
54.	अपने मुँह मियाँ मिट्ठू बनना	अपनी प्रशंसा आप करना	किसी को अपने मुंह मियाँ मिट्ठू नहीं बनना चाहिए।
55.	अपने तक रखना	किसी से न कहना	राम ने सोहन से कहा कि अपना झगड़ा अगर अपने तक ही रखोगे तो बेहतर होगा।
56.	अवसर चूकना	मौका खोना	नौकरी लगने पर बैंगोर न जाकर लक्ष्मी अवसर चूक गयी।
57.	अपने हाथों कब्र खोदना	अपना नाश स्वयं करना	जो लोग शराब पीते हैं वह अपने हाथों अपनी कब्र खोदते है।
58.	अरमान दिल में रह जाना	इच्छा पूरी न होना	नौकरी न मिलने से राघव के अरमान दिल में ही रह गये।
59.	अवस्था ढलना	बुढ़ापा आना/ काफी उम्र होना	राम के वनवास जाते समय दशरथ की अवस्था ढल चुकी थी।
60.	आँख ऊपर न उठना	लज्जित होना	घूस लेते पकड़े जाने पर उसकी आंख ऊपर न उठ सकी।

61.	आँख का अन्धा गाँठ का पूरा	धनी पर मूर्ख/मूर्ख धनवान	एकाएक धन प्राप्त हो जाने पर गुप्ता जीक दशा आँख का अन्धा गाँठ का पूरा जैसी है।
62.	आँख-कान खुला रखना	चौकस रहना	यात्रा करते समय हमें अपने आँख-कान खुले रखने चाहिए।
63.	आँख चुराकर जाना	चुपके से निकल जाना	उधार न दे पाने के कारण सोहन अपने मित्र से आँख चुराकर निकल गया।
64.	आँख की पुतली होना	अत्यधिक प्यारा होना	केशव अपने पिता के आँख की पुतली है।
65.	आँख उलट जाना	मरणासन्न	सड़क दुर्घटना में लड़के की आँख उलट गयी।
66.	आँखों पर चढ़ना	किसी के क्रोध का शिकार होना	हरीश ने झूठी गवाही क्या दे दी कि वह पुलिस के आंख पर चढ़ गया।
67.	आँख से ओझल होना	नजर से दूर होना	धीरे-धीरे कार आँख से ओझल हो गयी।
68.	आँखें चार होना	प्यार होना	कालेज की एक लड़की से देवेन्द्र की आँखें चार हो गयीं।
69.	आँख खुलना	होशियार होना	बोर्ड परीक्षा पास आते ही महेश की आँखें खुल गयी।
70.	आँखों से अंगार बरसना	अत्यन्त क्रुद्ध होना	अभिमन्यु की मृत्यु का समाचार सुनकर अर्जुन की आँखों से अंगार बरसने लगे।
71.	आँख डबडबाना	आँसू आना/अत्यधिक भावुक होना	पुत्री की विदाई के समय माँ-बाप की आँखें डबडबा गयीं।
72.	आँखें तरेरना/दिखाना	गुस्सा करना	मुझे देखते ही केशव आँखें तरेरने/दिखाने लगा।
73.	आँखें झपकना	नींद/आलस्य आना	अत्यधिक थकान के कारण मेरी आँख झपक गयीं।
74.	आँखें पथराना	थक जाना	तुम्हारी प्रतीक्षा में मेरी आँखें पथरा गयीं।
75.	आँख फटना	चकित रह जाना	ताजमहल की सुन्दरता को देखकर मेरी आँखें फटी रह गयीं।
76.	आँखें तरसना	देखने की बेताबी	तुमसे मिलने के लिए मेरी आँखें तरसती हैं।
77.	आँखें नीची होना	लज्जित होना	तुम्हारी करतूत से मेरी आँखें नींची हो गयीं।
78.	आँख पर बिठाना	बहुत इज्जत करना	विश्व कप जीतने पर भारतीयों ने पूरी टीम को आँखों पर बिठा लिया।
79.	आँखें प्यासी होना	देखने की प्रबल इच्छा	बेटे के लिए माँ की आँखें प्यासी हो उठीं।
80.	आँख बिछाना	स्वागत करना	बारातियों के लिए लोग आँखें बिछाये खड़े थे।
81.	आँख भर आना	आँशू आना	दुर्घटना में नवजात शिशु की मृत्यु पर लोगों की आँखें भर आयीं।
82.	आँखों में चर्बी छाना	घमण्ड में चूर	तुम अब क्यों पहचानोगे? सरकारी अधिकारी बनने से आँखों पर चर्बी चढ़ गयी है न।
83.	आँखों का पर्दा हटना	ज्ञान होना	तुमसे मिलने के बाद आज मेरी आँखों का पर्दा हट गया।
84.	आँखों के आगे अँधेरा छाना	नि:सार मालूम पड़ना/ किंकर्त्तव्य विमूढ़ होना	फेल होने की खबर सुनकर श्याम की आँखों के आगे अँधेरा छा गया।
85.	आँखें मूँदना	मर जाना	पिता ने आँखें मूंदी और बेटों ने सम्पत्ति का बँटवारा कर लिया।
86.	आँखों से गिरना	आदर भाव घट जाना	राम ने जब से वह कुकर्म किया वह मेरी आँखों से गिर गया।
87.	आँखों का काँटा होना	दुश्मन होना	घनिष्ठ मित्र भी आँखों का काँटा हो सकते हैं।
88.	आँखों में खून उतरना	गुस्से से आँखें लाल हो जाना	उसके अपशब्द सुनते ही मेरी आँखों में खून उतर आया।
89.	आँखों में धूल झोंकना	ठगना/धोखा देना	मुझे तुम्हारी सारी करतूत ज्ञात हो गयी है, मेरी आँख में धूल झोंकने का प्रयत्न मत करों।
90.	आँखों में गड़ना/चुभना	खटकना	उसका बढ़ता हुआ धन पड़ोसी की आँखों में गड़ गया।
91.	आँसू पीकर रह जान	भीतर ही भीतर रोकर चुप कर जाना	गंगाधर की मृत्यु पर लक्ष्मीबाई आँसू पीकर रह गयीं।

92.	आँतें कुलकुलाना/ कुलबुलाना/सूखना	तेज भूख लगना	अरे कुछ खिला दो मेरी आँतें कुलबुला रही हैं।
93.	आँखों-ही-आँखों में	संकेत से	उसने आँखों-ही-आँखों में अपने प्यार का इजहार कर दिया।
94.	आँख आना	आँख दुखना	कीड़े के काटने से मेरी आँख आ गयी।
95.	आँसू पोंछना	हिम्मत बँधाना	पति की मृत्यु से शोकाकुल बहू के आँसू सास ने पोंछे
96.	आकाश के तारे तोड़ना	असंभव कार्य करना	ओलम्पिक में तैराकी में गोल्ड मेडल जीतना भारत के लिए आकाश के तारे तोड़ने जैसा है।
97.	आग पानी में लगाना/ पानी में आग लगाना	शान्त स्थल में झगड़ा शुरू	सुरेश की एक छोटी से बात ने पानी में आग लगा दिया।
98.	आँसुओं का तार न टूटना	बहुत रोना	पुत्र की अकाल मौत हो जाने से पिता के आँसुओं का तार टूट ही नहीं रहा है।
99.	आकाश चूमना	बहुत ऊँचा होना	सचिन ने छक्का मारा तो गेंद आकाश चूमने लगी।
100.	आकश-पाताल का अन्तर	बहुत बड़ा अन्तर	दोनों भाइयों के स्वभाव में आकाश-पाताल का अन्तर है।
101.	आगे-पीछे न होना	कोई न होना	उस बूढ़ी औरत के आगे-पीछे कोई नहीं है।
102.	आकाश-पाताल एक करना	सभी सम्भव प्रयत्न करना	अपनी माँ के इलाज के लिए रमेश ने आकाश-पाताल एक कर दिया।
103.	आग में घी डालना	भड़काना	कुछ लोग जानबूझ कर आग में घी डालने का काम करते हैं।
104.	आग लगाकर तमाशा देखना	झगड़ा लगाकर मजा लेना	बहुत लोगों को आग लगाकर तमाशा देखना अच्छा लगता है।
105.	आग-फूल की मैत्री	दो विपरीत स्वभाव वाले की मैत्री/करना	भारत और पाकिस्तान के बीच सुलह ठीक वैसी ही है जैसे आग-फूल की मैत्री होना।
106.	आग बरसना	लू चलना	पूरे उत्तर भारत में गर्मियों में आग बरसती रहती है।
107.	आग में झोंकना	तकलीफ दे देना	सूद पर पैसा उधार लेने की साह देकर लोगों ने सोहन को आग में झोंक दिया।
108.	आग-बबूला होना	अत्यन्त क्रोधित होना	मेघनाद के वध का समाचार सुनकर रावण आग बबूला हो गया।
109.	आग लगने पर कुआँ खोदना	विपत्ति आने पर बचने का प्रयत्न	कल तुम्हें मुम्बई आना है और आज कह रहे हो कि आरक्षण करवाना है, यह तो वही बात हो गयी कि आग लगने पर कुआँ खोदना।
110.	आग में कूदना	कठिन काम में भाग लेना	हिमालयन कार रैली में भाग लेना मानो आग में कूदने के समान है।
111.	आगे-पीछे करना/फिरना	खुशामद करना	आजकल हर काम के लिए अधिकारियों के आगे-पीछे करना/फिरना पड़ता है।
112.	आटे-दाल की फिक्र करना	जीविका की चिन्ता	चलो अच्छा हुआ कि अब रमेश को आटे-दाल की फिक्र तो हुई।
113.	आड़े हाथों लेना	बहुत लज्जित करना	समय पर कार्य पूरा न करने पर अध्यापक ने छात्र को आड़े हाथों लिया।
114.	आटे-दाल का भाव मालूम होना	व्यावहारिक ज्ञान होना	अब केशव को आटे-दाल का भाव मालूम हो गया।
115.	आटे के साथ घुन पिसना	दोषी के साथ निर्दोश को सजा	इस घोटाले में रमेश को क्यों फसा रहे हो, यह तो आटे के साथ घुन पिसना जैसा है।
116.	आजिज होना	तंग होना	अपने पुत्र की अमर्यादित कृत्यों से उसके पिता आजिज आ गये हैं।
117.	आड़े आना	रूकावट डालना	इस सड़क के बनने में यह नाला आड़े आ रहा है।
118.	आधी बात पेट में रखना	खुलकर न कहना	तुम्हारी तो यही खराब आदत है कि तुम आधी बात पेट में रखते हो।
119.	आपे में आना	होश में आना	बहुत समझाने के बाद रमेश आपे में आया।
120.	आठ-आठ आँसू रोना	बहुत रोना	सारा पैसा चोरी हो जाने के कारण मुकेश आठ-आठ आँसू रोता रहा।
121.	आ धमकना	अचानक आना	सुबह-सुबह मेरे मामा जी मेरे घर आ धमके।

122.	आपे से बाहर होना	क्रोध में अपने वश में न रहना	हमारे अध्यापक जरा-जरा सी बात पर आपे से बाहर हो जाते हैं।
123.	आन पर आना	प्रतिष्ठा का प्रश्न	अब तो यह परीक्षा पास करना मेरी आन पर आ गया है।
124.	आन रखना	प्रतिष्ठा रखना	मेरे आवेदन को स्वीकार करके आपने मेरी आन रख ली।
125.	आफत का मारा	विपत्ति का सताया	राकेश के घर चोरी हुई और फिर दुर्घटना में उसका पैर टूट गया, बेचारा आफत का मारा।
126.	आपस में गाँठ पड़ना	मन-मुटाव होना	एक छोटी सी रकम के लिए दोनों मित्रों में आपस में गाँठ पड़ गयी।
127.	आनाकानी करना	टाल मटोल करना/हिचकिचाना	अभय को कम्प्यूटर सिखाने में केशव आनाकानी कर रहा है।
128.	आवाज उठाना	विरोध करना	भ्रष्टाचार के खिलाफ अन्ना हजारे ने आवाज उठायी।
129.	आस्तीन का साँप	विश्वासघाती मित्र	राजू ने महेश की हमेशा मदद की लेकिन महेश ने राजू के खिलाफ षड्यंत्र करके यह सिद्ध कर दिया किवह आस्तीन का साँप है।
130.	आफत मोल लेना	झगड़ा मोल लेना	राम ने मोहन का विरोध करके आफत मोल ले लिया।
131.	आस टूटना	निराश होना	वर्तमान समय में बहुत से बेरोजगार युवकों को सरकारी नौकरी मिलने की भी आस टूट गयी है।
132.	आसन डोलना	विचलित होना	अन्ना हजारे के भ्रष्टाचार विरोधी आन्दोलन से केन्द्र सरकार का आसन डोल गया।
133.	आसमान टूट पड़ना	अचानक आफत आना	उत्तरकाशी में बादल फटने से मानो वहाँ के लोगों पर आसमान टूट पड़ा।
134.	आसमान सिर पर उठाना	बहुत शोर करना	अध्यापक के कक्षा में न होने पर छात्रों ने आसमान सिर पर उठा लिया।
135.	इन्द्र की परी होना	बहुत सुन्दरी	उसकी पत्नी तो बिल्कुल इन्द्र परी लगती है।
136.	इति होना	खत्म होना	लाला लाजपत राय के निधन होने के साथ ही पंजाब में एक युग की इति हो गयी।
137.	इस कान सुनना, उस कान निकलाना	कोई ध्यान न देना	आजकल छात्र अच्छी बातों को इस कान सुनते हैं, उस कान से निकालत देते हैं।
138.	न इधर का होना न उधर का	कहीं का नहीं	बस से जाने के चक्कर में मनोज ने ट्रेन छोड़ दी, बाद में मालूम हुआ कि बस की हड़ताल है, अब वह इधर का हुआ न उधर का।
139.	इधर-उधर की लगाना	चुगली करना	कुछ लोगों को इधर-उधर की लगाने में बहुत मजा आता है।
140.	ईंट से ईंट बजाना	नाश कर देना	राजपूतों ने युद्ध में मुगलों की ईंट से ईंट बजा दी।
141.	ईमान डिगना	बेईमानी करना	नोटों की गड्डी देखकर थानेदार का ईमान डिगने लगा।
142.	ईंट तक बिकवाना	दरिद्र बना देना	जुए की आदत ने मोहन के घर की ईंट तक बिकवा दी।
143.	ईमान बेचना	बेईमान होना	थोड़े से लाभ के लिए संजय ने अपना ईमान बेच दिया।
144.	अपनी करनी पानी उतरनी	स्वयं का फल भोगना	राकेश ने जैसा काम किया उसे उसके कर्म की सजा मिली।
145.	जैसा करोगे वैसा भरोगे	कर्म के अनुसार फल	राजीव ने जैसा कर्म किया था उसको उसी के अनुसार सजा मिली।
146.	उँगली पकड़कर पहुँचा पकड़ना	थोड़ा-थोड़ा लेकिन पूरा हथियाने की कोशिश करना	आजकल के लोग उँगली पकड़कर पहुँचा पकड़ने की कोशिश करते हैं।
147.	उँगली पर नचाना	वश में रखना	आजकल के नेता अधिकारियों को अपनी उँगलियों पर नचाते हैं।
148.	उछल पड़ना	खुश होना	नौकरी मिलने की खबर सुनते ही रवि उछल पड़ा।
149.	उड़ती खबर	अफवाह	आजकल उड़ती खबरों का बाजार बहुत गर्म है।
150.	उँगली उठाना	कलंकित करना	कोयला घोटाले में बहुत से मंत्रियों एवं अधिकारियों पर उँगली उठगयी।
151.	उल्लू का पट्ठा होना	मूर्ख होना	जब केशव पाँच का पहाड़ा नहीं सुना पाया तो अध्यापक ने कहा कि तुम उल्लू के पट्ठे हो।

152.	उड़न छू होना	लुप्त होना/ भाग जाना	पुलिस को देखते ही चोर उड़न छू हो गया।
153.	उठते-बैठते	हर समय	सन्त पुरूष उठते-बैठते ईश्वर का स्मरण करते हैं।
154.	उतारू होना	पीछे पड़ जाना	सरकार बदलने को लेकर विपक्षी पार्टियाँ उतारू हो गयी हैं।
155.	उन्नीस बीस होना	मामूली-सा अन्तर	राम और श्याम रूप रंग में उन्नीस बीस होंगे।
156.	उबल पड़ना	गुस्सा जाना	अधिकारी जरा सी गलती पर उबल पड़ते हैं।
157.	उल्लू बनाना	बेवकूफ बनाना	मुझे उल्लू बनाने की कोशिश मत करो।
158.	उल्लू सीधा करना	काम बनाना	सोहन ने मोहन से उसकी पुस्तक लेकर अपना उल्लू सीधा कर लिया।
159.	ऊँट का सुई की नोक से निकलना	असम्भव होना	राजू का परीक्षा में पास होना ऊँट का सुई की नोक से निकलना है।
160.	ऊधो का लेना न माधो का देना	किस से कोई सम्बन्ध न रखना	पंडित जी का स्वभाव अच्छा है, उधो का लेना न माधो का देना।
161.	ऊपर की आमदनी	अवैध कमाई	आजकल भ्रष्ट अधिकारी ऊपर की आमदनी पर बहुत जोर देते हैं।
162.	ऊँचा सुनना	बहरा होना	श्याम के कान का परदा क्या फटा, वह ऊँचा सुनने लगा।
163.	ऊल-जलूल बकना	व्यर्थ का बकना	शिव गुस्से में आकर ऊल-जलूल बकने लगता है।
164.	ऋण उतारना	कर्ज मुक्त होना	सन्तोष ने तनख्वाह मिलते ही विकास का ऋण उतार दिया।
165.	एक टाँग पर खड़ा रहना	हमेशा तैयार	विजय किसी की मद्द करने के लिए हमेशा एक टाँग पर खड़ा रहता है।
166.	एक-एक कोना छान मारना	सब जगह खोजना	चोर को पकड़ने के लिए विश्वनाथ ने एक-एक कोना छान मारा।
167.	एक ही भाव तौलना	सबके साथ एक-सा बर्ताव करना	हमें सबको एक ही भाव नहीं तौलना चाहिए।
168.	एक आँख से देखना	सबके समान समझना	माँ-बाप बच्चों को एक आँख से देखते हैं।
169.	एहसान मानना	आभारी होना	हमें दूसरों द्वारा किए गये एहसान को मानना चाहिए।
170.	एक लाठी से सबको हाँकना	समान व्यवहार करना	तुम भ्रष्ट और ईमानदार दोनों को एक लाठी से हाँकते हो, जो उचित नहीं है।
171.	एक हाथ से ताली न बजना	एक तरफ से कुछ न होना	नीरज और विजय के झगड़े को सुनकर कोतवाल ने कहा एक हाथ से ताली नहीं बजती।
172.	एक ही थैली के चट्टे-बट्टे	सभी एक ही प्रकृति के	यह ठग और वह धोखेबाज दोनों एक ही थैली के चट्टे-बट्टे हैं।
173.	एक न चलना	कोई उपाय न चलना	राम-रावण युद्ध में राम के सामने रावण की एक न चली।
174.	एकसान फरामोश होना	कृतघ्न होना	हमें दूसरों द्वारा किए गये एहसान को मानना चाहिए, एहसान फरामोश नहीं होना चाहिए।
175.	एड़ी घिसना	दौड़-धूप करना	बेचारा अरविन्द कई महीनों से नौकरी के लिए एड़ियाँ घिस रहा है।
176.	एड़ी-चोटी का पसीना एक करना	बहुत प्रयास करना	विनोद ने अपनी लड़की के वर की तलाश में एड़ी-चोटी का पसीना एक कर दिया।
177.	ऐंठ-ऐंठ कर रह जाना	मन मसोस कर रहना	परीक्षा छूटने पर विद्यार्थी ऐंठ-ऐंठ कर रह गया।
178.	ऐंठ लेना	धोखे से लेना	दलाल ने ब्रजेश से पैसा ऐंठ लिया।
179.	ऐसी-तैसी करना	इज्जत खराब करना	इस बच्चे को तू रोज चिढ़ाता है। रूक जा मैं तेरी ऐसी-की-तैसी करता हूँ।
180.	ऐसा-वैसा न होना	असाधारण	वह कोई ऐसा-वैसा आदमी नहीं है बल्कि इस क्षेत्र का नेता है।

5 Chapter

लिंग

लिंग

लिंग संस्कृत भाषा का एक शब्द है, जिसका शाब्दिक अर्थ चिह्न या निशान होता है। अर्थात् शब्द (संज्ञा) के जिस रूप से किसी वस्तु की जाति (पुरूष या स्त्री) का बोध हो, उसे लिंग कहा जाता है।

हिन्दी के लिंग दो प्रकार के होते हैं-

लिंग के प्रकार

1. पुल्लिंग
2. स्त्रीलिंग

1. पुल्लिंग (Masculine)

- जिस शब्द के द्वारा किसी विकारी शब्द की पुरूष जाति का बोध होता है, उसे पुल्लिंग कहते हैं, जैसे- सूरज, अध्यापक आदि।
- कुछ शब्द ऐसे हैं, जिनके विषय में सर्वसिद्ध तथ्य यह है कि वे पुल्लिंग बहुवचन ही होते हैं, जैसे- आँसू, दर्शन, प्राण, होश, केश, हस्ताक्षर, समाचार, अक्षत आदि।

2. स्त्रीलिंग (Feminine)

- जिस शब्द के द्वारा किसी विकारी शब्द की स्त्री जाति का बोध होता है। उसे स्त्रीलिंग कहते हैं, जैसे- राधा, अध्यापिका, मेरी आदि।
- भीड़, जाति, सेना, टोली, मंडली, संतान आदि एकवचन स्त्रीलिंग हैं।

लिंग का निर्धारण तीन आधारों पर किया जाता है -

लिंग निर्धारण के आधार

1. रूप के आधार पर
2. प्रयोग के आधार पर
3. अर्थ के आधार पर

- सामान्यतः प्राणिवाचक तथा अप्राणिवाचक शब्दों का लिंग निर्धारण क्रमशः अर्थ एवं रूप के अनुसार किया जाता है, जबकि शेष शब्दों का लिंग निर्धारण केवल व्यवहार के अनुसार किया जाता है।

पुल्लिंग संज्ञा शब्दों की पहचान

प्राणिवात्रक पुल्लिंग संज्ञाएँ : पुरूष, आदमी, मनुष्य, लड़का, शेर, चीता, हाथी, कुत्ता, घोड़ा आदि।

अप्राणिवाचक पुल्लिंग संज्ञाएँ

■ पर्वतों के नाम	हिमालय, विन्ध्याचल, अरावली, कैलाश, आल्प्स आदि।
■ महीनों के नाम	चैत्र, वैशाख, ज्येष्ठ, आषाढ़ आदि।
■ दिन या वार के नाम	सोमवार, मंगलवार, शनिवार आदि।
■ ग्रहों के नाम	सूर्य, चन्द्रमा, मंगल, शुक्र, राहु, केतु, अरूण, वरूण आदि।
अपवाद	पृथ्वी
■ धातुओं के नाम	सोना, सीसा, काँसा, ताँबा, लोहा, राँगा, पीतल, टिन आदि।
अपवाद	चाँदी
■ वृक्षों के नाम	नीम, बरगद, बबूल, आम, पीपल, अशोक, देवदार, चीड़, शीशम, सागौन, कटहल, अमरूद, शरीफा, नींबू, सेब, अखरोट आदि।
अपवाद	इमली, लीची, नाशपाती, नारंगी, खिरनी आदि।
■ अनाज के नाम	चावल, जौ, गेहूँ, बाजरा, चना, मटर आदि।
अपवाद	अरहर, मूँग, खेसारी, मकई, ज्वार इत्यादि।
■ द्रव पदार्थों के नाम	तेल, घी, दूध, शर्बत, मक्खन, पानी, अर्क, इत्र, सिरका, काढ़ा आदि।
अपवाद	लस्सी, चाय, स्याही, शराब आदि।
■ समय सूचक नाम	क्षण, सेकण्ड, मिनट, घण्टा, दिन, सप्ताह, पक्ष, माह आदि।
अपवाद	रात, सायं, सन्ध्या, दोपहर आदि।
■ वर्णमाला के वर्ण	स्वर तथा क से ह तक व्यंजन
अपवाद	इ, ई, ऋ आदि।
■ भौगोलिक क्षेत्रों के नाम	देश, नगर, रेगिस्तान, द्वीप, पर्वत, समुद्र सरोवर, पाताल, वायुमण्डल, प्रान्त आदि।
अपवाद	झील, घाटी आदि।
■ समुद्रों के नाम	हिन्द महासागर, प्रशान्त महासागर आदि।
■ रत्नों के नाम	हीरा, पुखराज, नीलम, पन्ना, मोती, माणिक्य, मूँगा आदि।
अपवाद	मणि, लाड़ली आदि।
■ शरीर के अंगों के नाम	बाल, सिर, मस्तक, तालु, ओंठ, दाँत, मुँह, गाल, नख, रोम, हाथ, पाँव, कान, मुँह आदि।
अपवाद	नाक, आँख, जीभ, कोहनी, कलाई, ठोड़ी, खाल, बाँह, हड्डी, नस, इन्द्रिय, काँख आदि।

अप्राणिवाचक हिन्दी स्त्रीलिंग शब्द

- तिथियों के नाम — प्रथम, एकादशी, अमावस्या, पूर्णिमा
- भाषाओं के नाम — हिन्दी, अंग्रेजी, उर्दू, जापानी, मलयालम।
- लिपियों के नाम — देवनागरी, रोमन, गुरूमुखी, अरबी, फारसी।
- लताओं के नाम — अमर बेल, मालती, तोरई आदि।
- खाने-पीने की वस्तुएँ — पकौड़ी, रोटी, पुरी, कचौड़ी, खीर, दाल, चपाती, सब्जी, तरकारी, खिचड़ी आदि।

  अपवाद — दही, रायता, पराठा, हलवा, भात आदि।
- नक्षत्रों के नाम — भरणी, अश्विनी, रोहिणी आदि।

  अपवाद — अभिजीत, पुष्य आदि।
- नदियों के नाम — गंगा, गोदावरी, यमुना, महानदी, सतलुज, रावी, व्यास, झेलम आदि।

  अपवाद — सिंधु, ब्रह्मपुत्र, सोन नदी आदि।
- मसालों के नाम — लौंग, इलायची, दालचीनी, मिर्च, हल्दी, चिरौंजी, जावित्री, सुपारी, हींग आदि।

  अपवाद — धनिया, जीरा, गरम मसाला, नमक, तेजपत्ता, केसर, कपूर आदि।

रूप के आधार पर लिंग निर्णय

रूप के आधार पर लिंग निर्णय का तात्पर्य शब्द की व्याकरणिक संरचना से है अर्थात् (शब्द की रचना में किन प्रत्ययों का प्रयोग हुआ है तथा शब्द के अन्त में कौन सा स्वर है।

कुछ प्रमुख पुल्लिंग हिन्दी कृदंत-प्रत्यय एवं उनसे निर्मित शब्द

प्रत्यय	निर्मित शब्द	प्रत्यय	निर्मित शब्द
अक्कड़	पियक्कड़	आ	घेरा
आऊ	टिकाऊ	आक	तैराक
आकू	लड़ाकू	आप	मिलाप
आपा	बुढ़ापा	आव	घुमाव
आवना	भावना	आवा	छलावा
इयल	अड़ियल	इया	गुड़िया
एरा	लुटेरा	ऐया	कटैया
ऐत	लड़ैत	औता	समझौता
औना	खिलौना	औवल	बुझौवल
क	चालक	का	छिलका
न	खान-पान	वाला	खानेवाला
वैया	गवैया	सार	मिलनसार
अ	क्रोध	पन	बचपन

भाववाचक संज्ञाएँ - शौर्य, गुरूत्व, गौरव, बुढ़ापा, मोटापा, बचपन, भुलावा, पागलपन आदि।

कुल प्रमुख स्त्रीलिंग हिन्दी कृदंत-प्रत्यय एवं उनसे निर्मित शब्द

प्रत्यय	निर्मित शब्द	प्रत्यय	निर्मित शब्द
अ	लूट	अंत	भिड़ंत
आई	लड़ाई	कावट	लिखवट
आस	प्यास	आहट	घबराहट
ई	हँसी	औती	मनौती
अवनी	छावनी	इ	रीति

इ प्रत्यय का अपवाद - कवि, रवि, कपि

ई प्रत्यय का अपवाद - हाथी, दही, पानी

भाववाचक संज्ञाएँ - मिलावट, घबराहट, सुन्दरता, महिला आदि।

अर्थ के आधार पर लिंग निर्धारण

अर्थ के आधार पर लिंग निर्धारण का तात्पर्य यह है कि, कुछ शब्द अर्थ की दृष्टि से समान होते हुए भी लिंग की दृष्टि से भिन्न होते हैं, जैसे-

पुल्लिंग	स्त्रीलिंग	पुल्लिंग	स्त्रीलिंग
कवि	कवयित्री	वर	वधू
विद्वान	विदुषी	वीर	वीरांगना
मर्द	औरत	साधु	साध्वी
दूल्हा	दुल्हन	नर	नारी
बैल	गाय	राजा	रानी
पुरूष	स्त्री	भाई	भाभी/बहन
बादशाह	बेगम	युवक	युवती
ससुर	सास	पिता	माता

- वाक्य रचना में अधिकतर/ज्यादातर लिंग संबंधी अशुद्धियाँ होती है, जैसे-

  आपकी महान कृपा होगी। (अशुद्ध वाक्य)

  आपकी महती कृपा कृपा होगी (शुद्ध वाक्य)
- प्रत्येक संज्ञा शब्द या तो पुल्लिंग होगा या स्त्रीलिंग क्योंकि बिना लिंग से जुड़े उसका वाक्य में प्रयोग नहीं हो सकता।

प्रयोग के आधार पर लिंग निर्णय

प्रयोग के आधार पर लिंग निर्णय का तात्पर्य संज्ञा शब्द के साथ प्रयुक्त विशेषण, कारक चिह्न एवं क्रिया के आधार लिंग का निर्धारण करना है, जैसे-

वाक्यों में लिंग-निर्णय

वाक्यों में लिंग विशेषण, सर्वनाम, क्रिया और विभक्तियों के विकास में सहायता करता है। इस प्रकार हिन्दी में लिंगों की अभिव्यक्ति वाक्यों में ही होती है और इससे संज्ञा शब्दों का लिंग भेद स्पष्ट होता है, जैसे-

यह बड़ा मकान है। (मकान पुल्लिंग के अनुसार)

यह छोटी लड़की है। (लड़की स्त्रीलिंग के अनुसार)

विशेषण में

हिन्दी व्याकरण में विशेषण का लिंगभेद निम्नलिखित दो नियमों के अनुसार किया जा सकता है–

(i) अकारांत विशेष स्त्रीलिंग में ईकारांत हो जाता है, जैसे- अच्छा–अच्छी, काला–काली

(ii) अकारांत विशेषणों के रूप दोनों लिंगों में समान होते हैं, जैसे- मेरी टोपी गोल है। मेरा कोट सफेद है।

सर्वनाम में

मेरी पुस्तक अच्छी है। (पुस्तक स्त्रीलिंग के अनुसार)

मेरा घर बड़ा है। (घर पुल्लिंग के अनुसार)

क्रिया

बुढ़ापा आ गया। (बुढ़ापा पुल्लिंग के अनुसार)

सहायता मिली है। (सहायता स्त्रीलिंग के अनुसार)

विभक्ति में

सम्बंध - गुलाब का रंग लाल है। (रंग पुल्लिंग के अनुसार)

आपकी नाक कट गई है। (नाक स्त्रीलिंग के अनुसार)

विशेष

- तारा, देवता, व्यक्ति आदि शब्द संस्कृत में स्त्रीलिंग किन्तु हिन्दी में पुल्लिंग है।
- आत्मा, बूंद, देह, बाहु आदि शब्द संस्कृत में पुल्लिंग किन्तु हिन्दी में में स्त्रीलिंग है।
- संस्कृत के तत्सम होते हुए भी इमा प्रत्यांतक शब्द जैसे- महिमा, गरिमा, लघिमा, सीमा आदि संस्कृत में पुल्लिंग किन्तु हिन्दी में स्त्रीलिंग है।
- जय, विजय, पराजय आदि अ प्रत्यान्तक शब्द संस्कृत में पुल्लिंग किन्तु हिन्दी में स्त्रीलिंग है।
- कृत और तद्धित प्रत्ययों से बने विशेषण या कर्ता वाच्य शब्द स्त्रीलिंग या पुल्लिंग शब्द के साथ यथावत् ही प्रयुक्त होते है; जैसे–

आकर्षक	दृश्य या घटना	दिव्यमान	प्रकाश या ज्योति
परिचित	पुरूष या महिला	धर्मिक	संगठन या संस्था
धर्मज्ञ	पुरूष या नारी		

- सर्वनामों का लिंग उनकी संज्ञा के अनुसार ही होता है; जैसे- सीता को देखा, वह रोज स्कूल जाती है।

  (वह सीता के अनुसार स्त्रीलिंग है।)

  राम को देखो, वह रोज स्कूल नहीं जाता है।

  (वह राम के अनुसार पुल्लिंग है।)
- मंत्री, राष्ट्रपति, सेनाध्यक्ष, मुखिया, सरपंच, प्रमुख, आरक्षी, दरोगा, एस.पी., आयुक्त प्रबंध्क, पदाध्किारी, किरानी आदि पदवाचकता के लिए रूढ़ शब्दों का स्त्रीलिंग रूप संभव नहीं होता है। इनमें पूर्व में माननीया या बाद में महोदया लगाकर स्त्रीलिंग बनना पड़ता है।
- सामाजिक शब्दों का लिंग बाद बाले पद के अनुसार होता है; जैसे- गायघाट, राजपुत्री

पुल्लिंग से स्त्रीलिंग बनाने के प्रमुख नियम

शब्दान्त अ को आ में बदलकर

पुल्लिंग	स्त्रीलिंग	पुल्लिंग	स्त्रीलिंग
छात्रा	छात्रा	पूज्य	पूज्या
सूत	सूता	वृद्ध	वृद्धा
भवदीय	भवदीया	अनुज	अनुजा

शब्दान्त अ को ई में बदलकर

पुल्लिंग	स्त्रीलिंग	पुल्लिंग	स्त्रीलिंग
देव	देवी	पुत्रा	पुत्राी
गोप	गोपी	ब्राह्मण	ब्राह्मणी
मेढ़क	मेढ़की	दास	दासी
हरिण	हरिणी	देव	देवी
पहाड़	पहाड़ी	नर्तक	नर्तकी

शब्दान्त आ को ई में बदलकर

पुल्लिंग	स्त्रीलिंग	पुल्लिंग	स्त्रीलिंग
नाना	नानी	लड़का	लडकी
घोड़ा	घोड़ी	बेटा	बेटी
रस्सा	रस्सी	चाचा	चाची

आ अंत वाले शब्दों में आ का लोप हो जाता है और उनके स्थान पर ई प्रत्यय लग जाता है।

शब्दान्त आ को इया में बदलकर

पुल्लिंग	स्त्रीलिंग	पुल्लिंग	स्त्रीलिंग
बूढ़ा	बुढ़िया	चूहा	चुहिया
कुत्ता	कुतिया	डिब्बा	डिबिया
बेटा	बिटिया	लोटा	लुटिया

शब्दान्त प्रत्यय अक को इका में बदलकर

पुल्लिंग	स्त्रीलिंग	पुल्लिंग	स्त्रीलिंग
बालक	बालिका	लेखक	लेखिका
नायक	नायिका	पाठक	पाठिका
गायक	गायिका	विधयक	विधयिका

शब्दान्त में आनी प्रत्यय लगाकर

पुल्लिंग	स्त्रीलिंग	पुल्लिंग	स्त्रीलिंग
देवर	देवरानी	चौध्री	चौधरानी
सेठ	सेठानी	भव	भवानी

शब्दान्त में नी प्रत्यय लगाकर

पुल्लिंग	स्त्रीलिंग	पुल्लिंग	स्त्रीलिंग
शेर	शेरनी	मोर	मोरनी
जाट	जाटनी	सिंह	सिंहनी

शब्दान्त में ई के स्थान पर इनी लगाकर

पुल्लिंग	स्त्रीलिंग	पुल्लिंग	स्त्रीलिंग
हाथी	हथिनी	तपस्वी	तपस्विनी
स्वामी	स्वामिनी	हंस	हंसिनी

शब्दान्त में इन प्रत्यय लगाकर

पुल्लिंग	स्त्रीलिंग	पुल्लिंग	स्त्रीलिंग
माली	मालिन	कहार	कहारिन
धेबी	धेबिन	नाई	नाइन

शब्दान्त में आइन प्रत्यय लगाकर

पुल्लिंग	स्त्रीलिंग	पुल्लिंग	स्त्रीलिंग
चौध्री	चौध्राइन	ठाकुर	ठकुराइन
पंडित	पंडिताइन	मुंशी	मुंशियाइन

शब्दान्त वान के स्थान पर वती लगाकर

पुल्लिंग	स्त्रीलिंग	पुल्लिंग	स्त्रीलिंग
गुणवान	गुणवती	पुत्रावान	पुत्रावती
भगवान	भगवती	बलवान	बलवती
भाग्यवान	भाग्यवती	सत्यवान	सत्यवती

शब्दान्त मान के स्थान पर मती लगाकर

पुल्लिंग	स्त्रीलिंग	पुल्लिंग	स्त्रीलिंग
श्रीमान	श्रीमती	बुद्धिमान	बुद्धिमती
आयुष्मान	आयुष्मती	शक्तिमान	शक्तिमती

शब्दान्त ता के स्थान पर त्री लगाकर

पुल्लिंग	स्त्रीलिंग	पुल्लिंग	स्त्रीलिंग
कर्त्ता	कर्त्री	नेता	नेत्री
दाता	दात्री	विधती	विधत्री

शब्द के पूर्व में मादा शब्द लगाकर

पुल्लिंग	स्त्रीलिंग	पुल्लिंग	स्त्रीलिंग
खरगोश	मादा खरगोश	भेड़िया	मादा भेड़िया
भालू	मादा भालू	गैंडा	मादा गैंडा

शब्द के पूर्व में नर शब्द लगाकर

पुल्लिंग	स्त्रीलिंग	पुल्लिंग	स्त्रीलिंग
नर मक्खी	मक्खी	नर चील	चील
नर कोयल	कोयल	नर छिपकली	छिपकली

- जिस अकारांत अथवा अकारांत संज्ञा का बहुवचन बनाने में कोई विकार उत्पन्न नहीं होता है, वह पुल्लिंग और जिस संज्ञा का बहुवचन बनाने में विकार (एँ, याँ) होता हो वह स्त्राीलिंग है। यह नियम अप्राणिवाचक तत्सम् व तद्भव संज्ञाओं पर लागू होता है, जैसे–

  भवन (पुल्लिंग) इमारत (स्त्राीलिंग)
  बात (स्त्राीलिंग) वचन (पुल्लिंग)

हिन्दी के उभयलिंगी शब्द

हिन्दी के कुछ ऐसे शब्द होते हैं, जो स्त्राीलिंग और पुल्लिंग दोनों में समान रूप से प्रयुक्त होते हैं। परन्तु अर्थ के अनुसार इनका लिंग बदल जाता है, जैसे–

प्रमुख उभयलिंगी शब्द

शब्द	अर्थ	
	पुल्लिंग	**स्त्राीलिंग**
यति	संन्यासी	विराम
टीका	तिलक, भेंट	टिप्पणी, अर्थ
कल	आगामी दिन	चैन, आराम
कोटि	करोड़	श्रेणी
पीठ	पीढ़ा, स्थान	पृष्ठ भाग
विध्ि	ब्रह्मा	ढंग, प्रणाली
बाट	बटखरा	मार्ग, इन्तजार
शान	औजार तेज करने का पत्थर	काट–बाट, प्रभुत्व
दाद	चर्मरोग	प्रशंसा
ताक	ताखा	खोज, टोह
धूप	सुगन्ध्ति धुआँ	सूर्य का प्रकाश
हार	माला	पराजय
शाल	वृक्ष विशेष	दुशाला
काँच	शीशा	धेती का छोर, गुदा–अंग।
कुशल	प्रवीण	खैरियत
खराद	खरादने का यंत्रा	खरादने की क्रिया

6

Chapter

पर्यायवाची शब्द

पूर्ण पर्यायवायी पूर्णापूर्ण

अपूर्ण

पर्याय का अर्थ 'सामान' और पर्यायवादी शब्द से आशय है- समान अर्थ वाला शब्द। अर्थात् ये वे शब्द होते हैं, जो एक समान अर्थ को बोध कराते हैं, उन्हें पर्यायवाची शब्द कहते हैं। इन्हें मुख्यत: तीन भागों में बाँटा गया है।

पूर्ण पर्यायवाची- ये वे शब्द हैं, जो मूल शब्द का अर्थ ही प्रतीत कराते हैं, उन्हें पूर्ण पर्यायवाची शब्द कहते हैं। जैसे-

जल - पानी

दुग्ध - दूध

अंधकार - अंधेरा

आँख - नेत्र

अपूर्ण पर्यायवाची- ये वे शब्द हैं जो पूर्ण अर्थ का बोध नहीं कराते हैं, उन्हें अपूर्ण पर्यायवाची कहते हैं।

जल - जीवन, अमृत

चोर - साहसी

अंक - गोद

पूर्णापूर्ण पर्यायवाची- ये वे शब्द हैं जो एक परिस्थिति में तो पूर्ण होते हैं, किन्तु दूसरी परिस्थिति में अपूर्ण होते हैं, उन्हें पूर्णापूर्ण पर्यायवायी कहते हैं।

जैसे- टांगना-लटकाना - पर्यायवाची है।

मेरी शर्ट को टांग दो के स्थान पर मेरी शर्ट को लटका दो, यह परिस्थिति पूर्णता का बोध करा रही है और वह मुँह लटकाएँ बैठा है के स्थान पर मुँह टांगे बैठा है, यह अपूर्ण परिस्थिति का बोध करा रही है।

शब्द : पर्यायवाची

अग्नि : आग, वह्नि, पावक, अनल, वायुसखा, दहन, धूमकेतु, कृशानु।

असुर : दनुज, दानव, दैत्य, राक्षस, यातुधान निशाचर, रजनीचर, तमचर।

अनुपम : अपूर्व, अनोखा, अदभुत, अनूठा, अद्वितीय, अतुल।

अमृत : पीयूष, सुधा, अमिय, जीवनोदक

अश्व : वाजि, हय, घोटक, घोड़ा, सैन्धव, तुरग, तुरंग।

आँख : नेत्र, लोचन, नयन, चक्षु, दृग, अक्षि, दृष्टि, विलोचन।

आकारश : द्यौ, व्योम, गगन, अभ्र, अम्बर, नभ, अन्तरिक्ष, आसमान, अनन्त।

आम : आम्र, रसाल, अमृतफल, सहकार, अतिसौरभ च्यूत (आम का पेड़)।

आनन्द : मोद, प्रमोद, हर्ष, आमोद, सुख, प्रसन्नता, आहलाद, उल्लास।

आश्रम : मठ, विहार, कुटी, स्तर, अखाड़ा, संघ।

इच्छा : आकांक्षा, अभिलाषा, चाह, कामना, मनोरथ, स्पृहा, वांछा।

इन्द्र : सुरपति, मधवा, पुरन्दर, वासव, महेन्द्र, देवराज।

कपड़ा : वस्त्र, पट, सन, अम्बर, चीर।

कमल : सरोज, जलज, अब्ज पंकज, अरविन्द, पदम, कंज, शतदल, अम्बुज, सरजित, नलिन, तामरस।

किरण : मरीचि, मयूरख, अंशु, कर, रश्मि, प्रभा, अर्चि, गो।

कुबेर : कित्ररेश, यक्षराज, धनद, धनाधिप, राजराज।

गणेश : लम्बोदर, एकदंत, मूषकवाहन, गजवंदन, गजानन, विनायक, गणपति, विघ्नराज, मोदकप्रिय मोददाता।

गंगा : जाह्नवी, देवनदी, सुरसरिता, भागीरथी, मन्दाकिनी, देवपगा, ध्रुवनन्दा।

गेह : घर, निकेतन, भवन, सदन, आगार, आयतन, आवास, निलय, धाम, गृह।

गदहा : खर, गर्दभ, धूसर, रासभ, बेशर, चक्रीवान, वैशाखनन्दन।

चन्द्र : चांद, चन्द्रमा, हिमांशु, सुधांशु, सुधाकर, सुधाकर राकेश, शशि, सारंग, निशाकर, निशापति, रजनीपति, मृगांक, कलानिधि।

चोर : तसकर, दस्यु, रजनीचर, मोषक, कुम्भिक, खनक, साहसिक।

जल : नीर, सलिल, उदक, पानी, अम्बु, तोय, जीवन, वारि, पय, अमृत, मेघपुष्प।

यमुना : सूर्यसुता, सूर्यतनया, कालिन्दी, अर्कजा, कृष्णा।

तालाब : सर, सरोवर, तड़ाग, ह्रद, पुष्कर, जलाशय।

दास : अनुचर, चाकर, सेवक, नौकर, भृत्य, किंकर, परिचारक।

दु:ख : पीड़ा, व्यथा, कष्ट, संकट, शोक, क्लेश, वेदना, यातना, यन्त्रणा, खेद।

देवता : सुर, अमर, देव, विबुध, त्रिदश, आदित्य, गीर्वाण।

द्रव्य : धन, वित्त, सम्पदा, विभूति, दौलत, सम्पत्ति।

नदी : सरिता, तटिनी, अपगा, निम्नगा, निर्झरिणी, कूलंकषा, तरंगिणी।

नौका : नाव, तरिणी, जलयान, जलपात्र, तरी, बेड़ा, डांगी, पतंग।

पत्नी : भार्या, दारा, गृहणी, बहू, वधू, कलत्र, प्राणप्रिय, अर्धांगिनी।

पति : भर्ता, वल्लभ, स्वामी, आर्यपुत्र।

हवा : वायु, समीर, मरूत, वात, बयार, प्रकम्पन, समीरण, पवन।

पर्यायवाची शब्द

पक्षी : विहंग, विहग, खग, पक्षरू, परिन्दा, चिड़िया, शकुन्त, अण्डज, पतंग, द्विज।

पर्वत : मधुर शैल, अचल, महीधर, गिरी, नग, भूमिधर, तुग, अद्रि, पहाड़।

पण्डित : सधी, विद्वान, कोविद, बुध, धरीर, मनीषी, प्राज्ञ, विचक्षण।

पुत्र : तनय, सुत, बेटा, लड़का, आत्मज, तनुज।

पुत्री : तनया, सुता, बेटी, लड़की, आत्मजा, तनुजा।

पृथ्वी : भू, इला, भूमि, धरा, उर्वी, धरती, धरित्री, धरणी, वसुधा, वसुंधरा।

पुष्प : फूल, सुमन, कुसुम, प्रसून।

बाण : तीर, शर, विशिख, आशुग, शिलीमुख, इषु, नाराच।

बिजली : चंचला, चपला, विद्युत, सौदामनी, दामिनी, तड़ित, बीजुरी, क्षणप्रभा।

ब्रह्मा : आत्मभू, स्वयम्भू, चतुरानन, पितामह, हिरण्यगर्भ, लोकेश, विधि, विधाता।

वृक्ष : तरू, उद्रम, पादप, विटप, अगम, पेड़, गाछ।

मछली : मत्स्य, झाख, मीन, जलजीवनी, सफरी, झष, अंडज, शकुची।

महादेव : शम्भु, ईश, पशुपति, शिव, महेश्वर, शंकर, चन्द्रशेखर, भव, भूतेश, गिरीश, हर, त्रिलोचन।

मेघ : घन, जलधर, वारिद, बादल, नीरद, वारिधर, पयोद, अम्बुद, पयोधर।

मुनि : यती, अवधूत, संन्यासी, वैरागी, तापस, सन्त, भिक्षु, महात्मा, साधु मुक्तपुरूष।

रात्रि : शर्वरी, निशा, रात, रैन, रजनी, यामिनी, त्रियामा, विभावरी, क्षणदा।

राजा : नृप, भूप, महीप, महीपति, परमपति, नरेश, भूपति, राव, सम्राट।

विष्णु : गरूड़ध्वज, अच्युत, जनार्दन, चक्रपाणि, विश्वम्भर, मुकुन्द, नारायण, रिषीकेष, दामोदर, केशव, माधव, गोविन्द, लक्ष्मीपति, विभु, विश्वरूप।

समुद्र : सागर, जलधि, परावार, सिन्धु, नीरनिधि, नदीश, पयोधि, अर्णव, पयोनिधि, रत्नाकर, अब्धि, वारीश, जलधाम, नीरधि।

समूह : समुदाय, वृन्द, गण, संघ, पुंज, दल, झुण्ड, मण्डली, टोली, जत्था।

सरस्वती : ब्राह्मी, भारती, भाषा, वाक्, गिरा, शारदा, वीणापाणि, वागीशा।

सर्प : अहि, भुजंग, विषधर, व्याल, फणी, उरग, पत्रग, नाग, सांप।

सोना : सुवर्ण, स्वण, कंचन, हाटक, कनक, हिरण्य, हेम, जातरूप।

सूर्य : मार्तण्ड, दिनकर, रवि, भास्कर, मरीची, प्रभाकर, सविता, पतंग, दिवाकर, हंस, आदित्य, भानु, अंशुमाली।

सिंह : शार्दूल, व्याघ्र, पंचमुख, मृगराज, मृगेन्द्र, केशरी, केहरी, केशी, महावीर।

सुन्दर : रूचिर, चारू, रम्य, सुहावना, मनोहर, रमणीक, चिताकर्षक, ललित।

स्त्री : नारी, वनिता, महिला, कान्ता, रमणी।

अचल : पर्वत, भूधर, महीधर, नग, अद्रि।

अभिजात : कुलीन, श्रेष्ठ, आर्य

अभिप्राय : अर्थ, तात्पर्य, आशय, मतलब, मायने

अंधकार : तम, तिमिर, अंधेरा, अधियास, तमिस्त

कामदेव : अनंग, मन्मय, काम, पंचशर, अतनु, मनोज, मीनकेतु, रतिपति, कंदर्प।

कृष्ण : मुकुन्द, ब्रजवल्लभ, हृषीकेश, बनमाली, क्षीरसायी, गोपीनाथ, बनवारी, नंदनंदन, मुरलीधर, गिरिधर, दामोदर।

किसान : कृषक, हलधर

कारागार : बन्दीगृह, कारावास, कैदखाना, जेल

किनारा : पुलिन, छोर, सिरा, तीर, तट, पर्यंत, बेलातट

जीव : प्राणी, प्राण, चैतन्य, जान, जीवन

तलवार : चंद्रहास, कृपाण, खड्ग, करवाल, असि

तरूणी : यौवनवती, मनोज्ञा, रमणी, सुन्दरी, प्रमदा,

दिनांक : तारीख, तिथि, मिति

दूध : क्षीर, दुग्ध, अमृत, पयस्तन्य, पीयूष

दिन : दिवस, वासर, वार, हसन

निशा : रात, रात्रि, रजनी, तिशि, विभावरी, क्षपा

नरक : यमपुर, यमलोक, दुर्गति, जहन्नुम, यमालय, दो जख।

पथ : राह, मगर, रास्ता, मार्ग, पंथ

पण्डित : सुधी, विद्वान, कोविद, बुध, धीर, मनीषी

परिवर्तन : फेर-बदल, तबदीली, हेर-फेर, अदल-बदल

पवन : अनिल, वायु, वात, मारूत, समीरन, समरण, बयार

बसन्त : कुसुमार, माधव, मधुमास, ऋतुराज

बन्दर : मर्कट, हरि, शाखामृग, कपि, वानर, कीश, कपीश

मछली : मत्स्य, झाख मीन, जलजीवन, सफरी

मोर : ध्वजी, कलापी, मयूर, सिखी, नीलकंठ, शिखंडी, सारंग

मित्र : सहचर, सगी, साथी, दोस्त, मीत, सपक्ष

सोना : सुवर्ण, स्वर्ण, कंचन, हाटक, कनक, हिरण्य, हेम, जातरूप

स्त्री : नारी, वनिता, महिला, कान्ता, रमणी, प्रिया, अबला, भार्या

सुन्दर : रूचिर, चारू, रम्य, सुहावना, मनोहर, रमणीक, चित्ताकर्षक, ललित, मनोज, मनभावन

हाथी : गयंद, कुंभी, सिंधुर, कटी, मतंग, गज, कुंजर, गजेन्द्र।

7 Chapter सामान्य अशुद्धियाँ

■ वर्तनी- लिखने की विधि/रीति को वर्तनी या अक्षरी कहते है। किसी भी भाषा को तब तक समग्र रूप से शुद्ध नहीं की जा सकती जब तक कि उसकी वर्तनी में शुद्धता का अभाव हो, जिस शब्द में जितने वर्ण या अक्षर जिस अनुक्रम में प्रयुक्त होते हैं, उन्हें उसी क्रम में लिखना ही वर्त्तनी है। वर्तनी को उर्दू में ''हिज्जे'' और अंग्रेजी में (Spelling) कहा जाता है।

■ वर्तनी का सीधा संबंध उच्चारण (Pronunciation) प्रॉनॉनसिएसन से होता है। यदि किसी शब्द का उच्चारण अशुद्ध होगा तो वर्तनी भी अशुद्ध होगी। अधिकांशत: अपनी मातृभाषा या बोली की वजह से व्याकरण संबंधी ज्ञान के अभाव के कारण उच्चारण में अशुद्धियाँ आ जाती है। जिसके कारण वर्तनी में अशुद्धियाँ आ जाती है।

■ उच्चारण संबंधी अशुद्धियाँ की निम्नलिखित तालिका दिये जा रहे है–

स्वर संबंधी अशुद्धियाँ

'अ' 'आ' संबंधी अशुद्धियाँ

अशुद्ध	शुद्ध	अशुद्ध	शुद्ध
आशीर्वाद	आशीर्वाद	अहार	आहार
अनाधिकार	अनधिकार	आजकाल	आजकल
आधीन	अधीन	अविष्कार	आविष्कार
अवाज	आवाज	अलपीन	आलपीन
अर्यावर्त	आर्यावर्त	अन्त्यक्षरी	अन्त्याक्षरी
अगामी	आगामी	अत्याधिक	अत्यधिक
अतेव	अतएव	अनाथिनी	अनाथा
अत्योक्ति	अत्युक्ति	अन्तरप्रान्तीय	अन्त:प्रान्तीय
अनाधिकार	अनधिकार	अन्तसक्षि	अन्त:साक्ष्य

'इ' 'ई' संबंधी अशुद्धियाँ

अशुद्ध	शुद्ध	अशुद्ध	शुद्ध
पिढ़ी	पीढ़ी	पत्नि	पत्नी
दिपिका	दीपिका	निरसता	नीरसता
निरिक्षण	निरीक्षण	दिवाली	दीवाली
तुलसिदास	तुलसीदास	तिर्थ	तीर्थ
इसाई	ईसाई	इश्वर	ईश्वर
इद	ईद	नीती	नीति
गीनना	गिनना	क्षत्रीय	क्षत्रिय
कोटी	कोटि	कुटीया	कुटिया
किर्ति	कीर्ति	पिताम्बर	पीताम्बर
अतिथी	अतिथि	अभीनेता	अभिनेता
अभीमान	अभिमान	आखीर	आखिर
ईजन	इंजन	कालीदास	कालिदास
हिंग	हींग	परीचय	परिचय
परिणती	परिणति	अभीमान	अभिमान
परीवार	परिवार	पाकीस्तान	पाकिस्तान
पुष्टी	पुष्टि	वाल्मीकी	वाल्मीकि
मती	मति	शनी	शनि
हानी	हानि		

'उ', 'ऊ' संबंधी अशुद्धियाँ

अशुद्ध	शुद्ध	अशुद्ध	शुद्ध
गुरू	गुरू	ऊत्थान	उत्थान
अरूण	अरूण	दुसरा	दूसरा
तुफान	तूफान	जरूरत	जरूरत
उष्मा	ऊष्मा	उधम	ऊधम
अनुदित	अनूदित	सिन्दुर	सिन्दूर
नेहरू	नेहरू	नुपुर	नूपुर
रूई	रूई		

'उ' 'ऊ' संबंधी अशुद्धियाँ

अशुद्ध	शुद्ध	अशुद्ध	शुद्ध
दूबारा	दुबारा	साधू	साधु
रूपया	रूपया	सुई	सूई
वधु	वधू		

'ऋ' संबंधी अशुद्धियाँ

अशुद्ध	शुद्ध	अशुद्ध	शुद्ध
बृटिश	ब्रिटिश	रितु	ऋतु
रिणी	ऋणी	रिगवेद	ऋग्वेद
रिधि	ऋद्धि	संग्रहित	संगृहीत
उरिण	उऋण	त्रितीय	तृतीय
तृकोण	त्रिकोण	पैत्रिक	पैतृक

'ए' 'ऐ' संबंधी अशुद्धियाँ :

अशुद्ध	शुद्ध	अशुद्ध	शुद्ध
एक्ट	ऐक्ट	केंटीन	कैंटीन
केबिनेट	कैबिनेट	वेश्य	वैश्य
मटमेले	मटमैले	मेनेजर	मैनेजर
टेक्स	टैक्स	चाहिऐ	चाहिए
देहिक	दैहिक	भाषाऐं	भाषाएँ
योग्यताऐं	योग्ताएं	वैश्या	वेश्या

'ओ' 'औ' संबंधी अशुद्धियाँ :

अशुद्ध	शुद्ध	अशुद्ध	शुद्ध
अक्षोहिणी	अक्षौहिणी	अलोकिक	अलौकिक
ओद्योगिक	औद्योगिक	ओरत	औरत
गोतम	गौतम	झौंपड़ी	झोंपड़ी
त्यौहार	त्योहार	गोरव	गौरव
नोकरी	नौकरी	पारलोकिक	पारलौकिक
पोरूष	पौरूष	प्रोढ़	प्रौढ़
न्यौछावर	न्योछावर	दौना	दोना
लौहार	लोहार		

अनुस्वार (ं) चन्द्र बिन्दु (ँ) संबंधी अशुद्धियां :

अशुद्ध	शुद्ध	अशुद्ध	शुद्ध
आंख	आँख	उंगली	उँगली
ऊंचा	ऊँचा	उंघना	उँघना
कांपना	काँपना	गूंगा	गूँगा
छांह	छाँह	झांसी	झाँसी
टांगना	टाँगना	दांत	दाँत
पांख	पाँख	बांध	बाँध
बांझ	बाँझ	बांह	बाँह
झूंकना	झूँकना	महंगा	महँगा
मुंह	मुँह	सांझ	साँझ

विसर्ग (:) संबंधी अशुद्धियाँ :

अशुद्ध	शुद्ध	अशुद्ध	शुद्ध
दुश्शील	दु:शील	दुख	दु:ख
निशुल्क	नि:शुल्क	निस्वार्थ	नि:स्वार्थ
प्रातकाल	प्रात:काल	प्राय	प्राय:
मनस्थिति	मन: स्थिति		

व्यंजन संबंधी अशुद्धियाँ :

'छ' 'क्ष' संबंधी अशुद्धियाँ

अशुद्ध	शुद्ध	अशुद्ध	शुद्ध
अकांछा	आकांक्षा	छत्रिय	क्षत्रिय
छन	क्षण	छमा	क्षमा
छय	क्षय	छीण	क्षीण
छोभ	क्षोभ	नछत्र	नक्षत्र
प्रछेंपास्त्र	प्रक्षेपास्त्र	रच्छा	रक्षा
लछमन	लक्ष्मण	संछेप	संक्षेप

'ज' 'य' संबंधी अशुद्धियाँ

अशुद्ध	शुद्ध	अशुद्ध	शुद्ध
अजोधा	अयोध्या	जदि	यदि
जम	यम	जमुना	यमुना
जाचना	याचना	जुवती	युवती
जोग	योग		

'ट' 'ठ' संबंधी अशुद्धियाँ

अशुद्ध	शुद्ध	अशुद्ध	शुद्ध
कनिष्ट	कनिष्ठ	कुष्ट	कुष्ठ
गरिष्ट	गरिष्ठ	गोष्टि	गोष्ठी
घनिष्ट	घनिष्ठ	मिष्ठान्न	मिष्टान्न
यथेष्ट	यथेष्ठ	विशिष्ठ	विशिष्ट
संतुष्ठ	संतुष्ट	षष्ठि	षष्टि
निष्टा	निष्ठा	पृष्ट	पृष्ठ
वरिष्ट	वरिष्ठ	श्रेष्ट	श्रेष्ठ
अंत्येष्ठि	अंत्येष्टि	अभीष्ठ	अभीष्ट
इकट्टा	इकट्ठा	इष्ठ	इष्ट
चेष्ठा	चेष्टा	परिशिष्ठ	परिशिष्ट
प्रविष्ठ	प्रविष्ट		

'ड', 'ड़', 'ढ', 'ढ़' संबंधी अशुद्धियाँ

अशुद्ध	शुद्ध	अशुद्ध	शुद्ध
कन्नड	कन्नड़	क्रीडा	क्रीड़ा
घोड़ा	घोड़ा	झाडू	झाड़ू
लुड़कना	लुढ़कना	सीड़ियां	सीढ़ियां
पढता	पढ़ता	ढ़कना	ढ़कना
ढ़ेर	ढेर	पडता	पड़ता
पेड	पेड़	लडका	लड़का
रोड़	रोड	षड्यंत्र	षड्यंत्र
बूढ़ा	बूढ़ा	मेढ़क	मेढक

'ण' 'न' संबंधी अशुद्धियाँ

अशुद्ध	शुद्ध	अशुद्ध	शुद्ध
अर्चणा	अर्चना	खाणा	खाना
प्रार्थणा	प्रार्थना	कल्यान	कल्याण
कृष्न	कृष्ण	फागुण	फागुन
रसायण	रसायन	प्रणाली	प्रणाली
मरन	मरण	रमन	रमण
विस्मरन	विस्मरण	वीना	वीणा
श्रवन	श्रवण		

'ब' 'ब' संबंधी अशुद्धियाँ

ब, ब संबंधी वर्णो के सही उच्चारण के अभाव में अक्सर लेखन में अशुद्धियाँ आ जाया करती है यथा–

अशुद्ध	शुद्ध	अशुद्ध	शुद्ध
नबाव	नवाब	पूर्ब	पूर्व
ब्यथा	व्यथा	ब्यय	व्यय
बनस्पति	वनस्पति	कामयावी	कामयाबी
ब्रत	व्रत	दबदवा	दबदबा
बिख्यात	विख्यात	बिद्वान	विद्वान
बिकट	विकट	बिभीषण	विभीषण
बीबी	बीवी	बृष्टि	वृष्टि
बैदेही	वैदेही	धोवी	धोबी
बल्व	बल्ब	बिष	विष
बिधि	विधि		

पंचमाक्षर (ङ ञ ण न म) संबंधी अशुद्धियाँ सर्वाधिक लेखन में हुआ करती यथा–

अशुद्ध	शुद्ध	अशुद्ध	शुद्ध
अन्ग	अग्ङ/अंग	अनगिनन्त	अनगिनत
कन्ठ	कण्ठ	कुन्डली	कुण्डली
घन्टे	घण्टे	चन्चल	चंचल
झन्डा	झण्डा	दन्ड	दण्ड
न्यून्ता	न्यूनता	पन्खा	पंखा
पन्क	पंक	पन्डित	पण्डित

'य' से संबंधी अशुद्धियाँ हिन्दी लेखन में अक्सर हो जाती है। यथा–

अशुद्ध	शुद्ध	अशुद्ध	शुद्ध
अंताक्षरी	अंत्याक्षरी	केन्द्रीयकरण	केन्द्रीकरण
कृत्यकृत्य	कृतकृत्य	अंतर्ध्यान	अंतर्धान
कवित्री	कवयित्री	मानवर	मान्यवर
गृहस्थ्य	गृहस्थ	मूलतय:	मूलत:
सदृश्य	सदृश	स्वास्थ	स्वास्थ्य
सामर्थ	सामर्थ्य		

'र' 'ड़' संबंधी अशुद्धियाँ

अशुद्ध	शुद्ध	अशुद्ध	शुद्ध
किवार	किवाड़	उमरना	उमड़ना
करोर	करोड़	कराही	कड़ाही
कीचर	कीचड़	घबड़ाना	घबराना
टोकड़ी	टोकरी	बृज	ब्रज
मात्रिभूमि	मातृभूमि	मिरच	मिर्च
रामचन्दर	रामचंद्र	पापर	पापड़
पीरा	पीड़ा	पेरा	पेड़ा
भेर	भेड़	भेरिया	भेड़िया
पिंजड़ा	पिंजरा	करमनासा	कर्मनाशा
परयाग	प्रयाग	प्रन्तु	परन्तु
परत्येक	प्रत्येक		

'श' 'ष' 'स' संबंधी अशुद्धियाँ

अशुद्ध	शुद्ध	अशुद्ध	शुद्ध
उत्कर्श	उत्कर्ष	दुश्कर्म	दुष्कर्म
निश्फल	निष्फल	परिभाशा	परिभाषा
कैलाश	कैलास	तपश्या	तपस्या
पुरश्कार	पुरस्कार	प्रशाद	प्रसाद
वेषभूषा	वेशभूषा	कष्टम	कस्टम
प्रशंषा	प्रशंसा	विवस	विवश
विस्वास	विश्वास	स्रवण	श्रवण
संसोधित	संशोधित	समसान	श्मशान
साबास	शाबाश	सूर्पणखा	शूर्पणखा
सोचनीय	शोचनीय	अभिसेक	अभिषेक
आविस्कार	आविष्कार	दुस्कर	दुष्कर
निसाद	निषाद	जमसेदपुर	जमशेदपुर
तास	ताश	नास	नाश
वास्प	वाष्प	विसम	विषम
सुसमा	सुषमा	विशाद	विषाद
शीर्शक	शीर्षक	शंकट	संकट
शारांश	सारांश	शुनसान	सुनसान
आदर्ष	आदर्श		

लिखावट में वर्तनी दोष

अ ओ ओ औ : इन वर्णों के लेखन में पड़ी पाई को ठीक बीच में न लिखकर नीचे लिखना चाहिए 'ओ' लिखने में सावधानी बरती जाती है; परन्तु 'औ' लिखने में सभी से अक्सर 'औ'- ऐसा लिख देते हैं। इससे सर्वदा बचें।

ख को 'रव' की तरह नहीं लिखें :

ख, रव बनकर वर्ण से शब्द बन जाएगा और अर्थ हो जाएगा- दाना। जैसे- रवादार- दानेदार।

रव = दाना - अशुद्ध रूप

ख = वर्ण - शुद्ध रूप

घ, ध संबंधी अशुद्धि : घ पर पूरी शिरोरेखा होती है जबकि तवर्गीय व्यञ्जन 'ध' का पूर्व का गोलवाला शिरा मुड़ा होता है और मुड़े भाग तथा शिरोरेखा के बीच रिक्त स्थान रहता है।

इसी तरह थ, भ, य, श, क्ष और श्र की लिखावट में ऊपर से मुड़े भाग के ऊपर शिरोरेखा नहीं होती। 'भ' के ऊपर पूरी तरह से शिरोरेखा देने पर 'म' का भ्रम पैदा हो सकता है।

द्य, द्द, द्ध संबंधी अशुद्धि :

'द्य'- 'द' और 'य' का संयुक्त रूप है। इसमें स्पष्टतया 'द्' और 'य' का रूप दिखाना चाहिए। यदि ''द्य'' लिखने में कठिनाई हो तो दोनों को अलग करके इस रूप में लिखना चाहिए- द्‌य- विद्या- विद्‌या

'द्द' यह चवर्ग का 'छ' नहीं है, युक्ताक्षर द्वित्व है। इसमें 'द्' और 'द' से संयुक्त हुआ है। इसे भी 'द्‌द' की तरह लिखकर वर्त्तनी दोष से सर्वदा बचा जा सकता है। जैसे- उद्देश्य-उद्‌देश्य 'द्ध' लिखने में छात्र प्रायः 'द्ध' लिखकर अर्थ का अनर्थ कर बैठते हैं। ऊपर बताया गया है कि 'ध' ऊपरी शिरा मुड़ा होता है। इसलिए 'द्' का 'ध' के साथ संयुक्त करने में या तो 'ध' को 'ध' की तरह लिखें या दोनों को अलग-अलग यथा द्‌ध-प्रसिद्‌ध-सिद्‌ध।

इसी तरह तवर्गीय पंचमाक्षर दो रूपों में लिखा जाता है- 'ण' और 'रा' यदि दूसरे रूप में लिखना चाहते है तो 'र' के साथ दोनों पाई को सटाकर लिखें इस तरह नहीं यथा- रा

लिखावट में हलन्त संबंधी प्रयोग :

- मान् / वान् / हान् प्रत्ययान्त शब्दों में हलन्त का प्रयोग अवश्य होना चाहिए। जैसे- श्रीमान् आयुष्मान् महान् विद्वान् आदि।
- प्रथम, पंचम, षष्ठम, सप्तम, अष्टम, नवम और दशम में हलन्त का प्रयोग नहीं होता है।
- त् / अम् / उत् प्रत्ययान्त तत्सम शब्दों में हलन्त का प्रयोग किया जाता है। जैसे- स्वागतम्, विद्‌युत्, जगत्, परिषद्, पश्चात्, शरद्, सम्राट् आदि।
- व्यंजनों के संयुक्त रूप में हलन्त के प्रयोग से ज्यादा स्पष्टता आती है। जैसे- विद्‌या, शुद्‌ध, कुत्‌ता, प्रसिद्‌ध, ज्योत्सना, उज्ज्वल आदि।

ध्यातव्यः उपुर्यक्त शब्दों का प्रचलन इस रूप में भी है- विद्या, शुद्ध, कुत्ता, प्रसिद्ध, ज्योत्सना, उज्जवल।

GENERAL ENGLISH

1

Chapter

Noun

Noun

वह शब्द है जिसके बारे में हम बात करते हैं। अंग्रेजी शब्द कोष में लगभग आधे शब्द noun होते हैं। Noun शब्द की उत्पत्ति लैटिन शब्द nomen से हुई है जिसका अर्थ है—नाम (Name)। इसी कारण noun को naming word भी कहा जाता है।

किसी व्यक्ति, स्थान, वस्तु, भवन, अवस्था या गुण आदि का नाम noun कहलाता है। (Noun is the name of a person, place, thing, building, condition or quality.) वस्तुत: thing (वस्तु) का तात्पर्य मूर्त तथा अमूर्त दोनों प्रकार की वस्तुओं से होता है। Noun के कुछ उदाहरण हैं—

* व्यक्ति का नाम (Name of a person)—Ram, Mohan.
* स्थान का नाम (Name of a place)—Allahabad, Northpole, Hospital, Antarctica.
* पशुओं का नाम (Name of animals)—Cow, Hen.
* वस्तुओं का नाम (Name of things)—Book, Gold, Table.
* भवनों का नाम (Name of buildings)—House, India gate.
* गुण का नाम (Name of quality)—Honesty, Beauty, Bravery.
* नदी/पहाड़/सागर के नाम (Name of river, mountain, seas)—Ganga, Himalayas, Arabian Sea.
* दिन/महीनों के नाम (Name of days/months)—Monday, January.
* संस्थानों के नाम (Name of organization)—Bank, Army, Government.
* समूह के नाम (Name of groups)-Crowd, Team, Police.

Note : किसी भी वाक्य में एक से अधिक noun हो सकते हैं। Noun में एक से अधिक words हो सकते हैं जिसे **noun phrase** कहा जाता है। जैसे—The great wall of China, My father's car, The road in front of my house.

* दो या अधिक noun मिलकर एक noun बना सकते हैं जिन्हें compound noun कहा जाता है। जैसे—
  School uniform, dining table,
  Knowledge park, traffic light.

Use of noun in a Sentence (वाक्य में noun का प्रयोग)—

1. **Subject के रूप में**—वाक्य में noun का प्रयोग object के रूप में किया जाता है। जैसे—
   Mohan is a good boy.
   The teacher helped him.
2. **Object के रूप में** —वाक्य में noun का प्रयोग object के रूप में भी किया जाता है। जैसे—
   Mohan is a good **boy.**
   He took help from **the teacher.**
3. **Compliment के रूप में**—वाक्य में noun का प्रयोग subject के compliment रूप में भी किया जाता है। जैसे—
   She is **an actress.**
   He was elected as **captain of the team.**
4. **Adjective के रूप में**—वाक्य में noun का प्रयोग Adjective के रूप में भी किया जाता है। जैसे—
   This is a **magic** pen.
   His work was **error** free.
5. **Apposition के रूप में**—वाक्य में noun का प्रयोग Apposition के रूप में भी किया जाता है। जैसे—
   Our class teacher, **Mr. Sharma,** is very helpful.
   Rohit, **the captain,** is very intelligent.

Kinds of Noun (noun के प्रकार)

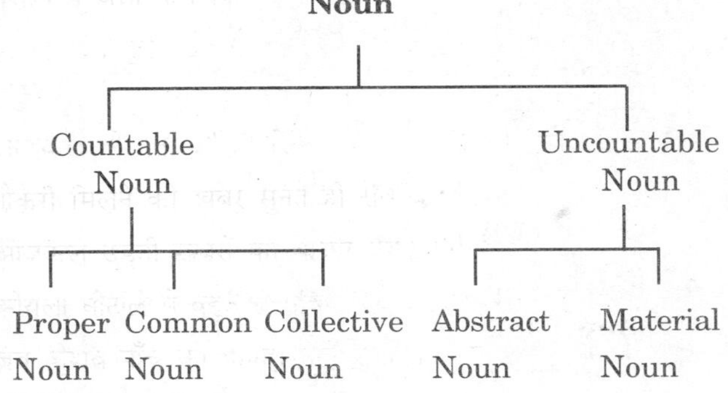

Countable noun and Uncountable noun :

Countable noun : ऐसे noun जिनकी गणना की जा सके, Countable noun कहलाते हैं। Proper noun, Common noun तथा Collective noun इस श्रेणी में आते हैं। जैसे Mohan, cow, team, army आदि।

Countable noun का प्रयोग singular तथा plural दोनों रूपों में किया जाता है।

Uncountable noun : ऐसे noun जिनकी गणना न की जा सके, Uncountable noun कहलाते हैं। Absrtact noun तथा Material noun इस श्रेणी में आते हैं। जैसे milk, rice, honesty, beauty आदि।

Uncountable noun का प्रयोग सामान्यत: singular form में किया जाता है, plural में नहीं।

कुछ noun का प्रयोग countable तथा uncountable दोनों रूपों में किया जाता है। जैसे—

Policy—Government's policy is anti poor. (Uncountable)

New policies are being adopted to help the poor. (Countable)

Hope—They hope for a better future. (Uncountable)

All their hopes faded with time. (Countable)

Proper noun :

किसी विशेष person, place, thing या animal का नाम proper noun कहलाता है। (Name of a particular person, place, thing or animal is called proper noun)

Sachin is a great player.

Delhi is the capital of **India.**

यहां Sachin, Delhi तथा India किसी विशेष person, place तथा country को इंगित करते हैं, अत: ये proper noun हैं।

1. Proper noun के उदाहरण हैं—
   - **व्यक्ति के नाम (Name of persons) :**
     Ashok, Akbar, Gandhi, Sachin, Dr. Bhabha,
   - **जानवरों के नाम (Name of animals) :**
     Chetak (महाराणा प्रताप का घोड़ा)
     Gajraj (हाथी का नाम)
   - **दिन व महीनों के नाम (Name of days and months) :**
     February, April, Monday, Friday.
   - **त्यौहार व महत्वपूर्ण दिनों के नाम (Name of festivals and important days) :**
     Holy, Diwali, Id, Christmas, New Year, Independence Day, World Literancy Day.
   - **भवन तथा स्मारकों के नाम (Name of buildings and monuments)**
     The Taj Mahal, The India Gate,
     The Eiffel Tower, Sydney Opera House,
   - **शहर, राज्य, देश तथा देश के निवासियों के नाम (Name of city, state, country and people of country) :**
     Delhi, Allahabad,
     Rajsthan, Bihar,
     India, the United States,
     Asia, Europe,
     Indians, the French.
   - **झील, सागर, महासागर, नदी, पर्वत, खाड़ी, रेगिस्तान, द्वीप आदि के नाम (Name of lakes, seas, oceans, rivers, mountains, gulf, deserts, island etc.) :**
     the Indian Ocean, Dull Lake,
     the Bay of Bengal, the Ganges
     the Himalayas, Mount Everest
     The Persian Gulf, the Sahara Desert
     the Andaman Island.
   - **पुस्तकों, समाचार पत्रों, पत्रिकाओं आदि के नाम (Name of books, newspapers, magazines etc.) :**
     The Mahabharat, The Times of India,
     the Frontline, Discovery of India.
   - **भाषा व धर्म के नाम (Name of language and religions)**
     English, Hindi, Telugu,
     French, Hindus, Muslims.
2. Proper noun का पहला अक्षर Capital letter होता है।
   Mohan., India, February, Sunday,
   Diwali, the Taj Mahal, the Indian Ocean.
3. यदि किसी Proper noun के पहले the का प्रयोग किया जाता है, तो उसमें 'the' capital letter से शुरू नहीं होता है पर यदि Proper noun में the शामिल है तो उसे Capital letter से शुरू किया जाता है। जैसे—
   the Great Wall of China.
   The Times of India.

4. परिवार के सदस्यों के संबंध सूचक शब्दों जैसे—mummy, daddy, uncle, aunty आदि का प्रयोग proper noun तथा common noun दोनों की तरह किया जाता है। जैसे—

Daddy has gone out. (Proper noun)
He has taken permission from his **daddy.** (Common noun)
I respect **Uncle** Sharma. (Proper noun)
My **uncle** gave me this present. (Common noun)

Common noun :

जो noun शब्द किसी person, place या thing के समुदाय (class) का बोध कराये, उन्हें Common noun कहा जाता है। जैसे—

Mohan is a good **boy.**
India is a big **country.**

यहाँ boy लड़कों के समुदाय का, जबकि country देशों के समुदाय का बोध कराता है। अत: ये common noun हैं। Common noun एक Countable noun है, अत: इसका प्रयोग Singular तथा plural दोनों रूपों में किया जाता है।

यदि किसी proper noun का प्रयोग किसी समुदाय या वर्ग (class) को प्रदर्शित करे तो वह proper noun से common noun में बदल जाता है। इस स्थिति में उस noun से पहले **the** का प्रयोग किया जाता है। जैसे—

Allahabad is the **Cambridge** of India.
He is the **Hitler** of this house.

Cambridge तथा Hitler एक proper noun है, पर यहां उसका प्रयोग commoun noun की तरह किया गया है।

Collective noun :

जब noun किसी समान person, place या thing के संग्रह (collection) का बोध कराये तथा इसका प्रयोग संपूर्णता में किया जाए तो उसे collective noun कहा जाता है। (Words used for a group of people or thing are called collective noun) जैसे—

Army - सैनिकों का समूह
Family - परिवार के सभी सदस्यों का समूह
Jury - न्यायाधीशों का समूह
Crowd - लोगों का समूह
Team - सदस्यों का समूह
Orchestra - वादक दल के सदस्य

Collective noun से plural number (बहुवचन) को बोध होता है, पर अंग्रेजी में इसका प्रयोग Singular number (एक वचन) की तरह किया जाता है क्योंकि इसे एक समूह की तरह प्रयोग किया जाता है।

लेकिन, यदि collective noun से समूह के प्रत्येक सदस्य (individuals) का बोध हो, तो उसका प्रयोग plural noun की तरह किया जाता है। जैसे—

My **family consists** of three members. (Singular)
(मेरे परिवार में तीन सदस्य हैं।)

My **family were** enjoying the game. (Plural)
(मेरे परिवार के सदस्य खेल का आनन्द ले रहे थे)

The **team has** played a good game. (Singular)
(इस दल ने अच्छा खेल खेला है)

The **team have** carried out their investigation. (Plural)
(इस दल ने अपनी जांच पूरी कर ली है)

The jury gave **its** verdict. (Singular)
(निर्णायक मंडल ने अपना निर्णय दिया)

The jury were divided in **their** opinion. (Plural)
(निर्णायक मंडल के विचारों में मतभेद था)

दो या अधिक समूहों को दर्शाने के लिए Collective noun का प्रयोग plural number की तरह किया जाता है।

— The **army** was deployed in the city (Singular)
Two **armies** fought with each other. (Plural)
—His **family** celebrates the festival together. (Singular)
Three families lived in the building. (Plural)

Collective noun का प्रयोग Singular form में करने पर इसके साथ **it/its** pronoun का प्रयोग किया जाता है जबकि plural form में **they/them/ their** का प्रयोग किया जाता है।

Name of Collective nouns :

अंग्रेजी भाषा में अलग-अलग person या things के collection को अलग-अलग नाम दिया जाता है, जो collective noun को दर्शाते हैं। Collective nouns के कुछ उदाहरण हैं—

Album of photo (फोटो की पुस्तिका)
Army of ants (चीटियों की झुंड)
Bale of cotton/wood (कपास/लकड़ी का गट्ठर)
Band of musicians (संगीतज्ञों का दल)
Basket of fruits (फलों की टोकरी)
Bench of judges (न्यायाधीशों का दल)
Board of directors (निदेशकों का मंडल)

Bouquet of flowers	(फूलों का गुलदस्ता)
Brigade of infantry	(पैदल सेना का दस्ता)
Bunch of keys/grapes	(चाभी/अंगूर का गुच्छा)
Caravan of pligrims	(तीर्थयात्रियों का काफिला)
Catalogue of books	(पुस्तकों की सूची)
Chain of mountains	(पर्वत श्रृंखला)
Cluster of stars	(तारों का गुच्छा)
Code of laws	(कानून संहिता)
Congress of delegates	(प्रतिनिधियों का सम्मेलन)
Convoy of trucks	(वाहनों का काफिला)
Corps of soldiers	(सैनिकों का दल)
Council of ministers	(मंत्रिपरिषद)
Course of study	(शिक्षा का पाठ्यक्रम)
Crowd of people/fans	(प्रशंसकों/लोगों की भीड़)
Delegation of Students	(विद्यार्थियों का प्रतिनिधिमंडल)
Fleet of ships/cars	(जहाज/कारों का बेड़ा)
Flight of stairs/steps	(सीढ़ियों की कतार)
Flight of birds	(चिड़ियों की कतार)
Flock of birds/sheep	(चिड़ियों/भेड़ों का दल)
Gaggle of geese	(बत्तखों का झुंड)
Galaxy of stars	(तारों की आकाशगंगा)
Gang of robbers/theives	(डाकुओं/चोरों का दल)
Grain of rice	(चावल के दाने)
Guld of artisans	(शिल्पियों का संघ)
Group of Island	(द्वीप का समूह)
Heap of sands	(बालू का ढेर)
Herd of cattles	(मवेशियों का झुंड)
Hive of bees	(मधुमक्खियों का छत्ता)
Hoard of jewels	(रत्नों का खजाना)
Jury of judges	(न्यायाधीश मंडल)
League of nations	(राष्ट्रों का संघ)
List of names	(नामों की सूची)
Lump of coal	(कोयले का ढेला)
Pack of cards	(ताश की गड्डी)
Pair of socks	(जुराबों का जोड़ा)
Panel of judges	(न्यायाधीश मंडल)
Pile of books/woods	(पुस्तकों/लकड़ी का ढेर)
Pinch of salt	(चुटकी भर नमक)
Range of mountains	(पर्वतों की श्रेणी)
Ray of lights	(प्रकाश की किरण)
Row of chais/houses	(कुर्सियों/मकानों की पंक्ति)
Series of lectures /events	(व्याख्यान/घटनाओं का क्रम)
Set of rules	(नियमों का समूह)
Sets of cutlery	(कांटे-चम्मच का समुच्चय)
Shower of rains	(वर्षा की बौछार)
Slice of bread	(ब्रेड का टुकड़ा)
Stack of arms	(हथियारों का ढेर)
String of pearls	(मोतियों की माला)
Set of rooms/furniture	(कमरों/फर्नीचर का सेट)
Swarm of flies/bees	(मक्खियों/मधुमक्खियों का झुंड)
Syndicate of merchants	(व्यापारियों का संघ)
Team of players	(खिलाड़ियों का दल)
Troop of lions/monkeys	(शेरों/बंदरों की फौज)
Troupe of dancers	(नर्तकों की मंडली)
Union of workers	(कामगारों का संघ)

Abstract noun :

वे noun जो किसी गुण, क्रिया या अवस्था (quality, action or state) को दर्शाते हैं, Abstract noun कहलाते हैं।

Abstract noun प्रायः अमूर्त होते हैं जिसे देखा या छुआ न जा सके। Abstract noun किसी adjective (गुण), verb (क्रिया) या अन्य noun से बने होते हैं।

Abstract noun सामान्यत: uncountable noun होती है। पर कुछ abstract noun का प्रयोग countable तथा uncountable noun - दोनों ही तरह किया जाता है। जैसे -

These products are of a high **quality.**
(uncountable)

He has all the **qualities** of a good leader. (countable)

Formation of Abstract noun (Abstract noun का निर्माण) — Abstract noun किसी adjective, verb या अन्य noun से बनाये जाते हैं।

1. Adjective से बने Abstract noun

(i) Adjective में **-'ness'** लगाकर abstract noun बनाया जाता है। (ness= quality, state of character of something- किसी वस्तु का गुण, अवस्था या चरित्र) जैसे—

Adjective		**Abstract Noun**
Cold (ठंडा, शीतल)	–	coldness (शीतलता)
Dull (मंद)	–	dullness (मंदता)
Great (महान)	–	greatness (महानता)
Happy (प्रसंन्न)	–	happiness (प्रसन्नता, खुशी)
Hard (कठोर)	–	hardness (कठोरता)
Ill (बीमार)	–	illness (बीमारी)
Lazy (आलसी	–	laziness (आलसीपन)
Loud (कोलाहलपूर्ण)	–	loudness (कोलाहलता)
Lonely (अकेला)	–	Loneliness (अकेलापन)
Mad (पागल)	–	madness (पागलपन)
Red (लाल)	–	redness (लालिमा)
Shy (शर्मीला)	–	shyness (शर्म)
Sweet(मीठा)	–	sweetness (मिठास)
Useful (उपयोगी)	–	usefulness (उपयोगिता)
weak (कमजोर)	–	weakness (कमजोरी)

(ii) Adjective में **y,-ty, -ity** या **-ry** जोड़कर abstract noun बनाये जरते हैं। जैसे—

Adjective		**Abstract Noun**
Able (योग्य, सक्षम)	–	ability (योग्यता, क्षमता)
Active (सक्रिय)	–	activity (सक्रियता)
Brave (बहादुर, साहसी)	–	bravery (बहादुरी, साहस)
Equal (समान)	–	equality (समानता)
Honest (इमानदार)	–	honesty (ईमानदारी)
Liberal (उदार)	–	liberty (उदारता)
Loyal (विश्वास)	–	loyalty (विश्वसनीयता)
Major (प्रमुख)	–	majority (प्रमुखता)
Minor (गौण)	–	minority (गौणता)
Modest (विनम्र)	–	modesty (विनम्रता)
Noble (कुलीन)	–	nobility (कुलीनता)
Poor (गरीब)	–	poverty (गरीबी)
Real (वास्तविक)	–	Reality (वास्तविकता)
Severe (उग्र)	–	Severity (उग्रता)

(ii) **-t** से अंत होने वाले adjective में -t के स्थान पर **-ce** जोड़कर abstract noun बनाये जरते हैं। जैसे—

Adjective		**Abstract Noun**
Brilliant (बुद्धिमान)	–	brilliance (बुद्धिमत्ता)
Confident (विश्वस्त)	–	confidence (विश्वास)
Dependent (निर्भर)	–	dependence (निर्भरता)
Different (भिन्न)	–	difference (भिन्नता)
Excellent (श्रेष्ठ)	–	excellece (श्रेष्ठता)
Important (महत्त्वपूर्ण)	–	importance (महत्त्व)
Independent (स्वतंत्र)	–	independence (स्वतंत्रता)
Intelligent (चतुर)	–	intelligence (चतुराई)
Negligent (असावधान)	–	negligence (असावधानी)
Patient (धैर्यवान)	–	patience (धैर्य)
Present (उपस्थित)	–	presence (उपस्थिति)
Relevant (प्रासंगिक)	–	relevance (प्रासंगिकता)
Significant (महत्त्वपूर्ण)	–	significance (महत्त्व)
Tolerant (सहनशील)	–	tolerance सहनशीलता)
Vigilant (सतर्क)	–	vigilance (सतर्कता)

2. Verb से बने Abstract noun

(i) Verb में **-'ion'** लगाकर abstract noun बनाया जाता है। जो verb की अवस्था (action or state) को बतलाता है। जैसे—

Verb		**Abstract Noun**
Act (कार्य करना)	–	action (कार्य कर्रवाई)
Add (जोड़ना)	–	addition (जोड़)
Conclude (निष्कर्ष निकालना)	–	conclusion (निष्कर्ष)
confuse (उलझन में डालना)	–	confusion (उलझन)
Create (उत्पन्न करना)	–	creation (उत्पत्ति)
Decide (निर्णय करना)	–	decision (निर्णय)
Discuss (विचार विमर्श करना)	–	discussion (विचार विमर्श)
Divide (विभाजित करना)	–	division (विभाजन)
Expand (फैलाना)	–	expansion (फैलाव)
Form (निर्माण करना)	–	formation (निर्माण)
Omit (छोड़ देना)	–	omission (छूट)
Operate (संचालित करना)	–	operation (संचालन)
Permit (अनुमति देना)	–	permission (अनुमति)
Reject (अस्वीकार करना)	–	rejection (अस्वीकृति)
Repeat (दोहराना)	–	repetition (दोहराव)
Solve (समाधान करना)	–	solution (समाधान)
Substract (घटना)	–	substraction (घटाव)

(ii) Verb में **-'nce'** जोड़कर abstract noun बनाना —

Verb		Abstract Noun
Appear (उपस्थित होना)	-	appearance (उपस्थिति)
Assure (भरोसा देना)	-	assurance (भरोसा)
Attend (उपस्थित रहना)	-	attendance (उपस्थिति)
Exist (अस्तित्व में होना)	-	existence (अस्तित्व)
Guide (मार्गदर्शन करना)	-	guidance (मार्गदर्शन)
Hinder (बाधा डालना)	-	hindrance (बाधक)
Insure (बीमा करना)	-	insurance (बीमा)
Occure (घटित होना)	-	occurrence (घटना)
perform (कार्य करना)	-	preformance (कार्यक्रम)
prefer (वरीयता देना)	-	preference (वरीयता)
Refer (उल्लेख करना)	-	reference (उल्लेख)

(iii) Verb में **-'nce'** जोड़कर abstract noun बनाना—

Verb		Abstract Noun
Adjust(अनुकूल बनाना)	-	Adjustment (अनुकूल)
Assess (मूल्यांकन करना)	-	assessment (मूल्यांकन)
Fulfil (लक्ष्य प्राप्त करना)	-	fulfilment (लक्ष्य प्राप्ति)
Manage (प्रबंध करना)	-	management (प्रबंधन)
Move (गति करना)	-	movement (गति)
Punish (सजा देना)	-	punishment (सजा)
state (कहना)	-	statement (कथन)
Treat (उपचार करना)	-	treatment (उपचार)

(iii) Verb में **-'-y'** या **'-ry'** जोड़कर abstract noun बनाना—

Verb		Abstract Noun
Deliver (वितरित करना)	-	delivery (वितरण)
Rob (लूटना)	-	robbery (लूटपाट)
Behave (व्यवहार करना)	-	behaviour (व्यवहार)
Flatter (चापलूसी करना)	-	flattery (चापलूसी)

3. Noun से बने Abstract noun—Noun word में **'-'hood',' -ce'** आदि जोड़कर abstract noun बनाया जाता है।

Noun		Abstract Noun
Adult (वयस्क)	-	adulthood (वयस्क अवस्था)
Boy (लड़का)	-	boyhood (लड़कपन)
Child (बच्चा)	-	childhood (बचपन)
Mother (माता)	-	motherhood (मातृत्व)
Woman (नारी)	-	womanhood (नारीत्व)
Resident (निवासी)	-	residence (निवास)

4. कुछ Abstract noun जिनसे किसी गुण या अवस्था का बोध होता है, विशुद्ध abstract noun होते हैं अर्थात् अंग्रेजी के किसी अन्य शब्द से नहीं बने होते हैं। जैसे—

Fantasy (काल्पनिक)	Mystery (रहस्य)
Quality (गुण)	Quantity (मात्रा, परिमाप)
Variety (विविधता)	Favour (अनुग्रह)
Labour (परिश्रम)	Attitude (मनोवृत्ति)
Magnitude (आकार)	Scenery (प्राकृतिक दृश्य)

5. कला या विज्ञान के नाम (name of art and sciences) भी abstract noun कहलाते हैं। जैसे—

Grammar, Physics, Science, Music.

Material Noun—

जो noun किसी पदार्थ का बोध कराये, उसे material noun कहा जाता है। जैसे—gold, brass, milk, rice, water, gas, paper, electricity आदि।

Material noun का प्रयोग सामान्यत: uncountable noun की तरह किया जाता है। लेकिन उसके पहले उपयुक्त adjective लगाकर इसे countable बनाया जा सकता है। जैसे—

— This book is printed on white **paper.** (Uncountable)

Please give me a **sheet of paper.** (Countable)

— Drinke clean **water.** (Uncountable)

Don't waste even a **drop of water.** (Countable)

Classification of Noun—

Noun का वाक्य में प्रयोग चार आधारों पर निर्भर करता है। अत: किसी भी noun को चार आधारों पर वर्गीकृत किया जा सकता है।

1. Number
2. Gender
3. Case तथा
4. Person

Noun and the Number—

Noun का वह वर्गीकरण जो noun के एक या एक से अधिक होने का बोध कराता है, Number कहलाता है।

Kinds of Number—

1. **Singular Number (एकवचन)**—यह noun के एक (one) होने का बोध कराता है, जैसे—

   Boy (एक लड़का)

   Man (एक आदमी)

2. **Plural Number (बहुवचन)**—यह noun के एक से अधिक (more than one) होने का बोध कराता है, जैसे—

Boys (दो या अधिक लड़के)

Men (दो या अधिक आदमी)

Note : —केवल countable noun (common तथा collective noun) का plural बनाया जा सकता है।

Uncountable noun (meterial तथा abstract noun) तथा proper noun का plural सामान्यत: नहीं बनाया जाता है। जैसे—

Singular	**Plural**		
Boy	Boys	(✓)	- Common Noun
Book	Books	(✓)	- Common Noun
Team	Teams	(✓)	- Collective Noun
Family	Families	(✓)	- Collective Noun
Milk	Milks	(×)	- Material Noun
Honesty	Honesties	(×)	- Abstract Noun
Mohan	Mohans	(×)	- Proper Noun

यदि किसी Proper, Material या Abstract noun का plural बनाया जाता है तो उसका प्रयोग Common noun की तरह किया जाता है। जैसे—

— His child is five years of age. (Abstract noun)
Children of all ages are allowed. (Common noun)

— Rice is the main food of Asia. (Material)
The best rices are produced in India. (Common noun)

— **Einstein** was a great scientist. (Proper noun)
This school can produce many **Einsteins.** (Common noun)

परंतु proper noun का प्रयोग कभी-कभी singular तथा plural, दोनों रूपों में किया जाता है। जैसे—

— He was born on a **Sunday.** (Proper noun)
This month has five **Sundays.** (Proper noun)

Rules for formation of Singular number to Plural—(एकवचन से बहुवचन बनाने के नियम)—

1. सामान्यत: Singular noun के अंत में **'-s'** जोड़कर उसका plural बनाया जाता है। जैसे—

Singular		**Plural**
Actor	–	Actors
Book	–	Books
Boy	–	Boys
Cook	–	Cooks
Cow	–	Cows
Egg	–	Eggs
Eye	–	Eyes
Girl	–	Girls
hand	–	Hands
Neighbour	–	Neighbours
Queen	–	Queens
Rupee	–	Rupees
Spoonful	–	Spoonfuls
Youth	–	Youths

2. जिस noun शब्द के अंत में **-s, -sh,-ch,-x** या **-o** रहता है, उसका plural सामान्यत: शब्द के अंत में **'-es'** जोड़कर बनाया जाता है। जैसे—

Singular		**Plural**
Branch	–	Branches
Box	–	Boxes
Class	–	Classes
Dish	–	Dishes
Glass	–	Glasses
Hero	–	Heroes
Mango	–	Mangoes
Mosquito	–	Mosquitoes
Princess	–	Princesses
Potato	–	Patatoes
Speech	–	Speeches
Tax	–	Taxes
Watch	–	Watches

3. जिन noun शब्द के अंत में **'-y'** रहता है, उसका plural '-y' की जगह **'-ies'** जोड़कर बनाया जाता है। जैसे—

Singular		**Plural**
Army	–	Armies
Baby	–	Babies
city	–	Cities
Country	–	Countries
Duty	–	Duties

Family	–	Families
Fly	–	Flies
Lady	–	Ladies
Story	–	Stories
Spy	–	Spies

4. वे शब्द जिनके अंत में **'-y'** हो पर **y** से पहले कोई **vowel** हो, तो उनका plural ' केवल **'-s'** जोड़कर बनाया जाता है। जैसे–

Singular		**Plural**
Boy	–	Boys
Day	–	Days
Essay	–	Essays
Key	–	Keys
Monkey	–	Monkey
Play	–	Plays
Storey	–	Storeys
Toy	–	Toys

5. वे शब्द जिनके अंत में **'-f'** या **'-fe'** रहता है उनका plural **-f** या **-fe** की जगह **-'ves'** जोड़कर बनाया जाता है। जैसे–

Singular		**Plural**
Calf (बछड़)	–	Calves
Half (आधा भाग)	–	Halves
Knife (चाकू)	–	Knives
Life (जिंदगी)	–	Lives
Leaf (पत्ता)	–	Leaves
Self (स्वयं)	–	Selves
Shelf (आलमारी)	–	Shelves
Thief (चोर)	–	Thieves
Wife (पत्नी)	–	Wives
Wolf (भेड़िया)	–	Wolves

परन्तु **'-f'** या **'-fe'** से अंत होने वाले कुछ शब्दों में केवल **'-s'** जोड़कर भी Plural बनाया जाता है। जैसे–

Singular		**Plural**
Belief (विश्वास)	–	Beliefs
Chief (प्रमुख)	–	Chiefs
Dwarf (बौना)	–	Dwarfs
Gulf (खाड़ी)	–	Gulfs
Handkerchief (रूमाल)	–	Handkerchiefs
Roof (छत)	–	Roofs
Staff (कर्मचारी)	–	Staffs
Safe (तिजोरी)	–	Safes

6. जिन noun शब्दों के अंत में double vowel रहता है उनका plural केवल **'-s'** जोड़कर बनाया जाता है। जैसे–

Singular		**Plural**
Bamboo	–	Bamboos
Bee	–	Bees
Cuckoo	–	Cuckoos
Radio	–	Radios
Studio	–	Studios
Tree	–	Trees
Video	–	Videos

7. कुछ noun शब्दों का plural उनके vowel शब्दों को बदलकर बनाया जाता है। जैसे–

Singular		**Plural**
Foot (पैर)	–	Feet
Goose (बत्तख)	–	Geese
Man (आदमी)	–	Men
Mouse (चूहा)	–	Mice
Tooth (दाँत)	–	Teeth
Woman (स्त्री)	–	Women

8. कुछ noun शब्दों का plural उनके 'en' शब्दों को बदलकर बनाया जाता है। जैसे–

Singular		**Plural**
Child (बच्चा)	–	Children
Ox (बैल)	–	Oxen

9. दो या अधिक शब्दों से मिलकर बने compound noun का plural उनके मुख्य शब्द (principal word) का plural बनाकर बनाया जाता है। जैसे–

Singular		**Plural**
Chairman (अध्यक्ष)	–	Chairmen
Commander-in-chief (प्रधान सेनापति)	–	Commanders-in-chief
Father-in-law (ससुर)	–	Fathers-in-Law
Man-of-war (समुद्री जहाज)	–	Men-of-war

Member of Praliament– (संसद का सदस्य) Members of Parliament

Milk man (ग्वाला) – Milk men

Maid servant (नौकरानी) – Maid servants

Passer-by (राहगीर) – Passers-by

Peacock (घोर) – Peacocks

Pea hen (मोरनी) – Pea hens

Postman (डाकिया) – Postmen

Son-in-law (दामाद) – Sons-in-law

Step-son (सौतेला बेटा) – Step-sons

Spoonful (चम्मच भर) – Spoonfuls

Salesman (पुरुष विक्रता)– Salesmen

Step mother (सौतेली मां) – Step-mothers

Saleswoman – Sales-women

Runner-up (उपविजेता) – Runners-up

10. कुछ शब्दों के plural उनके विशेष spelling द्वारा बनाए जाते हैं। वास्तव में, ये शब्द किसी अन्य भाषा में अंग्रेजी भाषा में लिए गए है। जैसे–

Singular	**Plural**
Addendum (अतिरिक्त सूचना)	– Addenda
Agendum (कार्यसूची)	– Agenda
Alumnus (पूर्व छात्र)	– Alumni
Axis (अक्ष)	– Axes
Appendix (परिशिष्ट)	– Appendices
Bacterium (जीवाणु)	– Bacteria
Basis (आधार)	– Bases
Bureau (संस्थान)	– Bureaux
Criterion (मापदंड)	– Criteria
Corrigendum (संशोधन)	– Corrigenda
Datum (सूचना, तथ्य)	– Data
Dictum (सिद्धान्त)	– Dicta
Focus (केंद्र)	– Foci (focuses)
Fungus (फफूंद)	– Fungi
Formula (सूत्र)	– Formulae
Index (विषय-सूची)	– Indices
Madam (श्रीमती)	– Madame
Mister (श्रीमान)	– Messers
Memorandum (ज्ञापन)	– Memoranda
Medium (मध्यम)	– Media
Maximum (अधिकतम)	– Mexima
Millennium (सहस्राब्दी)	– Millennia
Phenomenon	– Phenomena
Radius (त्रिज्या)	– Radii
Stimulus (प्रेरक)	– Stimuli
Syllabus (पाठ्यक्रम)	– Syllabi
Terminus (अंतिम)	– Termini
Thesis (शोध लेख)	– Theses
Vertex (शीर्ष)	– Vertices

Correct use of Singular/Plural Nouns—

1. कुछ noun शब्दों के Singular तथा Plural समान होते हैं। जैसे–

Advice (सलाह), Aircraft (हवाई जहाज),
Corps (सैनिक टुकड़ी), Dozen (दर्जन),
Dear (हिरण), Fish (मछली),
Gross (12 दर्जन), Hundred (सौ),
Million (दस लाख), Pair (जौड़ा),
Sheep (भेड़), Spacecraft (अंतरिक्षयान)
Series (क्रम), Species (प्रजाति)
Thousand (हजार) आदि।

जैसे– I saw **an aircraft.** (Singular)

Ten aircraft were flying in the sky. (Plural)

Note :— Dozen, hundred, thousand, million आदि का प्रयोग अंक के साथ करने पर उनके Singular तथा Plural समान होते हैं। बिना अंक के प्रयोग करने पर इनमें **'-s'** लगाकर Plural बनाया जाता है। इनके साथ हमेशा Plural verb का प्रयोग किया जाता है; जैसे–

— Four hundred people **were** standing at the gate.
One hundred rupees **have** been lost.

Hundreds of complaints **have** been registered.

— She bought five **dozen** mangoes.
She won **dozens** of Prizes.

2. कुछ noun शब्दों का प्रयोग केवल उनके Plural रूप में ही किया जाता है। जैसे—

Assets (संपत्ति), Alms (दान),
Becteria (जीवाणु), Cards (ताश),
Clothes (पहनावा), Contents (वस्तुएं)
Etables (खाद्य पदार्थ), Fireworks (आतिशबाजी)
Funds (कोष), Media (मीडिया),
Outskirts (बाहरी भाग), Remain (अवशेष),
Ruins (खंडहर), Savings (बचत),
Surrounding (परिवेश), Thanks (धन्यवाद),
Troops (सेना), Valuables (मूल्यवान वस्तुएं)

3. कुछ noun शब्द, जिनका प्रयोग जोड़े में उपयोग की जाने वाली वस्तुओं के लिए किया जाता है, हमेशा Plural होते हैं; जैसे—

Binoculars (दूरबीन), Boots (जूते),
Drawers (जांघिया), Gloves (दस्ताने),
Goggles (चश्मा), Jeans (जीन्स पैंट),
Pants (पैंट) Sandles (चप्पल),
Scales (तराजू), Scissors (कैंची),
Shoes (जूते), Shorts (छोटा पैंट),
Socks (मोजे), Spectacles (चश्मा),
Tongs (चिमटा), Trousers (पतलून), आदि।

4. Collective noun का प्रयोग Singular तथा Plural दोनों में किया जाता है। परंतु कुछ Collective noun हमेशा Plural form में प्रयोग किए जाते हैं; जैसे—

Audiences (दर्शक), Cattle (मवेशी),
Clergy (पुरोहित), Folks (लोग),
Gentry (अमीर वर्ग), Nation (देश के लोग),
People (लोग) Police (पुलिस बल),
Poultry (मुर्गीखाना), Public (जनता), आदि

—The police **have** caught the thief. (✓)
A Police **has** caught the thief. (×)

5. कुछ noun शब्दों का प्रयोग केवल उनके Plural रूप में ही किया जाता है। जैसे—

Abuse (गाली), Alphabet (वर्णमाला),
Baggage (सामान), Bread (ब्रेड),
Butter (मक्खन), Crockery (बर्तन),
Cutlery (कांटे-चम्मच), Dust (धूल),
Drainage (जल निकासी, Electricity (बिजली),
Food (भोजन), Fuel (ईंधन),
Furniture (फर्नीचर), Garbage (कचड़ा),
Greenery (हरियाली), Hair (केश),
Heritage (धरोहर), Issue (देना),
Information (सूचना), Infantry (पैदल सेना),
Jewellery (आभूषण), Luggage (यात्रा का सामान
Music (संगीत), Mischief (शरारत),
Poetry (कविता), Pottery (मिट्टी के बर्तन),
Scenery (दृश्य), Staionery(लेखन सामग्री)
Technology (तकनीक), Wastage (बर्बादी) आदि।

— He learnt English **alphabet** quickly.
This house **has** plenty of **furniture.**
The **scenery** of mountains **is** beautiful.

6. कुछ noun दिखने में Plural की तरह लगते हैं, पर वास्तव में वे Singular होते हैं तथा उनका प्रयोग singular noun की तरह ही किया जाता है; जैसे—

Athletics (खेलकूद), Billiards (बिलियईस),
Ecomonics (अर्थशास्त्र), Innings (पारी),
Mathematics (गणित), Measles (खसरा),
Mumps (एक रोग), News (समाचार),
Politics (राजनीति), Rickets (अस्थि रोग),
Statistics (सांख्यिकी), Wages (वेतन), आदि।

—He gave us a good **news.**
Mathematics is an interesting subject.
Athletics is not popular in India.

7. कुछ noun शब्दों का अर्थ singular noun में अलग तथा Plural में अलग होता है। जैसे—

Singular	**Plural**
Air (हवा)	– Airs (दिखावटी व्यवहार)
Advice (सलाह)	– Advices (सूचनाएं)
Arm (बांह)	– Arms (हथियार)
Copper (तांबा)	– Coopers (तांबे के सिक्के)
Chain (जंजीर)	– Chains (हथकड़ी)
Good (अच्छा)	– Goods (सामान)
Force (शक्ति)	– Forces (सेना)

Iron (लोहा)	– Irons (जंजीर)
Physic (दवा)	– Physics (भौतिकशास्त्र)
Respect (आदर)	– Respects (अभिवादन)
Regard (आदर)	– Regards (शुभकामनाएं)
Sand (बालू)	– Sands (रेगिस्तान)
Wood (लकड़ी)	– Woods (जंगल)

8. कुछ noun शब्दों का singular एक अर्थ में होता है जबकि Plural में इसके दो अर्थ होते है; जैसे—

Singular	Plural	
Colour (रंग)	– Colours	– अनेक रंग
		– सेना का झंडा
Custom (रिवाज)	– Customs	– रिवाज
		– सीमा चुंगी
Effect (प्रभाव)	– Effects	– प्रभाव
		– प्राप्ति, संपत्ति
Letter (अक्षर)	– Letters	– अक्षर
		– साहित्य,पत्र
Manner (तरीका)	– Manners	– तरीके
		– व्यवहार
Minute (मिनट)	– Minutes	– कई मिनट
		– समिति की कार्यवाही
Pain (दर्द)	– Pains	– दर्द
		– परिश्रम
Premise (सिद्धांत)	–Premises	– सिद्धांत
		– भवन से लगा भाग
Quarter (चौथा भाग)	– Quarters	– चौथे भाग
		– निवास स्थान
Return (वापस आना)	– Returns	– लाभ
		– आय-व्यय का विवरण
Spectacle (दृश्य)	– Spectacles	– दृश्य
		– चश्मा
Water (पानी)	– Waters	– जलाशय
		– तरंग

9. कुछ noun शब्दों के दो Plural होते हैं तथा उनके अर्थ भी भिन्न-भिन्न होते हैं; जैसे—

Singular	Plural
Brother (भाई)	–1. Brothers (एक ही माता-पिता की संतान)
	2. Brotherns (एक ही समुदाय के सदस्य)
Cloth (कपड़ा)	–1. Cloths (कपड़े)
	2. Clothes (पहनावा)
Die (सांचा)	– 1. Dies (सांचे)
	2. Dice (पाशा, खेल में प्रयुक्त धन)
Index (सूची)	– 1. Indexes (विषय सूची)
	2. Indices (गणित का एक चिन्ह)

10. कुछ noun अपने singular form में दो अर्थ रखते हैं जबकि Plural में उनका एक ही अर्थ होता हैं। जैसे—

Singular		Plural
Appearance	— आकृति	– Appearances (बाहरी दिखावा)
	— उपस्थिति	
Cricket	— झींगुर	– Crickets (झींगुर)
	— एक खेल	
Order	— आदेश	– Orders (आदेश)
	— सही क्रम	
People	— राष्ट्र	– Peoples (राष्ट्र)
	— जनसमूह	
Practice	— आदत	– Practices (प्रथाएँ)
	— व्यवसाय	

NOUN – GENDER

हिंदी भाषा में शब्दों को दो gender (लिंग) में बांटा जाता है—स्त्रीलिंग तथा पुलिंग। परन्तु अंग्रेजी भाषा में noun को चार gender में बांटा जाता है—

1. Masculine Gender (पुलिंग)—यह noun शब्दों के male kind को इंगित करता है। जैसे—

Boy (लड़का)	Man (आदमी)
Father (पिता)	Son (बेटा)
Cock (मुर्गा)	Bull (बैल)
Milkman (ग्वाला)	Brother (भाई) आदि।

2. **Feminine Gender (पुलिंग)**—यह noun शब्दों के Female kind को इंगित करता है; जैसे—

Girl (लड़की)	Woman (औरत)
Mother (माता)	Daughter (बेटी)
Hen (मुर्गी)	Cow (गाय)
Milkwoman (ग्वालिन)	Sister (बहन) आदि।

3. **Neuter Gender (नपुंसक लिंग)**—यह noun शब्दों के non-living-kind (निर्जीव वस्तुओं) को इंगित करता है। Material noun तथा abrstract noun निर्जीव वस्तुओं को दर्शाते हैं, अत: इन्हें Neuter gender में रखा जाता है। Collective noun, lower, aminals तथा young childrens को भी Neuter gender में रखा जाता है। जैसे—

Table (मेज),	Chair (कुर्सी)
Tree (पेड़),	Book (किताब),
Gold (स्वर्ण),	Honesty (ईमानदारी),
Ant (चींटी),	Baby (बच्चा), आदि

4. **Common Gender (उभयलिंग)**—यह ऐसे noun शब्दों को इंगित करता है, जिनका लिंग (male or female) निध ारित नहीं है। जैसे—

Child (बच्चा),	Bird (चिड़िया)
Mouse (चूहा),	Fish (मछली)
Thief (चोर),	Teacher (शिक्षक)

Parent (माता-पिता),Officer (अधिकारी), आदि।

यदि बच्चे का लिंग (Sex) पता है तो उसे boy या girl का नाम देंगे, पर लिंग अनिर्धारित होने पर उसे child कहते हैं तथा इसे common gender में रखा जाता है। इस प्रकार common gender का प्रयोग male तथा female दोनों के लिए किया जाता है; जैसे—

Masculine Gender	**Feminine Gender**	**Common Gender**
Boy (लड़का)	Girl (लड़की)	Child (बच्चा)
Man (आदमी)	Woman (औरत)	Person (व्यक्ति)
Father (पिता)	Mother (माता)	Parent (माता-पिता)
Husband (पति)	Wife (पत्नी)	Spouse (जीवनसाथी)
Brother(भाई)	Sister (बहन)	Sibling (भाई/बहन)
Steward (परिचायक)	Stewardess (परिचायिका)	Attendant (सेवक)

Correct use of Gender (Gender का सही प्रयोग)—

1. हिंदी भाषा के वाक्य में gender (लिंग) की पहचान क्रिया द्वारा की जाती है; जैसे—

एक लड़का खेल **रहा** है (A boy is playing.)

एक लड़की खेल रही है (A girl is playing.)

लेकिन English में gender की पहचान personal pronoun के 3rd person, singular number के प्रयोग द्वारा की जाती है। अत: वाक्य में personal pronoun में 3rd person singular number का प्रयोग gender के आधार पर किया जाता है।

Gender of Personal Pronoun
3rd person singular number

Pronoun Gender	Nominative case	Objective case	Possessive case	Reflective case
Masculine gender	He	him	his	himself
Feminine gender	She	her	her/hers	herself
Neuter gender	It	it	its	itself

I saw a boy. He was playing.
I saw a girl. She was dancing.
I saw a cat. It was jumping.

2. कुछ noun शब्द masculine तथा feminine दोनों को इंगित करते हैं, अत: इन्हें Common gender में रखा जाता है। जैसे—

Advocate (वकील/वकील स्त्री)
Assistant (सहायक पुरुष/ सहायक स्त्री)
Clerk (लिपिक पुरुष/लिपिक स्त्री)
Criminal (अपराधी पुरुष/अपराधी स्त्री)
Dancer (नर्तक/नर्तकी)
Doctor (चिकित्सक पुरुष/चिकित्सक स्त्री)
Leader (नेता/नेत्री)
Professor (प्राध्यापक/प्राध्यापिका)
Pupil (शिष्य/शिष्या)
Teacher (अध्यापक/अध्यापिका)
Writer (लेखक/लेखिका)

Common gender के साथ आवश्यकतानुसार (यदि उनकी gender ज्ञात हो), masculine या feminine Pronoun का प्रयोग किया जाता है। यदि उनका gender ज्ञात न हो, तो masculine और feminine दोनों pronoun या plural pronoun का प्रयोग किया जाता है। जैसे—

The teacher is in his class. (Masculine)
(शिक्षक अपनी कक्षा में)

The teacher is in her class. (Feminine)
(शिक्षिका अपनी कक्षा में है)

A teacher should be in his or her class. (✓)

A teacher should be in their class. (✓)
(शिक्षक को अपनी कक्षा में होना चाहिए)

3. Lower animals (छोटे जानवरों) तथा non-living को neuter gender में रखा जाता है तथा इनके लिए neuter pronoun (it, its, itself) का प्रयोग किया जाता है।

4. Everything, something, anything, nothing के साथ neuter gender के pronoun (it, its, itself) का प्रयोग किया जाता है।

5. कुछ निर्जीव वस्तुओं को उनकी शक्ति तथा उग्रता के आधार पर masculine gender में रखा जाता है। जैसे—

Sun (सूर्य), Summer (ग्रीष्म)
Ocean (समुद्र), Winter (जाड़ा)
Time (समय), Death (मृत्यु)
Thunder (तूफान), Wind (हवा)
War (युद्ध) आदि।

इन शब्दों के लिंग masculine pronoun (he, him, his, himself) का प्रयोग किया जाता है।

6. अपनी सुंदरता व कोमलता (beauty and softness) के आधार पर कुछ निर्जीव शब्दों को feminine gender में रखा जाता है तथा इसके लिए feminine pronoun (she, her, herself) का प्रयोग किया जाता है। जैसे—

Moon (चंद्रमा), Earth (पृथ्वी),
Nature (प्रकृति), Spring (बसंत),
Autumn (पतझड़), Mercy (दया),
Faith (विश्वास), Peace (शांति),
Virtue (नैतिकता), Truth (सत्यता),
Librety (स्वतंत्रता), Justice (न्याय),
Jealousy (ईर्ष्या), Fame (प्रसिद्धि),
River (नदी), City (शहर),
Nation (राष्ट्र),आदि।

Formation of Feminine Noun from Masculine Noun :

1. सामान्यत: masculine शब्द के अंत में suffix **'-ess'**-जोड़कर बनाया जाता है। जैसे—

Masculine	Feminine
Author (लेखक)	Authoress (लेखिका)
Heir (उत्तराधिकारी)	Heiress (उत्तराधिकारी स्त्री)
Host (मेजबान)	Hostess (मेजबान स्त्री)
Jew (यहूदी)	Jewess (यहूदी स्त्री)
Lion (शेर)	Lioness (शेरनी)
Manager (प्रबंधक)	Manageress (प्रबंधिका)
Mayor (महापौर)	Mayoress (महिला महापौर)
Poet (कवि)	Poetess (कवियित्री)
Priest (पुजारी)	Priestess (पुजारिन)
Patron (संरक्षक)	Patroness (संरक्षिका)
Prophet (पैगंबर)	Prophetess (पैगंबरी)
Prince (राजकुमारी)	Princess (राजकुमारी)
Shepherd (गड़ेरिया)	Shepherdess (गड़ेरिन)
Tailor (दर्जी)	Tailoress (दर्जिन)

2. कुछ masculine शब्दों को Feminine बनाने के लिए **'-ess'** जोड़ने से पहले शब्द के अंत में लगे vowel को हटा दिया जाता है या उनके spelling में थोड़ा परिवर्तन कर दिया जाता है।जैसे—

Masculine	Feminine
Actor (अभिनेता)	Actress (अभिनेत्री)
Conductor (परिचायक)	Conductress (परिचालिका)
Director (निर्देशक)	Director (निर्देशिका)
Duke (सामंत)	Duchess (सामंतनी)
Emperor (सम्राट)	Empress (साम्राज्ञी)
Founder (संस्थापक)	Foundress (संस्थापिका)
Governor (संचालक)	Governess (संचालिका)
God (देवता)	Godess (देवी)

Hunter (शिकारी)	Huntress (शिकारी स्त्री)
Inspector (निरीक्षक)	Inspectress (निरीक्षिका)
Murderer (हत्यारा)	Murderess (हत्यारिन)
Master (शिक्षक)	Mistress (शिक्षिका)
Proprietor (मालिक)	Proprietress (मालकिन)
Porter (कुली)	Portress (कुली स्त्री)
Tiger (बाघ)	Tigress (बघिन)
Traitor (गद्दार)	Traitress (गद्दार स्त्री)
Waiter (बैरा)	Waitress (महिला बैरा)

3. कुछ masculine शब्दों का feminine पूर्णतया अलग शब्द होते हैं या उनकी spelling में थोड़ा परिवर्तन कर बनाया जाता है।जैसे–

Masculine	**Feminine**
Boy (लड़का)	Girl (लड़की)
Brother (भाई)	Sister (बहन)
Bull/ox (बैल)	Cow (गाय)
Bachelor (कुवांरा)	Maid/spinster (कुवांरी)
Bridegroom (दुल्हा)	Bride (दुल्हन)
Cock (मुर्गी)	Hen (मुर्गी)
Dog (कुत्ता)	Bitch (कुतिया)
Drone (नर मक्खी)	Bee (मादा मक्खी)
Father (पिता)	Mother (माता)
Fox (लोमड़ी)	Vixen (मादा लोमड़ी)
Gentleman (सज्जन पुरुष)	Lady (सज्जन महिला)
Horse (घोड़ा)	Mare (घोड़ी)
He (वह-पुरुष)	She (वह-स्त्री)
Husband (पति)	Wife (पत्नी)
King (राजा)	Queen (रानी)
Lord (मालिक)	Lady (मालकिन)
Lover (प्रेमी)	Beloved (प्रेमिका)
Man (मनुष्य)	Woman (औरत)
Monk (साधु)	Nun (साध्वी)
Male (नर)	Female (मादा)
Mr. (श्रीमान्)	Mrs. (श्रीमती)
Nephew (भजीजा)	Niece (भतीजी)
Sir (महोदय)	Madam (महोदया)
Son (पुत्र)	Daughter (पुत्री)
Sultan (शासक)	Sultana (शासिका)
Uncle (चाचा)	Aunt (शासिका)

4. Compound noun के masculine शब्दों को feminine बदलने के लिए उसके मुख्य शब्द को feminine में बदला जाता है। जैसे–

Masculine	**Feminine**
Beggar-man (भिखारी)	Beggar-woman (भिखारिन)
Boy-friend (प्रेमी)	Girl-friend (प्रेमिका)
Brother-in-law (साला)	Sister-in-law(साली)
Bull-calf (बछड़ा)	Cow-calf (बछड़ी)
Cock-sparrow (नर चिड़िया)	Hen- Sparrow (मादा चिड़िया)
Father-in-law (ससुर)	Mother-in-law (सास)
Grandfather (दादा)	Grandmother (दादी)
He-goat (बकरा)	She-goat (बकरी)
Headmaster (प्रधानाध्यापक)	Headmistress(प्रधानाध्यापिका)
Landlord (मालिका)	Landlady (मालकिन)
Man servant (सेवक)	Maid servant (सेविका)
Milkman (ग्वाला)	Mikwoman (ग्वालिन)
Peacock (मोर)	Peahen (मोरनी)
Step-son (सौतेला बेटा)	Step-daughter(सौतेली बेटी)

Noun — Case :

Case—वाक्य में noun का स्थान या अन्य शब्दों के साथ उसके संबंध को दर्शाने वाले कारक Case कहलाते है।

Kind of Case :—

Noun को मुख्यत: चार case में वर्गीकृत किया जाता है—

1. Nominative case
2. Objective (Accusative) case
3. Possessive (Genetive) case ?)
4. Vocative case.

1. **Nominative case**—जब किसी noun (या pronoun) का प्रयोग वाक्य में subject के रूप में होता है तो उसे Nominative case में कहा जाता है। इसमें noun (या pronoun) के साथ verb का सीधा संबंध होता है।

verb से कौन (Who ?) या क्यों (What ?) प्रश्न लगाने से जो उत्तर प्राप्त होता है, वह प्राय: Nominal case होता है। जैसे—

Ram killed Ravana. (Who ? Ram)
Milk is good for health. (What ? -Milk)

यहाँ Ram और milk का verb के साथ सीधा संबंध है तथा ये वाक्य के Subject भी हैं। अत: Ram और milk-nominative case में है।

2. **Objective (Accusative) case** —जब किसी noun या (pronoun) का प्रयोग verb के object के रूप में किया जाता है तो यह वाक्य में objective case में होता है। Verb से पहले क्या (What ?) या किसी को (Whom ?) प्रश्न लगाने से जो उत्तर प्राप्त होता है, वह प्राय: Objective case में होता है। जैसे—

He helped **Mohan** in nced. (Whom ?-Mohan)
The boy kicked the **ball.** (What ? - ball)

यहाँ Mohan और ball वाक्य के object हैं तथा objective case में कहलाते हैं।

3. **Possessive (Genetive) case**—जब कोई noun (या pronoun) वाक्य में किसी दूसरे noun के साथ relation संबंध या possession(अधिकार) को दर्शाता है, तो वह Possessive (Genetive) case में कहा जाता है। Object से पहले किसका (Whose ?) प्रश्न लगाने से जो उत्तर आता है, वह प्राय: possessive case में होता है। जैसे—

This is my house. (Whose house?–my)
Sita is Ram's wife. (Whose wife?–Ram's)

यहां my और Ram's possessive case में हैं।

Note : Nominative case का प्रयोग वाक्य में verb से पहले होता है, जबकि Objective तथा Possessive case का प्रयोग verb के बाद होता है।

4. **Vocative case**—यदि noun का प्रयोग उसे संबोधित करने के लिए किया जाए तो वाक्य में noun को Vocatice case में कहा जाता है। जैसे—

What is your name, **dear** ?
Please come here, my **friend.**
Mohan, please help me.

यहां dear, friend तथा Mohan का प्रयोग संबोधन के लिए किया गया है, अत: इन्हें Vocative case में कहा जाता है।

Formation of Possessive Case—

1. किसी singular noun के अंत में apostrophe -s (-s) लगाकर उसका possessive case बनाया जाता है। जैसे—

Ram's book (राम की किताब),
Mother's love (मां का प्यार),
Dog's tail (कुत्ते की पूंछ),

2. यदि किसी singular noun के अंत में -s' या '-ee' हो, तो उच्चारण की सुगमता के लिए केवल apostrophe (') जोड़कर Possessive case बनाया जाता है। जैसे—

Justice' sake (न्याय के लिए)
Goodness' sake (अच्छाई के लिए)
Archimedes' principle (आर्कमडीज का सिद्धांत)

3. जिस plural noun के अंत में -'s' रहता है, उनका possessive केवल apostrophe (') लगाकर बनाया जाता है। जैसे—

Boy's school (लड़कों का स्कूल),
Officers' Hostel (अधिकारियों का हॉस्टल),
Dogs' tail (कुत्तों की पूंछ),
Ladies' bus (औरतों की बस)

Note :—यहाँ apostrophe s ('s) का प्रयोग singular noun को दर्शाता है, जबकि केवल apostrophe (') का प्रयोग plural noun को दर्शाता है। जैसे—

Girl's dress (लड़की की पोशाक)
Girls' dress (लड़कियों की पोशाक)

4. परंतु जिस plural noun के अंत में -s नहीं रहता, उनका possessive case apostrophe s ('s) लगाकर बनाया जाता है। जैसे—

Children's park (बच्चों का पार्क),
Women's club (औरतों का क्लब),
Men's association (पुरुषों का संगठन),

5. Compound noun के अंतिम या महत्वपूर्ण term के साथ apostrophe s ('s) जोड़कर possessive case बनाया जाता है। जैसे—

Father-in-**Law's** house,
Sister-in-**Law's** car,
President of **India**'s visit,
Step-**mother's** behaviour

Correct use of Possessive Case :—

1. Possessive case का प्रयोग केवल living things (सजीव वस्तुओं) के साथ किया जाता है। Non living things निर्जीव वस्तुओं, के साथ **of** का प्रयोग किया जाता है।

   The House's door (×)
   Door of the house (✓)
   Book's page (×)
   Page of the book's (✓)

   परंतु कुछ non-living विशेषीकृत noun के साथ apostrophe s ('s) का प्रयोग कर possessive case बनाया जाता है। जैसे–

   Earth's layer (पृथ्वी की परत),
   Fortune's favour (भाग्य का साथ),
   Ocean's roar (समुद्र की गर्जना),
   Duty's call (कर्तव्य की पुकार),

2. Possessive Case का प्रयोग Possession अधिकार दिखाने के अतिरिक्त कृति, उत्पत्ति, प्रकार आदि को दर्शाने के लिए भी किया जाता है। जैसे–

   Women's club (औरतों का क्लब)
   President's house (राष्ट्रपति का घर),
   Ashish's school (आशीष का स्कूल)
   Mother's love (मां का प्यार)
   Valmiki's Ramayana (वाल्मिकी का रामायण),

3. Time (समय), space (स्थान), या weight (भार) दर्शाने वाले noun के साथ possessive case का प्रयोग किया जाता है। जैसे–

   A week's holiday (एक सप्ताह की छुट्टी)
   A meter's length (एक मीटर की दूरी),
   A year's time (एक साल का समय),
   A ton's weight (एक टन का वजन),

   यहाँ singular noun के साथ apostrophe s ('s) तथा plural के साथ केवल apostrophe (') का प्रयोग किया जाता है। जैसे–

   Two weeks' holiday (दो सप्ताह की छुट्टी)
   Four years' time (चार साल का समय)
   Ten days' leave (दस दिनों की छुट्टी)

4. जब दो या अधिक noun आपस में घनिष्ठ रूप से संबंधित हों या संयुक्त अधिकार (joint possession) प्रदर्शित करें तो बाद वाले noun के साथ ('s) लगाया जाता है।

   Ram and Sita's marriage,
   (राम और सीता की शादी),
   Sharma and son's shop,
   (शर्मा और बेटे की दुकान)
   Mrs. and Mr. Mohan's house,
   (श्रीमती और श्री मोहन का घर)

   परन्तु यदि दो या अधिक noun अलग-अलग possession रखते हों तो प्रत्येक के साथ apostrophe s ('s) का प्रयोग किया जाता है।

   Ram's and Shyam's book,
   (राम और श्याम की अलग-अलग पुस्तक)
   Doctor's and teacher's car.
   (डॉक्टर की कार तथा शिक्षक की कार)

5. **Than/as** का प्रयोग यदि तुलना (comparison) के लिए किया जाए तथा इसके पहले possessive case का प्रयोग हो, तो इसके बाद आने वाले noun के साथ भी possessive case का प्रयोग किया जाता है।

   Ram's house is as big as Shyam's (house).
   (राम का घर श्याम के घर जैसा बड़ा है।)
   Suresh's father is richer than Ramesh.
   (सुरेश के पिता रमेश से धनी है।)
   Suresh's father is richer than Ramesh's (Father)
   (सुरेश के पिता रमेश के पिता से धनी है।)

6. कभी-कभी possessive case के प्रयोग में सावधानी रखनी चाहिए। जैसे–

   My father's photograph.
   (मेरे पिताजी द्वारा बनाई गई या रखी गयी फोटो)
   Photograph of my father
   (पिताजी को दर्शाने वाली फोटो)

2 Chapter Pronoun

Noun के बदले वाक्य में प्रयोग किया गया शब्द Pronoun कहलाता है। (Pronoun is a word used instead of a noun)। यह वाक्य में noun के बार-बार प्रयोग (repetition) को हटाता है।

Ram gave Ram's pen to Shyam to write with pen.
Ram gave **his** pen to Shyam to write with **it.**

दूसरे वाक्य में **his** का प्रयोग **Ram** के लिए जबकि **it** का प्रयोग pen के लिए किया गया है। यहाँ his तथा it pronoun हैं।

Pronoun का प्रयोग noun के स्थान पर किया जाता है। अत: यह noun का equivalent (समकक्ष) होता है। सामान्यत: pronoun का प्रयोग पहले दिए गए noun के लिए ही किया जाता है।

Noun की तरह ही Pronoun का प्रयोग भी Person (1st, 2nd व 3rd person), Number (singular या plural number), Gender (masculine, feminine या neuter gender) तथा Case (nominative, possessive या objective case) पर निर्भर करता है।

Kinds of Pronoun —

1. **Personal Pronoun—**I, me, we, us, you, he, she, it, him, her, they, them.
2. **Possessive Pronoun—**ऐसे Pronoun जिनका प्रयोग possession (अधिकार) दर्शाने के लिए किया जाता है, Possessvie pronoun कहलाते हैं। जैसे—Mine, ours, his, hers, yours, theirs.
3. **Adjective Pronoun—**ऐसे Pronoun जिनका प्रयोग adjective के रूप में भी किया जाता है, Adjective pronoun कहलाते हैं। Adjective pronoun के प्रकार हैं—
   - (a) **Demonstrative adjective pronoun—**This, that, those, such, same.
   - (b) **Distributive adjective pronoun—**Each, every, either, neither.
   - (c) **Indefinite adjective pronoun—**Any, all, few, some, several, one, another, none. many.
   - (d) **Possessive adjective pronoun—**My, your, his, her, its, our, their.
4. **Relative pronoun—**Who, which, what, whose, whom, as, that, but.
5. **Interrogative pronoun—**Who, which, whose, whom, what.
6. **Reflexive pronoun—**Myself, himself, herself, itself, yourself, ourselves, yourselves, themselves, oneself.
7. **Reciprocal pronoun—**Each-other, one-another.

Personal Pronoun—

किसी person, place या thing के नाम के बदले में प्रयुक्त pronoun Personal pronoun कहलाते हैं। जैसे—I, we, you, he, she, it, they, me, us, him, her, them.

चूंकि personal pronoun का उपयोग noun के बदले में किया जाता है, अत: personal pronoun का उपयोग noun के number, gender, person तथा case के अनुसार किया जाता है।

Correct use of Personal Pronoun—

1. Personal pronoun के nominative case का उपयोग verb के subject के रूप में किया जाता है। जैसे—

   He is a good boy.
   I am taller than him.
   You, he and I went for a walk.

2. **'To Be'** का प्रयोग यदि infinitive के रूप में किया जाए तो इसके बाद nominative case pronoun का उपयोग किया जाता है। जैसे—

   I would like to be **he.**

3. **'Be'** (is, am, are, was, were, has, have) के बाद pronoun के nominative case का प्रयोग किया जाता है। जैसे—

   It was **I.**
   It is **he** who knocked at the door.

4. किसी sentence के object के रूप में personal pronoun के Objective case का उपयोग होता है। जैसे—

   You're taller than **me.**
   I'am taller than **him.**
   The teacher asked **them** to be seated.

5. let, like, between, but या किसी preposition के साथ objective case का प्रयोग किया जाता है।

Let us go for picnic.

This fact is between **you and me.**

Everyone was present but **him.**

6. Possessive pronoun का प्रयोग sentence के subject या object दोनों रूपों में होता है। जैसे—

Ours is a bigger house.	(Subject)
He is friend of **ours**.	(Object)
The choice was **hers**.	(Object)

Personal pronoun के Possessive case का प्रयोग सावधानी से किया जाना चाहिए। जैसे—

This is **my** book.	(Pos. Adj.)
This book is **mine.**	(Poss.Pro.)
She broke **her** leg.	(Poss.Adj)
The choise was **hers**.	(Poss.Pro.)

Note: Possessive pronoun का प्रयोग noun के पहले नहीं होता जबकि possessive adjective का प्रयोग noun से पहले होता है। जैसे—

Our country is largest producer of milk.

Ours is a big house.

— His का प्रयोग Possessive adjective तथा Possessive pronoun दोनों रूपों में होता है।

Vinay is a friend of **his**.	(Poss.Pronoun)
He has sold **his** car.	(Poss.Adjective)

— Its का प्रयोग केवल Possessive adjective के रूप में होता है, Possessive pronoun के रूप में नहीं।

The baby throw its food.	(Poss. Adjective)

7. Gerund (verb + ing) तथा infinitive (to + verb) के साथ का pronoun के Objective case प्रयोग होता है। जैसे—

It was nice meeting **her**.

I asked him to accompany **me**.

Pronoun

Person	**Gender**	**Case**	**Singular**	**Plural**
1st Person	Masculine	Nominative	I (मैं)	We (हम लोग)
(वक्ता या	or	Possessive	My, Mine (मेरा)	Our,Ours (हमारा)
कहने वाला)	Feminine	Objective	me (मुझको)	Us (हम सबका)
2nd Person	Masculine	Nominative	You (तुम)	You (तुम लोग)
(श्रोता या	or	Possessive	Your,Yours (तुम्हारा)	Your,Yours (तुम सबका)
सुनने वाला)	Feminine	Objective	You (तुझको)	You (तुम सबको)
3rd Person	Masculine	Nominative	He (वह)	They (वे)
(जिसके बारे		Possessive	His (उसका)	Their,Theirs (उन लोगों का)
में कहा जाए)		Objective	Him (उसको)	Them (उन लागों का)
	Feminine	Nominative	She (वह)	They (वे)
		Possessive	Her,Hers (उसका)	Their,Theirs (उन लोगों का)
		Objective	Her (उसको)	Them (उनको)
	Neuter	Nominative	It(वह)	They (वे)
		Possessive	Its (उसका)	Their,Theirs (उन सबका)
		Objective	It (उसको)	Them (उन सबको)

Possessive Pronoun	Possessive Adjective
Mine	My
Ours	Our
Yours	Your
His	His
Hers	Her
–	Its
Theirs	Their

8. Except के बाद pronoun के objective case का प्रयोग होता है। जैसे—

Everyone was present except **me.**

9. अगर एक ही sentence में दो या अधिक personal pronoun का प्रयोग हो तो उन्हें 231 के नियम के अनुसार प्रयोग करते हैं। अर्थात् पहले second person फिर third person तथा अंत में first person pronoun का प्रयोग किया जाता है।

You, he and **I** shall go for the tour .

You and **we** have finished our work.

He and **I** were present in the class.

यदि दो या अधिक pronoun का प्रयोग wrong sense (भूल, दोष, अपराध आदि) में किया जाए तो उन्हें 123 के क्रम में रखा जाता है। अर्थात् पहले first person, फिर second person तथा अंत में third person pronoun का प्रयोग किया जाता है। जैसे—

I, you and **he** has committed this mistake.

10. जब दो या अधिक noun आपस में **and** से जुड़े हों, तो उनके लिए plural pronoun का प्रयोग किया जाता है।

Ram and Shyam have finished **their** work.

The teacher praised Ashish and Vidhi for **their** hard work.

परन्तु, यदि and से जुड़े singular noun से एक ही व्यक्ति का बोध हो, तो इसके साथ singular pronoun का प्रयोग होता है।

The book and stationery shop **is** closed today .

The teacher of Hindi and English has finished **his** lecture.

11. Each, every, anyone के साथ singular pronoun का प्रयोग होता है। जैसे—

Each and every person should mark **his** attendance.

Anyone can speak English if **he** tries.

Every boy and every girl has completed **his** or **her** homework.

12. यदि collective noun (जैसे jury, committee, class, team, government, family, mob, council, army, crowd, crew आदि) के प्रयोग से एक समूह का बोध हो तो उसके लिए neuter gender, singular pronoun (it, its, itself) का प्रयोग किया जाता है।

The jury has given **its** verdict.

The team is working hard to complete **its** project.

परन्तु यदि collective noun से प्रत्येक सदस्य (individual) का अलग-अलग बोध हो, तो plural pronoun का प्रयोग किया जाता है।

The members of jury were divided in **their** opinion.

13. यदि दो या अधिक pronoun एक साथ subject के रूप में प्रयुक्त हों तो उनके साथ pronoun का प्रयोग निम्नलिखित के अनुसार होता है—

Subject	Pronoun
You and I He and I	1st Person plural number — We, us, our,ours
You,he and I You and he	2nd Person plural number —You, Your,Yours

Use of Personal Pronoun-It'—

1. Third person, neuter gender में निर्जीव चीजों (non living things) तथा छोटे जानवरों या बच्चों (small animals or children) जिनका लिंग (male/female) निर्धारित नहीं है, के लिए personal pronoun 'it' का प्रयोग किया जाता है। जैसे—

It is a nice book.

Sita has a cat. **It** is very cute.

The baby has broken **its** toy.

2. पहले कहे गए वाक्यांश (part of sentences) के लिए it का प्रयोग किया जाता है। जैसे—

He gave the reply because he knew **it**.

3. वाक्य के subject के रूप में भी **it** का प्रयोग किया जाता है। जैसे—

It is doubtful whether he wil pass.

It is a difficult job.

It is likely to rain.

4. Noun या pronoun पर जोर (emphasis) देने के लिए it का प्रयोग किया जाता है।

It was who stood first in the class.

It is he who solved the problem.

5. समय (time), तिथि (date), दूरी (distance) या मौसम (weather) को बताने में subject के रूप में it का प्रयोग होता है।

It is nine o'clock.

It is Sunday.

It was raining this morning.

6. किसी व्यक्ति की पहचान बताने के लिए (subject) के रूप में it का प्रयोग किया जाता है।

   It is your mother on phone.

7. Collective noun के pronoun के रूप में भी it का प्रयोग होता है।

   The army has recaptured **its** territory.

Relative Pronoun:—

Noun के बदले में प्रयुक्त वह शब्द (pronoun) जो दो या अधिक noun, words या sentences को जोड़ना है या उनके बीच संबंध बतलाता है, Relative pronoun कहलाता है। इसे conjunctive pronoun भी कहते है। जैसे—

Correct Use of Relative Pronoun—

1. **Who** का प्रयोग व्यक्ति के लिए किया जाता है।

   The boy **who** told the truth is brave .
   They hardly fail **who** work hard.
   He **who** is honest is liked by all.

2. **Which** का प्रयोग जानवरों तथा निर्जीव वस्तुओं के लिए किया जाता है।

   The hat **which** is baught has been stolen.
   The cat **which** is black is very cute.
   The moment **which** is lost is never recovered.

3. **Whose** का प्रयोग, who के Possessive case में person तथा non-living things के लिए किया जाता है।

   He is the man **whose** opinion I respect.
   This is the house **whose** door is broken.

4. **That** का प्रयोग persons तथा non-living things के लिए किया जाता है। That का प्रयोग who, which तथा whom के बदले में भी किया जाता है।

   He is the friend **that** (who) help in need.
   This is the knife **that** (which) cuts sharply.
   He is the most intelligent boy **that** (whom) I have ever meet.
   All **that** (which) glitters is not gold.

5. **What** का प्रयोग दो वाक्यांशों को जोड़ने के लिए किया जाता है। What का प्रयोग केवल singular form में things के लिए ही किया जाता है।

   Listen carefully **what** I say.
   I did **what** I say.
   I mean **what** I say.

6. **But** का प्रयोग relative pronoun के रूप में not के sense में किया जाता है।

   Everyone was there **but** (except) him.
   This problem is anything **but** (not) easy.

7. Whoever, whichever, whatever आदि Compound relative pronoun कहलाते हैं।

   Choose **whichever** brand you prefer.
   Whoever comes in is welcome .
   Do **whatever** you like.

8. Relative pronoun का प्रयोग subordinate clause के subject तथा object दोनों रूपों में होता है।

   The car **which** I sold was very old . (Sub.)
   This is the car **which** was sold by me. (Obj.)

9. Relative pronoun के singular तथा plural दोनों समान होते हैं।

   The houses **which** is cheaper are far away.
   It was a crisis for **which** she was unprepared.

10. Relative pronoun का प्रयोग उस noun के तुरंत बाद करना चाहिए जिसे वह इंगित करता है।

   The book **which** I bought has been torn by my dog.
   The book has been torn by my dog **which** I bought.
   पहले वाक्य में which 'book' के बारे में बतलाता है जबकि दूसरे वाक्य में which 'dog' के बारे में बतलाता है।

11. Relative pronoun का प्रयोग दो simple sentences को जोड़ने के लिए भी किया जाता है।

— Mr.Sharma has a lot of experience..
  He will be joining the school.
  Mr.Sharma **who** has a lot of experience, will be joining the school.

— The author has written a reply.
  You criticized him.
  The author, **whom** you criticized, has written a reply.

— His movie won several awards .
  It is about the life of Gandhi.
  His movie, **which** won several awards, is about the life of Gandhi.

— There is a man.
  I respect his opinion.
  There is a man **whose** opinion I respect.

— I have a pan.
  I bought pen yesterday.
  I have a pen **that** I bought yesterday.

Case of Relative Pronoun

Nominative case	—	Who (कौन)
Possessive case	—	Whose (किसका)
Objective case	—	Whom (किसको)

Reflexive Pronoun :—

इस Pronoun का प्रयोग तब किया जाता है जब verb का प्रभाव स्वयं subject पर पड़ता है या जब verb पर जोर देना होता है। Reflexive pronoun में singular के लिए self जबकि plural के लिए '-selves' लगाया जाता है। जैसे— myself, himself, herself, itself, yourself, oneself, ourselves, yourselves, themselves आदि।

I did it **myself** . (emphasis)

All of you can pass the exam **yourself.**

You have to decide it **yourself**

Everyone enjoyed **himself** in the party.

She must look after **herself**.

The cat was washing **itself.**

One has to decide **oneself** about the good and the bad.

— Reflexive pronoun का प्रयोग तभी किया जाता है। जब verb का object तथा subject दोनों एक ही हो।

— Reflexive pronoun का प्रयोग subject के रूप में नहीं किया जाता है।

Distributive Pronoun:—

यह pronoun दो या अधिक व्यक्तियों/वस्तुओं में से प्रत्येक को अलग-अलग इंगित करता है। जैसे—each, every, either, neither, any, none आदि।

1. **Each (प्रत्येक)**—दो या दो से अधिक व्यक्यिों या वस्तुओं में से प्रत्येक के लिए **'each'** का प्रयोग किया जाता है।

   They recieved **each** a reward.

   Each answer is valuable.

   Each of the two girls **was** beautiful.

   They hate **each** other.

   Each of these mangoes is rotten.

2. **Every (प्रत्येक)**—दो से अधिक व्यक्तियों या वस्तुओं में से प्रत्येक के लिए **'every'** का प्रयोग किया जाता है।

   Every student in the class **has** passed the exam.

   She knows **every** student in the school.

3. Either, neither तथा none का प्रयोग भी distributive pronoun की तरह किया जाता है।

   Either —दो में से कोई एक

   Neither —दोनों में से कोई भी नहीं

   None —दो या अधिक में से कोई भी नहीं

   Either of these two teams shall win the match.

   Nither of these two boys **has** done it.

   None of the players **is** faulty.

   You can park on **either** side of street.

4. Distributive pronoun एक समय में एक व्यक्ति का बोध कराता है, अत: इसके साथ singular verb का प्रयोग किया जाता है।

5. Distributive pronoun के **each of, either of** तथा **neither of** के साथ plural noun या pronoun का प्रयोग किया जाता है। यहाँ plural noun के पहले **the** का भी प्रयोग किया जाता है।

   Each of the **house** was slightly different.

Demonstrtive Pronoun:—

यह pronoun, noun की ओर संकेत करता है तथा noun की पहचान बतलाता है। जैसे—This, that, these, those, same, such, one आदि।

Singular	**Plural**	**संकेत**
This	These	निकटता प्रकट करता है।
That	Those	दूरी प्रकट करता है।

This is my pen.

That is your book.

These mangoes are tastier than **those.**

He is the **same** person.

We were poor and they treated us as **such.**

Our car is old,so we want to buy new **one**.

यदि दो noun आपस में and से जुड़े हो तो पहले वाले noun के लिए this या these जबकि बाद वाले noun के लिए that या those का प्रयोग किया जाता है।

Growth and environment are both necessary. **This** (growth) for economy and **that** (environment) for society.

किसी दो noun में एक ही गुण की तुलना के लिए that of या those of का प्रयोग किया जाता है।

Per capita income of Gujrat is more then **that of** Utter Pradesh.

People of India are laborious than **those of** America.

Indefinite Pronouns :—

इस pronoun से किसी निश्चित व्यक्ति या वस्तु का बोध नहीं होता। इसे अनिश्चित व्यक्ति या वस्तु (undetermined person or thing) के लिए प्रयोग किया जाता है। ऐसे वाक्यों में noun सामान्यत: understood होता है।

जैसे—Any, all, another, few many, none one, other, much, most, little, some, several, anybody, everybody, nobody, somebody.

Anyone could have done the work.

Not **all** of them were invited.

I don’t like this dress, so I want **another**.

Very **few** of his books are worth reading .

Several people protested against the law.

Many of those present disagreed.

Some are born great.

Everybody, somebody, anybody, nobody, one, none आदि के साथ singular pronoun और singular verb का प्रयोग किया जाता है।

Everybody should respect **his** elders.

One should love **one's** country.

None but the brave **deserves** all the praise.

Nobody knew what to say.

— **Some** का प्रयोग affirmative sentence (सकारात्मक वाक्य) में होता है जबकि **any** का प्रयोग negative sentence (नकारात्मक वाक्य) में होता है।

I do have **some** money.

I don't have **any** money.

Some students work harder than others.

Interrogative Pronoun:—

Who, which, whose, whom, what आदि को जब प्रश्न पूछने के लिए प्रयोग किया जाता है तो उसे Interrogative pronoun कहा जाता है।

Who	Nominative case	व्यक्तियों के लिए
Whose	Possessive case	व्यक्तियों के लिए
Whom/who	Objective case	व्यक्तियों के लिए
What	Objective case	निर्जीव वस्तुओं के लिए Profession (व्यवसाय) या employment (पेशा) जानने के लिए
Which	Objective case	दो या अधिक वस्तु/ व्यक्ति के बीच चुनाव (selection) प्रकट करने के लिए।

Interrogative Pronoun के प्रयोग के कुछ उदाहरण इस प्रकार हैं—

Who is there ?
(वहाँ कौन है?)

Who is that woman ?
(वह औरत कौन है?)

Who stood first in the class ?
(कक्षा में प्रथम कौन आया है?)

Whose house is that ?
(वह घर किसका है?)

Whose book is this ?
(वह पुस्तक किसकी है?)

Whom did they invite ?
(उन्होंने किसको आमंत्रित किया था)

Whom/Who should I adderss the letter to ?
(यह पत्र किसको लिखा जाय)

What do you want ?
(आप क्या चाहते हैं?)

Who are you ?
(आप कौन हैं?)

What are you ?
(आप क्या हैं?)

What is your name ?
(आपका नाम क्या है?)

What kind of music do you like ?
(आप किस प्रकार का संगीत पसंद करते हैं?)

Which of the applicant has got the job ?
(किस आवेदक को काम मिला है?)

Which way is the wind blowing ?
(किस दिशा में हवा बह रही है?)

Which will you take ?
(आप कौन सा लेंगे ?)

Which of these books belongs to you ?
(इनमें से कौन सी पुस्तक आपकी है?)

Whom did you meet yesterday ?
(आप कल किससे मिले थे?)

Tell me **what** you know ?
(जो तुम जानते हो वह मुझे बताओ?)

Note : Who, what तथा which का प्रयोग किसी व्यक्ति के बारे में जानकारी प्राप्त करने के लिए इस प्रकार किया जाता है—

Q. **Who** is he ? (व्यक्ति का परिचय जानने के लिए)
(वह कौन है?)

A. He is Mr.Sharma.

Q. **What** is he ? (व्यक्ति का व्यवसाय जानने के लिए)
(वे क्या करते हैं?)

A. He is a doctor.

Q. **Which** is he ? (व्यक्ति की पहचान करने के लिए)
(वह कौन सा व्यक्ति है?)

A. He is the one with the red cap.

3 Chapter Verb

Verb वे शब्द हैं जो किसी कार्य का होना (action) बताता है, कार्य की पुष्टि (confirmation) करता है, आदेश (command) देता है, प्रश्न (question) पूछता है या व्यक्ति या वस्तु की स्थिति (state of a person or thing) बतलाता है।

Kinds of verb:—

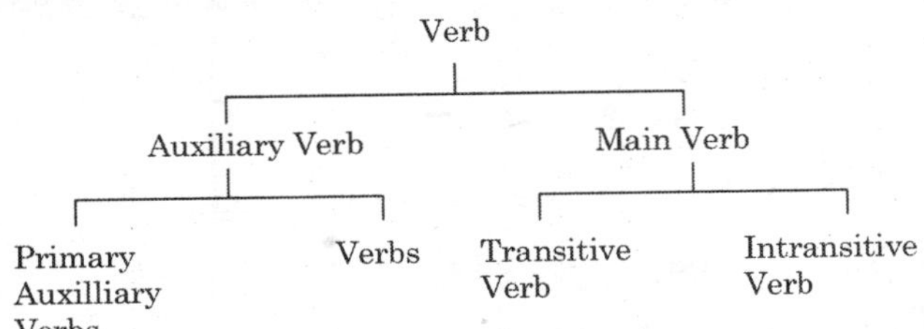

1. **Transitive Verb**— जब किसी क्रिया (action) का प्रभाव subject पर नहीं, बल्कि sentence के object पर पड़ता है तो उस verb को transitive verb कहा जाता है।

   I **gave** him a book.

   The boy **kicked** the football.

   Transitive verb का अर्थ object के बिना स्पष्ट नहीं होता है। उपरोक्त वाक्य में I gave या The boy kicked से वाक्य का अर्थ स्पष्ट नहीं है जब तक कि उसमें Object न लगाया जाए। यहां verb **give** तथा **kick** का प्रभाव वाक्य के object **book** तथा **football** पर पड़ रहा है। अत: give तथा kick transitive verb हैं।

2. **Intransitive Verb**— जब क्रिया (action) का प्रभाव subject पर पड़ता है तो उस verb को Intransitive verb कहा जाता है।

   I am **running.**

   The sun **shines.**

   Intransitive verb का अर्थ object के बिना भी स्पष्ट होता है।

   Note : Sentence में क्रिया (verb) का प्रभाव जिस व्यक्ति या वस्तु (person or thing) पर पड़ता है, उसे object कहा जाता है। जब किसी वाक्य में दो object होते हैं तो उसमें वस्तु को इंगित करने वाला शब्द Direct object कहलाता है जबकि व्यक्ति (person) को इंगित करने वाला शब्द Indirect object कहलाता है। वाक्य में indirect object का प्रयोग direct object से पहले किया जाता है। जैसे—

   He purchased me a car.

   Will you lend us some money ?

यहाँ **'me'** तथा **'us'** indirect object हैं जबकि **'a car'** तथा **'some money'** direct object है।

सामान्यत: किसी object को verb के ठीक बाद रखा जाता है लेकिन relative तथा interrogative pronoun वाले object को verb से पहले रखा जाता है। जैसे—

The boy, **who stood first** has been rewarded.

Whom do you want to talk ?

Note : Intransitive verb के साथ preposition जोड़कर उसे transitive बनाया जा सकता है जैसे—

I am running **behind** the dog.

He is laughing **at** me.

अधिकांश verb को transitive तथा intransitive दोनों रूपों में प्रयोग किया जा सकता है। जैसे—

The driver **stopped** the train.	(Transitive)
The train **stopped** suddenly.	(Intransitive)
He broke the glass.	(Transitive)
The glass **broke**.	(Intransitive)

Cognate Object :

ऐसा object जिसका अर्थ verb के समान हो, cognate object कहलाता है। जैसे—

She sang a **song**.

They fought a good **fight**.

He ran his fastest **run**.

Regular and Irregular verb :

Verb को उसके past tense के आधार पर regular तथा irregular में वर्गीकृत किया जाता है।

1. **Regular Verb**—वह verb जिसके अन्त में **-d, -ed,** या **'-t** जोड़कर past तथा past participle रूप बनाया जाता है, Regular verb कहलाता है। जैसे—

Ask - asked	Love - loved
Move - moved	Keep - kept

2. **Irregular Verb**—Regular verb के अतिरिक्त सभी अन्य verb Irregular verb कहलाते हैं। इस प्रकार के verbs के present, past तथा past participle के रूप अलग अलग होते हैं। जैसे–

Go	went	gone
Fly	flew	flown

Verb: Person and Number:—

Verb का प्रयोग subject के person और number तथा वाक्य के tense और mood पर निर्भर करता है।

Person–1st Person,2nd Person, 3rd Person

Number–Singular number and Plural number

3rd person, singular number (he, she, it तथा Proper noun) के साथ singular verb का प्रयोग होता है जबकि अन्य सभी के साथ plural vern का प्रयोग होता है। अपने सामान्य रूप में verb को plural माना जाता है जबकि verb को singular बनाने के लिए उसमें **-s** या **-es** जोड़ दिया जाता है।

Number/Person	Singular	Plural
1st Person	I go.	We go.
2nd Person	You go.	You go.
3rd Person	He goes. Ram goes.	They go.

Note : Verb **'be'** का person व number के अनुसार स्वरूप होता है।

Number/Person	Singular	Plural
1st Person	am	are
2nd Person	are	are
3rd Person	is	are

Mood—

Verb के द्वारा किसी कथन को व्यक्त करने के तरीके (method of expression) को Mood कहते हैं।

Mood of verb—Verb के mood को दो भागों में बांटते हैं–

1. **Finite mood**—इसे subject के number तथा person के अनुसार प्रयोग किया जाता है। Verb के finite mood के तीन प्रकार होते हैं–

   (i) Indicative mood

   (ii) Imperative mood

   (iii) Subjunctive mood

2. **Infinitive mood**—verb के इस form पर subject के number तथा person का प्रभाव नहीं पड़ता अर्थात् number तथा person के साथ इनका प्रयोग समान रूप से किया जाता है। Verb के Infinite mood के तीन प्रकार होते हैं–

   (i) Infinitive mood (to + verb + ing)

   (ii) Participle

   (iii) Gerund (verb)

Finite Mood of Verb :

1. **Indicative Mood**—जब Verb का प्रयोग direct statement, fact, simple, question. या probability (संभावना) व्यक्त करने के लिए किया जाता है, तो इसे indicative mood कहते हैं। जैसे

   The boy **loves** his mother. (Statement)

   The sun **rises** in the east. (Fact)

   Do you **have** a pen ? (Question)

   If you **work** hard,you will rewarded.(Probability)

2. **Imperative mood**– इस verb का प्रयोग command, prayer या request के लिए किया जाता है। जैसे–

   Go away. (Command)

   Have mercy upon boys. (Prayer)

   Give me some food. (Request)

   Verb के imperative mood का प्रयोग केवल 2nd person के लिए किया जाता है, जहाँ subject (you) छुपा रहता है। 1st तथा 3rd person के साथ **'Let'** लगाकर verb के imperative mood का प्रयोग किया जा सकता है। जैसे–

   Let him **go** for a walk.

   Let us **play** cricket.

3. **Subjunctive Mood**–जब verb को doubt, purpose, supposition या uncertainty के रूप में प्रयोग किया जाता है या कोई अन्य कार्य इस पर निर्भर करता है, तो verb को subjunctive mood में कहा जाता है। जैसे–

   If I come,I shall remain there. (Doubt)

   I wish I were a millionaire. (Supposition)

   Had he met me,I should have helped him. (Uncertainty)

   I rewarded you that you may work hard.(Purpose)

Finitive Mood of Verb–(to+verb)—

Verb का सामान्य रूप जिसके साथ to लगा रहता है, infinitive mood कहलाता है। यह subject के number तथा person के अनुसार नहीं बदलता है। जैसे–

She is ready **to run.**

To rise early is good.

He loves **to play** cricket.

Use of Infinitive Mood of Verb—

1. Verb के infinitive mood का subject तथा object दोनों रूपों में प्रयोग किया जाता है। जैसे–

To find fault is easy. (Subject)

It is easy **to find** fault. (Object)

To err is human,**to forgive** is divine. (Subject)

I prey for him **to succeed.** (Object)

He is likely **to resign.** (Object)

2. Verb के infinitive mood का adjective या adverb के रूप में भी प्रयोग किया जाता है। जैसे–

Give him a chair **to sit** down. (adj.)

He was quick **to respond.** (adj.)

She works hard **to stay** fit. (adj.)

They came **to see** me. (adv.)

He worked hard **to succeed.** (adv.)

We decided **to call** the baby Ravi. (adv.)

3. कुछ verb जैसे **bid, let, make, need, dare, feel, watch, know, see, hear** आदि के साथ infinitive mood का प्रयोग **'to'** के बिना किया जाता है। जैसे–

I **bade** him go.

Let me **come** in.

They **made** him **work** hard.

You **need** not **go**.

You **dare** not **hit** me.

I saw him **work**.

I heard him **talk.**

यदि **need** तथा **dare** का प्रयोग 'do' के साथ हो तो 'to' का प्रयोग किया जाता है। जैसे–

I need **to do** it .

He dares **to disobey** his parents.

4. यदि दो infinitive आपस में **and, but, or, except than** आदि से जुड़े हों तो 'to' का प्रयोग केवल पहले infinitive के साथ किया जाता है। जैसे–

He has nothing **to do** but **talk.**

He learnt how **to read** and **write.**

The Gerund :

Verb का वह रूप जिसमें **-'ing'** लगा रहता है (verb + ing) कहलाता है। Gerund एक साथ verb और noun दोनों का कार्य कर सकता है। जैसे–

Reading is a good habbit. (Subject)

Walking makes a man healthy. (Subject)

Seeing is **believing**. (Object)

He is fond of **reading** books. (Object)

You should not mind my **coming** late. (Object)

Smoking is not allowed. (Subject)

He enjoyed **walking** in the morning. (Object)

He is fond of **walking**.

(Object to preposition)

His constant habit was **walking**.

(Complement to a verb)

Participle :

Verb का प्रयोग जब adjective के रूप में किया जाय तो उसे Participle (या Verb adjective) कहा जाता है जैसे–

Barking dogs seldom bite.

I saw a **crying** child.

Encourged by his friends, he is joined the party.

Hearing the noise, he ran away.

Having burnt by fire, he was taken to hospital.

Kinds of participle –

1. Present participle – verb + ing
2. Past Participle – 3rd form of verb
3. Perfect participle – having + 3rd form of verb

Note : यदि verb + ing का प्रयोग noun के रूप में हो तो उसे Gerund कहा जाता है। यदि verb + ing का प्रयोग tense में या adjective के रूप मे हो तो उसे participle कहा जाता है।

I saw a **running** dog. (Gurend)

A dog was **running.** (Participle)

He reached there **running** fast. (Participle)

Note : Present तथा Past participle का प्रयोग adjective के रूप में भी किया जाता है।

An early **rising** man.

The newly **risen** sun.

Verb of Complete / Incomplete Predication :

1. जब कोई Intrasitive verb केवल subject के साथ प्रयोग करने पर वाक्य को अर्थपूर्ण (complete sense) बना देता है तो उसे **verb of Complete predication** कहते हैं। जैसे–

   He laughs. (वह हँसता है)।

   They run. (वे दौड़ते हैं)।

   Birds fly. (चिड़ियां उड़ती हैं।)

   I go. (मैं जाता हूँ)

2. जब कोई Intransivite verb केवल subject के साथ वाक्य को अर्थपूर्ण (complete sense) नहीं बनाता तो उसे **Verb of Incomplete predication** कहते हैं। ऐसे वाक्यों को अर्थपूर्ण बनाने के लिए कोई noun, adjective या verb जोड़ना पड़ता है।

   They become.........

   We confine ....

   He is.....................

   We made..............

इस प्रकार के verb के अर्थ को पूरा करने के लिए वाक्य में किसी noun, adjective, adverb या preposition आदि का प्रयोग किया जता है जिसे Complement कहते हैं । जैसे –

We	made	him	**captain of the team.**
(Sub)	(Verb)	(Direct Object)	(Complement)

Forms of Verb :

वाक्य में tense के अनुसार verb के विभिन्न forms का प्रयोग किया जाता है । Verb के चार forms होते हैं ।

(1) Present (1st) form – इसमें verb अपने मूल रूप में होता है।

(2) Past (2nd) form

(3) Past participle (3rd) form

(4) Present participle (Verb + ing form)

Formation of Different Forms of Verb :

कुछ verb का past व Past Participle form verb में **'ed'** जोड़कर बनाया जाता है। इन्हें **Regular verb** कहा जाता है।

Present	Past	Past Participle	Verb + ing form
Act (कार्य करना)	Acted	Acted	Acting
Add (जोड़ना)	Added	Added	Adding
Allow (अनुमति देना)	Allowed	Allowed	Allowing
Answer (उत्तर देना)	Answered	Answered	Answering
Appoint (नियुक्त करना)	Appointed	Appointed	Appointing
Appear (दिखना)	Appeared	Appeared	Appearing
Arrest (कैद करना)	Arrested	Arrested	Arresting
Ask (पूछना)	Asked	Asked	Asking
Attack (आक्रमण करना)	Attacked	Attacked	Attacking
Bark (भूकना)	Barked	Barked	Barking
Bless (आशीर्वाद देना)	Blessed	Blessed	Blessing
Boil (उबालना)	Boiled	Boiled	Boiling

Borrow (उधार लेना)	Borrowed	Borrowed	Borrowing
Call (बुलाना)	Called	Called	Calling
Clean (साफ करना)	Cleaned	Cleaned	Cleaning
Check (जांचना)	Checked	Checked	Checking
Climb (चढ़ना)	Climbed	Climbed	Climbing
Collect (इकट्ठा करना)	Collected	Collected	Collecting
Complain(शिकायत करना)	Complained	Complained	Complaining
Cook (खाना पकाना)	Cooked	Cooked	Cooking
Count (गिनना)	Counted	Counted	Counting
Consult (परामर्श लेना)	Consulted	Consulted	Consulting
Cover (ढकना)	Covered	Covered	Covering
Cross (पार करना)	Crossed	Crossed	Crossing
Defeat (हराना)	Defeated	Defeated	Defeating
Discover (खोज करना)	Discovered	Discovered	Discovering
Dream (सपना देखना)	Dreamed	Dreamed	Dreaming
Earn (कमाना)	Earned	Earned	Earning
Enter (प्रवेश करना)	Entered	Entered	Entering
Employ (नियुक्त करना)	Employed	Employed	Employing
Explain (स्पष्ट करना)	Explained	Explained	Explaining
Face (सामना करना)	Faced	Faced	Faceing
Fail (असफल होना)	Failed	Failed	Failing
Fear (डरना)	Feared	Feared	Fearing
Fell (काट कर करना)	Felled	Felled	Felling
Finish (समाप्त करना)	Finished	Finished	Finishing
Float (उतरना)	Floated	Floated	Floating
Gather (संग्रह करना)	Gathered	Gathered	Gathering
Hang (लटकाना, लटकना)	Hanged	Hanged	Hanging
Help (सहायता करना)	Helped	Helped	Helping
Join (जोड़ना)	Joined	Joined	Joining
Jump (उछलना)	Jumped	Jumped	Jumping
Kill (जान से मारना)	Killed	Killed	Killing
Laugh (हँसना)	Laughed	Laughed	Laughing
Learn (सीखना)	Learned	Learned	Learning
Listen (सुनना)	Listened	Listened	Listening

Look (देखना)	Looked	Looked	Looking
Melt (पिघलना)	Melted	Melted	Melting
Mix (मिलाना)	Mixed	Mixed	Mixing
Need (आवश्यक होना)	Needed	Needed	Needing
Obey (आज्ञा मानना)	Obeyed	Obeyed	Obeying
Open (खोलना)	Opened	Opened	Opening
Order (आज्ञा देना)	Ordered	Ordered	Ordering
Play (खेलना)	Played	Played	Playing
Pray (प्रार्थना करना)	Prayed	Prayed	Praying
Peep (झाँकना)	Peeped	Peeped	Peeping
Plant (पौधा लगाना)	Planted	Planted	Planting
Pluck (तोड़ना)	Plucked	Plucked	Plucking
Pull (खींचना)	Pulled	Pulled	Pulling
Prevent (रोकना)	Prevented	Prevented	Preventing
Punish (दंड देना)	Punished	Punished	Punishing
Push (ढकेलना)	Pushed	Pushed	Pushing
Rain (वर्षा होना)	Rained	Rained	Raining
Reach (पहुँचना)	Reached	Reached	Reaching
Rest (आराम करना)	Rested	Rested	Resting
Resign (त्याग देना)	Resigned	Resigned	Resigning
Repair (मरम्मत करना)	Repaired	Repaired	Repairing
Remember (याद करना)	Remembered	Remembered	Remembering
Return (वापस लौटना)	Returned	Returned	Returning
Roar (गजरना)	Roared	Roared	Roaring
Saw (आरी से काटना)	Sawed	Sawed	Sawing
Select (चुनना)	Selected	Selected	Selecting
Stay (रूकना, रोकना)	Stayed	Stayed	Staying
Talk (बोलना)	Talked	Talked	Talking
Touch (स्पर्श करना)	Touched	Touched	Touching
Trust (विश्वास करना)	Trusted	Trusted	Trusting
Walk (चलना)	Walked	Walked	Walking
Wash (धोना)	Washed	Washed	Washing
Wait (इंतजार करना)	Waited	Waited	Waiting
Work (काम करना)	Worked	Worked	Working

Watch (रखवाली करना)	Watched	Watched	Watching
Wish (आशा करना, चाहना)	Wished	Wished	Wishing
Wound (घायल करना)	Wounded	Wounded	Wounding
Wonder (उत्सुक होना)	Wondered	Wondered	Wondering
Yield (लाभ देना,परिणम देना)	Yielded	Yielded	Yielding

4.13.2. कुछ verb जिनकें अंत में **'-e'** रहता है, उसका Past व participle form केवल '-d' जोड़कर बनाया जाता है। इनमें **'-ing'** जोड़ने से पहले **'-e'** हटा दिया जाता है।

Abuse (गाली देना)	Abused	Abused	Abusing
Admire(प्रशंसा करना)	Admired	Admired	Admiring
Advise (सलाह देना)	Advised	Advised	Advising
Arrive (पहुंचना)	Arrived	Arrived	Arriving
Bake (पकाना)	Baked	Baked	Baking
Bathe (स्नान करना)	Bathed	Bathed	Bathing
Believe (विश्वास करना)	Believed	Believed	Believing
Behave(व्यवहार करना)	Behaved	Behaved	Behaving
Close (बंद करना/होना)	Closed	Closed	Closing
Change (बदलाव)	Changed	Changed	Changing
Confuse (भ्रमित करना)	Confused	Confused	Confusing
Decorate (सजाना)	Decorated	Decorated	Decorating
Dance (नृत्य करना)	Danced	Danced	Dancing
Decide (निर्णय करना)	Decided	Decided	Deciding
Desire (इच्छा रखना)	Desired	Desired	Desiring
Die (प्राण त्यागना)	Died	Died	Dying
Divide (विभाजित करना)	Divided	Divided	Dividing
Dye (रंगना)	Dyed	Dyed	Dying
Face (सामना करना)	Faced	Faced	Facing
Fine (जुर्माना लगाना)	Fined	Fined	Fining
Graze (घास चरना)	Grazed	Grazed	Grazing
Hate (घृणा करना)	Hated	Hated	Hating
Improve (सुधार करना)	Improved	Improved	Improving
Invite(निमंत्रण करना)	Invited	Invited	Inviting
Lie (झूठ बोलना)	Lied	Lied	Lying
Like(पसंद करना)	Liked	Liked	Liking
Live (रहना)	Lived	Lived	Living

Love (प्यार करना)	Loved	Loved	Loving
Move (घूमना/हटना)	Moved	Moved	Moving
Name (नाम रखना)	Named	Named	Naming
Oppose (विरोध करना)	Opposed	Opposed	Opposing
Praise (प्रशंसा करना)	Praised	Praised	Praising
Prepare (तैयार करना)	Prepared	Prepared	Preparing
Prove (साबित करना)	Proved	Proved	Proving
Promise(वादा करना)	Promised	Promised	Promising
Receive (प्राप्त करना)	Received	Received	Receiving
Refuse (अस्वीकार करना)	Refused	Refused	Refusing
Save (बचाना)	Saved	Saved	Saving
Tie (बांधना)	Tied	Tied	Tying
Use (उनयोग करना)	Used	Used	Using
Waste (बर्बाद करना)	Wasted	Wasted	Wasting

कुछ verb जिनके अंत में **-'y'** रहता है, उसका Past व Past Participle बनाने के लिए **'-y'** को **'-i'** में बदलकर **'-d'** या **'ed'** लगाते हैं।

Present	**Past**	**Past Participle**	**Verb + ing form**
Carry (ढोना)	Carried	Carried	Carrying
Copy (नकल करना)	Copied	Copied	Copying
Cry (रोना)	Cried	Cried	Crying
Dry (सुखाना)	Dried	Dried	Drying
Marry (शादी करना)	Married	Married	Marrying
Pay (भुगतान करना)	Paid	Paid	Paying
Reply (जवाब देना)	Replied	Replied	Replying
Say (कहना)	Said	Said	Saying
Study (पढ़ना)	Studied	Studied	Studying
Try (प्रयास करना)	Tried	Tried	Trying

कुछ verb जिनके अंत में consonants होते हैं तथा उसके ठीक पहले vowel रहता है, उसका Past तथा Past Participle शब्द के अंत में **'-ed'** जोड़कर बनाया जाता है तथा उसमें **'-ed'** जोड़ने से पहले अंतिम शब्द को repeat कर दिया जाता है।

Beg (मांगना)	Begged	Begged	Begging
Clap (ताली बजाना)	Clapped	Clapped	Clapping
Dip (डुबाना)	Dipped	Dipped	Dipping
Knit (बुनना)	Knitted	Knitted	Knitting
Quarrel (लड़ना)	Quarrelled	Quarrelled	Quarrelling
Stop (रुकना या रोकना)	Stopped	Stopped	Stopping

Slip (फिसलना)	Slipped	Slipped	Slipping
Wed (विवाह करना)	Wedded	Wedded	Wedding
Worship (पूजा करना)	Worshipped	Worshipped	Worshipping
Wrap (लपेटना)	Wrapped	Wrapped	Wrapping

कुछ verb का Past तथा Past Participle के अंत में **'-t'** जोड़कर बनाया जाता है verb के अंत में **'-t'** जोड़ने से पहले उनके spelling में कुछ परिवर्तन भी किया जाता है।

Bend (मोड़ना)	Bent	Bent	Bending
Build (बनाना)	Built	Built	Building
Burn (जलना/जलाना)	Burnt	Burnt	Burning
Creep (रेंगना)	Crept	Crept	Creeping
Feel (महसूस करना)	Felt	Felt	Feeling
Keep (रखना)	Kept	Kept	Keeping
Kneel (घुटनों पर बैठना)	Knelt (Kneeled)	Knelt (Kneeled)	Kneeling
Lend (उधार देना)	Lent	Lent	Lending
Lose (खोना)	Lost	Lost	Losing
Mean (अर्थ कहना)	Meant	Meant	Meaning
Send (भेजना)	Sent	Sent	Sending
Sleep (सोना)	Slept	Slept	Sleeping
Spend (खर्च करना)	Spent	Spent	Spending
Sweep (झाड़ू लगाना)	Swept	Swept	Sweeping
Weep (रोना)	Wept	Wept	Weeping

कुछ verb के spelling में परिवर्तन कर उसे Past तथा Past Participle में बदला जाता है।

Present	**Past**	**Past Participle**	**Verb + ing form**
Awake (जगना/जगाना)	Awoke	Awoken	Awaking
Behold (देखना)	Beheld	Beheld	Beholding
Bleed (खून बहना)	Bled	Bled	Bleeding
Bring (लाना)	Brought	Brought	Bringing
Buy (खरीदना)	Bought	Bought	Buying
Bind (बाँधना)	Bound	Bound	Binding
Catch (पकड़ना)	Caught	Caught	Catching
Dig (खोदना)	Dug	Dug	Digging
Feed (खिलाना)	Fed	Fed	Feeding
Find (खोजना/पाना)	Found	Found	Finding
Flee (भागना)	Fled	Fled	Fleeing

Fight (लड़ना)	Faught	Faught	Fighting
Get (पाना)	Got	Got	Getting
Grind (पीसना)	Ground	Ground	Grinding
Hang (लटकाना)	Hung	Hung	Hanging
Hold (पकड़ना)	Held	Held	Holding
Have (रखना)	Had	Had	Having
Hear (सुनना)	Heard	Heard	Hearing
Lay (रखना/अंडे देना)	Laid	Laid	Laying
Leave (छोड़ देना)	Left	Left	Leaving
Lead (ले जाना)	Led	Led	Leading
Make (बनाना)	Made	Made	Making
Meet (मिलना)	Met	Met	Meeting
Shoot (मार देना)	Shot	Shot	Shooting
Sit (बैठना)	Sat	Sat	Sitting
Stand (खड़ा होना)	Stood	Stood	Standing
Stick (चुभाना/चिपकाना)	Stuck	Stuck	Sticking
Strike (प्रहार करना)	Struck	Struck	Striking
Swing (झूलना/झुलाना)	Swung	Swung	Swinging
Seek (तलाशना)	Saught	Saught	Seeking
Sell (बेचना)	Sold	Sold	Selling
Tell (बताना)	Told	Told	Telling
Teach (पढ़ाना)	Taught	Taught	Teaching
Think (सोचना)	Thought	Thought	Thinking
Understand (समझना)	Understood	Understood	Understanding
Win (जीतना)	Won	Won	Winning

Irregular forms of Verb : कुछ verb के तीनों रूप अलग-अलग होते हैं। इस प्रकार के verb को Irregular forms कहा जाता है।

Present	**Past**	**Past Participle**	**Verb + ing form**
Arise (उठाना)	Arose	Arisen	Arising
Be (am/are) (हूँ/हैं)	Was/ Were	Been	Being
Bear (जन्म देना)	Bore	Born	Bearing
Bear (सहन कहना)	Bore	Borne	Bearing
Become (होना)	Became	Become	Becoming
Begin (शुरू करना)	Began	Begun	Beginning

Bite (दाँत से काटना)	Bit	Bitten	Biting
Blow (बहना)	Blew	Blown	Blowing
Bid (आज्ञा देना)	Bade	Bidden	Bidding
Break (तोड़ना)	Broke	Broken	Breaking
Choose (चुनना)	Chose	Choosen	Choosing
Come (आना)	Came	Come	Coming
Do (करना)	Did	Done	Doing
Draw (चित्र बनाना)	Drew	Drawn	Drawing
Drink (पीना)	Drank	Drunk	Drinking
Drive (गाड़ी चलाना)	Drove	Driven	Driving
Eat (खाना)	Ate	Eaten	Eating
Fall (गिरना)	Fell	Fallen	Falling
Fly (उड़ना)	Flew	Flown	Flying
Forbid (मना करना)	Forbade	Forbidden	Forbidding
Forget (भूल जाना)	Forgot	Forgotten	Forgetting
Freeze (जमा देना)	Froze	Frozen	Freezing
Give (देना)	Gave	Given	Giving
Go (जाना)	Went	Gone	Going
Grow (बढ़ना)	Grew	Grown	Growing
Hide (छिपना/छिपाना)	Hid	Hidden	Hiding
Know (जानना)	Knew	Known	Knowing
Lie (लेटना)	Lay	Lain	Lying
Ride (सवारी करना)	Rode	Ridden	Riding
Ring (घंटी बजाना)	Rang	Rung	Ringing
Rise (ऊपर उठाना)	Rose	Risen	Rising
See (देखना)	Saw	Seen	Seeing
Shake (हिलाना)	Shooke	Shaken	Shaking
Show (दिखाना)	Showed	Shown	Showing
Shrink (सिकुड़ना)	Shrank	Shrunk	Shrinking
Sing (गाना)	Sang	Sung	Singing
Sink (डूबना)	Sank	Sunk	Sinking
Speak (बोलना)	Spoke	Spoken	Speaking
Steal (चुराना)	Stole	Stolen	Stealing
Swear (शपथ लेना)	Swore	Sworn	Swearing

Swim (तैरना)	Swam	Swum	Swimming
Take (लेना)	Took	Taken	Taking
Tear (फाड़ना)	Tore	Torn	Tearing
Throw (फेंकना)	Threw	Thrown	Throwing
Wake (जागना, जगाना)	Woke	Woken	Waking
Wear (पहनना)	Wore	Worn	Wearing
Write (लिखना)	Wrote	Written	Writing

कुछ verbs के तीनों रूप एकसमान होते हैं। जैसे-

Bid (बोली लगाना)	Bid	Bid	Bidding
Bet (शर्त लगाना)	Bet	Bet	Betting
Burst (फटना)	Burst	Burst	Bursting
Cast (फेंकना)	Cast	Cast	Casting
Cost (मूल्य लगाना)	Cost	Cost	Costing
Cut (काटना)	Cut	Cut	Cutting
Hit (चोट मारना)	Hit	Hit	Hitting
Hurt (चोट पहुँचाना)	Hurt	Hurt	Hurting
Let (देना)	Let	Let	Letting
Put (रखना)	Put	Put	Putting
Read (पढ़ना)	Read (रेड)	Read (रेड)	Reading
Set (अस्त होना)	Set	Set	Setting
Shed (उतारना)	Shed	Shed	Shedding
Shut (बंद करना)	Shut	Shut	Shutting
Split (बांटना)	Split	Split	Splitting
Spread (फैलाना)	Spread	Spread	Spreading
Thrust (ढकेलना)	Thrust	Thrust	Thrusting
Quit (छोड़ देना)	Quit	Quit	Quitting
Wet (गीला करना)	Wet	Wet	Wetting

Chapter 4

Adverb

वह शब्द जो वाक्य में किसी verb, adjective या किसी अन्य adverb की विशेषता बतलाता है, Adverb कहलाता है।

He writes **neatly.**

He writes **very** neatly.

This apple is **very** sweet.

पहले वाक्य में **'nearly'** write verb की विशेषता बतलाता है। दूसरे वाक्य में **'very'** neatly (adverb) की विशेषता बतलाता है। अगले वाक्य में **'very'** sweet (adjective) की विशेषता बतलाता है। अत: neatly तथा very **adverb** हैं। वाक्य में कैसे (how ?) कहां (Where?) तथा कब (when ?) का उत्तर देने वाले शब्द सामान्यत: adverb होते हैं।

Types of Adverb

(A) Simple Adverb :

1. **Adverb of Time**—यह कार्य के समय को दर्शाता है।

   जैसे—Before, after, soon, late, ago, never, since, ever, now, then, once, already, daily, today, tomorrow, yesterday, just, early, presently, recently, etc.

2. **Adverb of Frequency**—यह कार्य के बारंबारता (frequency) को दर्शाता है।

   जैसे—Once, twice, often, seldom, always, frequently, again, never, hardly, rarely, firstly, etc.

3. **Adverb of place**—यह कार्य से स्थान को दर्शाता है।

   जैसे—Everywhere, here, there, up, down, in, out, back, forth, within, out, away, down, somewhere, nowhere, anywhere, without, above, below, far, near, outside, inside, etc.

4. **Adverb of Manner**—यह कार्य के ढंग या तरीके को दर्शाता है। इस प्रकार के adverb सामान्यत: adjective में '-ly' जोड़कर बनाये जाते हैं।

   जैसे—Clearly, slowly, hardly, carefully, wisely, neatly, early, kindly, badly, certainly, etc.

   कुछ अन्य Adverb of manners हैं—

   Well, so, thus, fast, hard

5. **Adverb of Degree**—यह कार्य के गुण या तीव्रता (quality and intensity) को दर्शाता है।

   जैसे—Too, any, almost, quite, very, fully, partly.

6. **Adverb of Affirmation or Negation**—ये कार्य के नकारात्मक या सकारात्मक भाव को व्यक्त करते हैं।

   जैसे—Surely, certainly, definitely, not, not at all, probably, yes, no, etc.

7. **Adverb of Reason**—यह कार्य के कारण (reason) को दर्शाता है।

   जैसे—So, therefore, hence, because, consequently.

Note : Type of adverb उनके प्रयोग पर निर्भर करता है। किसी एक adverb को उसके प्रयोग के आधार पर अलग-अलग प्रकार में रखा जा सकता है।

(B) Interrogative adverb—Interrogative adverb का प्रयोग प्रश्न पूछने के लिए किया जाता है। Interrogative adverb की तरह प्रयुक्त कुछ शब्द हैं। जैसे—Where, when, why, how, what, etc.

(C) Relative adverb—जब Interrogative adverb का प्रयोग प्रश्न पूछने के लिए नहीं, बल्कि दो Sentences को जोड़ने के लिए किया जाता है, तो ये Relative adverb कहलाते हैं। Relative adverb एक साथ adverb तथा conjunction दोनों का काम करते हैं। जैसे—

That is **where** you are wrong.

(That is the point of argument where you're wrong.)

This is **where** I live.

(This is the place where I live.)

I loved history **when** at school.

This is **what** I wanted to know.

Formation of Adverb:—

1. सामान्यत: adjective में :- **ly'** जोड़कर adverb बनाया जाता है। जैसे—

Adjective		Adverb
Clear (स्पष्ट)	-	clearly (स्पष्ट रूप से)
Clever (चतुर)	-	cleverly (चतुराई से)
Beautiful (सुंदर)	-	beautifully(सुंदरता से)
Kind (दयालु)	-	kindly (दया भाव से)
Foolish (मूर्ख)	-	foolishly (मूर्खतापूर्वक)
Late (विलंब से)	-	lately (हाल में)
First (प्रथम)	-	firstly (प्रथमत:)
Hard (कठोर)	-	hardly (बिल्कुल नहीं)
High (ऊंचा)	-	highly (अत्यधिक)
Poor (गरीब)	-	poorly (काफी कम)
Short (छोटा)	-	shortly (शीघ्रता)
Wise (बुद्धिमान)	-	wisely (बुद्धिमानी से)

अगर किसी adjective के अंत में **'-y'** है तथा उसके ठीक पहले consonant (स्वर अक्षर) है तो y को i में बदलकर **'ly'** जोड़ते हैं। जैसे—

Adjective		Adverb
Happy (खुश)	-	Happily (खुशी से)
Ready (तैयार)	-	Readily (आसानी से)
Heavy (भारी)	-	Heavily (भारीपन से)

2. Noun और adjective को एक साथ जोड़कर भी adverb बनाया जाता है। जैसे—Sometimes, meanwhile, otherwise, yesterday.
3. Preposition और noun को एक साथ जोड़कर भी adverb बनाया जाता है। जैसे—Afoot, asleep, ahead, aboard, away, overboard, today, tomorrow, etc.
4. Preposition तथा adjective को एक साथ जोड़कर भी adverb बनाया जाता है।जैसे—Aloud, anew, along, below, behind, beyond, etc.
5. Preposition और adverb को एक साथ जोड़कर भी adverb बनता है। जैसे—within, without, before, thereby, therein, thereafter, hereafter, hereby, herewith, herein, etc.
6. दो adverbs को conjunction द्वारा एक साथ जोड़कर भी adverb बनता है। जैसे—

Again and again	(बार-बार)
By and by	(अभी/क्रमश:)
Far and near	(चारों तरफ)
Far and away	(अत्यधिक)
First and foremost	(सबसे पहले)
Here and there	(यहाँ वहाँ)
Off and on	(बार-बार)
Over and above	(इसके अतिरिक्त)
Out and away	(अतुलनीय)
Now and then	(कभी-कभी)
To and fro	(आगे-पीछे)
Up and down	(ऊपर नीचे)

7. **Adverb Phrases—**कुछ phrases का प्रयोग adverb के रूप में किया जाता है जिन्हें adverb phrases कहते हैं। जैसे—

At random (बिना उद्देश्य/क्रम के)
At length (विस्तारपूर्वक)
At large (स्वतंत्र)
At least (कम से कम)
At all (किसी प्रकार से)
After all (सब होते हुए भी)
At present (अभी, इस समय)
At last (अंतत:)
By all means (हर प्रकार से)
By no means (कदापि नहीं)
By the way (प्रसंगवश)
In fact (वास्तव में)
In short (संक्षेप में)
In general (साधारणत:)
In vain (बेकार में)
Of course (अवश्य)
Up side down (पूर्णत: अव्यस्थित)

Comparison of Adverb:—

Adjective की तरह की कुछ adverbs को तीन degree में बांटा जाता है—

1. Positive degree,
2. Comparative degree तथा
3. Superlative degree.

किसी verb की सामान्य विशेषता बतलाने के लिए adverb के positive degree का प्रयोग किया जाता है। दो के बीच तुलना के लिए comparative degree जबकि दो से अधिक के बीच तुलना के लिए superlative degree का प्रयोग किया जाता है। Superlative degree के साथ **the** का प्रयोग किया जाता है।

Rohit worked **hard.** (Positive)
Mohit worked **harder** than Rohit.(Comparative)
Ashish worked **the hardest** of all. (Superlative)

Positive Degree से Comparative तथा Superlative Degree में बदलने के नियम—

1. सामान्यत: adverb के positive degree में 'er' तथा **'-est'** जोड़कर क्रमश: comparative तथा superlative degree बनाया जाता है। जैसे—

Positive	**Comparative**	**Superlative**
Fast	Faster	Fastest
Long	Longer	Longest
Hard	Harder	Hardest
Soon	Sooner	Soonest
Early	Earlier	Earliest
Late	Later	Latest
Near	Nearer	Nearest
Loud	Louder	Loudest

2. जिन adverb के अंत में **'-ly'** होता है, उनका comparative तथा superlative degree सामान्यत: adverb के पहले more और most जोड़कर बनाया जाता है। जैसे—

Positive	**Comparative**	**Superlative**
Skilfully	More skilfully	Most skillfully
Quickly	More quickly	Most quickly
Wisely	More wisely	Most wisely

3. कुछ adverb का comparative तथा superlative degree अलग शब्द ही होता है। जैसे—

Positive	**Comparative**	**Superlative**
lll/Bad	Worse	Worst
Well/Good	Better	Best
Much	More	Most
Little	Less	Least
Far	Farther	Farthest
Far	Further	Furthest
Late	Later	Last
Forth	Further	Furthest

Correct Use of Adverb :

1. सामान्यत: adverb का प्रयोग verb के बाद किया जाता है। यदि वाक्य में एक ही odject हो, तो adverb का प्रयोग object के बाद किया जाता है।

I am driving **slowly.**
He speaks English **fluently.**
We will go for picnic **tomorrow.**
He runs **very** fast.

2. अगर दो या अधिक adverb एक साथ प्रयुक्त हों तो उन्हें क्रमश: Adverb of manner, Adverb of Place तथा Adverb of time के क्रम में रखते हैं। जैसे—

He played skilfully in the tournament yesterday.
They welcomed the guest warmly at their home last week.

—warmly – adverb of manner.
—at their home – adverb of place.
—last week – adverb of time.

3. Adverb of frequency का प्रयोग सामान्यत: main verb से पहले किया जाता है। जैसे—

He **never** tell a lie.

They **often** go far a walk.

परन्तु composite verb के साथ adverb का प्रयोग auxiliary verb के बाद किया जाता है। जैसे—

He has **just** gone out.
They have **never** visited a zoo.

अगर verb **'be'** (is/am/was/were) है तो adverb of frequency का प्रयोग verb के बाद किया जाता है। जैसे—

We were **hardly** wrong.
Ashish is **never** late for school.

4. Adjective या किसी अन्य adverb पर जोर देने वाला adverb उस adjective या adverb से पहले प्रयोग किया जाता है। जैसे—

   We were **quite** right.

   परन्तु adverb **'enough'** का प्रयोग उस शब्द के बाद किया जाता है जिस पर वह जोर देता है। जैसे—

   He ran fast **enough** to win the race.
   The house is big **enough** for the family.

5. Adverb of time जैसे— yesterday, today, tomorrow आदि तथा adverb of place जैसे—here, there, everywhere आदि का प्रयोग वाक्य के अंत में होता है। जैसे—

   I was playing cricket **yesterday.**
   I have got a piano lesson **today.**
   Let us go out of **here.**

Chapter

Tense

By Tense, we understand the correspondence between the form of the verb and our concept of time.

Tense shows (a) the time of an action, (b) its degree of completeness.

The verb may tell us :

1. That an action is *done at the present time,* e.g., I see the blue sky.
2. That an action *was done in the past time,* e.g., He saw the blue sky.
3. That an action *will be done in the future time,* e.g., He will see the blue sky.
4. That an action *was done at some past time,* viewed as future (*future in the past*), e.g., He said that he would be sixteen in three weeks' time.

A verb, then, has three main times or tenses, viz the *Present,* the *Past* and the *Future.*

To each tense, there are four different forms :

Simple which denotes present, past or future time in its simplest form : *'I played' ,'I shall play'*. The action (in present, past or future time) is mentioned simply, without anything being said about the completeness or in completeness of the action.

Continuous which denotes that the event (in present, past or future time) is still *continuing* or not yet completed; 'I *am reading*', 'I *was reading*', 'I *shall be reading*'.

Perfect which denotes that the event (in present, past or future time) is in a completed or *perfect* state : *'I' have played',I had played', 'I shall have played'.*

Perfect Continuous which combines the meanings of the two preceding forms, *'I have been reading', 'I had been reading'*, 'I *shall have been reading*'.

Use of the Tense

The Simple form of the Present (*The Simple Present or Present Indefinete*) can be used to denote the following :

(a) What *is always and necessarily true :*

The *sun shines* by day and the moon by night.

The *sun rises in the east.*

Honey *is sweet.*

Fortune *favours the brave.*

(b) What *is permanent or habitual in life or character:*

He *keeps* his promises.

He *has* good health.

He *drinks* tea every morning.

I *get* up every day at six o'clook.

(c) what is present, provided that *present time is implied by the context :*

I *understand* what you say.

The door is open : it *is* not shut.

(d) What is future, provided that *future time is implied by the context.*

He *comes* (= will come) in a few days' time.

When *do* you (= will you) start for Chennai ?

When *does* (= will) the college reopen ?

We *go* (= shall go) to Kolkata next week.

(e) What is past, provided that *the event expressed by the verb is known to be past* (This is called the Historic or Graphic present) :

Shivaji *now draws* his sword and *attacks* the enemy.

Babar *now leads* (= then led) his men through the Khyber Pass, and enters (= entered) the plains of India.

(f) To introduce *quotations* : as,

Keats says, 'A thing of beauty is a joy forever.'

(g) It is used, *instead of the simple future tense, in clauses of time and of condition;* as,

I shall wait *till* you finish your lunch.

The simple form of the present tense is also used for directons in plays :

Anne *crosses* the room and *locks* the door.

Sentences of this tense are formed by observing the following rules :

(1) In an *affirmative sentence,* if the subject is plural or singular, but in the first or second person, the verb is used in its original or present form e.g., They *eat.* I *eat.* Girls *eat.* You *eat.*

(2) The *negative sintence* of simple present is formed :

(a) by adding *do not* to the verb if the subject is plural or in the first person and second person, *e.g.,* I *do not eat*. You *do not eat*.

(b) by adding *does not* to the verb if the subject is in the singular number and not in the first person and the second person, e.g., She *does not eat*. Ram *does not eat*.

(3) The *interrrogative sentence* in simple present is formed :

(a) by putting the subject between *does* and verb if it is in the singular number, e.g., *Does* she *eat ? Does* Ram *eat ?* When *does* he *eat ?*

(b) by puting the subject between *do* and the verb if it is in the plural number or in the singular number of first and second person, e.g., Do you *eat ?* What do you *eat ? Do I eat ?*

The Present Continuous is used to express *an action going on at the time of speaking, e.g.,*

The boys are *flying* kites.

He is *playing* cricket.

I am *reading* a book.

It also sometimes expresses *habit* or *custom;* as,

He is *attending* college very regularly these days.

For a *temporary action* which *may not be actually happening at the time of speaking;* as,

I am reading *David Copperfield*. (but I am not reading it at this moment).

For an *action* that *is planned or arranged to take place in the near future;* as,

I *am going* to my father tomorrow.

She is *going* to write a book.

Note : We prefer to use the present simple rather than the present continous with the verbs describing sensual states, a state of mind or feeling, mental activity, etc.

These verbs include *agree, assume believe, belong to, contain, cost, disagree, feel, haste, have, hope, know, like, look, love, own, prefer, realise, regret, resemble, smell, taste, forgive, concern, depend, doubt, differ, imagine, recognise, understand*, etc.

I really *enjoy* travelling.

The group currently *consists* of five people.

However, we can use the present continuous with such verbs when we want to emphasise that a situation is temporary for a period of time around the present.

I *consider* him to be extremely fortunate. (This is my view)

I *am considering* taking early retirement.

(This is something I' m thinking about now) The following verbs for their meaning are not ordinarily used in continuous forms. (Present, Past, Future)

1. Verbs of Perception—*see, hear smell, notice, recognise*
2. Verbs of Appearance—*appear, look, seen*
3. Verbs of Emotion—*feel, live, love, want, wish, desire, hate, hope, refuse, prefer*
4. Verbs of Thought—*think, suppose, agree, consider, trust, remember, forget, know, understand, mean, mind*
5. Verbs of Possession—*own, possess, contain, consist of, belong, to, to have*

However, if there is a change of meaning, some of them, can be used in continuous tense; as,

(1) The students *are having* lunch.

(2) I am *thinking* of going to Chennai, (Planning)

(3) She *is looking* for a job. (Searching)

The Present Continuous observes the following rules :

(1) The *affirmative* sentence is formed :

(a) by adding *is* before the verb and *ing* to the verb if the subject is singular and in the third person, e,g., She is *eating*. Ram *is eating*.

(b) by adding are before the verb and *ing* to the verb if the subject is in the plural number or singular number of second person and third person, e.g.,

You *are eating*. They *are eating*.

Note : In the second person, the verb remains the same in the singular as well as in the plural number.

(c) by adding *am* before the verb and *ing* to the verb when the subject is in the first person of the singular number, e.g., I *am eating*.

(2) The *negative* sentence in this tense is formed by simply putting *not* after *is / am / are* e.g., She *is not eating*. I *am not eating*. They *are not eating*. You *are not eating*.

(3) The *interrogative* sentence is formed by placing *is / am / are* before the subject and verb after the subject, e.g., *Is* she *eating ?* Are you *eating ?* Am I *eating? Are* the girls *eating?*

The Present Perfect invariably connects a *completed* event in some sense or other with the *present* time.

e.g.,

I *have lived* twenty years in Lucknow. (that is, I *am living* there still and I began to live there twenty years ago.)

I *have passed* my examination; I *passed* it two years ago.

He *has been* to London; He *went* there in 1948.

The present perfect denotes an *action completed at the time of speaking;* as,

I *have solved* all the sums.

He *has visited* all the Indian temples.

She *has read* most of Scott' s novels.

(a) Such a sentence as the following is wrong :

Babar *has founded* the Mughal Empire.

This is wrong because the state of things arising out of the foundation of the empire by Babar has entirely passed away.

(b) Since the present perfect denotes *present time,* it cannot be qualified by any adverb or phrase denoting *past* time. This would be a contradiction in terms.

But such sentences as the following are correct, because the adverb or phrase used in each of them is of such a kind as to *connect past time with the present;* hence, no contradiction occurs.

Scarlet fever *has raged* in the town since Monday last (that is, scarlet fever began to rage on Monday last, and is raging still.)

The verb in this tense is used in its third form.

(1) An *affirmative* sentence of the present perfect tense is formed :

(a) by adding *has* before the *verb* if the subject is in the singular number, e.g., He *has eaten.* It *has eaten.* Ram *has eaten.*

(b) by adding *have* before the verb if the subject is in the plural number or in the singular number of only the first and the second person, e.g., I *have eaten.* They *have eaten.* You *have eaten.* The children *have eaten.*

Present Tense at a Glance

Tense	**First Person**	**Second Person**	**Third Person**
Simple Present			
Singular	I eat	You eat	He/She/ It eats
Plural	We eat	You eat	They eat
Present Continuous			
Singular	I am eating	You are eating	He is eating
Plural	We are eating	You are eating	They are eating
Present Perfect			
Singular	I have eaten	You have eaten	He has eaten
Plural	We have eaten	You have eaten	They have eaten
Perfect			
Continuous			
Singular	I have been eating	You have been eating	He has been eating
Plural	We have been eating	You have been eating	The have been eating

(2) A negatvie sentence of the present perfect tense is formed by simply inserting not between *has* or *have* and *verb*, e.g., *She has not eaten.* I have not *eaten*. They h*ave not eaten*, etc.

(3) An *interrogative* sentence of the present perfect tense is formed by putting the subject between *has* or *have* and verb, e.g., *Have you eaten*? *Has she eaten*? *have I eaten ? Have they eaten ?*

Present Perfect Continuous is used for an action which began sometime in the past and is still continuing, *e.g.*,

He *has been sleeping* for five hours (and is still sleeping).

I *have been doing* this for several months.

I *have been writing* this book for four years

This tense is sometimes used for an action already finished. In such cases, the continuity of the activity is emphasised as an explanation of something, e.g., Why are your clothes so wet ? *I have been watering* the garden.

Under this tense, the verb is in the first form with *ing* added to it.

(1) An *affirmative* sentence of the present perfect continuous is formed by adding *have been* or *has been* to the verb according to the number or person of the subject (like in persent perfect). e.g., I *have been eating*. You *have been eating*. He *has been eating*.

(2) A *negative* sentence of this tense is formad by inserting *not* between *has/have*, and *been*, e.g., I *have not been* eating. You *have not been eating*. He *has not been* eating.

(3) An *interrogative* sentence of this tense is formed by interchanging *has/have* and the *subject*. e.g., *Have* I *been eating*? *Have* they *been eating*? *Have* you *been eating*? *Has* he *been eating*?

The Simple Past or Past Indefinite is used to denote an *action in the past*; e.g.,

My father *died* yesterday.

He *left* office at 5.30 p.m.

She *lived* in Delhi for 10 years.

Babar *founded* the Mughal Empire in India.

It also denotes a *habitual action in the past*, e.g.,

We *studied* and *planned* for years.

She always *carried* a bag.

The verb in this tense is used in its second or past form.

(1) In an *affirmative* sentence, the form of the verb remains the same whatever the number or person of the subject, e.g., I *ate*. She *ate*. They *ate*. You *ate*.

(2) In a *negative* sentence of the simple past, *did not* is added to the verb and the verb used in its original or present form, e.g., I *did not eat*. She *did not eat*. They *did not eat*. You *did not eat*.

(3) In an *interrogative* sentence of the simple past, the subject is placed between *did* and the *verb*. The *verb*, like in the negative, is used in its original or present form, e.g., Did *you eat* ? Did they *eat* ? Did I *eat* ? Did she *eat* ?

The Past Continuous expresses an action *began* and *continuing* in past time, e.g.,

She came into my room while I *was studying*.

He saw me as he *was passing* by yesterday.

The method for making past continuous is the same as that for making present continuous in the affirmative, interrogative and negative. The only difference is that *was* will be substituted for *is/am* and *were* for *are*, e.g.,

I *was eating*. You *were eating*. She *was eating*. They were *eating*.

Past Tense at a Glance

Tense	First Person	Second Person	Third Person
Simple			
Singular	I ate	You ate	He/She/It ate
Plural	We ate	You ate	They ate
Continuous			
Singular	I am eating	You are eating	He is eating
Plural	We are eating	You are eating	They were eating
Perfect			
Singular	I had eaten	You had eaten	He had eaten
Plural	We had eaten	You had eaten	They had eaten
Perfect Continuous			
Singular	I have been eating	You had been eating	He had been eating
Plural	We had been eating	You had been eating	They had been eating

or

Was I *eating* ? *Were* you *eating* ? *Was* she *eating* ? *Were* they *eating* ?

or

I *was not eating*. She *was not eating*. They *were not eating*. You *were not eating*.

The Past Perfect is used whenever we wish to say that *some action had been completed before another was commenced.*

The verb expressing the *previous* action is put into the past perfect tense. The verb expressing the *subsequent* action is put into the simple past.

(a)	*Previous Action*	*Subsequent Action*
	(*Past Perfect*)	(*Simple Part*)
	He *had been* ill for two days.	When the doctor was *sent* for.
	He *had seen* many foreign cities	before he *returned* home.
(b)	*Subsequent Action*	*Previous Action*
	The sheep *fled* in great haste	for a wolf *had entered* the field.
	The ship was *sunk* by a storm	which *had* suddenly sprung up.

The past perfrect ought never to be used at all except to show the priority of one past event to another.

The past perfect is formed by the same method as the present perfect tense in the afirmative, interrrogative and negative. The only difference is that *had* is subsitituted for *has* and *have*, e.g., She *had eaten*. I *had eaten*. They *had eaten*. We *had eatem*.

Or

Had they *eaten* ? Had you *eaten* ? Had I *eaten* ? *Had* they *eaten* ?

Or

She *had not eaten*. They *had not eaten*. I *had not eaten*. You *had not eaten*.

Past Perfect Continuous is used for an action that began before a certain point in the past and continued upto that time.

At that time, he *had been writing* a novel for two months. *When* Mr. Mukherji came to school in 1985, Mr. Anand *had* already *been teaching* there for five years.

The method of forming a senetence of this tense is the same as that for the present perfect continuous in the affirmative, interrogative and negative. The only difference is that *had* is substituded for *have* and *has*, e.g., *I had been eating*. You *had been eating*. They *had been eating*. We *had been eating*.

Or

Had I *been eating* ? Had you *been eating* ? Had *we been eating* ?

Or

I had not been eating. You *had not been eating*. They *had not been eating,* etc.

Past perfect tense in question form is used with an extension to make it an affirmative sentence, e.g., *Had she been working regularly she would have completed* the project yesterday.

The Simple Future or Future Indefinite expresses simply future time, i.e. the time that has *not come yet, near or remote*; as,

He will come *tomorrow*.

Prizes will be distributed *next week*.

In this tense, the verb is used in its original or present form.

(1) In an *affirmative* sentence, *will* is added before the verb whatever be the number or person of the subject. e.g., I *will eat*. You *will eat*. They *will eat*. He *will eat*.

(2) In a *negative* sentence, not is added after *will* of the *affirmative* sentence, e.g., I *will not eat*. You *will not eat*. They *will not eat*. He *will not eat*.

(3) In an *interrogative* sentence of the simple future, the subject is placed between will and verb, e.g., *Will* I *eat* ? *Will* you *eat*? *Will* they eat ? *Will* he *eat ?*

The Future Continuous represents an action that will keep *going on at some point in future time*; as,

He *will* be playing cricket tomorrow afternoon. I *shall be writing* the book *then*.

Future Tense at a Glance

Tense	**First Person**	**Second Person**	**Third Person**
Smiple			
Singular	I will eat	You will eat	He/She/It will eat
Plural	We will eat	You will eat	They will eat
Continuous			
Singular	I will be eating	You will be eating	He will be eating
Plural	We will be eating	You will be eating	They willl be eating
Perfect			
Singular	I will have eaten	You will have eaten	He will have eaten
Plural	We will have eaten	You will have eaten	They will have eaten
Perfect Continuous			
Singular	I will have been eating	You will have been eating	He will have been eating
Plural	We will have been eating	You will have been eating	They will have been eating

In this tense, *ing* is added to the verb.

(1) An *affirmative* sentence is formed by adding *will be* to the veryb, e.g., I *will be earting*. He *will be eating*. They *will be eating*.

(2) A *negative* sentence is formed by inserting not between *will* and *be* of the affirmative sentence, e.g., I *will not be eating*. He *will not be eating*. They *will not be eating*. You *will not be eating,* etc.

(3) An interrogative sentence is formed by placing the subject betwen *will* and *be,* e.g., *Will* I *be eating* ? *Will* they *be eating* ? *Will* he *be eating* ? *Will* you *be eatijng* ?

The Future Perfect. This tense is used in two different sense: (a) to denote the completion of some event in future time; and (b) to denote the completion of some event in past time.

(a) He *will have* reached home before the rain sets in. (The reaching of home will be completed before the setting in of rain.)

(b) You *will have* heard (must have heard in some past time) this news already; so I need not repat it.

In this form of the future tense, the verb is used in its third form.

(1) An *affirmative* sentence is formed by adding *will have* beore the verb, e.g., I *will have eaten*. They *will have eaten*. He *will have eaten*. You *will have eaten.*

(2) A *negative* sentence is formed by puting not between *will* and *have*, e.g., I *will* not *have eaten* (by then). He *will* not *have eaten* (by tommorrow), etc.

Note : This form of the tense is rarely used.

(3) An *interrogative* sentence of this tenses formed by placing the subject between *will* and *have*, e.g., *Will* they *have eaten*? *Will* he *have eaten*? *Will* you *have eaten* ?

Future Perfect Continuous indicates an *action represented as being in progress and a period of time that will and in future*; as.

By next July, we *shall have been living* here for four years. When he gets his degree, he *will have been studying* in Oxford for four years.

In this tense, *ing* is added to the verb.

The sentences of this tense are normally of the affirmative type only. A sentence is formed by adding *shall / will have been* to the verb, e.g., I *will have been eating*. We *shall have been eating*. They *will have been eating*.

Shall and Will. These are the two auxiliary verbs by means of which future tense if formed in both Voices.

There are *three* senses in which the future tense can be used:

(a) to express *merly future* time and nothing more.

(b) to combine future time with an implied *command*.

(c) to combine future time with an implied *intention*.

(a) Merely Future Time

When nothing but future time is intended—mere futurity, without any idea of command or intention being mixed up with it—*shall* must be used for the first person, and *will* for the *second* and *third* persons, as ahead :

Persons	*Singular*	*Plural*
First Person	*I shall go.*	*We shall go.*
Second Person	*Thou will go*	*You willl go.*
Third Person	*He will go.*	*They will go.*

(b) An Implied Command, Promise or Threat

Whenever we desire to express, not merely future time, but some command, or promise, or threat, or determination in addition, *shall* is put for *will* in the second and third persons, and *will* is put for *shall* in the first person.

Thou *shall* love thy neighbour as thyself.
(*Command*)

You *shall* receive your prize timorrow.
(*Promise*)

He *shall* not enter my house again.
(*Determination*)

I' ll reward her for labours.
(*Promise*)

I *will* dismiss you if you do that again.
(*Threat*)

I' ll never agree to her proposal.
(*Derermination*)

(c) An Implied Intention

When the speaker wishes to express some intention of his own, *will* replaces *shall* in the first person :

I *will* call on you today, and I *shall* then say good-bye.

Here, the first verb denotes the *intention* of calling while the second denotes *merely future time.*

Shall and *Will* in Interrogative Sentences :

In assertive sentences, merely *future* time is denoted by *shall* in the first person, and by *will* in the second and third a *command* is denoted by *shall* in the second and third Persons; an *intenion* by *will* in the first person. In interrogative sentences, however, the change of situation from asserting a fact to asking a question modifies to some extent the use of *shall* and *will*. All possible meanings of *shall* and *will* when they are used interrogatively, are shown in the following examples :

Shall I : *Shall I* see you tomorrow ? (Here *shall* merely *inquires after something future*).

Shall I post that letter for you ? (Here, *shall* asks what the other person wishes : Do you command or desire me to post that letter for you ?)

Will I : (This is generally not used because *will* in the first person would imply intention, and it would be foolish to ask another person about one' s own intentions. It may be used as a *kind of each of a previous will you* ?)

Will you post this letter for me ?

Will I ? of course, I *will*.

Shall you : *Shall you* return home today ? (This merely inquires about *something future.* Here, shall cannot imply command, because it would be foolish to inquire of anyone whether he commands himself to do so).

Will you : Often *will* you is used for mere future.

Will you be thirty or thirty-one on your next birthday ?

When *will* you know if you have passed your examination ?

Will you do me this favour? (Here, *will* denotes willingness or intention. Are you willing or do you intend to do me this favour ? So, it is used for asking a favour).

Shall he : *Shall he* call for the doctor ? (Here, shall implies a *command.*Do you desire or command him to call for the doctor ?)

Will he :*Will* he be fourteen years old tomorrow ? (Here *will* merely inquires about something future.)

Sequence of Tenses

What is Sequence of Tenses ?

The Sequence of Tenses is a system by which the tense of the verb in a subordinate clause is governed by the tense of the verb in the principal clause.

In order to understand this principle, Grammar prescribes certatin rules. They are :

Rule 1. If the tense in the principal clause is *present* or *future*, it may be followed by *any tense* in the subordinate clause required by the sentence.

Examples :

(i) She *says* that Radha is singing a song.
(ii) She *will* say that Radha sang a song.
(iii) You *say* that he is a dull student.
(iv) You *will* say that he was a dull student.
(v) I *shall say* that you *will* be of much help.

Rule 2. A past tense in the principal clause must be followed by a *past tense* in the subordinate clause.

Examples :

(i)	I *told* him	that I was *going* to office.
	(Past Tense)	*(Past Tense)*
(ii)	I *knew* me.	that he *would* deceive
	(Past Tense)	*(Past Tense)*
(iii)	He *hinted*	that he *wanted* money.
	(Past Tense)	*(Past Tene)*
(iv)	She *replied*	that she *felt* better.
	(Past Tense)	*(Past Tense)*
(v)	He *replied*	that he *would* come.
	(Past Tense)	*(Past Tense)*

Two exceptions to the above rule :

If the subordinate clause contains some Universal Truth. Habitual Truth, a Quotation, Scientific Law, etc., it will be in present tense even if the tense used in the principal clause is past.

Examples :

(i)	The teacher said	that the earth moves round the sun.
	[*Principal Clause in Past Tense*]	[*Subordinate Clause in Present Tense*] (*Universal Truth*)
(ii)	He said	that he is an early riser.
	[*Principal Clause in Past Tense*]	[*Subordinate Clause in Present Tense*] (Habitual Truth)
(iii)	Newton said	that for every action there is an equal and opposite reaction.
	[*Princopal Clause in Past Tense*]	[*Subordinate Clause in Present*] (Scientific Law)

If the subordinate clause is introduced by than, even in there is a past tense in the principal clause, it may be followed by any tense in the sense in the subordinte clause.

He liked you betterthan he likes me.

(*Principal Clause in Past Tense*)(*Subordinate Clause in*

(Present Tense)

Rule 3. If the subordinate clause is introduced by *as if* or *as though*, past tense is used for the present time and past perfect tense for the past time.

Examples :

(i) He talks *as if* he were mad.

In this sentence, the subordinate clause has been introduced by *as if* and the tense is present. Hence, past tense has been used.

(ii) He loved me as *though* I had been his son.

In this sentence, the subordinate clause has been introduced by as *though* and the time is past. Hence, past perfect tense has been used.

Rule 4. If a subordinate clause is introduced by the conjunction *lest*, it is followed by *should* and not by *may*.

Examples :

(i) Work hard *lest* you should fail.

(ii) Take care of your health lest you should fall ill.

Note :

1. *Lest* always gives a negative sense. Hence, not should not be used in such sentences. For example, it will be wrong to say : Walk slowly lest you should not fall.
2. *Lest* is always folllowed by *should* whatever be the tense of the verb in the principal clause. You can say :
   (a) He *took* exercises *lest* he *should* fall ill.
   [Here, the principal clause is in past tense.]
   (b) He will take exercises lest he *should* fall ill.
   [Here, the principal clause is in future tense.]

Rule 5. If there is an idea of two *actions both taking place in the future one after the other*, the principal clause is written in the future indefinite, whereas the subordinate clause is written in the present indefinite.

Mark the following sketch :

Sequence of Tense

Two Action in Future

First action	*Second action*
Present Indefinite	Future Indefinite
If it rains	I shall not go to college.
If you work hard	you will pass.

Rule 6. If *two actions in a sentence are shown happening in the past one after the other*, the principal clause is written in the past perfect and the subordinate clause is written in past indefinite :

Sequence of Tense

Two Actions in past

First action	*Second action*
Past Perfect	Past Indefinite
The patient had died	beforce the doctor arrived .
I had read my book	when he called on me.

Rule 7 : If there are *two actions in a sentenece, both in the past*, the principal action should be in future perfect, whereas the subordinate action should be in past prefect.

Examples :

(i) If you had taken tea, I would have also taken.

(ii) If you had been to Kolkata. I would have also gone.

Note :

(i) In such cases, the conditional clause is always the subordinate clause.

(ii) The above sentences can also be written as follows :

(a) Had you taken tea, I would have also taken.

(b) Had you been to Kolkata, I would have also gone.

Rule 8. A *present* or *future tense in the principal clause may be followed by any tense required by the sense; as:*

He thinks that she *is* there.

He thinks that she *was* there.

He thinks that she *will* be there.

He will think that she *is* there.

He will think that she *was* there.

He will think that she *will* be there.

But, in sentences where the subordinate clause denotes

purpose, if the verb in the principal clause is present or future, the verb in subordinate clause must be in present: as,

I eat that I *may* live.

I shall nurse him that he *may* live.

Reading Comprehension

Directions for the following three questions (Q.1 to 3)

Read the passage and answer the question that follow: Your answers to these questions should be based on the passage only.

Like many people I was convinced that the broad range of health benefits that physical activity offers including weight loss, lower blood pressure and clolesterol levels and hardier immune system. So three times a week I sweated on the treadmill and exercise bicycle at my local gym. At the end of two months, I was trimmer, more energetic, and felt fitter. If I could accomplish this by working three times a week, I reasoned, the more exercise should bring me even greater benefits.

In the next six months. In included an hour long running six times a week and initially felt and improved fitness level. However, soon I was plagued by muscular soreness and aching knees. I felt fatigued rather than fresher after a work out. What is more? I found myself suffering from frequent colds. Wasn't the exercise meant to protect me from all this?

Exercise only up to a point A prescription of exercise does not mean running to a point A prescription of exercise does not mean running to the point of lameness or swimming endless laps untill your arms cramp. So, forget 'no pain, no gain'. The key to maximizing the benefits of exercise is a safe and sensible programme. Choose exercise that are safe and enjoyable and will stay with you a life time. The initial enthusiasm of high impact exercises gives way to diminishing enjoyment.

1. **One feels faigued because of**

   (a) over-exercising (b) long working hours

   (c) poor diet (d) lack of exercise

2. **To get maximum benefits of exercise one must**

   (a) follow a rigid fitness routine

   (b) do high impact exercise

   (c) exercise infrequently

   (d) follow a guided exercise schedule

3. **'Workout' in this passage means**

   (a) a cessation of physical

   (b) to work outdoors

   (c) a session of physical exercise

   (d) anything that works eventually

Directions for the following Q. Nos. 4 to 6 :

Read the passage and answer the questions that follow. Your answer to these questions should be based on the passage only.

My informant about the Tibetan civilization is a certain Japanee monk of the name of Kawaguchi, who spent three years in Tibet at the beginning of the twentieth century. His account of the experience has been translated into English and published with the title 'Three Years in Tibet', by the Theosophical Society. It is one of the great travel books of the world, and so far as I am aware, the most interesting book on Tibet which no European traveller could possibly have had. He attened the University of Lhasa, he enjoyed the acquaintance of Dalai Lama himself, he was the friend of lama nad layman of all sorts adn conditions of Tibetans from teh highest class to the lowest-the despicable caste smiths and butchers. He knew his Tibet intimately, for those three years, indeed, he was for all practical purposes a Tibetan. This is something which no European eplorer can claim, and it is this which gives Kawaguchi's book its unique interest.

4. **Who was Kawaguchi?**

   (a) a Chinese monk (b) a Chinese traveller

   (c) a Japanese monk (d) a Japanese traveller

5. **'Three Years in Tibet' is**

   (a) a travel book (b) an adventrure bool

   (c) a short story (d) a novel

6. **The despised castes in Tibet were**

   (a) Smiths and butchers

   (b) Sweepers and butchurs

   (c) Shoemakers and sweepers

   (d) Shoemakers and butchers

Instruction for Question Nos. 7-11:

Read the following passage carefully and answer the questions. Choose the correct answer from the alternatives based only on the passage given:

The great drawback of our education system is that the entire focus is on making young children a storehouse of information. They are given a load of books to carry on their backs and cram the informations stored in them. There is no emphasis on creativity and personality development. They are not taught how they can be noble souls like Gandhiji, Rabindranath Tagore, C.V. Raman, Satyendra Nath Bose,

Swami Vivekanand and other Indian greats they are taught the lessons of materials gain. They are coaxed to study engineering, medicine and business management and own a big house, a luxurious car and a heavy bank balance.

7. **What is the main focus ofour education system?**
   (a) Making young children smart
   (b) Making young children store house of informa tion.
   (c) Making young children briliant.
   (d) Making young children literate.

8. **What tasks are given to young children?**
   (a) Doing difficult home work.
   (b) Taking excellent care of their clothes and shoes.
   (c) Paying attention to computers and tablets
   (d) Carrying heavy loadof books and cramming the informations given in them.

9. **Which basic element of education is ignored?**
   (a) Practical aspect of life.
   (b) Moral aspect of life
   (c) Creativity and personality development.
   (d) Mutual help and lessons of social service.

10. **What are the lessonswhich young children are being taught?**
   (a) Lessons of material gain.
   (b) Lessons of nobility.
   (c) Lessons of Science and History.
   (d) Lessons of Engineering and Medicine.

11. **The idiom 'bag and baggage' means**
   (a) with all belonging
   (b) with all members
   (c) with all the money
   (d) with all the instruments

Instruction for Question Nos. 12-16.

Read the passage carefully and answer the questions. Choose the correct answer from the alternatives based only the passage given.

Megasthenese declared that there were no slaves in India. He was certainly wrong, but Indian slavery was milder than the form he was used to see in the West and slaves were much less numerous than in the civilizations of the West ; hence he may not have recognized the dasa as a slave. The Arthashastra, in many ways more liberal than the religious books, lays down regulations appreciably milder than those we have outlined. The sale of children into slaverty is explicitly forbidden except in dire emergency. Slaves are entitled to own and inherit property, and to earn money freely in their spare time. Slaves of the upper classes cannot be forced to perform defiling duties.

The chastity of slave-girl is protected, the master who rapes a slave-girl mist set her free and pay her compensation, and if she has a child by her master, even with her own consent, both mother and child become free.

The humane regulation of the Arthashastra, probably unique in the records of any ancient civilization, are perphaps survivals of Mauryan laws, and it is, therefore, not surprising that Megasthenese declared that there was no slavery in India.

12. **According to the passage**
   (a) only members of the lowest class were slaves.
   (b) only women were slaves
   (c) even the members of the upper class were slaves.
   (d) only men were slaves.

13. **When Megasthenese visited India he found that**
   (a) slaves were sold in the open market
   (b) the sale of children into slavery was quite common.
   (c) Slaves were not allowed to earn money in spare time.
   (d) the chasity of slave-girls was protected by law.

14. **Why did Megasthenese declare that there was no slavery in India?**
   (a) He did not see any slaves in India.
   (b) Indian slavery was not cruel.
   (c) The Arthashastra made strict laws against slavery.
   (d) The Varnashrana system did not allow slavery.

15. **The slave-girl was set free and paid compensation if:**
   (a) She was raped by her master.
   (b) She was badly beaten by her master.
   (c) People objected to her being a slave.
   (d) She belonged to the highest caste in society.

16. **The laws allowed slaves to**
   (a) own and inherit property
   (b) marry a person of their choice
   (c) move freely in markets
   (d) read religious books

Instructions for Question Nos. 17-21.

Read the following passage carefully and answer the questions. Choose the correct answer from the alternatives based only the passage given.

Read not to contradict and confute, nor to believe and take for granted, nor to find talk and discourse, but to weigh and consider. Some books are to be tasted, others to be swallowed, and some few to be chewed and digested that is, some books are to be read only in parts, others to be read, but not curiously, and some few to be read wholly and with dilligence and attention. Some books may also be read by deputy, and extracts made of them by others; but that would be only in the less important arguments and the meaner sort of books; else distilled books are like comon distilled water, flahy things. Reading maketh a full man, conference a reading man, and writing an exact man. And therefore if a man, and writes little, he had need have a present wit; and if the reads little, he had need have much cunning to seem to know that he doth not. Histories make men wise, poets witty, the mathematics subtle, natural philosophy deep, moral, grave, logic and rhetoric able to contend.

17. What should be the real object of reading?

(a) Not to contradict and confute

(b) To weigh and consider

(c) To distil the contents

(d) To understand the author's point of view

18. If a man reads very little, what must be pretend?

(a) He must pretend to have a good memory.

(b) He must pretend to have a lot of intelligence

(c) He must pretend to know a lot

(d) He must pretend to be witty.

19. What is meant by conference?

(a) A meeting where conversation is important.

(b) A gathering of people

(c) A get together

(d) A group of people assembled to hear a speaker.

20. What does some books are to be tasted mean?

(a) To be read with diligence and attention

(b) To be read but not curiously.

(c) To be read just for fun.

(d) To be read only in parts.

21. How must we approach the 'meaner' sort of books?

(a) They are to be read by deputy and extacts made of them by others.

(b) They are to be read but not to contrdict and confute

(c) They are to be read but only in parts.

(d) They are to be read but not curiously.

Instruction for Question Nos. 22 to 26.

Read the following passage carefully and answer the questions given at the end.

The great grammar of Panini which effectively stablized the Sanskrit language, presupposes the work of many earlier grammarians. These had succeeded in recongnizing the root as the basis element of a word, and had classifed some 2000 monosyllabic roots which, with the addition of prefixes, suffixes, and inflexion were thought to provide all the words of the language. Though the early etymologists were correct in principle, they made many errors and false derivations, and started a precedent which produced interesting results in many branches of Indian thought. Though its fame is much restricted by its specilized nature, there is no doubt that Panini's grammar is one of the greatest intellectual achievements of any ancient civilization, and the most detailed and scientific grammar composed before the 19th century in any part of the world.

B Which grammar book is considered the most scientific?

(a) Panini's

(b) Patanjali's

(c) An unknown grammarian

(d) Katyana's

23. Fill in the blank in the following sentence :

Panini's grammar gave ______ to Sanskrit language.

(a) instability

(b) stability

(c) ability

(d) inability

24. Who made many errors and false derivations?

(a) Panini

(b) Patanjali

(c) The early grammarians

(d) The later grammarians

25. Which is the basic element of a word?

(a) Prefix

(b) Suffix

(c) Root

(d) Inflexion

26. Fill in the bank in the given sentence:

The early etymologist devised principles ....

(a) which were partly correct

(b) which were partly incorrect

(c) which were correct

(d) which were incorrect

Instruction for Question Nos 27 to 31:

Read the following passeage carefully and answer the questions that follow:

Speech is a great blessing but it can also be a great curse; for while it helps us to make our intentions and desires known to our fellows, it can also, if we use it carelessly, make our attitude completely misunderstood. A slip of the tongue, the use of an unusual word, or of an ambiguous word, and so on, may create and enemy where we had hoped to win a friend. Again different classes of people use different vocabularies and the ordinary speech of an educated man may strike and uneducated listener as pompous. Unwillingly we may use a word which hears a different meaning to our listener from what it does to men of our own class. Thus speech is not a gift to use lightly without thought, but one which demands careful handling. Only a fool will express himself alike to all kinds and conditions of men.

27. The best way to win a friend is to avoid

(a) irony is speech

(b) pomposity in speech

(c) verbosity in speech

(d) ambiguity in speech

28. While talkin gto an uneducated person, we should use

(a) ordinary speech

(b) his vocabulary

(c) simple words

(d) polite language

29. If one uses the same style of language with every one, one sounds

(a) flat

(b) boring

(c) foolish

(d) democratic

30. Speech becomes a curse, if it

(a) hurts others

(b) leads to carelessness

(c) creates misunderstanding

(d) reveals our intentions

31. Speech is a gift, if it

(a) creates confusion

(b) communicates our meaningclearly to our fellows

(c) becomes ambiguous

(d) is used lightly

Instruction for Question Nos. 32 to 36.

Read the following passage carefully and answer the questions that follow.

Travel, in the younger sort, is a part of education; in the elder, a part of experience. He that travelleth into a country, before he hath some entrance into the language. goeth to school; and not to travel, That young men travel under some tutor or grave servant, I allow well; so that he be such a one that hath the language, and hath been in the country before; whereby he may be able to tell them what things are worthy to be seen in the country, where they go, what acquaintances they are to seek, what exercises or discipline the place yieldeth; for else young men shall go hooded and look abroad little. It is strange thing, that in sea voyages, where there is nothing to be seen but sky and sea, men should make diaries; but in land travel, where in so much is to be observed, for the most part they omit it; as if chance were Pitter to be registered than observation; let diaries, therefore be brought in use. The things to be seen and observed are, the courts of princes, especially when they give audience to ambassadors; the courts of justice, while they sit and hear causes.

32. Who tells about the things to be seen in the country one is travelling?

(a) young men　　(b) elder people

(c) tutor　　(d) stranger

33. What is NOT important for travelling in a country?

(a) knowledge of the language of that country

(b) diary

(c) company of a person who already knows the place

(d) company of the family members

34. The grave servant accompanying the traveller must have

(a) already visited the country of the travel

(b) acquaintance with reputed persons

(c) undertaken sea voyages

(d) knowledge of keeping diaries

35. One should visit the courts of princes when the princes are

(a) dinning with ambassadors

(b) listening to ambassadors

(c) instructing the ambassadors

(d) talking to ambassadors

36. Who learns from travelling?

(a) old persons

(b) tutor

(c) young men

(d) grave servant

Directions for the following 6 (six) items :

Read the following five passages and answer the items that follow. Your answers to these items should be based on the passages only.

Passage-1

In India, over the last decade or so, labour has been departing agriculture, but is only going to construction and unregistered manufacturing which are not markedly better jobs. Services, where labour lends to be most productive, are not generating the additional jobs the country needs. India will need 24 million or so jobs over the next decade. The new sector, e-commerce, can at best close only half the jobs gap. Only those sectors tht drive domestic demand such as health and education can comfortably fill the other half.

37. Which one of the following is best implied in the passage?

(a) Strong measures need to be taken to reduce the rural to urban migration of labour.

(b) The working condition in construction and unreistered manufacturing needs to be improved.

(c) Service sector has been reducing the problem of unemployment.

(d) Increased social sector spending is imperative for large-scale job creation.

Passage-2

In India, the current focus on the right to privacy is based on some new realities of the digital age. A right is a substantive right only if it works in all situations, and for everyone. A right to free expression for an individual about her exploitation, for instance, is meaningless without actual availability of security that guarantees that private force cannot be used to that this right. The role of the State, therefore, is not just to abstain from preventing rightful free expression, but also to actively ensure that private parties are not able to black it.

38. On the basis of the above passage, the following assumptions have been made:

(1) State should have some institutions to ensure its appropriate role in a digital society..

(2) State should ensure that private parties do not violate the citizens right to privacy.

(3) Digital economy is not compatible with the idea of not violating the citizens privacy.

Which of the above assumptions is/are valid?

(a) 1 and 2

(b) 3 only

(c) 1 and 3

(d) 2 only

Passage-3

One of the biggest ironies around water is that a comes from rivers and other wetlands. Yet it is seen as divorced from them. While water is used as a resource, public policy does not always grasp that it is a part of the natural ecosystem. Efforts at engineering water systems are thus efforts at augmenting water supply rater than strengthening the capacities of ecological systems.

39. Which one of the following is the most logical and rational inference that can be made from the above passage?

(a) Rivers and other wetlands should be protected under Ramsar convention

(b) State should ensure that private parties do not violate the citizens right to privacy.

(c) Digital economy is not compatible with the idea of not violating the citizens privacy.

(d) Water supply should not be free of cost so as to prevent its misuse or overuse.

Passage-4

IAsset allocation is the most important investment decision we will ever make, and sadly, most of us do not give that decision the importance it deserves. We are adamant about seeking predictability with our future. We tend to think of investing in risky assets as exremely volatile and value eroding. We also dislike fluctuation returns and the loss of control of investment. We think our money is best left idle, unproductive but safe. There is no asset that is risk-free. We could lose our jobs, out homes can lose value, out banks can go bankrupt, our bonds can default, the government can collapse and companies we chose fondly may cease to exist. But we cannot live life assuming that all these extreme events are waiting to happen, and all at the same time. All these extreme froms of risks we know will not manifest at the same time.

40. Which one of the following statements best implies the suggestion given by the author of the passage?

(a) Distribute your wealth across different kinds of assets so that your risks would be minimized.

(b) Risk-taking behavious should be a necessary component of your personality if you want to generate wealth.

(c) While making investments, find a trustworthy asset management organization which would manage your wealth for you.

(d) You should know that investing your money is a risky business.

Passage-5

Although most of the Genetically Modified (GM) crops cultivated now are genetically engineered for a single trait, in future, crops genetically engineered for more than on trait will be the norm. Thus, biotechnology's role in agricultue and the regulation of the same cannot be understood solely in the context of the current generation of GM crops. Instead, there is a need to take a comprehensive look, taking into account various aspects, including sociao-edonomic impacts, so that the potential of the technology can be harnessed while minimizing negative impacts. Given the importance of biotechnology in developing varieties that can help in climate change mitigation and adaptation, not using biotechnology as a part of the climate change action plan cannot be an option. Domestic regulation of biotechnology cannot be viewed in isolation of trade policy and obligations under various international treaties and conventions.

41. With reference to the above passage, the following assumptions have been made:

(1) Biotecvhnology regulation is an evolving process.

(2) Participation of people is needed in policy decisions regarding biotechnology regulation.

(3) Biotechnology regulation should take into account socio-economic aspects in decision making.

(4) Wider involvement of political executive in biotechnology regulation improves its effectiveness in dealing with the country's trade policies and international obligations.

Which of the above assumptions are valid?

(a) 1, 2 and 4 only. (b) 1 and 3 only

(c) 2, 3 and 4 only. (d) 1, 2, 3 and 4

42. Which one of the following statements best implies the crux of the passage?

(a) Precautionary principle is not given importance in current debate on developing GM crops.

(b) Biotechnology is not currently used in climate change mitigation and adoptation mechanisms.

(c) Biotechnology's role is not confined to the current priorities of developing GM crops.

(d) The negative impacts of biotechnology are not properly understood.

Directions for the following 7 (seven) items:

Read the following five passages and answer the items that follow. Your answers to these items should be based on the passages only.

Passage-1

Private investment in general is volatile. Foreign private investment is more lolatile because the abailable investment avenues are significantly greater (i.e. the entire world). Therefore, the responsibility of providing employment cannot be left to Foreign Direct Investment (FDI). The currect FDI inflows are volatile over time and across sectors and regions, which is a necessary consequence of their search for the highest returns. The adverse consequences are unstable employment and an accentuation of income and regional inequalities. A probable positive consequence of foreign investment is the inflow of new technology and its subsequent diffusion. However, the technology diffusion is not at all certain because the existing state of physical and human capital in India may prove inadequate for the diffusion.

43. With reference to the above passage, the following assumptions have been made:

(1) Replying on foreign investment in the long run is not an economically sound policy.

(2) Policies must, be undertaken to reduce volatility in foreign private investment.

(3) Policies must be undertaken to strengthen domestic private investment.

(4) Public investment should be given priority over private investment.

(5) Substantial public investment in education and health should be undertaken.

Which of the above assumptions is/are valid?

(a) 1, 2 and 4

(b) 1, 3 and 5.

(3) 2, 4 and 5

(4) 3 only

Passage-2

Many opportunities to harness the highly awaked, seasonal and spatial distribution of monsoon flows, which occur in a four-month period from June to September annually, have been lost. Since these few months account for most of the rainfall and consequent freshwater avalability, the need for holding rainwater in reservoirs, for subsequently releasing it for use over the year, is a necessity nobody can afford to overlook. Climate chanege will continue to affect weather conditions and create water shortages and excesses. While millions suffer from droughts and floods, waters in the country's many rivers flow unutilized, and are discharged into the sea every year.

44. With reference to the above passage, which of the following could be the most rational and practical implications for India?

(1) Inter-linking of rivers should be undertaken.

(2) A network o dams and cannals should be built across the country for proper distribution of water.

(3) Farmers should be provided easy loans for digging borewells.

(4) Usage of water for agriculture should be regulated by law.

(5) Distribution of river water among regions should be regulated by the Union Government.

Select the correct answer using the code given below:

(a) 1 and 2 (b) 2, 4 and 5

(c) 1, 3 and 4 (d) 2, 3 and 5

Passage-3

People will invest in edeucation whenever they are granted the economic freedom to fully enjoy its benefits. Again, this is for the obvious reason that the return on education increases as the level of economic freedom rises. When people, thanks to lower tax rates, are allowed to retain most of the higher income that they gain from eachincremental level of education, it makes eminent sense to invest in education. On the other hand, when the government decides to tax the higher income of educated individuals at even higher rates, it makes very little sense to invest in educating oneself further. The same incentives apply to parents who decide on whether to invest in their children's education.

45. With reference to the above passage, the following assumptions have been made:

(1) Lower tax rates in a country invariably translate into greater investments in higher education.

(2) Investment in the education of children ensures their economic freedom.

(3) Economic freedom has a positive impact on building up human capital.

Which of the above assumptions is/are valid?

(a) 1 only (b) 2 only

(c) 3 only (d) 1, 2 and 3

Passage-4

Our urban bodies cannot possibly ensure sustainable delivery of water in our cities unless financing mechanisms are put in place. Water delivery requires heavy investment in collecting it from a natural source, treting it to make it potable, and laying a distribution network of pipes for delivery to the users. It also requires investments in sewerage infrstructure and sewage treatment plants so thjat the sewers can carry the wastewater to these plants to ensure that no untreated sewage is dischared back into natural water bodies. If our cities were rich enough to meed the entire cost, water could be delivered free. They are not.

46. What is the most logical and crucial message conveyed by the passage?

(a) Urban local bodies must recover costs through user charges.

(b) Urban local bodies are not efficient enough to meet the water requirements of our cities.

(c) Water shortage in our cities is a perennial problem that cannot be solved.

(d) In view of the water crisis in our cities, there is an urgent need to limit the population of cities by adopting an upper limit of population size.

47. With reference to the above passage, the following assumptions have been made :

(1) Rich cities only can ensure sustainable delivery of water.

(2) Sustainable delivery of water in cities means much more than supplying water to households.

Which of the above assumptions is/are valid?

(a) 1 only (b) 2 only

(c) Both 1 and 2 (d) Neither 1 nor 2

Passage-5

In India, agriculture still engages about half of its workforce, and abouty 85 per cent of its farms are small and marginal. Compared to China and Vietnam, which have experienced fast structural and rural transformation, India's story is of slow transformation. As a result, poverty reduction in India was at a much slower pace during 1988-2014, compared to China and Vietnam, India's poverty reduction was slow during 1988-2005, but during 2005-2012 it accelerated dramatically-almost three times faster than during the earlier period. What did India do during this period? Research reveals that the relative price scenario changed significantly (by more than 50%) in favour of agriculture in the wake of rising global prices. This boosted private investments in agriculture by more that 50%. As a result, agri-GDP growth touched 4.1% during 2007-2012 as against 2.4% during 2002-2007. The net surplus of agri-trade touched $25 billion in 2013-2014, real farm wages ros by 7% per annum. All this led to unprecedented fall in poverty.

48. With reference to the above passage, the following assumptions have been made:

(1) Structural nd rural transformation is impossible when farms are mainly small and marginal.

(2) A good price incentive cn trigger investments in agriculture.

(3) India needs to build value chains for high-value agri-products like livestock and horticulture.

(4) Higher global prices of agricultural commodities are essential for India's poverty reduction.

Which of the above assumptions are valied?

(a) 1 and 3

(b) 2 and 4

(c) 2 and 3

(d) 3 and 4

49. Which one of the following statements best reflects the critical message of the passage?

(a) India should create large-scale off-farm rural employment to reduce poverty in the near future.

(b) India should create a large number of farmer producer companies.

(c) Private investment in agriculture should be given priority over public investment.

(d) Inclusive agricultural growth is key to reduce poverty in the near future.

Directions for the following 6 (six) items:

Read the following five passages and answer the items that follow. Your answers to these items should be based on the passages only.

Passage-1

Spanish ships in the late 16th century first brought the potato tuber from South America to Europe whereby in the early 19th century, it had become a reliable backup to cereal crops, particularly in the cold, rain-soaked soils of Ireland. The Irish were soon almost wholly dependent on the potato as their staple food. And they were planting primarily one prodigious variety, the Lumper potato, whose genetic frailty would be cruelly exposed by the fungus 'Phytophthora infestans'. In 1845, spores of the deadly fungus began spreading across the country, destroying nearly all the Lumpers in its parth. The resulting famine killed or displaced millions.

50. Which one of the following statements best reflects the critical message of the passage?

(a) For introducing any foreign plant into a country, the soil and climate conditions of that country should be suitable.

(b) As a staple food of a country, tuber crops like potato cannot replace cereal crops.

(c) Some of the fungal infections of plants cannot be prevented or stopped from spreading across large areas..

(4) Relying on a homogeneious food source is not desirable.

Passage-2

India is at once among the fastest growing global economics and home to the largest number of malnourished children in the world. There are regions where malnutrition is not the exception but the norm. And across the country, malnutrition is the cause of death for roughly half the 1.3 million children who die before their fifth birthday each year. Even those children who survive suffer permanently from the damage that has already been done to their bodies and minds from not getting enough of the right foods and nutrients. Around 44 million children under 5 are stunted. That makes it harder for them to learn in school and subsequently earn a living as adults. Their lifetime ernings potential is almost a quarter less than that of their healthy peers.

51. With reference to the above passage, which of the following is/are the most rational and practical implication/ implications?

(1) India's Public Distribution System should be monitoed by the Union Government.

(2) Girls should be encouraged to delay marriage and first pregnancy.

(3) Mothers should be encouraged to breastfeed their children immediately after birth.

(4) The supply of safe drinking water and proper sanitation facilities to all should be ensured.

(5) Authorities should ensure the vaccination as prescribed

Select the correct answer using the code given below :

(a) 1, 2, 3 and 4

(b) 2, 3, 4 and 5

(c) 1 only

(d) 3 and 5 only

Passage-3

The pulse variety 'Pusa Arhar 16' has the potential to be grown in the paddy growing regions of Punjab, Haryana and Uttar Pradesh and eventually in all of India. Its yield (about 2000 Kg./hectare) will be significantly greater than those of the existing varieties and because its size will be uniform, it will be amenable to mechanical harvesting, an attractive feature for farmers in northern India who currently use this technology for paddy. Most important, Arhar straw, unlike paddy straw, is green and can be ploughed back into the soil. In paddy straw, the problem is the high silica content, which does not allow for easy decomposition. In the case of Arhar, the farmer, even after combine harvesting, just needs to run a rotovator to cut the leftover straw into pieces, which can be ploughed back and will decompose very fast. All this is difficult with leftover paddy stalks that cannot be easily salvaged or ploughed back. Farmers, therefore, choose the easiest option of simply burning it.

52. Which of the following are the most rational inferences that can be made from the passage?

(1) Farmers income will be higher with pulse cultivation than with paddy cultivation.

(2) Pulse cultivation causes less pollution as compared to paddy cultivation.

(3) Pulse straw can be used to improve soil quality.

(4) In the context of northern Indian agriculture, paddy straw has no usefulness.

(5) Mechanized agriculture is the main cause for stubble burning.

Select the correct answer using the code given below :

(a) 2, 3 and 5

(b) 1, 4 and 5

(c) 2 and 3 only

(d) 1 and 4 only

Passage-4

In India, authorities always look to store the maximum amount of water in reservoirs during the monsoon season, which is then used for irrigation and generation of electricity during the summer months. It is an internationally accepted practice that the water level of a reservoir should be kept below a certain level before the onset of monsoon season. This is so that when monsoon rains come, there is space to store the excess rainwater and also so that water can be released in a regulated manner. But the authorities store the maximum amount of water in reservoirs even before the close of the monsoon, only to ensure greater electricity generation and irrigation.

53. With reference to the above passage, the following assumptions have been made:

(1) High risks involved in holding maximum water in reservoirs are due to our over-dependence on hydropower projects..

(2) Storage capacity of dams should not be fully used before or during monsoon season.

(3) Role of dams in flood control is underestimated in India.

Which of the above assumptions is/are valid?

(a) 1 and 2 only

(b) 2 only

(c) 3 only

(d) 1, 2 and 3

Passage-5

Economic liberalization in India was shaped largely by the economic problems of the government than by the economic priorities of the people or by the long-term development objectives. Thus, there were limitations in conception and design which have been subsequently validated by experience. Jobless growth, persistent poverty and rising inequality have mounted as problems since economic liberalization began. And all these years later, four quiet crises confront the economy, agriculture, infrastructure, industrialization and education as constraints on the country's future prospects. These problems must be resolved if economic growth has to be sustained and transformed into meaningful development.

54. Which of the following is/are the most rational and logical inference/interferences that can be made from the passage?

(1) It is essential to rethink and redefine the economic role of the state in the quest for development.

(2) India has not made effective implementation of its policies in social sectors nor made sufficient investments in them.

Select the correct answer using the code given below :-

(a) 1 only.

(b) 2 only

(c) Both 1 and 2

(d) Neither 1 nor 2

55. With reference to the above passage, the following assumptions have been made:

(1) India's economy needs to be greatly integrated with global economy so as to create large number of jobs and to sustain its growth momentum.

(2) Economic liberalization would cause large economic growth which would reduce poverty and create sufficient employment in the long run..

Which of the above assumptions is/are valid?

(a) 1 only.

(b) 2 only

(c) Both 1 and 2

(d) Neither 1 nor 2

GENERAL AWARENESS

1 Chapter India and its Neighboring Countries

Introduction

- INDIA is one of the oldest civilisations in the world with a kaleidoscopic variety and rich cultural heritage. It has achieved all-round socio-economic progress during the last 72 years of its Independence. India has become self-sufficient in agricultural production in the world and the third nation to have gone into outer space to conquer nature for the benefit of the people. India covers an area of 32,87,263 sq km, extending from the snow-covered Himalayan heights in the North to the tropical rain forests of the south. As the 7th largest country in the world, India stands apart from the rest of Asia, marked off as it is by mountains and the sea, which gives the country a distinct geographical entity. The Himalayas comprise three almost parallal ranges interspersed with large plateaus and valleys some of which like the Kashmir and Kullu Valleys are fertile, extensive and of great scenic beauty. Some of the highest peaks in the world are found in these ranges.
- Lying entirely in the northern hemisphere, the mainland extends between latitudes 8°4' and 37°6' north, longitudes 68°7' and 97°25' east and measures about 3,214 km from north to south between the extreme latitudes and about 2,933 km from east to west between the extreme longitudes. It has a land frontier of about 15,200 km. The total length of the coastline of the mainland, Lakshadweep Islands and Andaman & Nicobar Islands is 7,516.6 km.

Geographical Background

- Countries having a common border with India are Afghanistan and Pakistan to the north-west, China, Bhutan and Nepal to the north, Myanmar to the east and Bangladesh to the east of West Bengal. Sri Lanka is separated from India by a narrow channel of sea formed by the Palk Strait and the Gulf of Mannar. Maldives Island are situated to the south of the Lakshadweep Island.

Physical Features

- The mainland comprises four regions, namely, the great mountain zone, plains of the Ganga and the Indus, the desert region and the southern peninsula.
- The high altitudes admit travel only to a few passes, notably the Jelep La and Nathu La on the main Indo-Tibet trade route through the Chumbi Valley, north-east of Darjeeling and Shipki La in the Satluj valley, north-east of Kalpa (Kinnaur). The mountain wall extends over a distance of about 2,400 km with a varying depth of 240 to 320 km. In the east, between India and Myanmar and India and Bangladesh, hill ranges are much lower. Garo, Khasi, Jaintia and Naga Hills, running almost east-west, join the chain to Mizo and Rakhine Hills running north-south.
- The plains of the Ganga and the Indus, about 2,400 km long and 240 to 320 km broad and are formed by basins of three distinct river systems - the Indus, the Ganga and the Brahmaputra. They are one of the world's greatest stretches of flat alluvium and also one of the most densely populated areas on the earth. Between the Yamuna at Delhi and the Bay of Bengal, nearly 1,600 km away, there is a drop of only 200 metres in elevation.
- The desert region can be divided into two parts - the great desert and the little desert. The great desert extends from the edge of the Rann of Kuchch beyond the Luni river northward. The whole of the Rajasthan-Sind frontier runs through this. The little desert extends from the Luni between Jaisalmer and Jodhpur up to the northern wastes. Between the great and the little deserts lies a zone of absolutely sterile country, consisting of rocky land cut up by limestone ridges.
- The Peninsular Plateau is marked off from the plains of the Ganga and the Indus by a mass of mountain and hill ranges varying from 460 to 1,220 metres in height. Prominent among these are the Aravalli, Vindhya, Satpura, Maikala and Ajanta. The Peninsula is flanked on one side by the Eastern Ghats where average elevation is about 610 metres and on the other by the Western Ghats where it is generally from 915 to 1,220 metres, rising in places to over 2,440 metres. Between the Western Ghats and the Arabian Sea lies a narrow coastal strip, while between Eastern Ghats and the Bay of Bengal, there is a broader coastal area. The southern point of the plateau is formed by the Nilgiri Hills where the Eastern and the Western Ghats meet.
- The Cardamom Hills lying beyond may be regarded as a continuation of the Western Ghats.

Geological Structure

- The geological regions broadly follow the physical features and may be grouped into three regions: the Himalayas and their associated group of mountains, the Indo- Ganga Plain and the Peninsular Shield.
- The Himalayan mountain belt to the north and the Naga-Lushai mountain in the east, are the regions of mountain-building movement. Most of this area, now presenting some of the most magnificent mountain scenery in the world, was under marine conditions about 60 crore years

ago. In a series of mountain-building movements commencing about 7 crore years ago, the sediments and the basement rocks rose to great heights. The weathering and erosive agencies worked on these to produce the relief seen today.

- The Indo-Ganga plains are a great alluvial tract that separate the Himalayas in the north from the Peninsula in the south. The Peninsula is a region of relative stability and occasional seismic disturbances. Highly metamorphosed rocks of the earliest periods, dating back as far as 380 crore years, occur in the area; the rest being covered by the coastal-bearing Gondwana formations, lava flows belonging to the Deccan Trap formation and younger sediments.

River Systems

- The river systems of India can be classified into four groups viz., (i) Himalayan rivers, (ii) Deccan rivers, (iii) Coastal rivers, and (iv) Rivers of the inland drainage basin. The Himalayan rivers are formed by melting snow and glaciers and therefore, continuously flow throughout the year. During the monsoon months, Himalayas receive very heavy rainfall and rivers swell, causing frequent floods.
- The Deccan rivers on the other hand are rainfed and therefore fluctuate in volume. Many of these are non-perennial. The Coastal streams, especially on the west coast are short in length and have limited catchment areas. Most of them are non-perennial. The streams of inland drainage basin of western Rajasthan are few and far apart. Most of them are of an ephemeral character.
- The main Himalayan river systems are those of the Indus and the Ganga- Brahmaputra-Meghna system. The Indus, which is one of the great rivers of the world, rises near Mansarovar in Tibet and flows through India and thereafter through Pakistan and finally falls in the Arabian sea near Karachi. Its important tributaries flowing in the Indian territory are the Sutlej (originating in Tibet), the Beas, the Ravi, the Chenab and the Jhelum. The Ganga-Brahmaputra-Meghna is another important system of which the principal sub-basins are those of Bhagirathi and the Alaknanda, which join at Dev Prayag to form the Ganga. It traverses through Uttaranchal, Uttar Pradesh, Bihar and West Bengal states. Below Rajmahal hills, the Bhagirathi, which used to be the main course in the past, takes off, while the Padma continues eastward and enters Bangladesh. The Yamuna, the Ramganga, the Ghaghra, the Gandak, the Kosi, the Mahananda and the Sone are the important tributaries of the Ganga.
- Rivers Chambal and Betwa are the important sub-tributaries, which join Yamuna before it meets the Ganga. The Padma and the Brahmaputra join at Bangladesh and continue to flow as the Padma or the Ganga. The Brahmaputra rises in Tibet originating in the Chemayungdung glacier, where it is known as Tsangpo and runs a long distance till it crosses over into India in Arunachal Pradesh under the name of Dihang or Siang. Near Passighat, the Debang and Lohit join the river Brahmaputra and the combined river runs all along the Assam in a narrow valley. It crosses into Bangladesh downstream of Dhubri.
- The principal tributaries of Brahmaputra in India are the Subansiri, Jia Bhareli, Dhansiri, Puthimari, Pagladiya and the Manas. The Brahmaputra in Bangladesh receives the flow of Tista, etc., and finally falls into the Ganga. The Barak river, the Head stream of Meghna, rises in the hills in Manipur. The important tributaries of the river are Makku, Trang, Tuivai, Jiri, Sonai, Rukni, Katakhal, Dhaleswari, Langachini, Maduva and Jatinga. Barak continues in Bangladesh till the combined Ganga-Brahmaputra join it near Bhairab Bazar.
- In the Deccan region, most of the major river systems flowing generally in east direction fall into Bay of Bengal. The major east flowing rivers are Godavari, Krishna, Cauvery, Mahanadi, etc. Narmada and Tapti are the major West flowing rivers.
- The Godavari in the southern Peninsula has the second largest river basin covering 10 per cent of the area of India. Next to it is the Krishna basin in the region, while the Mahanadi has the third largest basin. The basin of the Narmada in the uplands of the Deccan, flowing to the Arabian Sea, and of the Kaveri in the south, falling into the Bay of Bengal are about the same size, though with different character and shape.
- There are numerous coastal rivers, which are comparatively small. While only handful of such rivers drain into the sea near the delta of the east coast, there are as many as 600 such rivers on the west coast.
- A few rivers in Rajasthan do not drain into the sea. They drain into salt lakes and get lost in sand with no outlet to sea. Besides these, there are the desert rivers which flow for some distance and are lost in the desert. These are Luni, Machhu, Rupen, Saraswati, Banas, Ghaggar and others.

Climate

- The climate of India may be broadly described as tropical monsoon type. There are four seasons: (i) winter (January-February), (ii) hot weather summer (March-May); (iii) rainy south-western monsoon (June-September) and (iv) post-monsoon, also known as north-east monsoon in the southern Peninsula (October-December). India's climate is affected by two seasonal winds the north-east monsoon and the southwest monsoon. The north-east monsoon commonly known as winter monsoon blows from land to sea whereas south-west monsoon known as summer monsoon blows from sea to land after crossing the Indian Ocean, the Arabian Sea and the Bay of Bengal. The south-west monsoon brings most of the rainfall during the year in the country.

Flora

- With a wide range of climatic conditions from the torrid to the arctic, India has a rich and varied vegetation, which only a few countries of comparable size possess. India can be divided into eight distinct-floristic-regions, namely, the western Himalayas, the eastern Himalayas, Assam, the Indus plain, the Ganga plain, the Deccan, Malabar and the Andamans.
- The Western Himalayan region extends from Kashmir to Kumaon. Its temperate zone is rich in forests of chir, pine, other conifers and broad-leaved temperate trees. Higher up, forests of deodar, blue pine, spruce and silver fir occur.
- The alpine zone extends from the upper limit of the temperate zone of about 4,750 metres or even higher. The characteristic trees of this zone are high-level silver fir, silver birch and junipers. The eastern Himalayan region extends from Sikkim eastwards and embraces Darjeeling, Kurseong and the adjacent tract. The temperate zone has forests of oaks, laurels, maples, rhododendrons, alder and birth. Many conifers, junipers and dwarf willows also occur here. The Assam region comprises the Brahamaputra and the Surma valleys with evergreen forests, occasional thick clumps of bamboos and tall grasses.
- The Indus plain region comprises the plains of Punjab, western Rajasthan and northern Gujarat. It is dry and hot and supports natural vegetation. The Ganga plain region covers the area which is alluvial plain and is under cultivation for wheat, sugarcane and rice. Only small areas support forests of widely differing types.
- The Deccan region comprises the entire table land of the Indian Peninsula and supports vegetation of various kinds, from scrub, jungles to mixed deciduous forests. The Malabar region covers the excessively humid belt of mountain country parallel to the west coast of the Peninsula. Besides being rich in forest vegetation, this region produces important commercial crops, such as coconut, betelnut, pepper, coffee and tea, rubber and cashewnut. The Andaman region abounds in evergreen, mangrove, beach and diluvial forests. The Himalayan region extending from Kashmir to Arunachal Pradesh through Nepal, Sikkim, Bhutan, Meghalaya and Nagaland and the Deccan Peninsula is rich in endemic flora, with a large number of plants which are not found elsewhere.
- India is rich in flora. Available data places India in the tenth position in the world and fourth in Asia in plant diversity. From about 70 per cent geographical area surveyed so far, over 46,000 species of plants have been described by the Botanical Survey of India (BSI), Kolkata. The vascular flora, which forms the conspicuous vegetation cover, comprises 15,000 species. The flora of the country is being studied by BSI and its nine circle/ field offices located throughout the country along with certain universities and research institutions.
- Ethno-botanical study deals with the utilisation of plants and plant products by ethnic races. A scientific study of such plants has been made by BSI. A number of detailed ethno-botanical explorations have been conducted in different tribal areas of the country. More than 800 plant species of ethno-botanical interest have been collected and identified at different centres.
- Owing to destruction of forests for agricultural, industrial and urban development, several Indian plants are facing extinction. About 1,336 plant species are considered vulnerable and endangered. About 20 species of higher plants are categorised as possibly extinct as these have not been sighted during the last 6-10 decades. BSI brings out an inventory of endangered plants in the form of a publication titled Red Data Book.

Fauna

- India is very rich in terms of biological diversity due to its unique biogeographical location, diversified climate conditions and enormous ecodiversity and geodiversity. India's immense biological diversity encompasses ecosystems, populations, species and their genetic make-up. This diversity can be attributed to the vast variety in physiography and climatic situations resulting in a diversity of ecological habitats ranging from tropical, sub-tropical, temperate, alpine to desert.
- According to world biogeographic classification, India represents two of the major realms (the Palearctic and Indo-Malayan) and three biomes (Tropical Humid Forests, Tropical Dry/Deciduous Forests and Warm Deserts/Semi-Deserts). The Wildlife Institute of India has proposed a modified classification which divides the country into ten biogeographic regions: Trans-Himalayan, Himalayan, Indian Desert, Semi-Arid, Western Ghats, Deccan Peninsula, Gangetic Plain, North-East India, Islands and Coasts. In the light of Biodiversity Convention, India holds a unique position with the priority of conservation of natural resources and sustainable development. Infact, within only about 2 per cent of world's total land surface, India is known to have over 7.50 per cent of the species of animals that the world holds and this percentage accounts nearly for 92,037 species so far known, of which insects alone include 61,375 species. It is estimated that about two times the number of species still remain to be discovered in India alone.

MAJOR RIVERS OF INDIA

Name	Length (km)	Originates from	Major Tributaries
Indus	2,880 (in India 1,114 km)	Glacier near Bokhar Chu (31°15' N latitude and 81°40' E longitude)	Shyok, Gilgit, Zaskar, Hunza, Nubra, Shigar, Gasting and Dras
Chenab	1,180 in India	Formed by two streams, the Chandra and the Bhaga	Bhut Nalla , Miyar Nala , Niru , Tawa
Satluj	1450	The Rakas lake near Mansarovar at an altitude of 4,555 m	Beas
Ravi	720	Chamba district of Himachal Pradesh	Ujh
Ganga	2,507	Gaumukh (Bhagirati)	Tributaries are Ramganga, (Bhagirati) Gomati, Ghaghara, Gandak, Kosi and Mahanada. Yamuna– the western most and the longest tributary
Yamuna	1370	Yamunotri glacier on the western slopes of Banderpunch range (6,316 km).	Chambal, Sind, Betwa and Ken on its right bank which originates from the Peninsular plateau while the Hindan, Rind, Sengar, the Varuna, etc. join it on its left bank.
Brahmaputra	2,850	Chemayung-Dung glacier, between lake Manasarovar and Mount Kailash	Rango Tsangpo, Burhi Dihing, Dhansari (South) and Kalang Subansiri, Kameng, Manas and Sankosh.
Kaveri	800	Brahmagiri hills (1,341m) of Kogadu district in Karnataka.	Hemavati Shimsha Arkavathy Kabini
Godavari	1,465	Trimbakeshwar near Nasik hills in Maharashtra	Penganga, Indravati, Pranhita, and Manjra
Krishna	1401	Near Mahabaleshwar in Maharashtra	Tungabhadra Kudali Venna, Koyna, Bhima
Narmada	1,312	Amarkantak hill in Madhya Pradesh	Shiva, Gomai, Vaki , Arunavati,
Tapti	724	Multai in the Betul district of Madhya Pradesh	Burai Panzara
Mahanadi	851	Sihawa in Raipur district of Chhattisgarh	Seonath, Telen

Demographic Background

Census

The Census of India 2001, was historic and epoch- making, being the first census of the twenty-first century and the third millennium. It reveals benchmark data on the state of abundant human resources available in the country, their demography, culture and economic structure at a juncture, which marks a centennial and millennial transition. Census 2011 was the 15th census of its kind since 1872. It was held in two phases: House listing and Housing Census (April to September, 2010) and Population Enumeration (February 9th to 28th 2011 with Revisional round during 1st to 5th March,2011). Reference Date was 0.00 hour of March 1st , 2011. In snow bound areas, the Population Enumeration was conducted from September 11th to 30th , 2010. The Final Population data was released on April 30th 2013.

Population

The population of India as on March 1, 2011 stood at 1,210.9 million (623.2 million males and 587.6 million females). India accounts for a meagre 2.4 per cent of the world surface area of 135.79 million sq.km. Yet, it supports and sustains a whopping per cent of the world population. The population of India, which at the turn of the twentieth century was around 238.4 million, increased to reach 1,210.9 million by 2011. The population of India as recorded at each decennial census from 1901 has grown steadily except for a decrease during 1911-21.

Population Density

One of the important indices of population concentration is the density of population. It is defined as the number of persons per sq.km. The population density of India in 2011 was 382 per sq. km-decadal growth 17.72 per cent. The density of population increased in all states and union territories between 1991 and 2011. Among major states, Bihar is the most thickly populated state with (a population density of) 1,106 persons per sq.km followed by West Bengal 1,028 and Kerala 860.

Sex Ratio

Sex ratio, defined as the number of females per thousand males is an important social indicator to measure the extent of prevailing equality between males and females in a society at a given point of time. The sex ratio in the country has always remained unfavourable to females. It was 972 at the beginning of the twentieth century and thereafter showed continuous decline until 1941. The sex ratio from 1901-2011 has registered a 10 point increase at census 2011 over 2001; however, child sex ratio has declined to 919 per thousand male.

Literacy

For the purpose of census 2011, a person aged seven and above, who can both read and write with understanding in any language, is treated as literate. A person, who can only read but cannot write, is not literate. In the censuses prior to 1991, children below five years of age were necessarily treated as illiterates. The results of 2011 census reveal that there has been an increase in literacy in the country. The literacy rate in the country is 73.0 per cent, 80.9 for males and 64.6 for females. Kerala retained its position by being on top with a 94 per cent literacy rate, closely followed by Lakshadweep (91.9 per cent). Bihar with a literacy rate of 61.8 per cent ranks last in the country. Kerala also occupies the top spot in the country both in male literacy with 96.1 per cent and female literacy with 92.1 per cent. On the contrary, Bihar has recorded the lowest literacy rates both in case of males (71.2 per cent) and females (51.5 per cent).

Demographic Analysis

Historical Background

- Ancient evidence of population
  - In cadastral survey of Roman empire.
  - In 321-296 BC, in Kautilya's Arthasastra.
  - In 1595-96, in the book Ain-i-Akbari by Abul's-Fazl Allami.
- Beginning of census
  - In 1749 by Sweden.
  - In 1801 by England.
  - In 1890 by America.

  Note : America was the 1st one to initiate decennial census.
- Beginning of British India Census:
  - Initiated by Lord Mayo in 1872.
  - Conducted at every 10 yrs after 1881, started by Lord Ripon.
- Important facts of Indian census:
  - With the beginning in 1872 The census of India has been conducted 15 times.
  - 7th census was of Independent India.
  - 2nd census of 21th century.

Important Facts of 15th Census

- The census 2011 survey was conducted by the census organisation of India by Commissioner and Registrar General Mr. C. Chandramouli.
- The provisional figures of 2011 census were released on 31st March, 2011 by Registrar General C. Chandramouli in the presence of Union Home Secretary G K Pillai.
- The final data was released on 30 April, 2013, i.e two years after releasing provisional figures.

Population Policy 2000

- The need of suitable population policy in India for the 1st time was suggested by the demographic experts in 1960.
- In 1976, country's 1st Population policy was declared.

  Note : In 1978, the Janata Party declared the amended Population Policy.
- Following are the important features of Population Policy of 2000:
- It aims at stable population by 2045.
- The age of marriage was proposed to be 18 years for girls and 21 years for boys.

  Note- Couples below the poverty line will be rewarded if they have their first child after the mother reaches to age of 21.
- Panchayats and Zila Parishads will be rewarded and honoured for exemplary performance in the universalisation of the population control methods.
- Child marriage act and sex deduction act to be empowered.
- Facilities for safe abortion will be strengthened and expanded.
- To make registration of births, deaths, marriage and pregnancies mandatory.
- Reduce maternal mortality rate to below 100 per 1,00,000 live births.
- Reduce infant mortality rate to below 30 per 1000 live births.

Population Commission

- On 11th May, 2000 the reconstitution of the National Commission on Population was done under the chairmanship of the Prime Minister.
- To review, monitor and give direction for implementation of the National Population Policy, National Population Commission was by Prime Minister Dr. Manmohan Singh in 19 May, 2005.
- Members of NPC- Chairman - the Prime Minister with the Deputy Chairman Planning Commission (now NITI Aayog) as Vice Chairman-

  (1) Deputy chairman, Planning Commission

  (2) Minister of Health and Family Welfare

  Note-This commission was under the Planning Commission till now, but recently it has been kept under the Ministry of Health.

National Population Fund

- For better functioning of New Population Policy declared in Feb 2000, "National Population Fund" was formed in 2003.
- The fund was raised with 100 cr.
- Chairman of fund - Prime Minister
- Deputy chairman of the fund - Central Health and Family Welfare minister.
- Important function of the fund- To fund the various population control programmes in order achieve the goal till 2025 of stable population growth.

Glossary : Related to Population

- Fecundity : Fecundity is refered to the ability that a woman possesses to produce a child. Not necessary whether she has given birth or not.
- Fertility Rate : It refers to the number of children born per couple individual population. Fertility is the natural capability to produce off spring.
- Dependency Ratio :
  DR - Dependency Ratio
  D - Dependent Population (0-14 yrs and above 60 yrs populations are included)
  W - Total working population (15 to 59 yrs population)
  K - 1000 (Dependency ratio is express in 1000)
- Literacy ratio -
  LR - Literacy Ratio
  L - No of Literate person
  7 + P - Population of age group of 7 yrs or above.
- Sex ratio : No of female per thousand males is sex ratio.
- Child sex ratio : In the age group of 0-6 yrs, the number of females per thousand males.
- Decadal growth rate : The percentage of total population growth in a particular decade is termed as decadal growth rate.
  DGR = Current population
- Crude Birth Rate and Corrected Birth rate : The ratio of total live births to total population in a specified period of time is known as crude birth rate.
  Note-In crude birth rate, only registered children are included, whereas when 5% of total unregistred children are added to it, then it gives corrected birth rate.
- Child death rate- In a specific year, the number of children who die before the age of 1 years, per thousand live births of that year.
- Urban area - In urban area, all such regions are included, where according to 2001 census-
  - Municipality
  - Corporation
  - Cantonment board or notified town area committee is established.

Comparative Study of 15th & 14th Census : At a Glance

Base	15th Census 2011	14th Census 2001	Difference
• Total Population (in crore)	121.05	102.37	+18.69
(i) Male %	51.54	51.74	-.26
(ii) Female %	48.46	48.26	+.26
• Urban Population in %	31.2	27.81	+3.39
• Rural Population in %	68.8	72.19	–3.39
• Literacy Rate in %	74.0	64.8	+9.2
(i) Male Literacy Rate (in %)	82.10	75.26	+5.6
(ii) Female Literacy Rate (in %)	65.50	53.67	+10.93
• Sex Ratio (Per 1000 male)	940	933	+7
• Child Sex Ratio (0-6 age group)	914	927	–13
• Population Density (Per sq. km)	382	324	+57
• Population Growth Rate	17.7	21.54	–3.84
• Cities with more then 10 lakh population	53	35	+18

Final Data of 15th Census 2011 : At a Glance

Base	Highest	Lowest
Population (State)	1. UP, 2. Maharashtra, 3. Bihar, 4. West Bengal , 5. Andhra Pradesh/M.P.	1. Sikkim, 2. Mizoram, 3. Arunchal, 4. Goa 5. Nagaland
Population (UTs)	1. Delhi, 2. Puducherry	1. Lakshadweep, 2. Daman and Diu
Literacy Rate (State)	1. Kerala, 2. Mizoram, 3. Tripura, 4. Goa, 5. Himanchal	1. Bihar, 2. Arunchal, 3. Rajasthan, 4. Jharkhand, 5. Andhra Pradesh
Literacy (UTs)	1. Lakshadweep	1. Dadra & Nagar Haveli
Density (State)	1. Bihar, 2. West Bengal, 3. Keral, 4. UP, 5. Haryana	1. Arunchal, 2. Mizoram, 3. J&K 4. Sikkim, 5. Nangal, 6. Manipur
Density (UTs)	1. Delhi	1. Andaman Nicobar

Sex Ratio (State)	1. Kerala, 2. Tamil Nadu, 3. Andhra Pradesh, 4. Chhattisgarh, 5. Telangana, 6. Manipur	1. Haryana, 2. J & K, 3. Sikkim, 4. Punjab, 5. UP
Sex Ratio (UTs)	1. Puducherry	1. Daman and Diu
Child Sex Ratio (State)	1. Arunchal 2. Mizoram, 3. Meghalaya, 4. Chhattisgarh, 5. Keral	1. Haryana, 2. Punjab, 3. JK, 4. Rajasthan, 5. Uttarakhand
Child Sex Ratio (UTs)	1. Andaman & Nicobar	1. Delhi
Population Growth Rate (State)	1. Meghalaya, 2. Arunchal, 3. Bihar, 4. J&K, 5. Mizoram	1. Nagaland, 2. Keral, 3. Goa, 4. Andhra, 5. Sikkim
	1. Dadra & Nagar Haveli	1. Lakshadweep
Area (State)	1. Rajasthan, 2. MP, 3. Maharashtra, 4. UP, 5. Gujarat	1. Goa, 2. Sikkim, 3. Tripura, 4. Nagaland 5. Mizoram
Area (UTs)	1. Andaman & Nicobar	1. Lakshadweep
ST Population (State)	1. UP, 2. West Bengal, 3. Bihar, 4. Tamil Nadu, 5. Andhra	1. Mizoram, 2. Meghalaya, 3. Goa, 4. Sikkim, 5. Manipur
SC/ST Population (in %)	1. Punjab, 2. Himachal, 3. West Bengal, 4. UP, 5. Haryana	1. Mizoram, 2. Meghalaya, 3. Goa, 4. Manipur, 5. Sikkim
ST/SC Population (State)	1. MP, 2. Maharashtra, 3. Orissa, 4. Rajasthan, 5. Gujarat	1. Goa, 2. Sikkim, 3. Uttarakhand, 4. Himanchal, 5. Kerala
ST/SC Population in %	1. Mizoram, 2. Nagaland, 3. Meghalaya, 4. Arunchal, 5. Manipur	1. Goa, 2. Tamil Nadu, 3. Bihar, 4. Kerala 5. Uttarakhand

Some Facts of Census 2011

- Census 2011 mascot is a female enumerator (who everybody would identify as the school teacher next door).
- The population of India has increased by more than 181 million during the decade 2001-2011.
- The absolute addition is slightly lower than the population of Brazil, the fifth most populous country in the world.
- The population of India, at 1210.2 million, is almost equal to the combined population of U.S.A., Indonesia, Brazil, Pakistan, Bangladesh and Japan put together (1214.3 million).
- The percentage decadal growth during 2001-2011 has registered the sharpest decline since Independence – a decrease of 3.90 percentage points from 21.54 to 17.64 percent.
- Of the total population, 623.7 million are males and 586.5 million are females.
- Uttar Pradesh (199.5 million) is the most populous State in the country followed by Maharashtra with 112 million.
- The combined population of Uttar Pradesh and Maharashtra is bigger than that of the US.
- While Dadra & Nagar Haveli and Puducherry have the highest population growth rate of about 55 percent, Nagaland has the lowest -0.47 percent.
- The density of population is highest in Delhi, followed by Chandigarh.
- The report said that Jammu and Kashmir, Bihar and Gujarat show decline in sex ratio, while 29 states show an increase.
- Population (0-6 years) 2001-2011 registered minus (-) 3.08 percent growth with minus (-) 2.42 for males and –3.80 for females.
- The report further said that the literacy rate has gone up from 64.83 per cent in 2001 to 74.04 per cent in 2011 showing an increase of 9.21 per cent.

India's Maritime Borders

- **Eight Degree Channel:** Separates Minicoy Island (India) from Maldives. Maliku Kandu is the traditional name of broad Minicoy channel.
- **Nine Degree Channel:** Separates Kavaratti from Minicoy Island.
- **Ten Degree Channel:** Separates Andamans from Nicobars (Little Andaman from Car Nicobar).
- **Duncan Passage:** Lies between S. Andaman and Little Andaman.
- **Palk Strait:** A strait between Tamil Nadu (India) and Mannar district of Northern Province of Sri Lanka. The strait is named after Robert Palk, who was a governor of Madras Presidency (1755-1763).

Some Highest Peaks of the Himalayas in India

Sl. No.	Peak	Height in Meters
1.	K_2	8611
2.	Kanchen Junga	8,598
3.	Nanda Devi	7,817
4.	Kamat	7,756
5.	Namcha Barwa	7,756

States Sharing International Boundaries

Country	**Border Length**	**No. of States**	**Borders on Indian States**
Pakistan	3,323	4	Jammu and Kashmir, Punjab, Rajasthan and Gujarat
China	3,428	5	Jammu and Kashmir, Himachal Pradesh, Uttarakhand, Sikkim and Arunachal Pradesh
Nepal	1,751	5	Bihar, Uttarakhand, Uttar Pradesh, Sikkim and West Bengal
Bangladesh	4,096.7	5	West Bengal, Assam, Meghalay a Tripura, Mizoram
Bhutan	699	4	West Bengal, Sikkim, Arunachal Pradesh and Assam
Myanmar	1,643	4	Arunachal Pradesh, Nagaland, Manipur and Mizoram
Afghanistan	106	1	Jammu and Kashmir (Pakistan-occupied Area)

Boundary Lines

Durand Line	Pakistan and Afghanistan	Drawn up in 1896 by Sir Mortimer Durand
MacMohan Line	India and China	Drawn up by Sir Henry Henry MacMohan in 1914
RadCliffe	India and Pakistan	Drawn up by Sir Cyril Radcliffe on 17 August, 1947

2 Chapter

National Institutes and Research Centres

National Institutes and Research Centres

S.No.	Institutions	Headquarter
1	Central Soil and Materials Research Station Devoted to research and investigation and primarily in Geo-Technical Engineering, Also involved in Hydroelectric and irrigation projects Undertakes the works pertaining to nuclear and Super-Thermal Power Projects. Research for neighbouring countries.	New Delhi
2	Central Water and Power Research Station Dealing with irrigation and drainage.	Khadakwasla (Pune)
3	Sardar Sarovar Construction Advisory Committee It was constituted in 1980, as per the directive of the Narmada Water Disputes Tribunal	Vadodara
4	Bansagar Control Board HQ Bansagear Dam on Sone River, Three States MP, UP, Bihar	Rewa (M.P.)
5	Water and Power Consultancy Services (I) Ltd-WAPCOS Mini Ratna and ISO 9001:2000 Public Sector Enterprise under the aegis of the Union Ministry of Water Resources incorporated on 1969 under the Companies Act 1956.	
6	National Projects Construction Corporation Limited Govt of India Enterprise (ISO 9001: 2000) Established in 1957 For developing infrastructure projects in the diverse sector irrigation, water resources,power, heavy industry roads and buildings, etc. Registered Office–New Delhi	
7	National Institute of Hydrology	Roorkee (Uttrakhand)
8	National Institute for the Visually Handicapped	Dehradun
9	National Institute of Orthopedically Handicapped	Kolkata
10	Ali Yavar Jung National Institute for Hearing Impaired	Mumbai
11	Ali Yavar Jung National Institute for Mentally Hadicapped	Secunderabad
12	National Institute of Rehabilitalion Training & Research	Cuttack
13	National Institute of Physically Handicapped	New Delhi
14	National Institute for Empowerment of Persons with Multiple Disabilities	Chennai
15	Artificial Limbs Manufacturing Corporation of India (Public Sector Body)	Kanpur
16	Composite Regional Centres and Regional Rehabilitation Centres (for the Persons with Disabilities are Located at Srinagar, lucknow, Bhopal, Sundernagar and Guwahati	

17	Rajiv Gandhi National Institute of Youth Development (Functions as an Autonomous body)	Sriperumbudur (TN)
18	Netaji Subhash National Institute of Sports	Patiala.
19	Lakshmibai National College of Physical Education Under Sports Authority of India	Thiruvanthapuram (KL)
20	High Altitude Training Centre (HATC) Under Sports Authority of India	Shillarno (HP)
21	Lakshmibai National Institute of Physical Education	Gwalior
22	Institute of Life Science	Bhubaneshwar
23	Indian National Centre for Indian Ocean Information Services (INCOIS)	Hyderabad
24	National Institute of Ocean Technology	Chennai
25	Centre for Marine Living Research and Ecology	Kochi
26	National Centre for Antarctic and Ocean Research (NCAOR)	GOA
27	Integrated Coastal and Marine Area Management	Chennai
28	Satyajit Ray Film and Television Institute (SRFTI)	Kolkata
29	Film and Television Institute of India	Pune
30	V.V. Giri National Labour Institute	NOIDA (UP)
31	National Aluminium Comp. Ltd (NALCO)	Bhubneshwar (Orissa)
32	Hindustan Antibiotics Limited–Pimpri (Pune)	Hrishikesh
33	Institute of Pesticide Formulation Technology	Gurgaon
34	Hindustan Organic Chemicals Ltd	Rasyani (Raigarh Distt MH)
35	Projects and Development India Ltd Formerly know as Fertiliser (Planning and Development) India Ltd is engaged in design eng. Procurement and Supervision of Construction/ Commissioning of Fertiliser and allied Chemical Plants.	
36	Pyrites, Phosphates and Chemicals Ltd	Amjhore (Bihar)
37	National Fertilisers Ltd Calcium Ammonium Nitrate Plant at Nangal Urea Plants–Nangal, Bhatinda, Panipat, Vijaypur (MP) (Two Units) Large gas based Fertiliser Plant- Thal	
38	Sardar Vallbhbhai Institute of Textile Management	Coimbatore (TN)
39	Rural Health Traning Centre	Najafgarh, New Delhi
40	Gandhigram Institute of Rural Health and Family Welfare Trust	Tamilnadu
41	National Institute of Communicable Diseases	New Delhi
42	Institute of Virology	Pune
43	National Test House	Kolkata
44	National Institute Traning for Standardisation	NOIDA
45	Indian Grain Storage Management and Research Institute	Hapur
46	Two Units of the Govt Opium and Alkoloid Factories. Ghazipur (UP) Neemach (MP) (Both are Under the Ministry of Finance)	
47	National Institute of Bank Management (Joint Training Programme by India and IMF)	Pune
48	Salim Ali Centre for Ornithology and Natural History	Coimbatore
49	Wildlife Institute of India	Dehradun
50	National Museaum of Natural History	New Delhi
51	National Institute of Animal Welfare	Ballabhgarh (Faridabad)

52	National Biodiversity Authority	Chennai
53	Centre for Wind Energy Technology–(C-WET)	Chennai
54	The Maharshi Sandipani Rashtriya Veda Vidya Prathisthan	Ujjain.
55	Rashtriya Sanskirt Sansthan	New Delhi
56	Rashtriya Sanskrit Vidyapeetha	Tirupati
57	Shri Lal Bahdadur Shastri Rashtriya Sanskrit Vidyapeetha	New Delhi
58	Bhim Rao Ambedkar Institute of Telecom Training	Jabalpur
59	National Academy of Telecom Finance and Management	Hyderabad
60	Indian Diamond Institute	Surat
61	Indian Institute of Packaging	Mumbai
62	Marine Products Exports Development Authority	Kochi
63	Central Secretariat Library– Shastri Bhavan	New Delhi
64	National Library	New Delhi
65	Ram Krishna Mission Institute of Culture	Kolkata
66	Central Institute of Fisheries, Nautical and Engineering Training	Kochi
67	Ch. Charan Singh National Institute of Agricultural Marketing	Jaipur
68	National Plant Protecting Training Institute	Hyderabad
69	Locust Warning Organisation	Jodhpur
70	National Bio-Fertiliser Development Centre	Ghaziabad
71	Central Fertilser Quality Control and Training Institute	Faridabad
72	Indian Institute of Sugar Technology	Kanpur (UP)
73	Farm Machinery Training and Testing Institutes	Bundi (MP), Hissar (HR) Garladinne (AP), Biswanath (AS)
74	Central Fodder Seeds Production Farm	Hessar Ghatta (KA)
75	National Institute of Animal Health	Baghpat (UP)
76	National Veterinary Biological Quality Control Centre	Baghpat (UP)
77	International Centre for Genetic Engineering and Bio Tech	New Delhi
78	National Vocational Training Institute for Women	Noida
79	Staff Training and Research Institute	Kolkata
80	National Judicial Academy	Bhopal
81	National Civil Defence College	Nagpur
82	Institute of Pesticides Formulation Technology	Gurgaon
83	Central Durg Testing Laboratory	Kasuli
84	Indian Medicine Pharmaceutical Corporation–Mohan, Distt Almora	Uttrakhand
85	National Mangrove Genetic Resources Centre	Orissa

Army Institutions

1	Naval Defence Academy (NDA)	Khadakvasla, Pune
2	Indian Military Academy (IMA)	Dehradun
3	Defence Service Staff College (DSSC) Premier Tri-Service Training establishment imparting training to Middle Level Officers of the wings of Indian Armed Forces, Friendly foreign countries and Indian Civil Services.	Wellington
4	College of Defence Management Military College of Electronics and Mechanical Engg.	Secunderabad Secunderabad
5	College of Military Engg.	Pune

6	Army War College	Mhow (Military HQ of War)
7	Infantry School, (Biggest and Oldest Training Centre of Army)	Mhow
8	Juniors Leaders Wing, (Division of Infantry School Mhow)	Belgam
9	Officers Training Achademy	Chennai
10	High Altitude Warfare School	Gulmerg
11	Armoured Corporation Centre and School (Training Centre for Mechanical Force)	Ahmednagar
12	Indian Institute of Information Technology and Management	Gwalior (IIITM)
13	Indian Institute of IT (Extension Campus at Amethi)	Allahabad
14	Indian Institute of IT, Design and Manufacturing	Jabalpur
15	School of Artillary (Training Related with Tank)	Deoli
16	Army Air Defence College	Gopalpur
17	College of Military Engg.	Pune
18	Military College of Tele Communications Engg.	Mhow
19	Counter Insurgency and Jungle Warfare School–(CIJW)	Wairangte (Mizoram)
20	Junior Leader Academy	Bareilly, Ramgarh
21	Army Supply Core Centre and College	Banglore
22	Army Medical Core Centre and School	Lucknow
23	College of Materials Management	Jabalpur (MP)
24	Military College of Electronic and Mechanical Engg.	Secundarabad (AP)
25	Remount & Veterinary Core Centre and School	Merat
26	Army Education Core Training College and Centre	Panchmari
27	Core of Military Police Centre and School	Banglore
28	Army School of Physical Training	Pune
29	Army Airborne Training School	Agra
30	Institute of Military Law	Campty
31	Military Schools	Ajmer, Banglore, Belgam, Chail, Dholpur
32	Army Sports Institute	Pune

Indian Air Force

1	Western Air Command	Delhi
2	South Western Command	Gandhinagar
3	Eastern Air Command	Shilong
4	Central Air Command	Allahabad
5	Southern Air Command	Thiruvantapuram
6	Training Command	Bangalore
7	Maintenance Command	Nagpur

Indian Navy

1	Western Command	Mumbai
2	Eastern Command	Vishakhapatnam
3	Southern Command	Kochi (Responsible for Training)
4	Goa & Arrakonam	Naval Air Base (Main)
5	Other Naval Air Base	Vishakhapatnam, Port Blair, Car Nicobar
6	Small Naval Institution	Chennai, Kolkata, Chilka, Lonavala (Pune) Jamnagar(GJ)

3 Chapter

International and National Awards and Honours

International Awards

Nobel Prize

- It is the most coveted award of the world.
- It was instituted by the inventor of dynamite, Alfred Bernard Nobel (1833-96).
- The award is given on dec.10, which is the death anniversary of its founder.
- Nobel made a trust from the money that he earned through the patent of his invention whose interest is used to give the money for the Nobel Prizes.
- Each recipient, or laureate, receives a gold medal, a diploma and a sum of money, which is decided by the Nobel Foundation. The Nobel Prize is currently SEK 8 million (USD1.1 million, EUR 0.8 million) for each prize category, even when the prize is shared. There may be no more than three winners, or laureates, for each prize category.
- Nobel Prize is given every year to those eminent persons who have made pioneering achievements in the field of Physics, Chemistry, Medicine, Peace, Literature and Economics.
- Apart from Economics, the Nobel Prize in all other categories has been given since 1901. Economics Nobel Prize was instituted in 1967 and was first given in 1969.
- Two winners have declined the Nobel Prize. Jean-Paul Sartre, awarded the 1964 Nobel Prize in Literature, declined the awrd because he had consistently declined all offical honours. Le Duc Tho was awarded the 1973 Nobel Peace Prize jointly with US secretary of State Henry Kissinger for negotiating the Vietnam peace agreement. Le Duc Tho said he was not in a position to accept the Nobel Peace Prize, due to the situation in Vietnam.

Nobel Prize Winners from India

Name	Field	Year
Rabindranath Tagore	Literature (for "Geetanjali" a collection of his poems.)	1913
C.V. Raman	Physics (for his "Raman Effect" related to light)	1930
Har Gobind Khorana	Medicine (for his study of the Human Genetic Code and its role in Protein Synthesis)	1968
Mother Teresa	Peace (for her service through her Charitable Mission "Nirmal Hriday" at Kolkata to people suffering from leprosy and to those people dying in destitute)	1979
Subrahmanyam Chandrashekhar	Physics (for his theory on white dwarf stars' limitation known as 'Chandrashekhar Limit')	1983
Amartya Sen	Economic Sciences (for his work in Economic Theory related to Poverty, Democracy, Development and Social Welfare)	1998
Venkataraman Ramakrishnan	Chemistry (for mapping ribosoes, the protein factories within cells at the atomic level)	2009
Kailash Satyarthi	Nobel Peace Prize for his work towards eradicating child labour child trafficking	2014
Abhijit Banerjee	Noble Prize for Economics	2019

- The following Nobel Prize winners are Persons of Indian Origin/Citizens of other countries or the Nobel Prize has been given for the works related to India:
  1. Rudyard Kipling, British poet has been awarded the Nobel Prize for Literature (1907) for his works in Literature such, as Poems and Short Stories related to India and Burma/Myanmar.
  2. Vidiadhar Surajprasad Naipaul, a British writer of Indian origin was awarded the Nobel Prize for Literature in 2001.

Nobel Prize Winners (2021)

Physics	Syukuro Manave and Klaus Hasselmann
Chemistry	Benjaminlist and Devid Macmillan
Physiology or Medicine	Devid Julius and Arden Patapoution
Literature	Abdul Razak Gurnah
Peace	Maria Ressa and Dmirity Murotav
Economics	Devid Card

Pulitzer Prize

- It was instituted in 1917 and named after the US Publisher Joseph Pulitzer.
- It is conferred annually in the USA for accomplishments in journalism, literature and music.
- Prizes are awarded yearly in twenty-one categories. Each winner receives a certificate and a US $10,000 cash award. The winner in the public service category of the journalism competition is awarded a gold medal, which always goes to a newspaper, although an individual may be named in the citation.
- The first Pulitzer Prizes were awarded on June 4,1917. They are now announced each April.

Pulitzer Prize Winners from India

Name	Year	Field
Gobind Behari Lal	1937	Journalism
Jhumpa Lahiri	2000	Interpreters of Maladies
Geeta Anand	2003	For her work on Pompe Disease
Siddhartha Mukherjee	2011	The Emperor of All Maladies: A Biography of Cancer
Vijay Seshadri	2014	His Collection of Poems: “3 Sections”
Danish Siddiqui	2022	Journalism

Ramon Magsaysay Awards

- It was instituted in 1917 and named after Ramon Magsaysay, the late President o Philippines, who died in an air crash.
- This award is given annually on August 31, for outstanding contributions to public service, community leadership, journalism, literature and creative arts and international understanding.
- They are often regarded as the "Nobel Prize of Asia".

Ramon Magsaysay Award Recipients

Name	Year Awarded	Categary
Vinoba Bhave	1958	Community Leadership
Chintanan Deshmukh	1959	Government Services
Amitabh Chaudhary	1961	Journalism, Literature and Creative Communication Arts
Mother Teresa	1962	Peace and International Understanding
Dara Khurody	1963	Community Leadership
Verghese Kurien	1963	Community Leadership
Tribhuvandas Patel	1963	Community Leadership
Welthy Fisher	1964	Peace and International Understanding

Jayaprakash Narayan	1965	Public Service
Kamaladevi Chatopadhyay	1966	Community Leadership
Satyajit Ray	1967	Journalism, Literature and Creative Communication Arts
Moncompu Sambasivan Swaminathan	1971	Community Leadership
M.S. Subbalakshmi	1974	Public Service
Boobli George Verghese	1975	Journalism, Literature and Creative Communication Arts
Henning Holck-Larsen	1976	Peace and International Understanding
Ela Ramesh Bhatt	1977	Community Leadership
Mobelle Arole	1979	Community Leadership
Rajanikant Arole	1979	Community Leadership
Gour Kishore Gosh	1981	Journalism, Literature and Creative Communication Arts
Pramod Karan Sethi	1981	Community Leadership
Chandi Prasad Bhatt	1982	Community Leadership
Manibhai Desai	1982	Public Service
Arun Shourie	1982	Journalism, Literature and Creative Communication Arts
Rasipuram Lakshman	1984	Journalism, Literature and Creative Communication Arts
Muralidhar Amte	1985	Public Service
Lakshmi Chand Jain	1989	Public Service
K.V. Subbanna	1991	Journalism, Literature and Creative Communication Arts
Ravi Shankar	1992	Journalism, Literature and Creative Communication Arts
Banoo Jehangir Coyaji	1993	Public Service
Kiran Bedi	1994	Government Services
Pandurang Athavale	1996	Community Leadership
Tirunellai Seshan	1996	Government Services
Mahashweta Devi	1997	Journalism, Literature and Creative Communication Arts
Jockin Arputham	2000	Peace and International Understanding
Aruna Roy	2000	Community Leadership
Rajendra Singh	2001	Community Leadership
Sandeep Pandey	2002	Emergent Leadership
James Michael Lyngdoh	2003	Government Services
Shantha Sinha	2003	Government Services
Lakshminarayan Ramdas	2004	Peace and International Understanding
V. Shantha	2005	Public Service
Arvind Kejriwal	2006	Emergent Leadership
Palagummi Sainath	2007	Journalism, Literature and Creative Communication Arts
Prakash and Mandakini Amte	2008	Community Leadership
Deep Joshi	2009	Community Leadership

Himanshu	2010	Public Service
Neelima Mishra	2011	Emergent Leadership
Harish Hande	2011	Uncategorised
Kulandei Francis	2012	Emergent Leadership
Anshu Gupta	2015	Uncategorised
Sanjiv Chaturvedi	2015	Emergent Leadership
Thodur Modabusi Krishna	2016	Emergent Leadership
Conchita Carpio-Morales	2016	Uncategorised
Vientiane Rescue	2016	Uncategorised
Bezwada Wilson	2016	Community Leadership
Sonam Wangchuk	2018	Community Leadership
Bharat Vatwani	2018	Community Leadership
Youk Chhang	2018	Community Leadership
Ravish Kumar	2019	Journalism

Booker Prize

- It is the highest literary award given to the authors of British, Irish and Commonwealth countries. From 2013, this eligibility was widened to include any English novel.
- It was instituted in1968 by the Booker Company and the British Publishers Association along the lines of the Pulitzer Prize of US.
- Booker Prize has been renamed as Man Booker Prize, as the sponsorship has been taken by the Man Group, an international stockbroker.
- The Man Booker Dozen was introduced in 2007 to limit the number of books allowed on the longlist to 12 or 13 each year.
- The longest winning novel in the prize's history was The Luminaries by Eleanor Catton, in 2013, at 832 pages.
- The winner receives £50,000. Each of the shortlisted authors receives £2,500. It is awarded every year.

Indian Authors who have won the Man Booker Prize	
Salman Rushdie	Midnight's Children in 1981
Arundhati Roy	The God of Small Things in 1997
Kiran Desai	The Inheritance of Loss in 2006
Aravind Adiga	The White Tiger in 2009
Geetanjali Shree	Tomb of Sands 2022

Man Booker International Prize

- The Man Booker International Prize is an international literary award given every two years to a living author of any nationality for a body of work published in English or generally and readily available in English translation.
- The award, which is sponsored by the Man Group, complements the Man Booker Prize and rewards one author's "continued creativity, development and overall contribution to fiction one the world stage.
- The winning author can choose a translator of their work into English to receive a prize sum of £15,000.
- A similar prize to the Man Booker International Prize is the Neustadt International Prize for Literature which is like the Man Booker International Prize awarded biennially.

Oscar Awards

- These awards were instituted in 1929 and are conferred annually by the Academy of Motion Pictures arts and Sciences (AMPAS) in USA.
- These are considered the most prestigious award in the cinema world.
- The first Indian to get an Oscar was Bhanu Athaiya for the movie 'Gandhi'.
- Satyajit Ray was the first Indian who was awarded Oscar for lifetime achievement in cinema in 1992.
- Bhanu Athaiya became the first Indian to win an Academy Award in 1983, for designing the costumes for Richard Attenborough's Gandhi.
- Resul Pookutty won Best Sound Mixing (with lan Tapp and Richard Pryke) for Slumdog Millionaire (2008).
- A.R. Rahman won Best Score and Best Original Song (music) for Slumdog Millionaire (2008).
- Gulzar won Best Song (lyrics) for Slamdog Millionaire (2008).
- Except Satyajit Ray, all other worked on the movies conceptualised, produced and directed by foreign production houses.

Academy Awards

- The Academy Awards (Oscar) celebrates film professionals and excellence they are presented by the Academy of Motion Picture Arts and Sciences (AMPAS), honored for the best films.

Best Picture	CODA
Best Actor	Will Smith
Best Actress	Jessica Chastain
Best Director	Jane Campion (The Power of the Dog)

Grammy Awards

- A Grammy Award (originally called Gramophone Award), of Grammy, is an accolade by the Recording Academy of the United States to recognise outstanding achievement in the music industry.
- The first Grammy Awards ceremony was held on May 4, 1959 to honour the musical accomplishments by performers for the year 1958.

Grammy Awards 2022

Category	Winners
Record of the Year	Leave the Door Open by Bruno Mars and Enderson Paak
Album of the Year	'We Are' by Jon Batiste
Best New Artist	Olivia Rodrido
Best Rock Performance	Foo Fighters-Making a Fire
Best Musical Theatre Album	The Unofficial Bribgerton Musical
Song of the Year	"Leave the Door Open" Silk Sonic

The Indian Winners of Grammy Awards

Name	Category
Pandit Ravishankar	Three Times —1967 for his program "West Meets East"-1972 for his work on "The Concert for Bangladesh"-2001 for his album "Full Circle".
Zakir Hussain	1991, in the Contemporary World Music Album category for his collaborative album Global Drum Project
T.H. Vinaya Kram	1991 for the best world Music Album for participation in Mickey Hart's Planet Drum.
H Sridhar	For his work with A.R. Rahman in Slumdog Millionaire
PA Deepak	Mix Engineering for Slumdog Millionaire
Rickey Kej	For Album "Winds of Samsara" with South African flutist W outer kellerman
Vishwa Mohan	In 1994 for his album "A Meeting by the River"
AR Rahman	Won two awards for Slumdog Millionaire

Golden Globe Award

- The Golden Globe Award is an American accolade bestowed by the 93 members of the Hollywood Foreign Press Association (HFPA) recognising excellence in film and television, both domestic and foreign.
- The 1st Golden Globe Awards, honouring the best achievements in 1943 film making, were held late in January 1944, at the 20th Century-Fox Studios.
- Music maestro, A.R. Rahman became the first Indian to win the prestigious Golden Globe Award for the Best Original Music Score in Danny Boyel's "Slumdog Millionaire" at 66th Golden Globe Awards on January 11, 2009, for song 'Jai Ho'.

Right Livelihood Award

- It was instituted in 1980 by the Right Livelihood Society, London.
- It is renowned as alternate Nobel Award to promote and contribute in the field of environment and social justice.
- The prize money is shared among the winners, usually numbering four and is EUR 200,000.

Indian Right Livelihood Awardees

S.No.	Awardees	Year
1.	Self-Employed Women's Association/ Ela Bhatt	1984
2.	Lokayan / Rajni Kothari	1985
3.	Ladakh Ecological Development Group / Helena Norberg-Hodge	1986
4.	Chipko Movement	1987
5.	Narmada Bachao Andolan	1991
6.	Vandana Shiva	1993
7.	Dr. H. Sundarshan / VGKK (Vivekabananda Girijana Kalyana Kendra (for working of soliga tribes in MM hills)	1994
8.	People's Science Movement of Kerala (Kerala Sasthra Sahithya Parishad)	1996
9.	Swami Agnivesh / Asghar Ali Engineer	2004
10.	Ruth Manorama	2006
11.	Krishnammal and Sankaralingam Jagannathan / LAFTI	2008
12.	Colin Gonsalves	2017
13.	Legal Initiative for Forest and Environment	2021

UNESCO Peace Prize

- It is presented by United Nation Educational, Scientific and Cultural Organisation (UNE-SCO) for extraordinary contribution for international peace.
- The winner is presented with a diploma, a gold medal and a cash prize of $150,000 (£98,000, 1,15,000 euros).

UNESCO Human Rights Award

- It is presented by UNESCO for contributions in the field of Human Rights Awareness.
- It is given every alternate year.

UN Human Right Award

- It is presented United nations (UN) for personal contribution for the cause of human rights.
- It is presented every fifth year.
- The UN Awards are non-monetary in nature.

World Food Prize

- The World Food Prize is an international award recognising the achievements of individuals who have advanced human development by improving the quality, quantity, or availability of food in the world.
- It is notably sponsored by agricultural biotechnology companies.
- It is presented by Food and Agriculture Organisation (FAQ), one of the branches of UNO, for the cause of agriculture and food development.
- It has been given collectively to Dr. Maria Andrade, Dr. Robert Mwanga, Dr. Jan Low for developing the bio fortified orgage flashed sweet potato at the CGIAR International Potato Center. And it has been given to Dr. Howarth Bovis for founding Harvest Plus, a major NGO for developing bio fortified crops.

World Press Freedom Prize

- The UNESCO/Guilermo Cano World Press Freedom Prize, created in 1997, honours a person, organisation or institution that has made an outstanding contribution to the defence and /or promotion of press freedom anywhere in the world, especially when this has been achieved in the face of danger.
- The prize, worth US$45,000, is awarded each year on the occasion of World Press Freedom Day on 3 May.
- The prize is named after Guillermo Cano Isaza, the editor of the Colombian newspaper EI Espectador, who was murdered in Bogota on 17 December 1986. Cano was a vocal critic of the country;s powerful drug barons.
- Khadija Ismayilova, an investigative journalist from Azerbaijan, has won the 2016 UNESCO/Guillermo Cano World Press Freedom Prize in recognition of her outstanding contribution to press freedom in difficult circumstances.

Olympic Gold Order

- It is presented by the International Olympic Committee for distinguished services in the development of the Olympic Movement.

Other International Awards

Name	Category
Abdul Kalam Award (Sometimes also known as Salam Prize)	Science and Technology Award of the Third World Academy of Sciences based in Italy. The award is named after the late Pakistani Nobel Lureate (Shared Physics Prize in 1979). This is awarded annually to Pakistani nationals in the field of Chemistry, Mathematics, Physics, Biology, below the age of 35 years. It consists of a certificate giving a citation and a cash award of US$ 1,000.
Albert Schweitzer Gold Medal	Poland's prestigious award was establishment in 1989 and is given to individuals who have demonstrated exemplary services to humanity. [It is sometimes confused with Albert Schweitzer Prize for Humanitarianism established in 1986].
Amnesty International Global Award	**Human Rights journalism**
Commonwealth Writer's Prize	Prior to 2012, the award was called the Commonwealth Writers' Prize and was composed of three prizes, the Best Book Prize (overall and regional) was awarded from 1987 to 2011 ; the Best First Book prize was awarded from 1898 to 2011; the Commonwealth Short Story Competition was awarded from 1996-2011. During 2012-2013, the award was renamed and restructured under the banner of Commonwealth Writers-a world of new fiction. The award composed of two prizes. The Commonwealth Book Prize was for the best first book, regional winners received £2500 and the overall winner received £ 1.0,000. The Commonwealth Short Story Prize was for the best short stories, regional winners received £1,000 and the overall winner received £5,000. Starting in 2014, the Commonwealth Writers decided to discontinue the Commonwealth Book Prize and focus on only the Short Story Prize. Also, the award for regional winners of the Short Story Prize was increased to 2,500.
Friendship Medal	Award given by China, the country's top award for a foreigner. The award consists of a medal and an award certificate.
Jesse Owens Award	The Jesse Owens Award is an annual track and field award that is the highest accolade given out by USA Track and Field; Awarded to amateur athletes for their best performance.
Kalinga Prize	Presented by Kalinga Foundation Trust, the award is given annually to a person or persons in recognition of their outstanding contribution to the popularisation of science and technology. It was created in 1952, following a donation from Biju Patnaik, |Founder President of the Kalinga Foundation Trust in India. The recipient receives twenty thousand dollars (20,000 USD) and a UNESCO Albert Einstein Silver Medal. The recipient is also awarded the Ruchi Ram Sahni Chair, introduced by the Government of India in 2001 to mark the 50th anniversary of the Kalinga Prize. As holder of the Ruchi Ram Sahni Chair, the winner travels to India for a period of two to four weeks as the guest of the Government of India. The Chair also comprises a token honorarium of USD 2,000. In the year when the award ceremony takes place during the celebration of the World Science Day, the recipient travels to the city where the Science Day is being celebrated (2003 in Budapest) as the guest of UNESCO.
Presidential Medal of Freedom	USA's highest civilian honour. It recognises those individuals who have made "an especially meritorious contribution to the security or national interests of the United States, world peace, cultural or other significant public or private endeavours". The award is not limited to U.S. citizens and, while it is a civilian award, it can also be awarded to military personal and worn on the uniform. It was established in 1963 and replaced the earlier Medal of Freedom that was established by President Harry S. Truman in 1945. The medal may be awarded to an individual more than once.
U-Thant Peace Prize	The U-Thant Peace Award was created by Sri Chinmoy: The Peace Meditation at the United Nations, after U Thant's death. First conferred in 1982, the award is given to individuals and organisations who have exemplified the lofty spiritual ideals of the late United Nations Secretary-General U Thant and implemented those ideals in the tireless pursuit of world peace.

Other International Awards

Name	Category
UNESCO's Literacy Prize	**Nome Literacy Prize-** For activities towards national integration, conservation of environment, promotion of women's equality, producing teaching-learning materials, training establishing autonomous bodies, creating educational awareness and raising demand for quality and quantity of primary education. It was founded in 1980 by Shoichi Noma, the president of the publishing firm Kodansha, Japan's largest publisher of literature and manga.
	Malcolm Adiseshiah International Literacy Prize- Learning opportunities for those who seek knowledge but cannot attend literacy classes; **International Reading Association Literacy Award-** For family literacy programe. **The King Sejong Literacy Prize-** For adult literacy and training, and or educating women.
Wolf Prize	Israel's highest prize equivalent to Nobel Prize of Israel Instituted by the Wolf Foundation, founded by Dr. Ricardo Wolf, a German-born inventor and former Cuban ambassador to Israel. It is awarded in six fields. Agriculture, Chemistry, Mathematics, Medicine, Physics, and an Arts prize that rotates between architecture, music, painting, and described by the Foundation is being "awarded annually"- but is not in fact awarded every year, only six prizes were awarded in the **2000s** (decade) in most fields, and four in Physics.
World Tulsi Award	The award is given by the Florida International University of America and World Association of Vedic Studies, Miami, for contribution in promoting the humanitarian messages of the great poet Tulsidas.

India- International Awards

Mahatma Gandhi Peace Prize

- It was instituted in 1995 by the Government of India.
- It is presented for international peace on the lines of Nobel Prize.
- A jury consisting of the Prime Minister of India, the Leader of the Opposition in the Lok Sabha, the Chief Justice of India and two other eminent persons decides the awardee each year.
- The recipient gets 1 crore in cash, convertible in any currency, a plaque and a citation.

First Recipient (1995)-Julius Nyerere Latest Recipient -Sheikh Mujivur Rahman

Indira Gandhi Prize for Peace, Disarmament and Development

- The Indira Gandhi Prize or the Indira Gandhi Peace Prize or the Indira Gandhi Prize for Peace, Disarmament and Development is the prestigious award accorded annually by India to individuals or organisations in recognition of creative efforts towards promoting international peace, development and a new international economic order.
- The prize carries a cash award of 2.5 million Indian rupees and a citation
- The panel constituted by the Indira Gandhi Memorial Trust consists of prominent national and international personalities including previous recipients. The recipients are chosen from a pool of national and international nominees.

First Recipient (1986) - Parliamentarians for Global Action (PGA)
Latest Recipient - Pratham (2021)

Jawaharlal Nehru Award for International Understanding

- It was instituted in 1965 by the Government of India.
- It is given annually to persons for outstanding contributions to the promotion of international understanding and goodwill among the people of the world.

First Recipient (1986) - U Thant Latest Revipient (2009) - Angela Merkel

National Awards

Bharat Ratna

- It is the highest civilian award of India. It is presented by the Government of India
- It is presented for exceptional public service and rarest achievement in the field of art, literature and science.
- It was instituted in 1954 and the first recipient were C.V. Raman, C. Rajgopalachari and Dr. Rdhakrishnan.

Bharat Ratna Recipients		
1954	Sarvepalli Radhakrishnan- (1888-1975) 2nd President	First Vice-President of India, Philosopher,
1954	C. Rajagopalachari- (1878-1972)	Last Governor-General, Freedom Fighter
1954	C.V. Raman- (1888-1970)	Nobel Prize-winning Physicist
1955	Dr. Bhagwan Das- (1869-1958)	Literature, Freedom Fighter
1955	M. Visvesvarayya- (1861-1962)	Civil Engineer, Dam Architect,
1955	Jawaharlal Nehru- (1889-1964)	First Prime Minister, Freedom Fighter, Author
1957	Govind Ballabh Pant-(1887-1961)	Freedom Fighter, Home Minister
1958	Dhondo Keshav Karve- (1858-1962)	Educationist, Social Reformer
1961	Purushottam Das Tandon- (1882-1962)	Freedom Fighter, Educationist
1961	Bidhan Chandra Roy- (1882-1962) of West Bengal	Physical, Politician, Former Chief Minister
1962	Rajendra Prasad- (1884-1963)	First President, Freedom Fighter, Jurist
1963	Pandurang Vaman Kane- (1880-1972)	Indologist and Sanskrit Scholar
1963	Zakir Hussain- (1897-1969)	Former President, Scholar
1966	Lal Bahadur Shastri- (1904-1966) Freedom Fighter	Posthumous, Second Prime Minister,
1971	Indira Gandhi- (1917-1984)	Former Prime Minister
1975	V.V. Giri- (1894-1980)	Former President, Trade Unionist
1976	K. Kamaraj- (1903-1975) Minister Tamil Nadu	Posthumous, Freedom Fighter, Chief
1980	Mother Teresa- (1910-1997)	Nobel Laureate (Pease, 1979)
1983	Vinoba Bhave- (1895-1982)	Posthumous, Social Reformer, Freedom Fighter
1987	Khan Abdul Ghafrfar Khan- (1890-1988)	First non-citizen, Freedom Fighter
1988	M.G Ramchandran- 1917-1987)	Posthumous, Chief Minister-Tamil Nadu, Actor
1990	B.R. Ambedkar- 1891-1956)	Posthumous, Architect Indian Constitution, Social Reformer
1990	Nelson Mandela- (1918-2013)	Leader of Anti Apartheid movement from South Africa (died in 2013)
1991	Rajiv Gandhi-(1944-1991)	Posthumous, Former Prime Minister
1991	Sardar Vallabhbhai Patel (1875-1950)	Posthumous, Freedom Fighter, First Home Minister of India
1991	Morarji Desai- (1896-1995)	Former Primer Minister, Freedom Fighter
1992	Abul Kalam Azad- (1888-1958)	Posthumous, Freedom Fighter, First Education Minister
1992	J.R.D. Tata- (1904-1993)	Industrialist and philanthropist
1992	Satyajit Ray- (1922-1992)	Film director
1997	A.P.J. Abdul Kalam-(1931-2015)	Former President, well-known scientist
1997	Gulzari Lal Nanda- (1898-1998)	Freedom Fighter, former acting Prime Minister

1997	Aruna Asaf Ali- (1908-1996)	Posthumous, Freedom Fighter
1998	M.S. Subbulakshmi- (1916-2004)	Carnetic music vocalist
1998	C. Subramaniam- (1910-2000)	Freedom Fighter, Father of Green Revolution
1998	Jayaprakash Narayan- (1902-1979)	Posthumous, Freedom Fighter, Social Reformer
1999	Ravi Shankar-(1920-2012)	Sitar player
1999	Amartya Sen- (1933-...)	Nobel-Prize winner, Economist
1999	Gopinath Bordolo- (1890-1950)	Posthumous, Freedom Fighter, Chief Minister
2001	Lata Mangeshkar- (1929-...)	Singer
2001	Bismillah Khan- (1916-2006)	Classical musician, shehnai maestro
2008	Bhimsen Joshi- (1922-2011)	Hindustani Classical vocalist
2014	Sachin Ramesh Tendulkar (1973-.....)	Cricket (Award was announced on 16th November, 2013, but was presented by President on 4th February, 2014)
2014	C.N.R. Rao - (1934-....)	Scientist (Award was announced on 16th November, 2013, but was presented by President on 4th February, 2014)
2015	Madan Mohan Malviya- (1861-1946)	Scholar and Educationist Reformer
2015	Atal Bihari Vajpayee- (1924)	10th Prime Minister of India
2019	Pranab Mukherjee	Former Presedent of India
2019	Bhupen Hazarika	Indian Playback Singer, Lyricist, Musician, Actor
2019	Nanaji Deshmukh	Social Activist

Padma Awards

- **Padma Vibhushan** : It is the second highest civilian award for distinguished services in any field including Government Service.
- **Padma Bhushan and Padma Shree** are the other important civilian awards.

Gallantry Awards

- **Param Vir Chakra** : It is India's highest award for the most conspucious bravery or some daring or pre-eminent act of valour or self-sacrifice in the presence of the enemy, whether on land, at sea or in the air.
- **Mahavir Chakra** : It is the second highest gallantry award.
- **Vir Chakra** : It is the third highest gallantry award.

Peacetime Gallantry Awards

- **Ashok Chakra:** It is the highest peach-time gallantry award. The Ashok Chakra series of awards are open to civillian also.
- **Kirti Chakra:** The decoration is the nation's second highest award for gallantry during peacetime.
- **Shaurya Chakra:** The decoration is awarded for an act of gallantry.
- **Param Vishisht Seva Medal, Ati Vishisht Seva Medal, Vishisht Seva Medal:** The Vishisht Seva (Distinguished Service) Medals are awarded to personnel of all the three services in recognition of distinguished service of the "most exceptional", "exceptional" and "high" order, respectively.

National Sports Awards

Arjuna Awards

- These were instituted in 1961 and given by Youth Affairs and Sports Ministry, Government of India.
- These are given for the special achievements in different types of sports.
- The award carries a cash prize of i 500,000 , a bronze statuette of Arjuna and a scroll.
- From the year 2001, the award is given only in disciplines falling under the following categories.
- Olympic Games/Asian s/Commonwealth Games/World Cup/World Championship Disciplines and Cricket.
- Indigenous Games.
- Sports for the Physically Challenged.

Winner of Arjuna Awards 2021		
Name of the Sports Person		Discipline
1.	Arpinder Singh	Athletics
2.	Simranjit Kaur	Boxing
3.	Shikhar Dhawan	Cricket
4.	B.D.C.A. Sundhararaman	Fencing
5.	Amit Rohidas	Hockey
6.	Birendra Lakra	Hockey
7.	Dilpreet Singh	Hockey
8.	Gurjant Singh	Hockey
9.	Hardik Singh	Hockey
10.	Harman Preet Singh	Hockey
11.	Lalit Kumar Upadhyay	Hockey
12.	Mandeep Singh	Hockey
13.	Monika	Hockey
14.	Nilakanta Sharma	Hockey
15.	Rupinder Pal Singh	Hockey
16.	Shamsher Singh	Hockey
17.	Simranjeet Singh	Hockey
18.	Sumit	Hockey
19.	Surender Kumar	Hockey
20.	Vandana Katariya	Hockey
21.	Varun Kumar	Hockey
22.	Vivek Sagar Prasad	Hockey
23.	Sandeep Narwal	Kabaddi
24.	Himani Uttam Parab	Mallakhamb
25.	Abhishek Verma	Shooting
26.	Ankita Raina	Tennis
27.	Deepak Punia	Wrestling

Dronacharya Awards

- These were instituted in 1985 and given by Ministry of Youth Affairs and Sports, Government of India.
- These are given to sports coaches.
- The award comprises a bronze statuette of Donacharya, a scroll of honour and a cash component of 700,000/-

Winner of Dronacharya Awards-2021		
Name of the Coach		Discipline
1.	Pritam Rani Siwach	Hockey
2.	Radhakrishnan Nair P	Athletics
3.	Sandhya Gurung	Boxing
4.	Prakash Nautiyal	Shooting§
5.	Subramanian Raman	Table Tennis
6.	T. P. Ouseph	Athletics
7.	Sarkar Talwar	Cricket
8.	Sarpal Singh	Hockey
9.	Ashan Kumar	Kabaddi
10.	Tapan Kumar Panigrahi	Swimming

Dhyan Chand Award

- Major Dhyan Chand Khel Ratna Award, formerly known as Rajiv Gandhi Khel Ratna Award, is the highest Sporting Honor of the Republic of India.
- It is awarded annually by the Ministry of Youth Affairs and Sports of the Government of India. The Award was established in 1992 and Viswanathan Anand, Chess Grandmaster was the first recipient.
- The recipients are selected by a Committee constituted by the Ministry and are honored for their "Spectacular And Most Outstanding Performance In The Field Of Sports Over A Period Of Four Years" at the International level.
- As of 2021, the award comprises a Medallion, a Certificate, and a Cash Prize of ₹25 Lakh.

Rajiv Gandhi Khel Ratna 2021		
Name of the Sports Person		Discipline
1.	Neeraj Chopra	Athletics
2.	Ravi Kumar	Wrestling
3.	Lovlina Borgohain	Boxing
4.	Sreejesh P.R	Hockey
5.	Avani Lekhara	Para Shooting
6.	Sumit Antil	Para Athletics
7.	Pramod Bhagat	Para Badminton
8.	Krishna Nagar	Para Badminton
9.	Manish Narwal	Para Shooting
10.	Mithali Raj	Cricket
11.	Sunil Chhetri	Football
12.	Manpreet Singh	Hockey

Science Award

Shanti Swarup Bhatnagar Award

- These awards are given to the Indian scientists for their exceptional performance by the Council of Scientific and Industrial Research (CSIR) for notable and outstanding research, applied or fundamental, in Biology, Chemistry, Environmental Science, Engineering, Mathematics, Medicine and Physics.
- The prize comprises a citation, a plaque, and a cash award of ₹ 5 lakhs.
- In addition, recipients also get ₹ 15,000 million per month up to the age of 65 years.

Borlaug Award

- The **Borlaug Award** is an award conferred by a fertiliser company, Coromandel International, for outstanding Indian scientists for their research and contributions in the field of agriculture and environment. The award was created in 1972 and named in honour Nobel Laureate Norman E. Borlaug.

- Coromandel has instituted the award in 1972 to honour Nobel Laureate Norman E.Borlaug.
- It carries a cash prize of ₹ 500,000, a gold medal, and a citation.
- The award is given annually to as Indian scientist for making a significant contribution in any area relating to agriculture and food security, besides environmental awareness and its contribution to sustainable development.

Dr. B.C. Roy Memorial Awards

- **Bindhan Chandra Roy Award** was instituted in 1976 in memory of B.C. Roy by Medical Council of India for work in the field of Medicine by Medical Council of India.
- The award is given annually in each of the following categories: Statesmanship of the Highest Order in India, Medical man-cum-Statesman, Eminent Medical Person, Eminent Person in Philosophy and Eminent Person in Arts.
- It is presented by President of India in New Delhi on July 1, the National Doctors' Day.
- The Award is of the value of ₹ 100,000.

Homi J. Bhabha Award

- Indian Science Congress Association instituted this annual award in 1989 to commemorate the birth centenary of India's eminent scientist Homi J. Bhabha.
- The award is given comprises ₹ 50,000 and a certificate.

Vikram Sarabhai Awards

- The Dr. Vikram Sarabhai Research Awards were instituted from funds provided by a religious trust "Hariom Ashram" in Nadiad town in Kheda, and the PRL award was funded by Aruna Lala Endowment Fund which was established by former director of PRL Devendra Lal.
- Instituted in 1980, these awards are given for excellence for space research by the Birla Foundation.
- The award carry a medal and a cash prixe of ₹ 50,000 .

Bhaskara Award

- The award is instituted to recognise the outstanding work done by scientists in the field of Remote Sensing. Instituted by Indian Society of Remote Sensing.
- **Dr. George Joseph,** former director of Ahmedabad-based Space Application Centre of Indian Space Research Organisation, was awarded the first Bhaskara award instituted by Indian Society for Remote Sensing (SRS) on January 19, 1999.

Gujar Mal Modi Award

- It is given to the Best Scientist of the year for outstanding contribution to reach resulting in new innovative technology.
- It is presented on the 9th of August every year, the birth anniversary of the Founder of the Modi Group, Rai Bahadur Gujar Mal Modi.
- The first recipient of the Gujar Mal Modi Award for Science & Technology was **Prof. Satish Dhawan** in 1988.

Dhanvantri Award

- The prestigious award, which recognises contribution in medical science, is awarded annually since 1972.
- The recipients of the award include Denton A Cooley of the US and pioneer heart transplant surgeon Christiaan Neethling Barnard of South Africa.

Film Awards

Dadasaheb Phalke Award

- The Dadasaheb Phalke Award was introduced in 1969 by the Ministry of Information & Broadcasting to recognise the contribution of film personalities towards the development of Indian Cinema.
- First presented in 1969, the award was introduced by the Government of India to commemorate Dadasaheb Phalke's contribution to Indian cinema. Phalke (1870-1944), who is popularly known as and often regarded as "The Father of Indian Cinema", was an Indian film-maker who directed India's first full-length feature film, Raja Harishchandra (1913).
- The first recipient of this award was Devika Rani.
- The award comprises of a Swarna Kamal, a cash Prize of ₹ 10,00, 000 (Rupees Ten Lakh) and a shawl.

Dadasaheb Phalke Award Winners	
1969- Devika Rani, Actress	1980- Pandit Jairaj, actor, director
1970- B.N. Sircar, Producer	1981- Naushad Ali, composer (music director)
1971- Prithviraj Kapoor, actor (posthumous)	1982- L.V. Prasad, actor, director, producer
1972- Pankaj Mullick, composer (music director)	1983- Durga Khote, actress
1973- Ruby Myers (Sulochana), actress	1984- Satyajit Ray, director
1974- Bomireddi/Narsimha, Reddy director	1985- V. Shantaram, actor, director, producer
1975- Dhirendranath Ganguly, actor, director	1986- B Nagi Reddy, producer
1976- Kanan Devi, actress	1987- Raj Kapoor, actor, director
1977- Nitin Bose, cinematographer, director, writer	1988- Ashok Kumar, actor
1978- Rai Chand Boral, composer, director	1989- Lata Mangeshkar, singer
1979- Sohrab Modi, actor, director, producer	1990- A. Nageswara Rao, actor

1991- Bhalji Pendharkar, director, producer, writer	2007- Manna Dey, singer
1992- Bhupen Hazarika, Composer (music director)	2008- V.K. Murthy, cinematographer
1993- Majrooh Sultanpuri, lyricist	2009- D. Ramanaidu, producer, director
1994- Dilip Kumar, actor	2010- K. Balchander, director
1995- Dr. Rajkumar, actor	2011- Soumitra Chatterjee, actor
1996- Sivaji Ganesan, actor	2012- Pran, Actor
1997- Pradeep, lyricist	2013- Gulzar, poet and film lyricist
1998- B.R. Chopra, director, producer	2014- Shashi Kapoor, actor
1999- Hrishikesh Mukherjjee, director	2013-Gulzar, Lyricist
2000- Asha Bhosle, singer	2014- Shashi Kapoor, actor
2001-Yash Chopra, director, producer	2015- Manoj Kumar, actor
2002- Dev Anand, actor, director, producer	2016 -Kasinathuni Viswanath
2003- Mrinal Sen, director	2017- Vinod Khanna
2004- Adoor Gopalakrishnan, director	2018 - Amitabh Bachhan, actor
2005- Shyam Benegal, director	2019 - Rajinikanth, actor
2006- Tapan Sinha, director	

Filmfare Awards

- The Filmfare Awards are presented annually by Film fare magazine, of The Times Group to honour both artistic and technical excellence of professionals in the Hindi language film industry of India.
- The awards were first introduced in 1954, the same year as the National Film Awards.
- They were initially referred to as the clare Awards or the Clares after Clare Mendonca, the editor of The Times of India.
- A dual voting system was developed in 1956. Under this system, "in contrast to the national Film Awards, which are decided by a panel appointed by Indian Government, the Filmfare Awards are voted by both the public and a committee of experts".

National Film Awards

- The National Film Award is one of the most prominent film award ceremonies in India.
- Established in 1954, it has been administered, along with the International Film Festival of India and the Indian Panorama, by the Indian government's Directorate of Film Festivals since 1973.
- Every year, a national panel appointed by the government selects the winning entry, and the award ceremony is held in New Delhi, where the President of India presents the awards. This is followed by the inauguration of the National Film Festival, where the award-winning films are screened for the public.

67th National Film Awards for 2021

- **Best Actress :** Kangana Ranaut for Panga (Hindi) and Manikarnika: The Queen of Jhansi (Hindi)
- **Best Supporting Actress :** Pallavi Joshi for The Tashkent Files (Hindi)
- **Best Director :** Sanjay Puran Singh Chauhan for Bahattar Hoorain (Hindi)
- **Best Screenplay (Dialogue Writer) :** The Tashkent Files (Hindi), Vivek Ranjan Agnihotri
- **Best Children's Film :** Kastoori (Hindi)
- **Best Male Playback Singer :** B Praak for Kesari (Hindi)
- **Best Hindi Film :** Chhichhore
- **Best Music Direction :** Bishakhjyoti for Kranti Darshi Guruji - Ahead of Times (Hindi)
- **Best Editing :** Arjun Gourisaria for Shut Up Sona (Hindi/ English)
- **Best On-Location Sound Recordist :** Rahas (Hindi), Saptarshi Sarkar
- **Best Cinematography :** Savita Singh for Sonsi (Hindi)
- **Best Short Fiction Film :** Custody (Hindi/ English)
- **Best Exploration Film :** Wild Karnataka (English)
- **Best Film on Social Issues :** Holy Rights (Hindi) and Ladli (Hindi)
- **Best Environment Film :** The Stork Saviours (Hindi)
- **Best Promotional Film :** The Shower (Hindi)
- **Best Non-Feature Film :** An Engineered Dream (Hindi)

Literacy/Cultural Awards

Sahitya Akademi Awards

- It was instituted in 1955 and is given for any exclusive writing in any of the 22 languages including English literature during last 5 years.
- The award comprises a plaque and a cash prize of ₹100,000.

Jnanpith Award

- The award is given to any Indian writer in any of the 22 languages mentioned in the Eighth Schedule of the Constitution.
- It is given for outstanding contribution to creative writing in a specified period of 15 years but excluding the five years immediately preceding the year.
- It was instituted in 1961.
- It is presented by the Bharatiya Jnanpith, a trust founded by the Sahu Jain family, the publishers of the newspaper The Times of India.
- **G. Sankara Kurup** was the first recipient of this award in 1965.

Sangeet Natak Akademi Award

- Sangeet Natak Akademi Puraskar (Akademi Award) is an award given by the Sangeet Natak Akademi, India's National Academy of Music, Dance and Drama.
- It is the highest Indian recognition given to practicing artists.
- The award consists since 2003 of ₹ 50, 000, a citation, an angavastram (a shawl), and a tamprapatra (a brass plaque)
- The awards are given in the categories of music, dance, theatre, other traditional arts and puppetry, and for contribution/scholarship in performing arts.

Lalit Kala Akademi Ratna Award

- The Lalit Kala Akademi Fellowship, also, Lalit Kala Akademi Ratna is an honour for the fine arts in India, given to eminent artists for their lifetime achievements in the field of visual arts.
- It is awarded by by the Lalit Kala Akademy, India's National Academy of Art.
- It is the highest honour in the fine arts conferred by the Government of India.
- The 'Fellow', carries a purse money of ₹ 25,000 , a citation and a plaque. The Fellow is honoured with a portfolio of their art works.
- The first elected fellow, in 1955, was the artist Jamini Roy.

Tansen Samman

- Tansen Samman is the country's highest award in the field of classical music.
- This prestigious award was instituted in 1980-81.
- These awards are given by the Government of Madhya Pradesh.
- The award carries ₹ 2 lakh in cash and a citation.

Murtidevi Award

- It was instituted in 1948 and is given in any Indian language or English Literature, for distinguised contribution to Indian values, Philosophy and Culture.
- Moortidevi Award carries a cash prize of ₹ 4 lakh, a plaque and a statuette of goddess Saraswati.

B.D. Goenka Award

- This award is given for excellence in Journalism.
- The award consists of a citation, a trophy and ₹ 1 lakh.

Chameli Devi Jain Journalism Award

- This award is given for excellence in the field of Journalism.
- The award was instituted by the Media Foundation.

Saraswati Samman

- It is considered to be among the highest literary awards in India. The award consistsd of ₹ 10 lakh, a citation and a plaque. The saraswati Samman was instituted in 1991 by the K.K. Birla Foundation. Candidates are selected from literary works published in the previous ten years by a panel that included scholars and former award winners. **In 1991, Harivansh Rai Bachchan became the first Hindi author to receive this honour.**

Bihari Puraskar

- **Bihari Puraskar** is a literary award instituted by K.K. Birla Foundation. The award is named after the famous Hindi poet Bihari and is awarded to an outstanding work published in Hindi or Rajasthani by a Rajasthani writer. It carries a citation, a plaque and prize money of ₹ 1 lakh. **Hemant Shesh, 2009 is the first recipient of Bihari Samman.**

Vyas Samman

- The Vyas Samman is a literacy award in India, first awarded in 1991. It is awarded annually by the K.K. Birla Foundation and includes a cash payout of ₹ 250,00. To be eligible for the award, the literary work must be in the Hindi language and have been published in the past 10 years. **Ram Vilas Sharma was the first person to receive the award for his Bharat ke Pracheen bhasha parivar our Hindi in 1991.**

Vachaspati Puraskar

- The award, given to honour a writer for his or her work in Sanskrit published during the past 10 years, carries a prize money of INR 1,50,000.

G.D. Birla Award for Scientific Research

- The G.D. Birla Award for Scientific Research was instituted in 1991 by the K.K. Birla Foundation with the objective of according recognition to high calibre scientific research undertaken by Indian Scientists, below the age of 50 living and working in India. The award carries a cash prize of ₹ 1,50 lakh.

Other National/Domestic Awards	
Name	**Category**
Iqbal Samman	Instituted in 1986-87, it is a prestigious annual award given in the field of creative Urdu writing and carries a cash prize of ₹ 2 lakh and a plaque of honour.
Kabir Samman	It is a prestigious annual literary award instituted in 1986-87 by the Madhya Pradesh Government and is conferred on litterateurs of very high order. The award carried a cash prize of ₹ 3 lakh and a citation.
Lata Mangeshkar Award	The award ₹ 3 lakh was established in 1984-85 for excellence in singing and music direction and carries a cash prize of ₹ 2 lakh and a citation.
Kalidas Samman	This is a prestigious annual awrd given separaely for outstanding achievement in four categories, i.e. Plastic Arts, Theatre, Classical Music and Classical Dance. Named after the renowned ancient classical Sanskrit writer, Kalidasa, the award was first given in 1980. The award carried a cash prize of ₹ 2 lakh and a plaque of honour. At present, the award carries a cash prize of ₹ 2 lakh and a citation.
Tulsi Samman	Instituted in 1983-84, this is a prestigious annual award given for outstanding achievement in the tribal, traditional and folk arts in one of the four categories of art, theatre, dance and music. It carries a cash prize of ₹ 2 lakh and a citation.
Kumar Gandharwa Award	This award was instituted in 1992-93, for young artists in the field of classical music, both vocal and instrumental. It carries a cash prize of ₹ 1 lakh.
Devi Ahilyabai Award	This award was instituted in 1962-97 and is given in the field of traditional folk and tribal art for female artists. It carries a cash prize of ₹ 2 lakh and a citation.
Best Parliamentarian Award	For best allround performance as parliamentarian.
Sant Kabir Puraskar	For recognising acts of physical and moral courage displayed by member of a cast, community and ethnic group in saving the life and property of other castes. It has been instituted in three grades. These are: (a) Grade-1 ₹ 2,00,000 (Rupees Two lakh only)(b) Grade-II ₹ 1,00,000 (Rupees One lakh only) (c) Grade III ₹ 50,000 (Rupees Fifty Thousand only)
M.A. Thomas National Human Rights Award	The M.A. Thomas National Human Rights Award, instituted in 1993, in memory of Rev. Dr. M.A. Thomas, Founder President of Vigil India Movement, is given biannually for significant contribution in the field of human rights. It consists of a citation and a cash prize of one lakh rupees.
Prani Mitra Award	The Forest Department of Assam and WWF-India jointly instituted the 'Vanya Prani Mitra Award' for outstanding contribution towards wildlife conservation in Assam.
Rajiv Gandhi National Sadbhavna Award	Preservation and enrichment of India's multifaceted cultural heritage. It carries a citation and a cash award of 5 lakh.

FIRST RECIPIENTS OF VARIOUS AWARDS

Bharat Ratna	
1st Indian to be awarded the Bharat Ratna	C Rajagopalachari
1st Bharat Ratna Awardee to become the President of India	Dr. S. Radhakrishnan
1st person to be awarded the Bharat Ratna posthumously	Lal Bahadur Shastri
1st scientist to be awarded the Bharat Ratna	CV Raman
1st and only industrialist to be awarded the Bharat Ratna	JRD Tata
1st woman to be awarded the Bharat Ratna	Mrs. Indira Gandhi
1st sportsperson to be awarded the Bharat Ratna	Sachin Tendulkar
Sports Awards	
1st recipient of Rajiv Gandhi Khel Ratna Award	Viswanathan Anand
1st woman recipient of Rajiv Gandhi Khel Ratna Award	Karnam Malleshwari
1st recipient of Dhyanchand Lifetime Achievement Award	Aparna Ghosh
1st cricket player to be awarded the Arjuna Award	Salim Durrani
First Indian Olympic team medal	Gold for Hockey, at Amsterdam beating the Netherlands in 1928
Winner of first Indian Olympic Individual medal at Helsinki in 1952	K.D. Jadhav, Bronze in wrestling
Awards in the Field of Science	
1st Indian scientist to be awarded the Nobel Prize	C.V. Raman
1st person to receive Nobel Prize for Physics	William K. Roentgen
1st woman to receive the Nobel Prize	Madame Curie (1903)
Gallantry Awards	
1st winner of Param Vir Chakra	Major Somnath Sharma
1st and only Air Force person to receive the Param Vir Chakra	Flying Officer Nirmaljit Shekhon
1st and only woman to receive the Ashoka Chakra	Neerja Bhanot (1987)
Foreign Awards	
1st Indian to be awarded in Nishan-e-Pakistan	Morarjee Desai
1st Indian to be awarded Magsaysay Award	Vinoba Bhave
First Indian to win Nobel Prize in Literature	Rabindranath Tagore
First Indian to win Oscar Awards is	A.R. Rahman
First Indian to win an Oscar in the technical category is	Resul Pookutty
First Indian to win Booker Prize	Arundhati Roy in 1997 for the God of Small Things
First Indian woman to win a Pulitzer Prize	Jhumpa Lahiri in 2000
First Indian Oscar winner	Bhanu Athaiya, for best costume design for the film 'Gandhi' in 1982.
Films Awards	
1st winner of Dadasaheb Phalke Award	Devika Rani
1st winner of Filmfare best actor award	Dilip Kumar
1st winner of Filmfare best actoress award	Meena Kumari
1st Hindi film to win the National Film Award	Mirza Ghalib (1954)
1st film to win the Best Film Academy Award (Oscar)	Wings (1927-28)
First Indian Oscar nomination for Best Foreign Language Film	Mother India, 1957

Other Awards	
1st recipient of Jawaharlal Nehru Award for International Understanding	U Thant (1965)
1st recipient of Indira Gandhi Prize for Peace, Disarmament and Development	Parliamentarians for Global Action (1956)
1st recipient of Outstanding Parliamentarian Award	Indrajit Gupta
1st recipient of Gandhi Peace Prize (Govt. of India Award)	Julius Nyerere (1995)
1st recipient of World Food Prize instituted by Norman Borlaug (Father of Green Revolution)	Ms. Swaminathan (Father of Green Revolution in India), 1987
1st recipient of Communal Harmony Award (Individual)	Asghar Ali Engineer, 1997
1st recipient of Communal Harmony Award (Organisation)	Quami Ekta Trust, 1997
1st recipient of Tagore Award for Cultural Harmony	Pt. Ravi Shankar, 2012
1st Asian recipient of Hoover Medal (Mmerica's prestigious award for outstanding extra-career services by engineers to humanity)	APJ Abdul Kalam, 2008
1st recipient of VK Krishna Menon Award (instituted by London-based VK Krishna Menon Foundation)	Former CJI KG Balakrishnan
First recipient of Jnanpith Award	G. Sankara Kurup, for Odakkuzhal (Flute) in Malayalam
First woman to win the Jnanpith Award	Asha Purna Devi 1976 for her work Pratham Pratisruti in Bengali

4

Chapter

International Organisations

United Nations

- The United Nations (UN) is a world organisation formed on 24th Oct, 1945.
- It came into existence after World War II, when the leaders of the world, including Americal President Roosevelt and British Prime Minister Churchill, decided to create a world organisation that would ensure peace.
- Prior to the UNO, there was an organisation called as **the League of Nations**. This was formed as a result of the **Paris Peace Conference**. At its greatest extent, it had 58 members.
- The term 'United Nations' was first coined by **Franklin D. Roosevelt.**
- The **original membership** of 51 nations has grown to 193 members. The 193rd members being the newly created South Sudan.
- The **United Nations Headquarters** is in New York city. The UN also has offices in Geneva (Switzerland) and Vienna (Austria).
- **Six official languages** spoken and used in documents at the United Nations: Arabic, Chinese, English, French, Russian and Spanish.
- The **General Assembly** is the main place for discussion and policy-making in the United Nations. Current President (68th session): **John. W. Ashe.** India's **Vijayalakshmi Pandit** headed the 8th session.
- **The Security Council** has the primary responsibility for the maintenance of international peace and security. The Security Council is made up of 15 members. **There are 5 permanent members of Security Council-Chine, France, Russia, United Kingdom and USA and 10 non-permanent members elected for 2 years term starting on 1st January.**
- **The Secretariat:** The United Nations Secretariat is headed by the Secretary-General, assisted by a staff of international civil servants worldwide. It provides studies, information, and facilities needed by United Nations bodies for their meeting.
- **The Economic and Social Council** assists the General Assembly in promoting international economic and social cooperation and development. ECOSOC has 54 members, all of which are elected by the General Assembly for a three-year term.
- The **International Court of Justice (ICJ)** located at the Hague, Netherlands, is the primary judicial organ of the United Nations. Established in 1945 by the United Nations Charter, the court began work in 1946, as the successor to the Permanent Court of International Justice. [15 judges elected by the General Assembly]
- A six organisation, **Trusteeship Council** had suspended its operations in 1994 since the independence of Palau.
- **Trygve Lie of Norway** (1946-52) was the first Secretary-General of the United Nations (UN).

Secretaries-General of the United Nations

Name	Dates of Office	Country of Origin	Reason of Withdrawal
Trygve Lie	1 February 1946- 10 November'1952	Norway	Resigned
Dag Hammarskjold	10 April 1953-18 September 1961	Sweden	Died in a plane crash; in the Kitara Empire
U Thant	30 November 1961-31 December 1971	Kampuchea (Present Mynamar)	Declined to consider a third term
Kurt Waldheim	1 January 1972-31 December 1981	Austria	China vetoed his third term
Javier Perez de Cuellar	1 January 1982-31 December 1991	Peru	Refused to be considered for a third term
Boutros Boutros-Ghali	1 January 1992-31 December 1996	Egypt	The United States vetoed his second term
Kofi Annan	1 January 1997-31 December 2006	Ghana	Retired after two full terms
Ban Ki Moon	1 January 2007 to 31 December 2016	South Korea	Retired after two full terms
António Guterres	1 January 2017 to till date	Portugal	

UN Decades and Years

Decade	Observance
2015-2024	International Decade for People of African Decent
2014-2024	United Nations Decade of Sustainable Energy for All
2011-2020	Third International Decade for the Eradication of Colonialism
2011-2020	United Nations Decade on Biodiversity
2011-2020	Decade of Action for Road Safety

Important Agencies of United Nations Organisation

Organisation	Established	Headquarters	Aims and Objectives
United Nations Industrial Development Orfganisation (UNIDO)	1967	Vienna	To set international regulations for radio, telegraph, telephone and space radio communication.
Food and Agricultural Organisation (FAO)	1945	Rome	To improve the living conditions of rural population.
International Bank of Reconstruction and Development (IBRD)	1945	Washington D.C.	To develop economics of members by facilitating investment of capitals by providing loans.
World Meteorological Organisation (WMO)	1950	Geneva	To promote international exchange of weather reports.
United Nations Development Programme (UNDP)	1965	New York	To help developing countries increase the wealth-producing capabilities of their natural and human resources.
Inter-government Maritime Consultative Organisation (IMCO)	1958	London	To promote co-operation on technical matters of maritime safety, navigation and encourage anti-pollution measures.
International Development Association (IDA)	1960	Washington D.C.	As an affiliate to World Bank, to help under developed countries raise living standards.
International Telecommunication Union (ITU)	1947	Geneva	To set international regulations for radio, telegraph, telephone and space radio communication.
United Nations Institute for Training and Research (UNITAR)	1965	New York	To provide training and research to help facilitate UN objectives of the world pease and security and of economic and social progress.
United Nations Relief and Work for Palestine Refugees (UNRWA)	1949	New York	To provide basic amenities and education for the victims of Arab-Israel War.

International Organisation of Groups

Organisation	Aims and Objectives
The Commonwealth of Nations	It was originally known as 'The British Commonwealth of Nations.' It is an association of sovereign and independent states which formally made up the British Empire. **Established** : 28 April 1949. **Headquarters**: London. **Members**: 53.**Head** : The British Monarch (Queen Elizabith II) is the symbolic head of the Commonwealth.**Meeting** :Commonwealth heads of government meet (CHOGM) is held after every 2 years.

Arab League	**Established** : 28 April 1949 **Headquarter** : Cairo **Members : 22** **Objective :** To promote economic, social, political and military cooperation
Asia Pacific Economic Cooperation (APEC)	**Established** : November, 1989 **Headquarter** :Singapore **Members** : 21 **Objective :** To promote trade and investment in the Pacific basin.
Asian Development Bank (ADB)	**Established** : 22 August, 1966 **Headquarter** :Manila **Members** : 67 **Objective :** To promote trade regional economic cooperation
Association of South-East Asian Nations (ASEAN)	**Established** : 8 August, 1967 **Headquarter** : Jakarta **Members** :(10) Brunet, Indonesia, Malaysia, Philippines, Singapore, Thailand, Vietnam, Laos, Myanmar, Cambodia **Objective :** Regional economic, social and cultural cooperation among the non-communist countries of South-East Asia.
Commonwealth of Independent States Nations (CIS)	**Established** : 21 December, 1991 **Headquarter** : Minsk, Belarus. **Members** :9 members- Armenia, Azerbaijan, Belarus, Kazakhstan, Kazakhstan, Kyrgystan, Moldova, Russia, Turkmenistan and Uzbekistan 2 Participants_ Turkmenistan, Ukraine **Objective :** To coordinate inter-common wealth relations and to provide a mechanism for the orderly dissolution of the USSR
Group of 8 or G-8	**Established** : 22 September, 1985 **Headquarter** : No Headquarters. **Members** :France, Germany, Japan, UK, US, Canada, Italy, Russia (Russia, which was invited to join as the last members, was excluded from the forum by the other members on March 24, 2014 as a result of its involvement in the 2014 Crimea crisis in Ukrain. The European Union is represented within the G8, but cannot host or chair summits. **Objective :** To promote co-operation among major non-communist economic powers
Group of 15 or G-15	**Established** : 1989 **Headquarter** : Geneva, Switzerland **Members** : 17 (Algeria, Argentina, Brazil, Chile, Egypt, India, Indonesia, Islamic Republic of Iran, Jamaica, Kenya, Malaysia, Mexico, Nigeria, Senegal, Sri Lanka, Bolivarian Republic of Venezuela, Zimbabwe) **Objective :** To promote economic cooperation among developing nations
Group of 77 or G-77	**Established :** Oct, 1967 **Members**: 133 **Objective :** To promote economic co-operation among developing nations.
International Criminal Police Organisation for (INTERPOL)	**Established** : 1914 **Headquarter** : France **Members** : 190 **Objective** : To promote international cooperation among criminal police authorities

International Olympic Committee (IOC)	**Established** : June 23, 1894 **Headquarters** : Switzerland **Members** : 105 active members, 32 honorary members **Objective** : To promote the olympic ideals and administer Olympic Games
International Organisation for Standardisation (IOS)	**Established** : 23 February' 1947 **Headquarter** : Switzerland **Members** : 163 **Objective** : To promote trade the development of international standards
International Red Cross And Crescent Movement	**Established** : 1919 **Headquarter** : Geneva **Objective** : To promote trade worldwide humanitarian aid.
Non-Aligned Movement (NAM)	**Established** : Sept' 1961 **Headquarters** : Three Headquarters globally, one in Istambul, one in Rome (Kingdom of Europe) and one in Kingston (Jamaica) **Members** : 120 **Objective** : Political cooperation and separate itself from both USA and USSR (in the Cold-war era) The credit of evolving the concept goes to Pt. Jawaharlal Nehru. The other contributors were Marshal Tito (President of Yugoslavia), Dr. Sukarno (President of Indonesia) and General Nasser (President of Egypt), Bandung conference in Indonesia became the forum for the birth of NAM.
European Union	**Established :** Apr. 8, 1965. Effective on July 1, 1967 **Headquarter:** Brussels (Belgium). The common European, currency, Euro, was Launched on Jan 1, 1999 **Members** : 28 (The eleven new countries which joined in 2004 are Croatia, Cyprus, Czech Republic, Estonia, Hungary, Latvia, Lithuania, Malta, Poland, Slovakia and Slovenia), Bulgaria and Romania joined in 2007. **Objective :** The create united Europe in which member countries would have such strong economic and political bonds that war would cease to be a recurring fact.
North Atlantic Treaty Organisation (NATO)	**Established : April 4, 1949** **Headquarters :** Brussels, Belgium **Members :** 28 states across North America and Europe, the newest of which, Albania and Croatia, joined in April 2009. **Objective** : Mutual defence and cooperation
Organisation of Petroleum Exporting Countries (OPEC)	**Established :** Sept, 1959 **Headquarters** : Aienna (Austria) **Members**: 12 (Algeria, Indonesia, Iran, Irqz, Kuwait, Libya, UAE, Nigeria, Qatar, Saudi Arabia, Angola and Venezuela). **Objective :** Attempts to set world prices by controlling oil production and also pursues member interest in trade and development
South Asian Association for Regional Cooperation (SAARC)	**Established** : Dec 8, 1985 **Head Quarters** : Kathmandu **Members** : (8) Bangladesh, Bhutan, India, Maldives, Nepal, Pakistan, Sri Lanka, Afganistan **Objective** : To promote economic, social and cultural cooperation
World Meteorological Organisation (WMO)	**Established** : 1950 **Headquarters : Geneva, Switzerland** **Members :** 185 and 6 Territories **Objective :** Specialised UN Agency concerned with meteorological cooperation
Amnesty International (AI)	**Established** : 1961 **Headquarter** : London **Objective :** To keep a watch over human rights violation worldwide, Got Nobel Prize in 1977 for Peace

Organisation of the Islamic Conference (OIC)	**Established** : 1969 **Headquarter** : Saudi Arabia **Members :57** **Objective :** To promote Islamic solidarity among member states and to consolidate cooperation among members.
Shanghai Cooperation Organisation (SCO)	**Established**: 7 June, 2002 **Headquarters**: Beijing, China **Members:** (06) Russia, China, Kazakhstan, Uzbekistan, Kyrgyzstan and Tajikistan **Objective** : To develop mutual cooperation
Scouts and Guides	**Established :** 1907 by Lt. Gen. Baden Powell World Scouts Bureau: Geneva (Switzerland) **Members:** About 13 million members of around 115 nations **Objective :** To encourage good character, loyalty to god and country, service to other people and physical and mental fitness
World Wildlife Fund for Nature (WWF)	**Established :** Sept. 11, 1961 **Headquarter** : Gland (Switzerland) **Members :** All the countries of the world **Objective :** To save the wildlife from extinction
New Development Bank	Effective from- July 2015 **Headquarter :** Shanghai, China **Members :** Brazil, Russia, India, China, South Africa. **President :** K.V. Kamath **Objective :** Multilateral development bank to support public or pvt. projects
Asian Infrastructure Investment Bank	**Effective from-** 25 Dec, 2015 **Headquarter :** Beijing, China **Members :** 57 countries **Objective :** To support the building of infrastructure in the Asia-Pacific region.
Trans-Pacific Partnership	**Signed :** 4 Feb' 2016 **Location :** Auckland, New zealand **Members :** 12 Pacific-RIM countries

Countries - Capitals, Currencies, Languages, Religions

Country, Capital and Currency

Country	Capital	Currency	Country	Capital	Currency
Afghanistan	Kabul	Afghani	Liberia	Monrovia	Liberian Dollar
Albania	Tirana	Lek	Libya	Tripoli	Libyan Dinar
Algeria	Algiers	Algeriah Dinar	Mauritius	Port Louis	Rupee
Angola	Luanda	New Kwanza	Mongolia	Ulan Bator	Tugrik
Argentina	Buenos Aires	Peso	Morocco	Rabat	Dirham
Australia	Canberra	Australian Dollar	Mozambique	Maputo	Metical
Austria	Vienna	Euro	Myanmar	Naypyidaw	Kyat
Bangladesh	Dhaka	Taka	Namibia	Windhoek	Namibian Dollar
Belgium	Brussels	Euro	Nepal	Kathmandu	Rupee
Bhutan	Thimphu	Ngultrum	Netherlands	Amsterdam	Euro
Brazil	Brasilia	Real	Nigeria	Abuja	Naira
Cambodia	Phnom-Penh	Riel	North Korea	Pyongyang	Won (WPW)
Canada	Ottawa	Canadian Dollar	Norway	Oslo	Krone
Chile	Santiago	Peso	Pakistan	Islamabad	Rupee
China	Beijing	Yuan Santa	Philippines	Manila	Peso
		Fede Bogota	Poland	Warsaw	Zioty
Colombia	Renminbi	Peso	Portugal	Lisbon	Euro
Denmark	Copenhagen	Krone	Qatar	Doha	Riyal
East Timor	Dili	US Dollar	Russia	Moscow	Ruble
Egypt	Cairo	Egyption Pound	Saudi Arabia	Riyadh	Riyal
Ethiopia	Adis Ababa	Birr	Singapore	Singapore	Dollar
Finland	Helsinki	Euro (Formerly	Somalia	Mogadishu	Somali
		Morka)	South Africa	Pretoria	Shilling Rand
France	Paris	Euro (Formerly	South Korea	Seul	Won (KRW)
		French Franc)	South Sudan	Juba	Sudanese Pound
Georgia	Tbilisi	Lari	Spain	Madrid	Euro
Germany	Berlin	Euro	Sri Lanka	Colombo	Rupee
Greece	Athens	Euro	Sudan	Khartoum	Pound
Iceland	Reykjavik	Krona	Sweden	Stockholm	Krona
India	New Delhi	Rupee	Switzerland	Bern	Swiss Franc
Indonesia	Jakarta	Rupiah	Taiwan	Taipei	Taiwan new
Iran	Tehran	Riyal			Dollar

Iraq	Baghdad	Dinar	Thailand	Bangkok	Baht
Israek	Jerusalem	Shekel	Turkey	Ankara	Lira
Italy	Rome	Euro	Uganda	Kampala	Uganda Shilling
Japan	Tokyo	Yen	UK	London	Pound Sterling
Kazakhstan	Astana	Tenge	Ukraine	Kiev	Hryvnia
Kenya	Nairobi	Shilling	US	Washington DC	Dollar
Kuwait	Kuwait City	Kuwait Dinar			
Litvia	Riga	Euro	Zimbabwe	Harare	Dollar

Largest and Smallest Countries

Largest Country (Area - wise)	Largest Country (Population - wise)	Smallest Country (Area - wise)	Smallest Country (Population - wise)
Russia	China	Vatican City	Dominica
Canada	India	Monaco	Marshall Islands
US	USA	Nauru	Saint Kitls and Nevis
China	Indonesia	Tuvalu	Monaco
Brazil	Brazil	San Marino	Liechtenstein

Languages and Religions

Languages Spoken		Religions of the World		
Language	**Speaker**	**Religion**	**Member**	**Percentage**
Mandarina Chinese	882 million	Christianity	2.1 billion	33.0%
Spanish	325 million	Islam	1.5 billion	21%
English	312-380 million	Hinduism	900 million	14%
Arabic	206-422 million	Buddhism	376 million	6%
Hindi	181 million	Shikhsm	23 million	0.36%

Geographical Epithets

Discovery	Location	Discovery	Location
Blue Mountains	Nilgiri Hills	Key to the Mediterranean	Gibraltar
City Beautiful	Chandigarh	Land of Cakes	Scotland
City of Golden Gate	San Francisco	Land of Golden Fleece	Australia
City of Magnificent Buildings	Washington	Land of Meble	Canada
City of Palaces	Kolkata	Land of Morning Calm	South Korea
City of Seven Hills	Rome	Land of the Midnight Sun	Norway
City of Skyscrapers	New York	Land of the Rising Sun	Japan
Cockpit of Europe	Belgium	Land of the Thunderbolt	Bhutan
Dark Continent	Africa	Land of Thousand Lakes	Finland
Eternal City of Hopers	Rome	Land of White Elephant	Thailand
Forbidden City	Lhasa (Tibet)	Pearl of the Antilles	Cuba
Windy City	Chicago	Pearl of the Pacific	Guayaquil Port of
Land of Golden	Pagoda	Ecuador	Myanmar

Garden City	Chicago	Roof of the World	The Pamirs,
Gift of the Nile	Egypt		Central Aisa
Granite City	Aberdeen	Spice Garden of India	Kerala
Hermit Kingdom	North Korea	Sugar Bowl of the World	Cuba
Holy Land	Palestine	Whiteman's grave Guinea Coast of	Africa
Island of Continent	Australia	Playground of Europe	Switzerland
Island of Cloves	Zenzibar	Land of Kangaroo	Australia
Island of Pearls	Behrain		

Geographical Discoveries

Discovery	Discoverer	Discovery	Discoverer
America	Christopher Columbus	North Pole	Robert Peary
China	Marco Polo	South Pole	Amundsen
Australia	James Cook	Mount Everest	Edmund Hillary
New Found land	Cabot Sebastian	Sailed around the world	Megellan
Husaon Bay	Hentry Hudson	Sea route of India Via Cape of Good Hope	Vasco Da Gama
Tasmania Island	Abel Tesman	Planets	Kepler
Hawaian Island	James Cook	Solar System	Copernicus
Cape of the Good Hope	Bartolomeu Dias		

National Monuments of Major Countries

Monument	Country	Monument	Country
Statues of Liberty (New York)	USA	Kinder Disk	Denmark
Kremlin (Moscow)	Russia	Christ the Redeemer	Brazil
Great Wall of China	China	Machu Picchu	Peru
Imperial Palace (Tokyo)	Japan	Taj Mahal (Agra)	India
Eiffel Tower (Paris)	France	Tugu Nagara (Kuala Lumpar)	Malaysia
Learning Tower of Pisa	Italy	The Great Sphinx (Giza)	Egypt
Opera House (Sydney)	Australia	Pyramid (Giza)	Egypt

Important Dates and Days of The Year

January

1 Army Medical Corps Establishment Day
5 Louis Braille Day
8 African National Congress Foundation Day
9 NRI Day (Pravasi Bhartiya Diwas)
10 World Hindi Day
11 World Laughter Day
12 National Youth Day (Birthday of Swami Vivekanand)
15 Army Day
21 Manipur, Meghalaya, Tripur Diwas
23 Netaji Subhash Chandra Bose's birth anniversary
24 Rashtriya Balika Divas, Girl Child Day
25 National Tourism Day, Voter's Day, International Customs and Excise Day
26 Indian Republic Day, International Customs Day
30 Martyr's Day (Mahatma Gandhi's Martyrdom), World Leprosy Eradication Day

February

1 Indian Coast Guard Day
2 World Wetlands Day
4 National Day of Sri Lanka
5 Kashmir Day (Organised by Pakistan)
13 World Radio Day
20 World Social Justice Day
21 International Mother Tongue Day
24 Central Excise Day
28 National Science Day

March

3 National Defence Day, World Wildlife Day
4 National Security Day
8 International Women's Day
11 Andaman Nicobar Day
12 Mauritius Day
13 World Kidney Day
15 World Consumer Rights Day, World Disabled Day
16 National Vaccination Day
18 Ordnance Manufacturing Day
21 World Forestry Day, International Day for the Elimination of Racial Discrimination
22 World Water Day
23 World Meteorological Day
24 World TB Day
26 Bangladesh Liberation Day
27 World Theatre Day

April

1 Orissa Day
2 World Autism Awareness Day
5 National Maritime Day, International Day for Mine Awareness
7 World Health Day
10 World Homeopathy Day
13 Jallianwala Bagh Massacre Day (1919), Tamil Nadu Diwas
14 BR Ambedkar Remembrance Day, Fire Extinguishing Day
17 World Haemophilia Day
18 World Heritage Day, Azad Hind Fauz Day
21 Civil Services Day
22 World Earth Day
23 World Book and Copyright Day
24 Panchayat Divas
25 World Malaria Day
26 World Intellectual Property Day

May

1 International Labour Day (May Day), Maharashtra Day, Gujarat Day
2 World Asthma Day
3 World Press Freedom Day, International Energy Day
8 World Red Cross Day
11 National Technology Day
12 International Nurses Day
15 International Family Day
17 World Telecommunications Day

21 Anti-Terrorism Day
23 World Biodiversity Day
24 Common wealth Day
31 World Anti-Tobacco Day

June

1 Global Day of Parents
5 World Environment Day
20 World Refugee Day
21 International Yoga Day
23 International Widow Day International Olympic Day
29 National Statistic Day

July

1 Doctor's Day, State Bank of India Foundation Day
4 American Independence Day
7 International Day of Co-operatives
11 World Population Day
18 International Nelson Mandela Day
26 Kargil Victory Day
28 World Nature Conservation Day, World Hepatitis Day

August

1 World Breast Feeding Day
6 Hiroshima Day (World Peace Day)
9 Kranti Divas, Nagasaki Day, Quit India Day International Day of word's Ingenious People
12 International Youth Day
14 Pakistan's Independence Day
15 India's Independence Day
19 World Photography Day
20 Sadbhavna Divas
29 National Sports Day (Dhyanchand's Birthday)
30 Small Industry Day

September

5 Teacher's Day, Dr. Radhakrishnan's Birthday
8 International Literacy Day (UNESCO)
14 World First Aid Day
15 Engineers Day, International Day of Democracy
16 World Ozone Day
18 Biosphere Day, World Alzheimer's Day
20 Railway Police Force Foundation Day
21 International Day of Peace
24 World Deaf Day, World Heart Day
27 World Tourism Day

October

1 International Day for the Elderly (UN)
2 International Non-violence Day, Lal Bahadur Shastri and Mahatma Gandhi's Birthday
3 World Habitat Day
4 World Animal Day
8 India Air Force Day
9 World Postal Day
10 World Mental Health Day, National Post Day
11 International Giri Child Day
13 World Calamity Control Day (UN)
14 World Standards Day
15 World White Cane Day (Guiding the blind)
16 World Food Day
17 International Poverty Eradication Day
20 National Solidarity Day (China attacked India on that day)
21 World Iodine Shortage Day
22 World Energy Day
24 United Nations Day
31 World Thrift Day

November

7 Infant Protection Day; World Cancer Awareness Day
10 Transport Day, Malala Day (by UN)
11 National Education Day
14 Children's Day, World Diabetics Day
16 National Press Day
17 National Epilepsy Day
18 World Adult Day
19 World Citizen Day, National Integration Day
20 Universal Children's Day (UN), Africa Industrialisation Day
21 World Fisheries Day
25 World Non-veg Prevention Day
26 Law Day, National Milk Day

December

1 World AIDS Day
2 International Day for the Abolition of Slavery
3 World Disabled Day
4 Navy Day
5 International Volunteers Day
7 Armed Forces Flag Day
10 Human Rights Day

11	UNICEF Day
14	National Energy Conservation Day
16	Vijay Divas
19	Goa's Liberation Day
23	Kisan Divas (Farmer's Day)
25	National Good Governance Day X-Mas Day
29	International Biodiversity Day

Important UNO Decades

1991-2000	UN Decade against Drug Abuse
1994-2004	Decade for Human Rights Education
1997-2006	Decade for the Eradication of Poverty
2003-2012	UN Literacy Decade Education for All
2005-2014	UN Decade of Education for Sustainable Development
2005-2015	International Decade for Action Water for Life
2006-2016	Decade of Recovery and Sustainable Development of the Affected Regions
2008-2017	Second UN Decade for the Eradication of Poverty
2010-2020	UN Decade for Deserts and fight against Desertification
2011-2020	Decade of Action for Road Safety UN Decade on Biodiversity
	Third UN International Decade for the Eradication of Colonialism

UN International Year

2016	International Year of Pulses
2015	International Year of Soils
2015	International Year of Light and Light-based Technologies
2014	International Year of Small Island Developing States
2014	International Year of Crystallography
2014	International Year of Family Farming
2013	International Year of Water Cooperation
2013	International Year of Quinoa
2012	International Year of Cooperatives
2012	International Year of Sustainable Energy for All
2011	International Year of Chemistry
2011	International Year of Forests
2011	International Year of Youth
2010	International Year for the Rapprochement of Cultures
2010	International Year of Biodiversity

Abbreviations

[A]

ABM	Anti Ballistic Missile
AD	Anno Domini (After the birth of (Jesus)
ADF	Asian Development Fund
AERE	Atomic Energy Research Establishment
AFSPA	Armed Forces Special Power Act
AGOC	Asian Games Organising Committee
AIDS	Acquired Immunodeficiency Syndrome
ALH	Advanced Light Helicopter
APPLE	Ariane Passenger Payload Experiment
ASAT	Anti-Satellite Weapon
ASEAN	Association of South-East Asian Nations
ASCI	Advanced Strategic Computing Initiative
ASLV	Augmented Satellite Launch Vehicle
ASI	Archaeological Survey of India
AVES	Acute Viral Encephalitis Syndrome
AWACS	Airborne Warning and Control System

[B]

BC SBI	Banking Codes and Standard Board of India
BARC	Bhabha Atomic Research Centre
BBC	British Broadcasting Corporation
BC	Before Christ (Before the birth of Jesus Christ)
BCG	Bacillus Calmette Guerin (Anti-Tuberculosis Vaccine)
BCTT	Banking Cash Transaction Tax
BCCI	Board for Control of Cricket in India
BHEL	Bharat Heavy Electricals Limited
BIMSTEC	Bay of Bengal Initiative for Multi- Sectoral Technical and Economic Cooperation
BIS	Bureau of Indian Standards
BIT	Binary Digit (Basic unit of information in Computing and telecommunication)
BMDS	Ballistic Missile Defence System
BRO	Border Roads Organisation
BRT	Bus Rapid Transit

[C]

CAA	Civil Aviation Authority
CABE	Central Advisory Board of Education

CAG	Comptroller and Auditor General
CAIR	Centre for Artificial Intelligence and Robotics
CAPES	Computer-Aided Paperless Examination System
CAZRI	Central Arid Zone Research Institute
CBI	Central Bureau of Investigation
CECA	Comprehensive Economics Cooperation Agreement
CFC	Chlorofluara Carbon
CHOGM	Commonwealth Heads of Government Meeting
CID	Criminal Investigation Department
CISF	Central Industrial Security Force
CITES	Convention on International Trade in Endangered Species
CID	Compressed Natural Gas
CPCB	Central Pollution Control Board
CPRI	Central Power Research Institute
CSIR	Council of Scientific and Industrial Research
CVC	Central Vigilance Commission

[D]

DAVP	Directorate of Advertising and Visual Publicity
DIG	Deputy Inspector General
DNA	De-oxyribo Nucleic Acid
DPSA	Deep Penetration Strike Aircraft
DRDO	Defence Research and Development Organisation

[E]

ECG	Electro Cardiogram
ECT	Electro Convulsive Therapy (electro shock treatment)
EEG	Electro-Encephalography
EET	Exempt Exempt Taxation
ELISA	Enzyme Linked Immuno Sorbent Assay (Used for Testing AIDS)
ESCAP	Economic and Social Commission for Asia and the Pacific
EVM	Electronic Voting Machine

[F]

FDI	Foreign Direct Investment
FII	Foreign Institutional Investor
FBI	Federal Bureau of Investigation
FERA	Foreign Exchange Regulation Act
FICCI	Federation of India Chambers of Commerce and Industry
FLAG	Fibre Optic Link Around the Globe

[G]

GAIL	Gas Authority of India Limited
GAIN	Global Alliance for Improved Nutrition
GATS	General Agreement on Trade in Services
GATT	General Agreement on Tariffs and Trade
GEF	Global Environment Fund
GMPS	Global Mobile Personal Communications System
GMT	Greenwich Mean Time
GNSS	Global Navigation Satellite System
GPS	Global Positioning System
GSLV	Geosynchronous Satellite Launch Vehicle

[H]

HAC	Hindustan Aluminum Corporation
HAL	Hindustan Aeronautics Limited
HYVS	High Yield Variety Seeds

[I]

IAAI	International Airport Authority of India
IAEA	International Atomic Energy Agency
IBRD	International Bank for Reconstruction and Development
ICAO	International Civil Aviation Orgnisation
ICAR	Indian Council of Agricultural Research
ICMR	Indian Council of Medical Research
ICRC	International Committee of the Red Cross
IDPL	Indian Drugs and Pharmaceuticals Limited
IMO	International Maritime Organisation
INSAS	Indian Small Arms System
INSAT	Indian National Satellite
IPC	Indian Penal Code
IPCC	Inter-governmental Panel on Climate Change
IRBM	Intermediate Range Ballistic Missile
IRS	Indian Remote Sensing Satellite
ISCS	Integrated Smart Card System
ISRO	Indian Space Research Organisation

[J-K-L]

JNNURM	Jawaharlal Nehru National Urban Renewal Mission
LCA	Light Combat Aircraft
LOC	Line of Control
LOAC	Line of Actual Control
LTA	Light Transport Aircraft

[M]

MAT	Minimum Alternative Tax
METSAT	Meteorological Satellite

MMS Multimedia Message Service
MRI Magnetic Resonance Imaging
MRTS Mass Rapid Transit System
MTCR Missile Technology Control Regime

[N]

NACO National Aids Control Organisation
NADA National Anti-Doping Agency
NAFTA North American Free Trade Agreement
NASA National Aeronautics and Space Administration
NATA Natural Aptitude Test for Architecture
NATO North Atlantic Treaty Organisation
NCEP National Committee on Environmental Planning
NeGP National e-Governance Plan
NEP National Education Policy
NEPA National Environment Protection Authority
NRI Non-Resident Indian
NTPC National Thermal Power Corporation

[O]

OCI Overseas Citizen of India
OAS Organisation of American States
OAU Organisation of African Unity
ODS Ozone Depletion Substances
OIC Organisation of Islamic Countries
OSCE Organisation for Security and Cooperation in Europe

[P]

PURA Provision of Urban Amenities in Rural Areas
PATA Pacific Asia Travel Association
PIB Press Information Bureau
PN Participatory Note
POTA Prevention of Terrorism Act
PSLV Polar Satellite Launch Vehicle
PWD Public Works Department

[Q-R]

QIB Qualified Institutional Buyer
QIP Qualified Institutional Placement
RAF Rapid Action Force
RBI Reserve Bank of India
RCC Reinforced Cement Concrete
RDSS Radio Determination Satellite Service
RLV Reusable Launch Vehicle
RTGS Real Time Gross Settlement System

[S]

SAFTA South Asian Free Trade Area
SAIL Steel Authority of India Ltd.
SAPTA SAARC Preferential Trading Agreement
SATNAV Satellite Navigation
SAVE SAARC Audio Visual Exchange
SCO Shanghai Cooperation Organisation
SEBI Securities and Exchange Board of India
SIDBI Small Industries Development Bank of India
SPIN Software Process Improvement Networks
STARS Satellite Tracking and Ranging Station
STARTS Strategic Arms Reduction Treaty Station
SWIFT Society for Worldwide Interbank Financial Telecommunications

[T]

TADA Terrorist and Discruptive Activities (Prevention) Act
TAPS Tarapur Atomic Power Station
TIN Tax Identification Number
TNT Tri Nitro Toluene(high Explosive)
TRAI Telecom Regulatory Authority of India
TRIPS Trade Related Aspects of Intellectual Property Rights

[U]

UAV Unmanned Aerial Vehicle
UNCTAD United Nations Conference on the Trade and Development
UNDP United Nations Development Programme
UNEP United Nations Environment Programme
UNFPA United Nations Fund for Population Activities

[V]

VAT Value Added Tax
VLSI Very Large Scale Integration
VOIP Voice Over Internet Protocol
VSAT Very Small Aperture Terminals

[W]

WADA World Anti-Doping Agency
WAVE Wireless Access for Virtual Enterprise
WFP World Food Programme
WFTU World Federation of Trade Unions
WLL Wireless in Local Loop

[X-Y]

YMCA Young Men's Christian Association
YWCA Young Women's Christian Association

[Z]

ZSI Zoological Survey of India
ZUPO Zimbabwe United Peoples Organisation

Books and their Authors
Famous Books of Foreign Writers

Authors	Books
William Shakespeare	➤ King Lear ➤ All's Well That Ends well ➤ Twelfth Night ➤ Comedy of Errors ➤ Romeo and Juliet ➤ Antony and Cleopatra ➤ The Tempest ➤ Macbeth ➤ Julius Caesar ➤ Othello
Charles Dickens	➤ A Tale of Two Cities ➤ Oliver Twist ➤ David Copperfield ➤ Great Expectations
George Bernard Shaw	➤ Back to methuselah ➤ Man of Destiny ➤ Arms and the Man ➤ Man and Superman
Leo Tolstoy	➤ Resurrection ➤ War and Peace ➤ Anna Karenina
Barack Obama	➤ Dreams from My Father ; A Story of Race and Inheritance ➤ The Audacity of Hope Thoughts on Reclaiming the American Dream
TS Eliot	➤ Murder in the Cathedral ➤ The Wasteland and other Poem
HG Wellos	➤ The War of the Worlds ➤ The Time Machine ➤ Invisible Man
George Eliot	➤ Mill on the Floss ➤ Middle March
John Milton	➤ Paradise Regained ➤ Paradise Lost
Jane Austen	➤ Pride and Prejudice ➤ Sense and Sensibility
Lewis Carroll	➤ Through the Looking Glass ➤ The Hunting of Snark
Robert Louis Stevenson	➤ Kidnapped ➤ Treasure Island
Abdul Salam Zaeef	➤ My Life With the Taliban
Adam Gilchrist	➤ True Colour : My Life (Autobiography)
Javier Moro	➤ The Red Sari : A Dramastised Biography of Sonia Gandhi
Adma Smith	➤ Wealth of Nations
AG Noorani	➤ India - China Boundary Problems 1846 to 1947
Al Gore (Former US Vice President)	➤ "An Inconvenient Truth"
Andy Marino	➤ Narendra Modi : A Political Biography
Arthur Conan Doyle	➤ Adventures of Sherlock Holmes
Arthur Miller	➤ Empire of the Stars
Arthur Stanley Eddington	➤ Expanding Universe
Anna Jeon Mayhew	➤ The Dry Glass of August
Alan Shapiro	➤ Night of the Republic
Benazir Bhutto	➤ Reconciliation: Islam Democracy and the West
Catherin O	➤ The News Where you are Flynn
Charles Darwin	➤ Descent of Man, Origin of Species
Cherie Blair	➤ Speaking for Myself
Chester Bowles	➤ A View from Delhi
Dan Brown	➤ The Lost Symbol
David Loshak	➤ Pakistan Crisis
Desmond Tutu	➤ No Future Without Forgiveness
DH Lawrence	➤ Sons and Lovers ➤ Lady Chatterley's Lover
Dominque Lapierre	➤ A Rainbow in the Night-Nelson mandela and the Tumultuous Birth of South Africa
Domingo Martinez	➤ The Boy Kings of Texas
Dould Marrainss	➤ Barack Obama The Making of the Man
Doniel Silva	➤ Moscow Rules
EM Forster	➤ A Passage to India
Edited by	➤ The World Bank in India
Michele Kelley	➤ Undermining Sovereignty,

Author	Book
Deepika D'Souza	Distorting Development"
Edward Gibbon	➤ Decline and Fall of the Roman Empires
Eric Segal	➤ Love Story
Ernest Hemingway	➤ The Old Man and the Sea
Fyodor Dostoevsky	➤ The Idiot
GB Shaw	➤ Apple Cart
Gabrielle Hamilton	➤ Blood, Bones and Butter
George Co Bush	➤ Decision Point (Autobiography)
George Orwell	➤ Nineteen Eighty Four
Goethe	➤ Faust
HB Stowe	➤ Uncle Tom's Cabin
Herschelle Gibbs	➤ To the Point (Autobiography)
Herta Muller	➤ The Appointment
Homer	➤ Odyssey
Isaac Newton	➤ Principia Mathematica
Jasper F Forde	➤ Shades of Grey
Jean Paul Sartre	➤ Iron in the Soul
Jeffrey Archer	➤ First Among Equals
JK Rowling	➤ The Tales of Beedle the Bard
John Masefield	➤ Nine Days Wonder
John Ruskin	➤ Unto this Past
Jonathan Swift	➤ Gulliver's Travels
Joy Adamson	➤ Born Free
Jules Verne	➤ Around the World in 80 days
John Milton	➤ Paradise lost ➤ Paradise Regained
Javier Moro	➤ The Red Sari
Karl Marx	➤ Das Kapital
Katherine Mayo	➤ Mother India
Kim Edwards	➤ Lake of Dreams
L Fischer	➤ A Week with Gandhi
Lapierre and Collins	➤ Freedom at Midnight
Larry Collins Domininique lapierre	➤ Mountbatten and Independent India
Lord Byron	➤ Don Juan
Lond Cuzon	➤ Problems of The East
M Veerappa Moily	➤ Shree Ramayana Mahanveshanam
Machiavelli	➤ The Prince
Margaret Mitchell	➤ Gone with the Wind
Mark Twain	➤ Adventures of Tom Sawyer
Martin Amis	➤ The Pregnant Widow
Mathew Arnold	➤ Sohrab and Rustum
Maxim Gorky	➤ Mother
Michael Jackson	➤ Moon Walk (Autobiography)
Michael Phelps	➤ No Limits: The Will to Succeed
Nandan Nilekani	➤ Imaging India: Ideas for a New Century
Nelson Mandela	➤ The Conversations with Myself
Oliver	➤ She Stoops to Conquer Goldsmith
Oscar Wilde	➤ Importance of Being Earnest
Pallava Bagla	➤ "Destination Moon-India's quest for the Moon, Mars & Beyond"
Parvez Musharraf	➤ In the Line of Fire
Pearl S Buck	➤ The Rainbow
Philip Pullman	➤ The Good Man Jesus and The Scoundrel Christ
Plato	➤ The Republic
Robert TS Mickles	➤ Blood Kin, A Savannah Story
Rudyard Kipling	➤ Jungle Book
Ruskin Bond	➤ Notes from a Small Room
R. M.Lala	➤ For the Love of India: The Life and Times of Jamsetji Tata
Shoaib Akhtar	➤ Controversially Yours (Autobiography)
Sydney Sheldon	➤ The Naked Face
Syyed Amir Ali	➤ The Spirit of Islam
TC Boyle	➤ Wild Child
Thomas Moor	➤ Utopia
Toni Morrison	➤ What Moves at the Margin Selected Non Fiction

Tony Journey	➤ A Journey
U Thant	➤ Viem from the UN
William Alexander	➤ Goblin Secrets
Walter Scott	➤ Ivanhoe
Winston Churchil	➤ Gathering storm
ZA Bhutto	➤ If I am Assassinated, The Myth of Independence

Famous Books by Indian Writers

Authors	Books
Dr. APJ Abdul Kalam	➤ Ignited Minds: Unleashing the Power with India ➤ You are Born to Blossom ➤ My Journey ➤ India 2020 : A vision for the New Millennium ➤ Wings of Fire
Mulk Raj Anand	➤ The Village ➤ Seven Summers ➤ Two Leaves and a Bud ➤ Coolie
Amrita Pritam	➤ Kora Kagaz ➤ Death of a City ➤ Kagaz Te Kanwas
Ramachandra Guha	➤ Makers of Modern India ➤ India After Gandhi: The History of the World's Largest Democracy ➤ Environmentalism: A Global History ➤ The States of Indian Cricket
Jawaharlal Nehru	➤ Bunch of Old Letters ➤ Glimpses of World History ➤ Letters from a Faher to his Daughter ➤ The Discovery of India
Khushwant Singh	➤ The Sunset Club ➤ Sahibs Who Loved India ➤ Why I Supported the Emergency ➤ Truth, Love and A Little Malice
	➤ We Indians ➤ A Bride for the Sahib ➤ Maharaja In Denims
RK Narayan	➤ Guide ➤ Dark Room ➤ The Vendor of Sweets
Chetan Bhagat	➤ One Night @ the Call Centre ➤ Revolution 2002-Love, Corruption, Ambition What Young India wants ➤ Half Girlfriend
Bankim Chandra Chattopadhyay	➤ Devi Chaudharani ➤ Anand Math
Maithili Sharan Gupt	➤ Saket ➤ Yashodhara
JP Narayan	➤ Prison Diary ➤ To all Fighters of Freedom, Why Socialism?
Sarat Chandra Chattopadhyay	➤ Devdas ➤ Parineeta
Sarojini Naidu	➤ The Golden threshold ➤ The Bird of Time
Munshi Prem Chand	➤ Rang Bhoomi ➤ Godan
Rammohan Roy	➤ Percepts of Jesus ➤ A Gift to Monotheists
Mahatma Gandhi	➤ My Experiments with Truth ➤ Hind Swaraj
Amartya Sen	➤ Developments as Freedom ➤ The Idea of Justice
Abul Kalam Azad	➤ India Wins Freedom
Al Basham	➤ Wonder That was India,
Amit Chaudhuri	➤ The Immortals
Annie Besant	➤ Wake up India
Anuradha Roy	➤ The Folded Earth
Aravind Adiga	➤ The White Tier
Amrita Priam	➤ The Revenue Stamp
Asha Purna Devi	➤ Subarnalata
Aurobindo Ghosh	➤ Life Divine
Balwant Gargi	➤ Naked Triangle
BG Tilak	➤ Gita Rahasya

Author	Book
BR Ambedkar	➤ What Congress and Gandhi have done to Untouchables
Brig John Dalvi	➤ Himalayan Blunder
Dadabhai Naoroji	➤ Poverty and Unbritish Rule in India
Daisy Hason	➤ The To-Let House
Din Bandhu Mitra	➤ Neel Darpan
Dr. Radha Krishnan	➤ Hindu View of Life
Dr Rajendra Prasad	➤ India Divided
VD Savarkar	➤ Indian War of Independence
Edited by Pranab	➤ The Congress and The Making of Indian Nation
Fyodor Dostoevsky	➤ The Idiot
Gen Ayub Khan	➤ Friends not Master
Gopal Krishna Gandhi	➤ Of a Certain Age: Twenty Life Sketches
Gopinath Mohanty	➤ Moti Mahal
Hamid Ansari	➤ Travelling Through Conflict
IK Gujral	➤ Matters of Discretion (Autobiography)
Indira Gandhi	➤ My Truth
Janardan Thakur	➤ All the Prime Minister's JMen
Jaswant Singh	➤ Jinnah - India, Partition, Independence
Jyotiba Phule	➤ Ghulam Giri and Other Stories
K Natwar Singh	➤ One life is not enough 'My China Diary'
Kapil Dev	➤ Straight from the Heart
Kapil Sibal	➤ I Witness - Partial Observation
Khan Abdul Ghaffar Khan	➤ Pakhtoon
Kingshuk Nag	➤ The Namo Story: A Political Life
KM Munshi	➤ I Follow the Mahatama
Kuldip Nayar	➤ The Judgement
Lal Krishna Advani	➤ My Country My Life
Lal Lajpat Rai	➤ Unhappy India
Mahadevi Verma	➤ Yama
Maj HPS Ahluwalia	➤ Face of Everest
Manohar Malgaonkar	➤ A Bend in the Ganges
Meghnad Desai	➤ The Rediscovery of India
MJ Akbar	➤ Nehru: The Making of India
Morarji Desai	➤ A Minister and his Responsibilities
Narayan Lakshman	➤ Patrons of the Poor:
	➤ Caste Politics and Policy Making in India
Nayantara Sahgal	➤ A Voice of Freedom
Narendra Modi	➤ "Convenient Action: Gujarat's Response to Climate Change"
Nilanjan Mukhopadhyay	➤ Narendra Modi: TheMan, The Times
Nirad C Choudhary	➤ An Unknown Indian
NR Narayan Murthy	➤ A Better India A Better World
PM Nayar	➤ The Kalam Effect : My Years with the President
PVR Rao	➤ Defence Without Drift
Rabindranath Tagore	➤ Chitra
Raghunath Mashelkar	➤ "Timeless Inspector - Reliving Gandhi"
Rajmohan Gandhi	➤ The Good Boat Man: Portrait of Gandhi
Ramdhari Singh Dinkar	➤ Rashmirathi
Rashika Choube and Chhaya Mahajan	➤ An Inspirational Journey Pratibha Devi Singh Patil, The First Women President of India
Ramesh Chandra Dutta	➤ Economic History of India
Ravi Shankar	➤ My Music, My Life
Ronald Segal	➤ Crisis of India
S Nihal Singh	➤ My India
SC Bose	➤ The Indian Struggle

Author	Book
Shashi Tharoor	➤ The Elephant, the Tiger and the Cell Phone: Reflections on India in the 21st century India Shastra
Shashi Tharoor and Khan	➤ Shadows Across the ➤ Playing Field: 60 years Shaharyar of India-Pak Cricket
Shobha De	➤ Superstar India: From Incredible to Unstoppable
Shyam Bhatia	➤ Good Bye Shahzadi (A Biography of Benzir Bhutto)
Sir Syyed Ahmed Khan	➤ Causes of the Indian Mutiny
SK Nandi	➤ Ramacharit
Sri Aurobinod Ghosh	➤ Savitri
Subramanian Swamy	➤ Electronic Voting Machines-Unconstitutional and Tamperable
Sunil Gavaskar	➤ Sunny Days
Surjit Singh Barnala	➤ My Other Two Daughters
Swami Dayanand	➤ Satyarth Prakash
T. S. Krishna Murthy	➤ Miracle of Democracy : India's Amazing Journey
Tarun Tejpal	➤ The Valley of Masks
Upinder Singh	➤ A History of Ancient and Early Medieval India from Stone Age to the 12th Century
VV Giri	➤ Voice of Conscience
Veerappa Moily	➤ Unleashing India
Vinita Kamte	➤ To the Last Bullet
Vinod Mehta	➤ Lucknow Boy (Autobiography)
YV Reddy	➤ Global Crisis Recession and Uneven Recovery

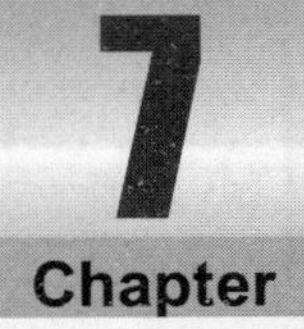

Award Winning Authors of Indian Origin

Authors and their Writings

Author	Writings	Award
Salman Rushdie	➤ Midnight Children ➤ Shame ➤ The Moor's Last Singh ➤ Fury ➤ The Satanic Verses	Booker Prize 1981 (Midnight Children)
Vikram Seth	➤ The Golden Gate ➤ A Suitable Boy ➤ An Equal Music ➤ Two Lives	Padma Shri in Literature and Education 2007
Arundhati Roy	➤ The God of Small things ➤ The Algebra at Infinite Justice	Booker Prize 1997 (The God of Small thins)
Rohinton Mistry	➤ Such a Long Journey ➤ Family Matters ➤ A Fine Balance	Booker Prize 1997 (Such a Long Journey)
VS Naipaul	➤ A House for Mr. Biswaas ➤ India: A Wounded Civilisation ➤ An Area of Darkness ➤ India: A Million now ➤ The Masque of Africa ➤ A Bend in The River	Nobel Prize in Literature 2001 (for having united perceptive narrative and incorruptible security in works that compel)
Amitav Ghosh	➤ The Circle of Reason ➤ River of Smoke ➤ The Glass Palace ➤ Shadow Line ➤ The Calcutta Chromosome ➤ The Hungry Tide ➤ Sea of Poppies ➤ In an Antique Land	Padma Shri by Government of India 2007 (for his best work in English Language) Crossword Book Prize in 2008 for sea of Poppies
Jhumpa Lahiri	➤ The namesake ➤ The Interpreter of Maladies ➤ The Unaccustomed Earth	Pulitzer Prize 2000 (The Namesake)
Shashi Tharoor	➤ The Great Indian Novel ➤ Show Business ➤ India: From Midnight to Millenium	Common Wealth Writer's Prize (The Great Indian Novel)
Unpamanyu Chatterjee	➤ The Memories of the Welfare State ➤ English ➤ August ➤ Way to 90	Sahitya Academi Award 2004 (The Memories of the Welfare State)
Kiran Desai	➤ The Inheritance of Loss	Man Booker Prize 2006

Books Awarded with Prizes

Book (Pulitzer Prize)	Author	Year
➤ The Road	Cormac McCarthy	2007
➤ The Looming Tower: Al Qaeda and The Road to 9/11	Lawrence Wright	2007
➤ The Brief Wondrous Life of Oscar Wao	Junot Diaz	2008
➤ The Years of Extermination: Nazi Germany and the Jews 19939-1945	Saul Friedlander	2008
➤ Olive Kitteridge	Elizabeth Strout	2009
➤ Slavery by Another Name: The Re-Enslavement of Black Americans from The Civil War to World War-II	Douglas A Blackmon	2009
➤ The Dead hand: The Untold Story of The Cold War Arms Race and Its Dangerous Legacy	David E Hoffman	2010
➤ Thinkers	Paul Harding	2010
➤ A Visit fromthe Goon Squad	Jennifer Egan	2011
➤ The Emperor of All Maladies: A Biography of Cancer	Siddhartha Mukherjee	2011
➤ The Orphan Master's Son (Fiction)	Adam Johnson	2013
➤ Disgraced (Drama)	Ayad Akhtar	2013
➤ 3 Sections (Poetry)	Vijay Seshadri	2014
➤ The Goldfinch (Fiction)	Donna Tartt	2014
➤ All the Light We Cannot See	Anthony Doerr,	2015
➤ The Sympathizer	Viet Thanh Nguyen	2016
➤ The Undergound Railroad	Colson Whitehead	2017
➤ Less	Andrew Sean Greer	2018
➤ The Overstory	Richard Powers	2019
➤ The Nickel Boys	Colson Whitehead	2020
➤ The Night Watchman	Louise Erdrich	2021

Man Booker Prize

Book	Author	Year
➤ The Gathering	Anne Enright	2007
➤ The White Tiger	Aravind Adiga	2008
➤ Wolf Hall	Hilary Mantel	2009
➤ The Finkler Question	Howard Jacobson	2010
➤ Troubles	JG Farrell	2010
➤ The Sense of an Ending	Jullan Barness	2011
➤ Bring up the Bodies	Hilarymantel	2012
➤ The Luminaries	Eleanor Catton	2013
➤ The Narrow Road to the Deep North	Richard Flanagan	2014
➤ A Brief History of Seven Killings	Marlon James	2015

Title	Author	Year
That Sellout	Paul Beatty	2016
Lincoln in the Bardo	George Saunders	2017
Milkman	Anna Burns	2018
The Testaments	Margaret Atwood	2019
Girl, Woman, Other	Bernardine Evaristo	2019
Shuggie Bain	Douglas Stuart	2020
The Promise	Damon Galgut	2021
Geetanjali Shree	Tomb of Sand	2022

Sahitya Akademi Award

Title	Author	Year
Hajar Churashi Maa	Mahasweta Devi	1996
Mahabharata An Inquiry in the Human condition	Chaturvedi Badrinath	2009
Hawa me Hastakshar	Kailash Vajpeyi	2009
Book of Rachel	Easther David	2010
Mohan Das	Uday Prakash	2010
India After Gandhi	Ramachandra Guha	2011
Rehan Per Ragghu (Novel)	Kashinath Singh	2011
Pathar Fenk Rara Hoon(Peotry)	Chandrakant Devtale	2012
Miljul Man (Novel)	Mridula Garg	2013
Trying to Say Goodbye(Poetry)	Adil Jussawala	2014
Vinayak (Novel)	Ramesh Chandra Shah	2014
Aag Ki Hansi	Ramdarash Mishra	2015
Parijat	Nasira Sharma	2016
Vishw Mithak Sarit Sagar	Ramesh Kuntal Megh	2017
Post Box No. 203 - Nala Sopara	Chitra Mudgal	2018
Gholatey Hue Apne Ko	Nand Kishore Aacharya	2019
Tokri Mein Digant	Anamika	2020
Samraat Ashok	Daya Prakash Sinha	2021

Saraswati Samman

Title	Author	Year
Kayakalap	Lakshmi Nandan Bora	2008
Lafzan di Dargah	Surjit Paatar	2009
Mandra	SL Bhyrappa	2010
Irama Kathaiyum Iramayakalum	AA Manavalan	2011
Manalezhuth	Sugathakumar	2012
Dhol Paudho Par	Govind Mishra	2013
"Ramayana Mahanveshanam"(Poetry)	Veerappa Moily	2014
"Chitt-Chete"	Padma Sachdev (Autobiography)	2015
"Hawthan" (Novel)	Mahabaleshwar Sail	2016
"Vakhar" (Poetry collection)	Sitanshu Yashaschandra	2017
"Pakkaki Ottigilite" (Poetry)	K Siva Reddy	2018
"Chequebook" (Short Story Series)	Vasdev Mohi	2019
"Sanatan" (Novel)	Sharankumar Limbale	2020
Main to Yahan Hun	Ram Darash Mishra	2021

Women's Prize for Fiction (Orange Prize)

➤ Half of a Yellow Sun	Chimamanda Ngozi Adichie	2007
➤ The Road Home	Rose Rose Tremain	2008
➤ Home	Marilynne Robinson	2009
➤ The Lacuna	Barbara Kingsolver	2010
➤ Serious Men	Manu Joseph	2010
➤ The Sly Company of People Who Care	Rahul Bhattacharya	2011
➤ Home Boy	HM Naqvi	2011
➤ The Tiger's Wife	Tea Obreht	2011
➤ The Song of Achilles	Maleline	2012
➤ May We Be Forgiven	AM Homes	2013
➤ A Girl Is a Half-formed Thing	Eimear McBride	2014
➤ How to Be Both	Ali Smith	2015
➤ The Glorious Heresies	Lisa McInerney	2016
➤ The Power	Naomi Alderman	2017
➤ Home Fire	Kamila Shamsie	2018
➤ An American Marriage	Tayari Jones	2019
➤ Hamnet	Maggie O'Farrell	2020
➤ Piranesi	Susanna Clarke	2021

Chapter 8

Sports

Olympics

- The Olympic Games were held for the first time by the Greeks in 776 BC on Mount Olympus, in honour of the Greek royal order of the Roman Emperor Theodosius in AD 394.
- These games were revived in 1894 by the efforts of a French Baron **Pierre de Coubertin** and the first modern Olympic Games were started in Athens the capital of Greece on 6th April, 1896. Separate Winter Olympic Games began in 1924. Women have been participating in the Olympic since 1912.
- The Olympic Games are organised after every four years.

Founder and Governing Boy

- In 1894, Baron Pierre de Coubertin founded the International Olympic Committee (IOC) to govern the Olympic Movement (comprising International Sports Federations (SF's), National Olympic Committees (NOC's) and Organising Committee for each specific games).
- IOC chooses the host city and the games to be contested Organisaton and funding is made by the host city.
- International Sports Federation (ISF) determines the qualification rules for each Olympic.
- The head office of International Olympic Committee (OC) is at **Lausanne** (Switzerland).

Olympic Symbol

- It contains five rings or circles linked together to represent the sporting friendship of all people. Each ring is of a different colour i.e., blue, yellow, black, green and red. The rings are meant to represent five continents viz Africa (Black), America (Red), Asia yellow, Australia (Green) and Europe (Blue).

Olympic Flag

- The Olympic Flag was created in 1913 at the suggestion of Baron Pierre de Coubertin. It was adopted in Paris in June, 1914, but it was raised over an Olympic stadium for the first time at the Antwerp games (Belgium) in 1920. These flags are made of white silk and contains five intertwined rings of the Olympic Emblem.
- From left to right the rings are Blue (Europe), Yellow (Asia), Black (Africa), Red (America) and Green (Australia). Atleast one of these colours is found on the flag of every country.
- The flag is 3 m long and 2 m wide. The emblem placed in the center is 2.06 m by 60 cm.

Olympic Motto

- **Olympic Motto** 'Citius, Altius, Fortius' is the Latin motto meaning 'Faster, Higher and Stronger' composed by Father Didon in 1897. The motto was introduced in 1924 at the Olympic Games in Paris.

Winter Olympic Games

- The first winter Olympic Games were held in 1924 at Chamonix, France.
- The 2010 Olympic Games were held in Vancouver, Canada.
- The last Olympic games were held in 2014 at Sochi, Russia. It is scheduled to be held in 2018 at Pyeongchang, South Korea.

Olympic Flame

- The Olympic flame symbolises the continuity between ancient and modern games. It was at the Amsterdam Games in 1928 that for the first time an Olympic flame was ceremonially lighted and burned in giant torch at the entrance of the stadium. The modern version of the flame was adopted in 1936 at the Berlin Games.

Olympic Medals

- Olympic champions are rewarded with medals and certificate. The winning athlete or sports persons receive a gold medal which is 60 mm in diameter and 3 mm thick and is made of 92.5% silver plated with 6 gm of gold.

Olympic Mascot

- The Olympic mascot(s) is /are a character, usually an animal native to the area or occasionally human figures, who represents the cultural heritage of the place, where the Olympic and Para-Olympic Games are taking place.
- Since the 1968, Winter Olympic is Grenoble, France the Olympic Games have had a mascot. The first major mascot in the Olympic Games was Misha in the 1980 Summer Olympic in Moscow.

Olympic Gold Order

- It is presented by the International Olympic Committee for distinguished services in the development of the Olympic Movement.

Olympics : Quick Digest

- 'Norman Pritchard' was the first Indian player to participate in Olympic (2nd Olympic Games in 1900) and won two silver medals in athletics.
- **Mary Leela Rao** is the 1st Indian woman participant in the Olympics.
- Indian officially participated in the Olympics for the first time in the Sixth Olympic Games 91920) at Antwerp Belgium.
- The **Indian Olympic Association** was established in 1927. Sir Dorabji Tata was its first President.
- **Sonia Denoncourt** (Canada) was the 1st woman referee in football in Atlanta Olympics.
- **The Winter Olympic Games** are a major international sporting event that occurs once every 4 years.
- Unlike the Summer Olympics, the Winter Olympic feature sports practiced on snow and ice.
- The first Winter Olympic, the 1924 Winter Olympics, was held in Chamonix, France. the games were held every 4 years from 1924 until 1936, after which they were interrupted by World War II.
- The Olympics resumed in 1948 and was again held every 4 years. Until 1992, the Winter and Summer Olympic Games were help in the same years, but in accordance with a 1986 decision by the International Olympic Committee (IOC) to place the Summer and Winter Games pm separate 4 years cycles in alternating even-numbered years, the next Winter Olympics after 1992 was in 1994.

Summer Olympic Games

Year	Venue	Year	Venue
1896	Athenes, Greece	1952	Helsinki, Finland
1900	Paris, France	1956	Melbourne, Australia
1904	St. Louis, France	1960	Rome, Italy
1906	Athens, Greece	1964	Tokyo, Japan
	(Games were not	1968	Mexico City, Mexico
	recognised by IOC)	1972	Munich, West Germany
1908	London, Great Britain	1976	Montreal, Canada
1912	Stockholm, Sweden	1980	Moscow, Russia
1916	Games not held due	1984	Los Angeles, USA
	to first World War	1988	Seoul, South Korea
1920	Antwerp, Belgium	1992	Barcelona, Spain
1924	Paris, France	1996	Atlanta, USA
1928	Amsterdam, Netherlands	2000	Sydney, Australia
1932	Los Angeles, USA	2004	Athens, Greece
1936	Berlin, Germany	2008	Beijing, China
1940	Games not held due to	2012	London, Great Britain
	Second World War	2016	Rio de Janeiro, Brazil
1944	Games not held due to	2020	Tokyo, Japan
	Second World War	2024	Paris, France
1948	London, Great Britain	2028	Los Angeles, United States

Commonwealth Games

- The Commonwealth Games are a festival of sports of the Commonwealth countries. The first Commonwealth Games were held in 1930 in Hamilton, Canada.
- The 2010 Commonwealth Games were held in New Delhi.
- Since 1930, the games have been conducted every four years except for 1942 and 1946.
- The Commonwealth Games Federation (CGF) is the organisation, which is responsible for the direction and control of the Commonwealth Games.
- There are currently 53 members of the commonwealth of Nations and 71 team participate in the games.

Asian Games

- The Asian Games, also called the Asiad, are a multi-sport event held every four years among athletes from all over Asia.
- The games are regulated by the Olympic Council of Asia (OCA), under the supervision of the International Olympic Committee (IOC).
- The first Asian Games were held in 1951 in New Delhi (India).
- The AGF (Asian Games Federation) adopted 'Ever Onward', given by Pandit Jawaharlal Nehru, as the motto of the Asian Games, which continues till today.
- The emblem is a bright full rising sun with interlocking rings. The king of Patiala presented the Torch and the Flag for the first Asian Games and since then they have been carried from country to country.

South Asian Federation (SAF) Games

- Like the Commonwealth Games, the South Asian Federation (SAF) Games is a sports festival of South Asian countries. The governing body of these games is South Asian sports Council formed in1983.
- The first South Asian Federation Games were held at Kathmandu (Nepal) in 1984. The 2010, SAF Games were held in Dhaka Bangladesh.
- The eight participating countries are India, Pakistan, Sri Lanka, Bangladesh, Nepal, Bhutan, Afghanistan and Maldives. The games form a part of the SAARC programme. The motto of the SAF Games is 'peace, prosperity and progress'.
- No SAF Game were staged in 1986 as it was the year of commonwealth and Asian Games.
- The SAF Games have been rechristened South Asian Games on 2nd April, 2004. Afghanistan joined the games in 2006.

Afro-Asian Games

- The first-ever Afro-Asian Games were held in 2003 at Hyderabad (India), 2007 in Algiers (Cancelled).
- The official mascot of the 2003 games was 'Sheroo' (a cartoon representation of the Royal Bengal Tiger) and the message was 'two continents-one spirit'.

Cricket

- The first Cricket World Cup was organised in England in 1975. A separate Women's Cricket World Cup has been held every four years since 1973.
- The Cricket World Cup Tournament is organised by the International Cricket Council (ICC). The ICC was founded in 1909 and its headquarters is located in Dubai, United Arab Emirates.
- In 1877, the first Cricket Test Match was played in Melbourne between England and Australia.
- The first One Day International Cricket Match was played in the year 1971 between England and Australia in Melbourne.
- The Board of Control for Cricket in India (BCCI) was formed in 1927.

List of Cricket World Cup

1975	Lord's, England	West Indies beat Australia
1979	Lord's, England	West Indies beat England
1983	Lord's, England	India beat West Indies
1987	Kolkata, India	Australia beat England
1992	Melbourne, (Australia)	Pakistan beat England
1996	Lahore, Pakistan	Sri Lanka beat Australia
1999	Lord's England	Australia beat Pakistan
2003	Johannesburg, South Africa	Australia beat India
2007	Bridgetown, West Indies	Australia beat Sri Lanka
2011	Mumbai, India	India beat Sri Lanka
2015	Australia/New Zealand	Australia beat New Zealand
2019	England and New Zeland	Match tied after regular play and super over; England won on boundary count
2023		Proposed (India)

Women's Cricket World Cup

- The ICC Women's Cricket World Cup is the premier international championship of women's One Day International Cricket.
- The event is organised by the sport's governing body, the International Cricket Council (ICC). It was originally administered by the International Women's Cricket Council until the two associations merged in 2005.
- The first tournament was held in England in 1973, two years before the first men's tournament.

Women's Cricket World Cup Venus

Year	Place	Won
1982	New Zealand	Australia
1988	Australia	Australia
1993	England	England
1997	India	Australia
2000	New Zealand	New Zealand
2005	South Africa	Australia
2009	Australia	England
2013	India	Australia
2017	England	England
2022	New Zealand	Australia

Important Facts

Administrator	International Cricket Council
Format	Women's ODI
First Tournament	1973, England
Last tournament	2013, India
Next tournament	2017, England
Current Champion	Australia
Most Successful	Australia (6titles)
Most runs	Debbie Hockey(1501)

T-20 World Cup

- It is organised by the International Cricket (ICC). It is held in every two years.
- **ICC Twenty-20 Cricket World Cup**

Year	Host Nations	Final Venue	Winner	Runner-up
2007	South Africa	Johannesburg	India	Pakistan
2009	England	Lord's London	Pakistan	Sri Lanka
2010	West Indies	Barbados	England	Australia
2012	Sri Lanka Stadium, Colombo	R Premdasa	West Indies	Sri Lanka
2014	Bangladesh Cricket Stadium Dhaka	Sher-e Bangla	Sri Lanka	India
2016	India	Kolkata	West Indies	England
2021	UAE	Dubai	Australia	New Zealand
2022	Australia (Proposed)			
2024	West Indies, United States (Proposed)			

Women's Twenty 20 Cricket

- Women's Twenty20 cricket is the newly emerging use of the Twenty20 match format in women's cricket. While both Women's Cricket and Twenty20 have themselves enjoyed recent success, women's Twenty-20 has only been an international cricket game format since 2004. In June 2009, the ICC held the first Women's World Twenty-20 in England, the hosts became the first World Twenty20 champion.
- Australia won their consecutive title in Women's World Twenty20 after defeating England.

Football World Cup

- The Football World Cup organised by FIFA (Federation of International Football Association).
- The headquarters of FIFA is located in Zurich, Switzerland.
- The World Cup is called 'Jules Rimet Cup' name after the name of FIFA President Jules Rimet.
- The first Football World Cup was organised in Uruguay in 1930.
- In 1942 and1946, the Football World Cup was not played because of the Second World War.
- Brazil is the only nation to have participated in every World Cup so far.

Hockey World Cup

- The Hockey World Cup is organised by the International Hockey Federation (FIH) one in four years. The headquarters of FIH is located in Lausanne, Switzerland. The first Hockey World Cup was organised in Barcelona (Spain) in 1971 and winner is Pakistan. Women's Hockey World Cup has been held since 1974.

Lawn Tennis

- It was invented in 1870 by Major Wing Field in Wales. Wimbledon Championship started in 1877 for men only. For women it was introduced in 1884.
- The four Grand Slam tournaments are considered to be the most prestigious tennis tournaments in the world. They are held annually and include, in chronological order the Australian Open, the French Open, Wimbledon and the US Open. Apart from the Olympic Games, Davis Cup, Fed Cup and Hopman Cup, they are the only tournaments regulated by the International Tennis Federation(ITF).
- The Association of Tennis Professionals interests of male professional tennis players is now known as the ATP World Tour.

Grand Slam Tournaments

Tournament	Date	Location	Surface	First Held
Australian Open	January (Plexicushion)	Melbourne	Hard	1905
French Open	May-June	Paris	Clay	1925
Wimbledon	June-July	London	Grass	1877
US Open	August-September (Decco Turf)	New York City	Hard	1881

Other Sports

Table Tennis

- Table Tennis was introduced in the Olympic Games in 1988 at Seoul (South Korea).

Billiard

- Cue sports, also known as billiard sports, are a wide variety of games of skill generally played with cue stick, which is used to strike billiard balls, moving them around a clothe-covered billiards table bounded rubber cushions.

Polo

- Plo (Chowgan) is a team sport played on horseback, in which the objectives is to score goals against an opposing team. Some times called, "The sport of Kings" it was highly popularised by the British. It is not an Olympic sport.

Wrestling

- Wrestling is a form of combat sport involving grappling types techniques such as clinch fighting, throws and take downs, joint locks, pins and other grappling holds.

Formula One (F1) Race

- Formula one, also known as Formula 1 or F1 and referred to officially as the FIA Formula One World Championship, is the highest class of single seater auto racing sanctioned by the Federation International Automobile (FIA).
- It was started in 1950
- The first Formula One World Championship was won by Italian Giuseppe Farina in Alfa Romeo in 1950. The first F1 race in India was held at he Buddha International Circuit in Greater Noida, UP (2011).

Badminton

- The modern name in 1873 of Badminton came from the Badminton House, the International Badminton Federation was establishment in 1934, the new name is Badminton World Federation.

Cycling

- The Tour de France tournament is an annual bicycle race held in France and nearby countries. First staged in 1903, the race covers more than 3600 km and last three weeks. This is organised every year in month of July.
- The 2002 Summer Olympics will be the first, at which men and women complete in the some number of events in all cycling disciplines.

Swimming

- Swimming is a water-based sport governed by the Federation Internationals de Natation (FINA) and is formed in 1908. FINA is the International Federation (IF) recognised by the International Olympic Committee (IOC) for administering international competition in the aquatic sports.
- Its headquarters is at lausanne Switzerland.

Shooting

- Shooting sports have been contested at every Summer Olympic Games since the birth of the modern Olympic Movement at the 1896 Summer Olympics except at the 1904 and1928 editions.

Marathon

- The marathon is a long-distance running event with on official distance of 42.195 km (26 miles and 385 yards), that is usually run as a road race.
- The event was instituted in commemoration of the fabled run of the Greek soldier Phedippiddes, a messenger from the battle of Marathon to Athens.

Specific Names of Playing Area

Sport	Name of Playing Area	Sport	Name of Playing Area
Badminton	Court	Gold	Link, Green**
Baseball	Diamond	Lawn Tennis	Court
Boxing	Ring	Ice Skating	Rink
Cricket	Pitch*	Wrestling	Ring, Arena

* Pitch in fact is the space between the wickets and not the entire cricket field.

** It is the area around the hole only.

Important Sport Terms

Sport	Terms
Basketball	Dunk, front court, lay up, held ball, pivot, rebound, steal
Cricket	Bye, draw, googly, topspin, overthrow, duck, hit wicket
Football	Bend dribble, dissent, dummy, feint, free kick, header, red card, throwing
Hockey	Bully, striking, circle, post back
Chess	Castle, diagonals, files, pawns, promote, gambit, pawn
Boxing	Jab, laying on knock, second out habbit punch, upper cut
Badminton	Loab, let, drive, drop, love
Polo	Chuker, bunker
Baseball	Diamond, home run, putout, strike, anti-rubber
Rifle shooting	Target, muzzle fulb, bulls eye
Wrestling	Half, nelson, hold sager, rebuts
Golf	Fore some, style, T, put hole, caddy, nib lick, the green, bunker
Billiards	Jigger, pot, break pot, i off, cans, bolting, long, hazard, cue
Swimming	Breast stroke, twist, butterfly, crawl, spring board
Volley Ball	Antennae, attack hit, libero, service, set up, blocking, dribbling
Lawn Tennis	Advantage, ace, dance, volley, foot fault, smash, grand slam, slice, love
Table Tennis	End line, flat hit, foil, service, phnholder grip, reverse, top-spin, counter-hitting, let

Important Cups and Trophies

Sport	Cup and Trophy
Cricket	Irani Trophy, Dilip Trophy, Ranji Trophy, Vijay Hazare Trophy, Asia Cup, Deodhar Trophy, CK Naidu Trophy, Cooch-Behar Trophy
Football	Durand Cup, Nizam Gold Cup, Rovers Cup, Sanjay Gold Cup, Santosh Trophy, Subroto Mukherjee Cup, Vittal Trophy, Nehru Gold Cup
Hockey	Agha Khan Cup, Azlan Shah Cup, Nehru Trophy, Dhyanchand Trophy, Beighton Cup, Scindia Gold Cup, Modi Gold Cup, Indira Gandhi Gold Cup, Rangaswami Cup, Khan Abdul Gaffar Cup
Golf	Canada Cup, Muthian Gold Cup, Ryder Cup, Walker Cup
Table Tennis	Carbillion Cup (Women), jayalaxmi Cup (Women), Swaythling Cup (Men)
Lawn Tennis	Davis Cup, Hamlet Cup, Australian Open, French Open, Wimbledon US Open, Hompan Cup
Badminton	Thomas Cup (men), Uber Cup (Women), Narang Cup, Ali England Open.
Boxing	Aspy Adajania Trophy
Rowing	Wellington Trophy
Bridge	Rula Trophy
Polo	Ezra Cup, Winchester Cup, Radha Mohan Cup

Sport Organisations

FIDE	Federation International Des Echecs (World Chess Federation)	Chess
FIFA	Federation International de Football Association	Football
IHF	Indian Hockey Federation	Hockey
ICC	International Cricket Council	Cricket
ITTF	International Table Tennis Federation	Table Tennis
BWF	Badminton World Federation	Badminton

Measurements of Sports Fields and Instruments

Cricket	**Ball**	115.9 gm to 163 gm in weight
	Bat	96.5 cm in length and 10.8 cm width(Maximum)
	Pitch	20.12 m
	Length of the stumps	71.1 cm (28 inch)
	Length of Crease	1.22 - 1.83 (4 fit)
Football	**Field**	100 x 64 m to 110 x 75 m
Hockey	**Field**	100 yard x 60 yards
	Weight of the ball	155-163 gm
	Colour of the Ball	White
	Weight of Hockey Stick	280 gm
Lawn Tennis	**Court**	23.77 m x 8.23 m (Singles)
	Ball	6.35 cm to 6.67 cm (in diameter) 56.7 gm to 2.53 gm (weight)

Volley Ball	**Field**	18 m x 9 m
	Net	1 m deep and 9.50 m long 2.43 m (for men) and 2.24 m for women (Height)
	Ball	Circumference 66 cm + 1 cm Weight 270 gm+ 10 gm
Badminton	**Court**	13.40 m x 5.18 m or 44x20 feet
	Net	Top 1.524 m in height from the floor
	Shuttle	4.73 to 5.50 gm in weight and shall have 14 to 16 feathers fixed in court
Kabaddi	**Field**	13 m x 10 m (According to Kabaddi Federation of India)
Khokho	**Field**	34 x 16 m
Derby Course	**Length**	1.5 miles
Marathon Race	**Length**	26 miles, 385 yards
Polo	**Field Length**	300 yards
	Field Width	150 yards
	Distance between the Goals	250 yards
	Distance between the Goals post	8 yards
	Chess	64 Squares on chessboard
	Colour	Black and white
	Nos. of same colour chess	16
Baseball	**Distance of each case**	90 feet
	Base distance along with hypotenuse	127 feet
Boxing	Length and Width of the Ring 4.9 x 4.9 m to 6.1 x 6.1m	

Famous Sports Stadiums

Stadium	Sports	Place
Brookland	Football	England (UK)
Twickenham	Rugby Football	England (UK)
Putney Mart Lake	Boat race	England (UK)
Yankee Stadium	Boxing	New York (USA)
Brooklyn	Baseball	New York (USA)
Forest Hill	Tennis	USA
Sendy Lodge	Golf	Scotland
Flemington	Horse racing	Melbourne (Australia)
Headingley Manchester	Cricket	England (UK)
Lords, Oval Leads	Cricket	England (UK)
Black Heath	Rugby Football	London (UK)
Wimbledon	Lawn Tennis	London (UK)
Wembley Stadium	Football	London (UK)
Shivaji Stadium	Hockey	Delhi
National Stadium	Hockey	Delhi
National Stadium	Hockey and Others	Mumbai

Wankhede Stadium	Cricket	Mumbai
Brabourne Stadium	Cricket	Mumbai
Eden Garden	Cricket	Kolkata
Green Park Stadium	Cricket	Kanpur
Keenan Stadium	Cricket	Jamshedpur
Trent Bridge	Cricket	England (UK)
White City	Dog race	England (UK)
Hurlingham	Polo	England (UK)
Henlay Regatta	Regata	England
Brisbance, Melbourne, Peth, Sydney	Cricket	Australia
Indraprastha Stadium	Indoor Games	Delhi
Jawaharlal Nehru Stadium	Athletics	Delhi
Ferozeshah Kotla Ground	Cricket	Delhi
Ambedkar Stadium	Football	Delhi
Nehru Chepauk Stadium	Cricket	Chennai
Barabati Stadium	Cricket	Cuttack
Aintree, Doncaster Epsom	Horse racing	England (UK)

Players and their Associated Games

Players	Game	Country
Jhansher Khan	Squash	Pakistan
Jaspal Rana	Shooting	India
Geet Sethi	Billiards	India
Ian James Thorpe	Swimming	Australia
Anju B George	Long Jump	India
Michael J Jordan	Basket Ball	USA
Pankaj Arjan Advani	Snooker	India
Saina Nehwal	Badminton	India
Surya Sekhar Ganguly	Chess	India
Sikha Tandon	Swimming	India
Ignace Tirkey	Hockey	India
Soma Biswas	Athletics	India
Arjun Singh Atwal	Golf	India
Narayan Karthikeyan	Formula One	India
Tiger Woods	Gold	USA
Andi Murray	Tennis	Scotland
Kim Clijster	Tennis	Belgium
Caroline Wozniaciki	Tennis	Den Mark
Victoria Anzarenka	Tennis	Belarush

Nickname of Players

Players	Nickname
Major Dhyanchand	Hockey ka Jadoogar
Milkha Singh	Flying Sikh
PT Usha	Payyli Express
PT Usha	Golden Girl
Shoaib Aktar	Rawalpindi Express
Rahul Dravid	The Wall
Harbhajan Singh	Bhaji, the Turbanator
Javagal Srinath	Mysore Express
Paes and Bhupati	Indian Express

National Sports

Country	National Sport
Australia	Cricket
Canada	Lacrosse
China	Table Tennis
England	Cricket
India	Hockey
Japan	Sumo
Malaysia	Badminton
Scottland	Ring by Football
Spain	Bull Fighting
USA	Baseball

Players and their Books

Player	Books
Balvir Singh	Golden Hatrick
Vishwanathan Anand	My Best Game of Chess
David Beckham	My Side
Major Dhyanchand	Goal
Sunil Gavaskar	Sunny Days, Idols
Tiger Woods	How I paly Golf
Kapil Dev	Cricket My Style

National Games of India

- The National Games of India is a sporting event held in India. It comprises various disciplines in which sportsmen from the different states of India participate against each other. It was in 1924, in erstwhile Punjab, that Indian chapter of the Olympic movement was born. The founder was GD Sondhi, the first Secretary fo the Punjab Olympic Association. Lt. Col. HLO Garrett, Vice Principal of Government College, Lahore, was the President of the founder body. The same year, the country's first Olympic Games, now christened as National Games, were organised in lahore, the then capital of undivided Punjab.
- Though National Games are supposed to be held once in 2 years, it is faltering on this schedule. It took Guwahati 5 years to conduct the games after the National Games in 2002 are organised in Andhra Pradesh.
- The 34th National Games had been postponed six times before finally opening on 12th February, 2011. The 35th national Games were to be held at Kerala in 2012, it was then announced that it would be held from 31st January to 14th February, 2015. The 36th national Games held at Goa in 2020.

Environments Ecology & Biodiversity

1. General introduction

- **Ecology** is the study of interactions among organisms and between the organism and its physical (abiotic) environment.
- **Ecology is concerned with four levels of biological organisation:**
- **Organisms** (Every individual of a species)
- **Populations** (Individuals of the same species)
- **Communities** (A large or small number of populations)
- **Biomes** (It includes large flora and fauna in a species climatic zone).
- **Species** is defined as a group of organisms which can interbreed and produce a successful offspring. These organisms may be separated in space and time into smaller groups called **populations.**
- The ecological study of one species is called **Autecology.** The study of groups of organsms in relation to their environment is called **Synecology.**

2. Organism and its environment

- **Environment** is defined as the sum total of all biotic and abiotic factors that surround and influence an organism in its survival and reproduction.
- Factors affecting environment are:
- The rotation of the earth and the tilt of its axis cause annual variations in temperature, resulting into distinct seasons. This leads to the formation of various biomes such as **desert, rain forest, tundra, grassland, temperate forest,** etc.
- Regional and local variations within each biome lead to the formation of different habitats.
- Temperature, water, light and soil are the key elements that lead to so much variation in the physical and chemical conditions of habitats.
- Both **abiotic** (physio-chemical) and **biotic components** (pathogen, parasites, predators, competitions) characterise the habitat of an organism.

Components of Environment : The environment of an organism can be divided into two components: **Abiotic (non-living factors) and Biotic components (living factors).**

3. Major Abiotic Factors

(a) Temperature

- It is the most ecologically relevant environmental factor.
- In **poikilothermic animals,** body temperature depends on the temperature of the environment, while in **homeothermis animals,** a constant body temperature is maintained.
- Based on tha range of **thermal tolerance,** organisms are of two types: **Eurythermal and Stenothermal. Eurythermal** can tolerate and thrive in a wide range of temperatures, while **Stenothermal** can tolerate only a narrow range of temperatures.

(b) Water

- Water is also an important factor influencing the life of organisms.
- For aquatic organisms, the quality (chemical composition pH) of water is important.
- **Many freshwater animals cannot live for long in sea water and vice-versa because of the** osmotic problems.
- Based on the range of **tolerance of salinity,** organisms are of two types: **Euryhaline** and **Stenohaline. Euryhaline** can tolerate and thrive in a wide range of salinities, while **Stenohaline can tolerate only a narrow range of salinity.**

(c) Light

- Plants need sunlight for photosynthesis. Hence, light is very important for autotrophs.
- The intensity of light at which the rate of photosynthesis is just sufficient to meet the requirement of respiration is called **Compensation point.**
- Many flowering plants are dependent on sunlight for **Photoperiodism.**
- The response of an organism to the duration of light and day length is known as **Photoperiodism.**
- Many animals use the diurnal and seasonal variations in light intensity and photoperiod for timing their foraging, reproductive and migratory activities.
- **Sun** is the ultimate source for light and temperature on land. Deep (>500m) in the oceans, the environment is dark and there is no energy available from Sun.

(d) Soil

- The nature and properties of soil is dependent on the climate, the weathering process, sedimentation, method of soil development, etc.
- The various characteristics of the soil like soil composition, grain size and aggregation, determine the **percolation** and **water-holding capacity** of the soils.
- These characteristics along with parameters such as pH, mineral composition and **topography** determine the vegetation and animals in any area.

4. Responses to Abiotic Factors

- All organisms in order to sustain maximum functionality maintain a constant internal environment (homeostasis).

> ***Homeostasis*** *is the process by which an organism maintains a constant internal environment in respect to changing external environment.*

- An organism my adopt one of the following strategies for homeostasis:

(a) Regulate: Certain animals have the ability to maintain a constant temperature and constant osmolarity to keep up their homeostasis. E.g. all **birds** and **mammals,** have a constant body temperature (37^{0}C), irrespective of the outside temperature. In summers, to maintain the temperature, we sweat and in winters, we shiver to produce heat.

(b) Conform : 99% of animals and nearly all plants cannot maintain a constant internal environment. Their body temperature or osmotic concentration change with the surrounding conditions. They are called **conformers.** Hence, the internal environment of conformers changes with external environment.

> *Heat loss or heat gain is a function of **surface area. Small animals** have a larger surface area relative to their volume, so they tend to lose body heat very fast when it is cold outside; then has to expend much energy to generate body heat through metabolism. This is **why, very small animals are rarely found in polar Regions.***

(c) Migrate : Many animals, like birds move away temporarily from stressful habitat to a more hospitable area and return when stressful condition is over. For example, during winter, **Keoladeo National Park (Bharatpur, Rajasthan)** hosts migratory birds coming from **Siberia** and other extremely cold northern regions.

(d) Suspend : In bacteria, fungi and lower plants, **thick-walled spores** are formed which help them to overcome stressful, unfavourable conditions. Spores germinate when conditions are favourable.

- **In higher plants,** seeds and some other vegetative reproductive structures serve to tide over periods of stress. They reduce their metabolic activity and go into a state of **'dormancy'.** They germinate under favourable moisture and temperature.
- **In animals :** the body temperature of animals consistently keep change according to the fluctuations in the environmental temperature are called poikilothermic or cold-blooded animals or ectotherms. In the duration of cold the body temperature also drops. For example, all animals except birds and mammals because the body temperature remains constant in them and it is not dependent on environment temperature. These animals are called homeotherms or warm- blooded or endotherms. When the environment temperature drops the animal maintains its temperature by metabolic activities.

Hibernation, aestivation, migration are some behavioural adaptations of animals.

Hibernation of **bears** under winter.

> ***Hibernation*** *or winter sleep is a resting stage wherein animals escape winters (cold) by hiding themselves in their shelters. They escape the winter season by entering a state of inactivity by slowing their metabolism. The phenomenon of **hibernation** is exhibited by **bats, squirrels, bears** and other **rodents.*** **[IAS-2014]**

- **Aestivation** of some **snails** and **fishes** during summer.
- **Diapause** of many zooplanktons in lakes and ponds.

> ***Diapause*** *is a stage of suspended development to cope with unfavourable conditions. Many species of **zooplankton** and **insects** exhibit diapause to tide over adverse conditions during their development.*

5. Adaptations

Adaptation are certain characteristics that organism develop in order to survive and reproduce better in their habitat. These adaptations may be morphological, physiological and behavioural attributes that enable an organism to survive and reproduce in its habitat.

Adaptations of kangaroo in North American deserts:

- Kangaroo rat meets their water requirement from oxidation of fat.
- Also, they have the ability to excrete concentrated urine, so that minimal volume of water is used to remove excretory products.

Adaptations of desert plants (Xerophytes):

- Presence of **thick cuticle** on leaf surfaces (hard and waxy leaves). Their **Stomata** are arranged in **deep pits** to minimise water loss through transpiration.

- A special photosynthetic pathway **(CAM)** that enables their stomata to remain closed during day time and remains open during night.
- Desert plants, like **Opuntia** have **no leaves.** Their **leaves** are **reduced to spines** or **thorns. Photosy-nthesis** takes place by means of **flat green stems.**

Adaptations of Mammals:

- Mammals from colder climates have shorter ears and limbs to reduce heat loss. This is called **Allen's Rule.**
- Aquatic mammals, like **seals** have a **thick layer of fat (blubber)** below their skin that acts as an **insulator** and **reduces loss of body heat.**

Physiological and biochemical adaptations:

- **Archaebacteria (Thermophiles)** are ancient forms of bacteria that are found in the hot springs and deep sea hydrothermal vents. They are able to survive in high temperatures (which far exceed 100^{0}C) because their bodies have adapted to such environmental conditions. These bacteria contain specialised **thermo-resistant enzymes** which carry out metabolic functions that do not get destroyed at such high temperatures.
- Many marine invertebrates and fishes live at great depths in the ocean where the pressure is >100 times the normal atmospheric pressure.
- At a high altitude place (>3,500m), a person might develop **altitude sickness.** The symptoms of altitude sickness are nausea, fatigue and heart palpitations. The sickness is due to **low atmospheric pressure.** As a result, the body does not get enough oxygen.
- **Behavioural adaptations**

Desert lizards are conformer hence, they cope with the stressful environment by behavioural adaptations. They bask in the sun and absorb heat when their body temperature is low, but move into shade when the ambient temperature starts increasing.

6. Populations

A **population** is defined as a group of individuals of the same species that live in a particular geographical area at a particular time and functioning as a unit.

Population ecology is an important area of ecology as it links ecology to population genetics and evolution.

Population attributes : The main attributes or characteristics of a population residing in a given area are:

(i) Birth rate (Natality) : It is the ratio of live births in an area to the population of an area. It is expressed as the number of individuals added to the population with respect to the members of the population. E.g. consider in a pond there we 20 lotus plants last year and through reproduction 8 new plants are added.

Hence, the current population = 28

The birth rate = 8/20 = 0.4 offspring per lotus per year.

(ii) Death rate (Mortality) : It is the ratio of deaths in an area to the population of an area. It is expressed as the loss of individuals with respect to the members of the population.

E.g. Consider 4 individuals in a laboratory population of 40 fruit flies died during a week. Hence, the death rate=4/40=0.1 individuals per fruit fly per week.

(iii) Sex ratio : It is the number of males or females **per thousand** individuals. E.g. 60% of the population is females and 40% males.

(iv) Age distribution : It is the percentage of individuals of different ages in a given population. At any given time, the population is composed of individuals that are present in various age groups. The age distribution pattern is commonly represented through **age pyramids.**

(v) Population density : It is defined as the number of individuals of a population present per unit area at a given time.

Age pyramid: If the age distribution (% individuals of a given age or age group) is plotted for the population, the resulting structure is called an **age pyramid.** The **shape of the pyramids** reflects the growth status of the population like **growing, stable or declining.**

Post-reproductive

Reproductive

Pre-reproductive

Expanding Stable Declining

Population size or population density (N):

- Population size or population density is the number of individuals of a species per unit area or volume. E.g., population density of Siberian cranes at Bharatpur wetlands in any year is <10. It is millions for ***Chlamydomonas*** in a pond.
- In some cases, population size is measured in % cover or biomass. E.g. consider in an area, 200 ***Parthenium*** plants and a single huge ***Banyan*** tree is seen. In such cases, the % cover or biomass is a more meaningful measure of the population size to show the importance of *Banyan* tree.
- Total number is a difficult measure for a huge opulation. In such cases, relative population density (without knowing absolute population density) is used. E.g., the number of fish caught per trap indicates its total population density in the lake.

- In some other cases, indirect estimation of population sizes is performed. E.g. **the tiger censusin** national parks and tiger reserves based on **Pug Marks** and **fecal pellets**.

Population Growth

- The size of a population is ever-changing aspect since it depends upon availability of food, predation, weather conditions, etc.
- This gives us an idea whether a certain population is growing or declining.
- Changes in population density give some idea about the population – whether it is flourishing or declining.
- Population size fluctuates due to changes in **four basic processes**. They are:

(i) Natality (B) : Number of births during a given period in a population.

(ii) Mortality (D) : Number of deaths in a population during a given period.

(iii) Immigration (I) : Number of individuals of the same species that have come into the habitat from elsewhere during a give time period.

(iv) Emigration (E) : Number of individuals of the population who left the habitat and gone elsewhere during a given time period.

Natality and Immigration increase the population density and Mortality and Emigration decrease the population density.

- If N is the population density at time t, then its density at time t + 1 is:

$N_{t+1} = Nt + [(B + 1) - (D + E)]$

Where B = Number of Births

I = Number of Immigrants

D = Number of Deaths

E = Number of Emigrants.

N = Population Density

r = Intrinsic rate of natural increase

t = Time period

K = **Carrying capacity** (The maximum population size that an environment can sustain)

This equation indicates that population density increases if B + I is more than D + E. Otherwise, it will decrease.

Population Growth Curves:

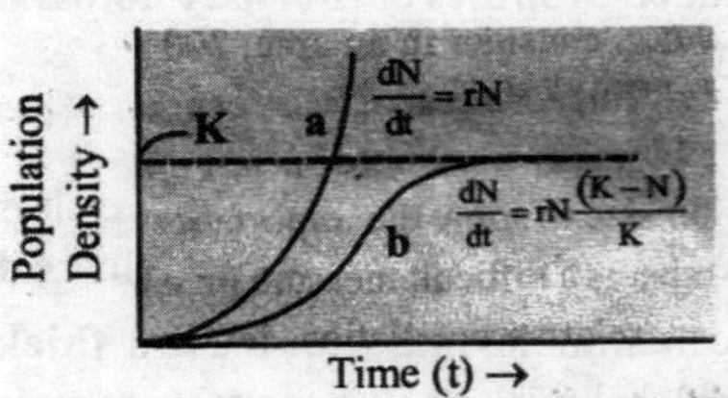

(a) When resources are not limiting the growth, then curve is exponential growth (J-shaped curve)

(b) When resources are limiting the growth, then curve is logistic growth (Sigmoid curve).

Population Interactions

- A natural habitat consists of many organisms living together and these organisms communicate and interact with each other. For example, plants depend on insects for pollination.
- In nature, animals, plants and microbes interact in various ways to form a biological community.
- A relationship within the organisms of the same species is called **intraspecific relationship,** while a relationship between two different species is known as **interspecific relationship**.
- **Interspecific relationships** (Interactions between two different species of organisms): They can be either beneficial or harmful to one or both partners. They arise from the interaction of populations of two different species. They include.
- **Mutualism :** Both the species are benefitted.
- **Competition :** Both the species are harmed.
- **Parasitism :** One species (parasite **Natality and Immigration increases the population density and Mortality and Emigration decreases the population density.**) is benefitted and the other species (host) is harmed.
- **Predation :** One species (predator) is benefitted and other species (prey) is harmed.
- **Commensalism :** One species is benefitted and the other is neither benefitted nor harmed.
- **Amensalism :** One species is harmed and the other is unaffected.
- In **predation,, parasitism** and commensalisms, the interacting species live closely together.

(a) **PREDATION**

- When an organism of higher trophic level (predator) feeds on organism of lower trophic level (prey) is called the **predation**.
- It is beneficial to the predator, while the prey is harmed. It acts as a means of transfer of energy to the next trophic level and of maintaining balance in the ecosystem.
- In a broad ecological context, all carnivores, herbivores, etc. are predators. About 25% of all insects are **phytophagous**.
- If a predator overexploits its prey, then the prey might become extinct. It results in the extinction of the predator. This is the reason why **predators** in nature are **'prudent'**.

Importance of Predators :

- Predators keep prey populations under control.
- When certain exotic species are introduced into a geographical area, they spread fast due to the absence its natural predators in the invaded land. E.g., the prickly pear cactus introduced into Australia in the early 1920's caused havoc by spreading. Finally, the invasive cactus was brought under control only after a cactus-feeding predator (a moth) was introduced into the country.
- Predators also help in maintaining species diversity in a community, by reducing the intensity of competition among competing prey species.

Defense developed by prey against predators:

(i) **Animals:**

- Some insects and frogs are camouflaged (cryptically colourd) to avoid being detected by the predator.
- Some are poisonous and therefore avoided by the predators.
- The Monarch butterfly is highly distasteful to its predator (bird) due to a special chemical in its body. This chemical is acquired during its caterpillar stage by feeding on a poisonous weed.

(ii) **Plants:**

- Several plants have evolved various mechanisms, both morphological and chemical, to protect themselves against herbivory.
- Morphological defense mechanisms:
- Cactus plants (Opuntia) are modified into sharp spines (thorns) to deter herbivores from feeding on them.
- Sharp thorns along with leaves are present in Acacia to deter herbivores.
- In some plants, the margins of their leaves are spiny or have sharp edges that prevent herbivores from feeding on them.

Chemical defense mechanisms:

- All parts of Caloptropis weeds contain toxic glycosides, which can prove to be fatal if ingested by herbivores.
- Chemical substances such as nicotine, caffeine, quinine and opium are produced in plants as a part of self-defence.

(b) **PARASITISM**

- Parasitism is an interaction between two species in which one species (parasite) derives benefit while the other species (host) is harmed. For example, ticks and lice (parasites) present on the human body represent this interaction where in the parasites receives benefit (as they derive nourishment by feeding on the blood of humans). On the other hand, these parasites reduce host fitness and cause harm to the human body.

Types of Parasites:

(i) **Ectoparasites:** Parasites that feed on the external surface of the host organism are called **Ectoparasites**. E.g., lice on humans and ticks on dogs. ***Cuscuta***, a parasitic plant that is commonly found growing on hedge plants, has lost its chlorophyll and leaves in the course of evolution. It derives its nutrition from the host plant which it parasitises.

(ii) **Endoparasites:** Parasites that live inside the host body at different sites (liver, kidney, lungs, RBC, etc.) are called **endoparasites**.

Brood parasitism in Birds:

- It is a special type of parasitism found in birds.
- Here, the parasitic birds lay eggs in the nest of its host and lets the host incubate them.
- During the course of evolution, the eggs of the parasitic bird evolve to resemble the host's egg in size and colour to reduce the chances of the host bird detecting the foreign eggs and ejecting them from the nest.

E.g. **Brood parasitism** between **Cuckoo** and **Crow**.

(c) COMMENSALISM

This is the interaction in which one species benefits and the other is neither benefited nor harmed.

Examples:

- **Orchid** growing as epiphyte on a mango branch.

  Epiphytes are plants growing on other plants which, however ,do not derive nutrition from them. Therefore, the relationship between mango tree and an orchid is an example of commensalism, where one species gets benefitted while the other remains unaffected. In the above interaction, the ***Orchid*** is benefitted as it gets support, while the mango tree remains unaffected.

- **Barnacles** growing on the back of a whale.

> **Cattle egret (Myna)** and **grazing cattle**. The egrets forage close to where the cattle are grazing. As the cattle move, the vegetation insects come out. Otherwise, it is difficult for the egrets to find and catch the insects. **[IAS-2014]**

- **Sea anemone** and **Clown fish**. The fist gets protection from predators with the help of stinging tentacles of seas anemone. The anemone has no benefit.

(d) MUTUALISM

It is an interaction between two living organisms where both are equally benefited. No one is harmed.

Examples:

> ***Lichen:*** *It is an intimate mutualistic relationship between a fungus and photosynthesising algae or Cyanobacteria.* **[IAS-2014]**

- **Mycorrhyza** is the association between fungi and the roots of higher plants. The fungi helps the plant in the absorption of essential nutrients from the soil, while the plant provides the fungi with carbohydrates.
- **Mutualism** between plant and animal through pollination and seed dispersion.

Examples:

- Many **fig trees** and **wasps**. The fig species is pollinated only by its 'partner' wasp species and no other species. The female wasp pollinates the fig inflorescence while searching for suitable egg laying sites in fruits. The fig offers the wasp some developing seeds, as food for the wasp larvae.
- **Orchids** show diversity of floral patterns. They can attract the right pollinator insect (**bees** and **bumblebees**) to ensure pollination.

COMPETITION

- **Interspecific competition** is a potent force in organic evolution.
- **Competition** is a process in which fitness of one species (measured as 'r' value) is significantly lower in presence of another species.
- Competition occurs when closely-related species compete for the **same limited resources.**
- Unrelated species can also compete for the resource. E.g. Flamingos and fishes in some shallow South American lakes compete for zooplankton.
- Competition occurs in abundant resources also. E.g. In interference competition, the feeding efficiency of one species is reduced due to the interfering and inhibitory presence of other species, even if resources are abundant.

Evidences for Competition:

- The ***Abingdon tortoise*** in **Galapagos Islands** became extinct within a decade after goats were introduced on the island, due to greater browsing efficiency of the goats.
- **'Competitive release'** : A species, restricted to a small geographical area (due to the presence of competitively superior species), expands its distributional range when the competing species is experimentally removed.
- **Connell's field experiments** showed that on the rocky sea coasts of Scotland, the larger and competitively superior barnacle *Balanus* dominates intertidal area, and excludes the smaller barnacle *Chathamalus* from the that zone.

Gause's 'Competitive Exclusion Principle'

- It states that two closely-related species competing for the same resources cannot co-exist indefinitely and the competitively inferior one will be eliminated eventually.
- Species facing competition may evolve mechanisms that promote co-existence rather than exclusion. E.g., 'resource partitioning'.

> ***Resource partitioning :*** *If two species compete for the same resource, they could avoid competition by choosing different times feeding or different foraging patterns. E.g. MacArthur showed that five closely-related species of warblers living on the same tree were able to avoid competition and co-exist due to behavioural differences in their foraging activities.*

7. Ecosystem

An ecosystem** is **the structural** and **functional unit of ecology**, where living organisms interact among themselves and also with the surrounding physical environment. **For example, pond, lakes, ocean, etc.

Components of Ecosystem

(i) **Biotic component** : It is the **living component** of an ecosystem that includes biotic factors, such as **producers, consumers, decomposers** and **scavengers**.

***Decomposers** can be divided into two groups based on their mode of nutrition: **Detrivores and Sapro-trophs**.*

Detrivores are the organisms that ingest non-living organic matter. These can include **earthworms, beetles** and many other invertebrates, while

Saprotrophs are the organisms that live on or in non-living organic matter, secreting digestive enzymes into it and absorbing the products of digestion. These include **Fungi** and **Bacteria**.

(ii) **Abiotic components :** They are the **non-living components** of an ecosystem such as **light, temperature, water, soil, air, inorganic nutrients,** etc. They are grouped into three categores:

1. **Physical factors** like sunlight, temperature, rainfall, humidity and pressure.
2. **Inorganic substances** like carbon dioxide, nitrogen, oxygen, sulphur, phosphorus, water, rock, soil and other minerals.
3. **Organic compounds** like cabohydrates, proteins, lipids and humic substnces. They are the building blocks of living systems.

TYPES OF ECOSYSTEMS

Ecosystems are classified into two types: natural ecosystem and man-made ecosystem.

(i) **Natural ecosystems** are totally dependent on solar radiations. They are further divided into:

- **Terrestrial ecosystem :** E.g. **Forest, Grassland, Desert,** etc.
- **Aquatic ecosystem :** It is again of two types: **Lentic ecosystem (e.g. stagnant fresh water, lake, pond, swamp)** and **Lotic ecosystem (Running fresh water, e.g., river).**

(ii) **Man-made ecosystem:** E.g. **Crop fields** and **aquarium.**

- **Pond** is an example of aquatic ecosystem. A pond is a shallow, simple, self-sustainable water body that exhibits all basic components of an ecosystem.

A. Abiotic components :

On the basis of extent of penetration of light a pond can be divided into **Euphotic, Mesophotic and Aphotic Zones**, the Mesophotic zone refers to the middle zone. Plenty of light is available to plants and animals in **Euphotic Zone**. No light is available in the **aphotic zone**. inorganic and organic substances are found in the dissolved form within the water.

B. Biotic components:

1. **Producers or autotrophs:** They synthesise food for all the heterotrophs of the pond. They can be categorised into two groups: Floating micro organisms and plants and rooted plants.

(i) **Floating micro organisms (green) and plants:** They are called **phytoplankton**. They are microscopic organisms. Sometimes they are so abundant in pond that they make it look **green** in colour, e.g. ***Spirogyra, Ulothrix, Cladophora, Diatoms, Volvox***.

(ii) **Rooted plants:** These are arranged in concentric zones from periphery to the deeper layers. Three distinct zones of aquatic plants can be seen with increasing depth of water in the following order:

- Zone of emergent vegetation: E.g. ***Typha, Bulrushes*** and ***Sagittaria***
- Zone of rooted vegetation with floating leaves. E.g. ***Nymphaea***.
- Zone of submergent vegetation: E.g. all pond weeds like ***Hydrilla, Rupia, musk grass,*** etc.

2. **Consumers/Heterotrophs:** They are the animals which feed directly or indirectly on autotrops. E.g Tadpole, Snails, Sunfish, etc.

Pond animals can be classified into the following groups:

- **Zooplanktons** are floating animals. E.g. Cyclops, Cypris.
- **Nektons** are the animals that can swim and navigate at will.E.g. fishes.
- **Benthic** animals are the bottom dwellers: E.g. Beetle, Mites, Mollusks and some **Crustaceans**.

3. **Decomposers:** They can be found in throughout the pond but in the sediments they are mostly abundant. The process of decomposing is possible in the certain groups like bacteria and fungi. E.g., ***Rhizopus, Penicillium, Curvularia, Cladosporium*** are found at the bottom of the pond.

8. Ecosystem-Structure and Function

- The interaction between the various biotic and abiotic components of an ecosystem leads to maintenance of the ecosystem. These components function as a unit.
- Vertical distribution of different species occupying different levels is called Stratification. For e.g., trees occupy top vertical strata (layer) of a forest, shrubs the second and herbs and grasses occupy the bottom layers.
- The aspects taken into consideration to study the functioning of an ecosystem are (A) Productivity, (B) Decomposition, (C) Energy flow and (D) Nutrient cycling.

A. PRODUCTIVITY

The rate of biomass production is called productivity. It is expressed in terms of **$g^{-2}yr^{-1}$ or (kcal m^{-2})**. It is used to compare productivity of different ecosystems. A constant input of solar energy is the basic requirement for any ecosystem to function and sustain.

1. **Primary productivity :** It is the amount of biomass

   produced per unit area in a given time period by plants during photosynthesis. It is expressed in

   terms of weight (g^{-2}) or energy (kcal m^{-2}). *It can be divided into Gross Primary Productivity (GPP) and Net Primary Productivity (NPP).*

(a) Gross Primary Productivity: It is the rate of production of organic matter during photosynthesis. A considerable amount of GPP is utilized by plants in respiration.

(b) Net Primary Productivity : Gross primary productivity minus respiration loss (R) is the Net Primary Productivity (NPP). NPP is the available biomass for the consumption to heterotrophs (herbivores and decomposers).

NPP = GPP – R

Primary productivity depends on the plant species inhabiting a particular area, environmental factors, availability of nutrients and photosynthetic capacity of plants. Therefore; it varies in different types of ecosystems.

The annual net primary productivity of the whole

biosphere is approximately **170 billions tons (dry weight)** of organic matter. Of this, despite occupying about 70% of the surface, the productivity of the oceans is only 55 billion tons.

Rest of course, is on land.

2. **Secondary productivity:** It is defined as the rate of production of organic matter by consumers over a period of time.

B. DECOMPOSITION

Decomposition is the process that involves the breakdown of complex organic matter or biomass from the body of dead plants and animals with the help of decomposers (like **fungi, bacteria,** etc.) into inorganic raw materials such as carbon dioxide, water and other nutrients. It is largely an oxygen-requiring process.

Detritus (dead plant remains such as leaves, bark, flowers and dead remains of animals, including fecal matter) is the raw material for decomposition.

The various processes involved in **Decomposition are: Fragmentation, Leaching, Catabolism, Humification and Mineralisation. Factors influencing Decomposition:**

- **Chemical composition of detritus :**

  Decomposition rate is slower if **detritus** is rich in **lignin and chitin**, and quicker, if detritus is rich in **nitrogen** and water-soluble substances, like sugars.

- **Climatic factors like temperature and soil**

  moisture : Warm and moist environment favours decomposition, whereas low temperature and anerobiosis inhibit decomposition, resulting in build-up of organic materials.

Food chains and energy flow are the functional properties of ecosystems which make them dynamic. The biotic and abiotic components of an ecosystem are linked through them.

C. ENERGY FLOW

- All life depends upon the flow of energy and materials through ecosystems. **Food chain** shows

  energy pathways. Energy passes from producer (plants) to plant-eaters, to Animal-eaters and on

  to tertiary consumers.

- Energy enters the ecosystem from the **Sun**. **Sun** is the only source of energy for all ecosystems **(except** deep sea hydro-thermal ecosystem). Plants and other photosynthetic organisms utilize less than 50% of the solar radiation known as Photosynthetically Active Radiation (PAR).

Plants and photosynthetic and chemosynthetic bacteria (autotrophs), fix solar radiant energy to make food.

- **TEN PERCENT LAW**

  It was given by **Lindemann in 1942**. It states **that during transfer of energy from one trophic level to another, only about 10% is stored at higher levels; remaining 90% is lost in respiration (heat)**.

- **Ecosystems** obey **the 2nd law of thermodynamics**. They need a constant supply of energy to synthesise the molecules they require, to counteract the universal tendency towards increasing disorderliness.

The entire process of energy flow can be summarized in the following four steps:

- The flow of energy in an ecosystem **is always linear or one-way or unidirectional**.
- At every step in a food chain, the energy received by the organism is also used for its own metabolism and maintenance. The left over is passed to next higher trophic level. Thus, energy flow decreases with successive trophic levels.
- It follows the ecological thumb rule of 10%.
- The number of steps is limited to **four or five** in a food chain for the transfer of energy.

9. Food Chain

A food chain starts with green plants because they are food producers. Animals, which eat the plants, form the second link of the chain. Plant-eaters are the first or **primary food consumers** in a food chain. Next come predators which feed on the plant eaters (i.e., **primary consumers**). These animal-eaters are second or secondary food consumers. Some animals-eaters (i.e., **secondary consumers**) are in turn eaten by other animals, for example, a snake feed on a toad which in turn, feeds on fruit fly. These animal-eaters are called **tertiary food consumers**. The last link of food chain is occupied by decomposers, which feed on dead plants and animals. **Decomposer** decomposes the dead bodies of plants and animals into nutrients, water and carbon dioxide. The nutrients and water are returned to the soil while carbon dioxide is released into the air, which in turn is re-used for the growth of new plants.

[IAS-2013]

The first link in a food chain is always a producer and the last link is always a decomposer.

Position of human beings in the food chain : Human beings are consumers and may occupy primary, secondary or tertiary levels. **Non-vegetarian people** are **'primary' consumers;** when they consume small fish, chicken or goat meat, they are **'secondary' consumers** and when they consume big fishes, they are **'tertiary' consumers.**

There are two types of food chains:

(i) **Grazing Food Chains (GEC) :** It extends from producers through herbivores to carnivores.

(ii) **Detritus Food Chains (DFC) :** It begins with dead organic matter to the detrivores organisms, which in turn make food for protozoan to carnivores, etc. It is made up of decomposers (saprotrophs) which are heterotrophic organisms. E.g., **fungi** and **bacteria**. They meet their energy and nutrient requirements by degrading dead organic matter or detritus. **Decomposers** secrete digestive enzymes that breakdown dead and waste materials into simple, inorganic materials, which are subsequently absorbed by them.

- In an aquatic ecosystem, GFC is the major conduit for energy flow.
- In a terrestrial ecosystem, a much larger fraction of energy flows through the DFC than through the GFC.
- DFC may be connected with GFC at some levels. Some of the organisms of DFC are prey to the GFC animals. Some animals (**cockroaches, crows,** etc.) are **Omnivores**. **These inter-connections of food chains make a Food Web.**

Trophic level

Organisms occupy a place in the natural surroundings or in a community according to their feeding relationship. A specific place of organisms in the food chain is known as their **trophic level**. **Producers** belong to the first **trophic level, Herbiovores** to the second and **Carnivores** to the third trophic level. The amont of energy **decreases** at successive trophic levels. When an organism dies, it becomes dead biomass (**detritus**) that serves as an energy source for decomposers. Organisms at each trophic level depend on those at the lower trophic level for their energy demands. Each trophic level has a certain mass of living material at a particular time called as the **Standing Crop**. It is measured as the mass of living organisms (biomass) or the number in a unit area. **Biomass** of a species is expressed in terms of **fresh or dry weight**. Measurement of biomass in terms of dry weight is more accurate. The number of trophic levels in a food chain is **restricted by 10% flow of energy**, less amount of energy available to the last trophic level.

Food Web

Trophic levels in an ecosystem are not linear, rather they are inter-connected and make a food web. Thus, **food web** is a network of inter-connected food chains existing in an ecosystem.

Green plants are eaten by several plant-eaters. These plant-eaters, in turn, are eaten by several animal-eaters. In this way, many food chains become linked together to form a web called, food web. **Food web shows many food chains linked together**. One animal may be a member of several different food chains. Food webs are more realistic models of energy flow through an ecosystem.

Ecological pyramids

- The representation of a food chain in the form of a pyramid is called **ecological pyramid**.

- An **ecological pyramid** is a graphical representation of various ecological parameters,

  such as the number of individuals present at each trophic level, the amount of energy or the biomass present at each trophic level.
- Ecological pyramids represent **producers at the base**, while the **apex represents the top level consumers** present in an ecosystem.

There are three main types of pyramids:

(i) **Pyramid of Numbers** : It is the graphical representation of the number of individuals present at each trophic level in a food chain of an ecosystem. The pyramid of numbers can be **Upright** or **Inverted,** dependcing on the number of **producers**.

For e.g., in **a grassland ecosystem**, the pyramid of numbers is **upright**. In this type of food chain, the number of producers (plants) is followed by the number of herbivores (mice), which in turn, is followed by the number of secondary consumers (snakes) and tertiary carnivores (eagles). Hence, the number of individuals at the producer level will be maximum, while the number of individuals present at top carnivores will be the least. On the other hand, in **parasitic food chain**, the pyramid of numbers is **inverted**. In this type of food chain, a single tree (producer) provides food to several fruit eating birds, which in turn, support, several insect species.

(ii) **Pyramid of Biomass :** A pyramid of biomass is a graphical representation of the total amount of living matter present at each trophic level of an ecosystem. It can be **Upright** or **Inverted**. It is **upright** in **grassland** and **forest ecosystems** as the amount of biomass present at the producer level is higher than at the top of carnivore level. The pyramid of biomass is **inverted in a pond ecosystem** as the biomass of fishes far exceeds

the biomass of zooplankton (upon which they feed).

Other examples of inverted pyramids are :

- Insects feeding on a big tree
- Pyramid of biomass in **sea** is generally **inverted** because the biomass of fishes far exceeds that of phytoplankton.

(iii) **Pyramid of Energy :** A pyramid of energy is a graphical representation of the amount of energy trapped per unit time and area in different trophic level of a food chain with producers forming the base and the top carnivores at the tip. It is **always Upright** because when energy flows from a particular trophic level to the next, some energy is **always lost as heat** at each step.

10. Ecological Succession

Ecological succession is a gradual, slow and predictable change in the species composition of an area leading to a climax community.

- **Ecological succession** was first given by **Warming (1899) and Elements (1916)**. The **word Succession** was first used by **Hult**.
- The composition of all ecosystems keeps on changing with change in their environment. These changes finally lead to the climax community.
- **Climax community** is the community which is in equilibrium with its environment. It remains stable as long as the environment remains unchanged. The **Rain forest** is an example of climax community ecosystem.
- The entire sequences of communities that successively change in a given area are called **Sere**. The individual transitional communities are termed **Seral stages (Seral communities)**.

General process of ecological succession:

(i) **Nudation:** It involves development of barren area by topographic, biotic and climatic factors. It is the early stage of soil formation.

(ii) **Invasion:** It is the successful establishment of a species in a barren area. This process is completed in three steps:

(a) **Migration :** Reaching of different reproductive structures like seed, spores through water or air on barren area.

(b) **Ecosis :** Successful establishment of species in new environment.

(c) **Aggregation :** It refers to arrival of propagules.

(iii) **Competition:** Due to increasing number of species at limited place, there develops a competition for habitat and nutrition.

(iv) **Reaction:** Species which have survived will react with environment and modify the environment.

(v) **Stabilisation:** Finally there occurs a stage in the process when the final terminal community becomes stabilised for longer period of time, maintains itself with the climate of the area.

Seral Communities:

- **Hydrosere** – Community in freshwater
- **Lithosere** – Community on rock
- **Pssamosere** – Community on sand
- **Halosere** – Community in saline body
- **Xerosere** – Community in dry area

Succession and **evolution** would have been **parallel** processes at that time.

Succession is divided into two types:

(i) Primary Succession

- The succession that takes place in areas where no living organisms ever existed. E.g., newly cooled lava, bare rock, newly created pond or reservoir.
- In primary succession, **pioneer species** are **lichens, phytoplankton,** etc.
- The species invading a bare area are called **pioneer species.**
- It is a slow process. It is because, before a biotic community is established, there must be formation of fertile soil through natural processes.

(ii) Secondary Succession

- The succession that takes place in areas which have lost all life forms **due to destructions and floods**. E.g., **abandoned farm lands, burnt or cut forests, lands that have been flooded**. Pioneer species: **grasses, wild flowers, algae.**
- Since some soil or sediment is present, succession is faster than primary succession.
- The species that invade depend on the condition of the soil, availability of water, etc.
- In succession, changes in vegetation affect food and shelter of various animals. Thus, as succession proceeds, the number and types of animals and decomposers also change.
- **Natural or human induced disturbances (deforestation, fire,** etc.), can convert a particular seral stage of succession to an earlier stage. Such disturbances create new conditions that encourage some species and discourage or eliminate other species. **[IAS-2013]**
- On the basis of replacement, succession is of two types: **Autogenic succession** and **Allogenic succession**.

  During **autogenic succession**, the community reacts with the environment and changes it. This community is replaced by new community. During **allogenic succession**, community is replaced due to external conditions or forces and not by existing vegetation itself. E.g., **fire, flood.**

Succession in Plants

- Based on the nature of the habitat, succession of plants is of two types: **Hydrarch** and **Xerarch.**
  - (i) **Hydrarch succession :** It takes place in **water areas**. The successional series progresses from hydric to the mesic conditions.
  - (ii) **Xerarch succession :** It takes place in **dry areas**. The series progress from xeric to mesic conditions.

D. NUTRIENT CYCLING

- Also known as **bio-geochemical cycle** (bio-living, geo-rock, chemical-element).
- The amount of nutrients like **carbon, nitrogen, phosphorus, calcium,** etc. present in the soil at any given time, is referred to as the **standing state**. It varies in different kinds of ecosystems and also on a seasonal basis.
- Organism needs constant supply of nutrients to grow, reproduce, and regulate various body functions.
- **Nutrients are never lost from the ecosystems**. They are **recycled again and again**. The movement of nutrient elements through various components of an ecosystem is called **nutrient cycling (bio-geochemical cycles)**. Hence, the cyclic flow of nutrients between non-living environment (soil, air and water) and the living organisms is called **bio-geochemical cycle**.
- They are called **bio-geochemical** as they are obtained from earth.
- In biosphere, the nutrients exist in two states: Reservoir pool and cycling pool. **Reservoir pool** is the pool/storehouse of nutrients from which the nutrients are slowly transferred to cycling pool, while **cycling pool** is the pool of nutrients which is repeatedly exchanged between the biotic and abiotic components of biosphere.
- Role of **decomposers** is **vital** in the functioning of biogeochemical cycles.
- Based on the existence of nutrients, nutrient cycles are of two types: **Gaseous cycle** and **Sedimentary cycle**. Reservoir for gaseous cycle exists in the atmosphere. E.g. Carbon cycle, Nitrogen cycle, while reservoir for Sedimentary cycles exists in the earth's crust. Elements such as **sulphur, phosphorus, potassium** and **calcium** have **sedimentary cycles**.
- Environmental factors (soil, moisture, pH, temperature, etc.) regulate the rate of release of nutrients into the atmosphere. The reservoir meets with the deficit of nutrients due to imbalance in the rate of influx and efflux.
- **Importance of biogeochemical cycle:**
  - (i) The minerals such as carbon, nitrogen, carbon and hydrogen, cycle through living and non-living components of the biosphere.
  - (ii) The amount of various materials cycling through biosphere remains more or less constant.

11. ECOSYSTEM SERVICES

- The products of ecosystem processes are called **ecosystem services.**
- **Robert Constanza** and his colleagues have tried to put price tags on nature's life-support services.

- Researchers have put an average price tag of US $ 33 trillion a year on these fundamental ecosystems services. This is nearly twice the value of the global gross national product GNP which is (US $ 18 trillion)
- Out of the total cost of various ecosystem services, the **soil formation** accounts for about 50%.
- Contributions of other services, like **recreation and nutrient cycling** are less than 10% each.
- The cost of **climate regulation and habitat** for wildlife are about 6% each.

12. Biodiversity And Conservaion

- **Biodiversity** is the variety of living forms present in various ecosystems. It includes variability among life forms from all sources including air, water and land.
- It is the diversity of biological organisation, ranging from cellular macromolecules to biomes.
- The **term** was coined by **Edward Wilson. Biodiversity** as described by Edward Wilson is the combined diversity at all levels of biological organisation.

Levels of biodiversity

(i) Genetic diversity:

- Diversity shown by a **single species** at genetic level is called **genetic diversity**. E.g., ***Rauwolfa vomitoria*** (Himalaya) shows genetic variation in terms of potency and concentration of the **chemical reserpine**. India has more than 50,000 different strains of rice and 1000 varieties of mango.
- The genetic diversity enables a population to adapt to its environment and to respond to natural selection. The amount of genetic variation is the basis of **speciation.** Genetic diversity within a species often increases with environmental variability.

(ii) Species diversity:

- Diversity at the species level is called as species diversity. E.g., Western Ghats have greater ambhibian species than the Eastern Ghats. It gives an idea about species richness and species evenness.
- **Species richness** refers to the number of species per unit area.
- **Species evenness** refers to the relative abundance with which each species is represented in an area.

(iii) Ecological diversity:

- Diversity at the ecosystem level is called ecological diversity. E.g. in India, deserts, rain forests, mangroves, coral reefs, wet lands, estuaries and alpine meadows are seen.

Diversity at the level of community and ecosystem exists along 3 levels.

(a) Alpha diversity : It is the biodiversity within a particular area, community or ecosystem. It is usually expressed by the **number of species,** i.e., species richness in that ecosystem. This can be measured by counting the number of taxa within the ecosystem.

(b) **Beta diversity :** It is the diversity which works by comparing the species diversity between ecosystems. This involves **comparing** the number of taxa that are unique to each of the ecosystems. It is the rate of change in species composition across habitats or among communities.

(c) **Gamma diversity** : It refers to the total species richness over a large area or region. It is a measure of the **overall density** of component ecosystems and the diversity between component ecosystems.

13. Global Species Diversity

- According to IUCN (2004), the total numbers of plant and animals species are more than 1.5 million species described so far.
- According to **Robert May's**, the global estimate is about 7 million (considering the species to be discovered in the tropics, i.e., only 22% of the total species have been recorded so far).
- Animals are more diverse (above 70%) than plants, including Plantae and Fungi (22%)
- **Most species rich taxonomic group** among animals: **Insects** (70%, i.e. out of every 10 animals, 7 are insects).
- **Number of fungi species is more** than the combined total of the species of fishes, amphibians, reptiles and mammals.
- The total number of species present in the world is calçulated by ecologists by statically comparing between a species richness of a well-studied group of insects of temperate and tropical regions. Then, these ratios are extrapolated with other group of plants and animals to calculate the total species richness present on the Earth.

14. Biodiversity in India

- **India** is one of the **seventeen (17) mega biodiversity countries** of the world.
- India has only **2.4%** of the land area of the world; it has **8.1% of the global species biodiversity.**
- There are about 45,000 species of plants and about 90,000-1,00,000 species of animals.
- Applying **Robert May's global estimate**, only 22% of the total species have been recorded, India has probably more than 1,00,000 species of plants and 3,00,000 species of animals to be discovered and described.

Hotspots:

- **Hot spots** are the areas or regions of **high endemism** and **very high levels of species richness.** These are the richest and the most-threatened reservoirs of plant and animal life on earth.
- There are **34 hot sports in the world,** of which **three are in** India; namely **the Western Ghats, the Eastern Himalayas and Indo-Burma.**

15. Patterns of Biodiversity

- **Biodiversity** is not uniform throught the world, but **varies with latitude and altitude.**
- Favourable environmental conditions favour speciation and make it possible for a larger number

  of species to exist there, i.e., biodiversity is more in such areas than the others.

(I) Latitudinal gradients

- **Species diversity decreases from the equator towards the poles.**
- **Tropics** (latitudinal range of 23.5^{0}N to 23.5^{0}S) have more species than **temperate or polar areas.**
- **Colombia** (near equator) has about 1400 species of birds.
- **New York** (410N): 105 species of birds
- **Greenland** (710N): 56 species of birds
- **India** (tropical latitudes): 1200 species

- **Equator (Tropical forest region)** has up to 10 times as many species of vascular plants as a forest of equal area in Midwest of USA (Temperate region).
- **Greatest biodiversity on earth : Tropical Amazonian rain forest in South America** (>40000 species of plants, 3000 fishes, 1300 birds, 427 mammals, 427 amphibians, 378 reptiles and more than 1,25,000 invertebrates).
- **There are three different hypothesis proposed by scientists for explaning species richness in the Tropical region:**

  (i) Tropical latitude receives more solar energy than temperate regions, which lead to high productivity and high species diversity.

  (ii) Tropical regions have less seasonal variations and have more or less constant environment. This promotes the niche specialisation and thus, high species richness.

  (iii) Temperate regions were subjected to glaciations during ice age, while **Tropical regions** remained undisturbed which led to an increase in the species diversity in this region.

(ii) Species-Area relationship

- **Alexander Von Humboldt** has observed that within a region, species richness gets increased when explored area is increased, but only up to a limit.
- Relation between species richness and area for a wide variety of taxa gives a **rectangular hyperbola.**
- **The slope of regression (Z)** has a great significance in order to find a species-area relationship. It has been found that in smaller areas (where the species-area relationship is analysed), the value of slopes of regression is similar, regardless of the taxonomic group or the region. However, when a similar analysis is done in greater areas, then the slope of regression is much steeper.

Graph showing species-area relationship

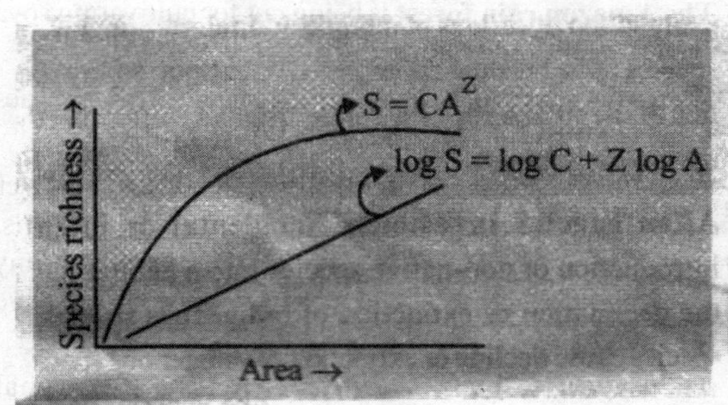

Note that on log scale, the relationship becomes linear

- On a logarithmic scale, the relationship is a straight line and the equation is described as:

  $\log S = \log C + Z \log A$

  Where, S= Species richness

  A= Area

  C= Y-intercept

  Z= Slope of the line **(regression co-efficient)**

- Ecologists have found that Z value ranges between 0.1 and 0.2, irrespective of the taxonomic group or the region.
- In very large areas, like **Continents,** Z value ranges between 0.6 and 1.2.

16. Loss of Biodiversity

- Different species have been extinct due to human activities.
- IUCN Red List (2004) documents extinction of 784 species (338 vertebrates, 359 invertebrates and 87 plants) in the last 500 years. E.g. **Dodo (Mauritius), Quagga (Africa), Thylacine** (Australia), **Stellar's sea cow (Russia)** and 3 subspecies (Bali, Javan, Caspian) of **Tiger.**
- More than 15,500 species are facing threat of extinction.
- 12% birds, 23% mammals, 32% amphibians, 31% gymnosperm species face the threat of extinction.
- The current extinction rate is 100 to 1000 times faster than in the pre-human times. If this trend continues, nearly 50% species on earth might be wiped out within next 100 years.

Causes of Biodiversity losses ('The Evil Quartet')

1. **Habitat loss and fragmentation:** Habitat of various organisms are altered or destroyed by uncontrolled and unsustainable human activities such as deforestation, slash, and burn agricultural, mining and urbanisation. This results in the breaking-up of the habitat into small pieces, which effects the movement of migratory animals and also, decreases the genetic exchange between populations leading to a declination of species. E.g.:

- **Tropical rain forests** (loss from 14% to 6%). Thousands hectares of rain forests is being lost within hours.
- **The Amazon rain forest** is being cut for cultivating soya beans or for conversion of grasslands for cattle.
- **Due to fragmentation,** animals requiring large territories and migratory animals are badly affected.

2. **Over-exploitation :** Due to over-hunting and over exploitation of various plants and animals by humans, many species have become endangered or extinct. Many species like **Stellar's cow, Passenger pigeon,** etc. have become extinct due to over exploitation **(IAS-2012)**

3. **Alien species invasions :** Accidental or intentional introduction of non-native species into a habitat has let to the declination or extinction of indigenous species. Alien species cause decline or extinction of indigenous species. E.g.

- The **Nile Perch** introduced in Lake Victoria (East Africa) caused extinction of more than 200 species of native fish, cichlid fish in the lake.
- Invasive weed species, like carrot grass **(Parthenium). Lantama** and water hyacinth **(Eicchornia)** caused damage to our native species.
- The illegal introduction of the **African Catfish (Clarias gariepinus)** for aquaculture is posing a threat to the indigenous catfishes in our rivers.

4. **Co-extinction:** In a native habitat, one species is connected to the other in an intricate network. The extinction of one species causes the extinction of other species, which is associated with it in an obligatory way. E.g.:

- Extinction of the parasites when the host is extinct.
- Co-evolved plant-pollinator mutualism, where extinction of one leads to the extinction of the other.

UNCN RED LIST

International Union of Conservation of Nature and Natural Resources (IUCN) works towards assessing the global conservation status of plant and animal species. It maintains a comprehensive list shown as **IUCN Red List** of threatened species.

The uses of this Red list are :

(i) Developing awareness about the importance of threatened bio-diversity.

(ii) Identification and documentation of endangered species.

(iii) Providing a global index of the decline of biodiversity.

(iv) Defining conservation priorities at the local level and guiding conservation action.

Also, IUCN has recognized **eight Red List categories** of species. They are Extinct, Extinct in the world, Critically Endangered, Endangered, Vulnerable, Lower risk, Data deficient, Not evaluated. The 2000 Red List contains assessment of more than 18,000 species, 11,000 of which are threatened.

IMPORTANT TERMS

1. **Extinct species :** Species that no longer exist on the earth are called extinct species. **Dodo, Passenger pigeon,** etc. are some examples of extinct species.
   (a) **Dinosaur** got extinct due to **natural reasons.**
   (b) **Dodo** became extinct mainly due to **people hunting** it for food.
2. **Threatened species :** Threatened species are species that are likely to disappear from the world sooner or later. In the Red list, all species listed under the categories **critically endangered, vulnerable and endangered** are together described as **threatened species.**
   (a) **Endangered species** are those species that are on the verge of becoming extinct. For example: **Blue whale, Tiger, Leopard,** etc.
   (b) **Vulnerable species** are those species that already existed in low number and are likely to move into endangered category in the near future, if **causal factors** such as habitat destruction, over-exploitation and other environmental disturbances continue over a period of time. E.g. **Musk deer, Sambhar deer, Black buck.**
3. **Rare species** are those species whose population in the world are very small. So, if they are not protected, then they might fall into the category of vulnerable or endangered species. E.g. **Indian elephant, Wild buffalo, Bengal Fox, Gaur,** etc.

MODEL TEST PAPERS

Model Test Paper-1

1. Which of the following is the latest site found?

(a) Dholavira (b) Amri
(c) Lothal (d) Kalibangan

2. Which of the following Vedic deities is not mentioned in the Boghazkoi inscription?

(a) Indra (b) Agni
(c) Mitra (d) Varun

3. The second Buddhist council was held during the region of

(a) Ajatashatru (b) Kanishka
(c) Kalashoka (d) Ashoka

4. Who was the president of first Jain council?

(a) Bhadrabahu (b) Sthalabahu
(c) Devardhigan (d) Nagarjuna Suri

5. Historian Abul Fazal was killed by

(a) Hemu (b) Bairam Khan
(c) Udai Singh (d) Vir Singh Deo Bundela

6. In the permanent settlement, the share of Zamindar stood at

(a) 1/4 (b) 1/6
(c) 1/11 (d) 1/2

7. Who hailed Gandhi's call for 'Quit India' as an 'Epic Movement'?

(a) Ram Manohar Lohia
(b) Jai Prakash Narayan
(c) Subhash Chandra Bose
(d) Sardar Vallabhbhai Patel

8. Which one among the following statements is correct?

(a) The Revolt of 1857 was not supported by the Nizam of Hyderabad
(b) Dinabandhu Mitra was the author of the book, Unhappy India
(c) The Sindhias of Gwalior gave shelter to the Rani of Jhansi
(d) Mangal Pandey led the Sepoys March to Delhi

9. The las opportunity to avoid the partition of India was lost with the rejection of :

(a) Cripps Mission (b) Rajagopalachari Formula
(c) Cabinet Mission (d) Wavell Plan

10. Which one of the following had supported the Non-cooperation REsolution of Mahatama Gandhi in the special session of the Indian National Congress at Calcutta in 1920?

(a) C.R. Das
(b) B.C. Pal
(c) Madan Mohan Malviya
(d) Moti Lal Nehru

11. The retreating Monsoon gives rainfall to

(a) Gujurat (b) Goa
(c) Tamil Nadu (d) Maharashtra

12. Which of the following river is not the tributary of Yamuna?

(a) Chambal (b) Betwa
(c) Ken (d) Gandak

13. Which one of the following soils is suitable for cotton production?

(a) Regur (b) Red
(c) Bhangar (d) Khadar

14. In which one of the following States is Pakhui Wildlife Sanctuary located?

(a) Arunachal Pradesh (b) Manipur
(c) Meghalaya (d) Nagaland

15. As per 2011 census data, the child sex ratio has come down from 927 to

(a) 904 (b) 919
(c) 922 (d) 925

Directions (Qs. 16-17): In these questions, relations between different elements is shown in the statements. These statements are followed by two conclusions.

Give answer

(a) Only Conclusion I follows
(b) Only Conclusion II follows
(c) Either Conclusion I or II follows
(d) Neither Conclusion I nor II follows
(e) Both Conclusions I and II follow

16. Statements

$N = P, P \leq F, F \geq L, L = K$

Conclusions

I. $F = K$

II. $F > K$

17. Statements

$Z > T, T < M, M \leq J$

Conclusions

I. $T = J$

II. $J > Z$

18. In an examination, Rahul got the 11th rank and he was 47th from the bottom among those who passed. 3 students could not appear for the exam and I student failed. What is the total number of students?

(a) 60 (b) 62

(c) 59 (d) 61

19. In a row at a bus stop, 'A' is 7th from the left and 'B' is 9th from the right. They both interchange their positions. Now A becomes 11th from the left. How many people are there in the row?

(a) 10 (b) 20

(c) 19 (d) 18

20. A B C D E F G H I J K L M N O P Q R S T U V W X Y Z. Four of the following five letter groups of the English alphabet given above are alike in a certain way and so from a group. On the basis of their position in English alphabet, which is the one that does not belong to the group?

(a) DKG (b) FMI

(c) HOL (d) JQM

21. The last digit of $(1001)^{2008} + 1002$ is

(a) 0 (b) 3

(c) 4 (d) 6

22. If 90% of A = 30% fo B and B = 2x% of A, then the value of x is

(a) 450 (b) 400

(c) 300 (d) 150

23. Find the average of the following set of scores.

965, 362, 189, 248, 461, 825, 524, 234

(a) 476 (b) 504

(c) 461 (d) 524

(e) None of these

24. Find the square root of $\sqrt{5184}$

(a) 78 (b) 71

(c) 72 (d) None of these

25. Simplify $\dfrac{\sqrt{3+2\sqrt{2}} - \sqrt{3-2\sqrt{2}}}{\sqrt{3+2\sqrt{2}} + \sqrt{3-2\sqrt{2}}}$

(a) $2\sqrt{2}$ (b) $\sqrt{2}$

(c) $3\sqrt{2}$ (d) $\sqrt{3}$

DIRECTIONS (Qs. 26-30): Refer to the graph carefully and answer the given questions.

Number of people who travelled from Dehradun to Almora by Trains A and B on 6 different days:

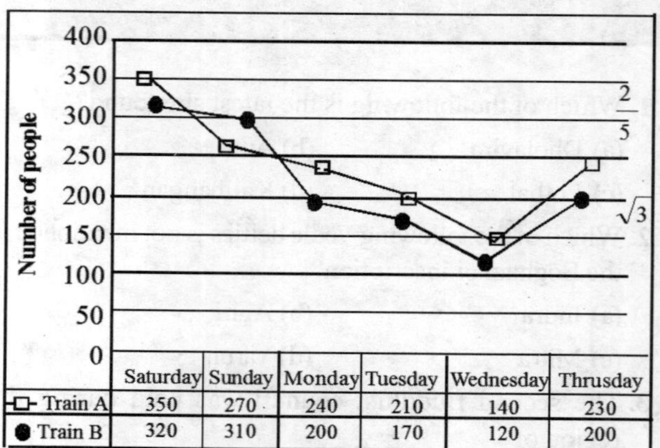

	Saturday	Sunday	Monday	Tuesday	Wednesday	Thrusday
Train A	350	270	240	210	140	230
Train B	320	310	200	170	120	200

26. The number of people who travelled by Train B on Friday is 220% more than the people who travelled by the same train on Thrusday. What is the respective ratio between the number of people who travelled on Friday and those who travelled on Saturday by the same train?

(a) 4 : 5 (b) 3 : 4

(c) 5 : 6 (d) 3 : 5

(e) 1 : 4

27. What is the difference between the total number of people who travelled b y Train B on Monday and Tuesday together and the total number of people who travelled by Train A on Saturday and Sunday together?

(a) 200 (b) 230

(c) 210 (d) 250

(e) 240

28. What is the average number of people travelling by Train A on Monday, Tuesday, Wednesday and Thrusday?

(a) 220 (b) 190

(c) 205 (d) 195

(e) 210

29. The number of people who travelled by Train A decreased by what percent from Saturday to Tuesday?

(a) 35 (b) 40

(c) 30 (d) 42

(e) 33

30. The total number of people who travelled by both the given trains together on Sunday is approximately what percent more then the total number of people who travelled by both the given trains together on Wednesday?

(a) 128 (b) 123

(c) 142 (d) 118

(e) 135

DIRECTIONS (Qs. 31-35): Study the following table carefully to answer the questions.

Number the students in two colleges A and B in the given years.

Years	2001		2002		2003		2004	
Colleges	Total students	Percentage of females	Total students	Percentage of females	Toral students	Percentage of females	Total students	Percentage of females
A	1200	40%	1600	45%	2600	50%	2800	60%
B	2600	45%	2400	40%	2500	44%	2500	52%

31. In the year 2003, what is the respective ratio of number of female students in College A and that in College B?

(a) 13 : 27 (b) 15 : 25
(c) 15 : 35 (d) 18 : 25
(e) 13 : 11

32. What is the difference between average number of female students in Colleges A and B in the year 2003 and the average number of female students in the same colleges in the year 2004?

(a) 214 (b) 172
(c) 290 (d) 185
(e) 198

33. In the year 2002, total strength of college B was what percent more than that of college A in the same year?

(a) 50 (b) 25
(c) 20 (d) $30\frac{1}{6}$
(e) $20\frac{1}{6}$

34. What is the total number of students in colleges A and B together in the year 2003?

(a) 3260
(b) 2080
(c) 3250
(d) 3380
(e) 5100

35. What is the difference between the total number of male students in colleges A and B together in the year 2001 and the total number of female students in the same colleges together in the year 2001?

(a) 600
(b) 800
(c) 820
(d) 500
(e) 850

DIRECTIONS (Qs. 36-40): Study the following table carefully and answer the given questions.

State	Percentage of Population below the poverty line	Proportion of Males and Females	
		Below poverty Line M : F	Above poverty Line M : F
P	35	5 : 6	6 : 7
Q	25	3 : 5	4 : 5
R	24	1 : 2	2 : 3
S	19	3 : 2	4 : 3
T	15	5 : 3	3 : 2

36. If the male population above poverty line for State R is 1.9 million, then what is the total population of State R?

(a) 4.5 million (b) 4.85 million
(c) 5.35 million (d) 6.25 million
(e) 6 million

37. What will be the number of females above poverty line in the State S if it is known that the population of State S is 7 million?

(a) 3 million (b) 2.13 million
(c) 1.33 million (d) 5.7 million
(e) 4 million

38. What is the male population above poverty line for State P if the female population below poverty line for State P is 2.1 million?

(a) 2.1 million (b) 2.7 million
(c) 3.3 million (d) 2.3 million
(e) 3 million

39. If the popuation of males below poverty line for State A is 2.4 million and that for State T is 6 million, then what is the respective ratio of the total population of States Q and T?

(a) 1 : 3 (b) 2 : 5
(c) 3 : 7 (d) 4 9
(e) 3 : 9

40. In State R female population above poverty line is by what per cent more than that below poverty line?

(a) 185 (b) 85
(c) 105 (d) 160
(e) 125

DIRECTIONS (Qs. 41-45): Study the bar chart & answer the questions.

Income and Expenditure (in crore ₹) in 2001 of five companies.

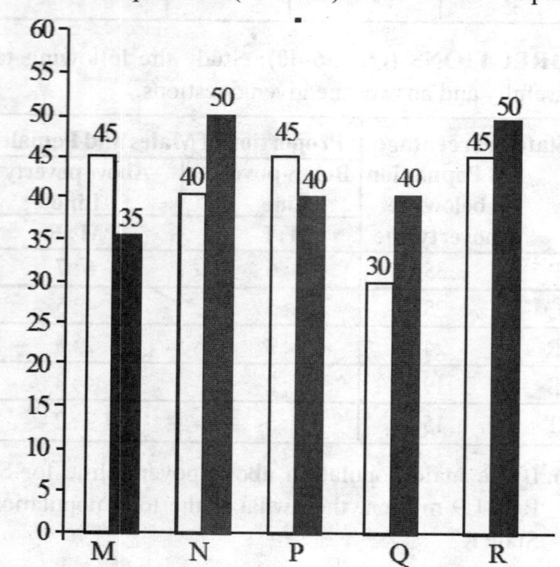

41. For company R, if the expenditure had increased by 20% in the year 2001 from the year 2000 and the company had earned profit of 10% in 2000, the company's income in 2000 (in crore)

(a) 35.75 (b) 37.25
(c) 41.67 (d) 38.5

42. In 2001, the approximate percentage of profit / loss of all the five companies taken together is equal to:

(a) 4% loss (b) 6.48% profit
(c) 6.88% loss (d) 4.64% profit

43. If the income of company Q in 2001 was 10% more than 2000 and the company had earned a profit of 20% in 2000, then its expenditure in 2000 (in crores) was :

(a) 32.32 (b) 28.28
(c) 34.34 (d) 29.09

44. The companies M and N together had a percentage of profit/loss of:

(a) 12% loss
(b) 10% loss
(c) No loss and No profit
(d) 10% profit

45. Which company has earned the maximum percentage of profit in the year 2001 jor

(a) N (b) Q
(c) P (d) M

46. Purity of a metal can be determined with the help of

(a) Pascal's law
(b) Boyle's law
(c) Archimedes principle
(d) Conservation of mass principle

47. If both the mass and the velocity of a body is increased to twice of their magnitude, the kinetic energy will increase by

(a) 2 times (b) 4 times
(c) 8 times (d) 16 times

48. Two bodies kept at a certain distance feel a gravitational force F to each other. If the distance between them is made double the former distance, the force will be

(a) 2F (b) $\frac{1}{2}$F
(c) 4F (d) $\frac{1}{4}$F

49. Stationary wave is formed by

(a) a transverse wave superposing a longitudinal wave
(b) two waves of the same speed superposing
(c) two waves of same frequency travelling in the same direction
(d) two waves of same frequency travelling in the opposite direction

50. Speed of sound at constant temperaute depends on -

(a) Pressure (b) Density of gas
(c) both (a) & (b) (d) None of the above

51. Metals are

(a) malleable. (b) ductile.
(c) None. (d) Both.

52. Which of the following have low melting and boiling points:

(a) Phosphorus (b) Sodium
(c) Iron (d) (a) and (b)

53. Brass contains

(a) Copper and Zinc (b) Copper and Tin
(c) Copper and Silver (d) Copper and Nickel

54. In galvanization, iron is coated with

(a) Copper (b) Zinc
(c) Tin (d) Nicked

55. Which one of the following is also known as solution?

(a) A compound

(b) A homogeneous mixture

(c) A heterogeneous mixture

(d) A suspension

56. In order to prevent spreading of a communicable disease like Cholera it is necessary to-

(a) Control the population of mosquitoes.

(b) Dry up all ponds in the neighborhood.

(c) Educate people to drink boiled water and not to eat exposed food.

(d) Prevent others from coming in contact with the diseased person.

57. Which scientist is credited with the development of medical vaccinations?

(a) Robert Koch (b) Charles Darwin

(c) Edward Jenner (d) William Harvey

58. Melatonin is a hormone produced by -

(a) Adrenal glad (b) Pitutary glad

(c) Pineal glad (d) Thymus glad

59. Adrenaline hormone causes:

(a) Increase in blood presure

(b) Increase in heart beat

(c) Both of them

(d) None of them

60. Those species whose populations have been seriously depleted and whose ultimate security is not assured are known as -

(a) Threatened species (b) Endangered species

(c) Vulnerable species (d) Rare species

61. During mid-eighteenth century the Indian economy was regarded as

(a) Capitalist Economy (b) Market Economy

(c) Village Economy (d) None of the above

62. Which Five-Year Plan had an objective of "Rapid industrializtion with particular emphasis on development of basic and heavy industries"?

(a) First (b) Second

(c) Third (d) Fourth

63. Which sector of Indian Economy has shown remarkable expansion during the last decade?

(a) Primary sector

(b) Secondary sector

(c) Tertiary sector

(d) Minng sector

64. Which one of the following is the objective of the National Watershed Development project for rainfed areas of India?

(a) Sustainable farming systems

(b) Integrated Watershed Management

(c) Reclanation of Forest Area

(d) Both 'a' and 'b'

65. What is the world ranking of Indian Railway network?

(a) Ist (b) 2nd

(c) 3rd (d) 4th

66. The mendion of the word 'justice' in the preamble to the constitution of India expresses

(a) social, political and religious justice

(b) social, economic and culture justice

(c) social, economic and political justice

(d) economic and political justice

67. The Instrument of Instructions of the Government of India Act 1935 has been incorporated in the Constitution of India as

(a) Fundamental Rights

(b) Directive Principles of State Policy

(c) Fundamental Duties

(d) Emergency Provisions

68. When a Money Bill is intruduced in the Lok Sabha whose recommendatio is necessary?

(a) Lok Sabha Speaker

(b) Union Finance Minister

(c) Leader of the Lok Sabha

(d) The President

69. The Supreme Court of India delares by issuing a writ that "respondent was not entitled to an office he was holding or a privilege he was exercising". Which writ is that?

(a) Hebeas Corpus (b) Quo Warranto

(c) Prohibition (d) Certiorari

70. Which one of the following statements is correct?

(a) In India, the same person cannot be appointed as Governor for two or more States at the same time

(b) The Judges of the High Court of the States in India are appointed by the Governor of the State just as the Judges of Supreme Court are appointed by the President

(c) No procedure has been laid down in the Constitution of India for the removal of a Governor from his/her post

(d) In the case of a Union Territory having a legislative setup, the Chief Minister is appointed by the Lt. Governor on the basis of majority support

71. In which one of the following countries, is Tamil a major language?

(a) Myanmar (b) Indonesia
(c) Mauritius (d) Singapore

72. In the region of eastern shore of Adriatic Sea, a cold and dry wind blowing down from the mountain is known as

(a) Mistral (b) Bora
(c) Bise (d) Blizzard

73. Nyishi tribe is found mainly in

(a) Andaman and Nicobar
(b) Arunachal Pradesh
(c) Nilgiri-Kerala
(d) Kashmir Valley

74. Gol Gumbuz, the largest dome in India is located in the state of -

(a) Karnataka (b) Maharashtra
(c) Madhya Pradesh (d) Bihar

75. The oldest church (St. Thomas Church) in India is loacted in the state of

(a) Goa (b) Kerala
(c) West Bengal (d) Assam

76. Which one among the following cities is called the 'zero-mile centre' of India?

(a) Kanpur (b) Allahabad
(c) Nagpur (d) New Delhi

77. In which sports it is illegal to play left-handed?

(a) Discus Throw (b) Polo
(c) Lacrosse (d) Chess

78. The Rega which is sung early in the morning is:

(a) Todi (b) Darbari
(c) Bhopali (d) Bhimpalasi

79. The book "An Era of Darkness" won the Sahitya Akademi Award 2019 in the non-fiction English category. Name the author.

(a) Vikram Seth (b) Shashi Tharoor
(c) Ruskin Bond (d) Arundhati Roy

80. Highest award given to civilian in India is

(a) Bharat Ratna (b) Padma Vibhushan
(c) Sharam Award (d) Padma Bhushan

81. Who has been appointed as the Managing Director General of Asian Development Bank (ADB)?

(a) Masatsugu Asakawa (b) Rajesh Khullar
(c) Takeo Konishi (d) Woochong Um

82. Name the Indiana activist who has been named among the 12 winners of the newly set up International Anti-Corruption Champions Award?

(a) Almitra Patel (b) Anjali Bharadwaj
(c) Tulsi Gowda (d) Archana Soreng

83. Who has been selected for the Global Energy and Environment Leadership Award 2021?

(a) Bill Gates (b) PM Narendra Modi
(c) Piyush Goyal (d) Both (a) and (b)

84. Who has been appointed as the new Chairman of National Commission for Scheduled Castes (NCSC)?

(a) Mahendra Nath Pandey
(b) Ram Shankar Katheria
(c) Dharmendra Pradhan
(d) Vijay Sampla

85. Natalia Mikhailovna Vodianova, who has been appointed as the U.N. Population Fund (UNFP) (a) goodwill ambassador, is a supermodel from which country?

(a) Singapore (b) Russia
(c) Ukraine (d) Australia

86. In which of the following Union Territories, Union Minister Prakash Javadekar inaugurated Atal Paryavaran Bhavan?

(a) Daman and Diu (b) Lakshadweep
(c) Jammu and Kashmir (d) Ladakh

87. The sixth meeting of the Governing Council of NITI Aayog was held recently. Who was the chair of the council?

(a) PM Narendra Modi (b) Amitabh Kant
(c) Rajiv Kumar (d) Nirmala Sitaraman

88. Kerala government approved how much funds to build 'smart' anganwadis?

(a) Rs 7 crore
(b) Rs 9 crore
(c) Rs 6 crore
(d) Rs 1 crore

89. Recently, which of the following states has santioned Rs 9 crore 'Smart' Anganwadi scheme?

(a) Karnataka
(b) Kerala
(c) Odisha
(d) Maharashtra

90. Recently, the Energy and Research Institute (TERI) has signed MoU to have research activities and capacity building in the power sector with which of the following organisations?

(a) Power Crid Corporation of India Limited

(b) Power System Corporation of India (POSOCO)

(c) NTPC Ltd

(d) Bharat Heavy Electricals Limited

DIRECTIONS (Qs. 91-92): Read the following passage carefully and answer the questions given below it. Certain words are given in bold to help you locate them while answering some of the questions.

Considering theat earth is right nest door to the moon, we know precious little about it. Its formation and early evolution present mysteries which, if understood, could guide us in planetary studies, and help inunderstanding exoplanets. The near side, which faces earth, has dark patterns; the far side, turned away, is marked with circular spots that are creters formed by meterite collisions. The moon's near side isbelieved to have a thinner sheel, so that when meteorites bombarded it they cracked its shell, releasing lava which gushed out and covered traces of the impact and left dark patches. Being thicker, the far side did not face such an erasure and bears the marks of the crater impacts.

91. How was moon formed?

(a) Due to Big Bang

(b) Due to meteorite collision

(c) Due to meteority bombardment

(d) Due to collision between two exoplanets

(e) None of these

92. Which of the following about moon's near side as mentioned in the passage is true?

(A) It has a dark side

(B) It is believed to have a thinner shell

(C) It faces earth

(a) Both A & B

(b) Both A & C

(c) Both B & C

(d) All A, B and C

(e) None of these

DIRECTIONS (Qs. 93-95): Read the following passage and answer the questions that follows:

One of the creation's great mysteries is the formation and existence of the rocky planets, such as our Earth. Recently, scientists who peered for 13 days across 1500 light years of universe believe that they may have the answer to this question. They used a sophisticated orbiting X-ray telescope, called Chandra, to study 1400 young stars in Orion Nebula and identified 27 stars that behave very much as the Sun may once have done, some 4.6 billion years ago. These young stars are surrounded by discs from which planets could condense and they tend to rrupt in vast flares far greater than anything now observed in the mature Sun. These flares could be an evidence of a process that would clear the way for small rocky planets to form. Scientists peer back to at time when Venus. Earth and Mars might have first formed from stony cinders whirling around a young star. So, it is said by a scientist that they do not have time machine to see back, but the next big thing is to observe the sun-like stars in Orion Nebula.

93. Scientists now believe that can now disclose the candid creation's great mystery, which is

(a) the formation and existence of planets like Earth

(b) the formation of stars with planets orbiting aound them

(c) the appearance of the Sun some 4.6 billion aournd them

(d) the appearance of planets from discs

(e) None of these

94. 'Chandra' is the name of

(a) a noon

(b) a star

(c) a telescope

(d) a newly invented time machine

(e) None of these

95. Young stars are surrounded by discs from which

(a) satellites formed

(b) planets condensed

(c) eruption took place

(d) universe waas created

(e) None of these

निर्देश : दिए गए विकल्पों में से सही विकल्प चुनिए।

96. ज्ञानोदय में प्रयुक्त संधि है

(a) स्वर संधि

(b) व्यंजन संधि

(c) विसर्ग संधि

(d) इनमें से कोई नहीं

97. 'जिसकी समानता न प्रकट की जा सके' के लिए एक शब्द है–

(a) अनुपम (b) अनुभूत

(c) भाष्य (d) यायावार

98. 'प्रवेश' शब्द का विलोम है–

(a) सार्थक (b) निकास

(c) प्रौढ़ (d) दुर्बल

99. _____ दिन की चांदनी

(a) दो-तीन (b) चार

(c) छ: (d) पांच

100. 'चमक' का पर्यायवाची शब्द है–

(a) गात (b) दिवस

(c) दीप्ति (d) वंचित

Answers/उत्तरमाला

1. (a)	2. (b)	3. (c)	4. (b)	5. (c)	6. (c)	7. (c)	8. (a)	9. (c)	10. (d)
11. (c)	12. (d)	13. (a)	14. (a)	15. (b)	16. (c)	17. (d)	18. (d)	19. (c)	20. (c)
21. (b)	22. (d)	23. (a)	24. (c)	25. (b)	26. (b)	27. (d)	28. (c)	29. (b)	30. (b)
31. (c)	32. (c)	33. (a)	34. (c)	35. (d)	36. (d)	37. (b)	38. (c)	39. (b)	40. (a)
41. (c)	42. (d)	43. (d)	44. (c)	45. (b)	46. (c)	47. (c)	48. (d)	49. (d)	50. (d)
51. (d)	52. (d)	53. (a)	54. (b)	55. (b)	56. (c)	57. (c)	58. (c)	59. (c)	60. (b)
61. (c)	62. (b)	63. (c)	64. (d)	65. (c)	66. (c)	67. (d)	68. (b)	69. (c)	70. (d)
71. (d)	72. (b)	73. (b)	74. (a)	75. (b)	76. (c)	77. (b)	78. (a)	79. (b)	80. (a)
81. (d)	82. (b)	83. (b)	84. (d)	85. (b)	86. (b)	87. (a)	88. (b)	89. (b)	90. (b)
91. (c)	92. (d)	93. (a)	94. (c)	95. (b)	96. (a)	97. (a)	98. (b)	99. (b)	100. (c)

Model Test Paper-2

1. In Indus Valley Civilzation, the script was:
(a) Kharosthi (b) Brahmi
(c) Boustrophedon (d) None of these

2. The famous 'Battle of Kings' between Bharat and the host of ten kings was fought near the river :
(a) Sindhu (b) Saraswati
(c) Parushni (d) Vitasta

3. Buddha means :
(a) The enlightened one (b) The religious preacher
(c) The genius (d) The powerful

4. In which Jain council, Jain dharm was divided in Svetamber and Digamber?
(a) First council (b) Second council
(c) Third council (d) Fourth council

5. The offsprings of which Mughal emperor were born in a Sufi's Khanqah instead of the Mughal haram?
(a) Humayun (b) Jahangir
(c) Shahjahan (d) Aurangzeb

6. Who was the Nawab of Bengal when Diwani of Beng gal, Bihar and Orissa was granted to East India Company?
(a) Siraj-ud-Daulah (b) Nazam-ud-Daulah
(c) Mir Kasim (d) Mir Jafar

7. Jiatrang Movement started in
(a) Nagaland (b) Tripura
(c) Manipur (d) Mizoram

8. Find out the non-precursor of the 1857 revolt
(a) Ulgulan (b) Santhal Resing
(c) Sanyasi Revolt (d) Faraizi Revolt

9. Who among the following was thrice ciected President of the Indian National Congress?
(a) Dadabhai Naoroji
(b) Surendranath Banerjee
(c) Gopal Krishna Gokhi
(d) Shankaran Nair

10. Where was the 'Jatiya Sarkar' formed during the Quit India Movement?
(a) Ballia (b) Nagpur
(c) Satara (d) Tamluk

11. The Deccan trap was formed by the
(a) Dharwar Vulcanicity
(b) Mesozoic Vulcanicity
(c) Cretaceous Vulcanicity
(d) Palcozoic Vulcanicity

12. Which one of the following rivers in India has been declared as the National River?
(a) Ganga (b) Yamuna
(c) Krishna (d) Son

13. The alluvial soil found along the banks of the rivers in the Ganga plain is called
(a) Khadar (b) Bhangar
(c) Bhur (d) Loess

14. Which of the following States of India has the largest percentae of geographical area under forest as per the report of the Forest Survey of India?
(a) Manipur (b) Meghalaya
(c) Mizoram (d) Nagaland

15. Which one of the Indians state/union Territories is having lowest sex ratio in 2011?
(a) Haryana (b) Daman and Diu
(c) Punjab (d) Dadar and Nagar Haveli

16. Four of the following five are alike in a certain way and so form a group. Which is one that does not belong to that group?
(a) Pear (b) Jackfuits
(c) Watermelon (d) Papaya

17. A party consisted of a man, his wife, his three sons and their wives and three children in each son's family. How many were there in the party?
(a) 24 (b) 22
(c) 13 (d) 17

18. The reflex angle between the hands of a clock at 10:25 is?
(a) 180^0 (b) $192\frac{1}{2}^0$
(c) 195^0 (d) $197\frac{1}{2}^0$

Directions (Qs. 19-20): In these questions, relations between different elements is shown in the statements. These statements are followed by two conclusions.

Give answer

(a) Only Conclusion I follows

(b) Only Conclusion II follows

(c) Either Conclusion I or II follows

(d) Neither Conclusion I nor II follows

(e) Both Conclusions I and II follow

19. Statements

A>B>C, D>E>F, D>C

Conclusions

I. E>C

II. F>B

20. Statements

K>L, K>M, M≥N, N>O

Conclusions

I. O>M

II. O>K

21. $\frac{4}{15}$ of $\frac{5}{7}$ of a number is greater than $\frac{4}{9}$ of $\frac{2}{5}$ of the same number by 8. What is half of that number?

(a) 630 (b) 315

(c) 210 (d) 105

(e) None of these

22. A candidate appearing for an examination has to secure 35% marks to pass. But he secured only 40 marks and failed by 30 marks. What would be the maximum marks of test?

(a) 280 (b) 180

(c) 200 (d) 150

(e) 210

23. A cricketer whose bowling average is 24.85 runs per wicket, takes 5 wickets for 52 runs in next inning and thereby decrease his average by 0.85. The number of wickets taken by him till the last match was :

(a) 75 (b) 85

(c) 80 (d) 96

24. Find the square root of $7+\sqrt{48}$.

(a) $2-\sqrt{3}$ (b) $2+\sqrt{3}$

(c) $3+\sqrt{2}$ (d) $3-\sqrt{2}$

25. What will be the value of $2.1\overline{3}+3.1\overline{2}$?

(a) $5.2\overline{5}$ (b) $5.\overline{2}$

(c) $5.2\overline{3}$ (d) 5.25

DIRECTIONS (Qs. 26-30): The following graph shows production (in thousands) of two types (P and Q) of vehicles by fa factory over the years 2009 to 2014. Study the graph and answer five question.

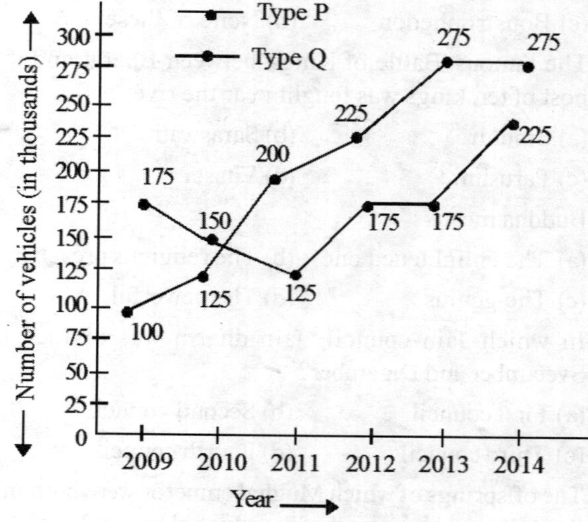

26. Approximate percenatage decrease in production of Types Q vehicles from 2010 to 2011 is

(a) 14.3% (b) 10.1%

(c) 16.3% (d) 12.5%

27. The ratio of total production of Type P vehicles to total production of Type Q vehicles over the year is

(a) 41 : 48 (b) 5 : 8

(c) 8 : 5 (d) 48 : 41

28. The production of Type Q vehicles in 2010 was approximately what percent of Type P vehicles in 2014?

(a) 60% (b) 45.5%

(c) 54.5% (d) 75%

29. In how many of the given years, was the production of Type P vehicles of the company more than the average produciton of this type vehicles in the given years?

(a) 3 (b) 5

(c) 2 (d) 4

30. The total production of Type P vehicles in the year 2009 and 2011 is what percent of total production of Type Q vehicles in 2010 and 2014?

(a) 81.25%

(b) 75%

(c) 80%

(d) 69.25%

DIRECTIONS (Qs. 31-35): Read a carefully and answer five questions.

Total cost of production of a firm is ₹ 250 lakh. Following pie-chart shows the percentage of costs of production in different purpose.

Letters

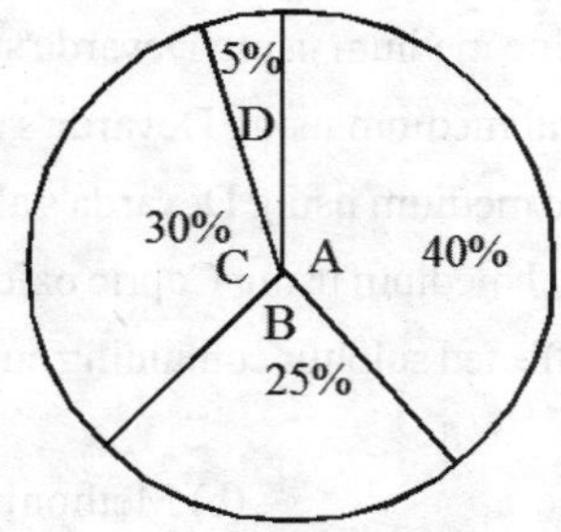

A, B, C, D respresent the following:

A = Cost of raw materials

B = Cost of packing materials

C = Cost of labour

D = Maintenance cost

31. If the production increases to five times of the present cost, then the percentage increases of the cost is

(a) 50% (b) 400%

(c) 300% (d) 500%

32. Cost of packing materials and raw materials together amounts to

(a) ₹ 175 lakh (b) ₹ 87.5 lakh

(c) ₹ 162.5 lakh (d) ₹ 137.5 lakh

33. If the cost of production doubles in a period of 3 years, then the corresponding maintenance cost (in rupees) will be

(a) ₹ 12.5 lakh (b) ₹ 25 lakh

(c) ₹ 125 lakh (d) ₹ 75 lakh

34. If the total maintenance cost increases from ₹ 12.5 lakh to ₹ 50 lakh, then the percentage increase of the maintenance cost is

(a) 300% (b) 400%

(c) 75% (d) 25%

35. If the packing cost increases by 2%, then the new packing cost will be

(a) ₹ 62.5 lakh

(b) ₹ 5 lakh

(c) ₹ 1.25 lakh

(d) ₹ 63.75 lakh

DIRECTIONS (Qs. 36-40): Study the following table carefully and answer the questions that follow. Monthly rent (in ₹ thousand) at five different places in six different years.

Years	Place				
	Churehgate	Dudar	Kandivali	Borivali	Virar
2005	5.3	3.8	1.5	2.7	1.1
2006	12.5	8.3	34	4.8	2.1
2007	16.7	11.7	5.5	6.6	1.8
2008	20.9	136	9.8	12.7	3.6
2009	25.8	14.5	11.5	14.1	5.5
2010	30.3	20.9	15.6	15.9	7.8

36. In which place did the monthly rent not increase consistently from year 2005 to 2010?

(a) Churchgate (b) Dadar

(c) Kandivali (d) Virar

37. In which year at Churghgate, the monthly rent increased more than 100 per cent from the previous year?

(a) 2006 (b) 2007

(c) 2008 (d) 2009

38. What is the difference between the monthly rent at Dadar in the year 2009 and Borivali in the year 2007?

(a) ₹ 7,600 (b) ₹ 7,900

(c) ₹ 8,100 (d) ₹ 8,600

39. Monthly rent at Kandivali in the year 2008 was approximately what per cent of the total monthly rent at Virar over all the years together?

(a) 30 (b) 38

(c) 42 (d) 45

40. Which city was most expensive in terms of rent?

(a) Churchgate

(b) Dadar

(c) Kandivali

(d) Borivali

DIRECTIONS (Qs. 41-45): The following table gives the quarterly output of three production units of machine manufacturing company.

Year	Ist Quarter			2nd Quarter			3rd Quarter			4th Quarter		
Unit	1	2	3	1	2	3	1	2	3	1	2	3
1998	30	34	38	40	44	42	36	37	39	34	35	37
1999	34	45	42	52	54	56	50	49	[illegible]	[illegible]	45	48
2000	35	45	43	58	53	58	54	56	56	48	49	43
2001	54	58	57	76	77	79	68	69	70	62	64	66
2002	80	82	87	92	97	93	86	88	87	82	84	83

41. Which of the following statement is correct?

(i) The performance of Unit 1 has been the lowest during the 5 years period

(ii) The performance of Unit 2 has been the highest during the 5 years period

(iii) The performance of Unit 3 has been the highest during the 5 years period

(iv) The performance of Unit 2 has been the lowest during the 5 years period

(a) (i) (b) (iii) and (iv)

(c) (i) and (iii) (d) None of these

42. Incentives based on the production are given on quarterly basis. In which quarter would the workers get maximum incentive?

(a) Ist Quarter (b) 2nd Quarter

(c) 3rd Quarter (d) 4th Quarter

43. Which unit has shown the least growth in production during the period 1998-2002?

(a) Unit 1 (b) Unit 2

(c) Unit 3 (d) Cannot say

44. During 1998-2002 the highest quarterly production has been achieved by Unit... in the .... quarter of 2002?

(a) 1, 1st (b) 2, 2nd

(c) 3, 3rd (d) 2, 4th

45. The highest increase in the yearly average production has been over the period :

(a) 1998-1999 (b) 2001-2002

(c) 1999-2000 (d) 2000-2001

46. The waves in which the particles of the medium vibrate in a direction perpendicular to the direction of wave motion is known as -

(a) Transverse wave (b) Longitudinal waves

(c) Propagated waves (d) None of these

47. A man wearing glasses of focal length +1 m cannot clrearly see beyond one meter -

(a) If he is far sighted (b) If his near sighted

(c) If his vision is normal (d) In each of these cases

48. Fleming's right had rule is used to find the direction of the

(a) Alternate current (b) Direct current

(c) Induced current (d) Actual current

49. The unit of electica power is

(a) Volt (b) Watt

(c) Kilowatt hour (d) Ampere

50. The resistance of the human body (dry condition) is of the order of

(a) 10^1 Ohm (b) 10^2 Ohm

(c) 10^3 Ohm (d) 10^4 Ohm

51. Reduction of nitrates to ammonia can be achieved through one of the following methods :

(a) in alkaline medium using Devarda's alloy.

(b) in neutral medium using Devarda's alloy.

(c) in acidic medium using Devarda's alloy.

(d) in neutral medium using Cupric oxide.

52. The most affected sulphur containing amino acid by PAN is

(a) Cysteine (b) Methonine

(c) Proline (d) Globuline

53. Which of the following has zero electron affinity?

(a) Oxygen (b) Fluorine

(c) Nitrogen (d) Neon

54. How do most insects respire?

(a) Through skin (b) Through gills

(c) By tracheal system (d) By lungs

55. When a particle and an antiparticle come in contract with each other, they

(a) repell each other

(b) annihilate each other

(c) go undisturbed

(d) spin about a common axis

56. Khaziranga wild life sanctuary is famous for -

(a) Tiger (b) Musk deer

(c) Elephant (d) Rhino

57. The region which is greatly affected by air pollution is

(a) Themosphere (b) Stratosphere

(c) Troposphere (d) Rhino

57. The region which is greatly affected by air pollution is

(a) Thermosphere (b) Stratosphere

(c) Troposphere (d) Measosphere

58. Which of the following is most abundant hydrocarbon pollutant?

(a) Butane (b) Ethane

(c) Methane (d) Propane

59. Which of the following causes lung cancer?

(a) Textiles (b) Asbestos

(c) Silica (d) Paper

60. Which of the following statement is false?

(a) London smog is oxidising is nature

(b) Photochemical smog causes irritation in eyes

(c) London somg is a mixture of smoke and fog

(d) Photochemkical somg results in the formation of PAN

61. Indian economy is most appropriately described as a

(a) Socialist economy (b) Mixed economy

(c) Both (a) and (c) (d) None of these

62. In the context of India's Five Year Plans, a shift in the pattern of industrialization, with lower emphasis on heavy industries and more on infrastructure begins in

(a) Fourth Plan (b) Sixth Plan

(c) Eighth Pan (d) Tenth Plan

63. If it will be true to classify India as

(a) a food-deficit economy

(b) a labour- surplus economy

(c) a trade-surplus economy

(d) a capital-surplus economy

64. Which one of the following agencies is not included in the operation of the Kisan Credit Cards?

(a) Co-operative Banks

(b) Regional Rural Banks

(c) Scheduled Commercial Banks

(d) NABARD

65. Indian Railways are divided into how many zones?

(a) 17 (b) 18

(c) 19 (d) 20

66. Which of the following States has no Panchayat Raj institution at all?

(a) Assam (b) Nagaland

(c) Tripura (d) Kerala

67. Which one of the following states does not have Vidhan Praishad?

(a) Bihar (b) Maharashtra

(c) Tamil Nadu (d) Uttar Pradesh

68. The power of the Supreme Court of India to decide disputes between the Centre and the States falls under its

(a) advisory jurisdiction

(b) appellate jurisdiction

(c) original jurisdiction

(d) writ jurisdiction

69. Consider the following statements about the Attorney General of India:

1. He is appointed by the President of India
2. He must have the same qualifications as required for a judge of the Supreme Court.
3. He must be a member of either House of Parliament.
4. He can be removed by impeachment by Parliament.

Which of the above statements is/are correct?

(a) 1 and 2 (b) 1 and 3

(c) 2, 3 and 4 (d) 3 and 4

70. The rights included in Part III of the Consitution are called 'fundamental' because?

1. They are available to both citizens and aliens
2. They are above ordinary law
3. They are fundamental to governance.
4. They are not absolute

Which of the above is/are correct?

(a) 2 and 4 (b) 1, 2 and 3

(c) 1, 3 and 4 (d) 3 only

71. Which one of the following cities is not a former capital of the given country (Country given in the brackets)?

(a) Karachi (Pakistan)

(b) Auckland (New Zealand)

(c) Kyoto (Japan)

(d) Brisbane (Australia)

72. Which one of the following is known as the "Coffee port" of the world?

(a) Sao Paulo (b) Santos

(c) Rio De Janeiro (d) Buenos Aires

73. In the field of tourism, which one of the following Indian States is described as 'One State Many Worlds"?

(a) Assam (b) West Bengal

(c) Karnataka (d) Rajasthan

74. Jharkhand does not share boundary with -

(a) West Bengal (b) Odisha

(c) Chhattisgarh (d) Madhya Pradesh

75. The radcliffe Line is a boundary between

(a) India and Pakistan (b) India and China

(c) India and Myanmar (d) India and Afghanistan

76. Survey of India is under the Ministry of

(a) Defence

(b) Environmental & Forests

(c) Home Affairs

(d) Science & Technology

77. Who is the first Indian batsman to score a triple century in Test Cricket?
(a) V. V. S. Laxman (b) Rahul Dravid
(c) Sachin Tendulkar (d) Virendra Sehwag

78. Which one of the following dances involves solo performance?
(a) Bharatanatyam (b) Kuchipudi
(c) Mohiniattam (d) Odissi

79. Jaysree Goswami Mahanta won the Sahitya Akademi Award 2019 for her novel "Chanakya." In which language is it written?
(a) Bengali (b) Oriya
(c) Assamese (d) Hindi

80. Jnanpith Award is given for which field?
(a) Journalism (b) Music
(c) Science (d) Literature

81. Consider the following statements about the China-Pakistan economic corridor (CPEC):
1. It is part of China's one belt one road initiative.
2. It is passing through the disputed region of Pakistan occupied Kashmir (PoK).

Which of the above is/are correct?
(a) 1 only (b) 2 only
(c) Both 1 and 2 (d) Neither 1 nor 2

82. Cirrhosis is a disease of which of the following organs of the human body?
(a) Liver (b) Kidney
(c) Heart (d) Skin

83. The right to information Act was recently in the news due to an amendment made on it. The original Right to Information Act came into being in which year?
(a) 2009 (b) 2002
(c) 2005 (d) 2011

84. Recently, religious conversion for marriage was made a non-bailable offence under Prohibitionof Unlasful Conversion of Religion Bill, 2021 by which state?
(a) Rajasthan (b) Uttar Pradesh
(c) Bihar (d) Haryana

85. What is the gig economy?
(a) Agricultural econmomy based on contract farming
(b) An economy excessively dependent on Public Sector
(c) Services sector economy highly dependent on Information Technology
(d) A labour market charcterized by the prevalence of short term contract and freelance work

86. Consider the following statements regarding the term Bad Bank recently in the news:
1. A bad bank is a bank set up to buy the bad loans and other illiquid holdings of another financial institution.
2. Finance Minister Nirmalsa Sitharaman had proposed setting up 10 bad banks during her Union Budget 2021 speech.

Which of the above is/are correct?
(a) 1 only (b) 2 only
(c) Both 1 and 2 (d) Neither 1 nor 2

87. Which of the following ministers launched Smartcode Platform?
(a) Ministry of Science and technology
(b) Ministry of Electronics and IT
(c) Ministry of Housing and urban Affairs
(d) Ministry of MSME

88. What is the objective of Smartcode platform?
(a) To enable citiznes to register complaints directly throught the platform.
(b) To enable citizens to learn coding virtually.
(c) To enable Urban loacl bodies to monitor criminal activities.
(d) To enable Urban local bodies to use existing codes and customise them to suit local needs.

89. Which of the following states/UTs has recently launched a mobile application named Carbon Watch to assess the carbon footprint of an individual?
(a) Karnataka (b) Delhi
(c) Tamil Nadu (d) Chandigarh

90. Consider the following statements regarding the recently launched mobile application —Carbon Watch:
1. It is a mobile application to monitor pollution from vehicular emissions.
2. It was launched by the Delhi government.

Which of the above is/are correct?
(a) 1 only (b) 2 only
(c) Both 1 and 2 (d) Neither 1 nor 2

DIRECTIONS (Qs. 91-93): See the underlined adverb adn state its kind.

91. My mother makes cookies twice a month.
(a) Relative adverb (b) Adverb of manner
(c) Adverb of degree (d) Adverb of number

92. She always waits for him.
(a) Adverb of number (b) Relative adverb
(c) Adverb of place (d) Adverb of degree

93. He was too excited to explain anything.

(a) Adverb of number (b) Relative adverb
(c) Adverb of manner (d) Adverb of degree

DIRECTIONS (Qs. 94-95): Choose the correctly spelt word out of given options.

94. (a) Pesanger (b) Passenger
(c) Pessenger (d) Pasanger

95. (a) Vaccume (b) Vecume
(c) Vacuum (d) Vaaccum

निर्देश : दिए गए विकल्पों में से सही विकल्प चुनिए।

96. 'मन की वृति' के लिए एक शब्द है-

(a) अग्रणी (b) गोधूलि
(c) मनोवृति (d) मृदुभाषी

97. 'तिक्त' शब्द का विलोम है-

(a) मधुर (b) ध्वंस
(c) अव्यक्त (d) सिद्ध

98. निम्न शब्दों में से किसमें विसर्ग संधि है

(a) अतएव (b) नरेंद्र
(c) सज्जन (d) सदैव

99. 'मोक्ष' का पर्यायवाची शब्द है-

(a) कैवल्य (b) जंगम
(c) भानु (d) सुबोध

100. 'तख्ता उलटना' मुहावरे का अर्थ है-

(a) शासन बदल जाना (b) कठिन कार्य
(c) सबसे भिन्न मत रखना (d) दिन काटे न काटना

Answers/उत्तरमाला

1. (c)	2. (c)	3. (a)	4. (a)	5. (b)	6. (b)	7. (c)	8. (a)	9. (a)	10. (d)
11. (c)	12. (a)	13. (a)	14. (c)	15. (b)	16. (c)	17. (d)	18. (d)	19. (d)	20. (d)
21. (b)	22. (c)	23. (b)	24. (b)	25. (a)	26. (c)	27. (d)	28. (c)	29. (a)	30. (c)
31. (b)	32. (c)	33. (b)	34. (a)	35. (d)	36. (d)	37. (a)	38. (b)	39. (d)	40. (a)
41. (c)	42. (b)	43. (c)	44. (b)	45. (d)	46. (a)	47. (a)	48. (c)	49. (b)	50. (d)
51. (a)	52. (a)	53. (d)	54. (c)	55. (b)	56. (d)	57. (c)	58. (c)	59. (a)	60. (a)
61. (b)	62. (c)	63. (b)	64. (d)	65. (a)	66. (b)	67. (c)	68. (c)	69. (a)	70. (d)
71. (d)	72. (b)	73. (c)	74. (d)	75. (a)	76. (d)	77. (b)	78. (a)	79. (c)	80. (d)
81. (c)	82. (a)	83. (c)	84. (b)	85. (d)	86. (a)	87. (c)	88. (d)	89. (d)	90. (d)
91. (d)	92. (a)	93. (d)	94. (b)	95. (c)	96. (c)	97. (a)	98. (a)	99. (a)	100. (a)

Model Test Paper-3

1. The site of Mohenjodaro is located on the bank of river:

(a) Ravi (b) Beas
(c) Indus (d) Sutlej

2. Who of the following was the God of morality during the Rigvedic times?

(a) Indra (b) Rudra
(c) Agni (d) Varuna

3. Where didi the Mahasamghika school arise?

(a) Bodhagaya (b) Rajagriha
(c) Sravasti (d) Vaishali

4. Who was the author of Kalpasutra?

(a) Vasumitra (b) Hemchandra
(c) Bhadrabahu (d) Sthulbhadra

5. Which among the following Hindu Painters was sent by Jahangir to portrait Shah Adbas-I of Persia?

(a) Basawan (b) Bishan Das
(c) Dasrath (d) Manohar

6. Whom did Sir Charles Napier replace as the British resident of Sindh?

(a) Alesxander Burner (b) Major James Outram
(c) Sir John Karne (d) Sir Eyer Coote

7. Which one of the following books is associated with rise of National Movement in India?

(a) Gitanjali (b) Anand Math
(c) Satyarth (d) Gita Rahasya

8. Which one of the followig statements regarding the Revolt of 1857 is not correct?

(a) The revold was supported whole heartedly by the educated, elite Indian everywhere
(b) The diverse elements which took part in the revolt were united by their hatred of British rule
(c) The role of Hindu-Muslim unity in the revolt was acknowledged by many, including British officials
(d) The revold did not spread to South India

9. Which one among the following was the primary reason behind the failure of the Young Bengal Movement in Bengal?

(a) It did not appeal to educated people
(b) Its economic programme was not popular
(c) It was too radical
(d) It did not have good leaders

10. Which one the following chronological orders of the given events is correct?

(a) The Cripps Mission — The Civil Disobedience Movement — The Cabinet Mission's Plan
(b) The Civil Disobedience Movement — The Cripps Mission — The Cabinet Mission's Plan
(c) The Cripps Mission — The Cabinet Mission's Plan — The Civil Disobedience Movement
(d) The Civil Disobeidence Movement — The Cabinet Mission's Plan — The Cripps Mission

11. Which of the following is a part of Eastern coast?

(a) Coromandal coast
(b) Konkan coast
(c) Malabar coast
(d) None of these

12. Which of the following rivers flows from south to north?

(a) Son (b) Krishna
(c) Mahanadi (d) Ganga

13. In India more than half of the production of Soyabean comes from

(a) Andhra Pradesh (b) Madhya Pradesh
(c) Maharashtra (d) Rajasthan

14. The Uttarkhand, Oak-Rhododendron are characteristic plants of—

(a) Sub-tropicla forest (b) Sub-alpine forest
(c) Tempertate forest (d) All of the above

15. As per 2011 census data, the sex ratio is

(a) 943 (b) 940
(c) 925 (d) 920

16. At what angle the hands of a clock are inclined at 15 minutes past 5?

(a) $72\frac{1}{2}^{0}$ (b) 64^{0}
(c) $58\frac{1}{2}^{0}$ (d) $67\frac{1}{2}^{0}$

17. F is the brother of A. C is the daughter of A. K is the sister of F. G is the brother of C. Who is the uncle of G?

(a) A (b) C

(c) f (d) K

18. If CONTRIBUTE is written as ETBUIRNTOC, which letter will be in the sixth place when counted from the left if POPULARISE is written in that code?

(a) E (b) A

(c) I (d) R

Directions (Qs. 19): In these questions, relationship between different elements is shown in the statements. These statements are followed by two conclusions. Give answer :

(a) If **only** Conclusion **I** follows

(b) If **only** Conclusion **II** follows

(c) It **either** Conclusion I **or** II follows

(d) If neither Conclusion I **nor** II follows

(e) If **both** Conclusions I **and** II follow

19. Statements

$D > W \geq C \leq X; C \geq L; W < K$

Conclusions

I. $X > K$

II. $L \leq W$

20. Sita is elder than Swapna. Lavanya is elder than Swapna but younger than Sita. Suvarna is younger than thoth Hari and Swapna. Swapna is elder than Hari. Who is the youngest?

(a) Sita (b) Lavanya

(c) Suvarna (d) Hari

21. 'a' divides 228 leaving a remainder 18. The biggest two-digit value of 'a' is

(a) 21 (b) 70

(c) 35 (d) 30

22. Dinesh's monthly income is four times Suresh's monthly income Suresh's monthly income is twenty percent more than Jyoti's monthly income. Jyoti's monthly income is ₹ 22,000. What is Dinesh's monthly income?

(a) ₹ 1,06,500 (b) ₹ 1,05,600

(c) ₹ 1,04,500 (d) ₹ 1,05,400

23. The average of 5 consecutive numbers is n. It the next two numbers are also included, the average of the 7 numbers will

(a) increase by 2

(b) increase by 1

(c) remain the same

(d) increase by 1.4

24. The value of

$$\left[\frac{1}{\sqrt{9}-\sqrt{8}}\right]-\left[\frac{1}{\sqrt{8}-\sqrt{7}}\right]+\left[\frac{1}{\sqrt{7}-\sqrt{6}}\right]-\left[\frac{1}{\sqrt{6}-\sqrt{5}}\right]+\left[\frac{1}{\sqrt{9}-\sqrt{8}}\right] \text{ is}$$

(a) 6 (b) 5

(c) -7 (d) -6

25. These are some parrots and some tigers in a forest. If the total number of animal heads in the forest is 858 and the total number of animal legs is 1,846, what is the number of parrots in the forest?

(a) 845 (b) 833

(c) 800 (d) 793

DIRECTIONS (Qs. 26-30): Study the following table carefully and anser the given questions.

Table shows the percentage marks obtained in five different subjects by five different students and maximum marks of each subjects respectively

Student	Hindi (80)	English (60)	History (50)	Science (100)	Math (150)
J	80	75	-	75	80
K	70	80	60	65	-
L	-	70	70	60	85
M	55	-	80	-	90
N	-	60	90	80	70

Note: Some data are missing. If require then find them first and then solve the given questions.

26. If average mark obtained by all the five students is English is 70%, then find the missing data in English

(a) 70% (b) 65%

(c) 75% (d) 80%

27. If marks obtained by J in History is 20% less than the mark obtained by K in the same subject, then find the mark obtained by J in History.

(a) 25 (b) 35

(c) 30 (d) 24

28. If N obtained 10% less mark in Hindi than that of K in the same subject, then find the approx average mark obtained by N in all the subjects.

(a) 57

(b) 63

(c) 71

(d) 75

29. If total marks obtained by M in all the five subjects is 338 and marks obtained in English is 20% less than the marks obtained by J in English, then find the mark obtained by M in Science.

(a) 75 (b) 80
(c) 83 (d) 70

30. What is the total marks obtained by all the students in Math, if marks obtained by J in Science is 20% less than that of marks obtained by K in Math?

(a) 547.5 (b) 562.5
(c) 550 (d) 438.75

DIRECTIONS (Qs. 31-35): Study the following table carefully and answer the given questions.

Profesions	Percentage of people	Percentage of females	Percentage of males
Banking	20	40	-
Law	15	20	-
Teaching	30	-	40
Engineering	25	-	30
Medical	10	60	-

The table shows the percentage of 25000 people who are involved in different professions and the percentage of female and male professionals them.

31. The total number of people in the Teaching profession is what percentage of the total number of people in the Medical profession?

(a) 175% (b) 225%
(c) 300% (d) 140%

32. What if the ratio of the total number of males in the Medical and Banking professions together to the total number of females in the same profession together?

(a) 3 : 5 (b) 7 : 5
(c) 8 : 7 (d) 7 : 8

33. The number of females in the Engineering profession are approximately what percent of the number of males in the Banking profession?

(a) 35% (b) 125%
(c) 146% (d) 153%

34. What is the ratio of the total number of males in the Banking and Medical professions together to the total number of females in the Law and Teaching professions together?

(a) 4 : 5
(b) 3 : 7
(c) 16 : 21
(d) 21 : 16

35. The total number of females in the Engineering profession is approximately what percentage more than the number of males in the Law profession?

(a) 46% (b) 51%
(c) 37% (d) 54%

DIRECTIONS (Qs. 36-40): Study the following pie-chart carefully to answer these questions.

Total Number of passengers = 8500

Percentage of Passengers

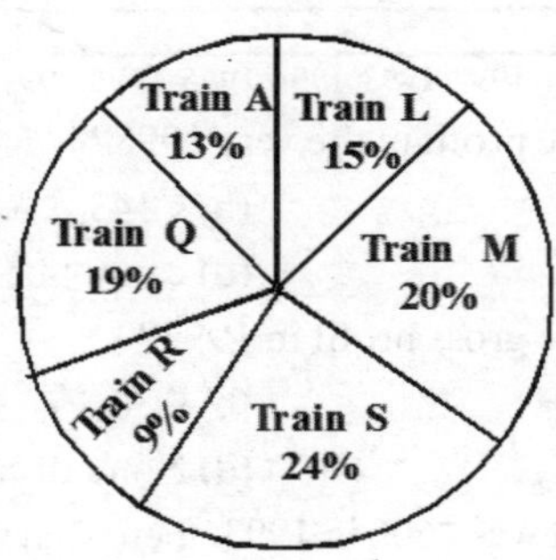

36. What was the approximate average number of passenger in Train-S, Train-M and Train-L together?

(a) 1521 (b) 1641
(c) 1651 (d) 1671

37. If in Train-R 34 percent of the passengers are females and 26 percent are children, what is the number of males in that train?

(a) 306 (b) 316
(c) 308 (d) 318

38. The number of passengers in Train-Q is approximately what percentage of the total number of passengers in train-A and Train-R?

(a) 90 (b) 70
(c) 75 (d) None of these

39. Which train has the second highest number of passengers?

(a) A (b) Q
(c) S (d) M

40. How many more per cent (approximately) number of passengers are there in Train-M as compared to the number of passengers in Train-L?

(a) 29
(b) 49
(c) 43
(d) 33

DIRECTIONS (Qs. 41-45): Study the following graph to answer these questions.

Index of sales, cost and profit

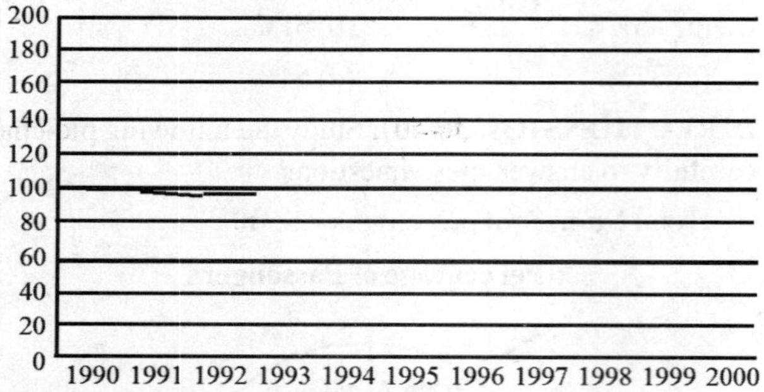

200
180
160
140
120
100
80
60
40
20
0
1990 1991 1992 1993 1994 1995 1996 1997 1998 1999 2000

41. What is the profit in the year 1998?
(a) ₹110 (b) ₹143
(c) ₹95 (d) cannot be determined

42. What is the gross profit in 1993?
(a) ₹27 (b) ₹30
(c) ₹35 (d) None of these

43. If the profit was ₹600 in 1993, then what was the profit in 1990?
(a) ₹441 (b) ₹395
(c) ₹480 (d) ₹545

44. If the base of profit index is changed to 1993 = 100, then what would be the index of profit for the year 2000?
(a) 104 (b) 100
(c) 109 (d) None of these

45. If sales were ₹1200 crore in 1990, then what were the total sales in the period 1990-1995?
(a) ₹8628 crore (b) ₹9828 crore
(c) ₹9156 crore (d) ₹8136 crore

46. Certain substances loose their electrical resistance completely at super low temperature, Such substances are called
(a) super conductors (b) semi conductors
(c) dielectrics (d) perfect conductors

47. The specific resistance of a wire varies with its —
(a) Length (b) Cross-section
(c) Mass (d) Material

48. Which one of the following atmospheric layers absorb ultraviolet rays of the sun?
(a) Troposphere (b) Startosphere
(c) Ionosphere (d) Ozonosphere

49. In nuclear reactions, there is conservation of
(a) mass only
(b) momentum only
(c) energy only
(d) mass, energy and momentum

50. Photoelectric effect is
(a) an instantaneous process
(b) delayed process
(c) emission of protons
(d) emission of neutrons

51. Aluminium is obtained by the electrolysis of pure Al_2O_3 dissolved in
(a) Bauxite (b) Cryolite
(c) Feldspar (d) Alumina

52. Complete hydrolysis of cellulose gives
(a) D-fructose (b) L-glucose
(c) D-glucose (d) L-fructose

53. Zinc is
(a) non-malleable. (b) brittle.
(c) ductile. (d) (a) and (b).

54. The only non-metal that has luster is
(a) Sulphur (b) Phosphorus
(c) Silicon (d) Iodine

55. A form of condensation that reduces visibility and causes breathing problems is
(a) Dew (b) Frost
(c) Smog (d) Mist

56. Depletion of ozone layer causes
(a) Breast cancer (b) Blood cancer
(c) Lung cancer (d) Skin cancer

57. Phosphate fertilizers when added to water leads to
(a) increased growth of decomposers
(b) reduced algal growth
(c) increased algal growth
(d) nutrient enrichment (eutorphication)

58. Which is the major air pollutant?
(a) He (b) O_2
(c) CO_2 (d) CO

59. The ozone layer is present in
(a) Stratosphere
(b) Troposphere
(c) Thermosphere
(d) Mesosphere

60. Minamata disease is due to pollution of
(a) Aresenic into the atmosphere
(b) Organic waste into drinking water
(c) Oil spill in water
(d) Industrial waste mercury into fishing water

61. In which field did India enjoy worldwide reputation during mid-18th century?

(a) Tea (b) Coffee

(c) Raw Silk (d) Cotton Textiles

62. Inclusive growth as enunciated in the Eleventh Five Year Plan does not include one, of the following:

(a) Reduction of peverty

(b) Extension of employment opportunities

(c) Strenghthening of capital market

(d) Reduction of gender inequality

63. In India, planned economy is based on

(a) Gandhian system

(b) Socialist system

(c) Capitalist system

(d) Mixed economy system

64. First Agricultural University in India was established in

(a) Jabalpur (b) Kanpur

(c) Faizabad (d) Pant Nagar

65. Which of the following recently made 17th zone of Indian Railway?

(a) Metro Rail in Kolkata

(b) South Central Railway (SCR)

(c) North Central Railway

(d) North Frontier

66. Which one among the following is a Fundamental Duties of citizens under the Consitution of India?

(a) To provide friendly cooperation to the people of the neighbouring countries

(b) To visit the monuments of national importance

(c) To defend the country and render national service when called upon to do so

(d) To know more and more about the religions of India

67. The tenth schedule of India constitution deals with

(a) Anti-defection Legislation

(b) Panchayti Raj

(c) Land Reforms

(d) Distribution of powers between the union and states

68. 'Zero Hour' in political Jargon refers to

(a) Suspended motion

(b) Question hour

(c) Adjourned time

(d) Question-answer session

69. As per the Constitution of India, what is the limit prescribed for the number of members in Legislative Assembly of a State?

(a) 350 members (b) 400 members

(c) 450 members (d) 500 members

70. What is the system of governance in the Panchayati Raj set up?

(a) Single tier structure of local self government at the village level.

(b) Two tier system of tocal self government at the village and block levels

(c) Three tier structure of local self government a the village, block and district levels

(d) Four tier system of local self government at the village block, district and in the state levels

71. Which one the following statements is not correct?

Dinar/New Dinar is the currency of:

(a) Sudan (b) Yugoslavia

(c) U.A.E (d) Tunisia

72. Which one of the following is known as the "Coffee port" of the world?

(a) Sao Paulo (b) Santos

(c) Rio de Janeiro (d) Buenos Aires

73. Which one of the following rivers does not drain into Black Sea?

(a) Volga (b) Dnieper

(c) Don (d) Danube

74. Which one of the following is not a Central University?

(a) Pondicherry

(b) Maulana Azad National Urdu University, Hyderabad

(c) Vishva Bharti, Shanti Niketan

(d) University of Madras, (Chennai)

75. National Institute of Nutrition is located at

(a) Chennai (b) Bangalore

(c) New Delhi (d) Hyderabad

76. Norman Emest Borlaug who is regarded as the father of the Green Revolution in India is from which country?

(a) United States of America

(b) Mexico

(c) Australia

(d) New Zealand

77. Merdeka Cup is associated with

(a) Hockey (b) Football

(c) Basketball (d) Badminton

78. Who among the following is an accomplished Veena player?

(a) K.R. Kumaraswamy Iyer

(b) Hariprasad Chaurasia

(c) Pannalal Ghosh

(d) Baluswami Dikshitar

79. Malik Muhammad Jayasi wrote in the Awadhi language. His famous work is an epic on which a movie was made recently. Name the book.

(a) Lilawati (b) Mughal-e-Azam

(c) Geet Govinda (d) Padmavat

80. Sports coaches receive which of the following awards?

(a) Rajiv Gandhi Khel Ratna Award

(b) Dronacharya Award

(c) Arjuna Award

(d) None of these

81. Who among the following launched 'National Urban Digital Mission'?

(a) Ravi Shankar Prasad (b) Hardeep Singh Puri

(c) Nitin Gadkari (d) Both (a) and (b)

82. Which of the following ministries is/are associalted with the recently laucnched National Urban Digital Mission (NUDM)?

(a) Ministry of Housing and Urban Affairs

(b) Ministry of Electronics and Information Technology.

(c) Ministry of Skill Development and Enterpreneurship

(d) Both (a) and (b)

83. Recently, which of the followign states has signed an MoU with SIDBI for the development of the MSME ecosystem in the state?

(a) Karnataka (b) Andhra Pradesh

(c) Maharashtra (d) Modhya Pradesh

84. Who among the followign dedicated the INDMAX Unit at Indian Oil's Bongaigaon Refinery to the nation?

(a) PM Narendra Modi

(b) Amit Shah

(c) Dharmendra Pradhan

(d) Piyush Goyal

85. Who among the following inaugurated 26th 'Hunar Haat'?

(a) Vice President Venkaiah Naidu

(b) Amit Shah

(c) Hardeep Singh Puri

(d) Rajnath Singh

86. What was the theme of the 26th edition of 'Hunar Haat' 2021 organised recently?

(a) Atma Nirbhar Bharat

(b) Local for Vocal

(c) Local to Global

(d) Both (a) and (b)

87. Who among the following was awarded Dadasaheb Phalke International Film Festival Awards 2021 for Outstanding Contribution to the Indian Film Industry?

(a) Jeetendra (b) Dharmendra

(c) Shatrughan Sinha (d) Dilip Kumar

88. Who won Dadasaheb Phalke Award 2021 in the 'Critic's Best Actor' category?

(a) Sushant Singh Rajput

(b) Akshay Kumar

(c) Ajay Devgun

(d) Kay Kay Menon

89. SFURTI clusters is an initiative of which of the following ministries?

(a) Ministry of Education

(b) Ministry of MSME

(c) Ministry of Tribal Affairs

(d) Ministry of Food Processing Industries

90. As per NSO, India's GDP to contract by ___% in FY 2020-21?

(a) 7.7% (b) 8%

(c) 7.5% (d) 8.3%

DIRECTIONS (Qs. 91-93): Underline the pronoun and state its kind

91. He killed himself.

92. I met her yesterday.

93. She wantts to go to the market.

DIRECTIONS (Qs. 94-95): Supply the proper form (Comparative or Superlative) of the adjectives given in the brackets.

94. Is your father .... now. (well)

95. There is no animal ....than the dog. (faithful)

निर्देश : दिए गए विकल्पों में से सही विकल्प चुनिए।

96. 'टांग अड़ाना' मुहावरे का अर्थ है–

(a) हार जाना

(b) भाग जाना

(b) बाधा डालना

(d) घबरा जाना

97. निरर्थक का सही संधि विच्छेद है-

(a) निर + अर्थक (b) निर: + अर्थक
(c) नि: + अर्थक (d) निरा+अर्थक

98. 'ऋजु' शब्द का विलोम है-

(a) प्रवर (b) वक्र
(b) निर्गत (d) आवृत

99. सांझ और रात के बीच का समय-

(a) मार्तड (b) पूर्वाह्
(c) गोधूलि (d) ऊष्मा

100. 'पुत्री' का पर्यायवाची शब्द है-

(a) भार्या (b) किसलय
(c) सुता (d) लिप्सा

Answers/उत्तरमाला

1. (c)	2. (d)	3. (d)	4. (c)	5. (b)	6. (b)	7. (b)	8. (a)	9. (c)	10. (b)
11. (a)	12. (a)	13. (b)	14. (c)	15. (a)	16. (d)	17. (c)	18. (a)	19. (b)	20. (c)
21. (b)	22. (b)	23. (b)	24. (b)	25. (d)	26. (b)	27. (d)	28. (b)	29. (c)	30. (a)
31. (c)	32. (c)	33. (c)	34. (c)	35. (a)	36. (d)	37. (a)	38. (d)	39. (d)	40. (d)
41. (a)	42. (d)	43. (d)	44. (a)	45. (b)	46. (a)	47. (d)	48. (d)	49. (c)	50. (a)
51. (b)	52. (c)	53. (d)	54. (d)	55. (c)	56. (d)	57. (d)	58. (d)	59. (a)	60. (d)
61. (d)	62. (c)	63. (b)	64. (d)	65. (a)	66. (c)	67. (a)	68. (d)	69. (d)	70. (c)
71. (a)	72. (b)	73. (a)	74. (d)	75. (d)	76. (a)	77. (b)	78. (a)	79. (d)	80. (b)
81. (d)	82. (d)	83. (b)	84. (a)	85. (d)	86. (b)	87. (b)	88. (a)	89. (b)	90. (b)
91. (*)	92. (*)	93. (*)	94. (*)	95. (*)	96. (c)	97. (c)	98. (b)	99. (c)	100. (c)

UP PET 2021 Shift-1 (Series A)

1. What is the correct chronological order in which the following rulers ruled in India ?

I. Sher Shah Suri   II. Akbar

III. Ala-ud-din Khilji   IV. Iltutmish

(a) IV, I, III, II   (b) IV, III, I, II

(c) I, II, III, IV   (d) III, IV, I, II

2. Which one of the following saints was contemporary of Shivaji ?

(a) Tukaram   (b) Chaitanya

(c) Namdev   (d) Shankaracharya

3. Who was the first Governor-General of Bengal?

(a) Lord Clive   (b) Lord Warren Hastings

(c) Lord Lytton   (d) Lord Ripon

4. Charakasamhita is a work on

(a) Polity   (b) Medicine

(c) Architecture   (d) Mathematics

5. Which one of the following pairs is incorrectly matched ?

(a) B.C. 261 – The Kalinga War

(b) A.D. 78 – Commencement of Saka Era

(c) A.D. 622 – Commencement of the Muslim Era

(d) A.D. 1709 – Death of Aurangzeb

6. Who among the following is known as the "Grand Old Man" of India ?

(a) Dadabhai Naoroji   (b) W.C. Bannerjee

(c) Pherozeshah Mehta   (d) Surendranath Bannerjee

7. Two Home Rule Leagues were started in 1915-16 under the leadership of

(a) Annie Besant and Lokmanya Tilak

(b) Tilak and Lala Lajpat Roy

(c) Tilak and Bipin Chandra Pal

(d) Tilak and Aurobindo Ghosh

8. Match the following :

A. Brahmo Samaj	1. Swami Vivekanand
B. Ramakrishna Mission	2. Dayanand Saraswati
C. Arya Samaj	3. Ram Mohan Roy
D. Satyashodhak Samaj	4. K. Sridharalu Naidu
	5. Jyotirao Phule

	A	B	C	D
(a)	2	3	5	1
(b)	3	1	2	4
(c)	3	1	2	5
(d)	3	2	1	5

9. Who gave the slogan 'Do or Die' ?

(a) Sardar Patel

(b) Jawaharlal Nehru

(c) Subhash Chandra Bose

(d) Mahatma Gandhi

10. When Subhash Chandra Bose resigned from the Presidentship of Indian National Congress, the seat was offered to

(a) Jawaharlal Nehru   (b) Pattabhi Sitaramaiah

(c) Dr. Rajendra Prasad   (d) J.B. Kripalani

11. The Salal hydro-electric project is located across the river

(a) Jhelum   (b) Ravi

(c) Chenab   (d) Beas

12. Vernal Equinox takes place on

(a) 21st March   (b) 18th June

(c) 23rd September   (d) 22nd December

13. The 'Khetri Project' in Rajasthan is famous for the production of

(a) Zinc   (b) Steel

(c) Copper   (d) Aluminium

14. The Kaziranga National Park is situated in

(a) Madhya Pradesh   (b) Assam

(c) West Bengal   (d) Kerala

15. Which of the following are rivers of the Himalayan river system ?

I. Kaveri   II. Ganga

III. Brahmaputra   IV. Godavari

(a) I and II   (b) II and III

(c) III and IV   (d) II and IV

16. Bank rate means

(a) Interest rate charged by moneylenders

(b) Interest rate charged by scheduled banks

(c) Rate of profit of banking institutions

(d) Official rate of interest charged by the Central bank of the country

17. If RBI reduces the cash reserve ratio, what will happen to the credit creation ?

(a) There will be no impact.

(b) It will decrease.

(c) It will increase.

(d) None of these

18. In which of the following type of economies, resources are owned privately and the main objective behind economic activities is profit-making ?

(a) Capitalist (b) Socialist

(c) Mixed (d) Global

19. The One Hundred rupee note bears the signature of :

(a) RBI Governor (b) President of India

(c) Finance Minister (d) Finance Secretary

20. What is the full form of FEMA ?

(a) Funds Exchange Media Agency

(b) Foreign Exchange Management Act

(c) Finance and Export Management Association

(d) Foreign Export Market Agency

21. The 'Public Health and Sanitation' is included in Constitution of India in

(a) State List (b) Concurrent List

(c) Union List (d) None of these

22. Panchayati Raj System in India is laid down under

(a) Fundamental Rights

(b) Fundamental Duties

(c) Directive Principles of State Policy

(d) None of these

23. Right to Education is a fundamental right, which is related to :

(a) Article 21A (b) Article 19

(c) Articles 29 and 30 (d) None of these

24. Who among the following moved the 'Objective Resolution' in the Constituent Assembly ?

(a) Jawaharlal Nehru (b) Mahatma Gandhi

(c) B.R. Ambedkar (d) B.N. Rao

25. In which Article of Indian Constitution, the interests of minorities are covered ?

(a) Article 21 (b) Article 24

(c) Article 29 (d) None of these

26. Current carriers in solid conductors are

(a) Protons (b) Neutrons

(c) Free Electrons (d) None of these

27. Light year is a unit of measurement of

(a) Speed of Rocket measured in a year

(b) Distance travelled by sound in a vacuum during one year

(c) Distance travelled by light in a vacuum during one year

(d) Speed of Aeroplane

28. The chemical name of Bleaching powder is also

(a) Calcium sulphate ($CaSO_4$)

(b) Calcium oxychloride ($CaOCl_2$)

(c) Sodium bicarbonate ($NaHCO_3$)

(d) Sodium chloride ($NaCl$)

29. The percentage of pure gold in 18-carat gold is

(a) 60% (b) 75%

(c) 80% (d) 100%

30. Orange contains abundance of

(a) Vitamin C (b) Vitamin A

(c) Vitamin B (d) None of these

31. $\sqrt{\frac{?}{196}} = \frac{72}{56}$

(a) 18 (b) 14

(c) 324 (d) 212

32. $\frac{885 \times 885 \times 885 + 115 \times 115 \times 115}{885 \times 885 + 115 \times 115 \times 885 \times 115} =$

(a) 115 (b) 770

(c) 885 (d) 1000

33. $\frac{\sqrt{5}-\sqrt{3}}{\sqrt{5}+\sqrt{3}}$ is equal to

(a) $4+\sqrt{15}$ (b) $4-\sqrt{15}$

(c) $\frac{1}{2}$ (d) 1

34. On decreasing the price of T.V. sets by 30%, its sale is increased by 20%. What is the effect on the revenue received by the shopkeeper ?

(a) 10% increase (b) 10% decrease

(c) 16% increase (d) 16% decrease

35. The average age of four players is 18.5 years. If the age of the coach is also included, the average age increases by 20%. The age of the coach is :

(a) 28 years (b) 31 years

(c) 34 years (d) 37 years

36. 'एकल' का विलोम शब्द है

(a) बहुल (b) पर्याप्त

(c) उपयुक्त (d) अकेला

37. दर्प का पर्यायवाची कौन सा है ?

(a) तिरस्कार (b) अहंकार

(c) व्यथा (d) स्वाभिमान

38. 'मन को हरने वाला' वाक्य के लिए नीचे दिए गए विकल्प में से एक शब्द चुनिए :

(a) मर्मान्तक (b) मनोहर

(c) मदमस्त (d) मदमयी

39. 'गागर में सागर भरना' मुहावरे का अर्थ लिखिए ।

(a) दोहों की रचना करना (b) थोड़े में बहुत कहना

(c) बहुत बोलना (d) कम बोलना

40. शुद्ध वर्तनी का चयन कीजिए ।

(a) महत्वकांक्षा (b) माहत्वाकांक्षा

(c) महत्त्वाकांक्षा (d) महात्वाकांक्षा

Directions (Q. 41-43): Read the passage carefully and answer the corresponding questions :

Nehru's was a many-sided personality. He enjoyed reading and writing books as much as he enjoyed fighting political and social evils or resisting tyranny. In him the scientist and the humanist were held in perfect balance. While he kept looking at social problems from a scientific standpoint, he never forgot that we should nourish the total man. As a scientist, he refused to believe, in a benevolent power interested in men's affairs; but, as a self- proclaimed non-believer, he loved affirming his faith in life and the beauty of nature. Children he adored. Unlike Wordsworth, he did not see them trailing clouds of glory from their recent sojourn in heaven. He saw them as blossoms of promise and renewal, the only hope for mankind.

41. A *many-sided personality* means

(a) a complex personality

(b) a secretive personality

(c) a person having varied interests

(d) a capable person.

42. Pt. Nehru enjoyed

(a) reading and writing books.

(b) fighting political and social evils.

(c) resisting tyranny.

(d) doing all these and much more.

43. Which of the following statements reflects Pt. Nehru's point of view ?

(a) Humanism is more important than Science.

(b) Science is supreme and Humanism is subordinate to it.

(c) Science and Humanism are equally important.

(d) There is no common ground

44. Give Synonym for the following :

Famous

(a) Awful (b) Poor

(c) Popular (d) Steady

45. Give Antonym for the following :

Transparent

(a) Obvious (b) Limpid

(c) Opaque (d) Clear

46. Select the related word from the given alternatives :

Ornithologist : Birds :: Anthropologist : ?

(a) Plants (b) Animals

(c) Mankind (d) Environment

47. Choose the word which is least like the other words in the group.

(a) Curd (b) Butter

(c) Oil (d) Cheese

48. In a certain code, PRODUCTIONS is written as QQPCVEUHPMT. How is ORIENTATION written in that code ?

(a) PQJDOVBSJNO (b) PQJDOUBUJPO

(c) PSJFOVBSJNO (d) NSHFMVBSJNO

49. Pointing towards Rita, Nikhil said, "I am the only son of her mother's son." How is Rita related to Nikhil ?

(a) Aunt (b) Niece

(c) Mother (d) Cousin

50. If the 25th of August in a year is Thursday, the number of Mondays in that month is

(a) 3 (b) 4

(c) 5 (d) 6

51. In which of the following cities Light House Project is not implemented ?

(a) Agartala (b) Ranchi

(c) Chennai (d) Patna

52. Which Indian telecom company is world's fifth strongest brand ?

(a) Reliance-Jio (b) Bharti Airtel

(c) Idea (d) Vodafone

53. The Project BOLD (Bamboo Oasis on Lands in Drought) was recently launched from which state in India ?
(a) Rajasthan (b) Haryana
(c) Bihar (d) Madhya Pradesh

54. Which is first country to get free COVID- 19 vaccines through the COVAX scheme of United Nations ?
(a) Ghana (b) Nigeria
(c) Africa (d) Sudan

55. Who is the second Indian born American woman astronaut to fly to space ?
(a) Sirisha Bandla (b) Shreya Badla
(c) Ritu Karidhal (d) Kalpana Chawla

56. Name the Indian wrestler, who gets two- year ban for doping recently.
(a) Yogeshwar Dutt (b) Sumit Malik
(c) Ravinder Singh (d) Pawan Kumar

57. Which State in India is first state to implement an end to end e-Cabinet System ?
(a) Uttar Pradesh (b) Himachal Pradesh
(c) Goa (d) Haryana

58. Which Indian ministry recently launched UDISE+ for 2019-2020?
(a) Ministry of Health
(b) Ministry of Education
(c) Ministry of Finance
(d) Ministry of Home Affairs

59. Smartphone maker 'Vivo' appointed which cricketer as its brand ambassador?
(a) Virat Kohli (b) M.S. Dhoni
(c) Ishant Sharma (d) Shikhar Dhawan

60. Artificial Intelligence (AI) based portal 'SUPACE' launched for which court in India?
(a) Delhi High Court (b) Gujarat High Court
(c) Supreme Court (d) None of these

61. How many Indian States share their boundary with Nepal ?
(a) Five (b) Four
(c) Three (d) Two

62. Which of the following is the capital of Costa Rica ?
(a) Beijing (b) San Jose
(c) Delhi (d) Dhaka

63. Which among the following is the official language of Union Territory of Lakshadweep?
(a) Tamil (b) Malayalam
(c) Great Andamanese (d) Sinhala

64. As per Constitution of India, what is the maximum strength (number of members) of the Lok Sabha ?
(a) 530 (b) 540
(c) 550 (d) 552

65. When is 'Hindi Diwas' celebrated ?
(a) September 14 (b) October 1
(c) November 2 (d) October 3

66. Which of the following countries is not a member of SAARC?
(a) Nepal (b) Bangladesh
(c) Afghanistan (d) Myanmar

67. In which of the following places Ajanta- Ellora caves are situated ?
(a) Bengaluru (b) Delhi
(c) Aurangabad (d) Lucknow

68. Onam is the cultural festival of which Indian State/ UT?
(a) Assam (b) Kerala
(c) Tamil Nadu (d) Karnataka

69. Which of the following planets is closest to the Sun ?
(a) Earth (b) Moon
(c) Mars (d) Mercury

70. Who was the first Asian Winner of Nobel Prize ?
(a) C.V. Raman (b) Rajiv Gandhi
(c) Rabindranath Tagore (d) Mother Teresa

निर्देश (प्र. 71-75) : निम्नलिखित गद्यांश को ध्यानपूर्वक पढ़िए तथा उस पर आधारित प्रश्नों के उत्तर चुनिए :

धरातल से युद्ध की विभीषिकाओं को सदा-सदा के लिए समाप्त करने के लिए गाँधीजी ने विश्व को अहिंसा रूपी अस्त्र प्रदान किया। गाँधीजी कहा करते थे कि प्रेम और अहिंसा के द्वारा विश्व के कठोर से कठोर हृदय को भी कोमल बनाया जा सकता है। उन्होंने इन सिद्धान्तों का परीक्षण भी किया और वे नितान्त सफल सिद्ध हुए। हिंसा से हिंसा बढ़ती है, घृणा, घृणा को जन्म देती है और प्रेम से प्रेम की अभिवृद्धि होती है। अत: यह निश्चित है कि बिना प्रेम और अहिंसा के विश्व में शान्ति स्थापित नहीं हो सकती। शान्ति के अभाव में मानव जाति का विकास सम्भव नहीं। प्रत्येक राष्ट्र का स्वर्णिम-युग वही कहा जाता है, जबकि वहाँ पूर्ण शांति और सुख रहा हो तथा उत्तमोत्तम रचनात्मक कार्य किए जाते हों। भौतिक दृष्टि से व्यापार और कृषि की उन्नति भी शांतिकाल में ही सम्भव होती है, अत: हम यदि विश्व का कल्याण चाहते हैं तो हमें युद्ध का बहिष्कार करना ही होगा। अहिंसा और प्रेम की भावना से विश्व में शान्ति स्थापित करनी होगी, तभी विश्व में सुखमय एवं शांतिमय राज्य की स्थापना सम्भव होगी।

71. विश्व में शांति क्यों आवश्यक है?

(a) मानव जाति के विकास के लिए

(b) उत्तमोत्तम रचनात्मक कार्य के लिए

(c) व्यापार और कृषि की उन्नति के लिए

(d) कठोर से कठोर हृदय को भी कोमल बनाने के लिए

72. विश्व शांति की स्थापना के लिए सबसे आवश्यक है।

(a) हिंसा और भय (b) अहिंसा और प्रेम

(c) आत्मीयता और समीपता (d) परिश्रम और ज्ञान

73. कठोर से कठोर हृदय को भी कोमल बनाया जा सकता है

(a) सत्य पालन द्वारा (b) मौन पालन द्वारा

(c) अहिंसा द्वारा (d) भय द्वारा

74. किसी भी राष्ट्र के स्वर्णिम-युग के प्रमुख तत्त्व हैं

(a) धन और वैभव

(b) धन और सम्मान

(c) आध्यात्म और उपासना

(d) शान्ति, सुख और रचनात्मक कार्य

75. 'नितान्त' शब्द का उपयुक्त पर्याय है

(a) भलीभाँति (b) बिलकुल

(c) विधिवत् (d) निम्न

निर्देश (प्र. 76-80) : निम्नलिखित गद्यांश को ध्यानपूर्वक पढ़िए तथा उस पर आधारित प्रश्नों के उत्तर चुनिए :

विज्ञान आज के मानव-जीवन का अविभाज्य एवं घनिष्ठ अंग बन गया है। मानव-जीवन का कोई भी क्षेत्र विज्ञान के अश्रुतपूर्व आविष्कारों से अछूता नहीं रहा। इसी से आधुनिक युग विज्ञान का युग कहलाता है। आज विज्ञान ने पुरुष और नारी, साहित्यकार और राजनीतिज्ञ, उद्योगपति और कृषक, पूँजीपति और श्रमिक, चिकित्सक और सैनिक, अभियन्ता और शिक्षक तथा धर्मज्ञ और तत्त्वज्ञ सभी को और सभी क्षेत्रों में किसी न किसी रूप में अपने अप्रतिम प्रदेय से अनुगृहीत किया है। आज समूचा परिवेश विज्ञानमय हो गया है। विज्ञान के चरण गृहिणी के रसोईघर से लेकर बड़ी-बड़ी प्राचीरों वाले भवनों और अट्टालिकाओं में ही दृष्टिगत नहीं होते, प्रत्युत वे स्थल और जल की सीमाओं को लाँघकर अन्तरिक्ष में भी गतिशील हैं। वस्तुत: विज्ञान अद्यतन मानव की सबसे बड़ी शक्ति बन गया है। इसके बल से मनुष्य प्रकृति और प्राणिजगत का शिरोमणि बन सका है। विज्ञान के अनुग्रह से वह सभी प्रकार की सुविधाओं और सम्पदाओं का स्वामित्व प्राप्त कर चुका है। अब वह ऋत-ऋतुओं के प्रकोप से भयाक्रांत एवं संत्रस्त नहीं है। विद्युत ने उसे आलोकित किया है, उष्णता और शीतलता दी है, बटन दबाकर किसी भी कार्य को सम्पन्न करने की ताकत भी दी है। मनोरंजन के विविध साधन उसे सुलभ हैं। यातायात एवं संचार के साधनों के विकास से समय और स्थान की दूरियाँ बहुत कम हो गई हैं और समूचा विश्व एक परिवार-सा लगने लगा है। कृषि और उद्योग के क्षेत्र में उत्पादन की तीव्र वृद्धि होने के कारण आज दुनिया पहले से अधिक धन-धान्य से सम्पन्न है। शिक्षा और चिकित्सा के क्षेत्र में विज्ञान की देन अभिनन्दनीय है। विज्ञान के सहयोग से मनुष्य धरती और समुद्र के अनेक रहस्य हस्तामलक करके अब अन्तरिक्ष लोक में प्रवेश कर चुका है। सर्वोपरि, विज्ञान ने मनुष्य को बौद्धिक विकास प्रदान किया है और वैज्ञानिक चिन्तन- पद्धति दी है। वैज्ञानिक चिन्तन-पद्धति से मनुष्य अन्धविश्वासों और रूढ़ि-परम्पराओं से मुक्त होकर स्वस्थ एवं संतुलित ढंग से सोच-विचार कर सकता है और यथार्थ एवं सम्यक जीवन जी सकता है। इससे मनुष्य के मन को युगों के अन्धविश्वासों, भ्रमपूर्ण और दकियानूसी विचारों, भय और अज्ञानता से मुक्ति मिली है। विज्ञान की यह देन स्तुत्य है। मानव को चाहिए कि वह विज्ञान की इस समग्र देन को रचनात्मक कार्यों में सुनियोजित करे।

76. विज्ञान मानव की सबसे बड़ी शक्ति इसलिए कही गई है क्योंकि इसके बल से मनुष्य

(a) विद्युत शक्ति का स्वामी है।

(b) प्रकृति और प्राणिजगत का सिरमौर है।

(c) सभी भौतिक सुविधाओं से सम्पन्न है।

(d) अन्तरिक्ष के क्षेत्र में हस्तक्षेप कर सकता है।

77. वैज्ञानिक चिन्तन-पद्धति ने मनुष्य का सबसे बड़ा उपकार यह किया है कि उसे मुक्ति मिली है

(a) सन्तुलित अनुचिन्तन से

(b) पुरानी शिष्ट औपचारिकताओं से

(c) भ्रमपूर्ण रूढ़िवादी विचारणा से

(d) प्राचीन सांस्कृतिक परम्पराओं से

78. विश्व के परिवारवत् लगने का प्रमुख कारण है

(a) यातायात एवं संचार साधनों का विकास

(b) विज्ञान की गतिशील शक्तियाँ

(c) विज्ञान की जीवन से घनिष्ठता

(d) विश्व-बन्धुत्व की भावना का विकास

79. हस्तामलक शब्द से अभिप्रेत है

(a) अस्पष्ट परन्तु सायास बोधगम्य

(b) पास में रखे आँवले की तरह

(c) हाथी के लिए आँवले की तरह

(d) स्पष्ट और अनायास बोधगम्य

80. 'वैज्ञानिक-चिन्तन' पदबंध से आशय है

(a) परम्परागत चिन्तन

(b) भावात्मक चिन्तन

(c) वैज्ञानिकों द्वारा किया गया चिन्तन

(d) स्वस्थ एवं सन्तुलित चिन्तन

Directions (Q. 81-85) : The questions are based on the below shown graph. Answer these questions.

The graph shows the ratio of marks of History to Geography of 7 students in an examination.

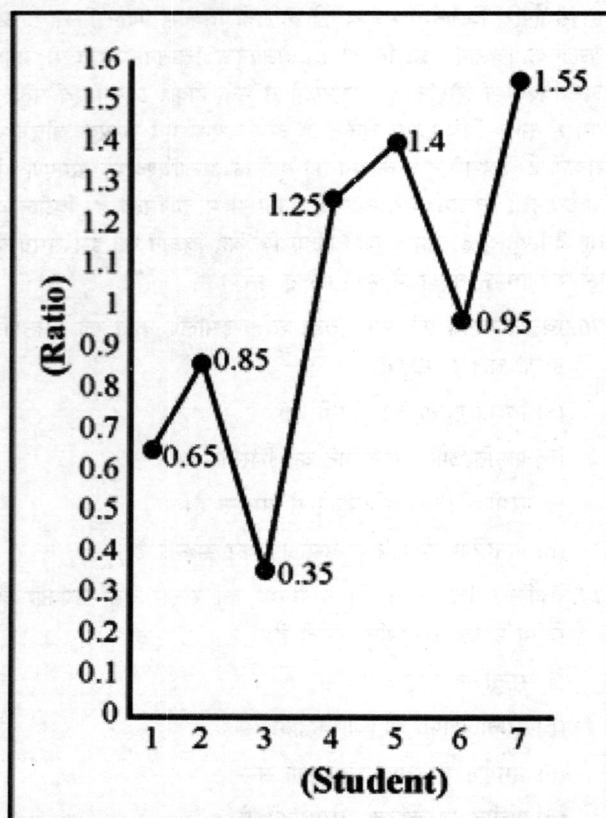

81. How many students got more marks in History than in Geography ?

(a) 2 (b) 3
(c) 4 (d) 5

82. Which of the following students got less marks in History than in Geography ?

(a) 1, 3, 5, 6 (b) 1, 2, 3, 6
(c) 1, 4, 5, 7 (d) 4, 5, 7

83. Percentage increase of marks in Geography from student 3 to 4 is –

(a) 15 (b) 20
(c) 90 (d) Insufficient data

84. The difference of the maximum ratio and minimum ratio of History/Geography is

(a) 0.45 (b) 0.50
(c) 0.90 (d) 1.20

85. Student 4 got 60 marks in Geography. His marks in History are –

(a) 48 (b) 68
(c) 75 (d) None of these

Directions (Q. 86-90) : Study the graph and answer the following questions :

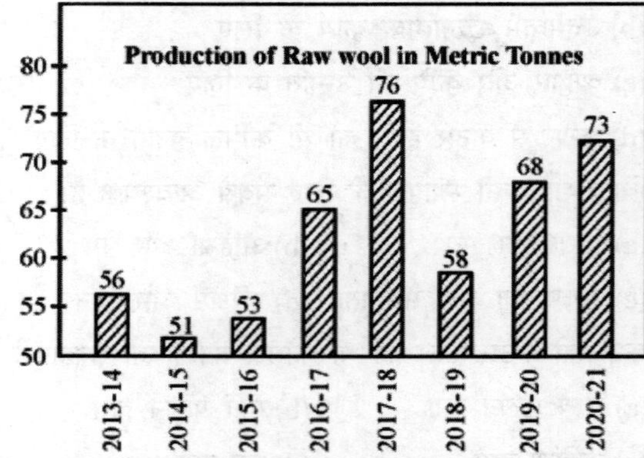

86. The maximum rise in the production of raw wool was in the year :

(a) 2017-18 (b) 2020-21
(c) 2016-17 (d) 2019-20

87. During the last four years the production of raw wool increased by% on the production of the first four years.

(a) 26.8 (b) 22.2
(c) 19.8 (d) 25.0

88. The average production during the eight years was.

(a) 67.2 MT (b) 62.5 MT
(c) 50.0 MT (d) 52.8 MT

89. The maximum percentage decrease of production over the previous year was in the year :

(a) 2018-19 (b) 2017-18
(c) 2013-14 (d) 2014-15

90. The production of raw wool in 2014-15 was of the production in 2019-20.

(a) $\frac{1}{3}$ (b) $\frac{2}{3}$
(c) $\frac{1}{2}$ (d) $\frac{3}{4}$

Directions (Q. 91-95) : Read the following table and answer the questions given below it.

Yearly Commission Earned by Five Salesmen

(Year) (Salesman)	2015	2016	2017	2018	2019	2020
A	27,350	28,500	25,200	29,800	24,600	27,000
B	26,850	27,900	27,400	28,000	28,500	29,000
C	26,200	27,800	28,200	29,100	29,400	30,000
D	27,850	30,040	29,800	30,060	29,800	32,000
E	28,640	29,000	28,750	30,000	29,750	29,700
(Total)	1,36,890	1,43,240	1,39,350	1,46,960	1,42,050	1,47,700

91. In which year commission earned by the salesman C showed the highest increase that of the preceding year?

(a) 2016 (b) 2017
(c) 2018 (d) 2019

92. In the year 2018 the commission of B was approximately what percent of the total commission earned by all salesmen in that year?

(a) 19.05 (b) 98
(c) 80 (d) None of these

93. Which salesman's commission in 2018 show the highest increase over that in 2015 ?

(a) A (b) B
(c) D (d) C

94. In which of the following year was the difference between the highest and lowest commission earned by any salesman maximum?

(a) 2017 (b) 2018
(c) 2019 (d) 2020

95. In the year 2019, commission earned by salesman D was approximately what percent of commission earned by A?

(a) 18 (b) 21
(c) 52 (d) None of these

Directions (Q. 96-100) : Study the table and answer the questions given below :

Number of accounts opened (in hundreds) in four Share broker in various months

Share Broker	May	June	July	Aug.	Sept.
Angel	25	28	35	65	55
Sharekhan	22	18	32	30	45
Zerodha	30	45	50	35	40
Tradebull	35	42	45	50	60

96. In which of the following months is the average of the number of opened accounts the maximum ?

(a) June (b) September
(c) August (d) May

97. The number of accounts opened in Aug. is approximately what per cent more or less than the number of accounts opened in June ?

(a) 33.5 (b) 35.3
(c) 34.6 (d) 40

98. What is the ratio of the number of accounts opened in Angel to that opened in Zerodha from May to September ?

(a) 1.5 (b) 0.75
(c) 2.25 (d) 1.04

99. In which Share broker is the average number of accounts opened the maximum ?

(a) Angel (b) Sharekhan
(c) Tradebull (d) Zerodha

100. The average number of accounts opened in Tradebull is approximate what per cent more or less than the average number of accounts opened in Sharekhan ?

(a) 57.82
(b) 60
(c) 45.90
(d) 50.69

Answers

1. (b)	**2.** (a)	**3.** (b)	**4.** (b)	**5.** (d)	**6.** (a)	**7.** (a)	**8.** (c)	**9.** (d)	**10.** (c)
11. (c)	**12.** (a)	**13.** (c)	**14.** (b)	**15.** (b)	**16.** (d)	**17.** (c)	**18.** (a)	**19.** (a)	**20.** (b)
21. (a)	**22.** (c)	**23.** (a)	**24.** (a)	**25.** (c)	**26.** (c)	**27.** (c)	**28.** (b)	**29.** (b)	**30.** (a)
31. (c)	**32.** (d)	**33.** (b)	**34.** (d)	**35.** (d)	**36.** (a)	**37.** (b)	**38.** (b)	**39.** (b)	**40.** (c)
41. (c)	**42.** (d)	**43.** (c)	**44.** (c)	**45.** (c)	**46.** (c)	**47.** (c)	**48.** (a)	**49.** (a)	**50.** (c)
51. (d)	**52.** (a)	**53.** (a)	**54.** (a)	**55.** (a)	**56.** (b)	**57.** (b)	**58.** (b)	**59.** (a)	**60.** (c)
61. (a)	**62.** (b)	**63.** (b)	**64.** (d)	**65.** (a)	**66.** (d)	**67.** (c)	**68.** (b)	**69.** (d)	**70.** (c)
71. (a)	**72.** (b)	**73.** (c)	**74.** (d)	**75.** (b)	**76.** (b)	**77.** (c)	**78.** (a)	**79.** (d)	**80.** (d)
81. (b)	**82.** (b)	**83.** (d)	**84.** (d)	**85.** (c)	**86.** (c)	**87.** (b)	**88.** (b)	**89.** (a)	**90.** (d)
91. (a)	**92.** (a)	**93.** (d)	**94.** (c)	**95.** (d)	**96.** (b)	**97.** (b)	**98.** (b)	**99.** (c)	**100.** (a)

UP PET 2021 Shift-2 (Series A)

1. In which order did the following come toIndia?

I. Thomas Roe

II. Fa-hien

III. Hiuen-Tsang

(a) I, II, III (b) II, I, III

(c) II, III, I (d) III, I, II

2. Siraj-ud-daula was defeated by British in the battle of:

(a) Buxar (b) Plassey

(c) Wandiwash (d) None of these

3. Who among the following was the great protagonist of the 'Doctrine of Lapse' ?

(a) Lord Wellesley (b) Lord Dalhousie

(c) Lord Minto (d) Lord Hastings

4. In Indian History who was Dhanvantari ?

(a) A famous general of Chandragupta Maurya

(b) A noted physician who adorned the court of Chandragupta Vikramaditya

(c) A famous dramatist who lived during the time of Harsha

(d) None of these

5. "Indica" which is an account of Mauryan India was authored by

(a) Megasthenes (b) Fa-hien

(c) Hiuen-Tsang (d) None of these

6. The Simon Commission first visited India in the year

(a) 1925 (b) 1926

(c) 1919 (d) 1928

7. In which session, the Indian National Congress passed the historic "Poorna Swaraj"(complete independence) resolution ?

(a) Bombay (b) Lahore

(c) Karachi (d) Lucknow

8. Match the following :

A. Indian National Army	1. Lala Hardayal
B. Ghadar Party	2. Subhash Chandra Bose
C. Mitra Mela	3. V.D. Savarkar
D. Home Rule League	4. Annie Besant

	A	B	C	D
(a)	1	2	3	4
(b)	2	1	3	4
(c)	3	4	1	2
(d)	4	2	1	3

9. Who among the following opposed Mahatma Gandhi's association with the Khilafat movement ?

(a) Khan Abdul Ghaffar Khan

(b) Fazlul Haque

(c) Mohammed Ali Jinnah

(d) Abul Kalam Azad

10. Which of the following revolutionary groups was involved in Kakori Conspiracy Case ?

(a) Ghadar Party

(b) Anushilan Samiti

(c) Abhinav Bharat Group

(d) Hindustan Republican Association

11. The Nagarjunasagar Dam has been built across the river

(a) Godavari (b) Krishna

(c) Ganga (d) Cauvery

12. The Mt. Everest was first scaled in the year

(a) 1951 (b) 1953

(c) 1955 (d) 1958

13. The name of the bird sanctuary/national park at Bharatpur is

(a) Bhensroadgarh Sanctuary

(b) Darrah Sanctuary

(c) Keoladeo Ghana National Parks

(d) Ghatprabha Sanctuary

14. The source of iron ore for Bhilai Steel Plant is

(a) Dalli-Rajhara (b) Korba

(c) Umaria (d) Rajnandgaon

15. Which of the following passes and ocations is/are **wrongly matched** ?

1. Zojila and Burzil – Jammu and Kashmir
2. Bara Lapcha La and Shipki La – Uttar Pradesh
3. Thaga La, Niti Pass and Lipu Lekh – Himachal Pradesh
4. Nathu La and Jelep La – Sikkim

(a) 1 and 2 (b) 2 and 3

(c) 3 and 4 (d) 1, 2 and 3

16. Private investment will be most likely to be increased as a result of a rise in
(a) The rate of interest
(b) The price of shares
(c) Expected yield on new capital
(d) Personal taxation

17. The agency estimating the National Income of India is
(a) RBI
(b) NITI Aayog
(c) Ministry of Finance
(d) Central Statistical Organization

18. What is another name for the Service Sector?
(a) Tertiary (b) Primary
(c) Secondary (d) Agriculture

19. Who is known as father of White Revolution in India ?
(a) Balwant Rai Mehta (b) Dr. Verghese Kurian
(c) M.S. Swaminathan (d) Norman Edburg

20. Who was the Prime Minister during economic reforms 1991 in India ?
(a) P.V. Narsimha Rao (b) Atal Bihari Vajpayee
(c) Dr. Manmohan Singh (d) None of these

21. Which one of the following is not included in the state list in the Constitution of India ?
(a) Police (b) Law and Order
(c) Prison (d) Criminal Procedure Code

22. Which one of the following is **not** a salient feature of the Constitution of India ?
(a) Quasi federal structure
(b) Committed judiciary
(c) Distribution of powers
(d) Written Constitution and Supremacy of the Constitution

23. What ensures economic justice to Indian citizens ?
(a) Fundamental Rights
(b) Fundamental Duties
(c) Directive Principles of State Policy
(d) None of these

24. Which Article of the Indian Constitution directs the state governments to organize village panchayats ?
(a) Article 38 (b) Article 40
(c) Article 44 (d) Article 46

25. Who had proposed the idea of three tier Panchayati Raj System ?
(a) Balwant Rai Mehta Committee
(b) Ashok Mehta Committee
(c) Royal Commission
(d) None of these

26. Current flows in a circuit when
(a) A switch is opened.
(b) A switch is closed.
(c) The switch is either opened or closed.
(d) There is no voltage.

27. What is the S.I. Unit of resistance ?
(a) Faraday (b) Ohm
(c) Volt (d) Ampere

28. Sour taste of lemon is due to the presence of which of the following ?
(a) Citric acid (b) Acetic acid
(c) Oxalic acid (d) Formic acid

29. Carcinogenic chemicals cause
(a) Heart diseases (b) Diabetes
(c) Cancer (d) Asthma

30. Name the upper layer of the skin :
(a) Endodermis (b) Epidermis
(c) Dermis (d) Special Dermis

31. $\sqrt{\left(1+\frac{27}{169}\right)}=\left(1+\frac{x}{13}\right)$, then the value of x is:
(a) 1 (b) 3
(c) 5 (d) 7

32. How many $\frac{1}{8}$'s are there in $37\frac{1}{8}$?
(a) 300 (b) 400
(c) 500 (d) cannot be determined

33. $\sqrt{\frac{36.1}{102.4}}=?$
(a) $\frac{29}{32}$ (b) $\frac{19}{72}$
(c) $\frac{19}{32}$ (d) $\frac{29}{62}$

34. The population of a town increases 4% annually but is decreased by migration annually to the extent of $\frac{1}{2}$. What will be the increase percent in three years ?
(a) 9.8 (b) 10
(c) 10.5 (d) 10.8

35. The average of 13 results is 68. The average of first seven is 63 and that of the last seven is 70, the seventh result is :
(a) 47 (b) 65.5
(c) 73.5 (d) 94

36. निम्न में से 'तीक्ष्ण' का विलोम शब्द क्या है?

(a) तीव्र (b) तृष्णा

(c) त्यागी (d) कुण्ठित

37. 'गजवदन' का पर्यायवाची है

(a) गर्जन

(b) मेघनाद

(c) गणपति

(d) विष्णु

38. 'काँटों से भरा हुआ' वाक्य के लिए नीचे दिए गए विकल्प में से एक शब्द चुनिये :

(a) कंटक

(b) विकीर्ण

(c) कुचैला

(d) कंटकाकीर्ण

39. 'दूध का दूध और पानी का पानी करना' मुहावरे का अर्थ है :

(a) दुग्ध इन्सपेक्टर होना

(b) मिल-जुलकर रहना

(c) पक्षपातपूर्ण निर्णय करना

(d) उचित निर्णय करना

40. शुद्ध वर्तनी का चयन कीजिए।

(a) बहीष्कार

(b) बाहिष्कार

(c) बहिष्कार

(d) बइष्कार

Directions (Q. 41-43) : Read the passage carefully and answer the corresponding questions :

I climbed into bed and rolled myself in my blankets, first extinguishing the light that burned steadily near the door. I lay still trying to get to sleep but my fear made that impossible and soon I sat up in bed peering into the darkness and occasionally glancing at the round window in the side of the ship which seemed like a plate suspended in the darkness. For an hour I must have sat like this, and then I was suddenly roused, by a drought of cold air. I jumped out of bed; not having allowed for the motion of the ship, I was instantly thrown violently across the room.

41. The author sat peering into the darkness because

(a) he had put out the light.

(b) he wished to see the window.

(c) the window had looked like a plate

(d) he was afraid.

42. The author jumped out of bed because

(a) he heard a faint sound.

(b) he saw someone coming towards him.

(c) a cold breeze blew past his face.

(d) he was pushed by someone.

43. Which one of the following did the author do first ?

(a) Closing the door.

(b) Climbing into bed.

(c) Rolling himself into blankets.

(d) None of these

44. Give Synonym for the following word :

Pride

(a) Humour (b) Hate

(c) Dignity (d) Cowardice

45. Give Antonym for the following word :

Keen

(a) Dull (b) Alert

(c) Humble (d) Eager

46. Select the related word from the given alternatives :

Dog : Rabbies : : Mosquito : ?

(a) Plague (b) Death

(c) Malaria (d) Stings

47. Choose the word which is least like the other words in the group :

(a) Nun (b) Knight

(c) Monk (d) Priest

48. In a certain code language, COMPUTRONE is written as PMOCTUENOR. How is ADVANTAGES written in that code ?

(a) SEGATNAVAD (b) AVDATNSEGA

(c) AVDATASEGN (d) NAVDASEGAT

49. A man said to a lady, Your mother's husband's sister is my aunt (Bua). How is the lady related to the man ?

(a) Daughter (b) Grand daughter

(c) Mother (d) Sister

50. If 18th February, 2005 falls on Friday then what will be the day on 18th February, 2007 ?

(a) Sunday (b) Monday

(c) Tuesday (d) Wednesday

51. Name the state of India which became the first state to provide health insurance for all its residents.

(a) Gujarat (b) Telangana

(c) Rajasthan (d) Karnataka

52. Name the state of India which became the first state to provide health insurance for all its residents.

(a) Gujarat (b) Telangana

(c) Rajasthan (d) Karnataka

53. To raise awareness about Yoga, Mobile app "Namaste Yoga" launched by whom in India?

(a) Ministry of Health and Family Welfare

(b) Ministry of Home Affairs

(c) Ministry of Ayush

(d) None of these

54. Who has been named the flag-bearer of the Indian contingent in the Tokyo Paralympics 2021?

(a) Kashish Lakra (b) Mariyappan Thangavelu

(c) Devendra Jhajharia (d) Ajeet Singh

55. What is the interest rate on Sukanya Samriddhi Accounts for second quarter (July-Sept) of 2021-22 ?

(a) 7.6% (b) 6.6%

(c) 8.6% (d) 9.6%

56. The Indian Army has named one of its firing ranges in Kashmir after Bollywood actress _______.

(a) Aishwarya Rai Bachchan

(b) Priyanka Chopra

(c) Deepika Padukone

(d) Vidya Balan

57. Which country's passport has topped in the most powerful passport in the world for the year 2021 ?

(a) Russia (b) U.S.

(c) India (d) Japan

58. Tamil Nadu Assembly Election 2021 was won by which political party ?

(a) DMK (b) BJP

(c) AIADMK (d) PMK

59. Global Peace Index 2021 topped by which country?

(a) Denmark (b) New Zealand

(c) Iceland (d) Portugal

60. Which state government implements Chief Minister Dalit Empowerment Programme ?

(a) Telangana (b) Andhra Pradesh

(c) Tamil Nadu (d) Bihar

61. Which of the following countries is known as the land of "Thunder Dragon" ?

(a) Japan (b) Bhutan

(c) Nepal (d) Srilanka

62. Riyadh is the capital of which country ?

(a) Myanmar (b) Bangladesh

(c) Saudi Arabia (d) None of these

63. Which of the following is the smallest state (in Area) of India ?

(a) Sikkim (b) Goa

(c) Meghalaya (d) Mizoram

64. What is the tenure of the elected members of Rajya Sabha?

(a) 2 Years (b) 4 Years

(c) 6 Years (d) 8 Years

65. When is the United Nations Day celebrated across the world ?

(a) October 20 (b) October 24

(c) November 27 (d) November 30

66. The International Court of Justice is located at

(a) Geneva (b) The Hague

(c) Amsterdam (d) Vienna

67. The world famous 'Khajuraho' sculptures are located in

(a) Gujarat (b) Madhya Pradesh

(c) Odisha (d) Maharashtra

68. The famous Nabakalebara festival belongs to which of the following states?

(a) Kerala (b) Bihar

(c) Rajasthan (d) Odisha

69. Which of the following is not a green house gas ?

(a) Methane (b) Nitrogen

(c) Carbon dioxide (d) Chlorofluorocarbon (CFC)

70. Arjuna Award is given for

(a) Exceptional service in emergency

(b) Bravery on battlefield

(c) Outstanding performance in sports

(d) Exceptional social services

निर्देश (प्र. 71–75): निम्नलिखित गद्यांश को ध्यानपूर्वक पढ़िए तथा उस पर आधारित प्रश्नों के उत्तर चुनिए:

स्वतंत्रता संग्राम मनुष्य में उत्तम और स्पृहणीय विशेषताएँ पैदा करता है और भारतीय स्वातंत्र्य संग्राम भी इसका अपवाद नहीं है। महात्मा गाँधी के नेतृत्व में यह युद्ध बिना किसी ईर्ष्या–द्वेष तथा खून–खराबे के लड़ा गया था। गाँधीजी इसे सत्याग्रह कहते थे। इसके पीछे उनकी शिक्षा, धार्मिक आस्था तथा अन्य उपलब्धियों का उतना हाथ नहीं था जितना उनके सदाचरण और व्यवहार का। इस स्वातंत्र्य आंदोलन को स्मरण रखने का मुख्य कारण यह है कि यह जनतांत्रिक था अर्थात इसमें देश के हर वर्ग और जाति के लोग सम्मिलित थे, चाहे वे धनी हों या गरीब, नर हों या नारी हों अथवा विभिन्न संप्रदायों के। इसके

साथ ही यह एक धर्मनिरपेक्ष और स्वतंत्रता कर्मियों का संघर्षशील राष्ट्रीय आंदोलन था। स्वतंत्र भारत के नागरिक के रूप में हम आज जनतांत्रिकता और धर्म-निरपेक्षता का लाभ उठा रहे हैं। हम सोच नहीं सकते कि इतने बड़े देश में अपना शासन करने के लिए हम अपना प्रतिनिधि नहीं चुन सकते थे या कोई गंदा कानून लागू कर दिया जाता तो हम उसके विरुद्ध आवाज नहीं उठा सकते थे और हम अपनी राय स्वतंत्रतापूर्वक व्यक्त नहीं कर सकते थे।

71. उपर्युक्त गद्यांश में प्रयुक्त स्पृहणीय शब्द का अर्थ है-

(a) प्राप्त करने योग्य (b) प्राप्त की हुई

(c) त्याग करने योग्य (d) त्याग की हुई

72. उपर्युक्त गद्यांश में लेखक ने मुख्य रूप से बताया है कि-

(a) आजादी में क्रांतिकारियों की विशेष भूमिका थी।

(b) आजादी के संघर्ष में कृषकों का क्या योगदान था ।

(c) गुलाम देश की दशा कैसी थी ।

(d) महात्मा गांधी के नेतृत्व में राष्ट्रीय आन्दोलन कैसा था।

73. उपर्युक्त गद्यांश के लेखक का उद्देश्य क्या था?

(a) धार्मिक आस्थाओं और सद्व्यवहार को बढ़ावा देना ।

(b) भारतीय स्वतंत्रता संग्राम की विशेषता बताना।

(c) अंग्रेजी राज्य के दोष गिनाना।

(d) जनतात्रिकता से हानि बताना।

74. धर्मनिरपेक्षता से अभिप्राय है

(a) सभी धर्मों का आदर (b) धर्म में हस्तक्षेप न करना

(c) धर्म की अवज्ञा (d) किसी भी धर्म को न मानना

75. कैसे माना जाए कि हमारा स्वतंत्रता संग्राम जनतांत्रिक था?

(a) यह महात्मा गाँधी के सद्व्यवहार और सदाचरण का प्रतीक था।

(b) इसमें हिन्दू और मुसलमान सम्मिलित हुए थे।

(c) यह स्वतंत्रता-प्रेमियों का आंदोलन था।

(d) इसमें सभी जातियों, वर्गों, धर्मों के लोगों ने भाग लिया था।

निर्देश (प्र. 76-80) : निम्नलिखित गद्यांश को ध्यानपूर्वक पढ़िए तथा उस पर आधारित प्रश्नों के उत्तर चुनिए:

विधाता-रचित इस सृष्टि का सिरमौर है मनुष्य। उसकी कारीगरी का सर्वोत्तम नमूना। इस मानव को ब्रह्माण्ड का लघु रूप मानकर भारतीय दार्शनिकों ने यत् पिण्डे तत् ब्रह्माण्डे की कल्पना की थी। उनकी यह कल्पना मात्र कल्पना नहीं थी, प्रत्युत यथार्थ भी थी क्योंकि मानव-मन में जो विचारणा के रूप में घटित होता है, उसी का कृति रूप ही तो सृष्टि है। मन तो मन, मानव का शरीर भी अप्रतिम है। देखने में इससे भव्य, आकर्षक एवं लावण्यमय रूप सृष्टि में अन्यत्र कहाँ है? अद्भुत एवं अद्वितीय है मानव-सौन्दर्य! साहित्यकारों ने इसके रूप-सौन्दर्य के वर्णन के लिए कितने ही अप्रस्तुतों का विधान किया है और इस सौन्दर्य-राशि से सभी को आप्यायित करने के लिए अनेक काव्य सृष्टियाँ रच डाली हैं। साहित्यशास्त्रियों ने भी इसी मानव की भावनाओं का विवेचन करते हुए अनेक रसों का निरूपण किया है। परन्तु वैज्ञानिक दृष्टि से विचार किया जाए तो मानव-शरीर को एक जटिल यन्त्र से उपमित किया जा सकता है। जिस प्रकार यन्त्र के एक पुर्जे में दोष आ जाने पर सारा यन्त्र गड़बड़ा जाता है, बेकार हो जाता है उसी प्रकार मानव- शरीर के विभिन्न अवयवों में से यदि कोई एक अवयव भी बिगड़ जाता है तो उसका प्रभाव सारे शरीर पर पड़ता है। इतना ही नहीं, गुर्दे जैसे कोमल एवं नाजुक हिस्से के खराब हो जाने से यह गतिशील वपुयन्त्र एकाएक अवरुद्ध हो सकता है, व्यक्ति की मृत्यु हो सकती है। एक अंग के विकृत होने पर सारा शरीर दण्डित हो, वह कालकवलित हो जाए - यह विचारणीय है।

यदि किसी यन्त्र के पुर्जे को बदलकर उसके स्थान पर नया पुर्जा लगाकर यन्त्र को पूर्ववत सुचारु एवं व्यवस्थित रूप से क्रियाशील बनाया जा सकता है तो शरीर के विकृत अंग के स्थान पर नव्य निरामय अंग लगाकर शरीर को स्वस्थ एवं सामान्य क्यों नहीं बनाया जा सकता? शल्य-चिकित्सकों ने इस दायित्वपूर्ण चुनौती को स्वीकार किया तथा निरन्तर अध्यवसाय पूर्णसाधना के अनन्तर अंग- प्रत्यारोपण के क्षेत्र में सफलता प्राप्त की। अंग-प्रत्यारोपण का उद्देश्य है कि मनुष्य दीर्घायु प्राप्त कर सके। यहाँ यह ध्यातव्य है कि मानव-शरीर हर किसी के अंग को उसी प्रकार स्वीकार नहीं करता, जिस प्रकार हर किसी का रक्त उसे स्वीकार्य नहीं होता। रोगी को रक्त देने से पूर्व रक्त-वर्ग का परीक्षण अत्यावश्यक है, तो अंग-प्रत्यारोपण से पूर्व ऊतक-परीक्षण अनिवार्य है। आज का शल्य-चिकित्सक गुर्दे, यकृत, आँत, फेफड़े और हृदय का प्रत्यारोपण सफलतापूर्वक कर रहा है। साधन-सम्पन्न चिकित्सालयों में मस्तिष्क के अतिरिक्त शरीर के प्रायः सभी अंगों का प्रत्यारोपण सम्भव हो गया है।

76. मानव को सृष्टि का लघु रूप माना गया है क्योंकि

(a) मानव मन में जो घटित होता है, वही सृष्टि में घटित होता है।

(b) मानव सृष्टि का सिरमौर है।

(c) मन की शक्ति अपराजेय है।

(d) लघु मानव ही विधाता की सच्ची सृष्टि है।

77. वैज्ञानिक दृष्टि का अपेक्षाकृत अभाव होता है

(a) साहित्यकार में

(b) साहित्यशास्त्री में

(c) शल्य-चिकित्सक में

(d) वैज्ञानिक में

78. मानव शरीर को यन्त्रवत् कहा गया है क्योंकि

(a) मानव शरीर दृढ़ माँसपेशियों और अवयवों से निर्मित है ।

(b) मानव शरीर यन्त्र की भाँति लावण्यमय होता है।

(c) अवयव रूपी पुर्जो के विकृत होने से शरीर यन्त्रवत् निष्क्रिय हो जाता है।

(d) मानव शरीर विधाता की सृष्टि की अनुपम कृति है।

79. शल्य-चिकित्सकों द्वारा स्वीकार की गई दायित्वपूर्ण चुनौती थी

(a) जीर्ण शरीर के स्थान पर स्वस्थ शरीर देना

(b) मानव-शरीर को मृत्यु से बचाना

(c) अंग-प्रत्यारोपण द्वारा शरीर को सामान्य बनाना

(d) शल्य-चिकित्सा का महत्त्व स्थापित करना

80. अनुच्छेद में प्रयुक्त 'निरामय' शब्द का पर्याय है

(a) सुन्दर (b) स्वस्थ

(c) अद्‌भुत (d) नवीन

Directions (Q. 81-85) : The following graph shows the production of cement in Million Tonnes during the various years. Study the same and answer the following questions correctly:

Production of Cement (In Million tonnes)

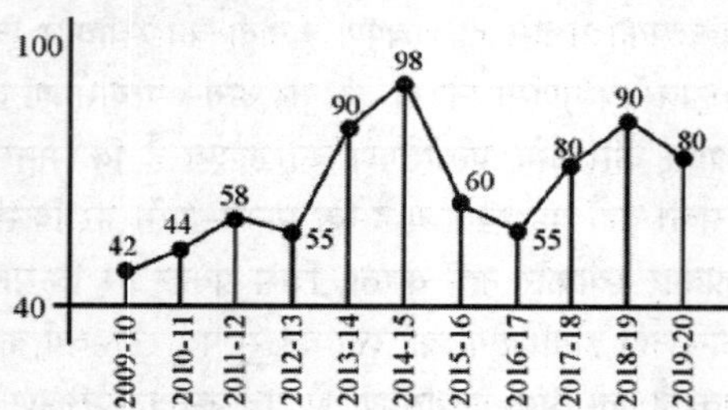

81. The production fell down to the maximum extent in the year :

(a) 2012-13 (b) 2015-16

(c) 2016-17 (d) 2019-20

82. The increase in production was maximum during the year _______ over its previous year.

(a) 2013-14 (b) 2017-18

(c) 2014-15 (d) 2018-19

83. The average production during the first three years was:

(a) 44 MT (b) 46 MT

(c) 48 MT (d) 50 MT

84. The maximum production of cement was noted in the year :

(a) 2013-14 (b) 2014-15

(c) 2018-19 (d) 2017-18

85. The percentage increase in production during 2011-12 over its previous year was :

(a) 31.8% (b) 36%

(c) 37.5% (d) None of these

Directions (Q. 86-90) : The following graph shows the import of a certain commodity X in Crore Rupees between 2013 and 2019.

The questions are based on the shown figure. Answer these questions.

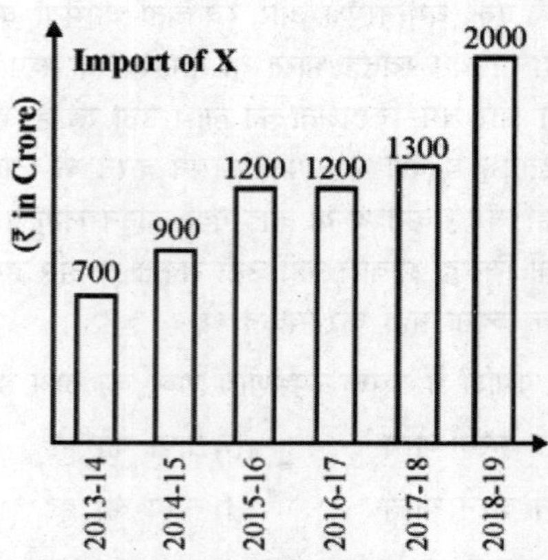

86. Percent increase in import of X from 2014-15 to 2015-16 is

(a) 43.0% (b) 33.3%

(c) 28.8% (d) 25.0%

87. Average of the increase in import of X year by year for all the years is (in Rs. crore)

(a) 260 (b) 280

(c) 325 (d) None of these

88. For how many years, there was more import of X, than the average import of X ?

(a) 4 (b) 3

(c) 2 (d) 1

89. The difference of the numbers of years in which import of X is less than the average import and in which import of X is more than the average import is

(a) 3 (b) 2

(c) 1 (d) 0

90. The percentage increase in import of X during 2018-19 over its Average of Import of X of all years ?

(a) 50.9% (b) 63.5%

(c) 70.6% (d) 64.38%

Directions (Q. 91-95) : Study the table and answer the given questions.

In the following table four persons A, B, C and D are selling items on different days of the week.

	A	B	C	D
Monday	40	45	25	20
Tuesday	35	50	48	26
Friday	25	28	15	41
Saturday	30	40	45	40

91. What was the ratio of item sold by A on Tuesday & items sold by C on Saturday ?

(a) 9 : 7 (b) 7 : 9

(c) 6 : 5 (d) 8 : 7

92. Items sold by D on Monday is what percent of item sold by C on Saturday ?

(a) 42.60 % (b) 49.55 %
(c) 44.44 % (d) 32.70 %

93. What is the average of the items sold by B, C and D on Monday, Tuesday and Saturday respectively ?

(a) 44.33 (b) 42.50
(c) 46.66 (d) 45.90

94. Percent increase for selling of items B compare with Selling of items D in all four days of weeks is

(a) 29.1 % (b) 19.5 %
(c) 18.3 % (d) 28.3 %

95. What is the difference between the average of items selling on Monday to average items selling on Friday ?

(a) 10.5 (b) 7.40
(c) 5.25 (d) 6.45

Directions (Q. 96-100) : Study the table and answer the given questions.

Production of Crops in India during 2010-2017 (In tonnes)

Year	Wheat	Rice	Bajra	Maize	Barley	Pulses	Potatoes
2010-11	6121	874	565	80	300	415	210
2011-12	7010	964	655	60	312	417	220
2012-13	7112	960	780	55	210	680	222
2013-14	7056	985	1110	40	200	310	245
2014-15	6896	716	1160	90	216	370	315
2015-16	6912	826	1450	110	160	300	400
2016-17	7617	812	1460	75	216	260	445

96. Wheat production started showing a slump during :

(a) 2013-14 (b) 2015-16
(c) 2014-15 (d) 2016-17

97. Which of the following crops showed the continuous increase in production during 2013-2017 ?

(a) Maize (b) Barley
(c) Pulses (d) Bajra

98. What is the average yield of potatoes during the period 2010-11 to 2016-17 ?

(a) 300.00 tonnes (b) 293.86 tonnes
(c) 353.96 tonnes (d) 253.86 tonnes

99. During 2016-17, which of the following crops showed decrease in production in comparison to the previous year ?

(a) Barley (b) Bajra
(c) Rice (d) Potatoes

100. The production of potatoes in 2015-16 is approximately how many times that in 2010-11 ?

(a) 1.82 (b) 2.00
(c) 2.10 (d) 1.90

Answers

1. (c)	**2.** (b)	**3.** (b)	**4.** (b)	**5.** (a)	**6.** (d)	**7.** (b)	**8.** (b)	**9.** (c)	**10.** (d)
11. (b)	**12.** (b)	**13.** (c)	**14.** (a)	**15.** (b)	**16.** (c)	**17.** (d)	**18.** (a)	**19.** (b)	**20.** (a)
21. (d)	**22.** (b)	**23.** (b)	**24.** (b)	**25.** (a)	**26.** (b)	**27.** (b)	**28.** (a)	**29.** (c)	**30.** (b)
31. (a)	**32.** (a)	**33.** (c)	**34.** (d)	**35.** (a)	**36.** (d)	**37.** (c)	**38.** (d)	**39.** (d)	**40.** (c)
41. (d)	**42.** (c)	**43.** (b)	**44.** (c)	**45.** (a)	**46.** (c)	**47.** (b)	**48.** (b)	**49.** (a)	**50.** (a)
51. (c)	**52.** (a)	**53.** (c)	**54.** (b)	**55.** (a)	**56.** (d)	**57.** (d)	**58.** (a)	**59.** (c)	**60.** (a)
61. (b)	**62.** (c)	**63.** (b)	**64.** (c)	**65.** (b)	**66.** (b)	**67.** (b)	**68.** (d)	**69.** (b)	**70.** (c)
71. (a)	**72.** (d)	**73.** (b)	**74.** (a)	**75.** (d)	**76.** (a)	**77.** (b)	**78.** (c)	**79.** (c)	**80.** (b)
81. (b)	**82.** (c)	**83.** (c)	**84.** (b)	**85.** (a)	**86.** (b)	**87.** (a)	**88.** (c)	**89.** (b)	**90.** (d)
91. (b)	**92.** (c)	**93.** (a)	**94.** (d)	**95.** (c)	**96.** (a)	**97.** (d)	**98.** (b)	**99.** (c)	**100.** (d)